THE MAZE OF URBAN HOUSING MARKETS

THE MAZE OF URBAN HOUSING MARKETS

THEORY, EVIDENCE, AND POLICY

Jerome Rothenberg, George C. Galster,
Richard V. Butler, and John Pitkin

The University of Chicago Press
Chicago and London

JEROME ROTHENBERG is professor of economics at Massachusetts Institute of Technology. GEORGE C. GALSTER is professor of economics and chair of the Urban Studies Program at the College of Wooster. RICHARD V. BUTLER is professor and chairman of economics at Trinity University. JOHN PITKIN is president of Analysis and Forecasting, Inc.

The University of Chicago Press, Chicago 60637
The University of Chicago Press, Ltd., London

Printed in the United States of America

00 99 98 97 96 95 94 93 92 91   5 4 3 2 1

Library of Congress Cataloging-in-Publication Data

The Maze of urban housing markets : theory, evidence, and policy /
Jerome Rothenberg . . . [et al.].
p. cm.
Includes bibliographical references and index.
ISBN 0–226–72951–6
1. Housing—Mathematical models. 2. Urban economics—Mathematical models. 3. Housing—United States—Econometric models.
I. Rothenberg, Jerome, 1924–
HD7287.5.M39 1991
363.5′1′0973—dc20   90–22756
CIP

∞The paper used in this publication meets the minimum requirements of the American National Standard for Information Sciences—Permanence of Paper for Printed Library Materials, ANSI Z39.48–1984.

Contents

Acknowledgments

The authors wish to thank the National Science Foundation (Grant GS-40769), the Federal Home Loan Bank Board, the Ford Foundation, the U.S. Department of Housing and Urban Development, the Lincoln Institute of Land Policy, the Joint Center for Urban Studies of MIT and Harvard University, the College of Wooster, and Trinity University for their financial support of a research agenda that at times may have seemed too ambitious. We are also grateful to the National Urban Coalition for its support of the research which first illuminated for us the complexity of urban housing markets and inspired us to investigate this complexity.

We would like to acknowledge three substantive contributions to the research. William J. Stull collaborated in the development of a prototype model which forms the foundation of this study; Larry Forgy brought new insights into the econometric analysis of housing prices; and Sunny Kim helped us specify the model of individual supplier behavior.

The demanding tasks of organizing and coding primary data on housing characteristics and sales were shared among several research assistants. Irene Jenkins's thoroughness and attention to detail were invaluable; Samuel Williams, Amy Philipson, Howard Leibowitz, and Allen Hemenway also assisted in these tasks. John M. L. Gruenstein, Kate Gasser, Doron Holzer, James Anderson, and Axel Boersch-Supan programmed the computers to process the data once it was encoded.

We are grateful to the staff of the Des Moines, Iowa, City Assessor's Office for making their property record data available to us, most especially to Chief Assessor Andy Regis and to Lyman Ellars for his patient assistance in helping us solve a myriad of practical problems. The People's Abstract Company of Des Moines generously allowed us access to their extensive records of property sales. Eva Ellars and Jerrine Andreni ably assisted our data collection efforts.

Ann F. Friedlaender and Dowell Myers offered helpful comments on early drafts of several chapters.

For their assistance in preparing the manuscript we thank Charlotte Wahl, Aju Fenn, Shirley Sartori, and Yvonne Cortright. David Garza expertly produced the figures. Kathryn Gohl provided painstaking copyediting.

Although primary responsibility for the drafting of different chapters was divided, every chapter embodies the fruits of an intellectual interplay which involved all of the authors over the course of a multiyear team effort. The views expressed herein are the authors' sole responsibility and do not necessarily reflect those of our employers or sponsors. In spite of our best efforts and the able assistance of all those whom we have mentioned above, it is inevitable that errors will remain in a work of this size and complexity. For these, the authors also accept sole responsibility.

1 Introduction

Most issues of interest to urban residents, investors, policymakers, and analysts are influenced profoundly by the operation of the metropolitan area's housing market. Housing occupancy and investment patterns influence such diverse concerns as industrial and commercial land uses, local government fiscal capacity, the well-being of various racial and ethnic groups, the location of transportation systems, and, of course, the deterioration, abandonment, or revitalization of neighborhoods. To understand the urban housing market is, thus, to understand that which fundamentally influences the well-being of most citizens.

This book provides what we hope is a significant analytical advance in our understanding of the maze that is the urban housing market. We see our primary goal here as the rigorous explication of a new theory of these markets. But we also provide results of various exploratory empirical models designed to test the veracity and power of the theory. In addition, we demonstrate the power and flexibility of our approach by applying it to analyze numerous contemporary urban housing problems and policies designed to ameliorate them.

Basic to our approach is the belief that there are distinctive features of urban housing markets that distinguish them from other types of markets. Any theory that hopes to provide a robust explanation for housing market dynamics and a framework for evaluating housing policy must take seriously these distinguishing features.

We believe that the concept of a *housing-quality submarket* is the foundation upon which such a theory of urban housing markets should be constructed. A submarket is a collection of all dwellings in a metropolitan area whose myriad attributes, though different, are evaluated as a whole by demanders and suppliers as closely equivalent. The metric collapsing of these attributes of the housing package, *quality,* is the basis for arraying the stock in a metropolitan area in a spectrum of submarkets, from highest- to lowest-quality levels. Within each submarket there is room for independent market adjustment. But also submarkets are interrelated to the degree that the quality differentials between them are small, due to the behaviors of both housing demanders and suppliers who view them therefore as close substitutes. The dynamics of urban housing markets can be understood by elucidating behaviors of households, builders of new dwellings, and converters of existing housing as they unfold in this segmented market complex. These dynamics may be characterized as *systematic but nonuniform,* and are central to an understanding of urban housing phenomena and policy options.

Our purposes in this chapter are twofold. First, we delineate the idiosyncrasies of housing and urban housing markets and indicate, in overview, how our approach attempts to deal with them both theoretically and empirically. Second, because the work is massive as well as written at various levels of complexity, we establish guideposts so that readers with particular interests or backgrounds can select the most appropriate chapters for perusal.

1.1 An Overview of the Approach

1.1.1 Theoretical Framework

Housing is a special kind of commodity, making the urban housing market a special kind of market. Housing is a spatially immobile, highly durable, multidimensionally heterogeneous, physically modifiable commodity, whose durability and expensiveness make extensive mortgage borrowing essential for an owner, and make an extensive rental market practicable. An owned dwelling is potentially an important asset in household portfolio management, and rental status significantly changes the portfolio situation. Further, changes in occupancy are highly costly. What do these distinctive features imply?

Spatial immobility means that its location is an intrinsic attribute of a dwelling. Because residents care deeply about differences in location as an aspect of socializing and status, of the consumption of private goods, of the differential availability of public goods, and of the accessibility to private goods, jobs, and other desired destinations, location can be an important determinant of housing quality, housing market value, and household welfare. The ingredients of locational attractiveness typically lie outside the control of the owner and/or occupier of a housing unit, however; therefore the urban housing market is inherently affected by neighborhood externalities of importance.

Extreme durability means that an overwhelming share of occupancies in each period is furnished by units built in the past; only a tiny fraction is due to newly produced units. But existing houses are modifiable in various ways. They can be physically changed in terms of their condition or various structural features, including size; the number of separate dwelling units they comprise can be changed; and the tenure status of occupants can be changed. So there are three distinct forms of supply in any period; that from unchanged existing dwellings, that from modified existing dwellings, and that from newly constructed dwellings. The last two represent competitive modes by which suppliers respond to changes in market conditions.

Supply does not take the form of modules of a homogeneous commodity. Housing units are enormously heterogeneous. They differ in numerous structural characteristics, in lot features, in the neighborhood, in local public services, and in accessibility to desired destinations. Occupants show by their behavior that differences in all these features are important. So housing is a *package* of many salient attributes, only some of which are under the control of the owner. And this heterogeneity makes for a wide spectrum of degrees of substitutability among dwellings. Housing is not, then, a single commodity but a complex of variously related commodities; the urban housing market is not one perfect market but a set of interrelated submarkets. The analysis of this market complex must deal with the pattern of substitutability among these housing variants and with its consequences.

Housing is a capital asset of importance. On the one hand, the extensive mortgage borrowing makes the housing sector highly vulnerable to macroeconomic effects on capital markets. On the other hand, the ownership of a housing asset represents a considerable portfolio investment. The uniquely large rental market in housing (relative to other consumer goods) that arises because of high durability and expensiveness makes for a tenure-choice decision between owner-occupancy and renting that depends on both consumption and portfolio investment considerations.

Finally, changes in occupancy/ownership are very costly. The considerable search warranted by the extreme heterogeneity and immobility of housing, complex legal and other transactional services (e.g., realtors' services), and moving services require a heavy outlay of time, effort, and money. Both current and capital cost aspects are mingled, and liquidity as well as income constraints are involved. An important consequence is that most households change occupancies only infrequently. Only a small percentage of households are actively on the demand side of the market in any period, those of them who are owners being both buyers and sellers simultaneously.

These distinctive features of housing are very difficult to model and are very rarely treated together. A unique aspect of our approach is to attempt to deal with all of them, albeit at different levels of completeness. In our theoretical studies, we attempt to deal with all of them at a reasonably penetrating level. Our econometric applications have had to compromise with the realities of data inadequacies and thus show uneven attention to these distinctive features.

Our approach involves a theoretical framework from which a number of variant models can be generated. The theoretical framework contains formal theories of urban housing market segmentation into submarkets, individual housing users (demanders), aggregate (spectral) demand, three different kinds of individual suppliers—owner-occupiers, landlords, and builders—aggregate (spectral) supply, and the dynamic working of the system of many related submarkets. Spectral demand and supply refer to the entire spectrum of aggregate demand for and supply of housing units in each of the various submarkets.

In the first element of our framework we attempt to come to grips with the heterogeneity of the commodity we call housing. In a large metropolitan area there can be literally thousands of somewhat different housing commodities that vary in the attributes of number of rooms, condition, structure type, architectural style and layout, lot size, neighborhood amenities, public services, access to employment, and so forth. This heterogeneity holds an implication central to our purposes: different houses likely represent only imperfect substitutes for one another, with degrees of substitutability varying from pair to pair. Thus, the market is likely to contain sets of housing clusters or submarkets, each one containing dwellings which are very close substitutes. The submarkets themselves differ in their degree of substitutability among one another, and this complex configuration of substitutability will influence the pattern of impulse propagation through the entire market—events spreading rapidly and completely within a submarket, with external repercussions dampening progressively as they reach submarkets of progressively lower substitutability.

Although this concept of segmentation is important inasmuch as it implies different forms of competitive interaction than in a single, perfectly articulated market, to discern an overall meaningful design in the multidimensional maze of components underlying these substitutability relationships is complicated. The basic approach used here is to assume that the market can be functionally segmented into an orderly structure of submarkets graduated according to quality level. *Quality level* refers to a hierarchical degree of substitutability according to demanders and suppliers in aggregate. For demanders, substitutability refers to overall attractiveness of a dwelling when all attributes of the package are evaluated. It is assumed that demanders implicitly evaluate the relative attractiveness of different packages as a function of their attributes and the balance among them, and that this attractiveness reflects their widespread willingness to trade off degrees of one attribute for additional degrees of another. For suppliers, substitutability refers to the cost of supplying a dwelling unit with one set of characteristics instead of some other unit with specified different characteristics. These cost tradeoffs depend on specific technological opportunities available to suppliers of new and existing units. Competition in the market by both demanders and suppliers promotes adjustment toward an equilibrium at which both bring their marginal tradeoffs across housing attributes into equality, thereby establishing approximately similar gradients of substitutability, and thus a set of implicit market prices for components.

Given the distribution of housing attributes over dwelling units, these gradients implicitly rank the housing stock by quality. Narrow ranges of this quality dimension may be considered submarkets wherein units are viewed as close substitutes by the market (although these aggregate evaluations will generally differ from those of individual demanders and suppliers). Units of radically different quality are considered relatively poorer substitutes. Thus, for instance, if the difference in quality between dwelling units in submarkets A and B is less than between A and C, then those in B are better substitutes for those in A than are those in C.

The market, then, is divided into submarkets differing in terms of quality and substitutability, the degree of which is established in the form of a single dimension of hierarchical linkage. Our method for empirically specifying this single quality dimension is, first, to use a hedonic index to derive weights of the various housing package attributes implicit in market valuations. This index then is used to estimate the *hedonic value* (or quality level) of each dwelling in the stock, which will be independent of subsequent rent or value changes. The hierarchical groupings of dwellings possessing hedonic values within relatively narrow ranges constitute the stock distribution across submarkets.

Having established a principle for dealing with heterogeneity via segmenting the market, our next theoretical component considers the individual household's demand. Variants of our model treat housing as a consumption good only (i.e., the case of a renter) or as a combination consumption good and portfolio asset (i.e., the case of an owner-occupant). Consider first the former case. The housing demand of the individual household is seen as a demand for a combination of the various attributes comprising the housing package. Individual attributes are traded off against one another and against the overall magnitude of the package of attributes (i.e., its quality level). And quality level of the package is traded off as well against other commodities. The household's utility is maximized where each set of tradeoffs equals the implicit relevant market price ratios for pairs of attributes, for attributes relative to quality level, and for housing quality level relative to nonhousing commodities.

The theory defines these various implicit prices. Those for attributes are defined in terms of a hedonic price decomposition of a housing package's rent or selling price. Because housing units are heterogeneous, durable, and only modifiable at a schedule of costs with nontrivial lags, housing units of different quality levels are only imperfect substitutes for one another. So in a particular time interval, dwelling units in any particular quality submarket may experience price or rent increases or decreases relative to those of other quality submarkets as a result of changing market forces within that time interval. At any particular time, therefore, implicit market valuations in a submarket represent an aspect of housing package price or rent not encompassed by the market valuation of individual attributes alone, and relative market valuations for different quality submarkets may change over time. Put differently, the quality or hedonic value of dwellings within a given submarket is determined by the dwellings' attributes and these attributes' implicit prices, but added components of observed market valuation will be created by demand and supply in the submarket within the period. Demands across the array of submarkets at each time period will be responsive to this submarket-specific aspect of total market valuation as well as to the attribute-specific aspect.

Utility maximization ideally defines potentially desired optimal packages, but not necessarily demander market behavior. The high costs of occupancy change will discourage most households from being willing to become active market participants in any particular period. By not actively searching for market opportunities, these households will not even know the availability of units or the set of attribute or quality-level prices, and will simply retain their present occupancy. Others, led by low-cost background information and a sense of significant disequilibrium—actually not rigorously definable except after a commitment to active market participation that generates considerable new information—become active participants, engage in costly search, and, as a result of that process, select a stochastically optimal housing package (which may be to remain in the present unit). The expected character of this package is described by the theory.

For the variant of our model wherein housing has both consumption and asset dimensions, the analysis must be formulated in multiperiod terms inasmuch as only in such terms does investment in a portfolio of any kind make sense. The utility function of the household demander depends on the multiperiod consumption of housing and nonhousing commodities and the holding of housing and nonhousing assets. Nonhousing assets affect utility by having a present capitalized value, and by generating current income, expected future income, and expected future capitalized values over time. Similarly, housing assets provide a present capitalized value and generate housing services in the present period, expected future services, and future capitalized values. In addition, mortgage borrowing for housing assets enters as a complication.

The analysis shows the utility-maximizing choice among different kinds of consumption at different dates and different kinds of portfolio investment at different dates. It then compares the effect that the dual consumption-portfolio asset character of housing has on both the consumption tradeoff between housing and nonhousing, and on the investment tradeoff between housing and nonhousing assets. In general this dual character affects the equilibrium configuration of both consumption and financial investment, and of their intertemporal distribution. A reasonable set of predictions is developed about the aggregate pattern of these configurational effects, their aggregate dynamic character, and the changing importance of housing in consumption and portfolio investment during inflationary processes. Explicit tax and other advantages and disadvantages of homeownership are included in the analysis, and the whole is integrated with our overall emphasis on stratification of the housing market complex. Finally, the analysis is applied to illuminating the tenure choice of households between being renters of housing or owner-occupiers.

Aggregate spectral demand is accomplished by summing quantities of each kind of housing package demanded (by both quality and tenure), both deterministically (by nonmovers) and stochastically through active search. Aggregation involves sequential demand adjustments by later adjusters as the decisions by earlier adjusters change the complex of market valuations.

The supply component of our theoretical framework contrasts modifiers of existing housing units and builders of new units. Since their respective dwellings are in principle capable of any degree of desired substitutability, they face the same spectral demand situation. But their cost functions differ with respect to construction type, inputs, and land (including locational availabilities). These differences have a systematic component based on degree of substitutability among alternative sets of origin-destination quality submarket modification pairs and measured by the size of the intersubmarket quality-level differences for each pair.

We assume that all suppliers attempt to maximize rates of return on present discounted value prospects. In the short run, market-period supply decisions consist only of whether to offer existing dwellings for rent or sale, or to hold them off the market. This choice is influenced by owner expectations about market valuation trends, holding costs, and occupancy costs. In a longer, medium-run framework, sufficient time exists for conversions and construction to be completed and thereby to affect the distribution of stock across submarkets. Each supplier regards the set of net payoffs from all the alternative supply options (at different quality submarkets and sets of attribute mix) and selects the one that maximizes rate or return. So each choice of a particular quality submarket/attribute mix is influenced by conditions in all other submarket/mix combinations. The cost function differences between builders of new dwellings and owners of existing dwellings lead them to different optimal choices, and the different origin-destination cost functions for existing dwellings in different starting submarkets lead their owners to make different choices as well.

In the market period, aggregate spectral supply is merely the summation of the existing dwellings that owners have chosen to offer in each submarket, at a given spectrum of market valuations. In the medium-run period, it is the sum of newly constructed dwellings plus dwellings converted into the particular submarket, minus those converted out of the submarket to another, to nonresidential uses, or to abandonment. Aggregate supply in response to a given aggregate spectral demand depends on the particular quality submarket distribution of existing dwellings at the beginning of the period, because this influences the aggregate conversion cost function for each submarket.

The urban housing market system as a whole operates as though degrees of substitutability represent *interactive distance*. The extent to which changes in one submarket are propagated to other submarkets depends on cross-submarket price elasticities of demand and supply, which are inversely related to interactive distance. The model thus views urban housing market dynamics in terms of *systematic nonuniformities*. Repercussions are systematic inasmuch as demanders and suppliers respond in predictable ways to changes in market valuations and rates of return, respectively. But because demand and supply elasticities are both finite and vary in different submarkets, shocks produce nonuniform effects both within and among submarkets, although, again, in systematic ways.

A key implication which follows from our theory of systematic, nonuniform submarket dynamics is that a market complex subject to various initial changes in one or more parts of the complex will show patterns of interactive repercussion that will in general result in a final configuration different from that of the initial impacts, sometimes considerably different. This is crucial for understanding the consequences of exogenous demographic or economic shocks and for predicting the effects of public policies: the reverberatory interplay among submarkets will frequently lead to a final outcome that differs markedly from the initial impacts generated by the shock or mandated by the policy. A "final" configuration is approached over sometimes considerable time in terms of a general equilibrium of demanders and suppliers, and thus among the marginal rates of use substitution and longer-run transformations for quality submarket/attribute mix combinations by different types of demanders and suppliers, respectively.

1.1.2 Empirical Investigation

In an attempt to assess the validity and power of the above theoretical framework, we have undertaken two distinct strands of empirical investigation: one is aggregate, cross-sectional for a number of standard metropolitan statistical areas (SMSAs);[1] the other is disaggregated, intertemporal for a single SMSA. In both strands we follow a similar strategy: (1) operationalize the degree of substitutability between houses in terms of quality as specified by a hedonic index; (2) partition the housing stock in each SMSA into quality-level/tenure submarkets according to this measure; (3) econometrically estimate parameters of functions describing static and dynamic behavioral relationships among these submarkets. Although both studies share these similarities, they offer important differences that we consider complementary insofar as each can answer questions the other cannot, as we shall see below. The studies are meant to be illustrative, however, not exhaustive. Indeed, we see our theory as opening up many more avenues of empirical investigation than have been undertaken here.

Our cross-sectional empirical work utilizes data from two samples of SMSAs: one for 1960 and 1970 (from U.S. Census data) and one for 1970 and 1975–76 (from Annual Housing Survey data). For both samples we estimated a hedonic index (separately by tenure) by regressing housing market prices (or rents) of units in various categories on a limited set of attributes relating to the structure. Properties of this index regarding the potential problems of aggregation and omitted variables biases are explored. Then the index is employed to partition each SMSA's stock in all years into quality submarkets by tenure, based on estimated hedonic values.

Demand and supply functions are specified and estimated with two-stage least squares techniques for all tenure/quality submarkets over two time periods—the immediate-run market period and the medium-run five-to-ten-year period. In the market period, the demand equations describe the proportion of all occupied dwellings in the SMSA that were in a given submarket, as a function of price proxies for the various submarkets, prices of nonhousing goods, and the SMSA's household income, racial, and age profiles. The supply equations describe the same proportion as above, but as a function of the proxy price in the given submarket relative to nonhousing prices, the size of the available housing stock, and past changes in average housing prices and in population (to reflect dynamic effects).

Medium-run period equations for aggregate stock supply and for the mix of conversion versus new construction modes are estimated with ordinary least squares for the 1960–70 and 1970–1975/76 periods for all tenure-quality submarkets. Aggregate proportional changes in submarket stocks are modeled as functions of beginning-of-period price proxies and housing stock conditions, intertemporal demand shifts in the given and in other submarkets, and competing housing supplies from the public sector. The excess of new construction over net conversions into a submarket, as a measure of supply mix, is specified similarly, but with different interpretations and expectations about parameters.

Our single-SMSA empirical investigations delve more deeply into particular kinds of qualitative improvement in the housing stock that were invisible in the aggregative, cross-sectional explorations. We collected a large, rich data base in Des Moines, Iowa, that provides a comprehensive picture of particular alterations in individual, owner-occupied parcels from 1963 to 1971. Specifically, in comparison with the cross-sectional approach, the Des Moines model utilizes more detail on the housing unit itself, including all significant structural features, quality of construction, physical condition, as well as size of lot. It also is more precise concerning the location of the housing unit and elaborates accessibility to the central business district (CBD), socioeconomic character of the neighborhood, and the physical condition of nearby buildings.

The single-SMSA model consists of a market stratification component and estimated medium-run supply adjustment relationships for owner-occupants of single-family homes. The stratification of the stock of housing into quality classes is effected as above by means of a hedonic index. In the Des Moines application of the theory, the hedonic index includes measures of the socioeconomic and physical character of the neighborhood, lot characteristics, and accessibility, in addition to many more detailed structural attributes than were available in our cross-SMSA model. The appropriate functional form of the relationship between variables is examined. The estimated index is then used to stratify the owner-occupied, single-family housing stock according to quality-level submarkets.

Supply adjustments are directly related to current market signals of returns and costs facing an owner of a particular structure in a given submarket. This contrasts with our cross-SMSA model, where revenues for an entire submarket were roughly proxied by beginning-of-period market valuations and within-period demand shifts, and costs by very general, beginning-of-period aggregate features of the entire SMSA housing market.

Relationships are specified for a variety of particular, medium-run supply changes on each of the sample parcels, such as additions of floor area, porches, plumbing, garages, air conditioning, or finished basements. In addition, an aggregate model is specified that explains the probability that any of the aforementioned additions are made and, if so, how much was spent by the homeowner.

These housing supply relationships depend on expected rate of return and owner characteristics. Market signals include both returns and costs. Returns are measured by the increment in hedonic value (quality) that the particular contemplated addition would yield for the particular unit, as estimated by the hedonic index. Costs are measured by an appraisal firm's estimates of the alteration contemplated. Owner characteristics are measured indirectly by the aggregate life-cycle stage, race, and socioeconomic characteristics of the census tract. Finally, other neighborhood characteristics are included to serve as proxies for areas most likely to be redlined by lenders and to face disinvestment in the face of prospective racial transition.

Both the theoretical and cross-SMSA empirical models stress the continuous nature of supply adjustments, the former because of its origin in neoclassical economic theory and the latter because of its aggregate nature. By contrast, as in many micro models, the single-SMSA Des Moines empirical model focuses on more lumpy, discrete adjustments. These changes are, therefore, appropriately measured by discrete behavior statistical techniques, such as multinomial LOGIT which we employ.

1.2 Guideposts for the Reader

This book should be of interest to a wide range of readers—academic economists, planner, policymakers, and housing professionals. Yet we realize that particular chapters, due to either their focus or the technical nature of their exposition, are more or less interesting to some. In the remainder of this chapter, we provide a road map to help each reader locate the portions of the book most relevant to his or her particular concerns.

Chapter 2 provides a context for our work. It reviews existing theoretical and empirical research on urban housing markets in five topical areas—the nature of housing, housing demand, new housing supply, supply from the existing housing stock, and housing market interaction models. In each area a contrast is made between extant work and our approach. Chapter 2 provides an overview of the field of urban housing economics and our contribution to it.

The first major subdivision of the book, part 1, consists of five chapters devoted to theoretical issues. Chapter 3–6 present our formal theory of urban-housing submarkets, demand, supply, and market adjustments and equilibrium, respectively. These chapters form the heart of our theoretical analysis and, as such, the major contribution to the field. They are, however, technical in nature. Chapter 7 provides a brief, nontechnical summary of the central conceptual elements and conclusions of the theory presented in these chapters. The central ideas are presented in the form of a graphic analysis that, although simplified, can be easily manipulated to generate powerful insights into the operation of urban housing markets.

The usefulness of our theoretical approach, especially in its simplified graphic version, is illustrated in parts 2 and 3, which are thus recommended for all those wishing a better understanding of urban housing phenomena, neighborhood dynamics, and public efforts to promote well-being through interventions in the housing market. Part 2 consists of two chapters delineating various applications of the model to urban housing phenomena. Chapter 8 analyzes determinants of changes in the quality and cost of housing, sheds new light on the conventional notion of filtering, and explores the origins of such contemporary urban housing problems as homelessness, rent burdens, and abandonment. Chapter 9 discusses the influence of the neighborhood on housing demanders and suppliers, and demonstrates how neighborhood change results from market adjustments propagating through the array of housing submarkets. Equity and efficiency implications of neighborhood dynamics are also considered, and suggestions for neighborhood stabilization are made.

The power of our approach in analyzing public policy interventions in urban housing markets is demonstrated in part 3. Chapter 10 analyzes demand-side approaches such as rent supplements. Chapter 11 analyzes the supply-side approaches of rehabilitation subsidies, new construction of high-quality dwellings followed by filtering, and new construction targeted for occupancy by low-income groups. Chapter 12 analyzes the market-regulation approach represented by rent control. In each chapter unique efficiency and equity implications are provided by our model, some of which contradict conventional wisdom. The policies are contrasted in terms of their comparative advantages in achieving particular programmatic goals and the particular features of the urban context which influence their success. We believe a major strength of our approach is its applicability for policy analysis and thus have designed chapters 10–12 to be accessible to a wide range of housing practitioners.

Part 4 consists of exploratory empirical studies which are based on our theoretical framework. Chapter 13 considers how housing quality may be defined operationally through the use of a hedonic index. Both inter-SMSA and intra-SMSA indexes are estimated, their statistical properties are investigated, and housing submarkets are specified with them. Those concerned about the specification of hedonic indexes and their application to defining housing-quality submarket will find this chapter of particular interest.

Empirical modeling of housing-submarket demand and supply relationships is described in chapters 14–16. The former two chapters employ an aggregated, cross-SMSA approach; the latter a disaggregated, single-SMSA one. Together they represent attempts to probe heretofore unexplored aspects of urban housing markets and, implicitly, to test the strength of our theoretical approach. As such they are recommended for those interested in econometric modeling and empirical estimates of housing market demand and supply parameters.

Finally, chapter 17 draws conclusions and implications from our analysis. We evaluate our work as to whether the theory has been coherent and complete, whether it has met the test of empirical plausibility, and whether it provides useful insights into contemporary phenomena and policy proposals. We close by identifying some fruitful directions for future research into the maze of urban housing markets.

Note

1. For periods when we gathered data for our empirical analyses the term *SMSA* was employed. We thus use this term throughout, even though it has now been superseded by *MSA*.

2 The Economics of Urban Housing Markets: Previous Work and New Directions

In this chapter we briefly summarize the disparate strands of research on the economics of urban housing.[1] We do not provide here a detailed account of previous theories, methods, or empirical findings; where relevant this is done in later chapters for appropriate components of the literature. Rather, having sketched our theoretical framework and related empirical investigations in chapter 1, we now undertake to establish a general understanding of existing work with which our approach may be compared and its uniqueness and significance assessed.

The housing market literature may be conveniently categorized into six broad areas: the nature of housing, the nature of housing markets and submarkets, housing demand, the supply of new housing, supply from the existing housing stock, and housing market interaction models. Each is reviewed in turn, in conjunction with a comparison with the relevant portion of our approach.

2.1 The Nature of Housing

2.1.1 Services versus Attributes

The earliest theoretical work on urban housing markets established a tradition of viewing housing in terms of abstract, one-dimensional units of housing services (see Alonso 1964; Muth 1969; Olsen 1969; Mills 1972; Evans 1973; and Brown 1985).[2] While unobservable, these services presumably flowed from the capital embodied in the dwelling structure and the parcel on which it was located. In long-run equilibrium in a competitive housing market, a precise measure of the housing services embodied in a given dwelling would be its market value or rent (see Olsen 1969). Similarly, in the long run, capital is considered perfectly malleable in form and location. Such extreme simplification of the heterogeneity, durability, and fixity of housing were mandated in these studies in order to derive tractable analytic solutions to long-run household accessibility/residential space tradeoff problems in an idealized monocentric city model (see Straszheim; 1975: ch. 2; and Maclennan 1982: ch. 1).[3]

Kain and Quigley (1975: ch. 2) and Straszheim (1975: ch. 2) have established a position contrary to this "housing services" view. They argue that by abstracting from the complexity of the housing commodity one assumes away many of the important and interesting housing market phenomena. Preeminent here are the processes by which dwellings are chosen by households who have different preferences for various structural, land, neighborhood, and public service attributes, and those by which durable structures are maintained, converted, or abandoned in the medium run.[4] Kain, Quigley, and Straszheim see housing not as homogeneous "housing services" but as an irreducible "vector of attributes," with components describing the dwelling's structural, quantitative, and qualitative features, neighborhood attributes, public services, and accessibility. Unfortunately, the emphasis on an irreducible heterogeneity comes at the cost of circumscribing the types of precise analytical solutions that are obtainable and the types of empirical applications that are tractable. One response has been to treat either an aggregated grouping or a selected subject of individual housing attributes as if they were distinct commodities capable of being purchased separately in the market (see Straszheim 1975: ch. 4; Kain and Quigley 1975: chs. 9, 10; and King 1976, 1977).

The key issue here, of course, is the appropriate level of complexity for performing analytic derivations, generating hypotheses about urban housing markets that are both interesting and empirically testable, and illuminating hypotheses generated from other approaches. The aforementioned positions provide two extreme answers.[5] Subsequent studies have taken various intermediate positions. Several theoretical investigations stemming from the Alonso-Muth framework have attempted to relax one or more of their simplifying assumptions about the nature of housing, while preserving the ability to derive analytic solutions concerning the impacts on, for example, residential densities and location patterns caused by changes in urban populations, transport costs, or incomes. Some models allow for infinitely fixed and durable housing stocks that are never demolished or altered (see Anas 1978; Fujita 1976, 1982). Others allow replacement without depreciation (Wheaton 1982a) or both replacement and depreciation (Muth 1976; Brueckner 1980; Vousden 1980; Robsen 1982), but stock adjustments are undertaken by developers who are myopic insofar as they respond only to current market conditions. Still others assume perfect developer foresight, but at the cost of some other simplification regarding durability and malleability of housing (see Arnott 1980; Brueckner 1981; Wheaton 1982b; Fujita 1982). Few consider heterogeneity in even a cursory way; for example, Robsen (1982) allows dwellings to be arrayed by age and quality, while Brueckner (1983) specifies distinct attributes of floor and yard space.

Another set of studies in the Alonso-Muth tradition has focused less on obtaining analytic solutions and more on deriving rich specifications for econometric modeling of neighborhood amenities. They deal with the heterogeneity aspect by adding separable neighborhood amenity terms to the structure/housing services term in the household's utility function (see Harris, Tolley, and Harrell 1968; McDonald 1979; Diamond 1980a; MacRae 1982).[6]

Other approaches have considered the supply of housing from the existing stock in nonspatial contexts, yet in a fashion distinct from the Alonso-Muth framework. These studies make durability the cornerstone, but typically slight the dimensions of fixity and heterogeneity. Models describing housing stock modifications (e.g., Ozanne and Struyk 1976; Ingram and Oron 1977), depreciation (e.g., Chinloy 1980; Margolis 1981), demolition and abandonment (e.g., Bender 1979), and housing maintenance (e.g., Moorhouse 1972; Dildine and Massey 1974; Asmus and Iglarsh 1975; Mendelsohn 1977; Mayer 1981) overwhelmingly employ the notion of "housing services." Only Ingram and Oron (1977), Bender (1979), Galster (1981b), and Galster and Hesser (1982) consider the influence of neighborhood quality, while Galster (1981a, 1987: ch. 3) and Shefer (1986) model housing services as jointly produced by structural capital and neighborhood physical and social dimensions.

Clearly, there has been a great deal of inconsistency of theoretical treatment concerning the nature of housing. Models have different purposes and employing different frameworks have made different simplifying assumptions. The question of which simplifications are justifiable is basically an empirical one.

This desire to isolate empirically those dimensions of housing that should be considered separable elements of household utility functions has spawned innumerable empirical estimates based on *hedonic indexes*.[7] Basically, such indexes attempt to discern econometrically the *implicit prices* (or *hedonic values*) possessed by various attributes of the housing package.[8] This is accomplished by regressing dwelling value or rent on a vector of dwelling package attributes, thus producing the sought-after parameter estimates. Seminal estimates of hedonic indexes were conducted by Nourse (1963), Ridker and Henning (1967), Ball (1973), King and Mieszkowski (1973), Grether and Mieszkowski (1974), and Kain and Quigley (1975). Attempts to collapse attributes into a limited number of dimensions via factor analysis have been made by, for example, Kain and Quigley (1970), Witte, Sumka and Erekson (1979), Krumm (1980), and Johnson (1982). These hedonic studies have indicated that the structure/lot nexus itself may be decomposed into numerous constituents and that other attributes related to neighborhood, condition, racial composition, air pollution, public services and taxes, and accessibility carry significant implicit prices.[9] Although recently there has arisen considerable discussion over the interpretation of these hedonic index results (see Rosen 1974; Lucas 1975; Muellbauer 1974; Quigley 1979:402–3; Diamond and Smith 1985) and their appropriate functional form (see Linneman 1980; Halvorsen and Pollakowski 1981; Murray 1983a), there appears to be a consensus that the multidimensional heterogeneity of housing is an empirical reality to which modeling efforts must be sensitive. Our attempts to grapple with this reality are described in chapter 13.

2.1.2 Our Approach

In this book we take the peculiar nature of housing seriously by allowing it to affect both the modeled market structure and the supply and demand relationships. This is the persistent theme of the first theoretical sections of the book. We attempt to deal with the multidimensionality of the housing commodity by employing the hedonic index technique in a unique way: to use estimated hedonic values of attributes to array the housing stock along the single dimension of *quality.* Thus, unlike the "housing services" approach, we derive a metric that both explicitly recognizes the heterogeneity of housing and is independent of temporal changes in overall market prices. Unlike the multidimensional "attribute vector" approach, however, our measure is used for a functional reduction of complexity that permits rigorous analytical manipulations in a neoclassical framework. In the process of estimating a variety of hedonic indexes for this purpose, we also incidentally make several important contributions to the hedonic literature by testing for aggregation and specification biases and for appropriate functional form.

The fixity of housing is treated in our theoretical exposition by including locational dimensions like neighborhood amenities and accessibility as components of housing quality affecting both demand and supply behaviors. In our single-SMSA empirical model we explore in chapters 13 and 16, respectively, how such locational dimensions appropriately enter the hedonic equation (especially how they interact with structural attributes), and how they independently affect various types of discrete changes in the standing stock. Our cross-SMSA model is too aggregated to treat space explicitly, but in chapter 13 we investigate the econometric consequences for hedonic estimations that arise from omitting spatial variables.

Finally, our approach explicitly considers the durability of housing. Our theoretical specifications (chs. 4–7) embody it on both the demand and supply sides of the market. Durability undergirds the asset dimension of housing that affects the consumption/tenure-choice decision of demanders. Owner behavior that alters the quality of dwellings in the existing stock is emphasized, along with the different technological possibilities and costs for such modifications that arise from differing degrees of stock malleability. Both cross-SMSA and single-SMSA empirical specifications focus on estimating parameters of functions describing alternative modifying investments in existing housing stocks.

2.2 The Nature of Housing Markets and Submarkets

The heterogeneity, durability, and locational fixity of housing hold powerful implications for the conceptualization of the urban housing market. Specifically, "the" market can be pictured more fruitfully as a set of distinct but interrelated submarkets containing dwellings differentiated by one or several alternative dimensions. These submarkets arise due to the joint nature of structural and locational attributes and the inelastic demands for and short-run supplies of housing over significant time periods. If, for instance, the stock of dwellings and neighborhood attributes were fixed, the equilibrating competition by households could result in the creation of quasi-rents for packages in particular locations that need not conform to accessibility cost differentials between them. Alternatively, with inelastic demand the competition among suppliers can permit the creation of quasi-rents over various types of dwelling categories up to the costs of new construction or conversion (delimited by the transformation possibilities embodied in the existing stock), and during the gestation periods of such supply responses.

On the supply side, inelasticity reflects the fact that stock conversions and new construction respond only after significant lags, given the imperfect malleability of housing and the nontrivial planning/production/marketing time for new construction. On the demand side, inelasticity results inherently from the high cost of changing occupancy. Additional sources derive from households desiring radically different housing attribute packages, or from subsets of households being choice-restricted by market imperfections such as discrimination (see Ball and Kirwan 1977; Schnare and Struyk 1976; and Quigley 1979:393). Empirically, one implication of submarkets is that the price of a given housing package may diverge from that predicted solely in terms of its attributes. Packages in "tight" submarkets will have prices higher, packages in "loose" submarkets will have prices lower, than what is predicted solely in terms of attributes. So both attributes and submarket conditions are needed in order to predict prices.

2.2.1 Spatial versus Dwelling-Type Submarkets

There is some agreement among urban economists that housing submarkets of some sort should be adopted as a working hypothesis (see Quigley 1979:393, 420 and Maclennan 1982:26). There is less agreement, however, as to whether the more important empirical dimension over which submarkets should be specified is spatial or according to dwelling characteristics.

Several empirical studies employing hedonic indexes have investigated the variation of housing prices over space, but differ in their criteria for spatial disaggregation and, hence, in their conclusions. Straszheim (1975) and Goodman (1981) identified significant implicit attribute and package price differences between political jurisdictions in a metropolitan area, although Schnare and Struyk (1976) did not. Lapham (1971), Kain and Quigley (1975), Straszheim (1975), and Galster (1979) all found significant differences in hedonic regression coefficients across observations stratified by race or by ghetto/nonghetto locations.[10] Ball and Kirwan (1977) were unable to find price differentials across spatial clusters containing households and dwellings of common characteristics. Palm (1978) analyzed space in the context of "information-search areas" over which there would be both probable exchanges of information between realtors and housing searches by households.[11] No implicit price differences between black, Chicano, and house-value stratifications were identified.

The alternative, nonspatial view of submarkets traces its heritage to the seminal work of Grigsby (1963: ch. 2). He defined submarkets in terms of "close substitutability" of dwellings and attempted some preliminary empirical categorizations by formulating matrices of household moves. Several closely related theoretical models have been developed based on Grigsby's principle of market segmentation according to substitutability (see Sweeney 1974c, 1974a; Schall 1981; and Braid 1981). They specified an abstract housing commodity "hierarchy" or "chain system," wherein there is unanimous agreement that all units at a given level have an infinite negative cross-price elasticity with all other units at the level but a positive cross-price elasticity with units in adjacent levels. From this framework they proved several theorems concerning short- and long-run equilibria and the comparative statics of the system. Grigsby's conceptualization has thus far stimulated no direct empirical investigations, although Johnson's (1982) work is closely related. He first used Q-factor analysis to group housing units according to similarity in thirteen variables, including package price of the unit and several structural, neighborhood, and jurisdictional attributes. The result was ten classes of dwellings that might be construed as submarkets (although Johnson does not claim this). He then estimated hedonic regressions for all ten classes and found different coefficient sets for each.

2.2.2 Our Approach

The approach we follow in this book is similar in spirit and fundamentally consistent with the theoretical treatments of Grigsby (1963), Sweeney (1974c, 1974a), Schall (1981), and Braid (1981). We go beyond them in two important ways, however. Initially, we not only posit housing market segmentation by substitutability as a principle, but suggest (in ch. 3) its reasonableness by grounding it in the underlying behaviors of households and suppliers and in housing technological supply constraints. Second, we develop for the first time an empirical method for operationally segmenting the urban housing market based on this principle (i.e., quality level as defined by a hedonic index), and actually perform such a partitioning in both a cross-SMSA and single-SMSA context. For the latter we then compare both quality level and spatial formulations of submarkets to see which is more robust. These explorations are described in detail in chapter 13.

2.3 Housing Demand

Urban economic literature on housing demand can be categorized into four general groups: models of the demand for housing services, the demand for individual attributes of the housing package, the demand for owner-occupancy, and demand as expressed by the spatial allocation of households.[12] Each is considered briefly in turn.

2.3.1 Demand for Housing Services

This approach, as applied to empirical models of demand, typically consists of regressing housing expenditures (a proxy for services) on measures of prices of housing services and nonhousing commodities, income, and demographic characteristics designed to capture preferences. A large number of studies have employed this basic approach, with numerous variants designed to improve upon earlier work. (For comprehensive reviews see DeLeeuw 1976; Quigley 1979:396–99; Mayo 1981; and Maclennan 1982:49–54.) The sources of disparity in these studies' empirical estimates can be traced to aggregation biases, measurement or specification errors, and sample selectivity (see Kent 1983).

Studies employing observations of individual households have, for example, obtained estimates of income and price elasticities considerably lower than those employing aggregate data. Attempts at reconciling these results generally have revolved around analyses of the omission or improper measurement of housing prices (Polinsky 1977, 1979; Polinsky and Ellwood 1979) and permanent income (Mayo 1981), but arguably are not completely convincing (Kain and Quigley 1975:171; Goodman and Kawai 1982).[13] To correct the measurement and specification errors identified in these critiques, a variety of techniques have been put forward for the measurement of both housing prices and permanent income. (For recent reviews and examples see Mayo 1981; Ihlanfeldt 1981; Goodman and Kawai 1982; and Cameron 1986.)

Several other issues concerning the specification of models using properly measured variables have arisen as well. Vaughn (1976) has noted that housing prices are jointly determined by demand and supply, so single-equation demand functions are likely to be subject to simultaneous-equations bias. MacRae and Turner (1981) have argued that ignoring the tax treatment of owner-occupied housing biases income elasticity measures upward, since increasing income not only directly augments purchasing power but also indirectly lowers the price of housing by reducing tax liabilities. Hamilton (1982) has demonstrated that, if there are differences in the present values of local public services and property taxes, those will be capitalized into house values and will yield lower estimates of income elasticities from models that employ such values as dependent variables. Finally, Kent (1983) and Gillingham and Hagemann (1983) have shown how models ignoring the choice of tenure made in conjunction with the choice of quality of housing produce upwardly biased results for income and price elasticities.

As for the problem of sample selectivity, several authors have questioned the notion implicit in the above studies that there is a single income or price elasticity of demand that is meaningful for all groups or over all periods of temporal adjustment. One form of empirical manifestation of this challenge has been the estimation of linear-expenditure systems based on implicit utility functions that allow elasticities to vary at different price and income levels[14] (see, e.g., Barton and Olsen 1976; Friedman and Weinberg 1981; MacRae and Turner 1981; and Andrikopoulos and Brox 1984). Another form has been to estimate conventional demand functions over samples stratified according to income and demographic criteria (see, e.g., Hanushek and Quigley 1979, 1982; and Gillingham and Hagemann 1983). A third form has criticized the equilibrium assumption implicit in the conventional approach (see Maclennan 1982: ch. 2) and has focused attention only on those households who have moved recently and thus are arguably closer to equilibrium (see, e.g., Aaron 1975; Roistacher 1977; and Hanushek and Quigley 1979, 1982). There remains disagreement, however, as to whether measured income elasticities are appreciably different between equilibrium and disequilibrium household subsamples (see Goodman and Kawai 1984; and Dynarski 1985). Yet another approach has been proposed by Harrington (1989), who shows that a lifetime intertemporal approach to housing demand yields a constellation of relevant intertemporal price parameters. Thus, he argues, the price elasticity as conventionally measured misrepresents households' true responses to changes in price.

The net result of the very considerable body of research alluded to above appears to be a consensus that, overall, housing demand elasticities with respect to price,[15] current income, and permanent income are significantly less than one in absolute value, with elasticities for permanent income considerably higher than for current income (see Quigley 1979: 396–99; Mayo 1981; and Harmon 1988). In addition, however, there is convincing evidence that all these elasticities vary significantly across different tenure, income, and demographic groups and that there are significant lags in the adjustments of households to changes in income or housing prices.

2.3.2 Demand for Individual Housing Attributes

The second approach to modeling housing demand follows from the notion of housing as described by a "vector of attributes" instead of a unidimensional metric of "services." Three distinct types of empirical investigations have ensued from this view.[16]

The first type uses hedonic regressions estimated over a metropolitan housing market to derive implicit (price) weights for the various attributes of housing packages. These weights are then used to collapse the wide array of attributes into four conceptually coherent and exhaustive "bundles": dwelling quality, interior space, exterior space, and neighborhood quality. Quantities embodied in the bundles consumed by individual households enter as dependent variables that are then regressed on household socioeconomic and demographic characteristics. In the Kain and Quigley formulation (1975: chs. 9, 10), prices of these bundles were assumed to be constant over the metropolitan area; in the King (1976, 1977) formulation they varied and were estimated by spatially-stratified hedonic indexes. Results of these studies indicated significant differences in income elasticities among various components of the housing package, systematic substitutions between housing attributes and nonhousing goods and among different attributes, and an attribute demand response to intermarket variations in their prices. Two more recent studies of this type produced somewhat divergent results. Bajic (1984) estimated a system of expenditure share equations for four composite housing attributes (structure characteristics, accessibility, lot size, and a proxy for neighborhood quality) employing an indirect translog utility function. He found that all four attributes were own-price elastic and fairly good substitutes. Parsons (1986) estimated on Almost Ideal Demand System for a slightly different four-attribute grouping (size, features, structure quality, and neighborhood quality). He concluded that the demand for these attributes was own-price inelastic.

The second type of study, while closely related to the first, is distinguished by a focus on particular subsets of individual housing attributes and by alternative specification and estimation of attribute prices. Straszheim (1975: ch. 4) and Quigley (1976, 1983) estimated intrametropolitan price variations that arise from household-specific work-site locations. These were then employed to estimate demands for various individual attributes: rooms, lot size, single-family homes (Straszheim), and a polytomous vector of discrete structure types (Quigley). Nelson (1978), Harrison and Rubinfeld (1978), Witte, Sumka and Erekson (1979), Linneman (1981), and Blomquist and Worley (1981) estimated nonlinear hedonic indexes that held the implication that implicit attribute prices varied across households according to quantities consumed. These prices were calculated for each household observation/attribute combination and used to estimate demand equations with robust cross-price elasticity effects among several attributes simultaneously.[17] Boehm (1982) considered the demands for dwelling size and quality contingent on the tenure choice. Besides conventional income, wealth and demographic measures, prices of large versus small units, and prices of high- versus low-quality units entered the two demand functions, respectively, but without any clear spatial referent or hedonically based origins. As with studies of the first type, these analyses have suggested that household demands for housing attributes are differentially responsive to income changes and to price variations in not only the given attribute but in substitute and complement attributes as well.

The third type of study, represented by Wheaton (1977) and Galster (1977,

1979), takes quite a different tack. This type extends the Alonso-Muth approach by considering bid-rent functions for a fixed, heterogeneous stock in the short run, instead of for a perfectly malleable, homogeneous stock in the long run. If households reside tolerably close to short-run equilibrium in a metropolitan market with a given housing stock, it follows from bid-rent theory that those with the same incomes, preferences, and work places will achieve comparable utility levels, even though they consume different vectors of housing attributes and pay different total housing prices. Relating the observed variations in these prices and attributes consumed for such a homogeneous group should thus reveal the group's implicit bid or demand for each attribute. Wheaton and Galster analytically derived various forms of estimating equations (corresponding to different possible utility functions) wherein income, commuting costs, and individual housing attributes were independent variables and annual housing expenditure was the dependent variable. Regressions for different household preference groups produced coefficients interpretable as utility function parameters for individual attributes.[18] Intergroup comparisons revealed, as before, important demand differences between income, life cycle, and racial classes. No estimates of income, own-price, or cross-price elasticities can be made with this approach, however. More recently, Gross (1988) used a similar bid-rent model to estimate households' willingness to pay for marginal changes in various housing attributes, the corresponding demand prices, and the probability of occupancy by different household groups. His parameter estimates differed significantly from those yielded by a utility-maximizing model. He concluded, however, that the stochastic element in the bid-rent function (due to variable specification problems and aggregation errors) may in the end be so large as to render such models ineffective.

2.3.3 Demand for Owner-Occupancy

The tenure-choice dimension of housing has received a great deal of attention in the literature. Early empirical work estimated the probability of homeownership purely as a function of household economic and demographic characteristics (see, e.g., Kain and Quigley 1972; Birnbaum and Weston 1974; McDonald 1979). Subsequent treatments have stressed the impotance of cross-tenure price differentials, especially as affected by federal fiscal and monetary policies (see, e.g., Struyk 1976; Rosen 1979a, 1979b; Brueggeman and Peiser 1979; Rosen and Rosen 1980; Hendershott 1980; and Dhrymes 1983). The effects of inflationary expectations on homeownership have been explored by, for example, Diamond (1980b), Ranney (1981), Boehm and McKenzie (1982), Follain (1982), Schwab (1982), Wheaton (1985), and Goodwin (1986). Recent developments have stressed the joint nature of the choice of housing quantity and tenure, and its implications for empirical specifications (see, e.g., Lee and Trost 1978; Boehm 1981, 1982; Gillingham and

Hagemann 1983; Rothenberg 1983; Kent 1983; Henderson 1985; Linneman 1985; Goodman 1988; Henderson and Ioannides 1983, 1989; and Börsch-Supan and Pollakowski 1990). Yet another approach has concentrated on the portfolio choice aspects of the tenure decision (see, e.g., Plaut 1987 and Haurin and Lee 1989). The consistent empirical findings of these studies have been that tenure choice is influenced not only by the household's income-wealth and life-cycle stage, but by taxes, interest rates, inflationary expectations, and other factors that alter relative tenure prices.

2.3.4 Household Spatial Allocation

A distinct approach to investigating housing demand is to investigate how households of various types distribute themselves over space and different housing types in response to market forces. Straszheim (1975: ch. 6) estimated for each of ten life-cycle stage/racial/tenure household groups the median income of that group across various zones in the San Francisco Bay area, as a function of the zone's housing stock age, average lot size, educational quality, employment access, racial composition, and (endogenous) price of a typical housing bundle. For virtually all groups he found prices and education to be significant, while lot size, housing age, access, and race were insignificant for owners' spatial distribution of income levels. Quite different results were obtained by Bradbury et al. (1977), who modeled 1960–70 changes in the resident population of three income groups in Boston SMSA zones as part of a larger simultaneous model that did not disaggregate by tenure.[19] Price changes (endogenous) proved of even modest significance only for the lowest income group, whereas (endogenous) vacancy rate changes were most important for the highest income group. Revealed preferences for lower density, newer, larger units with more bathrooms located in whiter zones with lower crime rates were directly related to income, but job accessibility was inversely so. Rabianski and Spitzer (1978) took a more aggregate approach and estimated a simultaneous model for cross-SMSA differences in occupancy of rented and owned dwellings.[20] Endogenous price elasticities were much higher than those obtained from studies cited in earlier sections employing only a single-equation model: -3.3 (renter) and -4.6 (owner) own-price, and 1.7 (renter) and 1.9 (owner) cross-price. Similarly, high income elasticities (especially for lower-income SMSAs) were found: 2.3 to 7.9 for owner stock and -3.6 to -7.2 for renter stock. (Of course these elasticities are not directly comparable to those in the demand for housing services section noted above because they deal with cross-tenure occupancy allocations and not quantities of housing consumed. In effect, they hold different things constant.) Adler (1987) argued that owner-occupiers have a higher demand for privacy than do renters. The spatial-distribution consequence of this difference is the familiar result that renters (on average) live closer to the city center than do owner-occupants—though it arises here for a new reason.

2.3.5 Our Approach

In contrast to previous studies of the demand for either housing services or particular housing attributes like unit size, location, or tenure, our approach deals with the household's dual choice of a tenure/quality submarket and an optimal attribute mix within that submarket, but concentrating on the former. That is, faced with a stock of heterogeneous owner- and renter-occupied dwellings arrayed according to our concept of quality, we posit the household choosing that submarket and attribute mix which yields the highest utility compared to the other polytomous alternatives. In this fashion we can consider both theoretically and empirically a rich set of potential responses to various prices: nonhousing prices, prices in the given tenure/quality submarket, prices in other quality submarkets of the same tenure, prices in other tenure submarkets, prices of different attributes. In our cross-SMSA empirical model (ch. 14) we estimate parameters of such aggregate household allocation functions in which all but the last of these prices are considered as endogenous in our simultaneous demand-supply system encompassing all submarkets. This model of demand is thus most similar to that of Rabianski and Spitzer (1978), although we consider household allocations over not only tenure but also quality-level submarkets. Our empirical model of conversion supply for a single SMSA (ch. 16) includes demand elements. Our explanatory specification includes prices of individual attributes as well as various submarket prices. Although the aggregate nature of our empirical modeling efforts precludes explicit treatment of portfolio, tax, and inflationary expectation effects on tenure choice, our theory (presented in ch. 4) does so rigorously.

2.4 The Supply of New Housing

In sections 2.4 and 2.5 we turn to studies concerning the supply side of the housing market. As in the case of demand, we consider in these sections studies that limit their focus to the topic of supplying either new or existing housing. More comprehensive treatments of supply and demand interactions are reviewed in section 2.6.

Aspects of the construction of new dwellings in metropolitan areas have been investigated in two quite different contexts: long-run equilibrium in a spatial model and medium-run adjustments abstracted from spatial considerations. Each is considered in turn.

2.4.1 Long-Run/Spatial Models

The first context centers on the seminal work of Muth (1969) and Mills (1972) that analytically derived expressions for the long-run equilibrium pattern of residential land use. Their common key assumptions were that (1) all households worked in the city center; (2) transportation was equally available at all locations; (3) housing could be expressed in terms of "housing service flows" that were produced by some function combining land and "nonland" (capital) inputs; (4) households chose sites based only on commuting costs and housing services consumed; and (5) all structures in the metropolitan area that provided such services were constructed at the same time.[21] The goal of these models was to explain the price, density, and spatial pattern of new residential development.

One of the key derivations generated in this body of work concerned the relationship between the price elasticity of housing services produced per unit of land and the elasticity of factor substitution between land and capital. An elasticity of substitution other than one implied that land/capital shares would vary with housing prices and thus that the density of housing should vary over space. The significance of the elasticity of substitution parameter in the theory has led to a large body of literature attempting to estimate its value empirically. Detailed reviews of these studies (see McDonald 1979: 77–88; Maclennan 1982: 101-2; and Grieson and Arnott 1983) and more recent work (Jackson, Johnson, and Kaserman 1984; Färe and Yoon 1985) suggest the likelihood of the estimate being somewhat less than unity.[22] This implies that, in response to lower land prices farther from the central city, the elasticity of housing services output per unit of land should increase with distance from the city center. This in turn means that as the urban population grows and land prices are bid up, relative residential densities should *increase* at more decentralized locations (i.e., "sprawl" should ensue).

Subsequent empirical work examining actual patterns of land prices and residential densities in metropolitan areas has produced evidence counter to the predictions derived from the above static models (see, e.g., Harrison and Kain 1974; and McDonald 1979: chs. 4, 8). In response, dynamic "vintage" models have been developed that replace the assumption of instantaneous/perfect malleability of housing with one in which particular dwellings are constructed during certain periods and housing service flows vary inversely with the age of the structure (see Muth 1973; Fisch 1977; Brueckner 1980). The numerous variants of these dynamic spatial models that have appeared differ primarily in their assumptions about the malleability and durability of dwellings, production technology, the endogeneity of depreciation, and the information available to builders.[23] It is beyond the scope of the present work to delve into the particular analytic results of these studies.

A notable recent advance in the formulation of long-run equilibrium spatial models has been provided by Brueckner (1983), who replaced "housing services" with distinct attributes of floor and yard space that can be supplied by developers in different proportions depending on household bids. He demonstrated theoretically that, as with the housing services approach, density should be inversely related to distance from city center. However, the behavior of floor and yard space is potentially more complex. Contemporaneous empirical work (Brueckner and Colwell 1983) in fact found floor space a nonincreasing function of distance, thus sharply contradicting the implications of the original Muth-Mills theoretical framework.[24]

2.4.2 Medium-Run/Nonspatial Models

DeLeeuw and Ekanem (1971) and Rabianski and Spitzer (1978) have attempted to estimate the supply of metropolitan rental housing using cross-SMSA data. Their formulations may be considered "medium run" since cross-SMSA differences in rents, input costs, incomes, and demographic factors arguably persist over relatively long periods. Thus, at a given moment, observed housing stocks should have been the result of accumulated supply responses to these nontransitory differentials. The specific empirical model of DeLeeuw and Ekanem (1971) involved the estimation of a reduced-form (combined supply-demand) equation between rents and prices of housing capital and operating inputs, number of households, real income, consumer prices, and vacancy rates. The solution of the estimated equation (assuming price and income elasticities of housing demand equaling unity in absolute value) implied very small supply elasticities with respect to rents, capital prices, and operating input prices. This study has, however, met with withering challenges on conceptual and empirical grounds (see Grieson 1973; Quigley 1979: 413; McDonald 1979: 85–88; and Follain 1979).[25]

Rabianski and Spitzer (1978) estimated a distinct rental supply function through simultaneous-equations techniques. The total rental stock in an SMSA was modeled as a function of (endogenous) median contract rents, the vacant rental stock, the population, and the number and median income of construction craft workers (their proxy for construction costs), all of which proved statistically significant and with the expected sign. The implied elasticity of supply with respect to median rents was 0.44. Of course, no attempt was made to adjust for quality differentials in rental stocks, so this estimate is highly suspect.

As part of their investigation cited above, Bradbury et al. (1977) analyzed decadal construction responses in various communities comprising the Boston SMSA. Their conceptual model posited supply elasticity as a function of the elasticity of supply of vacant land and the elasticity of substitution for land and capital. Empirical estimates confirmed that new construction supply elasticity varied with the availability of vacant land: from 0.87 in the outer suburbs to almost zero in the city of Boston, although, as with other studies, no controls for the quality of new construction were used. Nonprice (quantity) signals provided by vacancy rates and the intensity of competition by other land users also were inversely related to new construction responses, especially when considering single-family homes. Regressions estimating the fraction of construction represented by single-family units indicated an increasing rate of decline in this fraction associated with zones in which the ratio of vacant to total land area fell below 0.4.[26]

Two recent studies provide further support for the proposition that new construction supply elasticity is high. Stover (1986) estimated a cross-sectional translog cost function for single-family detached housing. His conclusion that the supply elasticity is infinite is consistent with the earlier findings (based on time series data) of Muth (1960) and Follain (1979). Smith (1989) formulated a nonspatial theoretical model of new construction supply response to an exogenous demand increase. Under somewhat restrictive assumptions, the model predicts that new construction would stimulate filtering and subsequent price adjustments until the original hedonic price level reemerged—once again, in effect, a horizontal supply curve.

2.4.3 Our Approach

In summary, past studies of new housing supply have demonstrated, in Quigley's (1979: 412) words, "relative lack of progress" compared to those dealing with housing demand. Most of the empirical difficulties can be traced to the unavailability of an unambiguous measure of the quantity/quality of housing constructed. Reliance on either market values or aggregate numbers of housing units built obscures relationships that are observable only if the bundle of attributes embodied by such units is considered. Our theoretical approach (in chs. 5 and 6) overcomes this shortcoming by positing how builders supply particular types of new dwellings in response to market revenues and construction costs associated with an array of alternative tenure/quality-level submarkets (and with attribute mix depending on relative attribute prices and costs). Not only the quantity of new units but also their tenure/quality distribution is thus modeled explicitly. In our more aggregate cross-SMSA empirical model (in ch. 15) we estimate parameters for functions describing the relative contributions made by new construction to five- and ten-year changes in the stocks of various tenure/quality submarkets.

2.5 Supply from the Existing Housing Stock

Being durable, the standing stock of housing is capable of supplying a continuing flow of useful attributes or services for many decades, depending on original building materials and the levels of structural maintenance undertaken by owners. Being modifiable, dwellings can also be converted so as to supply radically different sets of attributes and service levels.

2.5.1 Maintenance

Theoretical treatments of maintenance investigation have typically taken the "housing services" perspective for analytical tractability, though they have varied in their view of production technologies for these services.[27] Lowry (1960), Ingram and Kain (1973), Ingram and Oron (1977), Margolis (1981), and Mayer (1981) have developed optimal maintenance rules for landlord profit (or property value) maximization in a static context. Subsequent treatments using optimal control theory (e.g., Asmus and Iglarsh 1975) have derived the dynamic equivalent: maintain at all moments so that the discounted present value of all future rents gained from the marginal unit of maintenance equals the discounted value of the cost of that unit of maintenance.

Most theoretical investigations have applied these principles for absentee owners to the analysis of owner-occupants' maintenance behavior, that is, they have modeled owner-occupants as if they also were rate-of-return maximizers (see Winger 1973; Dildine and Massey 1974; Ozanne and Struyk 1976; and Segal 1980). Others have, however, recognized the dual investment-consumption role housing plays for owner-occupants and have modeled their maintenance decisions from a utility-maximizing standpoint (see Sweeney 1974b; Struyk 1976; Mendelsohn 1977; Galster 1981a, 1987: ch. 3). Such theoretical differentiation is appropriate, given the overwhelming empirical evidence indicating the superiority of owner-occupant over absentee-owner maintenance efforts (see Sternlieb 1966: 176, 227; Sternlieb and Burchell 1973: 306–8; Peterson et al. 1973: 46–47, 63; Schafer 1977; Mayer 1981; and Galster 1983).[28]

A variety of multivariate statistical analyses have tried to isolate characteristics of the dwelling, neighborhood, and owner which explain differences in maintenance investments (see Moorhouse 1972; Winger 1973; Mendelsohn 1977; Schafer 1977; Struyk and Soldo 1980; Chinloy 1980; Shear and Carpenter 1982; Galster and Hesser 1982; Myers 1984; and Galster 1987: ch. 9).[29] These studies have consistently found that intensity of maintenance was directly related to older frame structures, owner's income, nonelderly owners, and the degree to which the owner socially identified with others in the neighborhood. (For a more comprehensive critical review, see Galster 1987: ch. 9.)[30]

2.5.2 Quality Conversions

Ozanne and Struyk (1976), Ingram and Oron (1977), and Mayer (1981) have all developed similar static theoretical models for the optimal combination of operating inputs and more durable capital in the production of housing services from multiple-family rental dwellings.[31] Such models are relevant to the issue of conversions if the optimal choice involves significant capital changes, since it can then implicitly be considered as a discrete conversion in the quality level of the dwellings. Following up on the suggestions of Rothenberg (1978), Galster (1981a, 1987: ch. 3) developed a model that, unlike the above approaches, explicitly considered the distinct technological transformation possibilities as well as budgetary constraints associated with the upward or downward quality conversion options facing owner-occupants, as distinguished from the maintenance option.

Only a handful of multivariate studies have investigated empirically the issue of quality conversions, and little uniformity of results has occurred thus far.[32] Ozanne and Struyk (1976) used matched pairs of dwellings in a 1960–70 Boston sample to estimate changes in the flows of housing services from both owner-occupied and rental dwellings. Housing services embodied in dwellings were estimated with a rather crude hedonic index, and their supply prices were assumed to vary across spatial subdivisions in the metropolitan market. Conditional upon independent estimations of decadal changes in input prices, their estimated parameters suggested a quality conversion–price elasticity of 0.2 to 0.3 that was not significantly different across tenures. Quigley (1979: 417) has demonstrated, however, that these estimates are likely biased downward.

Several cross-sectional multivariate analyses have been conducted on the determinants of the likelihood of upgrading or rehabilitation expenditures on a given unit during a prior multiyear period. Galster (1981b), Shear and Carpenter (1982), Myers (1983), and Taub, Taylor, and Dunham (1984: ch. 6) examined single-family dwellings and found that several occupancy characteristics (higher education and income, rent in-movers, longer expected tenures, younger and larger families, those with greater social identification with neighbors) and structural characteristics (smaller homes fifteen to twenty-five years old but not more than thirty-five years old) were associated with higher probabilities of major alterations, additions, or quality improvements.[33] Mayer (1981, 1985) investigated structures containing one or more rental dwellings and found rehabilitation more likely for resident owners, buildings with initially poor exterior condition but sound mechanical system and structure, older buildings, and buildings in neighborhoods with solid public infrastructure, more white residents, but (surprisingly) more crime. Potepan (1989) modeled the household's demand for additional housing as a choice between moving and making improvements to its existing unit. He found that the probability of choosing to make improvements was positively associated with increases in current interests rates and negatively related to increases in household income. Particularly when fixed-rate mortgages predominate, this may explain why home-improvement booms tend to occurs in times of high interest rates and relatively slow economic growth.

Perhaps the most unsettled empirical issue here relates to the effect of neighborhood conditions on rehabilitation activity. The conventional wisdom that follows easily from the view of upgrading as an investment has been to posit a positive correlation here (see Grigsby 1963: ch. 6; Stegman 1972: 39; Goetze 1976, 1979; and Downs 1981: 16–17). But controlling for structure and owner characteristics, Mayer (1981, 1985), Galster (1981b), and Shear and Carpenter (1982) found the likelihood of upward quality conversions not to be significantly greater in neighborhoods with better housing conditions, lower densities, and less nonresidential land uses. Other, less rigorous studies suggested that both tenure and size of rental operation may affect the neighborhood condition/dwelling upgrading relationship. Sternlieb (1966: 93, 155, 223) and Sternlieb and Burchell (1973: 65–67), for example, found widespread opinions among tenement landlords that neighborhood problems were a significant inhibitor to property investments, whereas Ahlbrandt and Cunningham's (1979:159) survey revealed that only a small fraction of homeowners in deteriorating areas felt constrained by the neighborhood. Peterson et al. (1973: ch. 4) found that homeowners and small investors were more likely to rehabilitate and spent more doing so in higher-quality neighborhoods, but this pattern was reversed for large-scale landlords.[34] This is consistent with the evidence on large investors in slum areas gathered by Quinn et al. (1980). Still other researchers (Taub, Taylor, and Dunham 1984; Galster 1987: ch. 9) have found that current neighborhood conditions matter little for the housing investment decision compared to owners' expectations about the future of the area and the actions of other proximate property owners. The crucial importance of the availability of loans to finance apartment rehabilitation, and the relationship between such loans and the racial composition of the area, has been stressed by Mayer (1985). The relationship between housing-quality conversions and the quality of the surrounding neighborhood is thus probably not so straightforward or generalizable as predicted by existing theoretical models (see Galster 1981b). Yet, since none of the cross-sectional analyses above has used any explicit market-value-of-conversion variable, it remains unclear whether neighborhood variables serve as a proxy for this omitted factor or, alternatively, for (unmeasured) differences in deterioration of the given structures and thus in their "needs" for rehabilitation.

2.5.3 Housing Abandonment, Demolition, and Replacement

The abandonment (and possible demolition and subsequent replacement) of dwellings has been considered in a number of formal analytic models that, while primarily concerned with other aspects of the housing market, incidentally derive expressions for optimal dwelling lifetimes.[35] Of more interest to us here are models that focus directly on the abandonment-demolition-replacement process. Ingram and Kain (1973) and Bender (1979) have specified static optimization models for capital stock and lifetime of dwelling based on maximizing present values of net revenue streams, given exogenous depreciation rates and prices of housing services that are a function of neighborhood conditions.[36] Both models stress how fixed, imperfectly malleable capital may not be instantaneously adjusted to meet unanticipated changes in rents or in input costs. Bender (1979) has shown how abandonment of a structure without demolition/replacement by the owner can occur when the savings from property tax and operating cost avoidance exceeds the difference in present values of the optimal and current structure types, net of demolition costs.

Analogously, Bender (1979), Ingram and Oron (1977), and Arnott, Davidson, and Pines (1986) derived formal rules for optimal structural conversion, whether associated with demolition or not. They viewed the owner as constantly comparing the expected stream of net present values from the current structure with those from alternative structure types that the current structure might be replaced by or converted into. The replacement or conversion should occur when the difference in net present values between optimal and current structures exceeds transformation costs.

In their pathbreaking empirical study, Sternlieb and Burchell (1973: ch. 7) analyzed in a multivariate framework the predictors of abandonment in rental tenements. They found that high proportions of nonwhites in white-owned structures, deterioration and low socioeconomic status of adjacent areas, lack of any further mortgage responsibility, and, especially, property tax delinquency were directly related to the likelihood of abandonment. White's (1986) study of landlord housing abandonment in New York City also found the property tax to be a major determinant of abandonment rates. Bender's (1979) empirical model of cross-neighborhood abandonment levels employed a more limited set of variables, but found them directly related to median structural age, inversely related to large increases in median family income and the price of land, and only insignificantly inversely related to percentages of one-family structures and effective property tax rates. His results for private demolitions were the same for the area's average structural age and income growth, but were reversed for land price, single-family unit, and tax rate variables. Bradbury et al. (1977) specified separate 1960–70 net conversion-demolition equations for single-family, multifamily, and apartment units. Unlike in the above investigations, changes in vacancy rates, prices, and new private and public construction were considered endogenous. For all structure types, areas with greater proportions of deteriorating dwellings of the given type had much higher levels of losses (via demolition, abandonment, or conversion to another type). The stock built before 1960 was associated with net losses for single-family dwellings, but with net gains for higher density types. High and rising vacancy rates and new construction in areas with less vacant land contributed to net losses of single-family and multifamily units, presumably through demolition. Public housing construction led to losses in both multifamily and apartment segments.

Thus the limited evidence supports theoretical predictions. On the aggregate level, demolitions, abandonments, and structure-type replacement appear to be encouraged by factors serving as proxies for reduced gross revenues: lower dwelling prices, higher vacancies, intensified competition from new construction, and declining income levels of the neighborhood. The significant results for the age and condition of the existing stock suggest the importance of technological and cost factors. Finally, more disaggregate dimensions relating to the owner and tenant characteristics and to the tax status of the property also appear significant.[37]

2.5.4 Our Approach

The theoretical and empirical work in this book concentrates most heavily on the supply of housing from the existing stock. This is distinctive, for, as Smith, Rosen, and Fallis (1988) observe in their recent survey article, most microeconomic analysis of housing markets to date has made little or no distinction between this source of supply and new construction. Unlike previous treatments that take price per unit of housing services as either fixed at all levels of output or varied spatially, our theory posits the possibility of different implicit prices for bundles in different quality-level submarkets. We do not see a particular technology of supplying housing from the existing stock as invariant by structure type, age, or condition, as do most prior models. We emphasize the existence of a wide variety of technological transformation possibilities for structures with relevant subsets of these depending on the particular structure involved and on both the direction and magnitude of quality conversion being undertaken. Finally, instead of considering maintenance, quality conversions, and abandonment/replacement as distinct phenomena, we treat them as interactive components of an integral process of continuing housing management. In sum, our theory (in ch. 5) analyzes the various aspects of supply from the existing housing stock from the perspective of quality-level submarkets. The owner's operating and investment decisions are seen as arising from a complex but tractable optimization calculus involving comparisons of alternative revenue and technological-cost possibilities for different transformational "destinations" across the spectrum of submarkets.

Our empirical work in the cross-SMSA formulation (in ch. 15) models medium-run stock adjustments in ten tenure/quality submarkets and the relative contributions in each made by net conversions versus new construction. Variables which serve as proxies for the aforementioned alternative submarket revenue potentialities and technical transformational cost constraints embodied in the existing stock are utilized. Our single-SMSA model (see ch. 16) focuses on discrete, particular forms of quality conversions, involving additions, alterations, and improvements. Given its disaggregated nature, this formulation employs not only variables describing locational and ownership characteristics but also the aforementioned revenue and cost proxies. These latter variables represent the main departure from previous specifications: the rates of return prospectively attainable from undertaking particular structural improvements (and thereby implicitly moving into different submarkets with different market conditions) serve as prime predictors of such improvements.

2.6 Housing Market Interaction Models

Up to this point our review has considered almost exclusively theoretical and empirical studies that have examined only one dimension of the housing market. In this section we examine the few attempts that have been made to take a more comprehensive view. We first consider "filtering" models that deal with the interrelationships among household demands, new construction, and changes in the existing housing stock. Next we examine computer simulation models that treat complex demand-supply interactions. Finally, we briefly note prior simultaneous-equation econometric models of the housing market that explicitly recognize market interactions and grapple with them empirically.

2.6.1 Filtering Models

Substantial disagreement surrounds the notion of filtering in the housing literature. It has been used to refer both to life-cycle processes of housing units (changes in their price, or quality, or income level of occupant) and to life-cycle processes of households (changes in the quality of their housing which result from changes in the real housing prices they face or in their real income levels). Empirical analyses of filtering have typically focused on one of these indicators of change, for example, housing price declines (Lowry 1960), turnover of dwellings through "vacancy chains" (Kristof 1965), or the mobility of individual households through the stock (Myers 1975).[38] Whatever the focus, rigorous filtering analysis necessarily involves a (perhaps implicit) partitioning of the housing market into several distinct segments among which households and existing dwellings move in interplay with new construction. Four notable efforts have been made in this regard.

Grigsby (1963: ch. 2) conceptually partitioned the housing stock according to degrees of household substitutability, that is, groups of dwellings were "linked" by patterns of household mobility. Mobility, in turn, was seen as leading to changes in market values and, in consequence, in structure quality as well. The empirical form of Grigsby's seminal conceptualization was a matrix relating characteristics of recent home purchasers to the characteristics of their homes. Unfortunately, this operationalization has little behavioral content since it tells nothing about potential alternative submarkets for household movers, about why some households moved and others did not, and perhaps most critically, about how prices, maintenance, conversions, and new construction responded to moves.

Smith (1964) provided a framework involving a simple algorithm for assigning households to dwellings, within which a resulting new construction response could be analyzed. He partitioned the stock by specifying five archetypical dwellings, one at each quality level. Five households differing only in income were allocated to this stock in such a way that the aggregate of their rental bids was maximized: the lowest income in the lowest-quality unit, the highest in the highest, and so on. New construction was introduced by the specification of a cost function and an economic value function that varied across quality levels of potential construction. The latter function showed the change in the aggregate value of household rents that would result from the introduction of a new home at each quality level, based on the (assumed increasing) incremental bids households were willing to make for units of higher quality. Smith posited new construction occurring whenever the economic value function exceeded the cost function, and at the quality level where such occurred. In this framework, deterioration of the stock was seen as progressively lowering the cost function until eventually replacement occurred, while increases in either population or incomes augmented the value function, thereby generating new construction and (in the case of higher incomes) rendering the lowest-quality existing units vacant. While adding more behavioral richness on the new construction side, Smith's approach does not consider endogenous price changes in the various quality levels and how these changes influence household reallocations, variations in the deterioration rates of existing units, and possibly quality-level conversions of the existing stock.[39] Also, this approach implicitly assumes that the total number of units is constant and that household formation is not affected by housing prices.

The model by Sweeney (1974a, 1974c) and the subsequent extensions by Braid (1981) and Schall (1981) attempted to remedy the above shortcomings. These authors have conceptualized the housing market as a number of mutually exclusive commodities organized in a hierarchy or chain wherein there is unanimous household agreement on the commodities' quality ranking. It was assumed that within each level of the hierarchy all dwellings were perfect substitutes, between adjacent (nonadjacent) levels cross-price elasticities of demand were positive (zero), and prices across levels were directly related to hierarchy rank. Demand for a dwelling at a given level was a function of household tastes and income, and prices in other levels. The rate at which the existing stock at a given level deteriorated was directly proportional to the number of dwellings at that level and varied inversely with the average time a household occupied a dwelling at that level, that is, these factors influenced owners' maintenance decisions. The number of dwellings at a level was determined by the net numbers of units moving into (out of) the level via deterioration from higher (to lower) quality levels, and by new construction (normally presumed to occur only if the level is above some minimum). Dwellings in (lowest-quality) levels that could not command positive prices in equilibrium were abandoned or demolished.

Within this framework,[40] these authors analytically proved a variety of propositions concerning the nature, existence, and uniqueness of short- and long-run equilibria and derived comparative-static expressions. Perhaps of most relevance for the filtering issue, Sweeney (1974a, 1974c) and Schall (1981) demonstrated how new construction may or may not reduce the real price of housing at lower quality levels, depending both on the levels at which new construction occurred and on the demand and supply elasticities in these "target" levels and in lower levels. Thus, the Sweeney-Braid-Schall approach offers a provocative, robust formulation of housing market interactions, although, as noted by Quigley (1979: 420), some key results depend on very strong and unrealistic assumptions.[41] Despite this, there is empirical evidence supporting the basic theoretical results of the commodity-hierarchy models (see, e.g., Weicher and Thibodeau 1988).

An approach incorporating location has been developed by Arnott, Davidson, and Pines (1986), who modeled structural density, housing demand, and the construction/maintenance/demolition decisions in an explicit "developer-oriented" model of the filtering process. Their density-gradient results are generally consistent with those of, for example, Brueckner (1981), but they found no association between construction quality and location in the stationary state.

2.6.2 Simulation Models

An alternative to the above analytic approach to modeling market interactions is the simulation model. Basically, here one attempts to (1) specify a closed model with theoretically sound behavioral functions and equilibrium conditions, (2) assign plausible values to parameters (either on the basis of independent estimates or preliminary "calibration runs" of the simulation), and then (3) solve the model using a computerized algorithm. Housing market interactions are qualitatively described by the behavioral equations, and simulated comparative quantitative outcomes are estimated by solving the model with alternative values of the exogenous variables. In contrast to analytic approaches, the simulation approach can be seen as an attempt to model more realistic, hence more complex relationships, but at the cost of lost generality of solutions and of high developmental and computational expense.[42]

It is beyond the scope of this chapter to review in detail the major housing market simulation models of Ohls (1975), the Urban Institute (UI), and the National Bureau of Economic Research (NBER).[43] We do, however, provide a cursory sketch of how they view housing submarkets, demand, supply, and price formation.

All three share the conceptual position that the market may be functionally partitioned into submarkets, each exhibiting independent behavior while at the same time being related to other submarkets. Operational views are more distinct. Ohls sees "quality levels" representing different flows of housing services, abstracted from spatial considerations. The UI model specifies a submarket as an interval in the rent distributions of dwellings for a given spatial zone defined such that the numbers of dwellings in each interval in the zone are equal. The average rent in each interval is divided by a zonal price index to indicate the quality of housing service flows (see DeLeeuw and Struyk 1975: ch. 4). The NBER model posits within each residence zone the possibility of dozens of different housing bundles, each distinguished by its combination of structural dimensions (number of units in structure, number of bedrooms, lot size) and of five neighborhood quality dimensions (see Ingram, Kain, and Ginn 1972: 135–41) and Ingram (1979: 153).

As for demand, the Ohls model has households (arrayed along a log-normal income distribution) who maximize utility by consuming an optimal quantity of housing services, given rents, incomes, and total expenditure on housing constrained to equal 20% of income. Analogously, in the UI model, utility is a function of housing services and nonhousing goods consumed, prices of housing versus nonhousing goods, and zonal measures of accessibility, neighborhood quality, and racial composition (the latter two being endogenous). Utility parameters and income distributions differ across four age/race household groups (see DeLeeuw and Struyk 1975: 22–26, 76–80). Unlike the Ohls and UI approaches, where all households can adjust their housing during each iteration, the NBER model constrains the number of movers to rates appropriate to each of numerous household groups defined by family size, income, education, and race and age of head, and augments their demands with those of new households and immigrants to the city. For each household class in the mover group, demand equations predict the probability that a type of household at a given work place will choose a particular bundle type, given the availability of the type and its zonal "minimum gross price" determined by interzonal comparisons of housing, transportation, and racial discrimination costs (see Ingram, Kain, and Ginn 1972: chs. 6, 8).

The supply of housing in submarkets in all these simulation models is affected by alterations in the existing stock and by new construction. The Ohls formulation has maintenance expenditure needed to keep a dwelling in a given quality bracket directly related to housing services provided and time spent in the bracket. Below this expenditure dwellings will depreciate, but no quality upgrading is allowed via higher maintenance expenditure levels. New construction costs are a linear function of services, and construction only occurs above certain minimum quality levels determined endogenously. Buildings in the lowest quality level have no economic value and are presumably abandoned. The UI model assumes that owners of existing units make price/quantity offers according to initial service flows from a dwelling, its depreciation rate, and the price elasticity of the particular dwelling type's supply function. Builders have a perfectly elastic supply function but are constrained to operate in idealized "zones of new construction" in suburban areas. Abandonment occurs if an owner cannot find an occupant at a price sufficient to cover variable operating costs (see DeLeeuw and Struyk 1975: 17–22, 38–39). In the NBER model, maintenance investments are determined by a step function based on the ratio of the change in expected market price (between current quality class and another) to the associated costs. Dwellings not receiving the minimum maintenance deteriorate. The existing stock can also be modified into alternative structure-type categories. New construction can occur for numerous types/qualities of dwellings. Both stock transformation and construction alternatives are ordered by a "profit rate" (based on the most efficient combination of inputs, their costs, and expected prices of dwelling outputs) that determines priority of supply response, subject to the constraints of land-use zoning, available zonal vacant land, and an upper limit of the total forecasted demand for the metropolitan area (see Ingram, Kain, and Ginn 1972: 109–22).

As for price determination, Ohls's algorithm begins by arbitrarily choosing a quality level below which no new construction will occur and guessing at long-run competitive equilibrium levels of construction and market rents at this level. From this point the prices, rents, and time periods for remaining in the level may be calculated sequentially for all quality levels, based on nine equilibrium conditions. The initial arbitrary choices are iterated until the model produces a solution wherein all households have a dwelling, and dwellings at the lowest quality level have zero price and command just enough rent to cover maintenance. By focusing on long-run equilibrium price relationships, the Ohls approach thus does not allow one to explore shorter-run dynamic adjustments, for example, to see how maintenance or construction at a given quality level may be altered by comparative profits at other levels.

The UI model theoretically determines price simultaneously through demand and supply interaction in each submarket. The fundamental construct is a price per unit of service/quantity of housing services diagram (see DeLeeuw and Struyk 1975: 17–31). For each household class a "new housing [transformed] indifference curve" is derived representing the locus of price/quantity combinations for existing dwellings providing a comparable level of utility to that provided by consuming the optimal newly constructed dwelling. The area below (inside) this curve represents price/quantity combinations preferred over such an optimal new dwelling. Supply curves for existing dwellings of various submarkets are presented in normal fashion, upsloping for all prices above that minimum price needed to keep a dwelling in the housing stock. Those segments of existing stock supply functions that intersect the above preferred area indicate the range over which the given household type will choose. The curve is tangent at its maximum point to the long-run new housing supply function. However, in the UI solution algorithm used, the steps actually employed do not match the simultaneous solution posited in theory. The algorithm first sets prices for all existing dwellings above the price for new construction, then turns to the dwelling of highest initial quality and moves along its supply function until an occupant is found. The process continues for all existing dwellings. Given this price vector, demanders and suppliers adjust and another iteration follows in like manner. Thus, much of the spirit of simultaneous competition between builders and owners in a given submarket and between owners in different, substitute submarkets is lost.

In the NBER specification, prices that allocate demanders among submarkets and determine supply responses are not current prices but rather expected prices for which a weighted average of previous period prices serves as proxy. Once the demand and supply algorithmic outputs have been determined, the market-clearing mechanism matches movers to available units (provided through depreciation, conversion, and construction) of the type chosen by them. Each house type and submarket is solved separately via a linear programming algorithm that also generates end-of-period prices to be used in the next iteration (see Ingram, Kain, and Ginn 1972: 123–28). Thus demand, supply, and price in both a given submarket and in substitute submarkets are not determined simultaneously in the NBER approach.

2.6.3 Simultaneous-Equation Econometric Models

Filtering theories and simulation models stress the interrelationships between demand and alternative forms of supply in the housing market. Yet surprisingly few *empirical* studies have recognized this connection and specified their econometric models appropriately. Conventional, single-equation models are faced with a dilemma. If on one hand they include prices, vacancies, or various supply adjustments as regressors, the coefficients of these variables will be either subject to simultaneous-equations bias or, at best, difficult to interpret in a reduced-form context. If, on the other hand, they exclude such variables, their model is subject to specification error from omitted-variables bias.

Avoidance of this dilemma sets four econometric studies apart.[44] Inasmuch as their results have already been cited at the appropriate point in the sections above, only their overall specification is noted here. Straszheim (1975) estimated a simultaneous-equation model wherein the short-run allocations of various household groups across housing submarket zones and household prices in these zones were endogenous. Bradbury et al. (1977) estimated a more complex medium-run model in which cross-zone decadal changes in three different income groups, new construction, and gross conversions of three structure types were predicted. Changes in zonal prices, vacancy rates, structural sizes, population densities, welfare and black populations, and public housing construction were all endogenous. Rabianski and Spitzer (1978) specified a three-equation cross-SMSA model for occupied and total housing stocks in both tenures, with endogenous prices and rents. Finally, Witte, Sumka, and Erekson (1979) estimated simultaneous equations for both short-run demand (bid) and supply (offer) functions for the attributes of dwelling quality, dwelling size, and lot size, with endogenous attribute prices varying across space.

2.6.4 Our Approach

Our model offers a quantum leap forward in both the theoretical and empirical understanding of complex interrelationships in housing markets. In summarizing his review of the housing economics literature, Quigley states:

> In part, [the] relative lack of progress can be traced to the real analytical difficulties encountered by the unobservability of a single hous-

ing quantity. . . . Our lack of understanding of supply phenomena is partly attributable to the difficulty in observing the behavior of decision makers at the micro level; that is, individual landlords, the physical components they offer on the market, and their gross rentals and investment strategies. Finally, this lack of progress may be attributed, in part, to the difficulty in conceptualizing the ways in which the various segments of the housing market interact to produce price incentives. (1979: 412)

Our work deals directly with each of these assessed shortcomings. Instead of trying to specify demand and supply for housing services, we (like Grigsby 1963; Sweeney 1974a, 1974c; Braid 1981; Schall 1981) consider it in terms of dwellings in particular tenure/quality-level submarkets that are linked on both demands and supply sides by various degrees of substitutability. Both in our theoretical treatments and in our single-SMSA modeling effort we examine the behaviors of individual market agents, especially focusing on particular investment strategies pursued by particular owners of particular dwelling types. Finally, our approach provides for a rich variety of interactions: among quality levels of a given tenure, across tenures, and among competing forms of supply from the existing stock as well as from new construction. These interactions are essentially similar to those described in the simulation models. Unlike the simulation approach, however, we do not rely on calibration runs, independent evidence, or educated guesses to establish key parameter values, but estimate them econometrically. Our cross-SMSA efforts in this regard follow in the spirit of Bradbury et al. (1977) and Rabianski and Spitzer (1978).

2.7 Conclusion

Our approach to understanding the maze of urban housing markets takes several new directions. We take seriously the peculiar nature of housing—its heterogeneity, locational fixity, and durability. The multidimensional aspect of housing (including locational components) is rendered tractable by our unique application of a hedonic index—to use the implicit weights demanders and suppliers place on housing attributes (represented by hedonic coefficients) to array the stock along a single dimension of quality. Durability is central to our theories of the demand for owner occupancy and of conversion supply from the existing stock.

We not only posit housing market segmentation by quality (and tenure) as a principle, but suggest its reasonableness by theoretically grounding it in the notion of degree of substitutability as seen from the perspective of both housing demanders and suppliers. Relative magnitudes of intersubmarket repercussions thus can be modeled in terms of degrees of substitutability among them. In addition, we operationalize our submarket concept by partitioning urban housing stocks using an econometrically estimated hedonic index, comparing the result with spatial submarket approaches, and develop a variety of cross-SMSA and single-SMSA demand and supply models to test the concept empirically.

Our theoretical and empirical efforts and modeling the array of demands across submarkets are distinguished by their attention to a wide set of potential responses to a wide set of prices: prices in the given tenure/quality submarket, prices in other quality submarkets of the same tenure, prices in other tenure submarkets, and prices of nonhousing commodities (as well as a theoretical treatment of attribute mix demand responding to implicit attribute prices). In our approach to the study of supply of new housing we focus not only on the aggregate amount of new construction, but also on its tenure/quality distribution, as guided by the prospective rates of return available to builders across the submarket array. We emphasize, however, the role that conversions of existing dwellings—both upward and downward in quality—play in the overall supply response. We allow considerable complexity in our model of supply response from the existing housing stock: revenue possibilities vary in a nonlinear fashion across submarkets, and transformation possibilities in individual units (i.e., conversion costs) vary by structure type, age, and initial quality level; a particular optimal transformation is indicated for each unit.

Finally, we emphasize that demanders and suppliers respond to exogenous market shocks, not only in immediate short-run impact adjustments but as further secondary waves of longer-run repercussions spread in ever-dampened magnitudes across the submarket array from the point of initial impact. We show why these waves have systematic yet significantly nonuniform characteristics, resulting from a complex variety of interactions among submarkets, demanders, and both builders of new housing and converters of existing housing. With this structured arena of interrelationships we illuminate in a new way an extremely rich set of phenomena in the maze of urban housing markets.

Notes

1. For other recent reviews of the urban housing literature, see Quigley 1979; McDonald 1979: ch. 1; Maclennan 1982: ch. 1; and Smith, Rosen, and Fallis 1988.

2. With the exception of Olsen 1969, this notion of housing was embedded in the framework of the neoclassical "bid-rent" model. This approach has variously been labeled the "New Urban Economics" (Richardson 1977) the "traditional" view (Kain and Quigley 1975), and the "utility-space" approach (McDonald 1979). For a detailed review of this approach, see Wheaton 1977.

3. In the case of Olsen 1969, it was needed so that direct analogies between the housing market and the purely competitive model could be made. These analogies are strained if neighborhood externalities and attributes of housing that are not produced by the private market (e.g., public services) are admitted.

4. More specifically, Kain, Quigley, and Straszheim attack the realism of the im-

plicit assumptions made in the housing services model: (*a*) non-CBD work places are irrelevant; (*b*) housing capital is perfectly malleable; (*c*) neighborhood effects and non-market producible attributes are unimportant; (*d*) equally priced dwellings are equally attractive to all households and all housing suppliers; and (*e*) market imperfections, such as racial discrimination and redlining, are unimportant. A complementary critique is provided by Maclennan 1982: ch. 1. See also Quigley 1979: 394–95.

5. Murray 1978 has argued that there is more similarity between these two positions than might at first appear. He claims the use of "housing services" is no less general than the "vector of attributes" approach, since both formulations require separability and either homothetic preferences or the absence of joint production of housing characteristics.

6. After a critique of the two positions and supporting empirical evidence, McDonald concludes: "it seems that we can assume that the goods housing capital, operating inputs, maintenance and the residential lot produce a single characteristic, which I shall call housing. Other characteristics associated with the choice of residential location such as public services, air pollution, etc., cannot be conveniently aggregated" (1979: 28–29).

7. Hedonic indexes have become a conventional tool in urban economics and have been utilized in a variety of ways; see Maclennan 1977.

8. Intellectual impetus for this conceptualization was provided by Lancaster 1966 and Rosen 1974; both theorized about consumer demands for underlying characteristics in complex commodities and the resultant "implicit markets" for attributes.

9. For a review of these findings of the hedonic literature, see Quigley 1979: 379–405.

10. The former three studies attribute the result to discrimination against blacks in the housing market. Galster 1979 suggests it may also be due to systematic interracial differences in housing preferences.

11. Operationally, Palm defined these areas as one or more counties.

12. We do not consider here highly abstract models of long-run demand for residential sites in an idealized Alonso-Muth context. They analyze considerably different questions than those with which we concern ourselves in this book. For a review of these studies, see McDonald 1979: chs. 1, 5.

13. The Polinsky-Ellwood argument has been contradicted by evidence from Goodman and Kawai 1982. Kain and Quigley 1975 provides some additional rationalizations not noted here.

14. For a fuller description of this approach based on Stone-Geary utility functions, see Mayo 1981.

15. Two other distinct approaches to estimating price elasticities have produced similar estimates. One employs housing production functions (see the review by Quigley 1979) and the other wage and rent gradients (Eberts and Gronberg 1982).

16. See Quigley 1979: 405–10 for a more detailed review.

17. Witte, Sumka, and Erekson estimated "bid-price" instead of "attribute quantity" functions and thus were not able to estimate price elasticities.

18. Diamond 1980a utilized a related approach based on bid-rent theory to estimate the demand for neighborhood amenities.

19. Gross structural conversion and new construction equations closed the model.

20. Stock supply equations and identities closed the model.

21. Or, equivalently, that all housing was costlessly and perfectly malleable and

households adjusted instantaneously. For a more detailed discussion of these models, see Wheaton 1979; Quigley 1979: 413–14; Maclennan 1982: 100–102.

22. A closely related strand of this literature attempts to derive estimates of the elasticity of supply of the stock of dwellings of a particular quality or type (see Grieson 1974; Smith 1976; Grieson and Arnott 1983). For example, assuming households are indifferent to density and the marginal construction cost curve is linear, Grieson 1974 and Grieson and Arnott 1983 compute an elasticity of supply of apartment buildings ranging from about 2 (for a thirty-six story structure) to 7 (for an eight-story structure).

23. As illustration, Anas 1978 and Fujita 1976, 1982 assume that, once built, dwellings do not deteriorate nor can they be replaced. Wheaton 1982a permits replacement but not depreciation. Muth 1976, Robsen 1982, and Brueckner 1980, 1981 allow both. Arnott 1980 models dwellings as instantaneously and costlessly adjustable to any size. Anas 1978, Fujita 1976, Brueckner 1980, and Wheaton 1982a assume builders are myopic; Arnott 1980, Brueckner 1981, Fujita 1982, and Wheaton 1982b assume they have perfect foresight.

24. For another critique of the appropriateness of the long-run/spatial model for examining new construction, see Maclennan 1982: 102.

25. Using identical data, Grieson 1973 showed how an alternative, equally reasonable structural model yielded much higher elasticities. Quigley 1979 noted how the interpretation of the income coefficient rested on the assumption that there were no systematic measurement errors associated with income in the estimate of rent for a standardized dwelling across SMSAs. McDonald 1979 demonstrated that the assumptions made by DeLeeuw and Ekanem to identify the supply elasticity are not consistent with their empirical findings; when these assumptions are relaxed, the results suggest a zero elasticity. Finally, Follain 1979 used a variety of variable definitions, functional forms, and estimation procedures in an attempt to replicate a DeLeeuw-Ekanem type model. He was unable to reject the hypothesis of a perfectly elastic housing supply function.

26. For a critique of the Bradbury et al. 1977 model, see Quigley 1977.

27. The simplest view has services produced by "sunk" capital (that depreciates) plus operating inputs. See, e.g., Ingram and Kain 1973; Dildine and Massey 1974. Ingram and Oron 1977 distinguishes between "structural" (nondepreciating) capital, "quality" (depreciable) capital, and operating inputs, all of which are structure type-specific. Galster (1981a, 1987: ch. 3) models output of owner-occupied units as a function of structural capital (augmented by maintenance), neighborhood physical conditions, and neighborhood social interaction. Ingram and Oron 1977 and Rydell 1976 have attempted empirical estimations of maintenance production functions and claim there is some limited substitutability between operating inputs and capital.

28. The lone dissenting study is Ozanne and Struyk 1976. Their method is criticized by Galster 1983.

29. Stegman 1972, Sternlieb 1966, Sternlieb and Burchell 1973, Peterson et al. 1973, and Birch et al. 1979 have provided some bivariate and impressionistic evidence related to maintenance.

30. Other studies of individual owners have also stressed the importance of "noneconomic" factors that are not easily incorporated into our theories, such as racial antagonism between tenant and landlord. See Sternlieb 1966: 163; Stegman 1972: 42–46; Peterson et al 1973: 51.

31. Ingram and Oron's treatment is more robust insofar as two types of dwelling

capital are specified, the production technology varies according to structure type, and budgetary constraints are made a function of cash flow/borrowing considerations.

32. Several studies have considered the current physical condition of a dwelling and have estimated predictive relationships for a variety of variables. See Ozanne and Struyk 1976 and Sternlieb and Burchell 1973. These studies are difficult to interpret in the context of either maintenance or conversions because they look at the net result of a process to which numerous alternative factors besides maintenance and conversion investments contribute. See Galster 1983.

33. Galster 1981b also estimated the expenditure on upgrading conditional on its being undertaken and found it was directly related to expected length of tenure, age of dwelling, and youth of household head.

34. Although Mayer 1981 did not distinguish owners with different sizes of holdings, he did control for resident ownership, owner living nearby, corporate ownership, and number of units in a given structure and found only the first to be statistically significant. For more on scale-of-operation impacts, see Stegman 1972: 42–46, 102.

35. In the context of spatial models, see Hufbauer and Severn 1974; Anas 1978; Brueckner 1980, 1981; Vousden 1980; and Wheaton 1982a; in a nonspatial context, see Dildine and Massey 1974 and Muth 1973.

36. Ingram and Kain 1973 views "structural [housing] services" as produced by capital and operating units. Bender 1979 views housing services as produced by capital and "quality" (density/unit land area), with maintenance (potentially) offsetting depreciation.

37. Some of these idiosyncratic aspects may be very difficult to model formally or to estimate empirically. Stegman 1972: ch. 5, for example, cites "catastrophic damages" inflicted on a dwelling by a "problem tenant" as a possible precursor of abandonment.

38. See Grigsby 1963, Davies 1978, and Myers 1983 for detailed reviews of alternative definitions and the history of the concept.

39. Also, the reasonableness of Smith's assumptions concerning household bids for incremental quality and his assumption that all housing is owned and produced by one firm have been challenged by Davies 1978 and Edel 1972, respectively.

40. Plus other simplifying assumptions that vary somewhat across Sweeney, Braid, and Schall. Braid 1981, for example, examines only very short-run quality-level price responses generated by exogenous shocks, before any endogenous supply responses are forthcoming.

41. Quigley 1979: 420 especially attacks the assumption that dwelling lifetime is an increasing function of each level's price.

42. See Ingram 1979: 131–32 for a fuller comparison.

43. For a detailed discussion see Davies 1978 and Ingram 1979. For major descriptions of the UI model see DeLeeuw and Struyk 1975. For the original NBER model see Ingram, Kain, and Ginn 1972; Kain and Apgar 1982 indicates subsequent modifications in the model. For a generalization and extension of the market-clearing mechanisms in the UI and NBER models, see Anderson 1984.

44. Besides those mentioned here, Ozanne and Thibodeau 1983 specifies a simultaneous equation model but ends up estimating only a reduced-form equation for housing prices.

Part One: The Theory of Urban Housing Markets and Submarkets

3 The Stratification of Urban Housing Markets

Our model gives great emphasis to the segmented nature of urban housing markets. In this chapter, we describe how this segmentation arises naturally from the distinctive nature of housing units and how it can be embedded in a housing market model.

We begin by developing the implications of heterogeneity in the housing stock for market structure and the meaning of housing quality. Next, we show how the hedonic index technique can be used to represent the multidimensional nature of housing in a theoretically and empirically tractable model. We conclude with a discussion of the meaning and proper definition of housing submarkets.

3.1 Heterogeneity, Stratification, and Quality

3.1.1 The Implications of Heterogeneity

Urban housing units differ profoundly over a great many dimensions which the choices of households suggest are essential elements of consumer choice in the market. Different households have different tastes for the various components of the housing package, and typically each household conducts an extensive (hence costly) search for a unit appropriate to its tastes and income. Suppliers, responding to these heterogeneous tastes, produce and offer housing which is equally heterogeneous. In short, there are compelling reasons for modifying the standard assumption of a homogeneous commodity in models of housing market behavior.

Before proceeding to a discussion of how the heterogeneity of housing units might best be comprehended in models of urban housing markets, it is important to reach a clear understanding about the dimensions of this heterogeneity. Housing structures (and the housing units they contain) differ from each other with respect to condition, architectural style and features, size, plumbing facilities, and the like. Households are quite sensitive to such differences among housing units, as evidenced by their willingness to pay for more of a desirable feature such as size. However, a housing unit does not consist solely of a collection of rooms within some structure. The quality of housing services it offers is also influenced by its accessibility to other relevant parts of the urban area; by the size, shape, topography, and so forth of the lot of land on which it sits; and by the character of (and level of public services provided in) its neighborhood. The meaning of heterogeneity in housing is thus distinct from the usual heterogeneous product case in that the dimensions of heterogeneity in housing include some factors external to the housing unit itself, factors not controlled by suppliers. In particular, the neighborhood and locational components of the housing package are at best chosen by suppliers only when they acquire or construct a particular unit; these components may subsequently change due entirely to forces external to the suppliers and their immediate neighbors. For a clear understanding of housing market processes, then, it is necessary to distinguish between changes in housing quality undertaken by a supplier in response to market forces and changes in quality resulting from forces beyond his control. Economic models are able to differentiate between these two types of quality change only if they deal explicitly with the multidimensional nature of housing.

Perhaps the most significant implication of heterogeneity for housing market modeling is that it is a source of segmentation in the housing market. Since housing units are so diverse, they can be expected to exhibit a full range of substitution relationships, from near-zero to near-perfect. As a consequence, the urban housing market is most accurately represented as a collection of distinct yet interrelated submarkets. These submarkets constitute a market structure within which the forces of demand and supply interact. Housing market events and government policy initiatives which impact one submarket will have their primary effects in that submarket, with secondary effects appearing in other submarkets to the extent those submarkets are linked in substitution possibilities with the original target submarket. Changes in the demand for mansions, for example, will have a decided impact on the market for mansions, a lesser effect on the market for more modest homes, and virtually no effect at all in the market for tenements. This segmentation by substitutability is reinforced by another implication of heterogeneity. The great diversity of housing packages and the importance of differences among them mean that the amount of information needed (and hence the cost of information) for a satisfactory market transaction is high for both buyers and sellers. This forces demanders and suppliers to limit their search to a portion of the housing market (presumably that portion containing close substitutes for the housing or customers they desire to find), ignoring other parts of the market. Clearly, an understanding of the dimensions of heterogeneity underlying information costs, neighborhood externalities, and market segmentation is essential to any explanation of the functioning of urban housing markets.

3.1.2 Representing the Multidimensional Nature of Housing

In order to produce a tractable and interesting model of housing markets, the number of different "commodities" defined must be reduced from the many thousands of individual housing units while still retaining the essential heterogeneity of the housing stock. An important first step in this process is to enumerate those characteristics which play a significant role in distinguishing among various units in the market. The characteristics which have *some* influence on supplier or demander decisions probably number in the hundreds, but many of these (such as architectural style) are difficult to quantify and/or have only a miniscule (or ambiguous) impact on the market evaluation of units.[1] Still, the list of all the characteristics with significant and unambiguous market values is quite a long one. Witness, for example, the records of local property tax assessors, in which it is not uncommon to find a hundred or more housing characteristics recorded, all of which are alleged to contribute to market value. Hence, even if the set of descriptive characteristics is reduced to include only those with a discernible impact on market prices of units, it is still a very large set. Classifying all units by these characteristics alone would result in a number of "commodities" much smaller than the total number of units but still far too large for a tractable model.

This multidimensional characterization of housing quality can, though, be modified to serve as a workable basis for a housing market model. While a hundred-dimensional quality measure offers little advantage over the wildly impractical "every unit a separate commodity" model, representing housing units in a few more generally defined dimensions (such as size and condition) is a more promising approach. Even if the number of dimensions is reduced, though, two serious flaws remain: the multidimensional approach fails to comprehend the quite common phenomenon of joint consumption and production of certain housing characteristics, nor does it provide a convenient means of incorporating the tradeoffs demanders and suppliers make *among* characteristics.

The tied nature of housing characteristics, a pervasive feature of housing, arises from both supply- and demand-side jointness. This is so simply because households seek units with *configurations* of characteristics, not just a random assortment of them. In other words, many components of housing are complements; it is no accident, for example, that units with many rooms tend also to have multiple bathrooms. Thus, insofar as the multidimensional approach gives the impression that each possible combination of characteristics is equally likely to appear, it gives a misleading description of market conditions.

Furthermore, since in the multidimensional approach each dimension of the housing package is represented separately, there is no natural way to represent within it the cost and utility tradeoffs among characteristics made by market participants. To comprehend the substitution possibilities which determine the fate of both housing units and households in the market, an economic model must incorporate these tradeoffs. The multidimensional approach is unpromising in this regard, as in it each dimension implicitly has equal weight (which is hardly likely in the market).

3.1.3 The Meaning (and Measurement) of Housing Quality

The heterogeneity of housing also has important implications for the definition and measurement of housing quality. The quality of a housing unit is generally thought of as a transitive measure of that unit's essential character—its "goodness" or "badness," so to speak. Not only is this definition vague, but in a housing market with nonidentical buyers and sellers, such a measure cannot exist! The problem of aggregating the separate orderings of units arising from the heterogeneous preferences and costs (across characteristics) of individual market participants into a common, marketwide ordering is formally identical to the aggregation of individual utility functions into a social welfare function. Given heterogeneity of housing units, costs, and preferences, no aggregate ordering can reasonably be expected to correspond to the orderings of particular individuals. However, for economic modeling and public policy evaluation, just such an ordering—a transitive, monotonic representation of a unit's essential character or substitutive distance from other units—is needed. Accordingly, students of housing markets have devised a number of empirical approximations to meet this need. These measures are descriptive of market aggregates rather than the tradeoffs or welfare of individual households.[2] Marketwide measures of housing quality are thus bold, heroic constructs of model builders and policy planners. They do not arise naturally from the market process.

Quality measures commonly used in public policy discussions are of three basic types: market prices or rents; vectors of housing characteristics, with each characteristic carrying independent weight; and amounts of individual structure characteristics, such as structural conditions or presence of plumbing facilities. Each of these fails to represent accurately the market's evaluation of housing quality. The use of condition (or any other single characteristic) is the most obvious case. While condition has intuitive appeal as a quality measure, it is clearly inadequate for a heterogeneous housing stock since it represents only one of the many market-relevant aspects of housing quality. It is thus inherently incapable of representing either the jointness (e.g., with neighborhood characteristics or age of structure) or the market tradeoffs of condition with other housing characteristics. Vectors of characteristics are somewhat better since they explicitly recognize—at least to some extent—the heterogeneity of housing. However, since characteristic combinations are not constrained in the vector approach, jointness is ignored. Furthermore, since amounts of each characteristic implicitly carry equal weighting,[3] vectors provide an inadequate and misleading representation of the market tradeoffs among the included features (and an even more unsatisfactory treatment of those characteristics excluded from the vector). Market prices are inadequate quality measures because they do not classify housing units consistently over time. Prices may change due to exogenous events unrelated to the units' characteristics. In sum, the traditional approaches to measuring housing quality ignore some of the most important and unique features of housing markets and thus are seriously deficient.

3.1.4 The Hedonic Index: A Solution

Whether a housing-quality measure is needed for policy evaluation or to aid in understanding the interrelationships among the different submarkets in a housing market, the arguments of the preceding pages suggest that its definition should comprehend and incorporate the heterogeneity of housing units. Such a definition could, in principle, be arrived at in a number of ways, and there is nothing intrinsic to the notion of quality (as a market aggregate) which suggests that one of these ways is superior to the others. Each requires acts of faith, assumptions about how housing quality is defined, perceived, and agreed upon by participants in housing markets. For an economist, the natural choice among these is to assume the existence of a reasonably competitive market for reasonably quantifiable characteristics of housing units. Under appropriate and conventional (to economists) assumptions about the workings of such a market, it can (and shortly will) be shown that there exists a single-valued transitive function which translates the characteristics of a given unit into an index of overall quality. Using this function, housing units can be ordered along a continuum by degrees of sustitutability. Segmentation of the housing market can thus be represented (and, indeed, defined) by differences in the index, which is to say that the model can use the index to give consistent empirical meaning to the concept of segmentation. On the policy side, this same function can be used to create a hierarchical ordering of housing units according to their values of the index.[4]

The function in question is, of course, a hedonic index. As we demonstrate in the next section, equilibrium in a competitive housing market implies the existence of a relationship between market prices (or rents) of housing units and the characteristics of those units, that is,

$$p(H) = p(h_1, \ldots, h_n), \tag{3.1}$$

where $p(H)$ is the market value of a unit with characteristics $H = (h_1, \ldots h_n)$. This relationship reflects marginal tradeoffs on both sides of the market, so that (in the neighborhood of equilibrium) $\partial p(H)/\partial h_i$ equals both the marginal bid price of demanders and the marginal offer price of suppliers for housing characteristic h_i. Thus, at or near equilibrium, the prices and characteristics of housing units contain the information necessary to determine implicit prices of individual characteristics. These implicit prices can be used in turn to define a function (the hedonic index) which translates a vector of housing characteristics into a scalar representation of the overall quality perceived by the market for that bundle of characteristics.

The basic assumption of the hedonic method is that the vast number of individual models or versions of any commodity available in the market can accurately be characterized by a considerably smaller number of attributes or characteristics. Economists were originally attracted to this approach by its potential for studying technical change, since many (though not all) product changes may be viewed as producing not a new product but rather a new combination of the "old" characteristics. This representation of change has the obvious advantage that it greatly reduces the number of "commodities" which must be studied. The applicability of the hedonic concept to housing markets should be evident from the previous discussion. Housing is a prime example of a commodity whose individual units are greatly differentiated along identifiable dimensions (characteristics).

The hedonic technique has been available for a long time—indeed, the classic paper (Court 1939) is now more than a half-century old. However, current use of hedonic indexes really began in 1962, when the first of many papers using the technique to study the behavior over time of automobile prices (and those of other consumer durables) appeared.[5] These papers were intended primarily to provide a means for correcting price indexes of consumer durables for quality change. Applications of the hedonic approach to housing markets are in general much less concerned with price indexes and much more with housing quality itself; this literature is summarized and reviewed in chapter 2.

The hedonic approach has two significant advantages over alternative methods of measuring quality and defining commodities in housing markets. First, compressing the many characteristics of housing into one dimension allows the use of the homogeneous commodity assumption, with housing *quality* (and not particular characteristics of housing units) as the basis of measurement. Housing units differ from each other in this model not in several dimensions but only in the amount of housing quality they possess. Thus the hedonic construction avoids the complications and intractability of multicommodity models. Also, in doing so it retains and meaningfully comprehends the great heterogeneity of housing units. Since the hedonic index is in fact a composite of the many individual characteristics of units, it is sensitive to variations in any of these characteristics. Furthermore, the hedonic index reflects the marginal tradeoffs both suppliers and demanders make among characteristics in the market, so that differences in amounts of particular components will be given the weights implicitly prevailing in the marketplace. In short, the hedonic index of housing quality defines the "commodity" in housing markets in a way that makes economic analysis of such markets both possible and interesting. As an index of housing quality, it is free of the defects common to the other measures discussed above.

3.2 Hedonic Indexes and Housing Markets: Theory

In this section, we articulate the theoretical basis for the use of hedonic indexes to parameterize in one dimension differences in quality among differentiated housing units.

As it happens, the interpretation of hedonic indexes was for a time a controversial subject in the literature. Three distinct interpretations of the coefficients of the hedonic equation have been advanced: that hedonic indexes are basically a reflection of consumer preferences; that the coefficients arise from supply and cost conditions; and that the index arises from the market-clearing process and so reflects *both* supply and demand. We demonstrate that it is the third interpretation which is correct.

The derivation of hedonic indexes from household utility maximization was for many years the interpretation favored by most authors. The consumer-theory approach was a natural one given the preponderant use of hedonic indexes as a means of decomposing observed price changes into a "quality" component and a "pure price" component. Households, it was argued, purchase consumer durables not for final consumption but rather to provide a capital stock for their production of various services—housing services, for example. Under the assumption that the consumer capital good is completely represented by the specified characteristics, several authors have shown that in consumer equilibrium a hedonic-like relationship exists between durable goods prices and the quantity of each discrete characteristic, the weights (first derivatives of the hedonic relationship) being proportional to the marginal utilities of the various characteristics.[6] A related but distinct approach was developed by Houthakker (1951),[7] in which the household is assumed to face (as a price taker) a fixed tariff schedule. Under this assumption, the household's equilibrium can be shown to imply the existence of a hedonic relationship, with the coefficients again proportional to the relevant marginal utilities.[8] The demand interpretation of the index was implicitly assumed as the basis for the seminal Adelman and Griliches (1961) paper (which foreshadowed the hedonic revival of the early 1960s) and for many of the ensuing empirical studies.

An analogous hedonic relationship for suppliers can also be derived.[9] The difference is, of course, that when the problem is viewed as one of profit maximization by competitive firms, the weights (coefficients) are proportional to the relative marginal costs of producing the various embodied characteristics rather than the relative desirabilities of those components.[10] Otherwise, the derivation is essentially the same as that found in the consumer theory literature just discussed.

However, as Rosen (1974) and Lucas (1975) showed for hedonic indexes in general, *both* of these interpretations are valid at equilibrium; estimated hedonic indexes will not in general identify either demand or supply of the "product." The hedonic is, in effect, "a joint envelope of a family of value functions [of demanders] and another family of offer functions [of suppliers]" (Rosen 1974:44). In other words, the hedonic equation consists of the common (equilibrium) points of the value functions representing a particular utility map and budget constraint and the offer curves representing a given technology and set of factor prices. However, since *any* such envelope function is consistent with an infinitude of families of value and offer curves, the particular demand and supply functions giving rise to the equilibrium cannot be identified. In effect, then, the hedonic reveals a set of implicit characteristic prices which guide both buyers and sellers without exposing the underlying parameters of supply or demand.

In the remainder of this section, we derive the hedonic relationship in a competitive housing market[11] and discuss the consequences of our theoretical results. We assume that competition prevails among both buyers and sellers and that both buyers and sellers judge the utility and cost of housing units by the quantities of specified characteristics of those units. Sellers are presumed, then, to produce and offer housing units with the characteristics desired by buyers and to receive returns for doing so via a market mechanism. The hedonic index is shown to describe the terms under which transactions take place in this market.

In the derivations which follow, housing markets are in general assumed to conform to the standard competitive assumptions (exceptions are noted and discussed). While the applicability of certain of the standard assumptions remaining in the model is still subject to some question, these assumptions fit housing markets at least as well as they fit many other markets to which they are routinely applied. Consequently, the model which follows seems a reasonable description of housing market phenomena within the current state of the art of economic theory. One important assumption which *does* seem eminently reasonable in housing markets is that both buyers and sellers (in both rental and ownership markets) have zero weight in the market and thus are effectively price takers.

3.2.1 Initial Assumptions

Consider housing units as commodities which can be described as a vector of n characteristics,

$$H = (h_1, h_2, \ldots, h_n) \tag{3.2}$$

where each h_i is the amount of a particular housing characteristic such as floor space, condition, location, and so on. This defines a space in which each housing unit is identified by such a vector; transactions in housing units are thus seen as "tied sales" of bundles of characteristics. It is assumed that the vector $(h_1, \ldots, h_n)$ includes all attributes necessary to describe the housing unit completely and that each attribute is capable of objective measurement (though certainly households' subjective valuations of alternative combinations may differ). In addition, we assume that there exists a sufficient number of housing units on the market so that for all practical purposes choice among units (bundles) is continuous.[12] Finally, we abstract from the portfolio choice aspects of the housing decision by assuming that housing is purely a consumption good.[13]

Quoted market prices[14] for housing units implicitly define a function $p(H) = p(h_1, \ldots h_n)$ which relates these prices to particular bundles of characteristics. This function is, in effect, the hedonic relationship arrived at by households as they comparison shop the various units offered in the market. The $p(H)$ function indicates the *minimum* price found in the market for a given bundle of h_i's, since under competitive conditions buyers will have no reason to distinguish a particular seller's unit of given characteristics from any other unit having those characteristics and will therefore search only for the seller offering the lowest price. At the same time, sellers (assumed to be atomistic) will treat $p(H)$ as a parameter in their decision making, so they will not offer the bundle of characteristics $(h_1, \ldots, h_n)$ at any price below $p(h_1, \ldots, h_n)$. Consequently, $p(H)$, the set of market-clearing prices, will be determined as market-clearing prices usually are—by the distribution of substitution and transformation possibilities on the two sides of the market.

For the analysis which follows, we adopt the convention of measuring all h_i so that consumers would rather have more of them than less (i.e., they are "goods" rather than "bads"). Further, we assume that increasing the amount of any h_i will require additional resources. For these reasons, all the first partials of $p(h_1, \ldots, h_n)$ must be positive. The second derivatives of $p(H)$ are also assumed to exist and to be continuous.

Before proceeding to the detailed analysis, it should be noted that $p(H)$ is unlikely to be linear, that is, that the h_i may affect p interactively as well as separately. Intuitively, nonlinearity is likely because tastes and technology limit the market-relevant values of any one characteristic given a particular combination of the others. For consumers, tastes involve *configurations* of attributes, not simply collections; for suppliers, production of attributes is to a large extent joint, not separate. Linearity of $p(H)$ would be a surprise under these conditions. Nonlinearity, though, complicates some parts of the analysis (as will be seen shortly).

3.2.2 Household Equilibrium

Under the assumption that each household rents/buys one and only one housing unit at a time (certainly true for the vast majority of households), the household's utility function can be written in the usual way:

$$U = U(Z,H) \equiv U(Z, h_1, \ldots, h_n), \tag{3.3}$$

where U is assumed to be strictly concave (in addition to the other usual properties), and Z is the quantity of all other goods consumed. Following the usual convention, let Z be the numéraire, so income (Y) can be written

$$(3.4) \qquad Y = Z + p(H) \equiv Z + p(h_1, \ldots, h_n).$$

Utility maximization is achieved when a combination of Z and H meeting both the (nonlinear) budget constraint and the first-order conditions,

$$(3.5) \qquad \partial p / \partial h_i \equiv p_i(H) = U_{h_i} / U_z, \; i = 1, \ldots, n,$$

is selected. In other words, the household chooses a unit with the combination of characteristics that yields it the greatest satisfaction given its income and its relative tastes for each characteristic and for Z. Second-order conditions for utility maximization follow from the conventional assumptions about U, provided only that $p(H)$ is not sufficiently concave.[15]

Given the household's budget constraint and utility function, it is possible to derive a bid function for housing analogous to the bid function for urban land used in the Alonso (1964) model and its offshoots. This function $B(H, U, Y) = B(h_1, \ldots, h_n; \bar{u}, Y)$ is defined so that

$$(3.6) \qquad U(Y - B; h_1, \ldots, h_n) = \bar{u}.$$

That is, $\bar{u}$ is the utility level of the household when it spends B of its income to get housing with characteristics $(h_1, \ldots, h_n)$ and the remaining $(Y - B)$ on Z. This definition in equation (3.6) can be used to produce a family of indifference surfaces for the household between housing characteristics and Z foregone ("money"). Along each such surface the combinations of housing characteristics and Z that keep the household at some constant level of utility will be revealed. Differentiating equation (3.6), we have

$$(3.7) \qquad B_{h_i} = U_{h_i} / U_Z > 0; \; B_{\bar{u}} = -1 / U_Z < 0; \; B_Y = 1;$$

$$(3.8) \qquad B_{h_i h_i} = (U_Z^2 U_{h_i h_i} - 2 U_Z U_{h_i} U_{Z h_i} + U_{h_i}^2 U_{ZZ}) / U_Z^3 < 0,$$

where the inequality in equation (3.8) follows from the usual assumptions about the bordered Hessian matrix of U. Since U was assumed to be strictly concave, it follows that B must be concave in H.

What do equations (3.7) and (3.8) say about the B function? With respect to any housing characteristic h_i, B (the amount the household is willing to bid for the housing package described by the vector of characteristics $(h_1, \ldots, h_n)$ given its tastes and budget constraint) increases as the amount of h_i increases, but at a decreasing rate. B_{h_i}, the change in the household's bid resulting from a change in h_i alone, is thus its (implicit) marginal valuation of h_i given u and Y. (Alternatively, B_{h_i} can be seen as the marginal rate of substitution between h_i and money.)

At this point the household's utility-maximizing position can be described more concretely. Recall from the previous discussion that $p(H)$ is the minimum price that must be paid in the market for any housing unit H. The amount the household is willing to pay for H at a given income and utility level is the value of its bid function, $B(H; \bar{u}, Y)$. Therefore, utility maximization requires $p(H^*) = B(H^*; u^*, Y)$ and also $p_i(H^*) = B_{h_i}(H^*; u^*, Y)$, $i = 1, \ldots, n$, where H^* and u^* are the optimum housing choice and utility level, respectively. In geometric terms, the household's optimal location in h-space is at the tangency of the $B(H; u^*, Y)$ and $p(H)$ surfaces. Each household will of course have its own optimum; those households with especially strong preferences for some housing characteristic h_j will presumably settle on a unit offering more of h_j and less of the other h_i (and/or Z).

The nonlinearity of the budget constraint makes it difficult to generalize about comparative statics in this market. As Rosen points out for the general case, only under restrictive (and not very realistic) assumptions can it be concluded that higher-income households purchase greater amounts of all characteristics. Absent this conclusion, it is not necessarily true that higher incomes imply the consumption of higher-quality housing. In any event, to the extent that households with similar B functions and incomes select similar housing solutions, the housing market will naturally tend toward segmentation by quality—an insight which, as we have noted, is an essential organizing feature of urban housing markets.

3.2.3 Seller Equilibrium

We turn now to the question of the package of characteristics a seller of housing will assemble and offer on the market. At the outset, it should be made clear that the term *sellers* is somewhat different from the term *producers* used in most discussions of market equilibrium. The changes in both terminology and approach are necessitated by the great durability of housing. As a consequence of this durability, the vast bulk of housing services at any point in time is supplied by the existing stock of housing units; indeed, the production of new housing is but a small fraction of the total supply appearing on the market at any time. It is important also to remember that new construction is not the only means by which new or different packages of housing characteristics can be produced—the existing stock can be changed and adapted in response to market forces. Since a housing package of given characteristics can be produced either from scratch or by modifying an existing unit, the supply side of the market consists of many different types of entrepreneurs, with each type having its own technology and costs. These costs of responding to a market opportunity will determine which form of supply will predominate in a given section of the market. In fact, each has a portion of the housing market for which it is the low-cost source of supply.

Consider now the production decision of an individual firm. Following Rosen's approach, the "industry" is presumed to be a collection of atomistic sellers, each of which sells one and only one "design" (i.e., all the housing units it offers have the same vector of characteristics). This approach is chosen to avoid the complications arising from joint production in the multiproduct firm.[16] The total cost of the firm can be written as $C(N, H; \beta)$, where N is the number of units of specification H offered by the firm and C arises in the conventional manner from the firm's minimization of total factor costs subject to a joint production function relating H, N, and the factors of production.[17] The term β is a shift parameter representing exogenously determined inputs to the firm's cost-minimizing process such as factor prices and technology. C is assumed to be convex, with $C(0, H) = 0$ and the first derivatives C_N and $C_{h_i} > 0$ (i.e., it requires more real resources to produce either more units or better-quality units). These marginal costs are assumed to be nondecreasing (strictly increasing in the case of C_N) as well as positive.[18]

To maximize profit,

$$\pi = Np(H) - C(N,H), \tag{3.9}$$

the firm chooses the appropriate combination of characteristics H and number of units N. Note that the average revenue for units of design H is given by $p(H)$.[19] The first-order conditions are as follows:

$$P_i(H) = C_{h_i}(N,h_1, \ldots, h_n) / N, \; i = 1, \ldots, n \tag{3.10}$$

and

$$p(H) = C_N(N, h_1, \ldots, h_n). \tag{3.11}$$

The conditions can be interpreted in the usual manner. When the optimum combination of h_i is chosen, the marginal revenue from each attribute equals its marginal cost. Furthermore, given the optimal bundle of characteristics, this bundle will be offered in quantities up to the point where the price of the unit (which equals marginal revenue under competition) equals the marginal cost. As with the demand side, the convexity assumed for C does not produce the usual second-order conditions due to the nonlinearity of $p(H)$, and a stronger set of conditions is needed.

Proceeding as in the demand analysis, define now an offer function $F(h_1, \ldots, h_n; \bar{\pi}, \beta)$ for the firm indicating the price per unit it is willing to accept for units having specification $(h_1, \ldots, h_n)$ at a given profit level $\bar{\pi}$ and value of β (assuming that the optimal quantity of this design is chosen, that is, that the firm chooses the profit-maximizing N given β and F and thus earns profit $\bar{\pi}$). F defines a family of seller "indifference" surfaces which can be derived by substituting F into equations (3.9) and (3.11) to get

$$\bar{\pi} = NF - C(N, h_1, \ldots, h_n) \tag{3.12}$$

and

$$F = C_n(N, h_1, \ldots, h_n). \tag{3.13}$$

Equations (3.12) and (3.13) are the firm's profit and first-order conditions on quantity, respectively, given that it can sell at prices F. That is, equation (3.13) determines the N it is most profitable to sell if the F function is the relevant schedule of prices received by the firm.[20] The first derivatives of F can be found by differentiating (3.12):

$$(3.14) \qquad F_{h_i} = C_{h_i}/N > 0; \; Fp = 1/N > 0.$$

F_{h_i} is the marginal supply price of characteristic h_i (at constant profit).[21]

The conditions for supplier equilibrium can now be stated. Since $F(H;\bar{\pi}, \beta)$ is the offer price the seller is willing to accept on a unit of specification H at profit level $\bar{\pi}$, he maximizes profit by maximizing this offer price subject to the market price, $p(H)$, as a constraint; that is, profit is maximized when

$$(3.15) \qquad p(H^*) = F(h_1^*, \ldots, h_n^*; \pi^*, \beta).$$

Profit maximization requires a similar condition for each characteristic of the unit—its marginal offer price is maximized subject to a market constraint, or

$$(3.16) \qquad p_i(H) = F_{h_i}(h_1^*, \ldots, h_n^*; \pi^*, \beta).$$

The seller's equilibrium, in other words, occurs where the market-price surface for characteristics and a profit-characteristics indifference surface are tangent.

Just as with households, each firm will have its own optimum point, depending in this case on its value of β. In a formal sense, β serves the function with firms that income does for households—it is the parameter that determines the firm's ability to respond to various market opportunities. In practice, β can be seen as any factor which differentiates the cost curves of a given firm from those of other firms. Obvious examples are technology and factor prices; another might be factors external to the firm which influence the choice of technology, factor requirements, or characteristic combinations, such as the influence of weather and climatic conditions in the particular geographic area where the firm operates. The distribution of β across all potential suppliers will determine the family of offer functions that form the envelope of the market (hedonic) price function.

3.2.4 The Meaning of the Hedonic Index

The answer to the question What is the hedonic index? follows immediately when the above analysis is applied to describe the characteristics of market equilibrium. For households to be in equilibrium, $p(h_1, \ldots, h_n)$ must be the envelope of their bid functions; similarly, when sellers are in equilibrium, $p(h_1, \ldots, h_n)$ traces the envelope of their offer curves. A transaction will take place between buyer and seller where their respective bid functions and offer curves "kiss." At this point of tangency, the slopes of the two functions must be the same and equal to that of the market-clearing hedonic price function $p(h_1, \ldots, h_n)$.[22] The p function will be the locus of such transactions and thus can be seen to be a joint envelope of the offer and bid functions. The hedonic index therefore reveals nothing of the demand and supply conditions that generate it. Rather, it describes the terms of a particular market equilibrium. Like all envelope functions, it is consistent with an infinitude of possible bid and offer curves and contains no information which can be used to distinguish among these functions.[23]

Furthermore, as Lucas (1975: 174–75) points out, the common econometric technique of identifying supply or demand by means of exclusion restrictions—that is, by finding a characteristic which appears, say, in the supply function but does not affect demand—is useless since in equilibrium the vectors of characteristics relevant to the two sides of the market must be identical. This is so because in equilibrium a characteristic which is costly but yields no utility will disappear from the market, while one which is costless will have no influence on price. In short, the hedonic function does not contain any information which can be used to identify the supply and demand functions which give rise to a particular equilibrium.

A caveat is in order here. Note that the tradeoffs among characteristics implicit in the market-clearing hedonic price function are strictly valid only in the neighborhood of the market equilibrium that function represents. If market forces cause either the bid functions or the offer curves to shift, a new equilibrium position with a new set of market tradeoffs will result. For this reason, a hedonic relationship estimated at one point in time will be valid in another period only if market conditions are substantially the same.[24]

Even at a given equilibrium, hedonic prices measure *marginal* market tradeoffs among characteristics and not the *average* tradeoffs of any household or firm. To see why this is so, consider the relationship between two characteristics depicted in figure 3.1. In this figure, P is the "budget line" representing the relative market prices of characteristics h_i and h_j implicit in the equilibrium hedonic relationship, and I is a household's indifference curve for h_i and h_j. In equilibrium, I and P are tangent at point A, so that the household's marginal rate of substitution between h_i and h_j is equated to their market price ratio. Another combination of h_i and h_j such as that at point B involves the same marginal tradeoff as at A but clearly carries a different utility level for the household (since B is not on the same indifference curve as A). This has the important implication that units of the same hedonic value (value of $p(H)$) need not have the same level of utility for all households—hedonic value arises from the marginal tradeoffs of characteristics whereas the total utility of the household is a function of its own average tradeoffs. Thus the hedonic relationship, while quite useful for describing the workings of the housing market, will be less helpful in exploring the utility levels of individual households. Since this study is concerned with positive analysis of the market, such

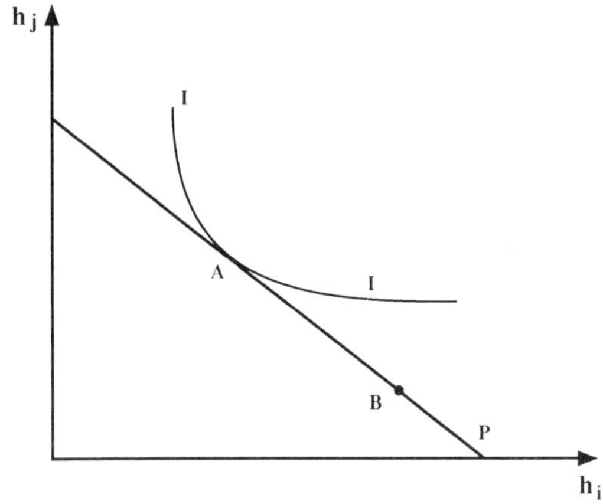

Figure 3.1. Marginal tradeoffs between housing attributes.

limitations on the welfare inferences possible from the results do not constitute a troublesome shortcoming.

3.2.5 Functional Form of the Hedonic Equation

The fact that $p(H)$ is the envelope of market transactions reflecting many different β's on the supply side and many different incomes and preferences on the demand side has an important implication for the functional form of estimated hedonic relationships. In particular, the slope of p ($= p_i$ with respect to attribute h_i) will not be constant over the range of values taken on by any h_i due to the interactions of h_i with other h_j's. For a variety of reasons, housing characteristics exist only in a limited range of combinations (recall the previous example of few one-bedroom, fourteen-bathroom units). Since the feasible (in a market sense) amounts of any h_i depend on the amounts of the other h_j present in the housing unit, a linear form, that is,

$$p(H) = a_0 + a_1h_1 + \ldots + a_nh_n, \tag{3.17}$$

is likely to be a relatively poor representation of reality.[25]

Given that some sort of interactive specification is desirable, what should the functional form be? Unfortunately, theory frequently offers little guidance about the form of the interactions. Absent such direction, researchers estimating hedonic indexes for a wide range of consumer durables have tended to regard the choice of functional form as an empirical question to be decided on the basis of plausibility, goodness to fit, and the like. Numerous investigators (dating back to Court 1939) have employed a semilogarithmic relationship between prices and characteristics, that is,

$$\log p(H) = b_0 + b_1h_1 + \ldots + b_nh_n, \tag{3.18}$$

though many have used the linear form (3.17) and still others have sought to identify the "best" functional form using Box-Cox techniques. In fact, none of these is likely to be the "correct" form since the true relationships among product characteristics are in general much more complicated and much less uniform than these forms imply.

In the case of housing, our theoretical arguments in chapters 4 and 5 have direct implications for functional form. There we argue that the correct specification of a hedonic index for housing should embody diminishing returns to each structural characteristic. Both demand-side (diminishing marginal utility of the occupants) and supply-side (increasing marginal costs of accommodating more of one feature while holding all others constant) forces drive the equilibrium hedonic relationship to this configuration. In chapter 13 we explore at greater length the empirical implications of this finding.

Interestingly enough, researchers who have compared different functional forms for hedonic indexes of housing have usually found surprisingly small differences among them. A perceptive explanation for this is offered by Dhrymes (1971:96). He suggests that clustering of the data (quite likely in the case of housing, as argued above) can so restrict the range of the sample that it covers only a relatively small portion of the (hypothetical) price surface. If such is the case, it would not be unreasonable for many forms to be equally good approximations to the true (and more complicated) surface over that limited range.

To summarize this discussion, one might say that theoretical considerations suggest a functional form for hedonic indexes of housing which incorporates at least some interactions among the various components of housing quality, and that no functional form which is practical for estimation can do better than approximate the true relationship. Since the choice is among approximations, choosing the best form for a particular application will doubtless continue to involve art as well as science.

3.3 Modeling the Stratification of Urban Housing Markets

3.3.1 Using the Hedonic Index

The hedonic index is but a first step toward understanding the workings of urban housing markets; for a complete description of how the market works, behavioral demand and supply equations must also be specified and estimated. The estimated marginal prices from the hedonic regression are used in the behavioral model to provide price information for the estimation of demand and supply, and to provide a basis for the segmentation of the housing market into its component submarkets.[26]

In practice, we proceed by first estimating the hedonic relationship for a housing market and then arraying the units in the housing stock in the order of their hedonic values. The segmented submarkets are then defined by partitioning this array into a number of groups of housing units having similar hedonic values (see ch. 13.) These submarkets—distinct but related "commodities," so to speak—serve as the basis for portraying the behavioral relationships of the housing market. Each submarket has its unique forces of supply and demand; these are influenced by events in other submarkets, with the strength of the influence directly proportional to the substitutive closeness of the other submarkets. Thus, the model includes a representation of the linkages among submarkets as well as the supply and demand relationships within each submarket.

How does the housing market structure just described differ from one using market prices of units as a quality metric? Due to the imperfect substitutability of housing units across submarkets, exogenous forces affecting particular submarkets will have their strongest impact on market prices there, with effects on other submarkets that diminish as substitution possibilities with units in the impact submarket become more remote. Accordingly, the advantage of using hedonic values rather than market values is that with the former a unit of given characteristics will continue to be classified in the same submarket so long as the preference/production tradeoffs of those characteristics with others are unchanged. Since relative market prices of different units *can* change without there being any changes in these tradeoffs, variations over time in market pressures or in the general level of prices will cause units to be misleadingly reclassified if market prices serve as the quality metric. In other words, the use of a hedonic index enables us to classify units consistently over time by separating the market evaluation of their objective characteristics from temporal movements in price unrelated to changes in those characteristics.

The hedonic definition of housing quality also permits the calculation of a submarket price variable which reflects the extent of exogenous pressures on that submarket. This is the price per unit of housing quality, that is, the ratio of average market value to average hedonic value for the units in a submarket. Differences in this ratio across submarkets act as a signal to suppliers and demanders, alerting them to unusual profit opportunities or bargains (and the reverse). Prices per unit of housing quality, then, are important factors in explaining the complex of linkages among submarkets.[27]

3.3.2 Are Submarkets Geographically Contiguous?

As we saw in chapter 2, some authors[28] have suggested that urban housing markets are best understood as a collection of a great many functionally independent geographic submarkets (perhaps even smaller than census tracts) differentiated by the characteristics of their housing units and/or the locations of the submarkets. In this view, systematic geographic variation of housing characteristics and prices within an urban area is "a fundamental characteristic of the urban housing market" (Straszheim 1975:23). If this is so, a unique hedonic relationship exists within each geographic submarket so that it is improper to estimate a single index for the entire market. This view is at variance with the conception of urban housing markets which underlies our approach. Our view, consistent with the way in which economists define markets in other contexts (e.g., defining the relevant market in an antitrust case), is that housing submarkets are defined on the basis of substitutability across *all* characteristics. That being the case, it is entirely conceivable that some close substitutes for a given group of housing units will not be geographically contiguous to those units. Households seeking to change units will generally search (at least initially) in more than one neighborhood, trading off structure, lot, neighborhood, and location characteristics of each. The difference between these views is important, for under our interpretation a marketwide hedonic relationship is the basis for describing segmentation by closeness of substitutability, while under the alternative view such an index should not even be estimated.[29]

It might seem that this argument could be settled econometrically, by subdividing a housing market into geographic "submarkets" and then testing whether the hedonic relationship varies significantly across these "submarkets." Attempts to do so almost invariably yield significant differences in the coefficients of the hedonic relationship, from which it is tempting to conclude that these "submarkets" should not be aggregated for the purpose of estimating a marketwide hedonic equation. There are, however, two good reasons to resist that temptation. First, as Schnare and Struyk (1976) showed, these coefficient variations often have only a minute impact on the explanatory power or predictive ability of the hedonic regression, so for many purposes (including ours) the differences among these "submarkets" probably have little practical significance. Second, and more importantly, it is highly unlikely that the observed variations are economically or statistically meaningful. Only if the submarkets defined a priori are in fact the relevant ones (in the usual economic sense of substitutability in the marketplace) can *any* conclusions be drawn about the cross-sectional stability of the hedonic relationship from these studies. Since, as argued above, closely substitutable units need *not* be geographically contiguous, *no* such stratification is likely to reflect the true structure of submarkets. Indeed, the only way to define submarkets which is consistent with economic theory—that is, by substitutability as determined in the market—is to begin with the marketwide hedonic index as we have suggested. Furthermore, as we demonstrate in chapter 13, submarkets so defined by quality do not appear to have meaningful geographic equivalents. Empirically, even small geographic areas generally contain wide varieties of dwelling quality.

3.4 Conclusion

In the first part of this chapter, we argued that a hedonic index is a convenient means for obtaining a transitive, one-dimensional, market-based scaling of the housing units in a given market. This scaling implicitly defines a hierarchy of units by providing a dimension along which units with different combinations of characteristics have locations. Since the scaling depends on consensual market tradeoffs, relative locations along the scale provide an approximate basis for judging degrees of substitutability among units. Units with similar values of the index should (by transitivity) be highly substitutable; units with greatly different hedonic values are presumably poor substitutes and belong in different submarkets. Hence, a hedonic index can function in a housing market model both to define submarkets of reasonably substitutable units and to assign each unit to the proper submarket.

In the second part of the chapter, we articulated the theoretical underpinnings of this argument. We demonstrated that equilibrium in a competitive housing market implies the existence of a hedonic relationship which describes the terms of trade for both sides of the market at that equilibrium position but which cannot be used to identify the underlying supply or demand functions.

Finally, we demonstrated how the hedonic index can be used to identify the appropriate submarkets for the analysis of demand, supply, and market equilibrium. In particular, we showed why defining submarkets as small contiguous geographic areas is inconsistent with our theoretical understanding of housing market segmentation.

Notes

1. For example, a Victorian structure may simultaneously have great appeal to some households and a strong negative impact on others; since the market valuation of the characteristic "Victorian style" will be the resultant of many conflicting opinions, no clear trend is likely to emerge. With such characteristics as bathrooms, however, it seems pretty safe to say that a unit with more of them will (ceteris paribus) be more highly valued.

2. The construction of such surrogates is hardly unique to housing. Consider, for example, the consumer price index, which is at best a crude approximation to any household's true cost of living. Despite its well-known failings, the CPI is used because a crude measure provides more useful information about consumer behavior and the workings of the economy than no measure at all. Just so, to understand housing markets it is necessary to invent aggregate quality measures even though no intrinsic ones exist.

3. The use of an arbitrary weighting scheme does not solve the problem, since it may still be unrelated to the true market relationships among characteristics.

4. While such an ordering is useful for drawing general conclusions about aggregates of households (much like the CPI), the efficacy of the index for evaluating the

welfare of individual households is quite limited. Values of the index are calculated from consensual marginal market tradeoffs among characteristics, while the total utility a household receives from any given combination of characteristics is determined by its own average tradeoffs. On the margin, all households must accept the relative valuations of characteristics that prevail in the market. But this does not mean that all households will rank housing units in the same order or that a given household will be indifferent among all housing units having the same value of the index. Diversity of preferences thus limits the ability of the aggregate market quality index to make accurate inferences about the welfare of individual households, even though it accurately reflects market tradeoffs.

5. For a representative sampling of this literature, see Fisher, Griliches, and Kaysen 1962; Cagan 1965; Dhrymes 1967; Triplett 1969; Cowling and Cubbin 1971; and Griliches 1971b.

6. See, for example, Muth 1966; Lancaster 1966, 1971; and Muellbauer 1974.

7. This approach has been extended and clarified by Muellbauer 1974.

8. For an empirical application in this tradition, see Dhrymes 1967, 1971.

9. See Rosen 1974 and Lucas 1975. These papers demonstrate the existence of the hedonic relationship from the supply side in the course of showing, as we do, that the correct interpretation includes both supply and demand.

10. One of the early empirical papers (Fisher, Griliches, and Kaysen 1962) assumes this interpretation of the hedonic index.

11. In doing so, we employ the basic theoretical structure of Rosen's (1974) model but adapt it to the special circumstances of urban housing markets.

12. But note that bundles themselves are indivisible; for example, two five-room houses are not the same as one ten-room house (on both the supply and demand sides of the market).

13. We introduce portfolio and tenure choice considerations and develop their implications at length in chapter 4.

14. *Prices* and *rents* (and other terms specifically applicable to either the owner or renter markets) henceforth are used interchangeably.

15. See Rosen 1974:38 and Intriligator 1971.

16. Such an assumption is probably less objectionable for housing than for most other markets since most sellers of housing offer only one unit and the biggest sellers (of new units) seek a relatively high degree of standardization in the units they produce.

17. Note again that the word *production* has a broader meaning in this market than in conventional discussions of firm behavior.

18. The set of feasible locations in h-space is further limited by technological and other constraints. For example, one cannot put a house with 5,000 square feet of first-floor area on a 4,000-square-foot lot; also, one seldom finds one-bedroom homes with fourteen bathrooms.

19. Note also that the assumption of competition can be maintained even though the marginal costs of characteristics (p_i) need not be constant, since all firms observe the same prices and treat them as parameters, i.e., $p(H)$ is still independent of any single firm's N.

20. It is thus possible to eliminate N from equations (3.12) and (3.13) by solving for N in equation (3.13) as an implicit function of F, then substituting this implicit function

into equation (3.12). The resulting expression defines F implicitly as a function of H, $\bar{\pi}$ and β.

21. As noted above, the assumed convexity of C does not insure that $F_{h_i h_i} > 0$ in this case.

22. That is, with respect to any one characteristic h_i, the slopes of both the bid and offer functions must be equal to the (marginal) market price p_i.

23. There are two cases in which the p function *can* reveal something of the underlying supply or demand conditions. (Neither of these cases is a realistic possibility in urban housing markets.) First, if all firms have the same β (face the same factor prices, use the same technology, etc.), the family of offer curves collapses to one curve, which must be everywhere coincident with $p(H)$. Similarly, if sellers differ but households are identical, the family of bid functions collapses to a single function which must coincide with $p(H)$, and $p(H)$ then identifies the demand side of the market.

24. Our empirical results suggest that changes in the relationship between 1960 and 1975–76 were not great (see ch. 13).

25. But note that the coefficients in a nonlinear form cannot be interpreted directly as implicit characteristic prices, though they certainly are related to those prices.

26. This is essentially the procedure suggested by Rosen 1974:50.

27. The concept of price per unit of housing quality has been used extensively in housing market research. See, for example, DeLeeuw and Struyk 1975, and Hirsch and Margolis 1977.

28. See, for example, Ingram, Kain, and Ginn 1972, and Straszheim 1973, 1974, 1975.

29. Note too that the model of segmented submarkets we postulate employs the marketwide index as the basis for structuring the linkage mechanisms among these submarkets. In contrast, the alternative approach views the submarkets it defines as having much greater degrees of insulation from each other and so does not require such elaborate consideration of intersubmarket linkages.

4 The Demand for Urban Housing and the Choice of Tenure

We have spoken of housing so far as purely a consumption good, and the consumption of it as the consumption of housing services. But one of the most distinctive features of the good is its extremely high durability. This durability is not simply the physical capability of the good to last, but its *market relevance* over a long period. This implies both a rather slow pace of technological improvement in the nature of the product (in providing services) and in the processes of its production, and a basically inessential character of the two kinds of advance. Product improvements in new houses can be retrofitted into old houses (like new equipment, heating and plumbing, etc.); productive process improvements are not decisive in creating comparable services at such lower costs as to render competitively necessary operating costs (plus maintenance and repairs) of older units higher than the costs of replacement by new units.

One important consequence of this durability is that the overwhelming proportion of current dwelling units occupied is supplied by units in the existing housing stock. Annual new production accounts for a minuscule proportion (2–3%).

A second important consequence is that housing units are a very expensive commodity. Very few households can afford to own them outright. Either they are purchased for ownership by means of borrowing a large portion of their cost via mortgage instruments, or they are not purchased for ownership at all, but their annual services are bought by rental. The rental market is very considerable—more than 35% of the urban market in the United States, and much above 50% in other developed countries.

A third consequence stems from both of these. In any short period, demand and supply are very closely linked together. In its owner-occupier market, the continued demand by a household for the services of its presently owned house implies that this house is not on the market for sale to another possible buyer. But when the household decides to move to occupy a different unit, this demand decision almost always is accompanied by the decision to offer its present unit for sale, that is, its demand decision is paired with a corresponding supply decision. Given the dominance of the existing stock over new construction, the number and identity of owner-occupier units on the market for sale depend largely on the number and identity of houses being offered for sale because their owners have decided to change their housing consumption. Basically the same can be said about the rental market. The rental units available for new occupancy in any period depend on which renters decide to change occupancy.

So ownership and rental supply depend on ownership and rental demand in a peculiarly intimate way. But this results in each decision being influenced by the other: owners do not blithely decide to change occupancy for demand reasons without having to be concerned about the prospect of selling their presently occupied unit on favorable terms, so that the *net effect* of both the purchase *and* the sale transaction makes them better off than staying. Somewhat similarly, renters do not decide to change rental occupancy without having the prospect of a more advantageous alternative into which to move; landlords do not force out present tenants without the prospect of a more advantageous alternative tenancy.

These linked decisions make a number of variables influential that do not usually appear in treatments of consumption demand. Among these are various frictions involved in changing occupancy: substantial search, transactions, and moving costs. Others concern availability and terms of mortgage credit. Still others involve the determinants of rental versus ownership tenure, and the resulting match in the relative numbers of rental and ownership units demanded and supplied.

All these complications should be brought to bear on the demand for housing as a pure consumption good. But these complexities pale beside the one that must finally be raised by recognition of the aforementioned special features of the housing commodity. As an expensive and durable good, ownership of it significantly affects the investment portfolio of most households. It thus constitutes a considerable kind of asset to be included—or excluded—from such portfolio, and therefore constitutes an important financial investment which must be integrated with all other financial investments that the household considers in deciding on an optimal financial portfolio at each moment in time.

So housing is not only a consumption good; it is also an investment good. The factors which must be considered to select an optimal pure consumption strategy are not necessarily the same as those relevant to deciding on an optimal financial investment strategy. To some extent the existence of a variety of financial instruments and a large rental market make reciprocal accommodation between the two possible. But there is no guarantee that a perfect accommodation will result.

In this chapter we begin with the conventional starting focus: housing as pure consumption. We deal with a number of the consumption complexities mentioned above, and place them within the larger consumption-investment ambiguity by assuming that financial instruments are varied and flexible enough, and the rental market extensive enough, and both essentially tenure-neutral (in a sense defined below) so that the user-household's choice of tenure leaves its consumption strategy unaffected. Sections 4.3 and 4.4 then explicitly examine the determination of tenure status in the real-world institutional setting and indicate the circumstances under which this tenure status decision affects the consumption strategy as well.

Section 4.1 treats housing as consumption, first in a strictly static context that abstracts from all of the complications listed above, then in a dynamic context that incorporates most of them. The latter treatment diverges so markedly from conventional treatments of housing as consumption that our treatment of housing as consumption *and* investment reverts to the simpler formulation of consumption choice so as to throw into sharp relief the effect that investment issues have on overall strategy when integrated with consumption.

4.1 Housing as a Consumption Good

4.1.1 Household Demand for Housing as Consumption: Static Analysis

In chapter 3 we described a housing unit as a vector of housing attributes (relating to structure, land, neighborhood, and location). However, because much of our succeeding analysis refers to quality-level submarkets, we now slightly modify that notation to facilitate this. The attributes are expressed in terms of three constructs—a ratio mix of attributes, the quality level embodying that mix, and the age of the structure. Age could have been subsumed within quality level and mix, but it is extracted separately because it is an important analytical variable in the theory of housing supply. Finally, we add to the description of the housing unit the tenure status in which it is occupied or is considered for occupancy. A significant part of our theory of demand argues that tenure status makes a difference: in the joint determination of tenure, attribute mix, and quality, the choice of tenure influences the other choices, especially quality level.

Any housing unit is therefore described as follows:

$$L = (H, [\mathrm{R}], AG, D), \tag{4.1}$$

where

L = housing unit;
H = the quality level;
$[R]$ = a matrix of ratios of the various housing attributes, with elements h_i/h_j—all i, j;
AG = age of structure; and
$D\ (= 0,1)$ = tenure status (0 for rental, 1 for owner-occupiership).

H is the output of a contour function, shown in equation (4.2):

$$H = H(h_1,h_2,\ldots,h_n), \tag{4.2}$$

where h_i is attribute of structure, and where the H function is the market hedonic function, *not* a particular household's indifference curve system (utility function). Figure 4.1 shows the relation between the definition of a housing unit in attribute terms and in terms of quality level and mix.

L_1 and L_2 are two housing units, with attributes (h_{11}, h_{21}) and (h_{21}, h_{22}), respectively. The market hedonic function, two relevant contours of which are shown by H_1, H_2, indicates that $H(L_1) = H_1 < H(L_2) = H_2$. The attribute mix of each is the tangent of the angle ($\tan \theta_i$) of the respective rays through L_1 and L_2. So L_1 and L_2 are translated into the terms of equation (4.1) as

$$\begin{bmatrix} L_1 = (H_1, \tan \theta_1 \ldots) \\ L_2 = (H_2, \tan \theta_2 \ldots) \end{bmatrix} \tag{4.3}$$

Individual Demand

Static analysis of demand for housing (as pure consumption) is in effect the implicit rental demand for a flow of services. If the household itself owns the housing unit that will provide the services, it is simply as though the household as user pays rent to itself as landlord—and the fact that the landlord *is* itself instead of some other makes no difference to its choice of unit to occupy. In such a model, therefore, there is no special reason why a household cannot own one unit but occupy a unit owned by someone else, renting out its own unit to a different household. There are no financial, transactional, tax, or inherent owner-occupier status factor that affect the household's achievable utility (via preference or budget constraints). Only (H, [R]) matters: owner-occupiership and housing ownership are independent of one another with respect to long-term utility maximization.[1]

We assume that each household knows (at near-zero cost) the availability

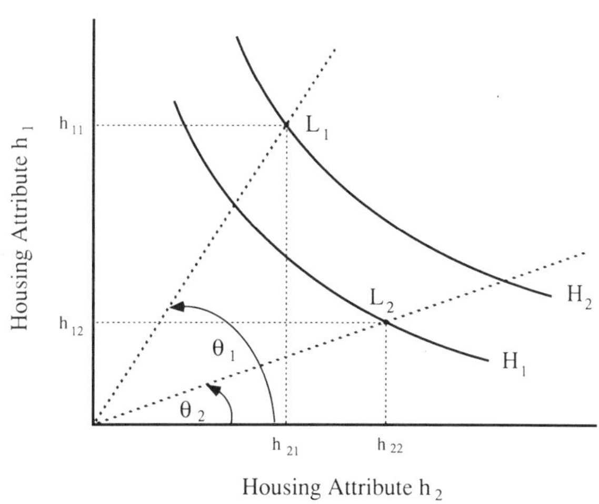

Figure 4.1. Housing units defined by attribute mix and quality level.

and characteristics of all housing units in the existing stock as well as all new units coming to market. In addition, transactions costs are assumed to be negligible. In this context, all units in the existing stock are essentially available for changed occupancy in each period. Accordingly, all units have an explicit market price (for units formally in the market) or a potential market price—an offer price (for units which may be induced by this offer to come into the market). We assume each household knows (also at near-zero cost) these prices.

Each household is assumed to have the utility function and budget constraint described in chapter 3, namely, in present terms:

$$U = U(Z, L) \equiv U(Z, h_1, h_2, \ldots h_n) \equiv U[Z, (H, [R], AG, D)] \tag{4.4}$$

$$Y = Z + p(L) \equiv Z + p\,(h_1, h_2, \ldots, h_n) = Z + f(p_1 h_1, p_2 h_2, \ldots p_n h_n)P(H), \tag{4.5}$$

where

Z = nonhousing (numéraire) good;

p = market price of the overall housing package L;

$p_1, p_2, \ldots, p_n$ = implicit prices of the attributes, as implied by the hedonic price relationship (i.e., $p_1 = \frac{\partial p(L)}{\partial h_i}$);

f = hedonic value of package L; and

P = positive or negative premium on attribute-explained price due to L's membership in quality class H

$$\left[\equiv \frac{\text{market value of packages in } H}{\text{hedonic value of units in } H}\right].$$

Equation (4.5) introduces attention to three different kinds of price for housing. As previously introduced, there is the market price of the housing package (L), $p(L)$. In addition, the market hedonic relationship generates, in the partial derivatives of the separate attributes, implicit prices for each of these attributes—attribute prices, (p_i). But housing packages sell as a whole, and while different attribute mixes can be obtained in a thick market by shopping among different whole packages, the packages are generally only imperfect substitutes for one another. In any particular period the number of units demanded at a particular quality level may exceed or fall short of the number of units supplied at the quality level, thereby either raising or lowering its prices of, in principle, all of the units currently supplied there, both absolutely and relatively to the prices of units at other quality levels. Because there are nonzero costs of converting existing units at other quality levels to this level, or from this level to others, or to build additional or fewer new units at this level, and since even when the net advantages of doing so are positive, the gestation period for making these adjustments are nontrivial, then some of the adjustments necessary to bring relative quality-level prices back to their initial level will not be made at all, and those that are made will take time. The result is that changing market conditions may well change relative prices across quality levels, and these changes may never be fully undone by market readjustments and may be partially undone only over the course of considerable periods of time. The concept of quality-level prices therefore reflects the possibility of such systematic market changes that are not essentially transitory. While a large part of some of them may be wiped out in the long run, in runs quite respectable in length such persistent changes are important to the understanding of how the housing market complex behaves.

The recognition that quality-level prices may be important analytic variables is tantamount to a recognition also that sets of housing units at different quality levels function as separate but related submarkets. Each submarket will have some play of relatively independent action and change, the degree of independence depending on the closeness of substitutability of such units in both demand and supply. The closer the substitutability, the less leeway there is for changes that persist relative to units in other quality-level submarkets. The real-world degree of imperfect substitution in urban housing is great enough to suggest that quality-level submarkets have an existence that must be heeded for proper analysis of the housing market complex.

Each household, then, faces a known set of housing units and a known set of three kinds of housing prices, along with its preferences and purchasing power constraint. It selects a utility-maximizing combination of L and Z: $\hat{L}$, $\hat{Z}$, where optimality refers to the size of Z and the quality level, attribute mix, age, and tenure status of L. This multiple optimization is similar to the case of profit-maximizing production for a firm with fixed productive capacity. It can be seen as a three-stage optimization process, of which one stage, that of tenure choice, is inessential in the present simplified model. In section 4.2, where the oversimplified assumptions that make tenure irrelevant to consumption choices are relaxed, this optimization is important, but cannot be separated from the two other stages. Stage one is to obtain an optimal attribute mix, where age is treated as an additional attribute and optimality consists of minimizing costs to achieve each possible quality level. This is akin to a firm's determining the optimal mix of productive inputs, that which minimizes production costs for each potential output level. The optimal mix there is not invariant over different output levels, and it is not invariant here over different quality levels. The second stage involves using the function of least-cost combinations of attribute mixes to determine the utility-maximizing quality level. This is akin to finding the profit-maximizing level of output, in terms of the cost-minimizing function of input mix over output level.

The first-order optimality conditions for attribute mix are those specified in equation (3.5) above, namely,

(4.6) $$\frac{Uh_i}{Uh_j} = \frac{\partial p_i}{\partial p_j} \text{ for } h_1, h_2, \ldots, h_n \text{ and } AG,$$

where p_i, p_j derive from the market's hedonic price functions. First-order optimality for quality level is based on the bid function $B(L, U, Y)$ as defined in equation (3.6), but translated into the reformulated model of this chapter, namely,

(4.7) $$\left.\frac{\partial U}{\partial H}\right| \frac{\partial U}{\partial z} = p\,\frac{\partial(L)}{\partial H} = f[(p_i h_i)]\,\frac{\partial P(H)}{\partial H} + P(H)\,\frac{\partial f}{\partial H}.$$

$\frac{\partial f}{\partial H} > 0$, because the optimal attribute quantities and so the attribute aggregate price must be larger for larger quality levels. $\frac{\partial P(H)}{\partial H} \gtreqless 0$, since a higher quality level may have a *different* price than the initial one, higher *or* lower. Thus, optimal mix requires relative amounts such that the preference tradeoff at the margin (the marginal rate of substitution) between any pair of attributes equals the ratio of their implicit prices, as defined by the market hedonic price function. The optimal quality is that for which the marginal cost of increasing quality is just equal to the marginal rate of substitution between quality and consumption of Z, at that original Z, H mix. These are perfectly straightforward results.

To flesh out these formal results empirically, we assume that both individual attributes (including age) and quality are somewhat, but not entirely, like normally superior goods: a higher attribute price discourages consumption of the attribute; a higher quality-level price discourages consumption of that quality level; moreover, often, but not always,

$$\frac{\partial U}{\partial h_i} > 0, \text{ but } \frac{\partial^2 U}{\partial h_i 2} < 0;$$
$$\frac{\partial U}{\partial H} > 0, \text{ but } \frac{\partial^2 U}{\partial H^2} < 0$$

That is, often the larger the amount of any attribute, all others remaining constant, the lower the amount of any other attribute the household would be willing to give up for an additional amount of it. This influence stems from a basic substitutive relationship for each pair of attributes. But the exception hinted at above stems from the fact that many groupings of attributes are complements: the balance or proportions among such attributes matter. There is a narrow range of multiple ratios that represents the most appropriate combinations of those attributes. Deviations from this range—*in either direction*—are less favored. Therefore, *higher* levels of some attribute, *given the particular amounts of its complementary group*, can result in an *increase* in the amount of an attribute outside the complementary group that the household would be willing to give up for a further increase in the complementary attribute. This occurs in the range where there is too little of the latter relative to the amounts in its complementary group. Only where increments in that attribute move the proportions in the whole complementary group *away from* the most appropriate interval do they have decreasing value relative to noncomplementary attributes.

One consequence of these complementaries is that, regardless of considerable differences in household housing preferences, appreciation for some basic proportions among groups of attributes are widely shared. So only moderate mix variations within these groups are likely to be observed in the market. In the case of extreme consensus, these groups of attributes would behave like joint components of a single attribute, and separate implicit prices would not be abstractable from market observations. Ratios of bedrooms to bathrooms, dining rooms to kitchens, garages to bedrooms are among the pairings for which notions of appropriate balance are likely to be important.

A special consideration applies to age of unit more than to other attributes. If it remains in the market at all, a given unit cannot change its age. Nor can new units be supplied at ages other than zero. For a given quality level, additional units at ages greater than zero can only be supplied through conversion of existing units at those ages in other quality submarkets. For other attributes, including neighborhood characteristics and accessibility, additional numbers can be supplied via new construction (e.g., increased construction of units in especially attractive neighborhoods) as well as via conversion.

An implication of this discussion of structural age is that, in a quality level where competition via conversion of existing units at other qualities is small, existing units of all ages may well survive by means of relative price adjustments, that is, a ten-year-old house may be widely believed to be worth twice as much as a twenty-five year-old house, so prices will adjust to this ratio. In like measure, most users will be indifferent among houses of all ages at that quality level, since relative prices for all the different ages will exactly offset perceived differences in consumption value among them. This age-related price adjustment would be less likely to occur with significant conversion activity from other quality levels. Contrary to the narrowing effect on real-world observable differences of attribute complementary, this adjustment produces *wider* observable differences. In the extreme, it is as if age were independent of all the other attributes, were truly separable.

A second major difference in static demand from ordinary markets concerns response to price changes. We have indicated that, like ordinary markets, rise in a price turns the household's demand away from the commodity whose price has risen. But the present demand is for *one out of a variety of related commodities*. If the price of one of these related commodities rises, the household will tend to favor a close substitute whose price relative to the first commodity has fallen. In the case of attribute prices the household will bring a different housing unit containing *less* of the attribute whose price has risen. In the case of quality-level prices, however, the situation is different. As we argued above, quality-level prices reflect excess demand conditions in different parts of the spectra of the market complex. A rise in the relative price of moderate-quality units does not require that the price of all units of higher quality rise relatively also, or that the prices of all units of lower quality rise relatively also. Changes in relative quality-level prices are nonmonotonic. The special circumstances of demand and supply in different parts of the quality spectrum can lead to highly idiosyncratic patterns of relative quality price changes.

In view of the irregularity of pattern for quality price changes, the change in price of one particular quality level may lead to what appears to be anomalous demand changes. Thus, if the price of units at some moderate quality level rises relative to both lower *and* higher quality levels, a particular household may decide to consume either lower *or* higher quality, depending on the exact new relative price/preference tradeoffs. Thus, among a group of slightly different households, some in the group may demand less quality and some demand more. This property of the choice of one out of a variety of substitutes significantly complicates the working of the market complex.

Aggregate Demand

Each household is assumed to face, and solve, the utility-maximizing exercise described in the last section. The result, for each, is the choice of a housing package, *L,* involving a particular tenure status, age of structure, attribute mix, and quality level. Together, then, when faced with a given set of available housing packages, given package prices, attribute prices (including a price gradient for age differences), and quality-level prices, there is a resulting set of housing packages demanded by the given population—a set with the joint attribute mix, quality level, tenure, and age characteristics mentioned. The aggregate demand, the sum of units demanded in an appropriate classification, is therefore the response of a particular population, with given number, preference, and income distribution, to prices and availabilities.

In this book we are particularly interested in the submarkets referring to quality level. Within each, there will be a wide variety of mix, tenure, age patterns. But all will be linked in a chain of high substitution clusters. Thus, for a population of given size, preferences, and income distribution, facing a given set of available housing units and three kinds of housing prices, utility-maximizing choice will generate an aggregate demand that will face the aggregate supply of units in each quality level, with the occurrence of actual transactions based on the matching of appropriate attribute mixes of units supplied and demanded within each submarket.

For given availabilities and prices, aggregate demand depends heavily on population characteristics. Thus, an outmigration of rich households and an equal inflow of poor households will lead to a decreased demand for high-quality units and an increased demand for low-quality ones. A uniform increase (decrease) in the population will lead to an increased (or decreased) number of units demanded in all quality submarkets. Similarly, changes in the distribution of tastes between housing and nonhousing, among quality levels, and among attributes, will lead to corresponding changes in aggregate demand for the affected characteristics (or for housing as a whole relative to nonhousing consumption).

A decrease (an increase) in the relative price of some attribute should lead to aggregate substitution in its favor (against it) relative to other attributes. An increase in a quality-level submarket price should result in fewer units demanded in that submarket, but some households will be induced to demand a unit in a lower quality level and some in a higher quality level. Much depends on the pattern of changes in several quality-level submarkets. Unlike attributes, quality-level submarkets have natural neighbors—adjacent higher and lower submarkets. Depending on the source of the price change, several adjacent levels are likely to experience change at the same, or nearly the same, time. The resulting pattern of demand switches depends crucially on the whole new pattern of these prices relative to those of unchanged submarkets. Only this entire spectrum of prices enables one to predict sometimes whether a given submarket price rise will lead to lower or higher quality demanded in the aggregate.

An important property of the matrix of aggregate demand over different-quality submarkets is that the demand for units in any particular one cannot be predicted solely in terms of market signals in that submarket; it depends on the pattern of both availabilities and prices in other submarkets and their changes. Since the submarkets are reasonably closely related to one another, it is rare that exogenous forces and events will impact only one submarket at a time. The complex of submarkets are initially affected in clusters, and, as we shall see in the chapters discussing market adjustments, initial impacts are subsequently spread differentially across the complex, both in degree and in promptness. These evolving changes affect the demand for different submarkets along the way and contribute to the market's overall adjustment process.

4.1.2 Household Demand for Housing as Consumption: Dynamic Analysis

The critical assumptions underlying static analysis are that households are always fully informed about market opportunities and that housing occupancy *change* entails negligible friction costs. While assumptions of this sort are never literally true of any kind of market, they are often tolerable approximations in getting to the heart of some markets. In urban housing, however, they constitute a serious misrepresentation of critical properties of that market. Information necessary to informed choice is extensive and expensive to obtain;

occupancy change entails very considerable frictions. The consequences of both propositions together are of great significance.

Individual Demand, Information, and Search Costs

Information and search costs are very substantial for urban housing. This stems both from the high degree and dimensionality of heterogeneity across urban housing units and from the physical immobility—the fixed spatial scattering—of such units. Housing units differ from one another in numerous ways, respecting all of the attributes of the package, not only the innumerable structure features including the structure's condition, but also those of the land, the neighborhood, and accessibility to desirable outside destinations. Neighborhood alone refers to the demographic profile in terms of identity and lifestyles, the array of government services rendered, public "goods" like crime, environmental quality and microclimate, prevailing condition of structures, and the availability of various private goods. Units not only differ in all these respects, but would-be users care deeply about a large percentage of these attributes.

Would-be participants in the housing market have to be aware of the array of different units that are available for their occupancy, know their properties as well as their prices. The availability of units is itself not a simple matter. For the very reasons we are explicating, a very large proportion of existing units is not actively available in the market at any one time. (This is elaborated at length below.) So effort must be expended just to discover what small subset of existing units *is* available for changed or new occupancy in the present period.

Informedness requires that a great deal be learned about each available unit, beginning with its availability. But many of these features cannot be known from summaries, descriptions, and photographs alone. They require face-to-face confrontation. Since housing units cannot be physically gathered together, such first-hand information requires separate, time-consuming, transportation-intensive visits (sometimes more than once for a single house). The result is that a serious housing search is very costly in terms of time, effort, and out-of-pocket costs.

Active participation in the market by a household that intends to change occupancy involves more than search. First, decision on an acquisition, especially owner-occupied purchases, requires negotiation and various technical procedures, legal and financial, which are necessary to conclude the transaction (like mortgage acquisition, deed search, etc). Second, once the transaction is concluded, the household has to move its possessions from its present occupancy to the new one. This is costly, in many instances prohibitively so. Where a long-distance move is involved, the transportation of members of the household is also a considerable enterprise. Third, if the change in occupancy involves shifting from a unit owned by the household, that unit must (almost always) be sold to make the purchase financially feasible for the household. This requires all of the aforementioned procedures in the role of seller instead of buyer/renter. Search efforts for the seller are formidable, but are not often appreciated because they are largely conducted by the seller's realtor agent, for the cost of which the owner must pay the realtor a significant commission upon successful completion of the search. Overcoming all these obstacles to an occupancy change is extremely costly in time, effort, and money costs, far in excess of what is involved in changed consumption for other commodities.

Call these the frictional costs of occupancy change. Their very considerable magnitude makes occupancy change an expensive action. Therefore, change will not be seriously considered unless the *net* improvement promised by an occupancy change is even more considerable than the frictional costs of change. For that to be true, the present occupancy must be seriously out of line with what the current market has to offer in meeting the household's current housing preferences. Small absolute disappointments with the present premises or small changes in new market availabilities and/or prices will not suffice to make occupancy change worthwhile.

Under what conditions, then, is a household likely to be ready for a serious effort at occupancy change? In answering this, a curious but important paradox must be faced. A household does not know or even surmise that some other available unit (together with its price and the price the household can obtain by selling its present unit) will on balance raise its utility—considering both units and the friction costs—unless it knows or has some substantial information about the availability, characteristics, and price of that other unit as well as the probable price it can obtain by selling its present unit and even the search costs it will incur in the process. But to know this information requires that the household engage in the search process. A small, informal search may be uninformative or misleading. So basically a formal full-scale search is in principle necessary in order to know firmly whether a full-scale search is warranted.

In fact, most households do not engage in full-scale search before they are ready to commit themselves to active participation in the market in the present period. But they do not commit themselves without information either. Our model assumes that this dilemma is resolved in a two-stage decision process. The process hinges on the existence of both relevant information that is cheap and easy to obtain and that which is more difficult and/or costly to obtain (Galster 1987: ch. 7). The former we refer to as "background" information, the latter as "foreground" information. Foreground information is information obtained by directed formal search of specific housing units, via realtor summaries and conferences, and on-site visits. It is costly in terms of time, effort, and travel cost. Background information is casual information obtained by word of mouth, newspaper advertisements, and accidental encounters while otherwise engaged, as well as more general information concerning housing construction, price trends, neighborhood changes, and so forth. This information can be considered essentially free.

Our model assumes that a household basically understands that change of occupancy represents a considerable household enterprise, involving heavy time, effort, and monetary costs as well as a substantial upset in living habits, social relations and accustomed locales, and public-private good accessibilities. So a household is not likely to be willing to engage upon occupancy change for light and trivial reasons. A move must promise very marked overall improvement in suitability (considering both attributes *and price,* along with sale prospects for the present premises) to be warranted. This could conceivably occur where the household was satisfied with its present occupancy, but extremely attractive new opportunities had emerged. But the differential suitability would have to be exceptional, not simply moderate, especially including price comparisons, to justify incurring the major human and monetary costs entailed in the process of a change. This factor depends of course on whether the occupancy change concerns rental or owner-occupier property. Occupancy-change costs for rental units are considerably smaller, though not trivial, than the emphasis in this paragraph, which refers chiefly to owner-occupier units. What this suggests is that large prospective overall improvements, especially in the absence of knowledge about specific more suitable accommodations, are most likely to occur where the household is actively dissatisfied with its present housing package (Galster 1987: ch. 8).

Economic analysis rarely finds *absolute* evaluations relevant to choice; it is almost always *relative* evaluations, comparisons between or among alternatives, that determine choice. This is not really a logical contradiction of that explanatory logic, for here we hypothesize that an absolute evaluation simply *initiates* a given direction in a sequential two-or-three-stage decision process. *If* the household is dissatisfied with its present housing, it is likely to pay more elaborate attention to the background information available about other housing possibilities, up to the reading of specific newspaper advertisements and asking friends and acquaintances. *Then, if* this systematic assembling of background information suggests that, compared to the present occupancy, important overall improvement in suitability[2] is highly likely to be achieved in an occupancy change, the household will formally enter the housing market as an active participant. Present dissatisfaction both initiates a preparation for informal comparison with dimly perceived alternatives and also raises the presumption that such comparison—and an eventual formal comparison—will probably indicate the advantage of moving.

To be an active participant in the housing market involves undertaking formal search for a new occupancy, engaging in negotiations with owners, incurring the costs of arranging and concluding transactions (including mortgage financing, deed searches, etc.), and, if successful in the above, moving possessions and selves to the new unit. What factors would lead a household to be willing to undertake this? A combination of unsuitability of the present occupancy and suitability of other possible occupancies suffices.

When a household moves into a new occupancy, it is to be expected that either the unit "exactly" fits the wants of the household at that very time or is planned to fit those wants progressively better over a foreseen short future as the household changes into an anticipated new stage (like planning to have three children over the next five years). During that period—the outset and at least a few years after in the first case, the next, say ten years in the second—the household will not be dissatisfied with its occupancy. Dissatisfaction sets in as the household changes—size, age cycle, income level, work location, housing and neighborhood tastes (with style of life). It will also set in as the condition of the house changes markedly, so that the quality of services and/or the cost of upkeep and repair alter for the worse. These factors will strengthen the longer the household has lived in the same housing unit. Against these, the passage of time in the same house increases emotional ties to both house and neighborhood. Where large life-cycle changes occur, however, some of these latter become obsolete, weaker, or obliterated—by death, friends moving away, changed tastes and capabilities. So on balance the passage of time in the same occupancy tends to increase net dissatisfaction with present occupancy.

The suitability of other occupancies similarly tends to grow with the duration of time the household has spent in its present occupancy. New units become built, relative prices change, often progressively, away from their original pattern at the beginning of the present occupancy, and neighborhood character and accessibility patterns have changed exogenously. The probability grows with time that some of these external changes will make new opportunities better than the increasingly unsatisfactory internal situation, and gradually better enough finally to offset the substantial costs of changing occupancy.

Thus the probability of a given household becoming an active participant depends on its current degree of disequilibrium, brought about by a combination of changes in the household's circumstances, in the situation of the housing package, or in the external market since the present occupancy was established. All of these are a positive function of occupancy duration and operate through changes in household income, size and age composition, housing availabilities and relative prices, in neighborhood and accessibility, in public sector services, and in new technical and geographic developments. We express the sense of this discussion in simplified form in equation (4.8):

$$\Delta U_{0i} = \mathrm{D}\,[\,\Delta Y^{i}(T_0^i),\ \Delta(\mathrm{p}_0/\hat{p}_i)(T_0^i),\ \Delta L(T_0^i)], \tag{4.8}$$

where

ΔU_{0i} = the expected change in housing utility for household i between its level at the outset of the present occupancy and that at the present time t_0;

T_0^i = the duration of household i's present occupancy at time t_0;

$\Delta Y^i(T_0^i)$ = the accumulated change in household i income as a function of present occupancy duration T_0^i;

$\Delta(p_0/\hat{p}_i)T_0^i)$ = the accumulated change in the ratio of prices of household i's present unit p_0 and its currently perceived optimal unit, $\hat{p}_i$;

$\Delta L(T_0^i)$ = the accumulated change in the character of the structure during the present occupancy (in various conversion actions and change in condition).[3]

We assume

$$\frac{\partial U^i}{\partial T_0^i} < 0 \text{ and } \frac{\partial |\Delta Y^i|}{\partial T_0^i} > 0.$$

The price change variable in equation (4.8) is an estimate *by* household i. Thus, it may differ in the same objective circumstances for another household. It represents a comparison of prices between $t_0 - T_0^i$ (i.e., the outset of i's current occupancy), and t_0 from household i's present unit and that unit which household i *now* perceives at its optimal unit—both price and identity being based, of course, on surmise, not actual knowledge. The optimum involved here will generally differ from what it would have been.

The probability of household i becoming an active participant in the housing market at t_0 is

(4.9) $$pr_0^i\ (D) = g^i\ (\Delta U^i(T_0^i),\ SC_0^i),$$

that is, where

pr_0^i = the probability that household i will become an active market participant in t_0; and

SC_0^i = i's perceived expected cost of successful search and other occupancy change cost at t_0.

Perceived expected-occupancy-change costs reflect attitudes toward risk by household i as well as objective components like moving and transactions costs. Under the same objective circumstances, therefore, *SC* may differ for different households. The $pr_0(D)$ will differ, then, for different households because of differences in both expected utility change from a shift in occupancy and the costs of effecting such a shift.

A household that has decided not to become an active participant in the housing market simply continues to occupy its present premises for at least another period. One that has decided to become active is a candidate for changing occupancy, but may not in fact do so if its formal search fails to conclude with an advantageous shift. We now examine the process of housing search for the latter households.

This book does not attempt to develop a special theory of housing search.

The literature contains a variety of such theories, but no consensus as to a definitive version.[4] We are content to append any of a number of suitable models from that literature. We suggest here, however, a theoretical context that seems appropriate to the kind of search that is involved.

Given the extravagant multidimensionality of the housing stock in the urban area and the importance of the quality level and mix (including land, neighborhood, and accessibility as well as structure) to the user, considerable information about market opportunities is required for informed choice. But to become fully informed, given the massive heterogeneity and the high unit cost of search, is prohibitively expensive. It is rational to become only partially informed. So degree of informedness becomes a decision variable, and housing search, which embodies this learning process, becomes an instance of optimal sampling, where both mode of selectivity and cut-off point are central. How many and which kinds of housing packages should be sampled?

Our theoretical approach to market segmentation suggests the behavioral importance of the stratified character of that segmentation. Housing quality is a salient perceptual feature of alternative housing packages. Not only does it imply a reasonably narrow band of utility, but it directly bears on the substitutability of housing as a whole with respect to other commodities by indicating a total monetary liability. We therefore hypothesize that the active searcher will first decide to focus the search on a narrow band of quality-level submarkets. He or she then searches specific packages within these submarkets for most appropriate attribute mix and price.

The strategy of optimal sample size has been discussed in some variety in the literature.[5] Two major approaches appear to dominate. One is based on reservation gain, the other on a gradient cutoff process. We suggest a variant of the gradient process, but indicate circumstances where the reservation gain approach may be more appropriate. Each housing package sampled registers a particular utility level. Gross utility gain is this level less that of the present occupancy. The cost of the search necessary to discover and learn about this package, plus the transactions and moving costs, constitutes the occupancy change cost. Subtracting this cost from gross utility gain gives net utility gain. The search cost is a function of both the number of packages that have been sampled before arriving at this particular package and the total elapsed time that would be required for occupancy change if the search stopped at this point. We assume that costs of search are approximately linear for number of items sampled and are approximately similar for different households, except for the utility loss of time directly spent in search. Elapsed time is not a measure of direct time spent in search, but the amount of total time including search, transaction closure, and moving that will have passed before a new housing occupancy can be begun if the search itself were stopped at this point. Some prospective moves have deadlines attached or other special inconveniences associated with postponing the desired occupancy shift. Households will differ markedly in this time measure of search cost. As an example of the difference between the two kinds of time cost, a household may have been "looking for" another house for a year, but during that year will have spent the equivalent of ten full days of actual search. Equation (4.10) summarizes the above:

$$(4.10) \qquad \Delta U(L_i, n_i, s_i) = (U(L_i) - U(L_0)) - U[S(n_i, s_i)],$$

where

$\delta U(L_{i0}) \equiv (U(L_i) - U(L_0))$ gross utility gain;

$\Delta U(L_i, n_i, s_i)$ = the net utility gain from package L_i, discovered as the nth item sampled, with expected overall elapsed time before occupancy change s_i;

$U(L_i)$ = the utility associated with package L_i;

$U(L_0)$ = the utility associated with the present package L_0;

$U[S(.)]$ = occupancy change cost, in utility terms with search of n_i items; and

s = elapsed time before occupancy change:

$$\frac{\partial U}{\partial n_i} > \frac{\partial U}{\partial s} > 0.$$

For a sequence of n items there will be a maximum value of δU among the items sampled, $\delta U^*(L_i, n_i, s_i)$. This value belongs to some L_j, encountered as the n_jth item, where $n_j \leq n_i$. It is assumed that the household can "return" to that L_j out of the first n_i items and proceed to negotiate a purchase transaction—in other words, that "implicit recontracting" is possible: a search can store recently sampled opportunities until ready to decide on which one to bid seriously. As n increases, δU increases. Consider the distribution of $\delta U(L)$ for the set of L in the entire housing stock. With specific information about this distribution we can, in principle, estimate a function showing the expected value of $\delta U^*(n)$—for different values of n, that is, $E\delta U^*(n)$—the expected maximum value function. Its likely shape is shown in figure 4.2. $E\delta U^*$ is likely to rise rapidly as n increases from low levels, because there are many housing packages "out there" that are superior to L_0 for our household at this early stage of search. As n increases further, exhausting the units "out there" that are better than L_0, the expected maximum value function rises more and more slowly, approaching the highest value of gross gain in the entire stock, δU^*, only asymptotically.

Figure 4.2 shows as well, the occupancy-change cost function (in utility terms). Only the search element is a variable, transactions and moving costs assumed to be constant.[6] The vertical distance, $E\delta U^* - U(S)$, measures expected net utility gain from occupancy change $E\Delta U^*$:

$$(4.11) \qquad E\Delta U^* \equiv E\delta U^* - U[S(n,s)].$$

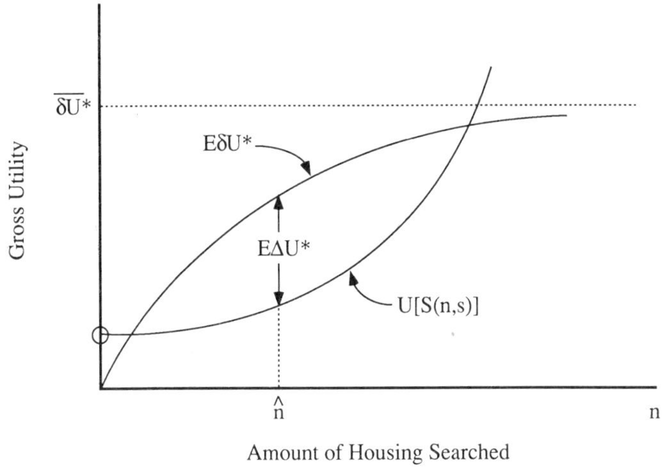

Figure 4.2. Optimal housing search.

EΔU* is maximized where

$$\frac{\partial E\delta U}{\partial n} = \frac{\partial U(S)}{\partial n}.$$

$E\Delta U$* is shown in figure 4.2 as the vertical distance between the $E\delta U$* and $U(S)$ curves. It is maximized where the slopes of the two curves are equal and $E\delta U^* > U(S)$. This occurs in figure 4.2 at $\hat{n}$, the optimal size of search. Figure 4.3 shows the effect of parametric changes on $\hat{n}$. δU_1^* indicates that either present occupancy is only moderately unsatisfactory or available alternatives are only moderately superior to it, δU_2^* that either present occupancy is quite unsatisfactory or available alternatives are considerably superior to it. $U(S_1)$ shows that per unit sampling costs are only moderate and/or that time elapse cost is only moderate (either search is conductible rapidly or only minor deadline and delay inconvenience exists). $U(S_2)$ shows larger per unit sampling costs and/or higher delay costs (slower search or delay is more inconvenient), while $U(S_3)$ shows highest per unit search costs and/or high delay costs.

When potential gross gains are only moderate ($E\delta U_1$*) but search costs are also low ($U(S_1)$), $\hat{n}_{11}$ is optimal search, which means high expected gross gains from occupancy shift. With the same schedule of expected gains but higher search costs ($U(S_2)$), optimal search is much less, $\hat{n}_{12}$, and hence expected gains from occupancy shift are much lower as well. Where search costs are quite high, ($U(S_3)$), the same gross gains schedule gives optimal search $\hat{n}_{13} = 0$. No search is prospectively warranted, and the household, although an active participant, ultimately remains in its present occupancy.

When potential gross gains are higher, because the present occupancy is more unsatisfactory and/or alternative opportunities are exceptionally attrac-

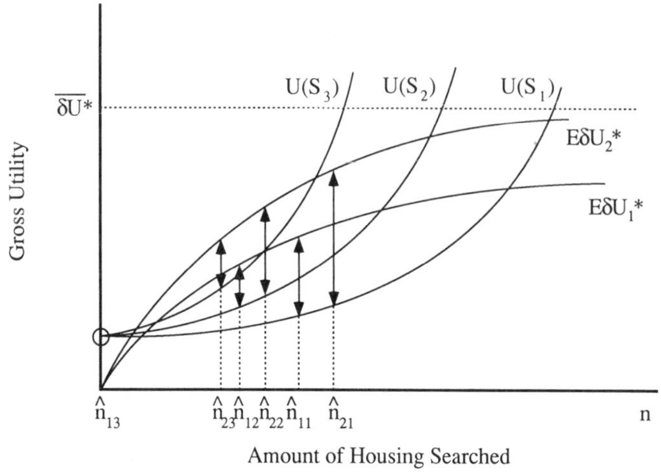

Figure 4.3. Effects of parametric changes on optimal search.

tive in their own right, $(E\delta U_2^*)$, even the highest search cost situation, $U(S_3)$, cannot discourage at least some search, $\hat{n}_{23}$. As expected, lower search costs, $U(S_2)$, give a higher optimal level of search, $\hat{n}_{22}$, in this particular example generating higher expected gross gains than with the lowest cost function under the $E\delta U_1^*$ regime. Finally, as expected, the lowest search cost–highest gross gain regime, $(E\delta U_2^*, U(S_1))$, gives the highest optimal level of search $\hat{n}_{21}$, and accordingly by far the highest expected level of gross gains.

In this analysis, the stopping point is decided on before search begins, rather than depending on the actual stochastic search experience, as under the reservation value approach. We are attracted to the above gradient approach because the long occupancy durations implied by our overall approach make possible significant irreversibilities and considerable gains, which together produce the possibility of considerable regret at a too precipitous leaping at the first good prospect that comes along, as may occur under the reservation value approach. *If* market conditions make it possible for a search to "save up" earlier seen prospects for subsequent action (within a reasonable time period, of course), then the gradient approach permits patience and more extensive scanning, making possible bigger gains. But market conditions may not permit this. A very tight seller's market is too competitive for buyers to permit them the luxury of postponing immediate action when they find something "acceptable." As soon as they find something "acceptable" they jump at it. This is the logic of the reservation value approach. In our context, it is not high search costs that make this an attractive analytic approach, but rather the market tightness that imposes the need for immediate clinching action. Thus, under some circumstances the one and under other circumstances the other search strategy seems more relevant. We believe that in normal market circumstances the gradient approach seems more fitting.

Can we predict the character of the *L* package that will actually result from optimal search? Since actual search involves inherently stochastic processes, we cannot predict the actual outcome of search at a particular time by a particular household. But for a group of similar households in similar circumstances we can predict expected characteristics of chosen *L*. Each household searcher in fact chooses an *L* package that diverges from its optimal package as defined under static, fully informed conditions. It gives a lower utility level than was theoretically possible. With respect to quality level it can diverge from the static optimum by being *either* higher *or* lower. There is no systematic reason to expect one or the other. Moreover, in such a presumed absence of systematic bias in chance or choice, the degree of divergence is likely to approximate a normal distribution (or a log normal). Similarly, the chosen package will diverge from optimality for each housing attribute. Here too there seems no grounds for expecting systematic bias either in direction or degree, so a normal (or log normal) distribution of divergences may well be appropriate here too. Thus, for a large enough group, the *expected* character of chosen packages (i.e., *(EH,* [*ER*], *EAG, ED))* should approximate that of the static optimum choice. This does not, of course, mean that the quantitative effect of actual dynamic choice on the configuration of submarket demand is the same as if all search households had made the static choice; its set of dynamic choices will have a nontrivial variance. Detailed analysis of intersubmarket impacts must use this variance pattern to allocate expected numbers of units demanded in the different submarkets. But the static package serves as the mean configuration chosen, the anchor submarket.

Aggregate Demand

The implications of the foregoing dynamic analysis of individual households on aggregate demand are profound. First, given the large occupancy-change costs, expected gross gains from such change must be quite large to warrant becoming an active market participant in the present period. The degree of individual disequilibrium is likely to change little year by year. Households who did not move last period are likely not to move again. Only gradually are household life-cycle changes and external availability/price changes likely to cumulate to the extent that incurring the steep costs of active participation in the market seems warranted. So in each period only a very small proportion of households is likely to become active in the market. Empirically, in the United States, which generally has the highest housing turnover rates in the developed world, average occupancy duration is more than five years for all tenures, implying that an average of less than 20% move in any year. For the important owner-occupier group, less than 9% or 10% move in any year. But even this understates the effect. Durations vary greatly among households. A small number of households moves much more frequently than the average and helps make the average as high as it is. In fact, a very small proportion of households do move in any one year, especially among owner-occupiers, for whom occupancy-change costs are very considerable and much higher than for renters.

So in any market period the demand side is represented by only a small sample of users. Are they representative of the rest? If one looks at the probability of active participation function in equation (4.9) in the context of equation (4.8), for the basis of self-selection of this small group, it is likely to be heavily made up of people who have been at their present occupancy a long time and/or have experienced important life-cycle changes recently. This household profile involves important stochastic elements. In addition, the information base that supports decisions about active participation has highly idiosyncratic elements. So these self-selected representatives of user interests represent in fact much randomness relative to the overall state of household housing preferences and income levels. They are both a small sample and not tightly systematically linked to the rest of the user population.

A second major implication stems from the fact that in housing markets, demand and supply are unusually intimately linked together. We have noted that the extreme durability of housing leads the existing stock overwhelmingly to dominate the supply of units occupied in any period. Occupancies supplied by newly built units make up no more than 2% or 3% of the total.[7] This means that the identity of the units which will be available for purchase or rental in any period depends overwhelmingly on which existing units are being released from their present occupancy by reason of their occupants deciding to become active participants for an occupancy change. As we have seen, the decision of owner-occupiers to become active is explicitly linked with their intention to put their present house on the market. With respect to renters, landlords rarely expel reasonable tenants who want to continue their occupancy; the availability of rental units on the market is generally the result of a tenant-initiated decision to vacate. Thus the market availability of units to buy or rent in any period—the active *supply* of housing—is predominantly determined by the *demand*-driven self-selection of active market participation. But this self-selection, as we have seen, is infused to an important degree with stochastic factors. Market demand *and* supply in any period therefore comprises only a very small sample of household users and housing units which is not strongly linked to the overall population of users or existing and potential housing units.

The further implication of both of these relates to price changes in the market. The prices that serve as market signals to the whole population of *potential* active demands and suppliers are in fact set in the active market in each of the kinds of periods we have just been describing. But these prices reflect the market adjustment to the impact of just those self-selected users and suppliers actively in the market in the period. The rest of the housing stock and user population exert only a broad framework constraint on these short-period price fluctuations. Some of the further implications of these market impacts are examined in the next few chapters, as we discuss first housing supply and then market adjustment. They are quite significant.

Now we turn to the more general situation of housing demand, where housing as an investment good is not neutral with respect to either tenure choice or the elements of pure consumption demand, for example, the quality of housing demanded.

4.2 Housing as Consumption and Investment

In the first section of this chapter we treated housing as a flow of consumption services, the demand for which was roughly akin to what derives from the standard theory of demand for a consumption good. This treatment assumed that the array of financial instruments and the existence of a large rental market were sufficient to allow consumption decisions to be made essentially independently of decisions about tenure status. But in the real world the capital market is not perfect, and changes in portfolio composition involving housing, as well as changes in housing occupancies, are neither nearly costless nor instantaneous. Search, monitoring, and transactions costs create nonneutral portfolio implications for consumption decisions and nonneutral consumption implications for tenure-choice decisions. In the present section we now treat housing as both a consumption and an investment good to examine whether and how this joint function may affect demand behavior: whether the two-way nonneutrality makes demand for an investment different than if housing were solely a portfolio asset, demand for consumption different than if housing were solely a consumption good (cf. Henderson and Ioannides 1986, 1987).

Because many new variables and relationships are required to illuminate the joint role, we modify the analysis so as to highlight the effect of the jointness. Accordingly, we simplify the earlier consumption-good analysis somewhat, onto which we add the investment role. We dispense with the multidimensional heterogeneity of the housing package, assuming continued equilibrium in attribute mix, and describe each given housing unit as varying only in terms of its quality level. This is consistent with our argument in chapter 3 that households trade off amounts of different attributes to achieve their desired quality level. In addition, there is reason to believe that the effect of the investment role of housing falls preponderantly on its "amount," not on its mix.

In this section we first examine what differences exist between the pure consumption and the mixed consumption-investment options, that is, what systematic differences obtain between a rental tenure and an owner-occupier tenure. (We are not concerned here with the producer orientation of house ownership purely for rental purposes, that is, landlord status. This is an aspect of housing supply, not demand, and is included under supply in later chapters.) Following this, we incorporate these features into a model of housing demand. Choice in this model is addressed both to the characteristics of the service flow relative to nonhousing consumption and to tenure status—rental or owner-occupier. Elaboration of this model permits us to delineate the kinds of impact the investment role of owner-occupancy has on housing demand.

Our treatment of housing investment is distinctive because it is placed within our basic context of the stratified array of housing submarkets. For this context we attempt to characterize not only the theory of housing consumption–investment of the individual household, but the pattern of the intersubmarket differences and adjustments, and the resulting configuration of choices. Much of this part of the analysis depends on the distribution of household differences in tastes, expectations, and wealth as well as on the degree of differentiation of institutional parameters.

4.2.1 Differences between Housing as Consumption and as Consumption-Investment

There are a number of differences between renting the flow of housing services and owning the stock from which those services flow. Some differences are highly inherent, some depend on slow-changing institutions, some on arbitrary, readily modifiable public policies. We have selected six that seem especially fruitful for our present purposes.

Mix of Portfolio Assets

Insofar as at least some part of the selling price of the housing unit is financed by the owner-occupier, there will be a change in the mix of assets held in the household's portfolio away from nonhousing assets and toward housing assets. In the United States, the housing asset dominates the portfolio for the majority of homeowners, so this shift of asset mix is likely to be very substantial. In the choice between rental and ownership tenure, therefore, an important consideration is the relative productivity of the housing and nonhousing assets available to each household.

Savings and Dissavings

Insofar as the purchase of a home is financed in part out of current income, nonhousing consumption and/or saving will be decreased. Typically the effect on saving is much larger, involving very heavy dissaving to the point of high indebtedness via large mortgage borrowing. Such heavy indebtedness (comprising for most U.S. homeowners their largest debt) considerably influences the intemporal allocation of consumption over a household's lifetime. So intertemporal choice is significantly involved in making tenure choice.

Consumption Aspects of Ownership Lifestyle

Premises occupied by tenants are treated differently than those occupied by owners in at least two aspects. An owner's use of property is basically unmonitored, unregulated by others. Physical usage; noise levels; strategy toward wear and tear, maintenance, repairs and replacement; modification through painting, minor structural changes, and so forth; privacy in an extensive sense—all these are far more under the control of the owner-occupier than of the tenant. These differences in the ways of using a housing unit can be significantly important to the user's satisfaction. Households may be attracted by the freedom, but repelled by the corresponding responsibility. Their net overall attitude will depend on the relative strengths of the two. Tastes probably vary markedly on this. Different households will be strongly or moderately or weakly positive, or strongly, moderately or weakly negative. For some families these attitudes, positive or negative, may be more important than many structural features; for others, less so; for others still, of little importance. Large differences in significance and direction have real implications for population self-selection in tenure choice. Another type of consumption element has been speculated on from the theory of imperfect contracts.[8] The above element stressed that owner-occupiers need not be responsible in their housing use to anyone else but themselves. They must take the full consequences of their manner of using their own property. Tenants, on the other hand, must inherently be responsible to someone else—the landlord—for their use of the property. But in the presence of imperfect contracts, where it is impossible for the landlord to predict some particular tenant's manner of using the premises and costly to monitor such use subsequently, rental contracts will be based on "average" use. Hence, less careful, less responsible tenants will benefit, more careful, responsible tenants will lose, relative to owning and residing in the property themselves according to their respective styles. So in terms of practicable financial and social-norm responsibility, ownership tenure is less, or more, attractive relative to rental tenure, depending on particular household characteristics.

The two tenures thus differ in the way housing services are consumed. The first kind empirically suggests that owner-occupier tenure involves for most households a positive good absent from the rental tenure, but one appraised differently by different households (even occasionally negatively). The second kind suggests a less preponderant appraisal: some households will find ownership status superior to, and possibly a comparable number inferior to, rental status. We speculate empirically that combining the two kinds of difference will leave ownership tenure with a net positive attraction for most households—other things being equal. Individual taste differences, however, will lead to a gradation of utility impacts, from significantly positive, declining toward zero, and even, for some few households, to negative.

Minimum Housing Investment

Zoning, building, health, and sanitary code regulations combine to make legally standard housing expensive in the United States. The urban supply of housing available for owner-occupancy, consisting until the recent condominium spurt of mostly one- and two-family houses and thus relatively easy to monitor publicly, usually contains few units of very low quality. In contrast, rental units in cities, preponderantly in multiple-unit structures, are much more difficult to monitor, and a much lower range of qualities is available.[9] So choice of owner-occupancy implies, in practical terms, that at a minimum, an investment of considerable size must be made to obtain an available owner-occupied house. This considerable capital value implies two things. First, it represents a large absolute amount to finance—out of assets, current income, and borrowing. It dislodges much in the household's finances and, for many households, may be outright prohibitive because of liquidity or overall wealth considerations. Second, the high market value capitalizes a stream of housing services that is at least of "standard quality"—in some supply circumstances (to be treated below) considerably higher than "standard." Thus, a modest-income household wanting owner-occupancy might well have to consume a considerably higher quality of housing than it would voluntarily choose in the absence of such constrained availability. Thus the effective floor on how little housing can be bought with owner-occupancy is a deterrence to that tenure relative to rental status for households wanting—due to taste, income, or wealth—housing in a lower range of quality. It is no deterrence to households whose unrestricted choice would have been for quality at least as high as the floor.

Real Estate Tax

The real estate tax is levied on real estate capital value. Regardless of its precise quantitative ultimate incidence, still academically unsettled,[10] this tax lowers the real rate of return on assets held in real estate form relative to non–real estate assets, which are not subject to such a tax, other things being equal. Moreover, the tax is nontrivial in magnitude, so it should exercise a nontrivial disadvantage to owning housing assets (and other real estate) rather than non–real estate wealth. This should influence the optimal portfolio of assets mentioned in the first item as inherent to the housing tenure choice. The degree of adverse tax treatment for real estate is modified by federal income tax treatment, as noted immediately below.

Income Tax Advantage

This factor has generally been treated as the paramount consideration influencing tenure choice.[11] We have left it for last to underscore that, while important, it is only one of a variety of considerations that influence tenure choice, some of which may be as, or even more, important to households, depending on the household and the circumstances.

The U.S. federal income tax favors owner-occupier over renter status in three ways: (1) it fails to tax the imputed value of the flow of housing services to owner-occupiers as income; (2) interest payments on a mortgage are deductible from taxable income while most other consumer interest payments are fully taxable; (3) state and local real estate taxes paid by owners are deductible from taxable income. On the other hand, renter payments for housing are not accorded advantageous treatment.

The first item is an outright subsidy to ownership tenure. The second is slightly less so, since its size depends on the discretionary decision about a mortgage. The third is actually a partial offset to the ownership *disadvantage* imposed by the different level of government. All three, however, boost the attractiveness of ownership tenure; the boost is greater the higher the income tax rate. If there are several tax rates, as a function of income, then the size of the effective subsidy is endogenous, since it depends on the relationships among income level, amount of housing demanded, and size of mortgage.

In the next section we spell out a model of housing demand (for quality and tenure) that incorporates all six of these differences. Our model is simple enough so that, except for the two interactive taxes, the effects of these differences are nearly linear and can be appreciated intuitively.

4.3 A Model of Housing Demand for Quality and Tenure

To capture the intertemporal character of the investment-consumption contrast we specify a two-period arena of choice: the present period and a future period. Households have a two-period welfare function that is made very simple to underscore the principal issue at hand. It is a log-linear function of two identical one-period utility functions, each of which is in turn log linear. The one-period utility functions are weighted exponentially to reflect time preference, the first-year function having a higher weight than the second.

Each one-year utility function has as its arguments amounts of the two consumer goods in the model, housing and all nonhousing consumption taken as a numéraire commodity, weighted by their utility elasticities. Housing is a complex commodity, as we have argued in this and earlier chapters. As we indicated above, however, to put the integration of consumption and investment into relief we focus only on the quality dimension of housing in this section, the rest being assumed to remain in equilibrium through variations in tenure choice. Let us consider, then, a housing unit in the following compact notation:

$$L = (H, [R], AG, D) \tag{4.13}$$

where

L = a particular housing unit;
H = the quality level of housing services (i.e., its quality submarket membership);
$[R]$ = the particular vector of the housing attribute mix = $(h_1, h_z, \ldots, h_n)$;
AG = age of structure in the first period; and
D = tenure: $D = 0$ is rental, $D = 1$ is owner-occupancy.

In what follows we assume a housing market in equilibrium with respect to attributes and age, and further simplify to assume that tastes are homogeneous for these dimensions; so in these dimensions every household pays at the margin for each tradeoff pair a relative price that equals the household's marginal rate of substitution between the pair. Thus every household pays appropriately for every age and every attribute combination. We assume moreover that the tenure choice is independent of these attribute mix patterns. So the central focus of the choice of D becomes the D/H interrelationship. We may therefore substitute (H, D) as a partial representation of housing. We do it by treating H as the housing "quantity" variable, but giving different utility weights to that for $D = 0$ and $D = 1$; moreover, giving a price of rental housing services, P_H, separate from the value of the ownership housing stock, I. We explicitly relate the two behaviorally below.

In the one-year utility function the distinction between $(H, D = 0)$ and $(H, D = 1)$ is reflected in the utility weights of the housing arguments. In view of our argument above that owner-occupier status represents a somewhat different consumption experience than renter status, we use a composite exponent for housing, that is, $\alpha_{hD} = \alpha_h + \alpha_s$ for $D = 1$ (ownership), $\alpha_s \geq 0$. For $D = 0$ (rental), $\alpha_s = 0$.

The welfare function is as follows:

$$W = W[U(H_1, Z_1), U(H_2, Z_2)] \tag{4.14}$$

for the general form, and the following for the particular specialization we employ in the next analysis:

$$W = B\left[H_1^{\alpha hD} Z_1^{\ \alpha Z}\right]^{g1}\left[H_2^{\alpha hD} Z_2^{\alpha z}\right]^{g2}, \tag{4.15}$$

where

W = welfare function of a household over the two periods;
U = welfare function of a household for one period (generic $U(H_1, Z_1)$ is first-period utility; generic $U(H_2, Z_2)$ is second-period utility; specialized $U = \bar{B}\, H^{\alpha hj}\, Z^{\alpha z)}$;
$B, \bar{B}$ = constants;
H = one-year housing service level;
Z = one-year nonhousing consumption level;

g_1, g_2 = intertemporal weights, $g_1 > g_2$; and

$$\alpha_{hD} = \alpha_h + \alpha_s \text{ where } \begin{cases} \alpha_s \geq 0 \text{ if } D = 1 \\ \alpha_s = 0 \text{ if } D = 0. \end{cases}$$

Below we are interested in household differences in tastes as well as in other determinants of choice. So we shall have a family of W^x, X = household 1, 2 . . . , where the functions differ in B, $\bar{B}$, α_h, α_s, g_2 ($g_1 = 1$).

There are budget constraints for each period, and the pair differs for the two tenures. We assume that the household receives a constant annual income, Y. In addition, there are two assets, a housing stock (comprising one housing unit), I, and nonhousing assets, A. These latter assets are expressed as capital values of expected flows of Z (since Z is the numéraire good).

In order to close the model over two periods, there is no terminal value which points beyond the second period (or for which a direct utility attribution would raise difficult questions). We simply require that all assets be fully consumed by the household. Since housing is highly durable we can interpret full consumption to mean either that period two is itself long enough to permit the physical housing stock to be used up by its end or, more modestly but arbitrarily, that period two is akin to the conventionally short period one, but that the household can only be an owner-occupier during the first period. It must sell its ownership right at the beginning of the second period and use the proceeds to rent housing services as well as nonhousing consumption during period two.

Though it seems a bit clumsy, we favor the second interpretation because we wish to permit differential price appreciation for the housing asset to result in either a financial gain or loss that impacts consumption levels in period two. Retention of owner-occupier status of an asset that appreciates markedly gives no utility gain, because the quality of the service remains unchanged despite the price change. In our simple financial model, only sale of the asset enables realization of the gain (there are no reverse equity mortgages).

So, in the first period, the household can decide to consume its housing as either renter or owner-occupier. But in the second period it must consume it solely as renter, having cashed in at the beginning of the period all of both kinds of assets held over from period one.

In both periods the household is subject to two kinds of tax—an income tax and a tax on the value of housing assets owned (but *not* on nonhousing assets). Both are fixed-rate taxes and are levied at the time when each period's consumption-investment actions are taken.

The purchase of housing assets is complicated by the presence of a mortgage market. A housing asset can be purchased with mortgage funds, but these funds have an upper limit for each housing asset purchased, so that the household must itself make a down payment. A mortgage interest rate, distinct from the rate of return on nonhousing assets, is charged for the loan, which is to be paid at the beginning of period one after a budget allocation is made.

Finally, the presence of two periods makes possible a change in prices between periods. Since in this model all decision making occurs at the beginning of period one, the prices in period two which influence that two-period strategy are prices *expected* when the household makes its choice at the beginning of period one, rather than actual realized prices. The prices referred to are those for housing and numéraire consumption services, and for both housing and nonhousing assets.

The decision is as follows. At the beginning of period one, the household observes period-one prices for consumer goods and assets, and tax rates, anticipates a set of period-two prices for these goods, and, on the basis of these, decides (1) whether to buy or rent housing in period one; (2) if ownership is decided on, how much money to borrow by mortgage; (3) how much housing to consume in period one; (4) how much of the nonhousing commodity to consume in period one; and (5) how much nonhousing assets to carry through period one. These explicit decisions, together with the expected changes in prices, determine an expected value of assets to be carried over into the beginning of period two, and thus the expected addition to consumption purchasing power they would represent over and above constant annual income after income tax in period two. Therefore, a further decision is made *at the same time:* (6) how much housing services to consume in period two; and (7) how much nonhousing commodities to consume in period two.

These period-two consumption allocations are extremely important for the overall strategy decisions made in period one, because the choice of owning or renting housing, together with the rest of the period-one package, determines an implicit expected set of period-two consumption opportunities, and optimizing on these opportunities tells the household *in period one* what maximum expected overall two-period welfare can be obtained for each resulting period one–period two combination.

Thus the nature of optimal choice can be pictured as follows. The household considers the set of first-period options in which housing is rented. For each possible allocation (involving level of housing and nonhousing consumption, and size of nonhousing assets to be carried over into period two), a set of expected period-two budget opportunities is implied. An *optimal* period-two allocation is then selected from this set, generating a best pair. So both period-one and period-two consumption are fully determined, and hence period-one and period-two utility levels. This in turn determines the highest level of two-period welfare attainable for each period-one choice. Every possible similar period one–period two best consumption pair is tried. That pair which gives the highest two-period welfare for period-one choice is designated as the optimal rental option. Next, the same winnowing process is performed on all the period-one opportunities in which the housing asset is *pur-*

chased. Along with consumption levels, mortgage, and nonhousing asset carryover, this determines for each such option an implicit set of period-two opportunities which, when subject to optimal consumption allocation, also determines a period one–period two best consumption pair. Each such best pair implies a best two-period welfare level. All ownership combinations are considered in this manner, and that one giving the highest welfare is designated the optimal ownership option. Finally, welfare levels of the optimal rental and ownership options are then compared, and that one giving the higher level is chosen. Thus, rental versus ownership tenure in period one is decided simultaneously with the optimal amounts of housing and nonhousing consumption in both periods (expected amounts for period two) and the optimal amounts of mortgage borrowing and nonhousing investment in period one. They all form elements of a single optimal choice.

We can now make explicit the model described. The two-period constraints for the rental option are as follows:

Period-One Rental Budget Constraint

$$P_{H1}H_1 + P_{z1}Z_1 + A_1 = Y(1 - t) + A_0 (1 + r(1 - t)), \tag{4.16}$$

where

P_{H1} = price of one unit of housing services in period one;
$P_{Z1}Z_1$ = price of one unit of nonhousing consumption in period one;
A_0 = initial value of nonhousing assets;
A_1 = value of nonhousing assets after period-one budgetary allocation made;
Y = annual income level (exogenous);
r = annual rate of return on nonhousing assets held; and
t = fixed rate of income tax (payable in each period).

Period-Two Rental Budget Constraint (Rental-Rental)

$$P_{H2}H_2 + P_{Z2}Z_2 = Y(1 - t) + A_1[1 + \beta(1 - wt)] \tag{4.17}$$

(no home ownership in period two; no retention of assets),

where

β = the expected rate of increase in the value of each nonhousing asset held;
P_{H2}, P_{Z2} = expected period-two prices of housing and nonhousing units of consumption; and
w = percentage of capital gains taxed as income.

The ownership budget constraints are as follows:

Period-One Ownership Budget Constraint

$$(I_1 - M_1) + P_{Z1} Z_1 + i M_1(1 - t) + I_1 \tau(1 - t) + A_1 = Y(1 - t) - A_0 (1 + r (1 - t)), \tag{4.18}$$

where

I_1 = value of housing asset owned in period one;
M_1 = value of mortgage loan to buy I, in period one;
i = mortgage interest rate (payable in period one); and
τ = rate of tax on housing real estate.

Period-Two Owner-Rental Budget Constraint

(4.19) $$P_{H2}H_2 + P_{Z2}Z_2 = Y(1 - t) + A_1[1 + \beta(1 - wt)] + I_1[wt + (1 + \tau)(1 - wt)] - M_1.$$

Auxiliary Constraints

(4.20) $$I \geq I^*.$$

If housing ownership is desired, the investment in a housing asset must be at least as great as level I^*. This minimum-quality constraint expresses our earlier discussion of relative supply unavailability of low-quality ownership housing in our hypothetical city with stringent zoning and code regulations for housing:

(4.21) $$g_1 > g_2.$$

This inequality expresses the existence of time preference in household intertemporal tastes.

(4.22) $$I = fP_{H1}H_1.$$

Capital values of housing assets as specified in (4.22) are simply the capitalization of the net gains from ownership, which include housing services and expected capital gains less mortgage interest, real estate tax, and fixed financial costs *(c),* all of which are modified by income tax treatment. The parameter f is the capitalization factor, obtained by capitalizing the two-period net financial gain from homeowning by the market cost of capital, *r,* and using the mean expected rate of capital appreciation of I in the population $\bar{\gamma}$, as the *market's* expectation.

(4.23) $$f = \frac{1}{G(1 - c)}$$

where

$G: = r + \bar{b};$
$\bar{b}$ = market average expected increase in value of A_1 between periods one and two;
c = capital transactions cost (a fixed percentage of capital value); and $0 < c \leq 1$.

This assumes that a normal mortgage situation transpires (i.e., $M = mI$, where m is a ceiling proportion of asset value) (see equation 4.28 below for explanation).

(4.24) $$P_{H2} = P_{H1}(1 + a),$$

where a is the expected rate of increase in the per unit price of housing services between period one and period two.

(4.25) $$P_{Z2} + P_{Z1}(a + b),$$

where b is the expected rate of increase in the per unit price of nonhousing consumption between period one and period two.

(4.26) $$I(1 + \gamma) = I(1 + a).$$

By the mathematics of our simple capitalization, the flow price appreciation equals the capital value appreciation.

Similarly for A:

$$A(I + \beta) = A(1 + b);$$

(4.28)
$$\begin{aligned} &M = 0, \text{ where } i > r \text{ and } A_0 \geq I; \\ &M = I - A_0 \leq mI, \text{ where } i > r \text{ and } A_0 < I; \\ &M = mI,\ 0 < m < 1, \text{ where } i < r \text{ and } A_0 \geq I(1 - m); \text{ and} \\ &M = 0, I = 0, \text{ where } A_0^* \leq I(1 - m) \\ &(A_0^* = A_0 \text{ supplemented out of } Y). \end{aligned}$$

Where the mortgage rate exceeds its opportunity cost, the rate of return on A, the household will try to finance I entirely out of A_0 (if $A \geq I$). If A_0 is insufficient, A_0 will be used up and the mortgage will equal the residual $I - A_0$, so long as this does not exceed mI, the maximum amount available from a mortgage. If $i < r$, the household will try to borrow as much as possible, which equals mI. The term $(1 - m)I$ is the minimum down-payment required by the mortgage. If the household cannot finance this out of A_0 (or, in the extreme, by A_0 supplemented by Y), an I this large cannot be purchased and no mortgage is obtained for this level of I.

Finally, to repeat equation (4.15):

$$\alpha_{hj} = \begin{cases} \alpha_h + \alpha_s \text{ where period-one housing is in ownership tenure} \\ \alpha_h \text{ where period-one housing is in rental tenure} \end{cases}$$

4.4 Optimal Tenure Choice in the Housing Model

Mathematical manipulation of equations (4.13)–(4.28) permits us to deduce several qualitative properties of the model. In the remainder of the chapter we examine them in turn.

4.4.1 Consumption Elements in Ownership

Other things equal, the presence of positive net consumption elements in ownership should increase the attractiveness of the ownership tenure relative to renting. Moreover, the larger the utility significance of these elements for any household, the greater the probability that the ownership tenure will be chosen. This means that if households differ appreciably in the utility weight of ownership (i.e., the size of α_{hs}), the probability of choosing ownership will be arrayed according to the sizes of α_{hsj} (j is each household), other things being equal.

This inference rests upon the notion that in purchasing housing services through ownership, a household is obtaining an extra commodity as well—"at no extra cost." In other words, the real price of housing services is in effect lower via ownership than via renting. But is ownership obtainable at no extra cost? No. There are two sources of cost to the owner stemming from the supply side and the demand side, respectively, and their treatment differs markedly.

The supply-side source is simple, and its treatment accordingly can be straightforward. In this model, housing units used for rental are identical with those used for ownership.[12] So they should be supplied (via either new construction or modification of existing units)[13] at the same cost. There is, however, one element of cost that is not accounted for by this assumption. It is the complex of legal-financial costs involved in transfer of a capital asset,[14] and any incremental costs of the more demanding search warranted where an important capital transaction is at stake. Fees for the services of realtors, lawyers, banks, and others are involved, making for a nontrivial one-time[15] cost over and above payment for the unit's annual flow of housing services. Since these costs are in practice approximately a fixed percentage of selling price, we can discount the transformation of the house's capital value into its flow of services (H) and price per unit of such services (P_H) by subtracting this capital transactions cost (c) from the capitalization factor (f) (see equation 4.22). Thus, in the absence of such a cost, the capital value (I) of the flow of service value ($P_H H$) is obtained, in this simplified financial market, by capitalization via the opportunity cost of capital in housing, assumed for simplicity to be the mortgage rate of interest (i). Thus,

$$I = FP_H H. \tag{4.29}$$

where F is a *gross* capitalization factor. However, if c percent of this capital value is a capital transaction cost, then only $I\,(1 - c)$ represents the capitalized value of the flow of housing services proper, that is,

$$I\,(1 - c) = F(1 - c)P_H H. \tag{4.30}$$

Let us call $I(1 - c)$ the operating housing stock, $\overset{o}{I}$. Then the conventional market capitalization process is reflected for $\overset{o}{I}$ directly, not I

$$Ia = \frac{1}{i} P_H H, \tag{4.31}$$

so:

$$\overset{o}{I}(1 - c) = \frac{1}{i}P_H H, \tag{4.32}$$

and thus:

$$I = \frac{1}{i}\frac{1}{1 - c}P_H H = f P_H H, \text{ where } f = \frac{F}{1 - c}. \tag{4.33}$$

So a given market value for the asset buys less housing quality than in the absence of this cost element, that is, ownership does carry a cost.

By this treatment, however, we can assume that the per service unit price of housing is the same for both rental and ownership units. Behaviorally, of course, there is a difference. Becoming an owner-occupier gives an extra commodity, D, with utility weight α_s, but at the cost of a penalty on the rate of return to housing assets relative to returns on nonhousing assets (approximately equal to $1 - c$). The net effect of D per se, therefore, is the difference between the welfare gain associated with $D = 1$ rather than $D = 0$, or $\frac{\partial w}{\partial \alpha_{hj}}\alpha_s$, an interactive function of the welfare function arguments, and the welfare cost associated with a penalty on the rate of returns of housing assets. The latter operates by both decreasing period-one housing consumption level by $1 - c$ percent for given total investment in housing,[16] *and* decreasing the value appreciation of the asset between periods one and two.

$$\text{(4.34)}\quad \text{a. } \overset{o}{I}_2 = \frac{P(1 + a)H}{i} = (1 + a)\overset{o}{I}_1 \text{ and } \overset{o}{I} = I, \text{ where } c = 0.$$

$$\text{b. } I_2 = \overset{o}{I}_2(1 - c) = (1 + a)(a - c)I_1, \text{ where } c > 0.$$

Thus, it decreases period-one consumption of housing and period-two consumption of both housing and nonhousing goods.

The conditions under which the net welfare effect is zero, that is, the household is indifferent between owning and renting, are complex, depending on many parameters and the resulting absolute size of H_1, Z_1, H_2, Z_2, but intuitively it depends directly on how important ownership instead of rental status is as a consumption good compared to ownership's transactions cost. The indirect effects of H–Z tradeoffs, period one–period two tradeoffs, and a–b, r–i differentials matter, but are more complex and likely to be secondary in importance.

The behavioral implication of this is that, since c is likely to be essentially equal for all households and housing units, there will be a self-selected degree of *net* attraction toward ownership based on individual differences in the size of α_s. Households with high appreciation of ownership for itself will be more attracted overall than those with lower appreciation. For some α_s, the household will be indifferent overall. For α_s lower than this, rental status will be more attractive on this score.

So far we have spoken only of the supply-side market adjustment, but there is a demand-side market adjustment as well. Indeed, the demand-side adjustment is likely to be the first to occur. Suppose a population has a given distribution of tastes for H, Z, and D, and a given stock of rental and ownership houses has come into being so that all markets clear in a general equilibrium, at equilibrium prices of rental and ownership units (both service flow and capital value prices). Now let a group of erstwhile marginal renters experience the same nontrivial increase in preference for ownership per se, that is, $\Delta\alpha_s > 0$.

For these households, ownership will now be preferable to renting, and they will shift their demands accordingly. As a result, prices of rental units will fall and those for ownership units will rise until the new price differential completely offsets the new preference advantage. Thus the new preference advantage will be exactly capitalized in the new price differential.

One implication of capitalization is that at these after-adjustment prices, one could not explain the ownership choice of the whole marginal shifting group—since they should be indifferent between tenures. Another is that one could not predict that a subsequent household experiencing the same shift in preferences would shift from rental to ownership.

Capitalization blurs the problem of predicting tenure shifts. It is especially serious when there is a large change in the identity of the marginal shifters because of the occurrence of large shifts. The problem is least serious when individual differences in taste are great and nearly continuous, so there are few large lumpy changes in the identity of marginal shifters. In this case, significant net advantages and disadvantages from shifting will remain for every price differential, because both intra- and extramarginal net advantages will be highly differentiated for most of the population. So here, except for the few households who are actually *at* the margin to begin with, our welfare analysis will clearly predict tenure choice for the rest of the population.

How reasonable is it to expect such capitalization to occur? Quite reasonable as a first-step market adjustment, but the adjustment does not stop there. The new relative prices for rental and ownership units will induce new supply adjustments, namely, an increase in the number of ownership units and a decrease in the number of rental units. This supply response will then *lower* ownership prices and *raise* rental prices. So at the adjusted prices the households at the presupply adjustment margin will now be intramarginal and will now clearly show a net advantage for ownership.

How much supply adjustment can be expected to occur? Additional relative supplies will be forthcoming until relative marginal costs of supplying the two types of units equal the market price ratio of the two. In discussing the supply side earlier we argued that these marginal costs to suppliers are in fact equal—the additional price of ownership referring only to financial costs to users, not to suppliers. With equality of marginal costs for the two types of unit, the market price will gravitate to equal supply prices, regardless of the disparity of user tastes. So any initial capitalization reflecting new net advantages to users will subsequently be wiped out by the resulting induced supply adjustments.

Therefore, we do not have to contend with the complexities inherent in variable degrees of capitalization. Differential taste situations will be reflected in differential tenure-supply distributions, not in differential prices alone or in differential tenure-price mixes.

4.4.2 Income Tax Treatment of Ownership-Rental

The analysis of consumption elements in ownership provides a model for the present category. Ownership carries not only an inherent consumption element with it; it also brings tax treatment referring to both consumption and investment which favors ownership over rental status. The value of housing services rendered by ownership does not have to be paid for; yet it is the imputed income from housing investment, and no income tax need be paid on it. Notwithstanding this lack of recognition for the returns, *costs* instrumental in making and maintaining the investment, mortgage interest, and real estate taxes *are* recognized as such and are therefore treated as if such investment were like any nonhousing investment.

Thus, in equation (4.17), this favorable treatment for housing investment makes the total purchasing power in period one greater than it would be for either a comparable level of housing services under rental or a comparable investment of resources in nonhousing assets. Associated with this housing investment option is therefore a complex tax advantage that has an income and a substitution effect in portfolio allocation; moreover, since this investment option is directly linked to consumption of housing services, there is also an advantage for housing over nonhousing consumption with both an income and substitution effect as well. Exact delineation of these effects is cumbersome because they operate not only for period one but for the composite of the two-period welfare function and thereby involve most of the arguments of the welfare function and of both period budget constraints. But the effect is clear: the income tax treatment raises the real rate of return on housing both absolutely and relative to nonhousing investment, and lowers the real price of housing service consumption both absolutely and relative to nonhousing consumption. So the welfare effect is to increase the maximum *potential* welfare level of the ownership option for everyone and to increase the *actual* welfare level for anyone already in ownership tenure and for anyone thereby induced to shift from rental to ownership tenure.

In terms of tenure choice, therefore, if, in the absence of these tax benefits, households were previously arrayed in terms of the decreasing welfare difference between ownership and rental tenure, with all those with positive difference already in ownership, the new appearance of these sizable benefits would offset even nontrivial negative welfare differentials for many households, and thus would shift the dividing line in tenure choice appreciably down the array toward a greater ownership proportion.

The above welfare differential array depends on the variety of household differences we mentioned earlier. In discussing the effects of consumption elements in ownership, we merely assumed relevant differences in tastes but did not attempt to link them to other aspects of the system. With this tax category under discussion, however, individual differences are strongly linked to a household characteristic that will be found to be strongly empirically linked as well to initial assets, to the effect of a required minimum size of housing investment, and even, in some real-world scenarios, to the size of the minimum mortgage rate available (as well as, effectively, to the size of the mortgage itself). The link is to household income. If the income tax is proportional, as in our explicit model, the absolute size of the housing benefits rises with income level. If the tax in the real world is progressive, this effect is even more pronounced.

Thus, whatever individual differences generate the ownership-rental welfare differential array when tax effects are excluded, admission of these differences will cause a tenure shift toward ownership that is strictly a positive function of income. Our discussion below suggests that the former (ex-tax effect) array is itself heavily affected by income level in the same direction. So while the effect of tax advantages is to extend the attractions of home ownership to everyone, practically speaking they give the greatest gains to those who already have ownership tenure and increase the number of households with ownership tenure strictly in accordance with income level—the higher the income level the larger the probability of inducing a shift to ownership. Nonshifters gain none of the tax benefits.

In terms of behavioral sensitivity to parameter values, the size of tax benefits is a positive function of the size of the tax rate. High tax rates generate much larger benefits from special treatment, and hence much larger behavioral adjustments, than low tax rates.

4.4.3 Minimum Required Housing Investment (I^*)

The two factors discussed above are linearly additive increments to the attractiveness of ownership over rental tenure. The present factor is also linear with these two, but has a negative effect on ownership.

Each level of I implies, via equations (4.22) and (4.23), a tied level of housing services, H. So I^* implies, for given P_H, i and c, a particular H^*. Suppose that a household, *if* it purchased I instead of H, were permitted to buy any level of I it desired, and that its unconstrained choice, $\hat{I}$, were less than I^*. Then the tied level $\hat{H}$ would fall short of H^*. Since $\hat{H}$ would maximize W for choice of I, imposition of the requirement that H be at least as great as

H^* would impose a lower W than with $(\hat{I}, \hat{H})$. If $\hat{H}$ were greater than H^*, $\hat{H}$ would be the permitted choice, so welfare under ownership would be maximized by free choice.

Therefore, where free choices generated H levels lower than H^*, any welfare gain from ownership would be offset by the welfare loss from the constrained minimum consumption of housing. The size of this welfare loss depends on the size of the difference between H^* and $\hat{H}$. This differential increases the lower is income level, since the latter is the major determinant of housing-level consumption. Thus, at low income levels, other things being equal (which are not inherently linked to income level), the welfare loss from the big differential between desired and required minimum H will be large, hence often more than enough to offset all possible advantages to ownership. Households at moderate income levels may still find a coerced increase in H necessary under ownership, but an increase so small that the associated welfare loss is less than the net attraction to ownership from all other sources. In other words, minimum required I^* progressively lessens the net attractiveness of ownership the lower is income level. For given tastes, there is a moderate income level at which the welfare loss from ownership (still positive: i.e., $\hat{I} < I^*$) is just equal to the net advantage from ownership from all other sources. We see this process by combining the linear effects of consumption elements (+), tax benefits (+), and minimum $I^*(-)$ in figure 4.4.

Four possible (D/t) functions are shown in figure 4.4, each for a different welfare weight given to the consumption elements of D: $\alpha_s^0 > \alpha_s' > \alpha_s'' > \alpha_s'''$.

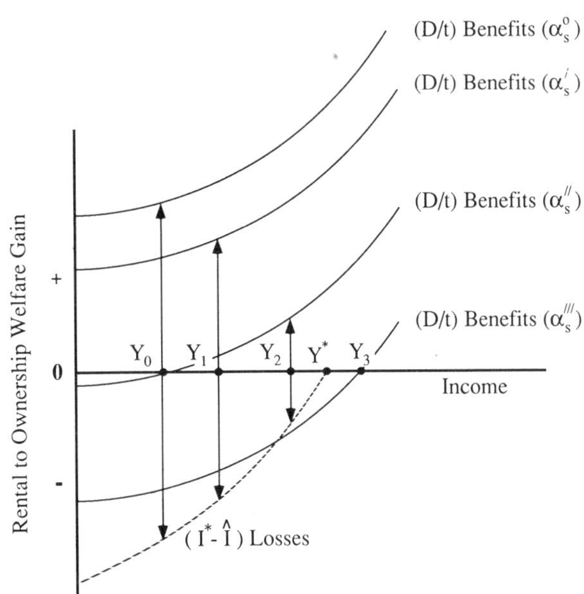

Figure 4.4. Demand/tax benefits and forced overconsumption.

Y^* is the level of income at which $H = H^*$, so beyond Y^* no coercion regarding H is required (and thus the welfare effect is zero for $Y \geq Y^*$). If the household has α_s^0, the income level at which I^* losses just equals (D/t) gains, and so the household is indifferent between ownership and rental, is Y_0. If it has α_s' the indifference level is Y_1 (higher than Y_0); if it has α_s'', the indifference level is Y_2; if it has α_s'', the indifference level is Y_3. To the right of each of these, ownership is sought, to the left, rental. The rising slopes of both (D/t) and $(I^* - I)$ functions show the positive income influence on tax and minimum H effects, and the parallelism of the three (D/t) functions shows the essential independence of D benefits from income.

Overall, figure 4.4 shows that income level demarcates tenure choice. Below a pivot level of income (Y_0, Y_1, Y_2, Y_3), all households of a corresponding level of α_s choose rental tenure, and above it all choose ownership. Location of the pivot depends on the level of α_s and on the slopes of the (D/t) and $(I^* - \hat{I})$ functions (generally unequal to one another). The diagram also shows that the pivot can be at a level of Y where H is either coerced (Y_0, Y_1, Y_2) or uncoerced (Y_3). It could conceivably by accident even equal Y^*, the minimum level of income at which H is not coerced. In each case the pivot is where the algebraic sum of the (D/t) and $(H^* - \hat{H})$ functions equal zero.

The common slope of the (D/t) functions is determined by the income linkage of tax benefits with income level. The slope of the $(H^* - \hat{H})$ function depends on the shape of the welfare functions—the form of the one-period utility function, and the time preference discounting of period two consumption relative to that of period one—and on relative prices. For example, the lower the taste for housing relative to nonhousing consumption, the steeper is the $(H^* - \hat{H})$ function.

The differentiation of tenure impact by income level has important implications for our basic emphasis in the book on household and market stratification. Each income level generates a different quality of housing demand, other things being equal. These different quality levels are embedded in the various—but *finite*—submarkets that reflect differing degrees of imperfect market relatedness among clusters of housing units, each submarket having some adaptational leeway independent of other submarkets. In this context, the tenure/income-level relationships imply that quality submarkets will contain nontrivial, sometimes quantum, monotonic differences in the percentage of households owning and renting housing. Tenure mix differences will be an accompanying characteristic of submarkets differing by quality.

4.4.4 Real Estate Taxation

Up to now we have dealt with explanatory variables whose joint effects were linear. Most of the remaining factors have nonlinear, interactive effects on tenure.

Real estate taxation has usually been thought of as one aspect of the income tax treatment of housing. In our model it has a more complex role. First, as we can see from equation (4.18), a real estate tax diverts available purchasing power away from all consumption and nonhousing investment, for any given I. Since nonhousing investment is not subject to such double taxation (i.e., added on to an income tax on the *returns* from investment), the existence of a real estate tax lessens the real rate of return on investment in housing relative to nonhousing assets. By so doing, it discourages a shift in portfolio from the latter to the former. Real estate taxation discourages owner-occupancy tenure.[17] The higher the real estate tax rate, the greater will be the discouragement about owner-occupier status.

In this context the treatment of real estate tax payments under the income tax is an offset to this discouragement. Equation (4.18) shows that the real estate tax τ decreases the diversion of purchasing power away from consumption and other investment. The size of this offset depends on the size of the income tax rate, increasing as the income tax rate increases. So the net discouragement effect against ownership is the multiplicative effect of the basic real estate tax drain as a percentage of I modified by a percentage of this as an income tax deduction. While our particular model specifies a single income tax rate t, more realistic scenarios using a progressive tax would have t rise as a function of Y: $t(Y)$, with $t' > 0$. So the size of the offset would be a positive function of Y. But the absolute size of the offset is a positive function of Y even with a proportional tax, since it depends positively on the size of I. In general, the higher the income, the higher will be desired H and so too desired I. More roundaboutly as well, higher annually recurring income strongly suggests a higher initial A_0 (via documented past savings), which is needed to finance the down payment on I and which, where the mortgage interest rate exceeds the rate of return on A, may be needed for all or most of the financing of I to make such investment attractive at all.

The above paragraph indicates that the net impact on ownership due to the real estate tax is highly likely to be negative, but that the size of this negative effect depends on Y, i, t, and A_0 as well. It is truly interactive with other factors, in complex relationships. Some appreciation of the impact of various parameter patterns is given in a later section of the chapter.

4.4.5 Mortgage Interest Rate and Rate of Return on A

Equations (4.16)–(4.18) show that the rate of return on A, that is, r, is part of the opportunity cost of investment in housing (along with current nonhousing consumption). Thus the higher r is, other things being equal, the less attractive I will be. There is an inherent competition between the substitute assets A and I. In addition to this direct effect is its indirect effect in influencing the marginal impact of income tax treatment on home ownership. A larger r lessens the attractiveness of ownership, but enhances the income tax encouragement to ownership by decreasing after-tax purchasing power of A proceeds by a larger absolute amount. The net encouragement from the direct and indirect effects of r is, of course, negative toward ownership since it gives back indirectly only part of what it takes away directly.

The mortgage rate of interest is a direct financial cost of investing in housing, since it is rare indeed that housing will be bought with 100% equity, even if the size of A_0 permits total internal financing. Our model permits a buyer to use 100% equity financing if the real, comparable term, risk-adjusted interest rate on mortgages is greater than the comparable rate of return on nonhousing assets, and if A_0 is adequate to cover I completely. In such a situation the tenure choice depends on the comparison between r and the rate of return on I, as well as the (H, Z) mix and that between present and future consumption. But if $i < r$ (assumed to refer to their real, comparable term, risk-adjusted values), then a mortgage will be sought for investment in I, and the tenure choice will depend on i as well as these other influences.

If $i < r$, so a mortgage will be sought to finance I; the higher i is, the lower will be the real rate of return on I, and so its attractiveness relative to rental will be lower. This effect can be treated either as raising the weighted opportunity cost of capital for I (i.e., mI costing i + $(1 - m)$ I costing r), or lowering the absolute net return on I $(P_H H - iM)$.[18]

At the value of i where it equals r there is a discontinuity. Values higher than this have no further discouraging effect on tenure choice so long as reliance on A_0 alone suffices to finance I wholly, since 100% equity financing will be sought. If $A_0 < I$, however, purchase of I would require some mortgage financing. All of A_0 would be used internally, and the balance, $I - A_0$, would be financed by mortgage. In this case, rising i would further dampen the attractiveness of ownership.

This analysis indicates that i, r, m, I, and A_0 are all interrelated for various regions of parameter values. This same interrelationship is seen when we discuss the size of housing demanded, H, below.

4.4.6 Income Level

The role of income has already been variously foreshadowed. Its effect on the attractiveness of ownership is unqualifiedly positive. It operates chiefly via three channels. First, the higher income is, the higher will be the level of housing services demanded. Incomes below the pivot level illustrated in figure 4.4 involve an $H < H^*$, thereby incurring a welfare loss under ownership due to the minimum consumption level required. This welfare loss increases the lower is Y, via a lower desired housing level, $H(Y)$. At and above Y^* (pivot Y), no welfare loss is incurred under ownership. This factor therefore acts with a discontinuity.

Second, the size of the absolute benefits from the income tax treatment of ownership is a continuous positive function of income. Even a flat rate tax makes both the mortgage interest and real estate tax deductions worth more the larger is income. The mechanism is that higher income induces higher H and therefore higher I as well; higher I implies a higher real estate tax assessment and thus tax liability, and presumes as well a higher mortgage M (via either $M = mI$, or $I - A_0 \leq mI$) and thus higher interest payments. These benefits grow throughout the range of Y.

Third, Y (as an annual recurring flow implicitly earned *before* our initial period) influences the size of initial nonhousing assets, A_0, which were presumably accumulated over time by savings out of that earlier, highly autocorrelated income flow trend. Savings grow as a function of Y in our model because of the need to balance intertemporal consumption levels. Thus the higher Y is now, the higher A_0 is likely to be. The size of A_0 is important to the attractiveness of ownership because, at the very least, a down payment on I must be financed predominantly from it (the remainder coming from new savings out of current income, a slender source, considering the amounts involved). So A_0 less than the minimum down payment $(1 - m)I^*$ will be an absolute bar to ownership. Less absolute is the scenario where $i > r$. A household would want to assume 100% equity. If $A_0 < I^*$, this is impossible. With $M = I - A_0$ $(\leq mI)$, the larger is M, the higher the cost of capital to finance I, since more has to be raised by mortgage at capital cost i and less at the lower r. So in its less extreme role, where $i > r$, the size of A_0 is again directly related to ownership attractiveness, thereby augmenting the overall direct and indirect positive relationship between income level and ownership.

In a previous section we drew some implications of this relationship concerning the pattern of tenure choice at different housing-quality submarkets. Quality submarkets will show disproportionate increases in the ratio of ownership to rental tenure as quality increases. Moreover, these will predominantly reflect welfare gains to households, since the attractions from ownership will not be significantly priced away via capitalization.

4.4.7 Initial Nonhousing Assets

We have essentially explained the effect of nonhousing assets above. A_0 is an adjunct to I, not a competitor—but the decision variable A_1, of course, is a competitor. A_0 permits, first, the absolute requirement for ownership, a down payment at least equal to $(1 - m)I^*$. Attempting to raise this primarily, or entirely, out of current income—at the sharp expense of period-one consumption—is likely to fail because of the large absolute size of the down payment. Second, a large A_0 permits financing ownership with flexibility over an interval beyond the I^* level; as the required down payment rises, the interval widens the larger is A_0.

This asset effect has not been mentioned yet, but could be important for some households. A household with high income but low A_0 would ordinarily want to consume a high level of H. But the household's A_0 suffices to finance only an I representing a much lower level of housing. In effect, A_0 constrains the household to much lower housing consumption through ownership than it could afford to buy through rental. This is the opposite of the kind of constraint on H wrought by the minimum I^* requirement. Ownership can thus constrain a household to consume *either* more *or* less housing than it would want to do—and could do unconstrainedly through renting. This represents a welfare loss and could in appropriate circumstances make ownership less attractive than renting.

A third impact of A_0 has been noted before. So long as $i < r$, the household planning to buy I would obtain a maximum-sized mortgage loan—mI. If, however, $i > r$, the household would try to finance I internally, through use of A_0. If $A_0 > I$, the household buys with 100% equity and sacrifices only r as the opportunity cost of the purchase. As A_0 falls progressively below I, a larger and larger proportion of the price must be raised by mortgage, and the per unit finance cost of the purchase, the weighted average of opportunity costs of capital, $C = \frac{A_0}{I}r + \frac{I - A_0}{I}i$, rises from r, where $A_0 \geq I$, to $(1 - m)r + mi$ (which exceeds r because $i > r$), where the maximum mortgage, mI, is obtained (m is usually a number $> .5$). As noted above, $A_0 - (1 - m)I^*$ raises the possibility of an absolute veto on ownership. A level of A_0 above $(1 - m)I^*$ but less than $(1 - m)\hat{I}$ (the unconstrained optimal level of H above I^*) avoids any absolute veto on ownership, but makes ownership less attractive by forcing a lower level of H than desired. And even a level of A_0 between $(1 - m)\hat{I}$ and $\hat{I}$ can decrease the attractiveness of ownership in situations where $i > r$. In this last case, the effect of A_0 is interactive with that of y, i, and r. In the second case, it is interactive with Y (in determining $\hat{H}$).

The effects of A_0, unlike that of tax rates and income, are discontinuous, having the various impact thresholds indicated above.

4.4.8 Expected Price Appreciations: *a* and *b*

These price appreciation variables are very important to the analysis. The real rate of return on A_1 and I as competing repositories of nonconsumed assets is their period-one flow of income plus their capital appreciation (+ or −) between the end of period one and the beginning of period two—appreciation that must be realized in our model by cashing in all assets at the start of period two. Parameters a and b are the main determinants of the differential in capital gains between I and A_1.

We must remember that a and b are not actual but *expected* appreciations. This distinction is significant in our model because we admit a population of households who differ in many respects—Y, A_0, tastes—and differ also in expectations about price changes. We employ these differences in order to illuminate the self-selection of different portfolio mixes during inflationary periods. In their absence, all households would have to be made indifferent between owning and renting in this regard via the adjustment of the market's capitalization of housing services alone. Securities buying and selling during asset appreciations seemed fueled not solely by consensual adjustments in relative prices but by genuine differences in opinion as well. We incorporate such differences of opinion as an additional influence on the diversity of tenure choice.

This source of diversity is not linked to our market stratification variables, like income or housing quality. It is largely orthogonal to these, being idiosyncratic like the differences in tastes also assumed. So our list of determinants results in some influences on tenure which are systematically related to the submarket complex, but also in some influences that cut across this complex.

We can see the specific influence of a and b on the rates of return of A_1 and I as follows. The real rate of return on A_1 is its one-period rate of interest flow after tax $r(1 - t)$, plus the after-tax capital gain rate, discounted to present (period one) value:

$$\rho_A = r(1 - t) + \frac{b(1 - wt)}{(1+r+\bar{b})} \tag{4.35}$$

where b is the particular household's expected appreciation of A and $\bar{b}$ is the market's average expectation.

The expression $1 + r + \bar{b}$ is the market's discount rate for money earnings. This return is a positive function of r, a negative function of t, and a positive function of $(b - \bar{b})$, the specific household's inflation expectation compared to that of the market—or simply a positive function of b, given $\bar{b}$.

The real rate of return on I is composed of the net benefits via housing services and discounted after-tax capital gains less financial costs (transactions costs, after-tax mortgage interest, and real estate tax—adjusted for income tax deductions), expressed as a percentage of equity investment in I. Thus,

$$\rho_I = \frac{G - (1 - c)}{(1 - m)} - \frac{G}{(1 + G)} + \frac{a\,(1 - wt)}{(1 - m)\,(1 - G)} - \left[\frac{(1 - t)\,(im + \tau) + c}{(1 - m)}\right], \tag{4.36}$$

where G = market discount rate = $r + \bar{b}$.

The first term shows the market's implicit rate of return of I in terms of P_HH, when discounted by G, as augmented by the leveraged purchase of I with only $(1 - m)\,I$ equity. This falls short of G because of the financial transactions cost, c. The second term, negative, is a penalty related to borrowing a mortgage and having to repay it later. As G rises this becomes a smaller negative number, because present value of the later repayment declines in importance. The third term is the discounted after-tax capital gains, augmented by the leveraged investment in I. The last term is the collection of after-tax costs (mortgage interest, real estate tax, and transactions charges), and this is also augmented by the leveraged investment. Leveraging affects both gains and costs proportionally, so *net* positive or negative gains will be enhanced equally.

The size of ρ_I thus depends strongly on capital gains a in addition to the other factors already discussed. It can be seen clearly in equation (4.36) that r and $\bar{b}$, i, τ, w and c unambiguously lower ρ_I, while t and a ambiguously raise it. The effect of m is likely to raise it when $i < r$, lower it in the opposite case. The effect of $\bar{b}$ in choice is more complex. While it lowers ρ_I, it also lowers ρ_A, so the net effect is less clear (working as it does, not only directly but also indirectly, on f via equation 4.23).

The rate of return on A_1 is not G, but G adjusted for taxes, which sets a wedge between it and the rate of return on I, because tax treatment differs markedly for the two types of investment.

(4.37)
$$\rho_{A_1} = r(1 - t) + \frac{b(1 - wt)}{(1 + G)}$$
$$(G = r + \bar{b}, \text{ not } r + b).$$

We can compare ρ_{A_1} and ρ_I as follows using equations (4.36) and (4.37):

(4.38)
$$\rho_I - \rho_{A_1} = r\left[\frac{(1 - c)}{(1 - m)} - (1 - t)\right] + \frac{(1 - wt)}{(1 + G)}\left[\frac{a}{(1 - m)} - b\right] + \frac{\bar{b}(1 - c)}{(1 - m)} - \left[\frac{(1 - t)(im - \tau) + c}{(1 - m)}\right] - \frac{G}{(1 + G)}.$$

The first term being greater or lesser than r depends on the size of the transactions cost of ownership (adjusted for leveraged purchase, $1 - m$) compared to the income tax rate. The former lessens the attractiveness of I, the latter of A_1 (since it, but not I, has its income subject to income tax). The second term is the present discounted after-tax difference in capital gains, that for I adjusted for leveraged purchase. The size of a relative to b clearly matters to differential rates of return, but not exclusively. The third term, $\frac{\bar{b}(1 - c)}{(1 - m)}$, is part of the rate of return embedded in the market capitalization of the income flow from I, namely, $P_H H$. The basic income flow difference in rates of return is really, therefore,

$$r\left[\frac{(1 - c)}{(1 - m)} - (1 - t)\right] + \frac{\bar{b}(1 - c)}{(1 - m)}.$$

In the comparison a substantial marginal income tax rate can more than offset the transactions cost of ownership, especially since the leverage of the I investment is advantageous due to the tax deductibility of interest payment, unless i and τ together are so large (i much larger than r) as to overwhelm even this, making leverage a disadvantage—and leading to a mortgageless scenario.

The fourth term lists the financial disadvantages of ownership, its distinctive costs: after-tax deducted mortgage interest payment and real estate tax and transactions cost—all adjusted for leveraged purchase. The higher is any one of these items, the lower is the relative attractiveness of ownership, with leveraging actually aggravating the deficiency (just as it enhanced its gain dimensions). The moderating effect of the income tax rate on this negativity due to deductibility is clearly seen here. The last term is a nonintuitive artifact of the time separation between the investment transaction and its closure.

4.4.9 Summary

Equation (4.38) is a good summary of the financial aspects of the tenure decision. Omitted from it, of course, are the welfare evaluations of different consumption mix and intertemporal mix tradeoffs—such as the consumption elements in ownership and the possibility of constrained under- or overconsumption of housing. Under ownership, tenure choice requires both sets of factors to be considered. We now turn, after a brief tabular summary of these parameter effects on tenure (see table 4.1), to the question What difference does a given tenure decision make to the consumption of housing?

4.5 Effect of Ownership on Consumption of Housing

Does tenure choice make a difference in the amount of housing consumption planned for the two periods? There are a number of ways such a difference might come about: (1) ownership over rental status carries an income effect, permitting more total two-period consumption without changing the housing-nonhousing mix; (2) ownership carries a substitution effect via a changed real price of housing relative to that of nonhousing, and this induces more housing relative to nonhousing; (3) ownership may require more housing consumption than wanted due to the I^* constraint and yet give higher welfare than renting; (4) ownership may not permit as much housing consumption as desired because of the inadequacy of initial assets to pay downpayment on the higher desired amount. The most important cases are the first two, not the binding constraint discontinuity ones. We concentrate on the former, but indicate under what circumstances the last two become important.

4.5.1 Income Effect

An income effect comes about in this model via the net financial effects of switching enough portfolio assets from nonhousing to housing to purchase the

Table 4.1. Effects of System Parameters and Household Variables in the Probability of Owner-Occupancy

	Direction of Effect	
	$r > 1$	$r < 1$
A. *System Parameter*		
1. Mortgage/value ceiling (1-Downpayment Rate)(m)	+	?
2. Mortgage interst rate (i)	−	−
3. Rate of return on nonhousing assets (r)	−	−
4. Market discount rate ($G \equiv r + \bar{b}$)	−	−
5. Transaction cost of housing asset transfer (c)	−	−
6. Income tax rate (t)	+	+
7. Percentage of capital gains taxed as income (w)	?	?
8. Property tax rate (τ)	−	−
9. Relative price of period-1 housing services (P_{H1})	−	−
10. Minimum conventional housing investment (I^*)	−	−
11. Market average expected increase in value of A_1 ($\bar{b}$)	−	−
B. *Household Variables*		
1. Relative taste for housing ($\alpha_h - \alpha_z$)	+	+
2. Taste for consumption elements of ownership (α_s)	+	+
3. Household income level (Y)	+	+
4. Size of initial nonhousing assets (A_0)	+	+
5. Relative rate of time preference (g_2/g_1)	+	+
6. Expected rate of increase in housing price (a)	+	+
7. Expected rate of increase in nonhousing price (b)	−	−

desired house. It consists of a difference between the rates of return to the two kinds of asset multiplied by the amount of assets to shifted. In the present nearly linear system, a given rate-of-return differential will be preserved over the range of different amounts of assets to traded. This means that on financial grounds alone, if the ownership asset carries a higher rate of return than nonhousing assets, the total financial gains will be greater the larger is the amount of housing purchased. The optimal amount of housing depends, however, on consumption mix and intertemporal mix considerations as well as on pure budgetary opportunities, so unlimited housing quality will not be bought.

Income effects will come about when the rate of return to housing ownership exceeds that to nonhousing assets. The conditions for this to hold are shown implicitly in equations (4.36)–(4.38). In the summary comparison of equation (4.38), it is clear from our whole discussion on the determinants of ownership tenure that just those factors that encourage ownership over renting increase the size of ρ_I relative to ρ_{A_1}. Thus, as the probability that ownership will be chosen increases, the probability that ρ_{I} will exceed $\rho_{\mathrm{A}I}$ increases as well. Indeed, the possibility of constrained over- and underconsumption of housing under ownership, or even of having to forego mortgage borrowing and buy on 100% equity under some circumstances, suggests that ownership may often not be preferred to renting *unless there is* a positive rate-of-return differential.

So ownership tenure is quite likely to be accompanied by *financial* gains, that is, by positive income effects. Examination of equation (4.38) also shows that the purchasing power gains are the results of cashing in a leveraged investment at the beginning of period two. Thus, the enhanced budget opportunities occur in period two, not in period one. So the income effect should result in higher consumption spending in period two over what would occur if the household rented in period one. However, our model prevents all of the effect from occurring in period-two consumption. The two-period welfare function depends on the balance between first- and second-period consumption—penalizing a big consumption disparity between the two periods. Moreover, due to time preference—expressed as $g_1 > g_2$ in the welfare function—second-period consumption is less valuable than first-period consumption. For both these reasons an *anticipated* increase in purchasing power that does not become available until the second period will lead to a two-period consumption strategy *mapped out at the beginning of the first period* under which the expected increase in two-period purchasing power will be shared between the two periods, that is, planned consumption will be greater in both periods. Since this concerns a price-neutral income effect, no adjustment need be made in the mix of housing versus nonhousing consumption: both will be increased according to their fixed elasticities of demand. Any change in the mix must stem from a change in relative prices, or else from an induced relaxation in the ownership constraints that generate over- or underconsumption of housing. The former is much more important, affecting a far larger percentage of owners. To this we now turn.

4.5.2 Substitution Effect

We must examine what happens to the price of housing services under ownership. This is not a straightforward matter because the owned house has no explicit price of housing services. We must make the explicit service price of rental housing comparable with the implicit service price of owned housing in order to compare them. Because of the financial complexity of the ownership transaction allocation, implying a portfolio asset shift, an intertemporal shift, and possibly a consumption mix shift, it is more convenient to translate the rental transaction in period one into a comparable set of shifts in these same dimensions and then to compare the overall financial implications.

We ask this question: What *increase* in housing investment is necessary to increase the flow of period-one housing by one unit of quality. It is this investment change, ΔI, that we subject to comparable treatment for rental and ownership status. The answer is found via equations (4.22) and (4.23).

$$\left.\begin{aligned} &(4.22) \qquad I = f P_{H1} H_1 \\ &(4.23) \qquad f = \frac{1}{G(1 - c)} \end{aligned}\right\} I = \frac{P_{H1} H_1}{G(1 - c)}$$

What is the net monetary cost to the household of making this additional investment under ownership? In what follows we assume the normal situation of seeking a maximum mortgage (mI), either because A_0 will not suffice to cover much more than the minimum down payment or because $i \leq r$, so a mortgage is not financially less attractive than cashing in one's nonhousing assets. Therefore, the amount of money actually to be spent to secure ΔI is only $(1 - m)\Delta I$. The investment increment, like the original investment, I, is leveraged through mortgage borrowing. This is not the net cost, because this investment will yield returns. We do not include the actual consumption services, because these are the basic welfare function consumption gains from the investment. Here we are concerned only with the financial returns, since it is these that influence budget opportunities. At the beginning of period two the investment will be cashed in. At that time the new value of ΔI will be received, $\Delta I\,(1 + a)$, but out of this the mortgage, $m\Delta I$, must be repaid and a tax must be paid on the realized capital gains. While the outlays—including additional ones to be mentioned below—are all made in period one, the cashed-in value, the capital gains tax, and the mortgage repayment must be made in period-two values, discounted back to period-one values via the cost of capital in the market, $1 + G$.

These outlays do not exhaust the net expenses associated with ΔI. In period one, interest must be paid on the mortgage, offset somewhat by the decrease in period-one income tax liability through interest deductibility. Similarly, local real estate tax at rate τ must be paid on the capital value, ΔI, and this too is offset somewhat here by the income tax deductibility of real estate tax payments. Finally, the financial transactions cost, at rate c, must be paid.

So in sum, the cost of providing one extra unit of service quality via ownership adds the equity cost of ΔI, the operating and transactions charges, and the repayment of mortgage, and subtracts the after-capital-gains-tax return of equity from liquidation as appreciated (in expectation!). This is shown in equation (4.39), where TCO is the total cost of ownership status:

$$(4.39)\quad TCO = \frac{(1 - m)\,P_{H1}}{G(1 - c)} \left\{1 + \left[\frac{(1 - t)\,(im + \tau) + c}{(1 - m)}\right] - \frac{a(1 - wt)}{(1 - m)\,(1 + G)}\right\} - \frac{(1 - m)\,P_{H1}}{G(1 - c)\,(1 + G)} = (1 - m)\,\Delta I \left\{\frac{G}{1 + G}\left[\frac{(1 - t)\,(im + \tau) + c}{(1 - m)}\right] - \frac{a(1 - wt)}{(1 - m)\,(1 + G)}\right\},$$

where $\frac{(1 - m)P_{H1}}{G(1 - c)} = (1 - m)\,\Delta I.$

The total cost for rental status, TCR, is comparably roundabout. We consider the same $(1 - m)\Delta I$ as above and ask what is the alternative use made of this by the renter. The renter spends P_{H1} of this to rent one extra unit of housing quality. The rest, $(1 - m)\Delta I - P_{H1}$ is spent on additional A_1. The cost of this in period one, after income tax, is $(1 - t)r$. We must further subtract the proceeds from liquidating the investment at the beginning of period two, which includes principal and capital gain, the latter diminished by capital gain tax, and both diminished by discounting to period-one values. The result is shown in equation (4.40):

$$(4.40)\quad TCR = P_{H1} + \left[\frac{(1 - m)P_{H1}}{G(1 - c)} - P_{H1}\right] \left[\frac{G}{1 + G} - r\,(1 - t) - \frac{b(1 - wt)}{1 + G}\right] = P_{H1} + ((1 - m)\,\Delta I - P_{H1}) \left[\frac{G}{1 + G} - r(1 - t) - \frac{b(1 - wt)}{(1 + G)}\right].$$

We calculate the excess total cost of rental over ownership, δ_{RO}, in equation (4.41):

$$(4.41)\quad \delta_{RO} = TCR - TCO = \Delta I\,(1 - m)\,r(1 - t) + \frac{(1 - m)\,\Delta I(1 - wt)}{(1 + G)}\left[\frac{a}{(1 - m)} - b\right] + P_{H1} - \left[\frac{G}{1 + G} - r(1 - t) - \frac{b(1 - wt)}{(1 + G)}\right] - \left[\frac{(1 - t)\,(im + \tau) + r}{(1 - m)}\right](1 - m)\Delta I.$$

To see how the value of δ_{RO} depends on typical parameter values we show the result of three scenarios in table 4.2, based on equation (4.41).

Scenario (A) mutes the most obvious advantages of ownership, namely, where $i < r$, making mortgage borrowing attractive, and $a > b$. In (A), $i = r$

Table 4.2. Excess Cost of Renting versus Owning

Parameter Value	Scenario (A)	Scenario (B)	Scenario (C)
c	.06	.06	.06
m	.7	.7	.7
G	.2	.2	.2
r	.1	.1	.1
i	.1	.05	.1
t	.4	.5	.3
P_{H1}	1.0	1.0	1.0
b	.1	.1	.1
a	.1	.2	.1
w	.5	.5	.5
τ	.02	.02	.02
Value of δ	.10	.18	.07

Note: δ is the excess cost of renting versus owning, expressed as an excess proportion over assumed ownership cost $P_{H1} = 1$.

and $a = b$. Despite this, the substantial size of t generates a strong net attraction for ownership. The real price of housing quality via ownership is fully 10% below that via renting. When the ownership advantages are augmented, as in scenario (B), where i is made less than r, and a is made larger than b, and t is increased to .5, the real price via ownership declines much more so that the real price via ownership is 18% less than that via renting. To show how powerful t alone is, scenario (C) returns to $i = r$ and $a = b$, and reduces t to .3. Despite this weakening of the advantages of ownership, the price for ownership is still 7% lower than the price for renting.

What we have seen is that the ownership option changes not only the overall budgetary opportunities available to households; it also changes the real tradeoff of spending opportunities between consumption of housing services and nonhousing consumption (i.e., the tradeoff between Z and H is different for rental than for ownership). In equation (4.41), δ_{RO} will equal zero only under very special circumstances. Moreover, the price change seems to be predominantly in one direction: to make housing services cheaper than they were (under renting) relative to Z. Since we assume a normal price elasticity of demand for quality, this implies that in calculating optimal budgetary allocations, a given household will be ready to buy more housing quality under its ownership option than under its rental option—even for some part of the parameter domain where rental is favored over ownership.

A brief mention should be made of the two other sources of difference in housing consumption under ownership and renting. They refer to the discontinuity constraints we have spoken about earlier: (1) where the minimum required I, I^* calls for higher H than would be selected under the rental option, and ownership is nonetheless chosen as on balance more attractive; (2) where the greatest minimum down payment requirement which can be afforded by the household, given its initial assets and current income, refers to a level of housing, H^0 (the counterpart of I^0, for which $I^0 - mI^0$ is barely affordable), which is less than it would buy under rental status—yet ownership is nonetheless chosen.

These circumstances may be important for some households, but they characterize a critical region, namely, where the household is close to indifference between the two options. Small parameter changes could lead to significant shifting across tenure boundaries by households in such circumstances. Because of this feature, the phenomena are important. They bear on the macrodynamics of the population. The tenure market, with its attendant effects on amount of housing quality consumed, probably does not operate smoothly under various kinds of exogenous changes. Households within these critical regions are likely to respond disproportionately to small changes in some signals, resulting in lumpy changes. We have more to say about this below.

We can now answer the paramount question of section 4.5: Does tenure choice influence the quality of housing consumed? Our analysis strongly suggests that the answer is yes. The mechanisms by which such an influence is generated are income and price effects, and the behavior discontinuities stemming from the constraint requiring minimum housing quality and downpayment for ownership. Our analysis indicates that under a wide variety of parameter values, ownership tenure confronts a household with a different opportunity set of housing-nonhousing consumption mixes than does rental tenure: the real budget constraint—"real income"—is different. Moreover, there do not appear to be dependable market processes forcing the two toward equality for any household. The same is true for price. The real price of housing service consumption relative to nonhousing consumption facing any given household will *generally* differ for ownership and rental tenures, and no market mechanisms appear to induce convergence between the two. Equality will be an accident, not the result of dependable adjustment. Moreover, no such adjustment mechanisms appear to push relative price differences to *offset* "real income" differences so as to equalize resulting housing demand under the two tenures. The sources of income and price differences are related, but only partially, *and even so, not compensatorily.* So these differences will exist, will persist, and may be of considerable magnitude. The result is considerable differences in housing consumption demand.

Minimum quality and downpayment requirements, with their opposite effects on housing consumption, also do bind, but less pervasively, in more specialized situations for particular households. Nonetheless, where they are relevant they also make housing consumption differ between ownership and rental tenure. Moreover, their occurrence is superimposed on—is simultaneous with—income and price differences. The behavioral result is a wide variety of differences in consumption over the population between the two tenures, the degree of variety abetted by the fact that price and opportunity set differences are partly due to households' own differences in future price expectations, that is, they are household-specific, thereby further evading any convergent effects of broad market adjustments. The resulting consumption differences may be considerable, and they constitute not only the housing-nonhousing mix but also the period-one/period-two mix for both forms of consumption (as we see immediately below).

4.5.3 Tradeoff Changes under Tenure Choice

The major question of our chapter has now been answered. The existence of an ownership option in addition to rental does lead to general differences in behavior. First, there is a socioeconomic stratification, although imperfect, of tenure status by quality submarket. Second, there are nontrivial income effects; third, there are nontrivial price/substitution effects (all in addition to the less general, more idiosyncratic discontinuity effects). We can ask for an overview of what kinds of behavioral tradeoffs are affected by these forces.

The income effects are predominantly financial gains stemming from favorable tax treatment of ownership transactions. In addition, they can reflect expected differential appreciation of capital values. As such, they primarily affect second-period budget opportunities. They go to increase second-period consumption above what it would have been with budget opportunities lacking such financial advantages. As we argued above, however, the form of the welfare function, with its advantage given to a close balance between consumption in the two periods, enables us to predict that some additional expected purchasing power will be used in a two-period allocation strategy that increases period-one consumption as well. But the second-period gain will be greater. So the first tradeoff change involved is that between present and future consumption, with the latter benefiting relative to the former when ownership is chosen.

The second tradeoff involved is that for housing versus nonhousing consumption. The ownership option involves a significant real price effect: ownership results in a lower price of housing services relative to nonhousing consumption than does renting. So the demand substitution effect should generate a greater consumption of housing services relative to nonhousing consumption under ownership. This price effect operates only in period one (when the ownership option can be taken), so it is in the first period that the consumption mix tradeoff is changed. Differential expected price appreciation for housing and nonhousing between periods one and two do affect relative period-two prices prospectively, and so too consumption plans, but in our model the effect refers only to rental use, because ownership is (for analytical convenience) not permitted in period two.

A third tradeoff is that between the attractiveness of nonhousing and housing assets in an investment portfolio. The distinctive features of housing investment generate a different rate of return for the two kinds of asset generally, and so their optimal mix. In general, ownership has distinctive financial advantages that make for a larger portfolio share than would otherwise obtain.

A fourth tradeoff is that between the consumption mix between the two periods. Second-period modification will arise largely from differential income elasticities, and first-period modifications largely from the substitution effect energized by the effect on period-one real prices. The difference here is less notable, however, because *some* of the real relative price effect is derived from anticipated period-two financial returns, which are related to—but not exactly the same as—the income effects discussed first. Thus the ownership option modifies most of the tradeoffs involved in both demand and investment choices. Its effects cannot afford to be ignored.

4.6 Summary of a Theory of Tenure Choice

4.6.1 Individual Choice and Its Aggregation

We are now able to put together elements of the analysis to delineate the determinants of tenure choice. We have established, for example, that I in effect unambiguously rises relative to Z_1 and A_1 with a rise in expected housing asset appreciation (a), income tax rate (t), taste for ownership as a consumption good α_s, income level (Y), and size of initial asset holdings (A_0). It falls unambiguously with a rise in mortgage interest rate (i), transactions cost of ownership (c), expected nonhousing asset appreciation (b), and rate of return on nonhousing assets (r). Other parameters have ambiguous effects, depending often on parameter interactions.

From the point of view of the present model, a theory of tenure choice consists in spelling out configurations of parameter values for which the model would predict that utility is maximized by one tenure choice or the other. Since so many parameters are involved, this can be fully accomplished only by substituting alternative whole sets of parameter values into the system's explicit solution. Some more intuitive illumination of the process may be obtained by taking advantage of an important feature of our approach—that aggregation of housing choice to a market level is accomplished by assuming the existence of a population that differs with respect to tastes (the utility function), budget size, and price expectations. Thus, at any one moment the population will make a variety of choices about both levels of housing H_1 and tenure status. The aggregate model is designed to predict the distribution of demand for housing submarkets and the tenure mix.

To illustrate the method it is not necessary to delineate complete sets of parameter configurations that determine the tenure split. It is instructive simply to let variables with unambiguous tenure effects vary systematically and track their consequences. Accordingly, let us trace the change in tenure choices as we hypothetically vary this set of variables so as to make optimal I_1, $\hat{I}_1$, rise systematically in each household's calculation of hypothetical optimal choice under the ownership option, monitoring the resulting rise in maximum W under ownership (relative to max W under the best rental allocation). Since $\hat{I} < I^*$ imposes welfare costs that can more than offset the normal financial advantages of ownership, rising $\hat{I}$ will decrease these costs until it reaches some level for which W max via ownership equals that for rental. We can start from $\hat{I}_1 = 0$, induce $\hat{I}_1$ to rise above 0 but considerably below I^*—so I_1 (actual) rises only "implicitly," since renting will be preferable. Continuing the process, $\hat{I}_1$ is induced to rise close enough to I^* so that ownership is finally preferred. Up to this point the household has remained a renter. Now actual I_1 leaps abruptly from 0 to I^* and the household becomes an owner-occupier. Further changes in the determinants of actual I_1 in the same direction keep the household in ownership status, but with higher and higher actual housing property investment.

The main effects of I_1 and its counterpart H_1 on nonhousing asset holding $(A)_1$ and nonhousing consumption $(Z)_1$, and on second-period consumption (H_2, Z_2) tradeoffs with I_1 and A_1, are continuous. But the effects of the switch-on/switch-off D, the min I^* requirement, and the minimum downpayment requirement are discontinuous. The discontinuity is important at the aggregate level because it leads to ranges within which modest changes in "conditions" (the determinants of I_1) can lead to large, abrupt changes in tenure choice. At the aggregate market level, households differ in the parameters of tastes, budget, and price expectations, but it is not a uniform distribution. Quantum changes in the situation may simultaneously push households over the tenure-choice threshold who began at different distances from that threshold. The number of households so pushed can jump widely up and down for similarly modest changes in conditions at different ranges of the population array. So irregular bunchings of switchovers in tenure choice is a distinct possibility.

Besides aggregate discontinuities, the differences among households in tastes and expectations will give rise at the market level to distinctive *sequences* of tenure changes, with households arrayed successively in terms of the attractiveness of I_1 under given conditions. As conditions change to increase the attractions of I_1, households shift to ownership status sequentially along this array.

4.6.2 Proportion of Home Ownership

We now deal explicitly with the market level, where many participants interact competitively. How will household intentions be translated into market outcomes?

We start with some set of initial conditions resulting in a given percentage of the population being owner-occupiers and the rest renters. Now let the determinants of I improve so that I rises for all. So a number of households at the head of the ownership-propensity queue will now want to shift to ownership tenure. Will they in fact succeed in doing so? We examine two cases: (1) no new production of dwellings, and (2) additional dwellings produced. Up to now we have assumed an effectively responsive market supply, leading to an absence of sustained market capitalization of ownership's benefits. We now relax this assumption to derive some explicit market dynamics.

Case 1: No New Production of Dwellings

The issue here hinges on whether the landlords of existing rental units will be willing to sell their houses to erstwhile renters. Will changes in conditions make these landlords comparably more determined to retain ownership of their properties, so that competition simply results, for the most part, in inflation of property values with little redistribution of ownership to renter households?

The market will, in fact, see a nontrivial shift in ownership. Previous renters in the ownership-propensity queue will be willing to assume ownership status because the complex of consumption elements and real financial gains raises ownership attractiveness above that of renting. So they bid up prices of houses to levels that encroach on the net advantages of owning over renting; but at those prices landlords, whose interest in the property is only financial (i.e., the consumption elements are irrelevant to them), can gain by selling their "excess" houses and buying *A*. Therefore, the proportion of owner-occupancy will rise under these circumstances.

It might be thought that our substantial population diversity would nonetheless preserve extensive, large intramarginal net gains for ownership despite market capitalization. This is not so. Different groups of prospective homeowners will cluster in the separate submarkets of the market complex, with substantial homogeneity in each. In each of the submarkets, prices would rise to reflect the much more highly similar potential gains of households attracted to that submarket. So most of the consumer surplus among the population would be bid away by differential capitalization in the different submarkets. Moreover, the effect of lowered real housing prices analyzed above in increasing housing-quality demand—by shifting to higher submarkets—would be frustrated. Most households would be at or close to the margin of indifference between owning and renting in the several submarkets.

In our analysis above we assumed away this case as being important in anything but the short run, partly just because such damaging capitalization creates an intense unfilled demand for additional supply to moderate the price squeeze. The effect of such demand is discussed in the next section.

Case 2: Additional Dwellings Produced

Renters at the top of the homeownership-propensity queue will bid up the prices of existing houses above the offer prices of landlords, and higher than before the strengthening of *I* determinants. So prospective profitability will rise for new construction, and additional units will be produced. These new units will compete with existing houses. The same competitive bidding process then ensues, with rental households high on the ownership queue outbidding existing landlords, the larger number of houses serving to moderate the absolute rise in dwelling prices, but not changing the relative valuations of renters and landlords. The process continues so long as the stronger demand can be met by new ownership units at the renter's supply price. Our assumption is that a highly elastic response is possible, and the bid-up prices are accordingly squeezed back down to their original levels. Empirical evidence suggests this is a reasonable assumption. In each submarket, therefore, most households retain substantial consumer surpluses, and only for the few households at the margin in each submarket are the surpluses effectively zero. So the percentage of owner-occupancy will rise nontrivially along with some households, sliding up to higher submarkets to consume more quality along with ownership.

4.6.3 Market Equilibrium

The market equilibrium in terms of tenure choice depends importantly on differences among market participants, which we classify as consuming households and landlords. Consuming households differ in several especially important respects: (1) tastes for housing services; (2) tastes for the consumption element in owner-occupancy; (3) time preference; (4) income level; (5) initial capital assets; (6) expectations about housing price appreciation (for rental and ownership units); and (7) expectations about price appreciation of other consumer goods and capital assets. Market participants in their role of landlords also differ in terms of their various price expectations.

Formal analysis of market equilibrium would require explicit distributional assumptions about these differences. For our present, less formal purposes it is enough to give a practical sense of what these differences signify for equilibrium.

With some given starting situation specifying housing supplies and ownership as well as the value of the determinants of household equilibrium, there will be an ordering of eagerness for ownership of houses for owner-occupier or landlord status. For similar expectations and nonhousing asset purchasing power, a household consumer will tend to have a higher bid price than a landlord because the former will take advantage of the consumption elements in owner-occupancy while the latter will not. But expectations differ: a landlord with higher expected a can outbid a household consumer with lower expected a.

Thus the market price and the allocation of owner-occupier status are determined by a competitive bidding among participants until the market clears. In terms of implicit (fictional) sequence, those most eager to own at least one dwelling outbid those less eager. If the supply of units exceeds the number of this group, less eager groups are required to own units in order to clear the market; so the price of ownership continues to fall (rate of financial return on I rises) until the marginally most eager are induced to own the last remaining units, at prices which equate their marginal evaluations. Intramarginal owners receive surplus returns in financial and consumption aspects.

Not all owners will be pure owner-occupiers; some will be landlords with higher than average relative price expectations favoring housing assets. Households who remain renters will tend to have lower than average expectations or be generally poorer households. Poorer households are likely to remain renters for a number of reasons (some of them discussed earlier): (1) most important of all, the likelihood that the minimum housing consumption requirement (via I^*) will seriously bind and thereby generate serious welfare losses to offset the potential financial gains of ownership; (2) an inability to make necessary downpayments because of an absence of adequate nonhousing assets; (3) the probability of lower than average α_s because of the greater urgency of inadequate Z consumption; and (4) a low enough level of period-one consumption as a whole to generate greater "impatience" and therefore a depreciation of the overall period-two budgetary gains possible under ownership.

Finally, the dispersed presence of pure owner-occupiers in the ordering of eagerness to own property suggests that some of them will be marginal at market equilibrium and will therefore have their own equilibrium conditions reflected in the market signals. As such, equilibrium prices will generate lower expected net rates of purely financial return on housing than on nonhousing assets for those who hold similar expectations, since they offset this financial deficiency with the enjoyment of consumption elements of ownership. Of course the same present prices can suggest different absolute and relative expected returns for those who hold different price expectations.

These sets of prices will remain unchanged if the supplies induced by them are sufficient to clear all markets. If not yet, additional supply will flow in and prices will differentially continue to sag in the manner we discussed just above until joint equilibrium is reached.

4.6.4 Inflation and Tenure Choice

Space permits only a brief mention of the applicability of the present analysis to behavior during inflation.

Suppose there is general inflation. Then expected a and b will be high. If there is no special reason for a to exceed b, ownership will nonetheless be stimulated so long as $i < r$, because then leveraged purchase of ownership will give ownership an increasing financial attractiveness. Of course, $i < r$ cannot be counted on in inflation. But housing inflation *may* exceed general inflation for a number of reasons. First, demographic trends and industrial-sector changes may suggest more stringent demand and supply pressure in this sector in the future (for demographic, migrational, financial, or building materials scarcity reasons) than for average industrial sectors. Second, the combination of physical durability of the asset and solidity of trends making for strong future excess demands may give prospective investors the perception of housing investment as safer than many other kinds of investment (thus, lower risk). Both grounds imply that in terms of our model, from an initial situation resulting in given appropriate household and landlord equilibrium, the determinants of I change, namely, mean a rises in the population relative to mean b. (A decrease in risk, for given expected mean return, implies a higher real risk–adjusted return.) Then owner-occupancy will rise more, even with a given stock of housing. The likely induced extra supply will not blunt this increase through lowered a, because its greater numbers is what is satisfying the greater demand for ownership. A chief factor that *could* throttle the increase is very substantial rises in mortgage interest rates. Detailed predictions of change require, of course, spelling out parameter distributions and specific initial conditions. The outline of the model presented here should suggest how a detailed analysis would proceed.

4.6.5 Aggregate Spectral Demand for Housing

In developing our integrated model of housing demand for consumption and investment we have said little explicitly about the distribution of demand among different-quality submarkets. Much of what pertains is similar to that for the model of demand for housing as consumption and needs little comment. The integrated model does have some systematic implications about the distribution of submarket demand, however. We briefly mention them here.

First, our discussion since section 4.1 explicitly stresses that a given package of housing attributes as a rental unit is *not* a perfect substitute for the same package as an ownership unit. Tenure makes a difference. The identity of a rental unit that would make some household A indifferent to a particular ownership unit will generally differ for households B, C, D, and so forth. It is for the overall market complex to determine which clusters of ownership and rental units have the same marginal tradeoffs in exchange to comprise the same or closely similar quality levels. The identity of these clusters is not obvious a priori. Therefore we do not attempt to make an inflexible a priori equivalence between rental and ownership submarkets. The two tenure sets of submarkets generate *approximate* parallel orderings, with only approximately regular correspondence across the two states. So when we discuss submarket distributions we indicate relative frequencies and their changes for rental submarkets separately from ownership submarkets without any attempt to identify explicit overall quality equivalences between the two sets.

Second, determinants of the demand for different quality levels (and for attribute mixes as well) will remain essentially the same as in the consumption demand model, except that now there is an additional preference component—taste for the consumption elements in ownership. Households that possess a higher than average level of this taste, other things equal, are empirically more likely to own than *comparable* households with lower levels of this taste. Therefore, given our analysis of the difference in effective prices of rental and ownership units, the former households are likely to consume a higher quality level of housing than the latter. The distribution of such tastes in the population will therefore have an effect on the distribution of occupancies at different quality levels. Since relative housing-nonhousing asset price expectations on the part of households have the same kind of impact on the likelihood of ownership versus rental, the distribution of these expectations in the population will also influence the distribution of quality-level demand.

This influence refers not only to a given distribution of tastes and asset price expectations but also to changes in those distributions. A rising relative frequency of high tastes for consumption elements of ownership, or an average increase in their level, other things equal, will tend to shift the distribution of demands toward higher quality levels. Corresponding changes in relative asset price expectations will have the same effects.

The same argument holds for the other determinants of tenure choice. Increases (decreases) in those factors that favor ownership (rental)—for example, income level, size of initial nonhousing assets, income tax rate (e.g., mortgage rate, rate of return on nonhousing assets, real estate tax rate)—will shift the distribution of quality levels demanded to cluster toward higher (lower) levels than would otherwise occur if only one kind of tenure existed.

4.7 Conclusion

Conventional treatments of housing demand have concentrated on housing as a consumption good. More recent attempts to do justice to tenure choice have dealt as well with housing as an investment good. These latter show how tenure choice and level of demand are determined, sometimes independently of one another, sometimes dependently. The analyses are often econometric models, concerned primarily with the effect of inflation, or taxes, or income, and so forth, on tenure choice, and there is rarely an explicit attempt to predict the systematic character of differences in the quality level of housing demanded along with the different tenures. Our treatment attempts to integrate the two aspects of housing in an essential way rather than adding them together. We find that the two tenures are considerably different and that choice of one is linked with other aspects of the demand for housing.

Our theory of demand emphasizes the multidimensional heterogeneity of housing and of housing preferences. Accordingly, the demand for housing is not a demand for a particular aggregate amount of housing; it is the demand for a distribution of occupancies in different quality/mix/tenure submarkets. These submarkets are collections of imperfect substitutes, graduated by the degree of closeness of substitution. We examine the simultaneous determinants of quality level, mix, and tenure status demand for each household and the aggregation of these demands over the complex of submarkets for the whole population.

While we do not explicitly present a dynamic version of our integrated model comparable with that of the consumption-alone model, a comparable version is certainly consistent with its spirit. So for both consumption-alone and consumption-investment demands there are important differences between a static and a dynamic perspective. Individual behavior is considerably different, aggregate performance is different, and the efficiency of the market mechanism differs markedly. Our treatment differs from most others in the nature and importance of these differences.

The second major difference in outcomes that our treatment establishes is a systematic divergence between quality-level demand under rental and ownership tenures. Not only is it necessary to incorporate investment portfolio considerations in order to explain tenure choice (as is the usual custom), it is necessary in order to explain the quality level of housing as well: quality demand and tenure choice are integrally connected.

The implications of these and other rather novel features of our treatment of demand are generated in the later chapter on market adjustment. To arrive there we must first develop the rather complicated theory of housing supply which our approach calls for. To this we now turn.

Notes

1. Long-run maximization, since portfolio investment refers to multiperiod intertemporal allocations.

2. Not necessarily "improved" housing, since what is more suitable for a particular household at a given time may be a housing unit of *lower* quality than presently occupied.

3. In ch. 5, devoted to supply, we deal with endogenous changes made in structures by their owner-occupier.

4. See, e.g., Courant 1978 and Clark 1982.

5. See the aforementioned works.

6. This is not strictly true. Some search processes have a number of near misses, instances where the transactions process actually began—i.e., search seemed completed but misfired—so search had to be resumed. For such situations, S would rise with n both because of more search *and* more transactions costs.

7. See President's Commission on Housing 1982: ch. 5.

8. Linneman 1986 provides seminal theoretical work here.

9. In the cities of many third world countries the predominance of poverty and the absence of stringent quality regulations make very simple, low-quality, owner-occupier units available as well.

10. See, e.g., Aaron 1975 and Yinger et al 1988.

11. See, e.g., Rosen 1979a, 1979b; Rosen and Rosen 1980; Boehm and McKenzie 1982, Diamond 1980a.

12. We assumed above that any attribute differences among units would be fully

relfected in utility-compensating price differences, a simplifying assumption that should be harmless for the issues being discussed.

13. See our discussion of housing supply in chs. 5 and 6.

14. Some of these costs are legally the buyer's responsibility, some the seller's. Since in our model a household that buys a house in period one will have to sell it in period two, it will incur both buyer's and seller's transfer costs in connection with ownership.

15. Actually a two-time cost, since part is incurred in buying and a later part in selling.

16. $I = \frac{1}{i} P_H H$, so $H = \frac{I_i}{P_H}$ where $c = 0$. Where $c > 0$, $I = \frac{1}{i\,(1 - c)} P_H H$, so $H = \frac{i\,(1 - c)\,I}{P_H} < \frac{i\,I}{P_H}$

17. It also discourages investment in housing ownership for landlord tenure because only some part of the tax, but not all of it, can be shifted, thereby lessening the supply of rental housing. The net effect is to decrease the supply of housing overall, relative to nonhousing good supply. This changes relative prices between housing (of all sorts) and nonhousing in favor of the latter and tends to decrease overall consumption of housing relative to nonhousing down to the level of the decreased housing supply. The further tenure mix effect discussed here is accordingly a second-order effect, based on differential transmissions of profit/utility changes due to the possibility of shifting part of the landlord's tax onto tenants, while no such possibility is available for owner-occupiers. The text's discussion of tenure mix changes therefore presupposes a net worsening of demand for owner-occupancy relative to landlord status.

18. The returns on I are discussed below.

5 The Supply of Urban Housing: New Construction and Conversion

This chapter presents our theory of the supply of housing units in the various submarkets comprising an urban housing market. We treat two distinct sets of housing suppliers—builders of new units, and owners of existing units who potentially can modify them in various ways, shifting them into different submarkets—and examine their relationship with one another.

The behavior of individuals within these two groups is analyzed in the very short run and over an intermediate period of response. In the short run, or market period, we model the owners' decisions to offer or withhold dwelling units for sale or rent as determined by the relationship between current market valuations and the owners' reservation prices. For the longer, medium-run period we focus on the role of alternative rates of return obtainable in different submarkets as guiding suppliers' responses.

The new construction supply response is influenced by the comparative rate of return obtainable to builders in the several submarkets and in nonhousing investments. The submarket conversion supply response is also fundamentally influenced by relative rates of return, where these comprise the same alternative submarket revenues as face builders, but costs of converting to each such submarket depend on the origin-destination pair and the specific characteristics of each potentially converting unit: for example, structure age, attribute mix, initial quality, and time lag of the particular conversion chosen. Through an aggregation of individual builder and converter responses we derive an aggregate, medium-run supply function for each housing submarket. The analysis demonstrates how the idiosyncracies of each metropolitan area's existing housing stock will yield different sorts of supply responses in reaction to exogenous demand factors. The distribution of the stock by type, age, attribute mix, and quality submarket influences the conversion costs and, thus, the aggregate conversion supply functions for all submarkets. Furthermore, the new construction supply response will be similarly influenced, inasmuch as new construction and conversion are substitute forms of supply.

This chapter concludes by considering dynamic aspects of the supply process that arise from the durability of the stock and time lags in the supply adjustment process. The former means that turnover of existing dwellings is a predominant form of supply, implying that demand decisions involving changing residences are intertwined with many supply decisions. The latter means that each decision maker's timing of supply adjustments will be based on considerable uncertainty about what other suppliers' projects are already underway and hence what market conditions will be evinced when the given adjustment comes to fruition. One interesting conclusion that follows from our dynamic analysis is that builders will construct units in a wider variety of submarkets than would have been predicted in the static analysis, due to wider variation in their predictions of future market conditions.

5.1 Individual and Aggregate Market-Period Supply from the Existing Stock

We first focus on the behavior of owners of existing dwellings over a relatively short period—their market-period supply. We define *market period* as an interval so short that there is insufficient time to convert the existing stock[1] (through undermaintenance, splitting, consolidation, or physical additions or other modifications) or to build new stock. Put differently, during the market period the only choice open to a dwelling owner, given the prevailing submarket valuation (sales price or rent, depending on tenure), is whether to sell or rent the unit in question or to hold it vacant for rent or sale during some future period. The relevant market valuations in question are, in turn, a function of the unit's quality H, attribute mix $[R]$ and age AG, that is, $MV(H,[R],AG)$.

5.1.1 Reservation Price

The central concept employed in the analysis of market-period supply is the *reservation price*—the minimum market valuation or bid that induces the owner of a given unit to rent or sell it. The determination of this reservation price is in principle straightforward, although in application difficult, extensively involving expectations. The owner must decide what is the lowest hypothetical present market valuation at which the discounted present value of net returns obtained by selling or renting the unit now at that market valuation is superior to the best discounted present value of net returns obtainable by postponing the sale or rental to various future periods at the valuations expected to prevail at those times. That lowest present offer/bid is the reservation price for the given unit at each present period. Since expected future market valuations in general will change as current market valuations change over time, "the" reservation price likely will change over time for any dwelling unit.

The reservation price can be specified more formally. In the case of owners of vacant units who are contemplating their sale, the reservation price P_0 is

$$P_0 = \max \left[P_T(1 + r)^{-T} - \sum_{t=0}^{T-1} {}^{H}C_t(1 + r)^{-t} \right], \tag{5.1}$$

$$\text{all } T,\ t = 1, 2, \ldots, T,$$

where

P_T = the expected selling price of the unit when sold during time T;
${}^{H}C_t$ = the per period cost of holding the unit vacant (security, minimal utilities, taxes, insurance, etc.); and
r = the owner's discount rate, presumably closely related to the market rate of interest.[2]

In equation (5.1) we assume that the potential seller may defer sale indefinitely, depending on future prospects. For potential landlords/owners of rental units the situation is different. Sale today precludes the sale at every other point in time. But renting one's property does not preclude keeping the property vacant at *any* time in the future beyond the present period, for subsequent rental. The gist of the difference is that the rental at any time involves only a one-period commitment for the property's use. At most, renting today precludes renting up to the beginning of the next period. So the bid price for rental today involves only comparison with next period's potential earnings. Therefore, for the owner of a rental unit, today's reservation price R_0 is

$$(5.2) \quad (R_0 - {}^{0}C_0)(1 + r)^{-1} = (R_1 - {}^{0}C_1)(1 + r)^{-2} - {}^{H}C_0(1 + r)^{-1}$$

or, simplified,

$$(5.3) \qquad R_0 = \max\,[(R_1 - {}^{0}C_1)(1 + r)^{-1} + ({}^{0}C_0 - {}^{H}C_0)],$$

where R_1 is the expected rent of the unit when rented during time t_1; ${}^{0}C_t$ is the per period cost of operating an occupied unit (increased repairs due to wear and tear, extra utility charges, rent collection, management costs, etc.).

Although the above reservation prices are easiest to comprehend when the absentee owner of a vacant home or apartment is considered, they also are applicable to the case of the owner-occupant of a unit. In each period each owner-occupier can be viewed as facing a three-way choice: (1) to continue to occupy the unit in the present period; (2) to put it on the market for sale or rental, while seeking a different unit to occupy; (3) to move out but withhold it from either sale or rental in the present period. Choice will depend on the relative sizes of the net benefits of each option: (1) excess of the owner-occupier's own bid price for a one-period consumption of the unit's services (and/or the present discounted net bid price for its lifetime services) over the present one-period market value of its services (and/or over its discounted capital value in the market); (2) excess of the one-period market value of its services over the owner's one-period bid price for its consumption plus the (positive or negative) excess of the owner's bid price for alternative one-period housing over its market price (for rental intentions; this calculation is expressed in capitalized value terms for sale intentions); (3) excess of present discounted market value of expected rental or sale value next period over the own bid price for this and the next period, plus the (positive or negative) excess of this and the next period's bid price for alternative housing over its market value during the same two periods. Reservation price in each of these is the base over which the excesses are calculated, but the concept is no longer a yes-no choice because three alternative excesses are involved. The option with the greatest excess will be chosen.

Options 1 and 2 both put the dwelling unit "on the market" now; option 3 removes it. But options 1 and 2 have quite different market behavioral impacts. Under option 2 there are two separate but linked market exchange relations involved: this unit changes occupancy between two households, with all its accompanying search and transactions costs, *and* another unit changes occupancy between two households (with the original owner-occupier taking part in both transactions) in the same way. Under option 1 the same number of units will be occupied, but *no* market transactions will take place. These circumstances are quite different because of the dynamic effect of the density of market activity in the quality of matchups between heterogeneous households and heterogeneous dwelling units (see ch. 4). In other words, option 2 may lead to a chain of improved matchups taking place in the market through the increased turnover, whereas option 1 will not.[3]

5.1.2 Individual Market-Period Supply

For each individual unit, then, a market-period supply function can be defined consisting of a dichotomous set of choices its owner can make: the choice not to supply the unit (corresponding to all market valuations below reservation price), and the choice to offer it (corresponding to all market valuations above the reservation price), as qualified for owner-occupier "supply choice" as described above. Symbolically, this supply function for unit j during market period t is[4]

$$(5.4) \qquad {}^{S}Q_{jt} = \begin{cases} 0 \text{ if } P_{jt} < P_{j0} \text{ or } R_{jt} < R_{j0} \\ 1 \text{ if } P_{jt} \geq P_{j0} \text{ or } R_{jt} \geq R_{j0} \end{cases}$$

Of course some units during any period may not be offered or may be withheld subject to the discretion of the owner. The most common examples would be those currently under long-term lease provisions for which eviction of occupants is illegal. Such units are constrained effectively to be "in the market," that is, planned to be used, for the given period.

5.1.3 Aggregate Market-Period Supply

By aggregating across all such constrained units and all units subject to the choice given in equation (5.4) within a given housing submarket in a metropolitan area, we can obtain the aggregate market-period t supply function for submarket i. This function shows the set of current market valuations MV_{it}

(sales prices or rents, as appropriate)[5] corresponding to the total number of units in submarket i that will be offered for use "to the market"[6]—${}^{S}Q_{it}^{\Sigma}$. For market valuations below the smallest of any unit's reservation price, only those units constrained to be on the market will be offered, $\Sigma^{S}Q_{it}^{\text{MIN}}$. For higher current market valuations, progressively more units will be placed on the market as progressively more of the array of reservation prices are exceeded. Since this part of the supply relationship is governed by the distribution of individual reservation prices, the function will have as parameters vectors of current and expected future values of unit operating costs, holding costs, market valuations, owner-occupier bid prices for consumption, and discount rates. Finally, if market valuations reach MV_{it}^{MAX} such that the entire stock in i $\Sigma^{S}Q_{it}^{\text{MAX}}$ is offered, the short-term constraints on expanding the stock render the relationship between quantity supplied and further MV increases perfectly inelastic. Symbolically,

$$(5.5)\quad {}^{S}Q_{it}^{\Sigma} = \begin{cases} \Sigma^{S}Q_{it}^{\text{MIN}} \quad \text{for } MV_{it} \leq \min P_0, R_0; \\ q(MV_{it}, [{}^{O}C_{it}, {}^{O}C_{it+1}, \ldots], [{}^{H}C_{it}, {}^{H}C_{it+1}, \ldots]; \\ [MV_{it+1}, MV_{it+2}, \ldots], [r_{t+1}, r_{t+2}, \ldots], \Sigma^{S}Q_{it}^{\text{MIN}}) \\ \qquad \text{for } \min P_0, R_0 \leq MV_{it} \leq MV_{it}^{*}; \\ \Sigma^{S}Q_{it}^{\text{MAX}} \quad \text{for } MV_{it} \geq MV_{it}^{\text{MAX}}. \end{cases}$$

Thus, subject to the limits of the size of the existing stock in the given submarket, the market-period supply will be larger (1) the lower the operating costs of occupied units; (2) the higher the holding costs of vacant units; (3) the more pessimistic the expectations owners hold about future market valuation trends; (4) the higher the discount (interest) rate; and (5) the better the present match between owner-occupant tastes and their current dwelling units. The entire array of functions like equation (5.5) across all i submarkets will be referred to as spectral market-period supply.

5.2 Individual Medium-Run Supply through New Construction

Over a longer period of time, the urban housing market can adjust more completely to prevailing market conditions than by simply offering existing units for rent or sale or not. Specifically, two alternative, competing modes of supply are available in this "medium-run" time frame: the construction of new dwelling units and the conversion of existing units in their attribute mix and/or from one quality submarket to another or out of the housing stock completely. In this section we first present our theory of the new construction supply response; in the next section we present the conversion response. First we present the parameters of the builder's choice problem: attribute prices, submarket market valuations for the spectrum of submarkets, new construction costs, and rates of return from nonhousing investments. Then we discuss the optimal choice of submarket(s) for new building.

5.2.1 The Builder's Choice Problem

Each potential builder of a new dwelling unit can produce at least one such unit with any attribute mix and for any submarket desired. In doing so, the resultant units can be rented or sold at the market valuation prevailing in the submarket for similar units. Each individual builder is assumed to be competitively small, so its output has no appreciable effect on market valuations. All builders have access to the same construction technology, and we assume that they will all choose the same, most efficient production function and lowest cost function. Their optimum choice of housing investment then has three aspects: (1) the least-cost attribute mix for any given quality submarket (H) desired; (2) the most profitable submarket H (defined by quality and/or tenure); and (3) the optimal number of dwelling units to build with that mix for that submarket. These choices are assumed to be made to maximize the rate of return on the builder's net assets:

$$(5.6) \qquad \max \gamma = [n\,(MV(H) - {}_{N}C(H) + \gamma'\,(T - n_{N}C(H))] \,/\, T$$
$$= (n[MV(H) - {}_{N}C(H)\,(1 + \gamma')] \,/\, T) + \gamma',$$
$$\text{subject to } T \geq n_{N}C(H)$$

where

γ = the rate of return on a builder's portfolio;
n = the number of housing units of the optimal investment defined by submarket and attribute mix;
MV = the per dwelling unit market valuation (or discounted present value of expected future net revenue streams) from the optimal unit;
${}_{N}C$ = the total cost per unit of the optimal dwelling unit built;
γ' = the net rate of return on total nonhousing investment and the builder's borrowing rate for the houses' residual cost; and
T = the builder's total net assets.

The first term in equation (5.6) can be interpreted as the net profit earned by the construction of n dwellings, the second as the opportunity cost of the funds invested in such construction. It is assumed that, since the borrowing and lending rates are equal, the builder is indifferent between borrowing part of the building cost or paying for it fully.

Our rationale for focusing on rate of return instead of absolute profit levels is as follows. Profit maximization in the present situation is subject to a form of budget constraint. Housing developers typically obtain most of their financing from specialized financial institutions. They compete for these funds against one another and against nonhousing sectors. Because of institutional characteristics of capital markets it is generally believed that there are effective ceilings for funds in the housing industry. Allocation within the sector rests on rate-of-return competition. So each builder's appropriate criterion for competitive success in obtaining funds is in terms of a rate of return on investment. Thus, suppose all builders could choose between an opportunity to invest \$300,000 at a 20% return or \$600,000 at a 15% return. The total profit of the second exceeds that of the first. But two developers choosing the first could outbid one developer choosing the second in seeking funding for the same total investment out of scarce overall funding resources. Thus, for each builder/developer the optimal submarket to target their new construction is that for which the rate of return is highest.

At each given time the builder faces a schedule of market valuations for units—new *or* existing—at each submarket H: $MV(H)$. The total cost ${}_{N}C$ of a new unit in any submarket is composed of two elements:

$$(5.7) \qquad {}_{N}C(H) = C_K(H) + C_U(H, AG=0),$$

where C_K is the construction cost (embodied capital) of a new unit in H; C_U is the discounted present value of the maintenance and repair cost of the unit in H with zero years of aging ($AG=0$), that is, the capital value of the expenditure stream needed to keep the unit at H quality indefinitely.

Our model does not include scale effects of construction for simplicity, so costs and revenues are linear for multiples of new units produced. Therefore portfolio rate of return will correspond to housing rate-of-return maximization: any resources invested in housing should seek that investment from which rate of return on those resources is maximized. Multiples of any quantum of investment in a particular kind of housing will earn the same rate of return as that quantum. So if any investment is to be carried out in housing, it should be for that type of unit for which rate of return on the unit investment is maximized.

By rearranging and simplifying equation (5.6), this rate-of return maximizing problem can be expressed as finding that H_i such that $MV_i - {}_{N}C_i$ is maximized. Differentiating with respect to H and setting the result equal to zero yields the first-order conditions:

$$(5.8) \qquad d\,MV / d\,H = (d\,{}_{N}C / d\,H)(1 + \gamma'),$$

that is, the usual marginal revenue (market valuation gain from selling a dwelling with an increment of higher quality) equals marginal cost (of building an increment of higher quality into a dwelling), but with costs adjusted upward to show the opportunity cost of capital.

The attribute mix that minimizes the total cost of reaching any H, or, alternatively, that maximizes the market value of any input bundle used, is that for which (analogously with housing demand)

$$(5.9) \qquad (\partial_{N}C / \partial h_i) / (\partial_{N}C / \partial h_j) = \partial p_i / \partial p_j.$$

Conditions (5.8) and (5.9) together determine the highest rate of return obtainable from new construction in housing. Let this be γ^H. The builder should build at least one such new unit or not as γ^H is greater than or less than γ', respectively. If γ^H is equal to γ', the builder is indifferent between housing and nonhousing investment. The amount of total housing investment undertaken by builders is assumed limited by the individual credit constraints they face.

5.2.2 Optimal Submarket for Construction—Statics

For each $MV(H)$, (γ'), ${}_NC(H)$ set, the builder will make a particular construction decision about the optimal number of dwelling units and submarket(s) in which to build. Changes in those parameters will change the decision.

To illustrate graphically, figure 5.1 shows a hypothetical situation facing an individual builder of new units who takes current housing market valuations, construction costs, and nonhousing rates of return as given. Alternative quality submarkets are shown on the horizontal axis, dollars of total costs and "present" market valuations on the vertical axis of figure 5.1.[7] The ${}_NC$ function shows the cost of producing a new unit for each submarket, as given by equation (5.7) *and* inflated by $(1+\gamma')$. (Here, and in all succeeding diagrams, we suppress the $(1 + \gamma')$ term for notational ease, although it is being included implicitly in all cost functions portrayed.) For simplicity here we assume that all builders are essentially similar; thus the same cost function faces all potential builders. The *MV* function shows the alternative market value opportunities that would result from selling or renting a new unit in each submarket; again the value is assumed to be the same for all builders.

Rate of return on housing investments is maximized at that submarket where marginal *MV* equals marginal ${}_NC$ (inflated by $1+\gamma'$, of course; see equation 5.8). Graphically this occurs where the slopes of the *MV* and ${}_NC$

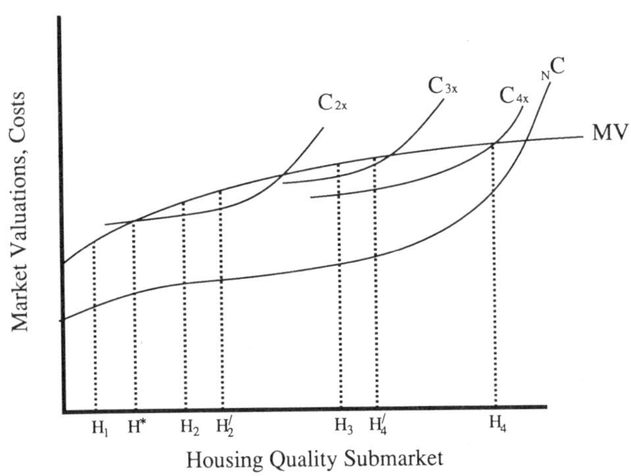

Figure 5.1. Rate-of-return maximization by submarket destination for new construction and conversion supply.

functions are equal. Here this occurs locally at both H_1 and H_3 and globally at H_3. (If any builder specialization exists, H_1 might also represent the effective global optimum for builders who specialize in low-quality units.)[8] Of course the returns from new construction at H_3 must be higher than those available from nonhousing investments, γ', before any building will be forthcoming.

As shown in figure 5.1, one or at most two submarkets will be the destination for new construction. This relatively limited set of alternative submarket targets for new units is characteristic of a highly competitive, nonspecialized building industry. It is in distinct contrast to the array of submarket targets to which optimal conversions of existing units are destined, as will be shown below. A wider-quality spread of optimal building can occur if there is significant builder specialization in the quality/tenure type of structure constructed. This would occur if there were significantly differential access to different technologies and inputs. Differences in the resulting ${}_NC$ functions would generate various construction targets in the spectrum of submarkets. While some specialization does exist in the residential construction industry (much more in nonresidential construction), the industry is highly competitive. Technologies, inputs, and financing are not notably unequal in accessibility. The most significant form of specialization may be between one- and few-unit structures and multiple-unit structures. This primarily concerns tenure type, not quality submarket focus. So the essential force of the result about few targets of new construction in this simple, nonspecialized, static case is empirically appropriate. A more important qualifying of its rigor is seen below when we discuss a dynamic framework for the theory.

A final word must be added concerning the choice of optimal submarket for new construction. In most U.S. cities there are zoning, health, and building codes that effectively specify both attribute mixes and quality levels that are illegal to construct, that is, they specify requirements for legality. In such cases, the feasible submarket choice set over which equations (5.8) and (5.9) can be maximized will be systematically constrained. In terms of figure 5.1, if H^* were the minimum legal submarket specified by local codes, builders who otherwise might have chosen to build in H_1 will be legally forbidden to do so.

5.3 Individual Medium-Run Supply through Conversion of Existing Units

Now consider the alternative form of supplying dwelling units—modifications of the previously existing stock. First we analyze the five alternative options that owners have for modifying their properties and discuss their implications for conversion costs. Next we show the basis for the optimal choice among these conversion options, based on comparisons of market valuations and conversion costs. Finally, we characterize the nature of intersubmarket housing conversions and consider how they depend on such factors as dwelling age, the time lags involved in conversion, and the dwelling's attribute mix.

5.3.1 Supply Options for Owners of Existing Units—Statics

In each period, owners of existing dwelling units have a number of options with respect to their property: (1) maintain it at the same quality level; (2) upgrade it to a higher level; (3) downgrade it in finite degree to a lower level; (4) abandon it to nonuse, ending its present provision of housing services; or (5) convert it to a nonhousing use (perhaps with the concomitant demolition of the current structure). The intersubmarket maximum in rate of return for a given unit will govern the choices among the first three options. The condition for choosing the fifth option is simply that the opportunity cost (i.e., returns from potential nonhousing uses) of using the capital embodied in the structure, and any further operational (maintenance and repair) resources for housing services, is greater than the highest return obtainable from any continued housing use (including temporary vacancy). For the fourth option, the choice condition is that the rate of return from using the structure (less any necessary complementary resources) is less for *any* use whatever than the opportunity rate of return of the necessary operational resources alone.

For all three housing options, owners face potential returns indicated in the same cross-submarket valuation function $MV(H,[R],AG)$ that confronts builders (and housing demanders). Their costs of achieving such returns, however, differ from those of builders. Each type of conversion, including sustaining the same quality level, has its distinctive production and cost functions.[9] These differences lie behind the choice by each owner of an optimal conversion action.

Maintaining the same quality level for a particular dwelling unit requires using operational resources for its maintenance and repair to the degree necessary to offset usage and passage of time. This, in turn, depends on the particularities of the attribute mix $[R]$ (materials, architectural style, etc.), initial quality H, and age AG.[10]

Upward conversion of a unit has three main routes: (1) physical additions, like the construction of porches, finishing a basement, adding a garage or swimming pool; (2) overmaintenance or alterations that enhance the unit's condition, like modernizing heating, cooling, plumbing or electrical systems, and remodeling and redecorating; (3) consolidating more numerous, smaller units in a structure into fewer but larger units.[11] These three have clearly different production functions and so different cost schedules, and are differentially affected by exogenous changes. Yet combinations of them are often used together in complementary packages.

Downward conversion of a unit has two dominant forms: (1) undermaintenance gradually to lower the condition of the unit, and (2) splitting of fewer, larger units in a structure into more numerous, smaller units. These two routes differ notably from one another and from the routes to upward conversion. Splitting involves investing resources deliberately to lower the quality of the resulting individual housing units within the structure, thereby deliberately lowering the market valuation of each. The action would be difficult to rationalize except that it results in a larger number of units in the affected structure and, if appropriately done as a response to changing market conditions, in a higher overall market value for the structure as a whole. This makes clear that the individual housing unit is not always the appropriate decision unit for housing investment. For some owners it is a whole house or even clusters of houses that form the real unit of decision making.

Undermaintenance is really gradual disinvestment in housing capital. Maintenance is a complementary input with capital that is necessary both to continue to provide housing services at an approximately constant quality and keep its future productivity relatively intact. Undermaintenance allows aging and use gradually to depreciate housing capital. It permits the lowering of housing quality in exchange for a saving on current outlays. The gain is the opportunity use of these resources elsewhere rather than in helping the given unit to provide housing; the loss is the permitted decline in service quality that leads to a decline in the unit's market valuation. An additional special element is involved in this form of conversion, namely, that undermaintenance is a considerably slower means of achieving significant quality declines than splitting. Actual decline cumulates—probably at an increasing rate—under the growing pressures of use and aging which are not offset by upkeep expenditures. It is like the negative of the process of creating wine—a considerable passage of time is needed for "destructive aging."

Any of the aforementioned maintenance, upgrading, or downgrading strategies may be accompanied by a conversion in tenure status from renter to owner occupancy, or vice versa. A change in tenure affects the rate of return by taking advantage of the lack of perfect substitutability between ownership and rental units otherwise highly similar. Sometimes a pure tenure change will not be accompanied by physical change. Usually, however, physical modification accompanies tenure change, because the imperfect substitutability across tenures is at least partly due to the competitive requirements for a higher degree of idiosyncratic tailoring to meet special consumption tastes in owner-occupied units than in rental units. Rental units are usually more staple and interchangeable across tastes, owner-occupied units more specialized. A tenure shift is thus likely to be accompanied by physical modification to make the unit more appropriate to its new market status. Such modifications may or may not change its quality level. We thus consider dwelling tenure change as a special case of quality submarket conversion.

5.3.2 Individual Conversion Cost Functions

The above discussion suggests that the appropriate concept of cost for supplying units from the existing stock will be complex. It is. This concept is summarized in equation (5.10) as a *total cost* function for some unit, $\propto$:

$$(5.10)\qquad {}^{\propto}C_{ijk} = C_K(H_i, [{}^{\propto}R]) + C^{ij}_M\,[M_k([{}^{\propto}R], {}^{\propto}AG)] + C_U(H_j,[{}^{\propto}R],{}^{\propto}AG) + C_T[M_k(H_i, H_j)],$$

where

${}^{\propto}C_{ijk}$ = total cost of converting unit $\propto$ from quality/tenure submarket i to submarket j by method k (when $i = j$ it is the cost of retaining $\propto$ at i, that is, C_i);

$C_K(\cdot)$ = the opportunity cost of the capital embodied in the unit (approximated by original construction cost), *or* remaining original cost not amortized, whichever is larger;

$C^{ij}_M\,[M_k(\cdot)]$ = the cost of modifying the unit from i to j by method k (this equals zero if a pure maintenance strategy is adopted);

$C_U(\cdot)$ = the (discounted present value of the) cost of maintaining the unit at destination submarket j (if no conversion occurs, it is the cost of maintaining the unit at origin i); and

$C_T(\cdot)$ = the opportunity cost of the time taken to convert the unit from i to j during which it is in suboptimal use (this equals zero if a pure maintenance strategy is adopted).

So the *incremental* cost of making the shift from submarket i to j, the difference in total costs between keeping it at the origin and shifting it to the destination submarket, is

$$(5.11)\qquad {}^{\propto}\Delta C_{ijk} = C^{ij}_M + C_U(H_j) - C_U(H_i) + C_T[\,M_K(\,H_i\; - \;H_j\,)\,],$$

where monetary units are adjusted upward, as with builders, to account for the opportunity cost of money in other investments or borrowing $(1+\gamma')$; that is, the incremental shift cost is composed of the explicit cost of the conversion itself, the *difference* in maintenance costs at the two submarkets, and the time conversion opportunity cost (during the transition period while the property's use is still imperfectly targeted, and so in disequilibrium use for a nontrivial period).

Thus the costs of supplying dwelling units from the existing stock are partly direct outlays and partly opportunities foregone. They depend, for any particular unit, on the quality differential between origin and destination submarkets, but also, as we shall see below, on the age of the unit, on its specific attribute characteristics, and on the method of conversion chosen for it.

5.3.3 Optimal Conversion Strategy

The owner of each housing unit will choose among all these conversion options on the basis of his or her ownership goals. Landlords who rent their dwelling's services to others will presumably want to maximize rate of return on their investment–whether expressed in flow or in capitalized value terms. Owners prepared imminently to sell their property will do likewise. Most housing units, however, are owner-occupied, with the owner not expressly on the verge of selling or renting, but interested in using the housing unit for its own consumption (as well as, perhaps, for its ultimate resale value).[12] We start by modeling the first two owner groups—the clearly "market-oriented" owners.

Market-Oriented Owners

Each market-oriented owner of housing chooses among the aforementioned conversion options—including the no-change (maintenance) option, which we have seen requires a specific kind of action as much as any other—on the basis of their respective expected rates of return. These are returns not only to any *additional* resources expended, but to the opportunity cost embedded in the unit's continued use to provide housing itself. The rate of return for each conversion option may be expressed in a form analogous to equation (5.6), with MV appropriate to each potential destination submarket and to the number of dwelling units lost and gained in the conversion, and the C function appropriate to the type of conversion, as specified in equation (5.10). Thus, for conversions to H_j using splitting or consolidation method k, where m is the new number of units per structure, the appropriate terms are mMV, and C_{ijk}. For maintaining the dwelling unit, the terms are MV_i and C_i; for upgrading or downgrading to H_j using method k and holding the number of units in the structure constant, they are MV_j and C_{ijk}. Abandonment and conversion to nonhousing use compete with the various housing retention alternatives, although for simplicity we do not formally model revenue and cost expressions for these options. The alternative with the highest rate of return is chosen; it specifies the optimal quality/tenure submarket destination (if any), the conversion method to be used to attain it, and any change in the number of units per structure.

Rate of return is maximized (for continuous $Cijk$ and MV functions) where

$$(5.12) \qquad d\,MV/d\,H = [(\partial^{\propto}C_{ijk}/\partial H)](1+\gamma') \\ \text{and } MV_j - MV_i > {}^{\propto}\Delta C_{ijk}(1+\gamma'),$$

that is, marginal conversion gains equal marginal conversion costs for increments in quality H, and total gains exceed the incremental costs of conversion. MV_i—the original housing market valuation—is in effect an opportunity cost of conversion because it is lost upon conversion. Thus, one also could express equation (5.12) as

$$MV_j > MV_i + {}^{\propto}\Delta C_{ijk}.$$

All owners of existing dwelling units face the same expected proceeds schedule for selling or renting, which is the same as that faced by builders. Although these expected benefits are similar across conversion suppliers, their costs differ significantly insofar as their units differ in original quality, age, and attribute mix. Cost will also vary dramatically depending on whether upward or downward conversions are contemplated, since the two are not symmetrical in costs. Thus, any two units starting in the same quality submarket may, though facing the same market valuation opportunities, select different conversions and end up in different destination submarkets, even in different *directions* of change. A fortiori, units beginning in different submarkets are quite likely to adopt different conversion choices. This means especially that conversions are not likely to concentrate heavily in one or a few destinations, unlike the previous case of builders of new dwellings.

This variation in conversion destinations can be illustrated graphically with the help of figure 5.1. It shows the hypothetical case of three owners of existing dwelling units currently in submarkets H_2, H_3, and H_4. The conversion cost functions corresponding to (opportunity-cost inflated) equation (5.10) that show the total costs of supplying each origin unit to various alternative destination submarkets are labeled C_2, C_3, C_4, respectively. The "present" market valuation attainable by any given conversion is shown by the MV function.

As indicated earlier, each owner will convert his or her unit to another submarket if this other submarket offers a superior (and positive) rate of return to that in the current submarket. Using the logic of rate-of-return maximizaton embodied in equation (5.12) above, this will occur where the slopes of the MV and C functions are equal.[13] Figure 5.1 shows that for the dwelling unit beginning at H_2, condition (5.12) is met by converting upward to submarket H_2'. Similar logic suggests that the dwelling unit at H_4 should be downgraded to H_4' and the unit at H_3 should be maintained at that submarket.

Figure 5.1 illustrates three important comparisons between medium-run supply through conversion and through new construction, as discussed earlier. First, there is a relatively wide spread of destinations for conversions of the existing stock compared to (here, only one global optimum for) new construction. In principle, there may be at least as many destinations as there are origins of existing units *and* different units from each origin, since, as we shall see below, different units at the same origin may end up in different destinations, due to the plethora of unit-specific conversion cost functions (associated with age and attribute mix differences). In contrast, since in our model builders face similar market valuation *and* cost prospects, many sets of housing prices can lead to overwhelming concentration of new construction in very few submarkets. Second, a given set of market signals, $MV(H)$, can simultaneously elicit upgrading, downgrading, and maintenance from owners of different units, whereas the construction response is more limited and near uniform in character. Third, younger existing units with origin submarket at a level which market conditions make a desirable destination for new construction (H_3 here) may not find any conversion destination preferable to its origin, but as we shall see below, older units at H_3 may well decide to convert.

The last result, and the specific character of the first two results, stems from the shape of the relevant conversion C_i functions relative to the new construction ${}_NC$ function. The basic relationship is simple: the marginal rate of transformation between any two quality levels is less via new construction than via modification of young existing units. It is more expensive to modify a unit from one submarket to another, where the original structure exercises various physical constraints concerning materials, architecture, configuration, size, and so forth than is the difference in building costs between those two quality levels via new construction, where capital is completely malleable and all inputs can be chosen and used together without prior constraint in the most efficient way that current technology permits.[14] So the family of total cost functions for converted units all have the property that they rise faster between an origin and an upgrading destination, or fall less fast between an origin and a downgrading destination, than the comparable segment of any new construction cost function. There is one exception to this generalization. As we shall see below, the cost functions for very old units may fall faster between an origin and a downgrading destination than that for new construction.

Non-Market-Oriented Owners

We have discussed the conversion behavior of market-oriented owners. What about owner-occupants, who are primarily interested in their housing unit for their own consumption use? Owner-occupants fall into two groups: those planning a change in housing consumption, and those planning a continuance of unchanged consumption. They differ in some respects, but they have this in common: for both groups, housing consumption characteristics can be obtained by either remaining in their present units *or* by moving elsewhere. *Both* groups may convert their dwellings in a market-oriented way (or sell to a new owner who will then do so) in the following scenarios: (1) no-consumption-change group—convert, and then sell or rent their present unit, and move elsewhere to duplicate the original housing package characteristics; (2) consumption-change group—convert, and then sell or rent their present unit and move elsewhere to obtain newly desired characteristics. Whoever does not move will diverge from rate-of-return maximization (equation 5.12) behavior in varying degrees.

Market-oriented conversion will be followed within the *no-move group,* too, however, if the expected utility value of the gain in expected future rate of return via such conversion exceeds the prospective present utility loss from search/moving costs, or from any highly prized unique features of the present dwelling, or for a possible temporarily unfavorable submarket valuation in the household's desired destination. Since market-oriented conversions from any initial position must compete with all other potential suppliers, for any particular unit to face a high potential rate-of-return gain for a particular conversion, there must be a combination of especially strong, unevenly distributed new demand pressures and a strategic market advantage for this particular unit to convert there from its given initial submarket. But some own-consumption owners will themselves constitute these demand pressures, and where only modest conversion of their present premises are necessary to attain their new consumption wants, these premises will possess competitive advantage in being the ones to convert. So their conversion will be indistinguishable from those of market-oriented owners.

Favorability of competitive conversion situations for desirable destination submarkets is likely to push even some households wanting unchanged consumption toward market-oriented conversion. Strong market-oriented indications to convert *away* from a particular submarket imply a combination of an origin submarket with loose market conditions and an easily accessible (i.e., low-cost) conversion destination with tight market conditions. An owner there can thus make sizable financial gains by converting from the weak to the strong submarket and then occupying other accommodations similar to the just-converted one on good terms, many unconverted dwellings usually remaining in the origin submarket (as we argue below).

Further approximations to market-oriented conversion are likely in the group focused on their own consumption. Most households do not know exactly how much longer they expect to occupy their present premises. They are thus concerned to preserve a modicum of "marketability" in their home in preparation for possible sale or rental. If the market-indicated conversion is in a direction of change conducive to their own desired change, they are likely to go beyond their most-preferred destination toward the market-indicated destination submarket as a form of inexpensive insurance. Conversely, they will likely refrain from undertaking conversions that, though attractive from a personal consumption standpoint, would render the dwelling highly idiosyncratic, or place it in a submarket of actual or potential great weakness, thus placing the household in a very risky situation.

Thus, strong market-oriented conversion indicators are likely to be influential in the conversion decisions of even owner-occupiers, in varying degrees, and for substantial (but varying) numbers in all submarkets. Because of this, and because the great majority of dwelling units and households will not warrant either market-oriented conversion or consumption change in any particular period, the absolute number of blatant countermarket conversions is not likely to be great in any such period. But some will occur. Nonetheless, the most likely predictive error in using a market-oriented theory of conversion is to underestimate the proportion of units that remain unchanged during the period, that is, to underestimate the conservatism born of transition costs, risk, and simple "let well enough alone" attitudes.

5.3.4 Conversion Costs, Structural Age, Time Lags, and Attribute Mixes

The conversion cost functions shown in figure 5.1 leave implicit several important aspects of conversion costs that were raised earlier in the context of equation (5.10). Unlike what we have characterized as a high degree of homogeneity among new construction firms, the "raw material" of conversion supply—the stock of existing units—is notably heterogeneous. Houses even in the same submarket differ in terms of age (AG), in their sets of housing attributes ($[R]$), and in their physical condition. All three have an impact on conversion decisions through their effect on equation (5.10). In particular, the conversion cost function from any origin submarket in figure 5.1 does not reflect conversion opportunities for all existing units at that origin. Different dwelling units will have different cost functions. So optimal conversion strategy will generally differ for units with different cost functions at the same origin submarket. Without explicitly considering the complete array of different cost functions, it is typically impossible to predict the *number* of units starting at each H_i that will convert to each possible submarket destination. In this section we examine four factors which we consider have especially important, systematic influences on conversion costs: structural age, time lags of conversion, attribute mix of the stock, and extent of quality conversion.

We begin with the effect of dwelling age on conversion costs. Though houses are very durable, as they age it becomes progressively more expensive to maintain them in any desired condition.[15] Indeed, the cost of upkeep that will maintain them for another period in the quality level at which they began the period—that is, the normal maintenance cost $C_U(H_i)$—rises at *every* quality level, and there is reason to believe that it rises *faster* with quality. Symbolically,

$$(5.13) \qquad \partial C_U(H,[R],AG)/\partial AG > 0;$$
$$\partial^2 C_U(H,[R],AG)/\partial AG\partial H > 0; \text{ and } \partial^2 C_U(H,[R],AG)/\partial H\partial AG > 0.$$

Graphically, these relationships can be portrayed as in figure 5.2. The functions AG_0, AG_1, AG_2 show the relationship between normal upkeep expenditures C_U and initial quality level H for new, moderately old, and very old units, respectively.

The implications of this for conversion cost functions can be seen by recalling that equation (5.10) includes a term for the cost of maintaining the unit at various destination submarkets (including the origin). Thus, ceteris paribus, increasing structural age is associated with steeper conversion cost functions because the difference in normal upkeep costs increases for all quality levels (but more so for higher than for lower) with increasing age.

This is illustrated in figure 5.3, where C_i^{AG} is the total cost of a unit converted from i in upward or downward directions, for age AG. The unit ages serving as parameters for these functions correspond to those in figure 5.2;

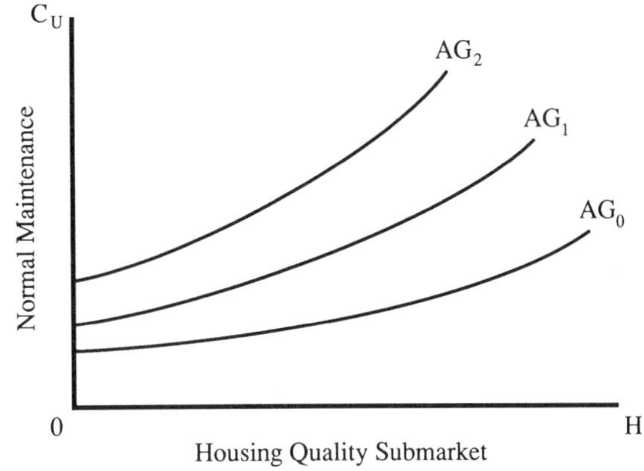

Figure 5.2. The effect of structural age on normal maintenance costs.

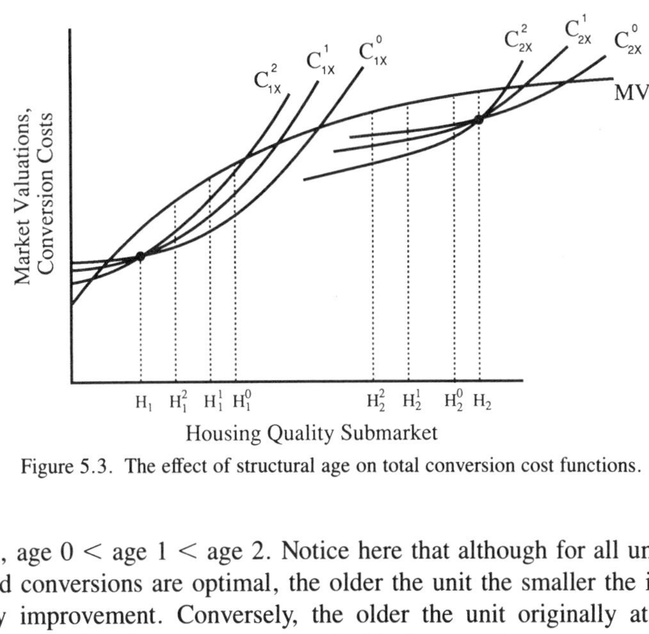

Figure 5.3. The effect of structural age on total conversion cost functions.

that is, age 0 < age 1 < age 2. Notice here that although for all units at H_1 upward conversions are optimal, the older the unit the smaller the indicated quality improvement. Conversely, the older the unit originally at H_2, the *larger* the quality *decrement* associated with downward conversion.

Thus, the nonparallel (nonproportional) rise in upkeep costs in progressively older units biases their conversion toward lesser upward, greater downward levels, and in general away from the upward and toward the downward direction. Indeed, in a simple example it can be shown that difference in age can lead to opposite conversion directions for units at the same origin. If, to highlight the effect of age, one assumes that both the C_i and MV functions are linear, it is easily proved that if the C_i and MV are normalized so that a δ shift upward or downward in quality is equally as profitable as remaining at the origin level for a dwelling unit of average age (at that origin), then (1) a δ shift upward is preferred to downward or to no shift for a dwelling unit of less than average age; and (2) a δ downward shift is preferred to upward or no shift for a dwelling unit of greater than average age. More generally, the greater steepness of C_{ix}^{AG} for older than for newer units will often tend to make a downward conversion optimal (here the *MV* function tends also to be steeper) for old units, while an upward conversion is optimal for newer units, since their flatter C_{ix}^{AG} slope is tangent to the *MV* function where it also tends to be flatter—at higher-quality submarkets.

The next factor to be considered is the time-lag cost associated with conversion—C_T in equation (5.10). The proposition here is that such costs tend to rise progressively as the differential between origin and destination submarkets grows (but both the fact and the amount depend on the particular conversion method M_k used), because the length of the gestation periods may also rise with the size of the conversions. Symbolically,

$$(5.14) \qquad (\partial C_T / \partial M_K)\ [\partial M_K(H_i, H_j) / \partial\ (|H_i - H_j|)_{|Hi}] > 0$$

for given conversion method M_K.

Figure 5.4 portrays this time-lag effect by indicating that larger C_T makes the conversion cost function more convex. That is, each C_{ix} portrays a cost function wherein the implicit conversion method M_K is very rapid so that there is only a small time-lag effect, regardless of how extensive a conversion is involved. ${}_LC_{ix}$, on the other hand, reflects a conversion method M_K^L that takes longer to accomplish, and time lag increases with the size of the quality change sought. Comparing C_{ix} and ${}_LC_{ix}$ shows that the marginal impact of increasing conversion distance, that is, quality differential, on both total conversion costs is positive. Notice that this effect is less for method M_K than for method M_K^L.

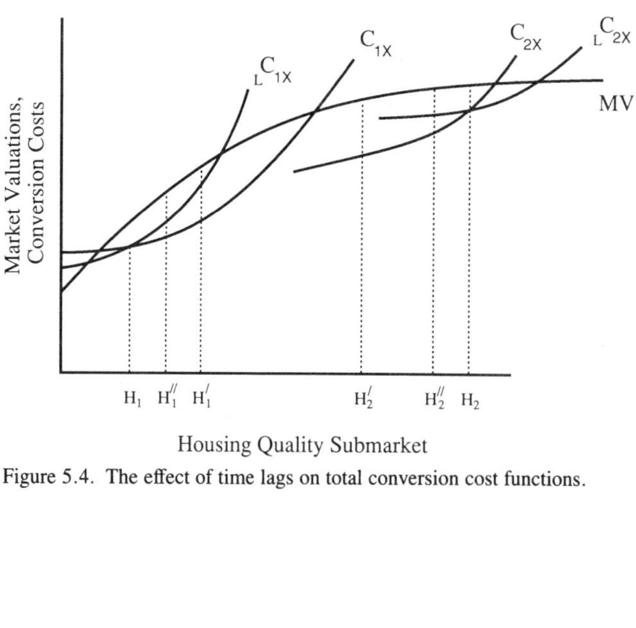

Figure 5.4. The effect of time lags on total conversion cost functions.

Here the optimal downward conversion for the unit originally at H_2 is attenuated from H_2' to H_2'' in the case of greater time-lag costs (i.e., from C_2 to ${}_LC_2$). Analogously, the upward conversion for the unit at H_1 is reduced from H_1' to H_1'' (i.e., via ${}_LC_1$ instead of C_1). Thus, time-lag costs involved in the conversion process tend to lessen the optimal origin-destination quality differential via conversion.

This consequence of time-lag costs has particularly important implications for downward conversions by means of the method of undermaintenance, since this involves very considerable elapsed time between the start of undermaintenance and the arrival at the destination submarket. As we have seen above, owners of older units may be especially prone to adopt this strategy. But this time-lag cost constitutes a limit to such a strategy for these units. Even the prospect of heavy continued savings via undermaintenance is offset by the delay in arriving at the target quality level where maximum net gains are obtainable. This does not mean that the undermaintenance policy is not profitable, but that in a static context of deciding *in advance* what is the best combination of conversion target *and* conversion method, undermaintenance may not be the *most* profitable. For example, in circumstances where a very large quality reduction seems most attractive, the optimal way to get there is likely to be a much faster route than continued undermaintenance. The most important such alternative is splitting of original units into a considerably larger number, each at a considerably lower quality than each of the original units. Time-lag costs thus are a factor that enters into the complex tradeoffs involved in determining the optimal mix of conversion target *and* method. The two are interrelated, not independent of one another, in this calculation.

The first influence on conversion costs related to one particular attribute of the housing package, its age. The second referred not to attributes but to conversion method and conversion "distance." Now we deal more generally with the heterogeneity of the existing housing stock. In equation (5.10) we have indicated that both the costs of modifying a unit C_M and intersubmarket differentials in normal upkeep costs C_U depend on its particular attribute mix [R]. Two units of the same initial quality, the same age, and undergoing the same conversion strategy will rarely possess the same technical capabilities for converting to any particular destination—certainly not to *all* other destinations. Their construction materials, architectural configuration, floor plan, mechanical systems, available yard space, and so forth may strongly influence the cost of achieving any or all potential conversions. To add even more complexity, one unit may be relatively cheaper to convert upward, another to convert downward. We suggest something of this complexity in figure 5.5.

Figure 5.5 shows that hypothetical units α, β, θ, and σ—all of the same age, sunk capital costs C_K, and initial quality—may well have different total costs of conversion for particular methods k_1, k_2 for potential upward and downward conversions, respectively. It also shows the possibility of asymmetries between upward and downward total conversion costs (that is, the

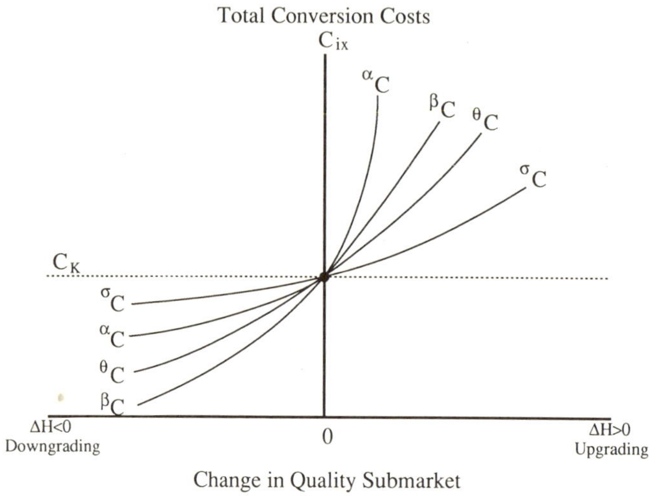

Figure 5.5. Families of representative conversion cost functions for units originally in submarket H_i.

order of cost functions upward is not necessarily the same as their order downward). Further realistic variation may be introduced by relaxing the assumption of equal embodied capital costs.

Finally, extent of conversion matters. We alleged above that in overall cost, conversion is inferior to new construction in that the initial structure embeds significant conversion possibility constraints, unlike the relative freedom of new construction. The more "distant" the conversion destination is from the origin submarket (i.e., the greater the quality differential), the more this disadvantage becomes—in effect a progressive flattening of the conversion cost (savings) function for downgrading and a progressive steepening of the conversion cost function for upgrading. Because conversions from each origin submarket must compete at each destination with conversions from every other origin submarket and (with the exception of the lower-quality submarkets) with new construction, the farther away an origin is the less competitive its converters will be with dwellings from both other sources. Moreover, the aforementioned time lags associated with conversion become more pronounced the greater the quality differential involved (especially for downgrading via undermaintenance), thus reinforcing the above relationship. So nearby origin submarkets, all other things equal, have competitive advantages at each destination submarket over more remote origins.

In sum, the heterogeneity of the existing stock in several dimensions—age, time lags in conversion, and attribute mix—and its specific distribution across quality submarkets suggest large variation in the array of cost functions to which owners refer when assessing conversion options. This, in turn, means that different owners considering whether to convert their dwelling units into the same destination submarket will likely have substantially different costs of doing so. "Nearness" in quality *and* structural age *and* speed of conversion *and* aptness of attribute mix thus all compete against one another for final determination of conversion action. Thus, a greater intersubmarket valuation differential is required to elicit conversion from farther- than from nearer-quality origins; from older than from newer units being upgraded, but from newer than older units being downgraded; and from less- than from more-apt and rapid converters. Such will be crucial for understanding the nature of *aggregate* and equilibrating conversions into any submarket, as is discussed in the next section. But the upshot at this point cannot be exaggerated: history matters. When and what sorts of dwellings were built in the past and how they have been converted since their construction crucially influence the character of the contemporary conversion supply response in an urban housing market.

5.4 Aggregate Static Medium-Run Supply through Construction and Conversion

Having discussed the factors that lead individual builders to construct new dwellings and individual owners of existing units to supply them to one submarket or another through maintenance or conversion activities, we are now in a position to derive aggregate supply functions for these two modes. When these two functions are added for each submarket target, over all submarkets, the aggregate, static medium-run supply function for that submarket is obtained, showing the relationship between submarket valuation and quantity of units supplied for given prices or rents in all other submarkets, after builders and converters have had adequate time to respond.

The meaning of "adequate time to respond" is not a simple concept in our theoretical approach, since we have emphasized that different forms of supply response may take quite different times to be achieved, with some requiring very considerable lags. So different adjustments will be completed at different times. Moreover, at any one time, different units may be responding to market signals generated in different past periods. Thus, the uneven temporal flow of responses may be quite important in this market. This subject is properly an aspect of market dynamics, and we return to it in section 5.6 below.

The aggregate static supply function ${}_{N}S$ for newly constructed units in submarket H_j is a straightforward aggregation of the individual construction decisions specified by equation (5.8). The aggregate number of builders who ascertain that H_j is their rate-of-return maximizing destination is a function of market valuations and construction costs in H_j compared to those in other submarkets, H_x, and the rate of return available from nonhousing investments. Symbolically,

$$(5.15) \qquad {}^{S}_{N}Q_j = {}_{N}S(MV_j, {}_{N}C_j, [MV_x], [{}_{N}C_x], \gamma') \\ x = 1, 2, \ldots, \neq j.$$

The derivation of the aggregate conversion supply for a submarket is considerably more complex, due to the inherently *inter*submarket impacts of any one conversion and to the aforementioned heterogeneity of dwelling-specific characteristics in the existing stock and, thus, conversion cost functions. Aggregate supply for any given submarket is the algebraic sum of the number of units starting there at the beginning of the period, plus the new construction additions to that submarket, plus the conversions to the submarket from all other submarkets, minus the conversions from the submarket to all other submarkets. Critical to the ability to determine aggregate conversion supply to the submarket is the ability to predict *net* intersubmarket flows. This requires an ability to indicate not only the strength of profitability differentials leading to shifts to particular other submarkets from a given origin and to there from other submarkets, but also to predict the resulting *size* of those flows. Net flows are very sensitive to the absolute sizes of the gross components. But these absolute flows require a prediction of how, in effect, the owner of *every* existing unit will decide to offer his or her unit to the market. Such a challenge is greatly complicated by the heterogeneity of the existing stock, since that diversity should be predicted to generate a wide variety of conversion responses. We must therefore look deeply to the treatment of conversion supplies from a notably heterogeneous stock. Because of this heterogeneity the predicted conversion of one unit from a particular origin submarket to a given destination submarket cannot be generalized to all units at this origin. However, the array of conversion cost functions displayed by units in various origin submarkets can be used to derive an aggregate supply function for each alternative destination submarket in principle.

From the array of different total conversion cost functions for units originating in submarket H_i, we can form an *aggregate cost function* that shows the *marginal* cost of converting upward the *least expensive* unit (or, in the case of downgrading, the unit with the greatest net cost savings) from some origin H_i to a common destination H_j as a *function of the total number of units converted* from H_i to H_j. For the marginal unit the relevant costs are given by equation (5.10): cost of maintaining at H_i equals C_i; cost at a new H_j equals C_{ij}. Now define the marginal conversion cost for the marginal unit converted from H_i to H_j, MC_{ij}, as

$$MC_{ij} \equiv C_{ij} - C_i. \qquad (5.16)$$

The locus of points of these MC_{ij} marginal costs and the corresponding number of units converted, Q_{ij}, yields the desired aggregate marginal conversion cost function: MC^{Σ}_{ij}. At each Q_{ij} where $H_j > H_i$, the function MC^{Σ}_{ij} shows the marginal cost of an upgraded unit from H_i to H_j for the *lowest*-cost converter remaining in H_i after Q_{ij} units have already been upgraded from H_i to H_j. Thus, the aggregate upward conversion process is seen as a sequence in which the lowest marginal cost converter goes first, the next lowest goes second, and so forth. Because higher Q_{ij} means that the marginal upward converter has higher marginal cost, the MC_{ij}^{Σ} function rises with Q_{ij}. Conversely, when $H_j < H_i$, MC_{ij}^{Σ} shows the marginal savings in upkeep (net of any modification and time-lag costs) associated with Q_{ij} downgraders from H_i to H_j. As the units with the greatest net cost savings (i.e., negative costs) are downgraded, the savings from downgrading associated with the marginal unit become progressively smaller (less negative).

Four representative MC_{ij}^{Σ} functions are shown in figure 5.6, where it is assumed that $H_1 < H_2 < H_j < H_3 < H_4$. The functions in the first quadrant pertain to upward conversions; those in the fourth quadrant to downward conversions. The larger the quality differential between lower-quality submarkets and H_j, the greater (on average)[16] the cost of converting the marginal unit, as shown in figure 5.6 by comparing MC_{1j}^{Σ} to MC_{2j}^{Σ}. Conversely, it is typically the case that the larger the quality differential between higher-quality submarkets and H_j, the greater the net costs savings from converting the marginal unit, although the higher time costs associated with this higher differential make this conclusion less certain.

The shape of the aggregate marginal conversion cost function has important implications for the competition among units in different submarkets. Suppose MV in a particular submarket rises from an initial equilibrium position. At these new relative cross-submarket valuations, existing units from several different origin submarkets may wish to convert into the now more profitable submarket. What will determine the origin mix of these? The answer depends on the interplay of quality differential between origin and destination submarkets, and on the number of converters between each origin and the given destination. The two factors have comparable effects on the marginal cost of conversion: MC_{ij}^{Σ} rises (or becomes less negative) both with increasing difference between H_i and H_j and with increasing Q_{ij}. Thus, a competitive advantage in conversion arising from a particular origin to a given destination situation is eroded by increasing numbers of such converters; a competitive advantage for

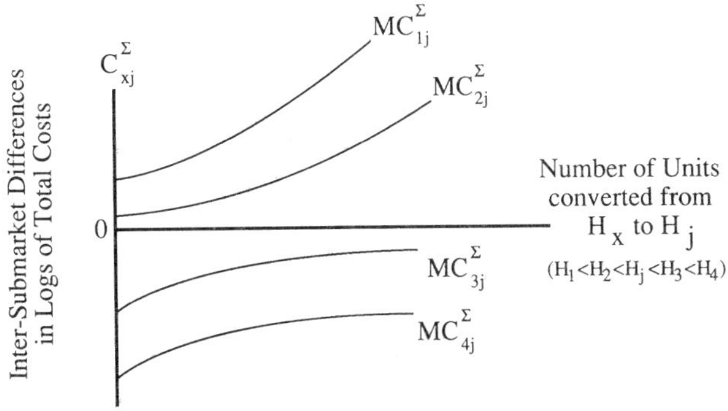

Figure 5.6. Cost of marginal conversion from H_x to H_j, as a function of the number of units converted.

a given number of converters is eroded as an increasing portion of that number comes from origins with increasing quality differential from that destination.

This relationship can be illustrated as follows. Assume for simplicity that the entire system of submarkets is in general equilibrium initially; that is, market valuations have adjusted such that no one has an incentive to build or convert any units, and households have no incentives to change occupancy.[17] We therefore can focus our attention clearly on the consequences that would transpire if the market valuation of some submarket H_j were to rise (due to some increase in demand for H_j) to some higher valuation, all other valuations remaining constant. We assume, for simplicity, that this new valuation represents a new, *medium-run equilibrium valuation.*[18] In particular, consider how this newly increased gap between MV_j and the market valuations in all other submarkets, MV_x, would induce conversions as a function of the relevant aggregate marginal conversion cost function between a partiular H_x and H_j. Note that since we are holding all other submarket valuations at their original levels but increasing MV_j absolutely, any and all conversions will be *into* H_j; none will be *out of* H_j.

This relationship is portrayed in figure 5.7. On the vertical axis we measure the intersubmarket valuation differential created by some given shift from initial equilibrium to another equilibrium valuation: $\Delta MV_{xj} \equiv MV_j - MV_x$, where x is the indicator of the origin submarket. Four representative differential market valuation functions are shown in figure 5.7, corresponding to potential conversions from origin submarkets H_1, H_2, H_3, and H_4.[19] The assumed ordinal ranking of quality for the relevant submarkets is $H_1 < H_2 < H_j < H_3 < H_4$. On the horizontal axis we measure the quantity of units in each origin x actually converted during the medium-run adjustment period into the given destination submarket H_j, Q_{xj}. Four representative marginal conversion cost functions similar to those portrayed in figure 5.6 are shown, again corresponding to the aforementioned four submarkets.

Since $\Delta MV_{xj} / (H_j - H_x)$ is the average slope of the MV function in the range between H_j and H_x (portrayed in fig. 5.1, for example) and $MC^{\Sigma}_{xj} / (H_j - H_x)$ is the average slope of the aggregate marginal conversion cost function in this same range, the condition for approximately optimal conversion between x and j is met when, at the marginal conversion,[20]

$$(5.17) \qquad \Delta MV_{xj} / (H_j - H_x) = MC^{\Sigma}_{xj} / (H_j - H_x)$$

or, simplifying, $\Delta MV_{xj} = MC^{\Sigma}_{xj}$.

Graphically, this condition is shown as the intersection of the marginal conversion cost and differential market valuation functions for the same origin submarket. In terms of figure 5.7, this means that at most, Q_{2j} units will find it profitable to upgrade during the adjustment period from H_2 to H_j, and no units from H_1 will find it optimal to upgrade to H_j here. Analogously, Q_{3j} units will downgrade from H_3, but none will downgrade from H_4.

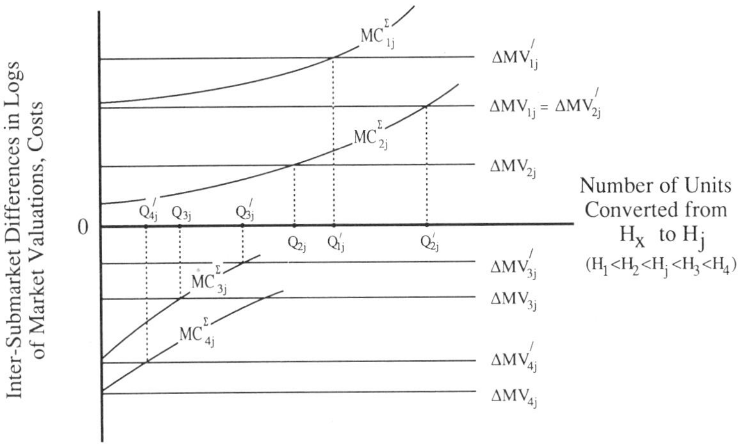

Figure 5.7. Marginal conversion costs and optimal conversions from different origin submarkets H_x to H_j.

Now suppose that, instead of the previous amount, MV_j rises by a larger initial amount to an even higher equilibrium position—all other valuations still remaining unchanged—so that, for graphical simplification, the relevant set of ΔMV functions is $\Delta MV'_{1j}$, $\Delta MV'_{2j}$, $\Delta MV'_{3j}$ $\Delta MV'_{4j}$ as shown in figure 5.7.[21] The optimal number of upgraded units to H_j rises from Q_{2j} to Q'_{2j} originating in H_2, and from zero to Q'_{1j} originating in H_1.[22] The optimal number of downgraded units into H_j rises from Q_{3j} to Q'_{3j} originating in H_3 and from zero to Q'_{4j} originating in H_4.

Thus, the relative numbers of these converters to a submarket destination such as H_j depend on the exact shapes of the aggregate marginal conversion cost functions and the relative intersubmarket (equilibrium) valuation differentials, ΔMV_{xj}. Different shifts in the MV_j function, or different MC^{Σ}_{xj} functions, will change the relative sizes of Q_{1j}, Q_{2j}, Q_{3j}, and Q_{4j}, but will not change the fact that a rise in ΔMV_{xj} will induce more units to undertake that conversion to H_j and will permit units to convert competitively to H_j from more distant-quality origins (that is, switch some situations with zero converters to one with a positive number—as here in the cases of H_1 and H_4).

Now consider the case where an initial equilibrium is upset by an absolute *decline* in MV_j to a lower, medium-run equilibrium level. In this instance we could construct a figure analogous to figure 5.7, except that the roles of origin and destination submarkets would be reversed. That is, $\Delta MV_{jx} \equiv MV_x - MV_j$, and the relevant marginal conversion cost function, MC^{Σ}_{jx}, is the cost of the marginal unit converting out of H_j into H_x. The crucial added distinction here is that units in H_j have more than one conversion option to choose from in order to attain their best rate of return. Thus the MC^{Σ}_{jx} function must be specified as involving only those units whose *highest* rate of return occurs with conversion from H_j to H_x. The intersections of the relevant marginal cost and valuation differential functions for upgrading from H_j to H_3 and H_4 would occur in the first quadrant and would thereby specify optimal numbers converted out of H_j to those destinations—Q_{j3} and Q_{j4}, respectively. Analogously, the marginal cost (savings) and valuation differential function intersections relevant for downgrading options would occur in the fourth quadrant and would specify the optimal number of H_j units downgraded to H_2 and H_1, Q_{j2} and Q_{j1}, respectively. Finally, conversions from H_j to abandonment and to nonhousing uses would be determined through the standard rate-of-return comparisons, although this cannot be easily shown graphically. Note that the conversion supply function for values below MV_{j0} is not symmetric to that associated with values above MV_{j0}; the former is based on the costs of converting units originally in H_j out of it, whereas the latter is based on the costs of converting units from all *other* submarkets into H_j.

Four important conclusions follow from the above analysis: (1) the greater the differential in the (equilibrium) $MV(H)$ function between the given submarket whose valuation has changed and other submarkets, the greater the quality differential for which it will pay competitively to convert a unit to the given destination, and the more units it will pay to convert from each such origin; (2) the percentage distribution of origins in a given total of conversions to a given destination will differ for various differentials in this $MV(H)$ function—less differential means more predominance of near-quality submarkets; (3) the percentage distribution of origins in a given total of conversions to a given destination will differ for different shapes of the MC^{Σ}_{xj} functions—the higher the costs (or the less the cost savings) for any Q_{xj}, the less its share of conversions into H_j; and (4) intersubmarket quality differential and numbers of converters from a given origin are competing (tradeoff) determinants of the attractiveness of different conversions.

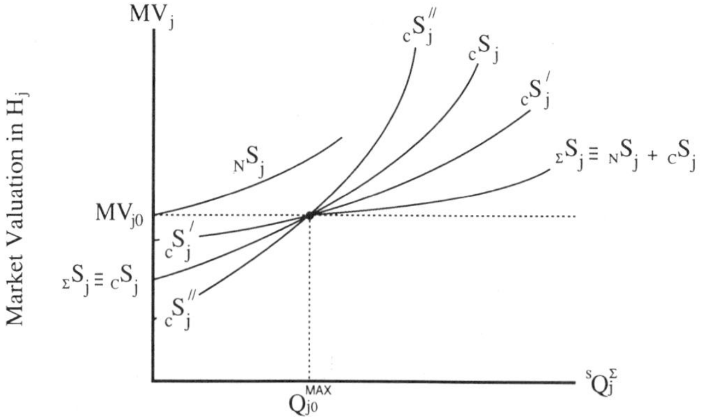

Figure 5.8. New construction, conversion, and aggregate supply functions to H_j.

The analysis embodied in figure 5.7 enables us to generate an aggregate, medium-run conversion supply function ${}_{C}S_j$ showing the relationship between *net* conversions *into* (or out of) each submarket H_j and various medium-run equilibrium market valuations $[MV_j]$, given some initial equilibrium position wherein the market valuation for H_j is MV_{j0}.[23] The ${}_{C}S_j$ function has three segments. As long as MV_{j0} (and all other market valuations, of course) remains constant, there will be no changes and the stock will remain at its initial level: Q_{j0}^{MAX}. If MV_j rises, the process of stock additions to H_j (via conversions) will occur, as described in the context of figure 5.7. If MV_j falls, the process of stock losses from H_j will occur, as described above. Symbolically, the total number of units supplied from the existing stock to a given submarket H_j in the medium run can be expressed as

$$(5.18) \quad {}_{C}Q_j^{\Sigma} = \begin{cases} -\sum\limits_{x \neq j} Q_{jx} - \sum\limits_{m} Q_{jm} & \text{for } MV_j < MV_{j0} \\ (= \sum\limits_{x \neq j} {}_{C}S_{jx}(MV_j, [MV_x], [MC_{jx}^{\Sigma}]) + \sum\limits_{m} {}_{C}S_{jm}(\gamma^H, \gamma') & \\ + Q_{j0}^{MAX} \quad \text{for } MV_j = MV_{j0} & \\ + \sum\limits_{x \neq j} Q_{xj} = \sum\limits_{x \neq j} {}_{C}S_{xj}(MV_j, [MV_x], [MC_{xj}^{\Sigma}]) & \text{for } MV_j > MV_{j0} \end{cases}$$

where ${}_{C}S_{jx}$ is the conversion supply function from j to other x submarkets, ${}_{C}S_{jm}$ is the conversion supply function to all m nonhousing uses and abandonment, and ${}_{C}S_{xj}$ is the conversion supply function from other x submarkets into j.[24]

Figure 5.8 portrays three such representative gross conversion supply functions for submarket H_j: ${}_{C}S_j$, ${}_{C}S_j'$, and ${}_{C}S_j''$. Each corresponds to a particular set of parameters that influence conversion supply through their embodiment of specifications of the distribution of the stock across submarkets other than H_j and the marginal conversion costs from each to H_j and vice versa. Thus, each conversion ${}_{C}S$ function has as an implicit parameter the distribution of *demands* across submarkets. An altered distribution of demands will lead to conversions which, by changing the configuration of the stock, will alter the aggregate conversion functions to all submarkets subsequently. To illustrate, suppose ${}_{C}S_j$ is the initial conversion supply function. Now if there were a permutation in the stock such that, *on average*, it had a *smaller* quality differential vis-à-vis H_j, and/or if one or more of the MC_{xj}^{Σ} conversion cost functions decreased, the supply to H_j would *increase* to ${}_{C}S_j'$ to the right of Q_{j0}^{MAX}. In other words, such circumstances would make it easier for other units to convert into H_j, should its valuation rise. If the opposite were to occur, conversion supply would *decrease* to ${}_{C}S_j''$ to the right of Q_{j0}^{MAX} in figure 5.8.

A permutation of the stock such that it is, *on average*, more similar in quality to H_j and/or a decrease in the costs of upward conversion (increase in savings from downward conversion) from H_j to other submarkets, MC_{jx}^{Σ}, will lead to a more rapid decrease in the H_j stock if market valuations drop below MV_{j0}, as shown by ${}_{C}S_j'$ in figure 5.8. The opposite assumptions would make it more difficult for owners in H_j to convert their properties out of H_j, and thus conversion supply would shift to ${}_{C}S_j''$ in figure 5.8.

Finally, the addition of newly constructed units during the period, as expressed in equation (5.16), to net conversions in equation (5.18), yields the *aggregate* (net) supply function for each submarket H_j during the medium run, ${}_{\Sigma}S_j$. In figure 5.8 this is shown as the horizontal addition of ${}_{N}S_j$ and ${}_{C}S_j$ to produce the ${}_{\Sigma}S_j$ shown.[25] Of course, new construction will only occur for $MV_j > MV_{j0}$, given our initial equilibrium assumptions. Thus the total stock supplied in the medium run in H_j may be expressed

$$(5.19) \qquad {}^{S}Q_j^{\Sigma} \equiv {}_{N}^{S}Q_j^{\Sigma} + {}_{C}^{S}Q_j^{\Sigma}$$

or,

$$(5.20) \qquad {}^{S}Q_j^{\Sigma} = \begin{cases} -\sum_{x \neq j} Q_{jx} - \sum_{m} Q_{jm} & \text{for } MV_j < MV_{j0} \\ (= \sum_{x \neq j} {}_{C}S_{jx}(MV_j, [MV_x], [MC_{jx}^{\Sigma}]) + \sum_{m} {}_{C}S_{jm}(\gamma^H, \gamma')) & \\ + Q_{j0}^{\text{MAX}} & \text{for } MV_j = MV_{j0} \\ + \sum_{x \neq j} Q_{xj} + {}_{N}^{S}Q^{\Sigma} & \text{for } MV_j > MV_{j0} \\ (= \sum_{x \neq j} {}_{C}S_{xj}(MV_j, [MV_x], [MC_{xj}^{\Sigma}]) & \\ + {}_{N}S_j(MV_j, {}_{N}C_j, [MV_x], [{}_{N}C_x], \gamma')). & \end{cases}$$

We refer to the entire array of functions like equation (5.20) across all j submarkets as static spectral medium-run supply.

5.5 Dynamics of Supply

Up to now we have been concerned with a static analysis of housing supply. But some of the elements dealt with strongly suggest that dynamic considerations are very important. Such considerations stem from such fundamental aspects as the durability and heterogeneity of housing, the modifiability of existing units, and the varied but considerable time necessary to make such physical modifications in existing units as well as to build new ones.

It is the great durability of housing that makes the stock of preexisting housing so overwhelming a source of present supply and this period's new construction so paltry. This leads to the fact that in each market period it is the turnover of existing units, and not the selling of new units, that is the most important source of market transactions. The most important source of "supply" is *demanders'* decisions: their decisions to move is what opens up most vacancies. This supply is either direct, for owner-occupier turnover, or indirect, via tenants' decisions to move. Thus, in the so-called market period, supply is largely the opposite side of the coin of demand. Even in the so-called medium-run period, the confounding of demand with supply is extensive. Conversions are carried out by owner-occupiers sometimes in the middle of their tenure to meet their changing wants, sometimes toward their tenure's end to promote a more advantageous sale, and sometimes as new purchasers to adapt the unit to their specific tastes at the outset of their tenure.

Supply is thus deeply bound up with demand. But demand, as we saw in chapter 4, is subject to very important participation lags (stemming heavily from the high costs of changing occupancy): demanders are only intermittently active participants in the market. In this chapter we have seen that demanders are engaging as well, also intermittently, in supply behavior—conversions—other than market transactions. So the various time-dependent sequences of events that characterize demand behavior also spill over into supply.

The second major source of dynamic considerations is the long, but varied, time required to make actual physical transformations in housing (including planning, financial mobilization, securing legal approvals, etc.)—both new construction and conversion. Its average length is important; so too is the high variance of gestation periods for the different types and methods of transformation, since this suggests an incidence of complex overlapping adjustment processes.

Thus, dynamics can be quite important for housing supply. In the present section we simply sketch some respects in which dynamical considerations modify the static viewpoint given above, and how these might fruitfully be treated. In chapter 6 we examine some of the implications of these issues for the meaning and significance of equilibrium and equilibrating processes.

5.5.1 Dynamics of Market-Period Supply

The market period appears to be only a deliberately still picture of possibly seething underlying processes. It seems unpromising to focus on explicit dynamic elements in something so temporary and changeable. Yet dynamics intrudes integrally even here. It intrudes fundamentally by making us ask what a market period is in fact and whether it is a worthwhile analytic construct. The question is important for the medium-run analysis as well, because in an important sense the latter begins where the former ends: one cannot really know the one without knowing the other. The problem of time demarcation for analytical periods is that, because of long and various supply gestation periods, some units are in process of *being* changed or of *coming* into existence altogether in each period; that is, what they are now is not what they are intended to be, or to become. The present short period—the market period—is not therefore a place of temporary rest, but rather an artificial truncation of a set of processes of change. This is especially true for unfinished new units still under construction and for units still in the process of being converted downward in quality by means of continued undermaintenance. Both processes have unusually long gestation periods. They represent supply adjustments already taken in the past in response to *previous* market conditions, but not yet completed. So present market signals will not adequately account for the character of present overall supply conditions.

Both biases have nonuniform locus of misrepresentation along the quality spectrum. For reasons of competitive advantage discussed below, new construction is likely to have a concentrated incidence in the quality submarkets comprising the top 30% to 40% of units. The uneven incidence for conversions stems more from an algebraic artifact than from competitive advantage. While downward undermaintenance conversion is the major source of continuous drift, upward conversion via mix of sequential physical improvements and overmaintenance also requires substantial gestation time and so will also contribute to the drift. Probabilistically, therefore, roughly middle-spectrum submarkets will have a larger percentage of their units involved in upward *or* downward drifts than will more extreme submarkets, because more such shifts will pass through the middle than through the extremes.

In sum, therefore, supply behavior during a market period is not adequately accounted for—modeled—by present market valuation signals (and their future projections). Dynamics matter. A dynamic treatment would add past market valuation signals as well to explain behavior of units identified as in flux, including new units still being constructed. In practice, of course, it is not always easy to identify units presently in flux—even sometimes via physical inspection. The ability to do so from data alone may be especially daunting. But inferential proxies, such as reports of recent modification outlays and actions, may often be available for tolerable effectiveness.

The second major issue stemming from continuous drift is the very meaning of the market period. It is *not* a period during which suppliers are constrained from doing anything other than either offering their units for or withholding them from use. Different suppliers may in fact be in various stages of shifting them from one submarket to another.The use/nonuse choice may therefore trivialize the complexity of what is really going on. If this is so, the convenient analytic advantage of the market-period conceptualization—namely, that "supply is fixed"—becomes dubious. How short a time, then, must one deal with in order for supply really to be fixed? Indeed, this apparently obvious question is in fact the wrong question here, the problem is that the time is *too short* to have permitted present units to become what they are intended to be. How *long* a time, then, should the market period be? Since the gestation periods responsible for the problem are often considerable, lengthening the period to include those periods completely would encroach seriously on the meaning of the *medium-run period*—for there would then be time for many kinds of supply change with shorter gestation periods to occur. We do not attempt to resolve this quandary at this point. Our purpose here is only to indicate that in a market characterized by such a rich menu of supply responses calling for explicit attention to dynamics, the very concepts of analytic adjustment periods become highly problematic. In chapter 6 we indicate the implications of this complexity of supply responses for the nature of equilibrium and equilibrating processes.

5.5.2 Dynamics of Medium-Run Supply

Our above discussion of market-period supply bears deeply on medium-run supply. In this section we go beyond the issues already mentioned to ones that stem from characteristics inherent to the medium-run period. This period is designed to illuminate deliberate responses by the various suppliers to changing market conditions, responses that include production of new dwelling units and modification of existing ones.

The first aspect of this medium-run period we call attention to is an important implication of long gestation periods necessary to accomplish some of these responses. We earlier noted the difficulty for an onlooker to predict how many new units targeted for each submarket are in the process of production or in the process of being converted there from other submarkets. The present problem is far more fundamental: how do the suppliers themselves decide how many units to target for each submarket, when their decisions must be based on present market conditions that may be changed significantly by the time the units so acted upon reach their assigned destinations? The problem is not simply that future market conditions must be predicted. It is that the most considerable changes to be predicted are those that are generated by the actions of the very same suppliers in committing themselves now to their chosen responses; that is, they are strictly endogenous changes.

This is, of course, the basic situation for which rational expectations solutions have been assumed to resolve the problem. In the markets we are discussing, such solutions are problematic. For accurate expectations to be formed the suppliers must know, or be able closely to estimate, what supply commitments are *in the works,* long before they have culminated in supplies reaching the market. This refers to both new construction and conversion projects, and the longer the gestation periods the greater potential aggregate magnitude of these unfinished projects. But such knowledge is rough at best. Estimates of it are likely to have high variance.

Our treatment carries the spirit of a rational expectation approach modified for the considerable uncertainty about what supply responses are in the works. Each supplier is assumed to estimate subjectively what is in the works and, on the basis of the predicted resulting endogenous market changes *for the time at which that supplier's response reaches the market,* to calculate the optimal rate-of-return supply response and commit himself or herself to begin it in the present. The subjective evaluations of incomplete supply changes currently in process (including other supply response decisions being made currently as well) have both a systematic and a random component. We assume that the closer in time to the present the supplier's response is completed, the closer expected market valuations will resemble those now obtaining. The random element permits various idiosyncratic information to be reflected in different estimates by different suppliers otherwise similarly situated, but does not invoke systematic bias. So each group of suppliers with equal gestation period is assumed to make estimates that are distributed normally, with common means for each submarket valuation, and standard deviations that are a positive function of length of gestation periods. The normal distributions for other groups have the same means, and standard deviations smaller or larger depending on the length of their gestation periods.

These subjective estimates of submarket valuations will, of course, influence the determination of optimal supply response for both new construction builders and potential converters of existing units. This determination is based on exactly the same logical basis as under perfect prediction in equation (5.8) for new construction and equation (5.12) for conversion, but with subjectively random estimated market valuations taking the place of uniformly predicted market valuations for all submarkets, as follows.

For builders,

$$(5.21) \qquad d\,MV^{V}/d\,H = (\,d\,{}_{N}C^{V}\,/\,d\,H\,)(\,1 + \gamma'\,);$$

for $(MV^{V}_{1}, MV^{V}_{2}, \ldots)\, MV^{V}_{i} \lesseqgtr MV^{x}_{i}$, all $X \neq V$ where MV^{V}_{1} is estimated market valuation for submarket i by builder V; ${}_{N}C^{V}$ is the cost function for builder V; ${}_{N}C^{V} = {}_{N}C^{1} = {}_{N}C^{2} = \ldots$ all builders.

$$(5.22) \qquad MV^{V}_{i} = G[\,MV^{o}_{i}, \sigma(\,g^{v}_{i}\,)\,],$$

where MV^{o}_{i} is the current value of MV_{i}; g^{V}_{i} is the gestation period for supply from builder V to submarket i; MV^{V}_{i} is a random variable distributed as $G(\mu, \sigma_{r})$ which is a normal distribution function with mean μ and standard deviation σ_{r}; $\sigma^{V} = \sigma(g^{V})$; $\quad \sigma' > 0$.

For converters,

$$(5.23) \qquad d\,MV^{\alpha}/d\,H = (\,\partial\,{}^{\alpha}C_{ijk}\,/\,\partial\,H\,)(\,1 + \gamma'\,);$$

for $(MV^{\alpha}_{1}, MV^{\alpha}_{2}, \ldots)\, MV^{\alpha}_{i} \lesseqgtr MV^{Y}_{i}$ all $Y \neq \alpha$ where MV^{α}_{1} is the estimated market valuation for converter of unit α; ${}^{\alpha}C_{ijk}$ is the cost of unit α converted from submarket i to submarket j via conversion method k.

$$(5.24) \qquad MV^{a}_{ik} = G_{i}[\,MV^{0}_{i}, \sigma(g^{\alpha}_{ijk})] \qquad \text{all } i, j, k,$$

where g^{α}_{ijk} is the gestation period for converting unit α from submarket i to j via conversion method k; MV^{α}_{i} is a random variable distributed as $G(\mu, \sigma^{\alpha}_{ijk})$ which is a normal distribution function with mean μ and standard deviation σ^{α}_{ijk} all i, j, k; $\sigma^{\alpha}_{ijk} = \sigma(g^{\alpha}_{ijk})$.

The formulations are basically similar for both new construction and conversion. They differ with respect to gestation periods. For practical purposes, in new construction we treat $g_i^V = g_i^x$, all $X \neq V$. We do allow $g_i \neq g_j$, because higher-quality housing will generally take longer to build than lower-quality housing.[26] In conversion, on the other hand, the relevant gestation period is specific not only to the destination submarket, but also to the origin submarket, the method of conversion being considered, *and* the particular unit being converted, since all four influence how long the conversion will take. Thus there is much greater dispersion of gestation periods for conversion than for new construction, and thus a much more varied spread of dynamically determined options over the static case for conversion than for new construction.

What are the consequences of this dynamic consideration for supply behavior? The most striking one affects new construction. In a static case we saw a total concentration of construction goals to a single submarket, so long as builders faced the same technology in a competitive market, that is, had the same cost function, and there was no chance mathematical multiplicity of optima. In the dynamic case this is changed. Even if all builders face the same cost curve, their predictions of future relevant submarket valuations will differ randomly from one another. All such differences will generate different optima among the builders. Moreover, since the average gestation period for new construction (including planning, input recruitment, financing as well as actual building), even for modest units, is more than a year, the variance of these disparate market valuations can be considerable. Therefore the spread of the resulting target optima can also be considerable. Moreover, the mathematical sensitivity to even small changes in the shape of the market valuation function can easily produce a considerable sprinkling of targets, rather than a tight band around the original concentrated target. So dynamic analysis rationalizes the more realistic experience of new construction at more than one submarket, but with some remaining variable interval of concentration.

Conversion is subject to a much larger variety of gestation periods, so a much broader set of variants in conversion targets will be evinced in the dynamic compared to the static case. But the average differences between the static and dynamic outcomes for each converter will be smaller, possibly much smaller, than for new construction. This is due both to the steeper conversion cost functions (which require much larger *changes* in the shape of the *MV* function to induce large changes in the identity of the optimal conversion) *and* to the shorter average gestation periods for conversion, which therefore generate a smaller dispersion of market valuation predictions around the current valuations. The one exception is downward conversion via undermaintenance. Such actions may display a considerable spectrum of targets in the dynamic context relative to the static targets.

The upshot of this dynamic modification of static outcomes, while very pervasive and highly variant, is difficult to characterize systematically, unlike in the new construction case. This is because the static conversion pattern already has very wide dispersion of targets overall, since there is a wide dispersion of conversion origins. No systematic directional or spread consequences are obvious.

The second major issue that deserves notice in the dynamic context refers to the *differences* in gestation periods. If we focus on any particular submarket, then a set of decisions taken today to supply newly constructed and converted units to that submarket will result in flows of additional units there that arrive at considerably different times. So at any time short of the completion of the longest of these targeted flows, examination of that submarket will misrepresent past supply decisions taken with respect to it. In the static case one could argue that counting numbers of units in different submarkets adequately described relative supply intentions toward them. In the dynamic case this is significantly misleading. Supply intentions are exhausted only after waiting out the longest delayed supply arrivals. But how does one know what that will be or how to recognize the last arrivals from all earlier ones?

Another, but related, confusion is that for those units which are converted by *shifting through* intermediate submarkets between origin and destination, a still picture of numbers of units in different submarkets will mislead one into thinking that although not everything that is ultimately to arrive at this submarket has yet arrived, everything that *is* here now belongs here. Some units currently in any particular submarket are in fact only temporarily there, in the process of shifting somewhere else.[27] How can these confusions be dispelled?

An approach that can in principle resolve these difficulties is to focus on sources of supply in each period, predict their supply decisions in that period (destination, number, method of getting there, and the predicted time of arrival), and from these aggregate the total multisource arrivals in each submarket at each subsequent period. Thus one has to be able to tag all origin units (including unconstructed ones) and predict both their ultimate destinations and their expected time of arrival in order to have a dynamic nonmisleading theory of relative submarket supply. This is, of course, difficult to accomplish stringently. In practical terms, rather gross approximations must be used.

One final complication concerning differential gestation periods should be noted. It is not only supply that is subject to significant—and variant—gestation periods. Chapter 4 indicates that in a dynamic context, demand too is subject to large differential lags in adjustment (i.e., destination arrivals)—largely due to highly uneven, sporadic instances of active demander participation in the market. Only a small percentage of users seeks occupancy change in any period. In each period some but not all of the units aimed at each submarket arrive there. Thus, in each period the active demand and supply agents in the market looking for one another are random variables, influenced by their different adjustment (gestation) periods. It is therefore important in understanding what happens in any particular submarket in any particular period to be able to predict just which supply and demand sources have fed this period's arrivals, and since when. This will be seen to be important to "overall equilibration" because of the relatively long-term constraint that results from each period's transactions. Resolution of this problem rests also with an ability to enumerate potential supply *and* demand *sources* and predict their optimal decision targets as well as how long it will take—and passing through what intermediate states, where this is relevant—to arrive there. Despite this possibility in principle, however, the complexity of its pattern of period-to-period adjustment raises the need to be sensitive to the specificity of period-by-period processes.

5.6 Conclusion

In the short-run market period the only supply choice faced by owners of existing dwelling units is whether or not to offer their units for rent or sale at the moment. They will offer them so long as the current market valuations or bids exceed their reservation prices. The locus of individual owners' reservation prices and the corresponding numbers of units they will offer to the market at these alternative prices define the aggregate market-period supply function for each submarket. The willingness to offer dwelling units will be greater (1) the lower the unit's operating costs, (2) the higher the unit's holding costs, (3) the lower the expected inflation of market valuations, and (4) the higher the discount rate.

Over a longer, medium-run period the stock of dwelling units in a given submarket potentially can be altered by both new construction and conversion activity. Builders are guided in their choice of submarket for construction by an intersubmarket comparison of market valuations and construction costs. To the extent that all builders face similar cost functions (and, of course, the same market valuation function), there will be a rough congruence in the quality submarkets into which new construction will be directed, that is, high concentration of intersubmarket construction. Housing construction will decline in aggregate as rates of return available from nonhousing investments rise relative to those available in the housing market.

Individual owners of existing dwelling units who are market-oriented are also guided by intersubmarket differentials in potential rates of return. Such owners strictly include landlords, but also include, though in less strict measure, a substantial portion of own-consumption-oriented owner-occupiers for various reasons. If positive rates of return can be gained neither from any submarket nor from conversion to nonhousing uses, the units will be abandoned. If rates of return from nonhousing uses of the property are superior to all alternative housing uses, a conversion to such a nonhousing use will ensue. But of most interest is the potential conversion of units across the quality/tenure submarket spectrum. The costs associated with maintaining a dwelling unit at its current submarket or converting it to another are highly unit-specific, depending especially on the unit's age, initial quality, conversion time-lag, and attribute mix. This means that there will be a comparatively wide range of submarket destinations for converters, even within sets of units that all originate from the same submarket. Costs for any dwelling unit (both out-of-pocket and opportunity costs associated with time lags) rise progressively for upgrading to progressively higher-quality submarkets; cost savings decline at a diminishing rate for downgrading to progressively lower-quality submarkets.

The current distribution of dwelling units across the quality submarket spectrum and the particular nature of the conversion cost functions possessed by the units in each submarket will, therefore, determine the aggregate conversion supply function into any given submarket, given some distribution of demands. If many dwelling units are of relatively similar quality to those in the given submarket, and if these same units can be converted to the given submarket relatively cheaply, the conversion supply response into the given submarket will be comparatively large (i.e., a high supply elasticity) for any increases in market valuations (over initial equilibrium levels) in the given submarket. Similarly, decreases in this submarket's valuation will produce conversions to other submarkets (and to nonhousing uses or abandonment), with an elasticity governed by the expense at which such units in the given submarket can be converted and the number of potential converting units. Aggregation of new construction plus conversions (both into and out of the given submarket) yields the aggregate, static, medium-run supply function for the submarket.

What all this means is that history matters. What kinds of dwellings were built, when they were built, and when and how they were converted crucially influence subsequent supply responses. Two metropolitan areas with the same current demand and cost conditions and initial submarket array of valuations, but with radically different initial distributions of housing characteristics, will generate very different conversion flows in response to similar exogenous shocks to the housing market. Therefore, also, since conversion and new construction are substitute forms of supply, they will generate very different new construction flows as well. The final quality distributions and market valuations of housing may well differ greatly as a consequence.

A dynamic point of view has rich application in the study of urban housing markets. We have drawn attention to only a few concerns, but they are central to some of the most distinctive features of such markets. In a very general sense they ask that we be vigilant to the actual passage of units supplied and user occupancies through real calendar time. More of the implications of this emphasis are drawn in the next chapter on market equilibrium and equilibrating adjustments.

Notes

1. Either to other housing submarkets or to nonhousing uses.

2. If the owner rented the unit between $t=0$ and $t=T$, the right-hand side of equation (5.1) would have an added term equaling the discounted present value of such rents, less operating costs, and holding costs would be adjusted accordingly.

3. The rationale behind this joint mobility/tenure-choice decision involves a complex amalgam of optimal consumption and portfolio considerations and housing search and moving costs. Much of the spirit of this calculus is presented in ch. 4. Also see Boehm 1981:375–89. For a review and synthesis of theoretical and empirical work on interurban mobility, see Galster 1987: ch. 7.

4. For owner-occupiers, solve the three-option inequalities above for the market valuation and express as the condition for which the greater of the two use surpluses exceeds the vacancy surplus.

5. We employ the term *market valuation* to render the analysis applicable to units both for sale and for rent. When rental units are considered, the periodic net rental stream should be understood as capitalized into discounted present values so as to make it commensurate with cost functions as well as sales prices.

6. Remembering the implicit sense in which a unit is "offered to the market" when an owner-occupier decides to continue occupancy.

7. "Present" refers to values expected to prevail when supply decisions taken today are ready to appear on the market. Because supply gestation periods actually vary for different types of suppliers, this is in fact an approximate concept only.

8. Builder specialization would actually be represented by i different ${}_NC$ functions. Global maximization for each group is where marginal MV equals marginal ${}_NC^i$, so a set of optimal choices is the result.

9. For a fuller analysis of these alternative production functions, see Galster 1987: ch. 3.

10. To a lesser extent it also depends on the character of occupancy. For a more complete model of maintenance determinants, see Galster 1983.

11. During 1973–80, 873,000 units were consolidated to create 466,000 larger ones; 885,000 were created by partitioning 378,000 larger ones (National Association of Homebuilders 1986).

12. See the discussion of the consumption goals of owner-occupancy in ch. 4, sec. 4.2.

13. For simplicity here we assume that choices of abandonment and conversion to nonhousing use have been judged less-profitable options, so we can concentrate only on optimal housing submarket choice.

14. Locational premia for land is ignored in this discussion; their inclusion would qualify the proposition.

15. For empirical evidence, see Galster 1987: ch. 9.

16. Given the heterogeneity of cost functions across units in different submarkets, it is possible that a few units in H_1 could be upgraded to H_j more cheaply than some (perhaps any) in H_2, but on the margin for the same Q_{ij} this is highly unlikely. For simplicity, then, we draw the MC functions as nonintersecting.

17. With the exception of conversion/construction so as to replenish retired stock but to maintain the overall distribution. The properties of general equilibrium are discussed in more detail in ch. 6.

18. In this manner we can focus on the comparative static characteristics of the initial and final situations. This is equivalent to assuming that all suppliers have perfect information and foresight about the intertemporal adjustment pattern of the stock to this new equilibrium evaluation in H_j. In reality, an increase in demand for H_j will boost short-run market valuations in H_j well above their medium-run equilibrium level, and suppliers will not always respond with equal speed or foresight about eventual

valuations that will be produced as the supply increases. Undoubtedly mistakes are made, and suppliers sometimes "overshoot" their response targets, considering what valuations ultimately result. These real-world complications need not, however, detract from the general (theoretical) nature of the medium-run supply response as described here.

19. The valuation differential functions not only embody the initial, equilibrium differential, but also the new, disequilibrating differential posited in the scenario.

20. These dwellings with lower marginal conversion costs than the marginal unit will, of course, represent an inequality in equation (5.17), with the right-hand side exceeding the left.

21. A given rise in MV means, of course, a larger shift for low than for high ΔMV in space.

22. An increase in several submarket valuations simultaneously complicates the graphical analysis by requiring comparisons among gains to different destinations. But an interval of H with generally rising prices will attract more converters as a whole from all other submarkets.

23. Note that such a pure function only can be defined if demands do not change in any other submarket. Indeed, the entire distribution of the stock must remain constant in order to define the pure conversion supply to the given submarket.

24. Note that all ${}_cS$ functions contain a probabilistic dimension, inasmuch as they will depend on the stochastic distribution of owners of existing units who are market-oriented with respect to conversion within the total duration of the medium-run adjustment period.

25. There is no necessary reason for the new construction supply function to be upsloped; this is done here for graphic clarity.

26. The chief possibility for $g^v_i \neq g^x_i$ is where builder V builds a significantly different number of units as part of the project than does builder X. Multiple-unit projects generally take considerably longer than single- or few-unit projects.

27. As we indicated in the last section, the misrepresentation is biased, not uniform, since middling submarkets are likely to be disproportionately occupied by these temporary units in comparison to extreme submarkets.

6 Housing Market Equilibrium

Having presented our theory of urban housing submarket spectral demand and supply in the previous two chapters, we are now in a position to discuss their interaction in the establishment of equilibrium in the market. During the market period the equilibration of demand and market-period supply specifies the portions of the existing stocks in each submarket that will be occupied and that will be vacant. Over a medium-run period, the interaction between demand and medium-run supply functions produces the equilibrium conditions across the quality spectrum. Of special interest to us here is the equilibrium market valuation and supply cost relationships, the equilibrium mix of new construction and conversion supplies to a submarket, and the intersubmarket equilibrium array of rates of return.

6.1 Market-Period Equilibrium: Static Analysis

During the short run, housing demanders are constrained to choose among existing dwelling units, and their owners are constrained to the single choice of either offering them for rent or sale or not. Based on the socioeconomic and demographic characteristics of households in the given urban housing market, the array of cross-submarket valuations and the prices for nonhousing goods, and the factors influencing optimal portfolio mix that affect tenure choice, an aggregate, market-period demand function for each submarket can be specified, as discussed in chapter 4, section 4.5. Analogously, given a set of initial units in quality level H_i with attribute mix $[R]$ and ages (AG), and their owners' corresponding reservation prices, an aggregate, market-period supply function can be specified, of the type defined in chapter 5 by equation (5.5).

We stress at the outset that *equilibrium* here is rather peculiar. Very small fractions of all households and owners come together in an active, market sense in the short run. Due to the costs of searching, transactions, and mobility,[1] most households are not active in any given market period. Analogous costs (information, transactions, turnover) for dwelling owners, plus prior occupancy commitments like leases, similarly remove most of them from such participation.[2] Thus any particular market-period equilibrium is characterized by the spectral demands and supplies produced by a randomly selected small subset of all demanders and landlords/sellers who are active in the given market period.

Each quality/tenure submarket i clears (i.e., market-period t equilibrium is reached in i) when the number of dwelling units with each attribute mix and age demanded equals the number supplied at a given submarket price or rent (market valuation), MV^*:

$$(6.1)\quad {}^{S}Q_{it}^{\Sigma}(H_i, [R], AG), (MV_{it}^*, [MV_{jt}], [p]) = {}^{D}Q_{it}^{\Sigma}(H_i, [R], AG), (MV_{it}^*, [MV_{jt}], [p]), j \neq i.$$

At market valuation $MV_i < MV_i^*$, demanders will wish to occupy more units in H_i than landlords/sellers of such units initially offer for rent or sale. These excess demands will be translated into higher bids for units and, concomitantly, an upward revision in units offered as these bids exceed the marginal suppliers' reservation prices. Thus, during the market period the supply offered will be adjusted upward until a market valuation is established which equals the bid of the marginal demander and the reservation price of the marginal supplier.[3]

This market-period equilibrium simultaneously establishes the occupied stock in the submarket, Q_{it}^*, and the vacant stock, ${}^{V}Q_{it}^*$:

$$(6.2)\quad {}^{V}Q_{it}^* \equiv \sum {}^{S}Q_{it}^{MAX} - Q_{it}^*$$

where $\Sigma^{S}Q_{it}^{MAX}$ is the total stock available in submarket H_i at the beginning of period t.

6.2 Market-Period Equilibrium: Dynamic Analysis

We have seen that for the market period it is the dynamic more than the static considerations that capture the really distinctive features of housing demand and supply. It is accordingly in dynamic terms that market equilibrium is more interesting.

Two issues are of paramount concern: user-housing matchups and supply-side adjustments to improve matchups. The first stems from the fact that demand and supply decisions are closely related to one another. There is no turnover at all among the existing stock of owner-occupied units unless their current users decide to change occupancy in the present period. These user-demander decisions to seek to occupy different units inherently create units available for sale or rent—they are user-supplier decisions as well. Moreover, rental unit turnover also generally is initiated by the decisions of present tenants to change their occupancy rather than by decisions initiated by landlords to evict their tenants. In chapter 4 we saw that the decision by users to change occupancy is understood best in a dynamic context. Housing and taste heterogeneity, and transactional complexities lead to very considerable frictional costs of changing occupancy. As a result only a small percentage of users entertains notions of shifting in any given period: in the high-turnover U.S. market, approximately one-tenth of owner-occupiers and somewhat more than one-quarter of renters shift annually.[4] So only a small minority of "demanders" are active participants in the market in any period. And since it is this active participation that creates unit supply availability in the market, only an accompanyingly small minority of housing units in the existing stock is actively available for turnover in the market. Annual new construction, comprising much less than 5% of the existing stock during even the best years for building, hardly changes this characterization of the relative size of annual active marketeering.

6.2.1 Market-Period Mismatching

What is the character of market-period equilibrium under these conditions? It is one of imperfect matchups between users and units. It is also one of only questionable household equilibrium. First, to examine the nature of the matching process we begin by simplifying to a situation of fixed population size and housing stock, with no housing retirements or additions. Households do, however, arrive in the local market, pass through a life cycle, and leave, their place being taken by others in exactly sufficient quantities. Let us dramatize the process through the life cycle of one hypothetical household arriving homeless in the local market area. Of one hundred houses in the stock, only ten are currently available for occupancy (sale of rental). None of these is among the top ten in the household's preferred list, the latter being subject to continued occupancy and thus not currently available on the market. So the household chooses unit A, which is the fifteenth on its list, considering attributes, quality, and price. If the house is bought for ownership it will not pay to shift from it for an extended period. Let us assume ownership, to sharpen the following account.

Three months after this transaction, three houses much preferred to unit A appear on the market. But our household cannot afford to be active in the market so soon again, even to get to know of the appearance of these units. So their occupancy does not change. More preferred units come onto the market and off, but our household still cannot afford to become active. Finally the household is ready, and some of the units originally preferred to A are now available; but passing through part of the life cycle, the household's housing preferences have changed somewhat. Of the houses most appropriate to its current needs, only its thirteenth most preferred is currently available on the market, so it shifts occupancy. But again, while raising its utility, the household does not improve its relative quality of matchup—its achieved utility level relative to its potential utility level—given the existing housing stock, and unchanged prices and incomes. This kind of scenario can be extended into further sequences for the household's remaining life.

The ironic unavailability of highly preferred units that actually exist is not an accident, but the result of inherent randomness. This can be generalized. The identity of the small percentage of units that are available in any given period is determined by the identity of the households that have decided—*at last*—to change occupancy. For any household this is sporadically infrequent: it is, from the viewpoint of other households, a random event. The preferences of particular households looking for particular kinds of housing packages do not significantly influence the identity or even the aggregate number of such kinds of units that become available. Those relatively few households seeking housing must select units whose availability is not in any significant way a response to the presence of their active demand: the availability of each other owner-occupied unit is the by-product of *its* owner's decision to seek its *own* preferred shift of occupancy, with little attention to the configuration of preferences of those few other households seeking their own preferred units. So these actively searching households can easily end up with units from the current available pool which are considerably less suitable than other units in the existing stock—at the same time *implicit* price—but which are not currently available. This possibility is not reserved for a few special households. Since it depends on the inherent randomness of the preferences of demander searches linked with the independent randomness of the characteristics of released units supplied, the mismatches can affect a large percentage of each year's shifting subset.

The foregoing analysis depends crucially on two elements that must be considered further: the substantial demand lags in the form of household market inactivity and the function of prices to elicit nonrandom housing availability. First, the substantial duration of inactivity. Chapter 4 argued that changes in occupancy generated high frictional costs, associated with costly search, explicit transactions costs, and substantial moving costs. The higher these are, the greater must be the expected gain from shifting occupancy to make it seem worthwhile *in advance* to become market-active—and so the less probable such opportunities will seem to exist in each period. As we indicate in chapter 4, the sheer passage of time raises that probability progressively by making the current occupancy increasingly less suitable to changing household circumstances. Eventually households are willing to move, but with an expected frequency that depends on both the frictional costs and the rate of change of household circumstances.

Frictional costs are presumed to be much greater for ownership than for rental tenure. Important financial transactions costs are present in the former but not in the latter. Even search costs are likely to be much higher for ownership than for rental transactions. First, more aspects of housing units must be examined when full ownership is being transferred than when only use is being transferred. Second, as an adaptation to expected longer tenure—less turnover—ownership units are more heterogeneous than rental units, the latter being much more staple to meet the expected preferences of a much larger number of successive tenants. The consequence of the difference in the frictional costs is much greater turnover for rental than for ownership households and housing units, and so comparable differences in length of demander lag. We thus can expect less mismatch in the rental part of the market. The more significant mismatch problem is in the ownership sector.

Prices have appeared in this account only casually. Yet in typical markets it is exactly prices that signal to the market participants which kinds of commodities are more wanted, which kinds less wanted, thereby eliciting the greater presence of the former, the lesser presence of the latter. Does not this signaling function operate here also, thereby improving matchups? The key to the effectiveness of prices in this function is widespread accurate information about them among actual and potential market participants. But this is exactly what is missing in the present situation. Most *potential* participants have cost incentives *not to become informed* about the prices of units available, that is, the prices of overall housing packages and, by complex inference, the implicit prices of separate housing attributes. Hence, they cannot know even the prices of their own inactive units *while they remain inactive,* and thus cannot compare either demand-side or supply-side opportunities open to them in the current market relative to their present occupancy. So the ongoing market process may be signaling frantically for additional units of particular sorts or additional household users with particular wants, but the widespread intentional uninformedness will prevent responses by the potential, inactive, suppressed part of the market. Since this is by far the largest part of the overall market, price adjustments during the market period will likely play a weak role at best in securing efficient household-housing matchups.

We have spoken about matchups in the market period. Would a succession of market periods suffice to wipe out the mismatch problem? We are accustomed to thinking about markets being temporarily out of equilibrium, but adjusting continually until equilibrium is achieved through converging processes. If this market were left undisturbed after an initial perterbation, would it gradually wipe out any initial mismatches?

Let us examine this by assuming a continuation of our population and housing stock fixity over several periods of adjustment. There is an exogenous shock to the system (e.g., new households enter as others leave). The resulting shuffle produces in a mismatch for households α, β, and Γ. Prices of active units adjust to show more excess demand (higher price) for the housing types most preferred by these households, less excess demand (lower price) for the housing types released by these three. What will happen in the second period? First, particular units and households that were active in the first period will not be active in the second. A new set of potential movers will arise who have different preferences than the earlier set; they will occupy a new set of units that may be released. The first set of mismatched households *and* units will *not* be hovering actively over the new market situation to see if an improved match can now be made. So the very same kind of random generation of searchers and units being searched for that occurred in the first period will occur now anew. The new market, despite the adjusted prices, will not carry much memory from last period's mismatches.

The chief exception to this statement will occur in the most rapid turnover portion of the rental market. Very highly mobile households may well be active in both periods, especially where they were badly mismatched in the first period. The price changes in that sector *will* gradually help to re-sort households for closer matches. Multiple periods here will tend to achieve reasonable convergence of matchup quality. This qualification is not an all-or-nothing affair. The rental sector as a whole has a spectrum of transition costs (based partly on heterogeneity and thus implicitly on quality level), and demand lags will accordingly differ with the size of these costs. Some portions of the rental market may involve frictional costs nearly as great as some portions of the ownership market.

The upshot of this analysis is that in each period the random generation of the small number of active demanders and units available will largely overwhelm the carryover dissatisfaction from the preceding period, so the market adjustment process will be very much like that of the first period, with its stochastic setting of mismatches. As period follows period, what transpires during one period will be largely independent of what transpired during the prior period; each new period will create its own new mismatches and fail systematically to correct earlier ones. The overall pattern of mismatches among both active and inactive participants will therefore depend preponderantly on chance and only slightly on any systematic self-correcting mechanism. Self-correcting market convergence is therefore not to be expected. So a long run composed of successive market-period adjustments will simply replay only a market-period outcome.

Since our last analysis explicitly ranged over a time period longer than that which is referred to in the definition of the market period, it is appropriate to adopt the full analytic paraphernalia of the longer period—the medium run—in our terminology. That means unfreezing the fixity of supply. We shall do this below. Our argument about a succession of market periods was merely designed to indicate that a market's self-correction via simple reshuffling over time alone is not adequate to correct the random flow of mismatches occurring at any time. Before we proceed explicitly to medium-run dynamics we must pause to relate the analysis of mismatches to the concept of equilibrium and disequilibrium.

6.2.2 Market-Period Equilibrium and Disequilibrium

What does the existence of significant demand lags, with consequences for the severity of mismatches, imply about the nature of market-period equilibrium and disequilibrium? The presence of mismatches may suggest that significant numbers of active participants are out of equilibrium since they could presumably do better for themselves than they are in fact doing in the market. Such a view would both overstate and understate the nature of the issue.

There is overstating because the concept of equilibrium is not usually taken to mean that all market participants do as well as they can (however well that may be in absolute terms), but only that they have no incentive to change from what they are doing. The difference between the two notions lies primarily in degree of informedness, although some would generalize it to the process cost of making an otherwise advantageous change from what they are doing. Thus, active participants who, after searching among available units, conclude a transaction think that they are doing the best they can. The mere fact that optimal search among this pool of available units stops considerably short of an exhaustive monitoring of the pool as a whole is not held to represent disequilibrium in other kinds of markets in which search is important, so why should it be here?

The problem here is, however, somewhat different. Active participants are unaware not only of the character of the unexamined portion of the available housing pool; they are much more seriously unaware of the vast bulk of the existing stock—the currently unavailable units—on no part of which they make offers to express their interests. And this unawareness—uninformedness—is importantly the result of occupants of the unavailable units deliberately deciding not to become aware of the pool of availabilities, and thereby considerably shrinking that pool. Thus, there is very marked uninformedness, and it is interactive between active and passive market participants: it is an endogenous lack of information. Mismatch in such a situation may more seriously partake of disequilibrium.

But even this seriously understates the extent of the problem. We have directed both the crude and the subtle notions of disequilibrium to those active market participants who conclude mismatch transactions. The more serious disequilibrium, however, applies to the much larger group of inactive participants. It will be remembered from chapter 4 that inactive participants will not even seek the degree of informedness necessary to determine whether they should become active unless they feel a substantial probability of improving their situation *net* of all the costs of being active and of shifting occupancy. In the presence of high overall frictional costs, most households will simply not believe it is worthwhile to become informed enough even to be *prepared* to initiate the active process. This may be so even though there are in fact advantageous opportunities out there and households are in fact nontrivially dissatisfied with their present accommodations and believe there may well be advantageous opportunities available in the market.

Schematically, households probably feel they are most suitably accommodated just after making an occupancy shift. This feeling erodes as family circumstances change and as obvious grossly observable market changes occur. But despite growing net dissatisfaction—absolute dissatisfaction with the present accommodation combined with growing suspicion that there are better opportunities available elsewhere—the high friction costs keep them inactive. Finally, as the former rises progressively and the latter suspicion grows gradually stronger, a threshold is passed and the household becomes active, seeks information, searches, and, possibly, concludes a change of occupancy at last.

Are these households in equilibrium or not during the period of their inactivity? Objectively they fare progressively worse as their lag extends. If they were trapped in this situation by the presence of transactions and moving costs, these latter, being real, would comprise true exogenous constraints and would rationalize their inactivity, that is, their inaction would constitute an equilibrium for them. But inasmuch as their inaction is constrained as well by their unwillingness *to find out* whether prospective gains would exceed the first set of constraints, the issue is more serious. Because this last is a self-constituted constraint, it is endogenous.

It is possible to argue, of course, that even this radical self-maintained uninformedness is an exogenous constraint inasmuch as the obtaining of adequate preliminary knowledge to make close calculation of active market status—and hence investment in future knowledge—worthwhile is itself costly. Such a position, however, would result in treating every degree of ignorance as optimal. That would surely strain beyond credibility the very notion of a household calculating that it does not want to change what it is doing. Such a position would trivialize the notion of individual equilibrium to uselessness. The upshot of this is that the presence of a large majority of households remaining inactive in the housing market each period, and each household becoming active only sporadically, while absolute and net suitability of its continued accommodation becomes avowedly weaker, suggests widespread and varied degrees of disequilibrium. This is considerably more serious than the sometimes awkward matchups consummated in active market transactions.

6.3 Medium-Run Dynamics

In our discussion of medium-run equilibrium we change our usual order of statics first and dynamics second. Instead we deal with dynamics first, both because it better sets the stage for handling studies with different forms of time dependency and because it facilitates a continuation of our examination in the last section of the nature of mismatches and equilibrium.

6.3.1 Unequal Lags and Gestation Periods

The key to medium-run dynamics is that the various demand and supply participants—active and potential—in the market have nontrivial and highly varied response lags. This has two facets. At any one time the current set of market signals will elicit a set of demand and supply responses from the various actors that will not appear in the market at the same time in the future, but rather at a wide spectrum of effective dates. The second is the same point from a different perspective. The current market will be affected by responses to market signals that obtained at different times in the past: (1) some actors (demanders and suppliers) will be completing their responses now to signals in the same past periods; (2) some will be completing their responses now to signals at different periods in the past; and (3) some will be in various stages of incomplete response to signals at different periods in the past. The two facets, taken together, mean that in any particular period some actors, who had already fully adjusted to past signals, are currently engaged in beginning a response to current signals, some others are completing in the current period responses begun in the past, still others are continuing beyond the present period into the future responses begun in the past, and the remainder are inactive. Except for the small minority who are both initiating and completing responses to present signals in the present period, an attempt to relate present market signals—prices, availabilities, vacancies—to present circumstances will be highly misleading. Too much of both the past (incompletions) and the future (intentions) is embedded in the present.

One implication is that the housing market *in every period* is inherently dynamic—it is in the process of changing all the time. New exogenous events do not politely wait the long times necessary for all the responses to have played out both their original impetuses and the subsequent readjustments necessary to make them finally mutually compatible with one another. So the concept of long-run equilibrium as the point of final, complete convergence of equilibrating adjustments must be seen as a hypothetical idealization rather than as an actual state of the market observable at a real point of time.

What, then, is the appropriate way to analyze market processes when demanders and suppliers are free to use and transform resources to meet their own consumption needs and take advantage of market opportunities? Our approach is first to predict (explain) which actors fall into each of the five classes of participants in each period: (1) inactive; (2) fully adjusted from the past and both initiating or completing adjustment in the present period to present signals;[5] (3) completing adjustment begun in the past in the present period; (4) continuing adjustment begun in the past through and beyond the present; and (5) beginning adjustment, not completing it, in the present. Second, we attempt to predict what will be the adjustments begun in the present, and which ones will be completed in the same period. Third, we predict the probable gestation periods for each of today's adjustments that extend into the future. Fourth, we perform the same prediction, but in reverse, for past-initiated adjustments that are completed in the present; that is, we track backward what was their gestation period and, hence, to what past signals they were responses, thus re-projecting forward to the present what is their probably final intention for the present. Finally, fifth, we do the same as this for adjustments still in process today; that is, we track them backward via gestation period to their initiation period, and from that predict both their ultimate intention in the future *and* their state of incompletion in the present period.

This approach really implies a matrix of recursive processes starting at various periods in the past and extending various periods into the future. Each period's events are a linear composite of processes initiated in the past and in the present, and of holdovers. So the unit of analysis is the focus on individuals and homogeneous groups. Predict for each of these what will determine its activity or inactivity, what its response will be to each set of influences, when that response will be initiated, how long it will take to complete, and what intermediate states it will assume during adjustment. Aggregation of these—for both demanders and suppliers—will enable prediction of a temporal progression of completions and incompletions over time and thus permit a prediction for each period of the aggregate behavior of all five classes of actors *in that period*—thus permitting the complete delineation of market behavior in each period, despite the complex time-dependencies involved.

6.3.2 New Construction and Conversion Responses to Market Mismatches

The second major question concerning medium-run dynamics is whether the supply responses permitted in this longer time period(s) affect market mismatches and individual disequilibria that occur in market periods, as described in section 6.2. Two forms of supply response are involved, and their effects are somewhat different, as we should by now expect. Accordingly, we discuss them separately. We begin with conversion of existing units.

Start with a mismatch. The household has just shifted to a unit better suited than it had, but not quite what it wanted. What is more natural, then, than for the new occupants to modify the unit so as to more closely fit its preferences? Under what circumstances will this be done? Neglecting whether the household can afford the additional expense, we discuss the question in terms of feasibility and cost effectiveness. If the modifications are minor, the required conversion is likely to be physically feasible and the cost of conversion is not likely to be high in absolute terms. But it is likely to be more costly than the implicit market price of those features, since the market price reflects a competitive squeezing down toward cost minimization. However, the market did not make those features available in an overall package otherwise suitable for the household as well—hence the mismatch to begin with. Despite the higher relative price, the household will likely make the conversion in this case, to offset the sheer market unavailability—as perceived by the household.

Some elements of mismatch cannot be physically changed by conversion. Locational goals, neighborhood characteristics, many parcel characteristics, and some extreme architectural features may be simply impossible to achieve with the given unit. Besides sheer feasibility, however, is a wider set of changes that are likely to be discouraged because they are expensive in absolute terms and their relative price is much higher via conversion than via market purchase in a different housing package. We argued in chapter 5 that conversions are likely to tend toward compatibility with good investment criteria. If the conversion investment is substantial, the household, not knowing how long it will remain in occupancy, will want to be sure that the change will be acceptable to prospective future buyers at a price reflecting its conversion cost. So conversion cost cannot be substantially out of line with the implicit present market valuation of the features involved. But many prospective conversions would be cost ineffective—and therefore represent a perilous investment.

The cost-effectiveness of a conversion depends on complementarities on supply and demand. The former refers to physically technical and configurational factors—like constraints on particular changes due to materials, architectural style, balance-of-scale features, and so forth. The latter refers to the demand attractiveness of various configurational features—like number of bathrooms relative to bedrooms, or upgrading to luxurious interiors with dilapidated exteriors or in impoverished neighborhoods. Additional market value will not be added linearly via conversion but based on the new configurations. Eccentric combinations relative to mainstream balances will result in value gains less than the cost of achieving them via conversion.

The upshot is that some initial mismatches will tend to be rectified via conversion by the new occupants themselves. Where so, this will represent a well-tailored adaptation to incomplete markets. But the incidence of such built-in corrections may not be high. They can be expected to occur mostly where the mismatch is minor. For more considerable mismatches, conversion will be possible but less frequent. Substantial prospective investment losses will inhibit them. Such inhibition is most likely where inappropriate location or lot or neighborhood is central to the mismatch; but factors for which important complementarities are involved will also deter conversion. In all such cases the household involved will tally the remaining mismatch as one of a set of dissatisfaction components whose growing magnitude over time will determine at what point it would be advantageous to reenter the market actively to change occupancy, since the poor present investment prospect implies that the desired features can be obtained at much less cost in a different housing package—via moving. Conversion that is undertaken by an owner with explicit intention to sell the property soon is like new construction for this issue and so is dealt with below.

In sum, consumption-oriented conversion is likely to improve market performance in a market where active participation induces prices to change to point to positive and negative excess demands. The combination of flexible, responsive prices and responsive self-helping conversion moderates the extent of disequilibrium in housing markets. But it only moderates such disequilibrium, it does not eliminate it. The serious barriers to conversion discussed above will prevent some of the most considerable mismatches from being corrected by this route. It remains to consider whether explicitly commercially oriented conversion and new construction can resolve most of the remaining problem.

New construction and market-oriented conversion work to correct mismatches not directly but indirectly by responding to changing market signals. Mismatches tend to generate price changes that reflect the mismatches approximately. Thus, where some particular feature is vainly sought for among available units by numbers of unsatisfied demanders, the price of that feature is likely to rise. The rise then attracts additional units via construction and conversion that emphasize that feature disproportionately, thereby lowering its subsequent price to announce its greater prevalence and so gradually induce occupancy shifts to diminish such feature-specific mismatches. But this process depends on the set of mismatches being due to a *net* deficiency of that feature whose scarcity accentuates the need for most efficient allocation among users: misallocations leading to significant disappointments. What if the mismatches are pure—the result of random pairing rather than net deficiencies? Then no particular features or configurations will be found in *net* deficit, so no diagnostic price changes will occur to guide supply responses, and whatever supply changes occur will not necessarily contribute to easing mismatches.

The situation is even more serious than the above qualification, however. The price changes envisioned above are responses to the active searches and transactions occurring in the market in each period. But these refer to only a very small percentage of users and existing housing units. The bulk are inactive. The attributes of these houses and the preferences of these households are largely hidden from the active market. Yet the identity of the active users and units changes from period to period—so supply responses, and hence price changes, elicited from last period's mismatches, even if they do accurately reflect those mismatches, may nowise contribute to diminishing *this* period's prospective mismatches for a different cast of active characters. A carryover tendency to ease this period's potential mismatches requires that net scarcities and redundancies be behind many of both period's mismatching—and that the net scarcities and redundancies be the same for both periods. This is really a situation of aggregate disequilibrium in the market. But any second-period net deficiencies may differ from those of the first period, or there may be no net deficiencies but only *pure* mismatching, which is the result of the randomness of the self-selection process by which the identity of active users and units is determined in each period, together with the stochastic, nonexhaustive search processes carried on among these participants. These pure mismatches occur even in the absence of aggregate deficiencies and redundancies. For both of these kinds of circumstances, first-period price change–induced supply responses will not help prevent second-period mismatches. Empirically, our earlier argument accounting for mismatches suggests that these circumstances are likely to be the generality; the uniform cross-period net deficit, net redundancy circumstance the exception. Hence, new construction and market-oriented conversions may be indispensable for rectifying aggregate disequilibria, but they may contribute little to allaying widespread mismatch. As such, they also will do little to ameliorate the widespread individual disequilibria that are directly implied by the very large percentage of users who are inactive in each period because of deliberate uninformedness, and the consequently long buildups of user dissatisfaction before occupancy shifts are sought.

In sum, high frictional costs and nonexhaustive stochastic searches can be expected to generate considerable mismatching and individual disequilibria even in the presence of medium-run supply adjustments. Supply adjustments, especially in the form of consumption-oriented conversions, will mitigate or even eliminate some instances, but widespread examples, especially serious ones, will continue to occur.

6.4 Medium-Run General Equilibrium

At the outset we should note that we eschew the conventional term *long run* when referring to the equilibrium established over time in a market. A long-run equilibrium is not supposed to depend on the path of adjustment, but to represent a period long enough for the outcome to be independent of path. In the case of urban housing, however, the intertemporal supply adjustments via conversion crucially depend on the characteristics of the initial stock, as we have seen in the previous chapter and the last section. The longer-term equilibrium thus depends in an important way on the particular path of adjustment over time undertaken by a particular initial stock. Indeed, the durability of housing is so great that to wait for a period long enough for the initial stock to have no effect on the character of the "final equilibrium outcome" easily could take a century or more. It therefore seems preferable to speak of a *medium run* here in terms of the gestation of occupancy, new construction, and conversion adjustments *in the context of a particular designated initial stock,* rather than to insist on a much longer time frame beyond which the initial stock would have no effect. In real time such a period could well involve a decade or more.

With our terminology thus clarified, we consider the medium-run equilibrium toward which the housing market in a metropolitan area adjusts from an initial, market-period equilibrium specified above. We assume that the spectrum of submarket aggregate demand functions obtaining at this initial period remains unchanged over the period of adjustment.[6] In the real world this would occur if, for example, new household entrants offset household withdrawals so as to keep aggregate demographic and socioeconomic characteristics unchanged over the period, and real incomes and prices for nonhousing goods held constant in the metropolitan area.

The array of market-period equilibrium market valuations established in equation (6.1) defines the *MV* function that specifies the opportunities available to builders and converters of housing. As discussed in chapter 5, suppliers' responses to the array of rates of return implicit in this function produce the medium-run aggregate supply function (equation 5.20). The medium-run general equilibrium occurs when all quality submarkets clear at a given set of submarket and attribute prices $[MV_i'][p']$:

$$(6.3) \qquad {}^{S}Q_i^{\Sigma}([MV_i'], [p']) = {}^{D}Q_i^{\Sigma}([MV_i'], [p']), \textit{ all } i.$$

At general equilibrium, all demanders are satisfied with their choice of quality levels and attribute mix, all builders have chosen their preferred quality level(s) and attribute mix targets, and all converters of existing units have made the most appropriate conversion decisions. No agent in the market can improve his or her situation with respect to consumption, building, or conversion.

This general equilibrium should not be treated as a static phenomenon, however. Although aggregate spectral demand remains constant, individual households may be moving into or out of submarkets. Similarly, aggregate spectral supply remains constant, but flows of retirements and conversions of individual dwellings are occurring which generate replacement demand filled by flows of new construction. General equilibrium, therefore, is best viewed as a static snapshot of a set of dynamic, though stable, flows.

A divergence from general equilibrium in any one submarket generally requires an adjustment of market valuations in all submarkets, as well generally of attribute prices, each adjustment calling for repercussions from others in a sequence. (We discuss these adjustments more fully below.) A mutually compatible adjustment configuration occurs through the typical adjustment convergence process of general equilibrium in an economy as a whole because all of the commodities are direct substitutes for each other; nonconvergence problems arising from complementarity are absent here. A complication to general equilibrium in our treatment must, however, be noted. It concerns asymmetry in the adjustment of attribute mix as opposed to quality level.

Structures in the existing stock were built at different times in the past, stretching over a long period. New structures built at any one time would be expected to have an attribute mix that accommodated closely to the set of relative attribute prices prevailing at that time—reflecting both cost conditions and taste factors stemming from the socioeconomic and demographic characteristics of the population—so the marginal cost-ratio-equals-attribute-price-ratio (equation 5.9) equilibrium condition would have held for that time. But as time passes such houses' attribute mixes fail to track the progression of changes in attribute prices. At any one such subsequent time the cost-revenue ratios may be unequal: strictly speaking the houses are out of mix equilibrium.

To see this proposition, begin with a stock of units at some time that is fully adjusted to current equilibrium attribute prices. Now, with the passage of time, production and taste factors change and thereby, through market clearing, relative attribute prices change. Three types of adjustment occur. Consumers change their desired housing configurations so as to satisfy the marginal utility-ratio-equals-attribute-price-ratio condition (equation 4.6) for the new prices. If we abstract from any supply transformation response, satisfying this condition is accomplished by shifts of households among the numerous, highly varied units of the existing stock, mutually advantageous shifting being guaranteed so long as there is taste heterogeneity among households. Such shifts alone, however, are not likely to reattain general equilibrium. They will be abetted by supply transformation responses of both new construction and conversion.

New dwelling units built in each period can be completely adjusted to whatever new set of attribute prices exists in that period, since rate-of-return maximization requires fulfillment of this condition (equation 5.9), and the technology is always assumed to be available to make fulfillment possible. But because of the small numbers of newly built units relative to the size of the existing stock, new construction too is not sufficient in general to produce equilibrium in attribute mix for the entire stock.

Conversion of existing dwelling units is the third adjustment forthcoming. Owners of existing units modify their units to bring attribute mix in closer accord with new attribute prices. Here is where the asymmetry lies. The technical constraints of existing units, in conjunction with conversion technology, often do *not* permit, or even make profitable, full adjustment to satisfy equation (5.9). Instead, many owners are trapped in corner solutions. So, for example, if it seems that the ratio of two attributes like yard space and interior space is too low relative to their price ratio, the owner may have no incentive to modify it; it may be too expensive to increase yard size and decrease interior space. Two kinds of discontinuity are likely to be involved. First, some market-perceived mix changes are likely to require lumpy conversion changes—sometimes even of an all-or-nothing character (e.g., a porch, or a garage, or none). The marginal conversion costs of such changes are likely to be high. So a nontrivial range of smaller price ratio discrepancies will not suffice to elicit such changes via return maximization, and smaller changes are not worth making. Second, some market-"appropriate" changes are simply physically infeasible: either they are of a type that cannot be accomplished at all with the given unit, or the degree of the change called for is too great for the unit. Architecture, major layout, lot size, and construction materials often impose stringent constraints on various potential conversions. The implication is that in any period a large number of units in the existing stock will not possess attribute mixes that reflect current implicit attribute prices the way one expects from a newly built unit. A consequence of a less-desired relative, even absolute, attribute mix for any such unit is a decline in market-perceived quality. Yet despite suffering a loss in market valuation, the owner of each is in equilibrium without "full" attribute adjustment because he or she can do no better with the unit in question at given quality and attribute prices.

The difference between quality level and attribute equilibrium, therefore, is that although consumers, builders, and owners of existing dwelling units are all presumed to be capable of smooth, pinpointed equilibrium adjustments for quality-level disequilibria, only the first two are presumed to be so capable for attribute adjustment. Owners of existing units may be trapped with mix discontinuities. In this case, therefore, the passage of time may find other structures, *still inside the boundary of incomplete adjustment,* with attribute mixes that become increasingly different from those being newly constructed. Such discontinuities throw heavier responsibility on new construction and consumer shifts to achieve general equilibrium.

In what follows we are concerned with the characteristics of medium-run general equilibrium for new construction and conversion. To simplify the analysis, we speak primarily of quality-level equilibrium, but this is not meant to preclude attribute-mix equilibrium. The treatment of quality level has its close counterpart in attribute mix and should be so understood. For the section where we examine systematic differences between new construction and conversion modes, we have already indicated the most salient difference under attribute-mix equilibrium, namely, new construction achieves precise, continuous adjustment whereas conversion is limited to discontinuous, incomplete adjustments, thereby placing additional responsibility for equilibrium adjustment not only on new construction but also on significant amounts of shifting by consumers among units.

We begin with the demand side of the market. For every set of submarket prices $MV(H) = (MV_1, MV_2, \ldots)$, there is a set of quantities of units at each quality level that the total population wants to occupy, the aggregate, medium-run demand function,

$$D(H) = D[\, MV(H)\,], \tag{6.4}$$

where $D(H) \equiv (D_1, D_2 \ldots)$, all submarkets H_i. The adjustment period involved is long enough so that all households are assumed to have taken the opportunity to be active participants in the market and thereby express their effective demand. This formulation draws attention to the fact that we speak below about an equilibrium in terms of prices *and* quantities simultaneously. Despite the complexity that follows, it is the adjusting variations of both prices *and quantities* among the submarkets that bring about the equilibrium.

Each set of market valuations $MV(H)$ elicits a total supply response, $S(H)$, expressing the set of units offered for occupancy at each quality-level submarket:

$$S(H) = S[\, MV(H)\,]. \tag{6.5}$$

As usual, at some initial $MV(H) = MV^0(H)$, there will be a resulting vector of excess demands (positive and negative):

$$X(MV^0) = D(MV^0) - S(MV^0). \tag{6.6}$$

Also, as usual, this vector $X(MV^0)$ will generate both changes in the components of $MV(H)$, that is, $\Delta MV(H)$ *and* induced changes pari passu with both $D(H)$ and $S(H)$. All submarkets i with positive excess demands will experience increases in MV_i; all submarkets j with negative excess demands will experience decreases in MV_j. But these price changes will elicit changes in both $D(H)$ and $S(H)$ in the usual directions, thereby moderating the size of the induced price changes required for a final, mutually consistent equilibrium set of sets for which $X(MV^*) = 0$, that is,

$$E(MV, D, S) \equiv [\, MV^*, D^*, S^* \mid X(MV^*) = 0]. \tag{6.7}$$

The nature of the demand adjustments is straightforward, so we turn our closer attention to the different components of supply.

6.4.1 Valuation and Cost Properties of Suppliers in General Equilibrium

As seen in chapter 5, the aggregate, medium-run supply to any quality submarket H_i includes four types of decisions: new construction in H_i, conversion of existing units from H_i to other submarkets (including abandonments, retirements, and shifts to nonhousing uses), conversion from other submarkets to H_i, and retention of units in H_i. In making a decision, each such decision maker has reconciled various possible tradeoffs with alternative decisions that might have been made. Moreover, each type of decision maker is competing against every other type of decision maker as well, and against every other decision maker of the same type.

New Construction

For every new builder, a decision to build in submarket H_i instead of any other H_j implies that the rate of return in H_i is higher: $\gamma_i > \gamma_j$, all j. Or, by rearranging equation (5.6),

$$MV_i - {}_NC_i(1 + \gamma') > MV_j - {}_NC_j(1 + \gamma'),\ all\ j. \tag{6.8}$$

While the total amount of new construction per period is a small percentage of the total stock, its high degree of concentration in a few parts of the submarket spectrum gives it a nontrivial impact on market valuations in those parts. Thus the $MV(H)$ set will be influenced by both the targeting and the magnitude of new construction. In addition, input costs may be a rising function of new construction size. We may rewrite equation (6.8) to express this dependence of MV and C on number and type of new units built:

$$\begin{aligned} MV_i({}_NS_i) - {}_NC_i({}_NS_i, {}_NS)\,(1 + \gamma') &> MV_j({}_NS_j) \\ &- ({}_NC_j({}_NS_j, {}_NS)\,(1 + \gamma'). \end{aligned} \tag{6.8'}$$

Notice that the cost functions ${}_NC$ show a dependence on both total construction activity and on construction activity in the specific submarket at issue. The latter is designed to capture bidding up the prices of any productive inputs that are specialized to this particular submarket.

Thus, as new construction of units proceeds and such units come onto the market, MV_i will be competed downward. In addition, if there is considerable builder and construction input specialization for H_i, the costs of construction, ${}_NC_i$ may be bid up.[7] The net result is that the left-hand side of equation (6.8′) is reduced until an equality is obtained in equilibrium. By rearranging the equality form of (6.8′), this can be expressed as

$$(6.9)\quad [MV_i({}_NS_i) - MV_j({}_NS_j)]/[{}_NC_i({}_NS_i) - {}_NC_j({}_NS_j)] = 1 + \gamma', \text{ all j.}$$

Thus, construction will occur across submarkets until for each pair the ratio of intersubmarket valuation differentials to intersubmarket construction cost differentials is constant.

What is more, we know that new construction must compete for capital with nonhousing investments, which earn a rate of return γ'. Construction will not occur in any submarket x unless $\gamma_x > \gamma'$. As all projects in all submarkets that meet this criterion are exhausted via increasing numbers of new construction, with housing prices and thus housing rates of return gradually declining, equilibrium will eventually be established where rates of return for builders of new units are equalized among one another and equated to those from nonhousing investments. From equation (5.6) this, in turn, means that for all such submarkets x where new construction can occur, the absolute equilibrium market valuation will be established:

$$(6.10)\qquad MV_x = (1 + \gamma')_N C_x.$$

Since MV_i and ${}_NC_i$ are functions of ${}_NS_i$, and MV_j and ${}_NC_j$ are functions of ${}_NS_j$, equation (6.9) determines the ratio between ${}_NS_i$ and ${}_NS_j$. When equation (6.10) is added, determining the absolute rate of return for ${}_NS_i$, together they determine the absolute values of ${}_NS_i$ and ${}_NS_j$. So the equilibrium described in equations (6.9) and (6.10) determines both the equilibrium market valuations MV_i^* and MV_j^* and the equilibrium quantities ${}_NS_i^*$ and ${}_NS_i^*$.

Conversions of Existing Units

An owner of a unit initially in submarket H_i will convert during the medium run to submarket H_j if a higher rate of return can be earned there, that is, if

$$(6.11)\qquad \begin{aligned} &MV_j - C_{ij}(1 + \gamma') > MV_i - C_i(1 + \gamma'), \\ \text{and } &MV_j - C_{ij}(1 + \gamma') > MV_k - C_{ik}(1 + \gamma'), \text{ all k,} \end{aligned}$$

where

C_{ij} = the cost of converting from i to j;
C_i = the cost of maintaining at i; and
C_{ik} = the cost of converting from i to k.

As we explained in chapter 5, conversion costs between the submarkets are not a constant even when the same conversion technique is used on successive units to be converted, let alone when different techniques are used. Units differ in their appropriateness for a particular submarket conversion. The most appropriate units are converted first (for competitive return maximization) and successively less appropriate ones follow in progression, with even the identity of the best conversion technique changing along the conversion queue. So C_{ij} is a rising function of number of units converting from i to j, for all i, j. Unlike new construction, however, we do not believe that (MV) is significantly influenced by ${}_CS_{ij}$, because, while the total number of shifters away from H_i to *all* destinations may well affect MV_i significantly, and the total of shifters from *all* origins to H_j may well affect MV_j significantly, the size of such pairwise transfer is likely to be too small to exercise much effect on either MV_i or MV_j. Nonetheless, for generality we rewrite equation (6.11) as follows:

$$(6.11') \quad MV_j({}_CS_{ij}) - C_{ij}({}_CS_{ij})\,(1 + \gamma') > MV_i({}_CS_{ij}) - C_i\,(1 + \gamma'),$$
$$\text{and } MV_j({}_CS_{ij}) - C_{ij}({}_CS_{ij})\,(1 + \gamma') > MV_k({}_CS_{ik}) - C_{ik}({}_CS_{ik})\,(1 + \gamma'), \text{ all } k.$$

As successive units actually convert from H_i to H_j, the marginal cost of each last unit converted rises according to equations (5.16) and (6.11′). To a lesser degree the market valuation in H_j is competed down and that in H_i is increased as the amounts supplied in the two submarkets rise and fall, respectively. All three adjustments tend to reduce the original inequality in equation (6.11′). But unlike the case for new construction, where an additional perfectly malleable unit can always be built on the margin if returns warrant it, here there is no guarantee that intersubmarket conversions will continue until (marginal) rates of returns for all owners' (market valuation/cost ratios) are equalized, due to the conversion heterogeneity of the existing stock. In fact, we demonstrate that only under extremely rare circumstances will this be the case. In addition, we demonstrate that only if a submarket is also supplied by new construction will its equilibrium market valuation be fully determinate.

To demonstrate, let us focus on an arbitrarily chosen pair of submarkets, H_i and H_j, where $H_j > H_i$ (thus $MV_j > MV_i$). At the point where conversions between the two submarkets in both directions have ceased, it must be the case that $\gamma_i \geq \gamma_{ij}$ or, for all remaining original owners inH_i,

$$(6.12) \quad MV_i({}_CS_{ji} - {}_CS_{ij}) - C_i(1 + \gamma') \geq MV_j({}_CS_{ij} - {}_CS_{ji}) - C_{ij}({}_CS_{ij})\,(1 + \gamma'),$$

and $\gamma_j \geq \gamma_{ji}$ or, for all remaining original owners in H_j,

$$MV_j({}_CS_{ij} - {}_CS_{ji}) - C_j(1 + \gamma') \geq MV_i({}_CS_{ji} - {}_CS_{ij}) - C_{ji}\,({}_CS_{ji})\,(1 + \gamma').$$

Through rearranging, equation (6.12) can be expressed as

$$(6.13) \quad (C_{ij} - C_i)\,(1 + \gamma') \geq MV_j - MV_i \geq (C_j - C_{ji})\,(1 + \gamma'),$$

suppressing for convience the conversion size influences on MV_i, MV_j, C_{ij}, and C_{ji}.

Since C_{ij} here represents upgrading costs and C_{ji} represents downgrading costs, all terms in equation (6.13) are positive. Only under the unlikely circumstance that $C_{ij} - C_i = C_i - C_{ji}$ for *all* owners of units currently in the given submarkets will all terms in equation (6.13) be equal and cross-submarket rates of return for owners of existing units be equalized at the margin.

If new construction does not occur (say due to housing code constraints) in either H_i or H_j (or both), the absolute level of equilibrium market valuations cannot be established in submarkets where building is absent. Assume construction occurs in H_j but not in lower-quality H_i. From equation (6.10), MV_j is determinate. From equation (6.13) it is clear that MV_i can be no lower than the difference between the cost of maintaining a unit in H_i (C_i) versus upgrading it to H_j (C_{ij}), multiplied by the opportunity cost of capital $(1 + \gamma')$, plus total returns potentially available from upgrading (MV_j). Conversely, it can be no higher than the difference between the costs of downgrading a unit to H_i (C_{ji}) versus maintaining it in H_j (C_j), multiplied again by opportunity costs, plus return MV_j. But within these bounds—established by the idiosyncratic features of the existing stock of units—the equilibrium value for MV_i is indeterminate with respect to the H_i, H_j pair. This is so even ignoring the likelihood that maintenance and conversion costs differ in both submarkets and from dwelling to dwelling.

The actual interval of indeterminacy is smaller, perhaps toward disappearance, however, when we consider additional submarkets. The valuations in submarkets H_i and H_j must be consistent not only with respect to conversions between H_i and H_j but also reciprocally between H_i and H_j, separately with other submarkets between H_i and H_j, as well as between all pairs of such intermediate submarkets *and* between all pairs of submarkets leading to H_i and away from H_j. If new construction takes place at any such submarkets, that further lessens the ultimate indeterminacy between H_i and H_j, or any pair in the spectrum. Thus, *all* successive values in the MV function are determined by a consistent overall, *simultaneous* meeting of the inequality pair conditions for all submarket pairs. Given the dense *network* of consistent intersubmarket balances involved, especially since new construction will occur in some submarket(s) to provide more determinate anchoring,[8] indeterminacy across the MV function will still remain but is not likely to be great—although it is likely to be uneven because of the notably uneven incidence of new construction.

To see this better, let us return to equation (6.13). We postulated that H_i and H_j are submarkets witnessing actual conversions in either or both directions. But this means that for any unit α so converted, this submarket pair represents the *best* origin-destination pair for this particular unit. Consequently, for a conversion from H_i to H_j,

$$(6.13') \qquad MV_j \,/\, C_{ij}^{\alpha}\,(1 + \gamma') > MV_k \,/\, C_{ik}^{\alpha}\,(1 + \gamma'), \text{ all k.}$$

Similarly for all units converting.

Actual conversions thus constrain relative submarket valuations both for submarket pairs actually involved in the conversion *and* for pairs linked to one of the former but not involving conversion. The constraint for the former pairs is stronger, involving equalities, while that for the latter pairs is weaker, involving only inequalities. But the network of overlapping conversion and nonconversion pairs is likely to be dense enough to give near determinacy to all submarket valuations.

In summary, the equilibrium conditions for owners of existing units are less precise in themselves, due to the heterogeneity of the cost functions these units possess, but are effectively tightened by the dense web of simultaneous, multilateral connections that must be satisfied competitively. Owners of existing units, whether they convert or not, are not required by equilibrium to earn the same rate of return at the margin, excepting in the unlikely circumstance where all owners' differences between maintenance and conversion costs are identical. Similarly, they are not required to earn (at the margin) the same rates of return as builders or those rates available from nonhousing investments. Some may earn considerably more than this opportunity rate of return,[9] especially in submarkets that are effectively incapable of being supplied by new construction. In such submarkets not only unit-specific costs but also equilibrium market valuations are somewhat indeterminate. Here it is possible for nonuniform rates of return to persist indefinitely if new builders are prevented from competing (by, e.g., building codes) and if the array of aggregate marginal conversion costs into the submarket is so high as to render any conversion supply unprofitable, given cross-submarket valuation differentials (see equation 5.18).

We have been speaking about equilibrium market valuations and rates of return. The equilibrium also involves relative supply quantities. Unlike market valuations and returns, however, equilibrium quantities are fully determinate. The conditions (equation 6.13) indicate stopping points for conversions, that is, the size of C_{ij} for the marginal converter. But this C_{ij}^{*} determines the identity of the marginal converter. While the size of his or her return compared to that of the next most appropriate potential converter in the queue may not be completely determined, the *identity* of both *is* established. Therefore, it is also established how many units did actually engage in each kind of conversion, namely, all those units higher on the queue in terms of appropriateness for converting from H_i to H_j—that is, all with C_{ij} lower than C_{ij}^{*}. This condition is true in all submarkets. The equilibrium conditions do then determine the whole pattern of conversions and hence the net change in total units in each submarket via conversion supply.

6.4.2 The Mix of New Construction and Conversion Supply in Equilibrium

In the previous section we saw the comparative static cost and valuation conditions that could be expected to prevail in a submarket in medium-run equilibrium and the resulting equilibrium supply quantities that are consistent with them. Here we extend this analysis to examine the mix of construction and conversion supply that contributes to the equilibrium.

Mix in a Single Submarket

To begin, we investigate the mix of supply adjustments for a single submarket viewed in isolation. Recall from the discussion in chapter 5 that, for some initial equilibrium situation embodying a particular distribution of stock across the submarket array, one can specify medium-run supply functions for new units ${}_{N}S$, for units supplied from the existing stock ${}_{C}S$, and for their aggregation ${}_{\Sigma}S$—equations (5.15), (5.18), and (5.20), respectively. Superimposition of an aggregate demand function ${}_{\Sigma}D$ for the given submarket on these supply functions produces the desired information about supply mix.

Graphically this is shown in figure 6.1, where a representative submarket H_j initially is in an equilibrium defined as (Q_{j0}^{MAX}, MV_{j0}). Suppose that the units in other submarkets (and their conversion cost functions) are distributed in such a way that the aggregate conversion supply into H_j for market valua-

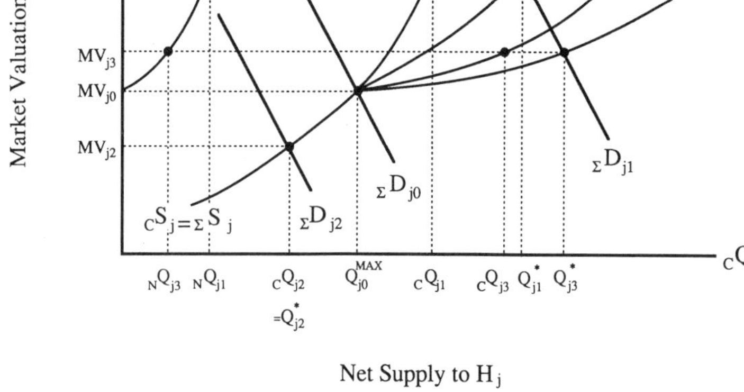

Figure 6.1. Equilibrium mix between new construction and conversion supply in a single submarket *j*.

tions greater than MV_{j0} is ${}_{C}S_{j1}$. Coupled with a new construction supply function ${}_{N}S_{j}$, this produces an aggregate medium-run supply function ${}_{\Sigma}S_{j1}$ (for $MV_{j} > MV_{j0}$). Suppose the conversion cost functions for units in H_{j} are such that the conversion supply function for $MV_{j} < MV_{j0}$ is ${}_{C}S_{j}$ ($= {}_{\Sigma}S_{j}$ since for such valuations new construction is zero).

Now if equilibrium demand for H_{j} were to decline to[10] (and remain at) ${}_{\Sigma}D_{j2}$, valuations would fall to MV_{j2}, and conversions of the stock in H_{j} to other submarkets, abandonment, and/or nonhousing uses would yield the medium-run equilibrium quantity supplied Q^{*}_{j2}. All of this (reduction in) supply would be accomplished through modifications in the existing stock in H_{j}. But if demand were to increase and remain indefinitely at ${}_{\Sigma}D_{j1}$, the resulting medium-run equilibrium would be (MV_{j1}). At this market evaluation it is clear from figure 6.1 that the total quantity supplied would be composed of ${}_{N}Q_{j1}$ newly constructed units, plus Q^{MAX}_{j0} units originally in the stock of H_{j} and ${}_{C}Q_{ji} - Q^{\text{MAX}}_{j0}$ additional units converted (net) into H_{j}. This comparative scenario illustrates an empirical generalization that submarket adjustments to declining demand will typically be dominated by adjustments in the existing stock (sometimes, as here, totally), while adjustments to rising demand will be accomplished by more nearly equal contributions from both supply modes.

The cross-submarket distribution of existing units and their respective costs of converting into H_{j}, relative to the cost of new construction, are the key determinant of the relative shares for the two modes as they adjust to rising demand. The lower the marginal conversion costs into H_{j} (i.e., the more elastic the conversion supply function) relative to marginal new construction costs, the larger will be the share of stock adjustment achieved by conversions. To illustrate, imagine that the existing stock in other submarkets has permuted such that, on average, it is more similar in quality to H_{j} than before. Thus the relevant conversion supply function is ${}_{C}S_{j2}$ and the relevant aggregate supply function is ${}_{\Sigma}S_{j2}$. Assume as before that demand is at ${}_{\Sigma}D_{j1}$. Such a change in supply would produce an equilibrium at (Q^{*}_{j3}, MV_{j3}). But because this equilibrium market valuation is lower than with initial supply, ${}_{\Sigma}S_{ji}$, namely, MV_{j3} instead of MV_{j1}, the *absolute* amount of new construction is lower (only ${}_{N}Q_{j3}$ instead of ${}_{N}Q_{j1}$), even though the total stock in H_{j} has grown larger: Q^{*}_{j3} instead of Q^{*}_{j1}. The *share* of new construction to the total number of units supplied is thus considerably lower.

Mix in Different Submarkets

In the last section we saw how the mix between new construction and conversion supply is determined in a single submarket. But is this same mix likely to occur in all submarkets, or is it entirely stochastic, or are there special forces that make for systematic differences in the mix in different submarkets? We examine this question in the present section. In order to give an intuitive characterization of this relationship it is helpful to simplify the commodity/

choice space considerably. Instead of a continuum of quality levels we shall deal with only two stylized levels—upper-quality (*U*) and lower-quality (*L*) submarkets. This facilitates graphical analysis.

The answer as to whether the ratio of units supplied by new construction and by conversion differs between *U* and *L* submarkets depends on some institutional and technical facts concerning the two modes. First, in most U.S. cities there are stringent code and zoning restrictions that establish rather high minimum standards for new housing structures in terms of materials, building techniques, safety, intensity of use, and so forth. This implies that few if any truly low-quality units can be legally built in each current period, at least as a first approximation. To enter the "low-quality" submarket via new construction requires "overbuilding," that is, building features appropriate to higher-quality submarkets, but aimed at clients who can afford only market valuations more appropriate to lower-quality submarkets (and thus viable in the market only with government subsidization of either users or builders—both of which are excluded from this example but are treated in chapters 10 and 11).

Second, features of the cost of maintenance and repair of existing units that we have already described are also influential. The cost of maintaining a unit during a given period at the submarket in which it began the period (its "normal maintenance") depends on a number of factors—materials, construction methods, architecture, nature of use, and so forth, as well as quality submarket and dwelling age. Normal maintenance cost rises with age, and very likely disproportionately so for higher-quality levels (see fig. 5.2).

The third consideration is that there is asymmetry between upward and downward conversion. While structural change, change in condition of structure, and consolidation of units within a single structure are all meaningfully available to upgrading, downgrading is mostly dependent upon change in condition and splitting of units within the given structure. For upgrading, consolidating of units within the structure has a strong, more flexible rival in structural change, which is akin to, but costlier than, new construction for comparable difference in quality level. For downgrading, splitting has no real structural change rival—and is capable of quicker and more radical change in quality than change in condition, but combinations of the latter two may be especially effective.

What these sets of factors together imply is that new construction has legal and technological difficulty building at low-quality submarkets, but downward conversion of some kinds of structures—especially old, large houses—is very inexpensive. Put differently, for new construction the salient factor is the legal need for overbuilding in some quality ranges; for converison it is the effects of age on the patterns of conversion costs and the asymmetries between upward and downward conversion. We attempt to introduce these features into two-dimensional *transformation functions*.

Let us begin with code/zoning restraints on new construction. Builders need to overbuild in some range of quality submarkets, but the degree of overhauling required—or perceived as desirable by builders—is not constant across this range. Above some clearly "acceptable" level H^{**}, no overbuilding is required; below some clearly "unacceptable" level H^*, no decrease at all in input quantities is permitted if a quality level lower than this is targeted. Between these two boundaries, however—within a "penumbra" of quality levels—the degree of overbuilding is discretionary, depending on builder judgment. Within this penumbra, if progressively decreasing quality levels are targeted, some inputs savings may be achieved, but not as much as if no legal restrictions were in effect. Overbuilding therefore occurs within the penumbra, and the degree increases continuously toward the lower boundary H^*, beyond which overbuilding is complete: no further input savings are possible. This is shown in figure 6.2.

The horizontal axis of figure 6.2 shows the range of quality submarkets, from lowest H_B to highest H_T. The vertical axis is the ratio of marginal cost associated with building in each quality level H_i to that of building in the highest level H_T. Moving left from H_T shows the input saving obtainable by targeting lower-quality destinations. In the absence of builder specialization or other systematic cost differences among builders, we expect the ratio to be a linear function. This occurs from H^{**} to H_T. Between H_B and H^*, legal restrictions are absolute; no input savings are possible for quality levels below H^*. Declines between H^{**} and H* permit nearly normal savings near H^{**}, but these decline continuously (i.e., degree of overbuilding increases continuously) as H^* is approached. So figure 6.2 shows increasingly unfavorable cost tradeoffs as output destinations decline below H^{**}.

To translate this essentially multiquality property into two quality levels cannot be done completely, but a flavor of it can be retained by the following

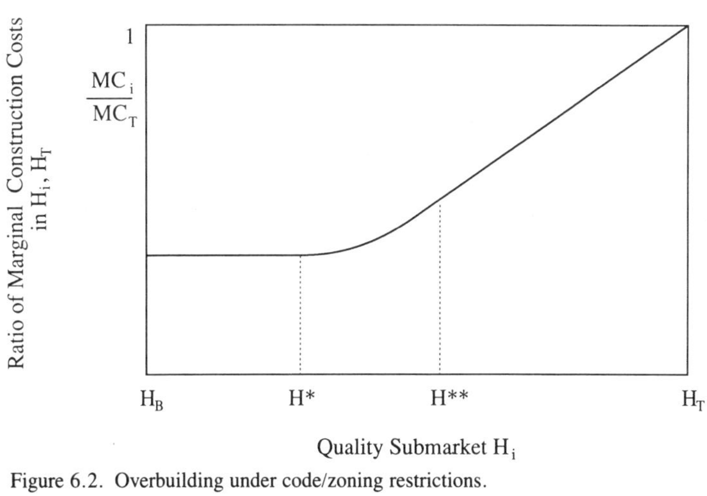

Figure 6.2. Overbuilding under code/zoning restrictions.

construction. Suppose we have only two quality-level submarkets—upper (U) and lower quality (L). A transformation function between them indicates the different combinations of the two achievable from a given total amount of productive resources, considering both production and normal upkeep costs. The slope at any point indicates the number of units of one that must be sacrificed if resources were optimally shifted to give one extra unit of the other. We define the slope of any particular mix, $(U/L)_i$ in the two-quality-level dimensional world, as the marginal tradeoff at an isomorphic location on the quality spectrum of the original multiquality-level dimensional world. In effect, we are equating the tradeoffs of "average" aggregate quality with those of *an* average quality. The correspondence between points in the two worlds is accomplished by the following transformation:

$$(6.14) \qquad U / (U + L)_i = (H_i - H_B) / (H_T - H_B).$$

That is, for example, $U/(U + L)_i$ equals .90 (so 90% of total units are upper quality, 10% lower), this point in two-commodity space corresponds to that location on the multiquality spectrum that is 90% of the distance from the lowest toward the highest quality level. The shape of the transformation function will generate a continuous series of unique ratios and so a unique correspondence with the quality spectrum. So the slope of the U–L transformation function at $U/(U + L)_i = .90$ is the same as the ratio of marginal costs at $H_i = H_B + [U/(U + L)_i] (H_T - H_B)$. That ratio is given in figure 6.2 above. For high values of $U/(U + L)$, shifts toward lower average quality have linear tradeoffs. They remain linear until "average" quality equals H** and thereafter the tradeoff worsens: the slope declines in absolute terms until, at "average" quality H^*, it becomes zero.

A transformation function registering these properties is shown in figure 6.3. Here the point (U^{**}, L^{**}) corresponds to average quality H^{**}.

A transformation function can be constructed for conversion supply also. Here, too, our construction involves translating situations from the multidimensional world into two dimensions, and here, too, the translation captures only a flavor of the issue. But the flavor suffices to enable us to characterize systematic differences between new construction and conversion.

We begin with an initial distribution of units across the different quality levels and a set of conversion cost functions. The initial distribution gives us a weighted mean quality level. This becomes translated into a point in U–L space in the same manner as with new construction (i.e., via $U/(U + L)$. The set of conversion cost functions, together with the distribution of units, generates submarket conversion supply functions where the "prices" in each are essentially ratios of market valuations across submarkets. The meaning of the transformation function tradeoff is the new "price ratio" that will attract enough additional units in the desired direction (i.e., toward U or L) so as to change the weighted average designated by the "unit change" in U–L space.

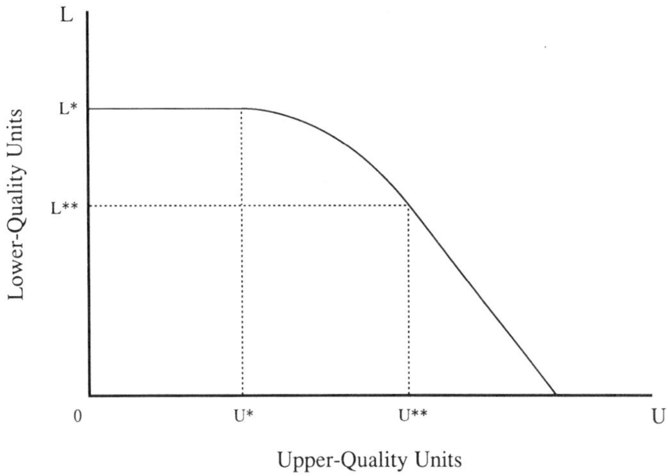

Figure 6.3. Aggregate transformation function for new construction in *U, L* commodity space.

The unfolding shape of the transformation function depends on how easy it is to elicit changes in relative submarket supplies. For a unit move in *U–L* space there are many possible combinations of multiple submarket shifts involving upward and downward conversions that will achieve the appropriate change in weighted mean quality. Each is associated with a new set of submarket valuations, and so a new weighted mean valuation ratio (using initial mean valuations as base). So the slope is itself a mean "price ratio" that will elicit the relevant supply quantities—unlike for new construction where it represented relative costs—but this is really an opportunity cost notion also.

The character of the shape of the conversion transformation function is determined by the fact that each move can come about through the competition among numerous suppliers with a wide variety of slightly differing cost circumstances. Small moves in either direction in *U–L* space should thus be essentially continuous and without great changes in shape. In orientation toward the *U* and *L* extremes, conversion costs for upward conversions to high-quality levels are likely to rise faster than for upward conversions to more modest quality levels, since the cost of making the conversion itself may be comparable for equal degrees of upgrading, but the differentially greater upkeep costs at high than at low levels did more to the cost of converted units at the former than at the latter levels. This factor makes downward conversions to very low-quality levels asymmetrically attractive relative to upward conversions to very high levels. So if the transformation has a tilt, it is to make higher and higher quality levels more difficult to attain, that is, a steeper slope as high *U*/*L* is approached.

Let us superimpose both new construction and conversion transformation functions in the same space to draw inferences about the respective quality

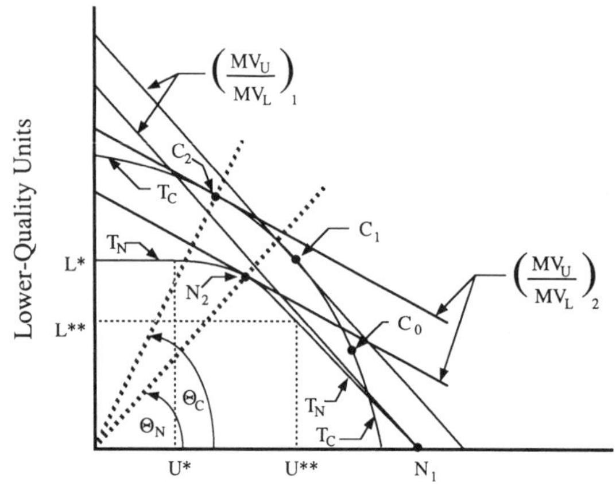

Figure 6.4. Upper/lower-quality mix for new construction and conversion.

specializations of the two supply modes. This is portrayed in figure 6.4. T_N and T_C are the transformation functions for new construction and conversion, respectively. Their shapes conform to the arguments given above. Their intercepts are the general equilibrium values determined over the medium run as described above.[11]

Suppose the initial distribution of existing units is at C_0, implying an equilibrium market valuation ratio (the tangent at C_0) for which the optimal new construction mix is at N_1 (as shown by a corner solution). Now let the new equilibrium market valuation (price) ratio be $(MV_U / MV_L)_1$, a ratio suggesting the relative strengthening of demand for L as against U. This new ratio is shown by the set of parallel lines so labeled in figure 6.4. Following the conventional rule, optimal mix for each supply mode is given by the point where the slope of the relevant transformation function equals the valuation ratio. Over the medium run the valuation ratio $(MV_U/MV_L)_1$ thus elicits conversion supply at C_1—a shift of the latter from C_0 to C_1 as conversions from U to L occur. Similarly, N_1 indicates the optimal ratio of U and L units supplied through new construction. Note that building will continue to focus exclusively on U (that is, a corner solution will persist) until the valuation ratio declines—that is, the valuation of L increases relative to that of U—to the point where it is less (in absolute value) than the slope of T_N in its linear range U^{**} to N_1. Of course one does not have to believe in strict linearity for so large a range of T_N to appreciate that even modestly favorable market valuations in upper-quality submarkets would result in substantial specialization in new construction of such units. Given our earlier analysis of the comparative superiority of construction over upward conversion, it is likely that a corner solution for new construction will persist for much smaller valuation ratios than would generate such corner solutions for conversions. That is, it is likely that the slope of the T_N function near the U axis is much less steep (absolutely) than the corresponding slope of the T_C function.

A less radical mix differential can be generated in figure 6.4 by valuation ratio $(MV_U/MV_L)_2$, suggesting an even stronger shift of relative demands toward L. The corresponding optimal mixes for conversion and construction are C_2 and N_2, respectively. It is clear here that in a scenario where a lower-quality submarket is a more prominent supply destination, conversion supply again produces a ratio of L to U (angle θ_C) greater than that produced by new construction (angle θ_N), despite the fact that starting point C_0 represents a *lower* ratio than N_2.

By continuing this exercise of rotating the valuation ratio lines in a counterclockwise direction, it can be seen that complete specialization to L will occur for conversion before a corresponding specialization of construction. Since legal restrictions render T_N horizontal in the range less than U^*, falling valuation ratios will produce a corner solution for conversion supply mix before they will for new construction mix.

The analysis therefore suggests that new construction will generate higher upper-quality/lower-quality mix ratios than will conversion, regardless of starting stock mixes and the presumed change in relative market valuations. Since the two modes are competitive, it is to some extent the superior strength of new construction at upper qualities that drives conversions largely elsewhere, and similarly the superior strength of conversion at lower qualities that drives new construction largely elsewhere.

This is not to suggest that the initial distribution of units does not influence equilibrium conversion mix. Quite the contrary, it does so by helping to determine the very shape of the T_C function (and therefore the location of tangency with the valuation ratio) as well as its equilibrium intercepts. Conversion supply functions to the various submarkets, as we saw in chapter 5, depend significantly on initial distribution, because this influences the marginal conversion cost functions on which conversion supply depends.

6.4.3 Determination of General Equilibrium Market Valuations

In the preceding sections we assumed an equilibrium set of market valuations across the submarkets and analyzed how builders and converters would respond. Now we examine how these equilibrium valuations are obtained through the interaction of spectral aggregate supply (both construction and conversion) and spectral demand. Again for simplicity we assume only upper- (U) and lower- (L) quality submarkets. Since the process of equilibration is analogous in both, our exposition focuses only on L. The graphic analysis is shown in figure 6.5.

Medium-run supply functions for new construction ${}_NS_L(MV_{Ui})$, for conversion ${}_CS_L(MV_{Ui})$, and for their sum ${}_\Sigma S_L\ (MV_{Ui})$ are portrayed as in figure 6.1, but now the fact that they have submarket valuations in the U submarket as a

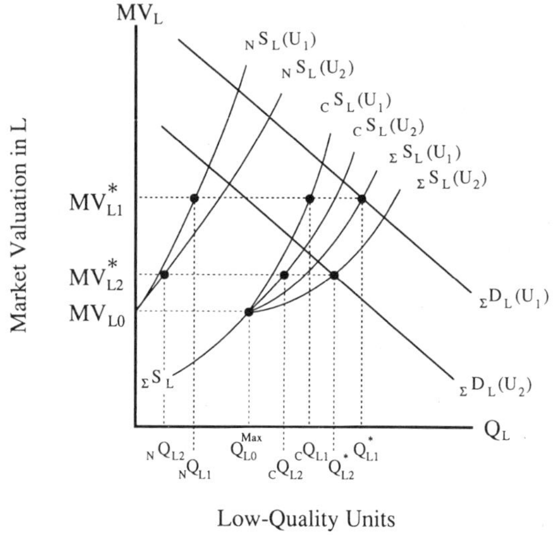

Figure 6.5. Equilibrium market valuation and quantity determination in low-quality submarket.

parameter is made explicit with the parenthetical terms. Similarly, the demand for L units is a function (among other things) of the market valuation in U: ${}_{\Sigma}D_L(MV_{Ui})$. The relationships between the two submarkets are substitutive on both supply and demand sides. That is, ${}_{\Sigma}D_L(MV_{U1}) > {}_{\Sigma}D_L(MV_{U2})$ since $MV_{U1} > MV_{U2}$. Analogously, higher valuations in U will siphon off erstwhile construction destined for L and encourage more net conversions into U as opposed to L. Symbolically, ${}_{N}S_L(MV_{U1}) < {}_{N}S_L(MV_{U2})$, ${}_{C}S_L(MV_{U1}) < {}_{C}S_L(MV_{U2})$, and ${}_{\Sigma}S_L(MV_{U1}) < {}_{\Sigma}S_L(MV_{U2})$ since $MV_{U1} > MV_{U2}$.

For any given valuation of U we can thus define both aggregate, medium-run demand and supply for L. For MV_{U1}, equilibrium in L gives Q^*_{L1} as aggregate equilibrium quantity, MV^*_{L1} as equilibrium valuation, and a supply mix of ${}_{C}Q_{L1}$ and ${}_{N}Q_{L1}$ for conversion and construction, respectively. For a lower valuation in U, MV_{U2}, supply to L *increases,* demand for L *decreases,* and market valuations of L *fall* to MV^*_{L2}. But aggregate equilibrium quantity is the net effect of opposing demand and supply shifts and thus cannot be specified a priori (the decreased quantity shown in fig. 6.5, Q^*_{L2}, is arbitrary). At the new equilibrium there will generally be a different ratio of construction and conversion to L.

The above analysis shows that if equilibrium valuation in one submarket assumes a certain value, equilibrium valuation in the other submarket will adjust to it, and vice versa. There is no unique pair of valuations at this stage of intersubmarket equilibrium. But if we start with a given valuation in L, valuation in U will adjust to it. Then valuation in L will adjust to that new valuation, and U will adjust yet again. Thus an interactive process occurs.

Will the process converge to a set of valuations that reciprocally support one another and bring about no further change?

We turn to analyzing this problem of convergence with the help of figure 6.6. The problem is the familiar one of conjectural variation. The market equilibrating combination in submarket *L* (MEC_L) is the locus of market-clearing combinations of MV_U and MV_L from the point of view of the *L* submarket adjustment. That is, for each value of MV_U, MEC_L shows the value of MV_L that achieves equilibrium in *L*. Similarly, MEC_U is the equilibrium adjustment locus for submarket *U*. Both functions are upward sloping, because *U* and *L* are substitutes.

The relative steepness of MEC_L and MEC_U depends on the demand and supply elasticities—direct and cross—for both *U* and *L*. As drawn in figure 6.6, the intersection of the two curves represents a stable general equilibrium: MV^*_U, MV^*_L. This is because stability requires—as is satisfied here—that any change in one market elicit a subsequent valuation change in the other which is less than the prior change, whichever is the submarket that changes first. If the elicited change exceeds the prior change, the relative slopes of the two curves are reversed and the system becomes unstable: once dislodged from the intersection, subsequent intersubmarket reverberations lead to wider and wider swings, never returning to the intersection.

In sum, general equilibrium relative market valuations for the spectrum of quality submarkets are determined by three groups of decision makers:

1. Marginal users of housing reach equilibrium choices for each pair of quality submarkets such that relative market valuations equal marginal rates

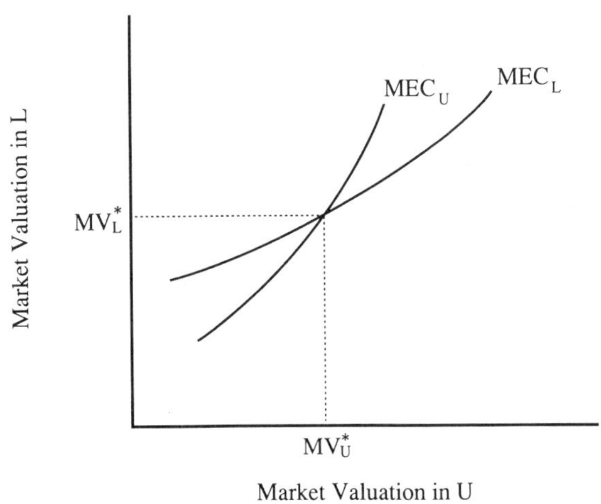

Figure 6.6. Intersubmarket general equilibrium convergence properties of upper- and lower-quality submarkets.

of substitution (infra-marginal users, not poised on the margin between any two, satisfy an inequality).

2. Builders of new housing reach equilibrium choices for each pair of submarkets actually targeted such that intersubmarket valuation differentials equal differentials in (opportunity cost-inflated) construction costs.

3. Groups of owners of each kind of existing dwelling select among possible downward conversion those destinations for which the market valuation differential between origin and lower-quality submarkets is at least as large as the differential between costs of maintaining the origin submarket and costs of downgrading, and for which this surplus exceeds that from any other destination; for upgrading options the inequality is reversed.

All three groups interact competitively; market valuations are determined by their interaction, not by the decisions of any one group.

In general, the demanders' marginal rates of substitution for any pair of quality levels are not constants; they vary with relative numbers of dwelling units consumed by the population. That is, they are a variable for each household and a variable across different households. Also, relative marginal costs for builders may vary with relative numbers of dwellings built at different quality levels, due to differences in input price pressures if builders specialize in construction at different levels. (Hitherto we have passed over such specialization lightly.) Finally, because of the structural differences among existing dwelling units of any origin quality level, conversion costs to each of the different destination submarkets for successive marginal converters will vary with the total number of conversions of each type from this origin to these different destinations. So any disparity in marginal tradeoff rates (substitution or transformation) among or within the three groups will be rectified by changing relative numbers of occupants or builders or converters: relative numbers and relative market valuations will simultaneously vary to establish the mutually consistent equilibrium balance overall.

One possible exception is if differences among builders of new units are minimal, especially in regard to building at different quality submarkets, and if building inputs are not specialized for construction at different submarkets. Then change in *absolute* numbers of new dwellings under construction may change input prices and so *absolute* construction costs, but changes in *relative* numbers of dwellings under construction at different submarkets will not change *relative* construction costs at those submarkets. If so, then the aggregate marginal rate of transformation via new construction between any two submarkets will be a constant. Under such a situation, general equilibrium will require that relative prices for any two quality submarkets to which new construction contributes in the present period be equal to this constant marginal rate of transformation. Corresponding marginal rates of substitution by demanders, and relative conversion costs where conversion supply contributes to those quality submarkets in the present period, must vary until they equal this same constant rate via changes in relative numbers.

This fixity of new construction transformation rates gives it a special influence in principle on relative market valuations. But such power is empirically constrained by the fact that, unlike users and modifiers who are likely to occupy and supply dwellings at all quality submarkets, new construction may supply dwellings to only a modest subset of submarkets. The very homogeneity of new construction options and constraints significantly narrows supply decisions relative to the wide disparities among households and owners of existing dwellings. As a result, for any of the many pairs of quality submarkets where new construction does not supply dwellings to *both* submarkets, relative market valuations are determined by interactions among the three kinds of decisions, as in the general case. Moreover, even in submarket pairs where new construction does occur, the total number of new units built in each period is likely to be too small to move valuations toward a full construction equilibrium.

6.5 Conclusion

In a short-run period the static equilibration of each submarket must be accomplished within the constraints of the initial dwelling stock. A market-period equilibrium is established when a cross-submarket array of market valuations has been established such that each submarket clears. At these valuations, any differences between units demanded and the total stock in the submarket specify the vacant stock.

The dynamics of short-run equilibrium have important differences from the static analysis. Significant supply gestation periods allow for a significant incidence of incomplete supply adjustments in the short-run period, thus misleading suppliers about the relationship between present numbers of units supplied across submarkets and present prices in each. The counterpart gestation phenomenon on the demand side, infrequent stochastic active participation in the market by users, leads to possibly important disequilibrium for many households as well as to a problematic process of improved user-unit matchups over time.

In a medium-run period, occupants, builders, and converters can adjust to market-period valuation differentials. The conversion cost functions implicit in the initial stock of units still impose constraints in this time frame. All demanders and suppliers are assumed capable of making smooth, complete adjustments to intersubmarket disequilibria, but converters may be prevented from adjusting fully to various attribute-mix disequilibria, due to the imperfect malleability of the existing stock. A medium-run equilibrium is attained when the cross-submarket array of market valuations creates a situation wherein no demanders have an incentive to move, and converters and builders have adjusted as much as they desire.

In the dynamic context, the supply adjustment process mitigates but does not wipe out either the possibility of continued user-unit mismatch over time or the possibility of household-user disequilibrium. Indeed, there is a remaining form of nonconvergence over indefinite periods that raises deep questions about the meaning of equilibrium in such markets and how usefully the concept serves for basic analysis. A useful empirical analysis has to take into account the various degrees of incompleteness of both supply and demand adjustments at any time.

For static analysis, in medium-run equilibrium the numbers and targets of new units bring about rates of return equal for all builders (at the margin) in all submarkets for which new construction is actually targeted, and equal to the opportunity rate of return from nonhousing investments. In submarkets that are supplied (at least partially) by new construction, the market valuations at equilibrium are equal to this opportunity rate of return, multiplied by the (opportunity rate of return–inflated) cost of constructing a new unit in the given submarket. However, even in such submarkets it is unlikely that the rates of return for all converters of units into them will be equal at the margin. In submarkets that are not supplied by new construction at all (due to housing code restrictions, etc.), the numbers and pattern of conversions generate market valuations that are not fully determinate, either absolutely or relatively. Here it is possible for owners to earn unequal rates of return in equilibrium, due to significant and pervasive differences in unit-specific conversion costs.

An equilibrium reduction in demand in a given submarket will tend to be met predominantly by stock conversions out of that submarket. An equilibrium increase in demand there will likely be met by a mix of new construction and net conversions into the submarket. The share of the increase generated by conversion will be greater the lower the marginal costs of converting into the submarket, compared to those of building in it, which depends on the distribution of the existing stock in the different submarkets at the beginning of the period.

If the particular increase in equilibrium demand occurs in a higher-quality submarket, new construction will assume a larger share of the increase in stock compared to conversion, and vice versa for lower-quality submarkets. The relative superiority of new construction over conversion at higher qualities is due to the difficulty (higher cost) of upgrading imperfectly malleable existing units compared to the cost of building perfectly malleable new units. Superiority of conversion over new construction at lower qualities, on the other hand, can be attributed to the necessity of more or less overbuilding in new construction due to building code and zoning requirements, contrasted with the ease of downgrading older, existing units. Over relatively wide ranges of intersubmarket valuation ratios a predominance of conversion supply to lower-quality levels will persist, even though accompanied by a virtual specialization of new construction in higher-quality levels. This, in turn, suggests that exogenous events and public policy interventions that differentially affect the costs of new construction and conversion will have dramatically differing impacts across the maze of urban housing submarkets.

Notes

1. And perhaps long-term leases.

2. Most homeowners are inactive on both sides of the market, for a combination of reasons cited above.

3. Note that should $MV_1 > MV_1^*$ occur, it implies that some owners overestimate the strength of demand and will be disappointed to discover no bids for their units, that is, unintended vacancies. We make no distinction between intended and unintended vacancies here.

4. Transactional frictions are much higher for ownership than for rental shifters.

5. Present signals include future predictions based on all signals from the past and including the present.

6. Understanding by this the set of both active and potential preference/income determinants, not simply the behavior of active participants in the market alone. In other words, the adjustment period extends long enough for all demand lags to be completed. Also implicit here are longer-run demand functions for each attribute mix (R). Here we are primarily interested in quality-level equilibrium, so we assume that the set of attribute prices remains essentially unaffected by inter-quality-level adjustments.

7. If construction costs *across the quality spectrum* are bid up, it will have no effect on the choice of most-preferable submarket for building.

8. But see the later qualification.

9. For those earning less than the opportunity cost of capital in their unit, we assume that they will sell in the medium run (even if a capital loss is incurred) and that the implied discount in sales price will produce a sufficiently small C_K for the subsequent owner to garner adequate returns. Those finding no buyers at any price (because they are earning *negative* returns on operating resources) will abandon their units.

10. All other submarkets' demands remaining constant, of course.

11. Normally the size of the standing stock is huge compared to potential stock added through construction over the medium run. But here for graphic convenience we scale the two transformation functions comparably.

7 Summary of the Theoretical Model

The goal of this chapter is to assist the reader in gaining a better intuitive, general understanding of our model of urban housing markets and submarkets. We summarize the major elements of our approach as explicated in chapters 3–6 and formulate them in a simplified, graphic fashion. This graphic version is employed in chapters 8–12 below, where numerous applications of the model are explored.

7.1 Housing-Quality Submarkets

The idiosyncratic nature of the housing commodity—heterogeneous, locationally fixed, imperfectly malleable—implies that the urban housing market should be treated analytically as a segmented, interconnected array of housing-quality submarkets. A submarket is a collection of all dwelling units in a metropolitan area whose myriad attributes, though different, are evaluated as a whole by demanders and suppliers as closely equivalent. The metric collapsing of these attributes of the housing package into a single dimension, *quality,* is the basis for arraying the housing stock in an urban area in a spectrum of submarkets, from highest- to lowest-quality levels.

Within each submarket, changes in demand and supply forces lead to adjustments in the submarket. But these are constrained by the fact that all the submarkets are interrelated with one another in varying degrees that depend on the quality differentials among them, since this determines the closeness of substitutability in the behaviors of both housing demanders and suppliers. Household users view submarkets as substitute options for occupancy. Builders and converters of existing units view submarkets as competing destinations for their supplies. By elucidating behaviors of households, builders of new dwellings, and converters of existing ones as they unfold in this segmented market complex, the dynamics of urban housing markets can be understood. Adjustments begun in one submarket will generate repercussions in others that tend toward the reestablishment of the original intersubmarket relationships, but will generally end with a somewhat changed set of relationships. Thus, each submarket has some independent play relative to the overall market complex.

7.2 Market-Period Demand

For any particular urban housing submarket comprising all dwellings of quality range *X*, there will be a function that relates the number of such dwellings that will be occupied by households to the market valuation charged for the dwellings (i.e., purchase price or rent), over some relatively short, "market" period. This "aggregate demand for submarket *X*" function represents an aggregation of the choices made by individual households in the urban housing market. Each household is assumed to select a quality submarket[1] so as to obtain the utility-maximizing mix of housing and nonhousing good consumption, within the constraints imposed by household income and wealth, and therefore dependent on the whole spectrum of submarket valuations. Because utility maximization requires that a smaller quantity of an item be consumed as its price rises relative to all other prices, the aggregate demand function for any submarket will demonstrate the usual inverse relationship between market valuation per dwelling in that submarket (MV_x) and the quantity of such dwellings occupied (Q_x) there. A representative aggregate submarket *X* demand function is shown as D_x in figure 7.1.

Even though housing is a necessity, there is still some sensitivity of quantity demanded to market valuation in any *given* submarket since households are free to switch to another, near-substitute one if the market valuation in the given submarket should rise dramatically (or even double up, dissolving their identity as separate households). One would predict that lower-income households occupying the lowest-quality submarkets would have the least flexibility in this regard: switching to a higher submarket may be especially burdensome

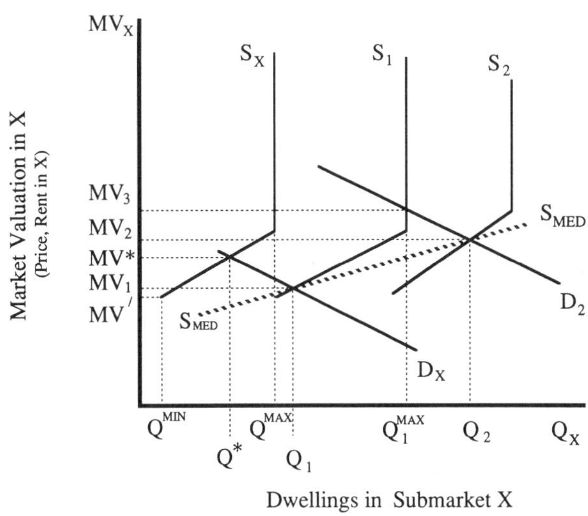

Figure 7.1. Illustrative market-period demand and supply functions for a submarket.

financially given limited discretionary income, and shifting to a lower-quality submarket is impossible.[2] Thus the (average) own-price elasticity of demand may be somewhat directly related to the quality of the housing submarket in question.

Additional market valuations shape the exact form of each submarket demand function as well. Market valuations in *other* quality submarkets in the metropolitan area are important influences since they pertain to substitutes of varying degrees of closeness to the submarket in question. As would be predicted for substitute relationships in general, changes in the market valuations in any of these other submarkets would lead to changes in the same direction in all other substitute submarkets, including the one in question. The size of the change in each is greater the closer the degree of substitution with the initiating submarket. For instance, if the market valuation of high-quality dwellings rose greatly, some occupants in the high-quality submarket may no longer be willing or able to devote such a large fraction of their income to housing expenditure, whereupon they may shift their demand to a lower-expense, lower-quality submarket. The number of such induced relocations would be larger to submarkets of closer substitutability than to those of weaker substitutability. Thus, cross-price elasticities would be inversely related to the quality differentials between pairs of submarkets.

Similarly, all other goods and services besides housing may be seen as "gross substitutes" as well in that they are competing for the limited budget of the consumer. If the prices of such nonhousing items as a group became relatively more expensive compared to housing, we would expect households at all income levels to buy more housing. This, in turn, would mean that some households at all income levels would "move up" to higher-quality submarkets all along the quality spectrum. The net result would be that demand in moderate-quality submarkets and above would rise, while the demand for the lower-quality submarkets would fall.[3]

The other central determinant of demand to be considered here is the distribution of households in a metropolitan area by preferences and purchasing power. Areas having a greater number of households at each income level who prefer to allocate relatively large fractions of their budget to housing will tend to have stronger demands for higher-quality submarkets, and vice versa for lower-quality ones. The same is true of areas with income distributions having greater numbers of households with higher real levels of income, fewer with lower levels.

In summary, at the static level, the demand for dwellings in a particular quality submarket depends upon several elements originating outside the housing market (income and preference distributions, prices of nonhousing goods) and upon others originating from within it (market valuations of substitute submarkets). It is the latter set that is particularly important for understanding housing market dynamics, for that provides one of the key mechanisms by which market signals are transmitted from one submarket to others.

On the dynamic level we emphasize that changes in occupancy involve substantial friction costs: considerable cost of search because of heterogeneity and inherent spatial dispersion of housing; significant transaction costs (legal, brokerage, debt aspects), especially for ownership transfers; and high moving costs. Households do not willingly incur these costs in any particular period unless they have strong prior grounds for expecting that, if they once entered into the active process of seeking to change occupancy in that period, they would be highly likely to improve on their current occupancy in overall *net* attractiveness by more than the high frictional cost of committing themselves to the process.[4] This condition is unlikely to be fulfilled recently after a prior change of occupancy, and its probability rises only gradually over time, as household circumstances and market conditions change progressively. Therefore, most occupancies last for long tenures—across many market periods. So in any one period only a small percentage of households are active participants in the market. This fact has great importance in interpreting the significance of what happens in the market in this brief period unit of analysis, as we shall see after discussing market-period supply.

7.3 Market-Period Supply

The behavior of the owners of existing dwellings (both absentee and occupant owners) over a short period of time is embedded in the notion of a market-period supply function. The *market period* is defined as that time interval too short to permit any substantive modifications of dwellings that would alter their quality submarket designation or for new dwellings to be built. By definition, then, the period relegates owner behavior initiated in that period to the choice of whether to offer a dwelling for rent or sale in that period and for what market valuation (rent or selling price). The market-period supply function (S_x) shows for any given submarket X the relationship between current market valuation in X (MV_x) and the number of existing dwellings currently in X that will be offered for rent or sale (Q_x).

Central to the formulation of the market-period supply function is the notion of a *reservation price*—the minimum price or rent that will induce a given owner to put the dwelling on the market. The reservation price will vary from owner to owner and will depend on two things—the relative costs of putting a dwelling on the market versus holding it vacant, and expectations of prospective benefits from both courses of action. As for the former, the higher are holding costs compared to occupancy costs, the lower is the reservation price. To illustrate, a developer currently holding a new, completed home may become willing to offer the unit for lower and lower prices, the greater become holding costs on the dwelling—debt servicing (or opportunity cost of capital), maintenance, utilities, security. The owner of an apartment building may prefer to hold an apartment vacant rather than leasing it at a rent that does not cover the extra variable costs associated with having a tenant in that dwelling (e.g., added repairs, utilities, rent collection, etc.). But if vacant units are prime targets for vandalism, holding cost considerations may predominate and reservation prices will drop.

Implicit in the aforementioned comparison of holding costs versus marketing costs is a set of expectations about future market potentialities, especially future submarket valuations. Whatever their current costs, owners will be more likely to hold their dwelling off the market if they expect rents or selling prices in the relevant submarket to rise substantially in the near future, and current commitment to lease or sale would preclude benefiting from those rises. Conversely, pessimism would lead to more owners trying to sell or rent their dwellings before the market "goes sour," whereupon reservation prices fall.

The upshot of the above discussion is that during any given market period each owner has established a reservation price based on the relevant costs and expectations. Those with low holding costs, high occupancy costs, and optimistic expectations will have relatively high reservation prices. Those with the opposite characteristics will have low reservation prices. Other owners will be arrayed between.[5]

The last consideration is that there is a limit to both the minimum and maximum number of dwellings that can be placed on the market. The maximum is the total stock of dwellings existing in the given submarket in the given market period. Since the market period is defined so as to disallow any alterations in the housing stock, the market-period supply function must be constrained to a maximum equaling the preexisting submarket stock (Q_x^{MAX}). The minimum is defined by the number of units in X (Q_x^{MIN}) held by the owner(s) in the submarket having the lowest reservation price (MV' in fig. 7.1). If the market valuation were to drop blow MV', no one would offer any dwellings for rent or sale during that market period.[6]

In concert, the minimum stock, the array of reservation prices, and the maximum stock define the market-period supply function for the submarket. As shown in figure 7.1, the function S_x indicates zero quantities supplied for all market valuations below MV' (from 0 to MV'). Finite supply begins at Q_x^{MIN}. This next segment is defined by adding to Q_x^{MIN} the total number of dwellings that will be offered for rent or sale in the given submarket at various hypothetical market valuations. The upward slope of S_x is determined by the distribution of reservation prices across the relevant group of owners and the number of dwellings each controls. Finally, S_x becomes perfectly inelastic at Q_x^{MAX}.

The above holds for a static analysis of supply. In the dynamic perspective, important qualifications occur. First is the distinction between supply as active market participation and as implicit continuation of current occupancy status.

A unit which is explicitly placed on the market for sale or rental has a far more direct impact on perceived market processes than one which is passively retained for continuing occupancy by current residents, whatever status that may be. Second, the overwhelming proportion of units in the stock falls in the latter category in each period, making units actively supplied a very small fraction of the total.

The third feature culminates the implications of the first two. Supply and demand are inextricably linked to one another—indeed, confounded together—in the market period. Since new construction is only a tiny percentage of total units, its addition to the market at the beginning of any market period is overwhelmed by turnover of units from the existing stock. But this turnover is based primarily on decisions by users to change their occupancy. This "demand" decision is what releases erstwhile occupied units to active supply states, whether for ownership *or* rental units. Thus, demand and supply decisions are united as the two sides of a coin. What is important about this is the character of the dynamic decisions made by users to change occupancy. As emphasized above, these are likely to be quite infrequent because of high friction costs, and therefore in any market period only a very small percentage of users will make that decision. These occur as a result of stochastic factors specific to the particular circumstances of each user. So the identity of the very percentage of households that become active demanders-suppliers in the market is essentially the result of stochastic processes. Similarly, the very small percentage of units that become actively available for new occupancy is likewise stochastically determined. This characterization of demand and supply will have important implications for the dynamic character of market-period equilibrium, as we shall see below.

The fourth complication that dynamics introduces relates to the fact that both new construction and various forms of conversion supply have considerable and varied gestation periods between the time of decision and the time of appearance of the units in question on the intended part of the market. Many of these intervals extend across several market periods. Therefore, *within* any such period the observed occupied stock in any submarket will *understate* the effect of past and present market valuations in that submarket (relative to other submarket valuations) by falsely *omitting* units intended for that submarket previously but not yet arrived via the two supply modes. It will *overstate* the valuation effects by falsely *including* units intended for other submarkets but still here, either because the actual conversions from here to elsewhere have not yet been initiated or completed, or because intended conversions from another submarket H_i to H_j involve transforming units *through* our submarket in question, and they have not yet passed through. Thus the "existing supply" in each submarket at any one market period is not necessarily predictable from the current set of submarket valuations, since the actual numbers in each may significantly misrepresent the numbers that past and present supply *adjustment* decisions have *intended* to appear in the future.

7.4 Market-Period Equilibrium

Given market-period demand and supply as shown in figure 7.1, the market will gravitate toward a market equilibrium position indicated by (Q^*, MV^*). This market equilibrium is defined by the market valuation MV^* for which the number of dwellings in submarket X that households wish to occupy equals the number of dwellings in X that owners wish to rent or sell. At market valuations below MV^*, more households would be seeking housing of quality X than would be willingly provided by owners. This would manifest itself as numerous bids on any dwelling offered and higher valuations offered due to the competition. This information about market strength would signal more and more owners with progressively higher reservation prices to offer their dwellings, until equilibrium was attained. Conversely, at market valuations above MV^*, many owners would find no buyers unless market valuations dropped enough to induce simultaneously more desired occupancies and fewer dwellings being offered.

Equilibrium not only specifies the number of dwellings that will be occupied in the submarket and their market valuations, but also delineates the number of dwellings that will be vacant during the market period: the total stock less the occupied stock; $Q^{MAX} - Q^*$ in figure 7.1. In principle it is possible for demand to be so great relative to the existing stock that the equilibrium could involve virtual 100% occupancy, that is, an intersection of D_x and S_x on the vertical segment of S_x.

Once again, admission of a dynamic perspective raises important complications, complications arising from the dynamic features of demand and supply that we discussed above. The complications concern the probability of user-unit mismatches and the meaning of equilibrium and disequilibrium.

If only a very small percentage of units and users are actively seeking one another in the market in each market period, and their identity depends heavily on both systematic and random factors that largely ignore the correspondence between what is wanted for new occupancy and what is available, and the actual turnover results require costly search, then there is a high probability that users will end up mismatched. A mismatch in this context means that a given user will obtain a new occupancy with less net advantage than was available in the current pool of active supplies, and with possibly much less advantage in the overall existing stock, that is, including the much larger inactive part of the stock. Such mismatches may well be pervasive in all submarkets and of significant degree. Moreover, a succession of market periods, allowing only for reshuffling of existing users and units but not for supply adjustments via new construction or conversion, is not likely to extinguish a large percentage of mismatches, because in each new period the stochastic forces that determine the identity of active participants will keep generating new sets of such active seekers, with no more guarantee of mutual conformity than before. Only supply adjustments over time are likely to ameliorate the degree of mismatching, but even these, as we argued in chapter 6, will not come close to resolving the problem fully.

The question of equilibrium and disequilibrium is seriously raised because active participants do not end up as well as they might, in an important sense. But even more, inactive participants presumably allow large discrepancies to grow between the net attractiveness of their current occupancies and that of what is potentially available—generally without even trying to discover whether it is worthwhile to find out whether this is true and what to do about it. While the information of active search necessary to reduce such mismatch is costly, and even the information about whether or not to engage in it is costly, the high voluntary degree of uninformedness, even in the face of outright dissatisfaction with an achieved or retained occupancy, suggests that one should characterize many users' end-of-period situations as disequilibrium. Insisting that the objective costs dissuading better adjustment warrant describing all such households as in equilibrium makes almost any degree of mistake by uninformedness definitionally equilibrium, and robs the concept of much of its predictive and explanatory relevance.

7.5 Longer-Run Demand, Supply, and Equilibria

The static market-period equilibrium described above specified the price or rent (i.e., market valuations) that users paid and property owners accrued from their dwellings in the quality submarkets they initially occupied. But it gave no indication whether these were consistent with a continuation of such behavior over time by users, or whether the implied rate of return on housing property in each submarket was superior or inferior to rates of return in other submarkets or to those gained from investments outside of the housing sector altogether. It is precisely these rate-of-return comparisons that guide longer-term housing supply decisions, since we view suppliers as attempting to maximize (risk-adjusted) rates of return on their portfolio of assets.

7.5.1 Demand

In a static analysis a housing user is deemed to maximize utility by fitting the appropriate quality and attribute mix of housing into an overall budgetary allocation. In a thick, highly competitive market with a large number of units being simultaneously traded, the many-faceted heterogeneity of these units permits formation of both a perceivable set of *implicit* individual attribute prices and a perceivable set of *implicit*[7] quality submarket prices.

Static utility maximization calls for each household user to choose a housing package that fits both his or her particular income level and housing preferences (for attribute mix and quality level) as follows: (1) optimal mix—the ratio of marginal utilities of any pair of attributes (their marginal rate of substitution in consumption) equals the ratio of their implied attribute prices; and

(2) optimal quality level—the marginal rate of substitution between housing quality and the numéraire good, nonhousing consumption equals the ratio of their implicit prices.[8] Such an optimal package is always available in the static market, so the household is assumed to occupy it, whether as a continuation of previous occupancy or by shifting occupancy to it. While population, household preferences, income levels, and the existing sock remain unchanged, this occupancy will then be continued indefinitely.

Dynamic considerations over this longer-run period enter intrinsically: households pass over time through a life cycle of preferences and income; they enter, age within, and retire from the market. Houses age, wear out, become obsolete; new units are introduced into the market; existing units are converted upward or downward in quality, and their attribute mixes are altered. Given time, then, specific households want to change occupancies because of a combination of changing life-cycle preferences and changing opportunities. But such desired static changes are constrained by the heavy friction costs of *changing* occupancy. These result in considerable lags between the formation of static directions and their ultimate achievement through market transactions, lags influenced heavily by dynamic obstacles. So in any one short period most households will not fully have achieved their static equilibrium position. It takes the longer run to allow for all such lags to have worked themselves out. Given the continuing process over time of life-cycle changes, this longer run during which a stable equilibrium is reached by all users is an idealization—used as an ideal reference situation rather than something that one can expect actually to observe in the real world.

For actual periods one will observe a continued set of stochastic, abrupt, lumpy changes made by subsets of households whose identity changes from period to period. The greater the length of the period being studied, the larger the percentage of households who will engage in at least one occupancy change during the period. But the longer the period, the greater is the chance that rising proportions of such shifters will be caught again after its last shift in the period in an uncompleted lag toward its next cumulatively desired static equilibrium position. The overlapping nature of these separate household lags makes choice of single ideal period to represent this effective longer run highly problematic.

A second major focus of demand in the longer run is the pertinence of tenure choice. Housing consumption is the use of a flow of services emanating from the housing package. This can be adequately characterized as a period-by-period rental, whether explicit or imputed, of such services. No question of actual tenant or owner tenure status need be relevant for a one-period analysis. But a multiperiod perspective makes a difference between the two tenures: ownership represents a capital portfolio situation that involves intertemporal tradeoffs different for that of tenant status.

We thus must explicitly treat tenure status in the context of the multiperiod *longer run.* The special importance of tenure choice in the present context is that the existence of an owner-occupier status, whether it is actually chosen or is simply available to be chosen, makes the household not simply a consumer of period-by-period housing service, but also a potential financial investor in one kind of overall portfolio rather than another. Our critical question is whether the availability of this joint consumer-investor role changed in any way the static consumption equilibrium developed in the pure consumer role case.

Our model of the joint consumer-investor role emphasizes that owner-occupancy differs from the pure consumption role in (1) creating a somewhat different consumer good; (2) being institutionally subsidized in terms of tax treatment of mortgage interest payments and state/local property taxes; (3) being empirically constrained to de facto nontrivial minimum investment requirements; (4) having to meet certain financial transaction costs; and (5) having to bear with significant minimum downpayment equity requirements. The result of these complications creates a complex decision for households. Some systematic conclusions from this complex decision matrix are (1) that ownership status is differentially attractive to different households, with preferences and income level especially important, higher-income households being especially more likely to own than lower-income households; and (2) that opting for ownership status generally lowers the implicit price of housing quality relative to nonhousing consumption in comparison with rental status, reductions that are sometimes quite considerable, and thus leads to a static equilibrium level of housing quality higher for owner-occupancy than for rental status, sometimes considerably higher.

7.5.2 Supply

The pattern of any period's newly formed equilibrium submarket valuations, in combination with the varied set of supply adjustment costs for new construction and different types of conversion, suggests a potentially new pattern of prospective rates of return from various supply adjustment strategies. Owners of existing dwellings may, for example, wish to intentionally modify them so as to convert them into a different quality submarket where rates of return now are prospectively superior to those in the original one. Some may now be unable to secure minimal rates of return from their dwelling regardless of its potential submarket, whereupon they may seek to convert it to nonresidential uses or, failing this, to retire it from the housing stock via abandonment. Builders of new dwellings may perceive rates of return in certain submarkets that exceed those potentially attainable in stocks and bonds, and therefore add to the housing stock in those submarkets. It is the sum total of these various actions, which over time modify the distributions of dwellings across the quality submarkets of a metropolitan area, that constitutes longer-run supply changes. We refer to this period as the *medium run*.[9]

The consequences of these adjustments can be portrayed with the help of figure 7.1. Suppose that, once it was achieved, the aforementioned market-period equilibrium (Q^*, MV^*) was associated with a prospective rate of return on housing supply investments that was superior to those available in other submarkets and for nonhousing investments for at least some suppliers. Those who are owners of existing dwellings in other submarkets will be induced to modify their dwellings (structurally and/or in condition) so as to convert them to quality-level X. Owners of dwellings initially of inferior quality may upgrade by making repairs, improving the heating, cooling, plumbing or electrical systems, building new additions, or consolidating smaller units into fewer, larger ones of quality X. Owners of dwellings initially of superior quality to X may downgrade by subdividing a former single-family unit into several rental units (each with fewer quantitative and qualitative amenities appropriate to X), or by passive undermaintenance—witholding normal upkeep activity over time. Finally, builders of new housing could add to the stock in X via construction, presuming that housing codes or other legal strictures would not prevent this.

In each short period during this medium-run process, we may think of a new market-period supply function as being relevant, as we do conventionally in microeconomic analyses of shorter- and longer-run supply. It would have the same qualitative appearance as S_x in figure 7.1, but would be shifted to the right to reflect the additional stock that had been added to X from the inception of the adjustment period to that given point of time. As shown in figure 7.1, this would be portrayed as a shift in the original market-period supply function for quality submarket X from S_x toward S_1, with a corresponding increase in the stock of such dwellings from Q^{MAX} toward Q_I^{MAX}.[10] As a result of this increasing supply, market-period-equilibrium market valuations will be progressively competed downward, thereby reducing the initial rates of return to further investment in submarket X. As dwellings are converted from other submarkets into X, supply will be lowered in these origin submarkets, thereby boosting market valuations and investment rates of return there. Concomitantly, as the most malleable units are converted, the costs of converting the marginal dwelling unit of progressively less appropriate units will rise continually. These adjustments simultaneously will act to slow and, eventually, to terminate the net incentives for adding further to the stock of dwellings in X through both forms of supply. All the while, households will have been altering their choices of optimal submarket in response to changing differentials in market valuations. When the point has been reached when there are no incentives for any households to change submarkets, no incentives for any owners of dwellings in any submarkets to alter the composition of the stock toward or away from submarket X, and no incentives for any further new construction in submarket X, X reaches its medium-run equilibrium. Generalizing, when this reverberatory process among all suppliers and demanders has reached a mutual resting place in all submarkets, then a general equilibrium has been attained in the urban housing submarket array.[11] Let this point be denoted in submarket X by (Q_1, MV_1) in figure 7.1, with the relevant (postadjustment) market-period supply indicated by S_1.

Even though for simplicity we have portrayed this equilibrium as if it were static, in reality equilibrium is but a static picture of a dynamic flow. The stability of the aggregate submarket demand and supply functions just described should not mask the reality that individual households are entering, exiting, and moving among submarkets and adjusting with their distinctively significant and varied lags, and moreover, that individual dwellings are being converted, built, or abandoned, also with characteristic significant and varied lags. Indeed, as we show in chapters 5 and 6, as dwellings age their conversion cost functions tilt so as to bias conversions toward downgrading and away from upgrading. We thus would expect in long-run equilibrium a general pattern (though by no means inexorable) of many dwellings moving downward in quality in response to their aging, and some even moving out of the housing market entirely, to be replaced by new construction at higher quality levels.

Suppose for illustration that this general equilibrium was now upset by an increase in the demand for quality X housing from D_x to D_2, as shown in figure 7.1 (all other submarkets unchanged initially). As vacancies fell in X and market valuations rose to MV_3, rates of return would again rise to extraordinary levels in submarket X, thereby inducing additional similar sorts of housing-stock supply adjustments as described above. This will lead to a new medium-run equilibrium (Q_2, MV_2) in figure 7.1, with the stock increment as embodied in the new market-period supply function S_2. It is the locus of such equilibrium pairs of market valuations and quantities that is generated by alternative demand shocks in submarket X (holding initial market valuations in all other submarkets constant), such as is represented by (Q_1, MV_1) and (Q_2, MV_2), that represents the medium-run housing submarket X supply function—S^{MED}. Again, it should be noted that the above is analogous to the standard microeconomic derivation of long-run competitive supply.

The costs of these various forms of medium-run supply adjustment—downgrading, upgrading, and new construction—influence the aggregate supply responsiveness to the given submarket X. Thus, for example, if there is little submarket specialization among builders and they do not significantly bid up construction costs in the metropolitan area as they increase building in X, the medium-run new construction component to S_{MED} will be highly elastic. Similarly, if the stock of existing units initially of lower quality than X can be, on average, cheaply upgraded to X and the stock initially of higher quality than X can be cheaply downgraded to X,[12] the aggregate conversion component to S_{MED} will be relatively elastic.

The determinants of these aggregate conversion supply functions are complex and depend heavily on the idiosyncracies of individual structures comprising a particular metropolitan area's stock, as well as the distribution of that stock across the submarket spectrum. But several general properties should be noted (see chap. 5). First, conversions are more costly absolutely, and relative to new construction, the wider the intersubmarket quality differential. Second, given the imperfect malleability of capital embodied in existing units, costs of upgrading (including costs of maintaining at new, higher qualities) rise progressively faster with increasing amounts of quality increment, again absolutely and relative to new construction. Conversely, the operating costs of downgraded dwellings fall at a decreasing rate for progressively greater decrements in quality. The aforementioned two relationships are even stronger for older dwellings. Thus, aggregate conversion supply response in X is more elastic when the existing stock (1) in higher-quality submarkets is older and "closer" or more similar (on average) in quality to X, and (2) in lower-quality submarkets is younger and "closer" or more similar (on average) in quality to X.

The mix of new construction and conversion modes of medium-run supply will not be the same in all submarkets (see chap. 6). Rather, conversion will tend to predominate in lower-quality submarkets, since downgrading is relatively inexpensive for most existing dwellings, whereas housing codes and zoning laws make it effectively too costly to build new housing at the low market valuations typically prevailing there. Conversely, new construction will tend to predominate in upper-quality submarkets, since it is generally more expensive to modify existing units than to build new units with the latest technologies that embody the desired combinations of dwelling attributes.

Finally, it is important to stress the properties of intersubmarket dynamics in our model. We describe these with the term *systematic nonuniformities* of responses. That is, we can predict how repercussions from some given exogenous shock in one submarket are propagated systematically throughout the submarket array, and the magnitude of the induced repercussions turns out to be systematically nonuniform across the array.

This special dynamic process results from both demand-side and supply-side features of the market outlined above. On the demand side, households will typically be induced to make switches to only modestly higher- or lower-quality submarkets in response to altered market valuations in their own or in such near-quality submarkets.[13] But since both own- and cross-price elasticities for all qualities of housing are likely to be much less than unity, the induced shifts in demand in near-quality submarkets will produce smaller secondary perturbations in market valuation than were present initially in the submarket bearing the brunt of the exogenous shock. These more modest perturbations will, in turn, induce further shifts in demand in still another set of submarkets further removed from the point of initial impact. These demand shifts will be, for reasons given above, further damped, until the successive waves of repercussions damp toward extinction, as ripples in a pond extending from the point of initial impact.

On the supply side, owners of existing dwellings find the cost of potential conversion directly related to the quality differential between origin and destination submarkets. Thus, an upset of equilibrium in one submarket will lead owners primarily to convert either out of it to near-quality submarkets or into it from near-quality ones. In either case the resulting alterations in market valuations in the submarkets to which converters in the initially impacted submarket flowed (or from which converters flowed) would be more modest than the initial disequilibration. This damping effect would be magnified to the extent that part of the response which served to increase the stock in a submarket took the form of new construction. A first wave of alterations would generate further waves, in more remote submarkets, as with demand repercussions, and these will progressively weaken with further repercussion stages, again toward extinction.

Thus, intersubmarket repercussions are damped progressively as they are transmitted to submarkets of quality increasingly dissimilar to that where the initial shock occurred, as a result of both demand and supply adjustments. While monotonic in degree with increased qualitative dissimilarity, they are nonuniformly so because neither the cross-price elasticities of demand nor the elasticities of medium-run aggregate supply are constant across pairs of submarkets in the submarket array. Cross-submarket variations in the incomes and preferences of their archetypical occupants, and idiosyncracies (especially structural age and attributes) of the existing housing stock at each point in the quality array which affect conversion costs for all submarkets, respectively, explain this second source of nonuniformity.

We now have in hand a comprehensive theory and a simplified graphic representation of urban housing submarkets and their interactions that produce dynamic market adjustments. We can proceed to demonstrate the power and utility of our model in the analysis of several important contemporary urban phenomena, the dynamics of neighborhood deterioration, and various urban housing policies. Chapter 8 considers housing decay and renovation, rent burdens, abandonment, and homelessness. Chapter 9 investigates the relationship between submarkets and neighborhoods, the sources and consequences of neighborhood decline, and policy options for stemming undesirable decline. Chapters 10, 11, and 12 critically evaluate demand-side, supply-side, and market regulation approaches to housing policy, respectively, with concluding comparative remarks provided at the end of chapter 12.

Notes

1. Submarkets can easily be thought of in terms of quality and tenure, if desired.

2. But they might well double up with others in the same lowest submarket, *decreasing* the real quality of housing for them, and decreasing the number of units occupied there *without* increasing occupancy in other submarket.

3. It is possible that only prices of nonhousing goods and services consumed predominantly by a subset of households change, in which case a more complex pattern of submarket demand shifts would ensue.

4. For a fuller theoretical and empirical analysis of household mobility behavior, see Galster 1987: ch. 8.

5. Owner-occupants also may be thought of as setting reservation prices, although the issue is complicated by the fact that they are simultaneously owners and tenants. In most periods, owner-occupants are in a situation where they choose to continue to "rent to themselves"; that is, they have a reservation price less than what they as tenants are willing to bid implicitly, and expect no net gain by renting to someone else at a higher bid when considering its net superiority in being thereby forced to rent or buy another unit for themselves. The choice to vacate the unit and offer it for rent or sale to someone else typically is motivated by exogenous forces like a change in family circumstances, age, size, and so forth, or a change in work place. In such circumstances the owner-occupant then behaves in a way analogous to a developer with a vacant unit, subject to the constraint of finding acceptable new housing.

6. This abstracts from owners who have previously committed to occupancy during the given market period by the writing of long-term leases. Such owners are analogous to owner-occupants: they can break contracts, but not for small gains. Like owner-occupied units, these former units are essentially off the market—with regard to both price and quantity.

7. These are both implicit in the sense that they abstract from raw observable prices.

8. The implicit price of nonhousing consumption is its perfect price index.

9. It is inappropriate to call it the *long run,* since such could imply to some that all existing dwellings have been replaced with newer, more adaptable structures—a process easily taking generations. Since in our model a key determinant of conversion supply responses is the array of features of the existing stock, we avoid this terminology.

10. One cannot predict in advance precisely what the slope and intercept of this new supply function will be; it will depend on the comparative reservation price(s) of the variety of new owners who enter the submarkets. For example, if all new entrants have a reservation price above MV', the intercept will remain the same; otherwise the new value corresponding to Q^{MIN} will take the value of the lowest of these new prices. Similarly, the price at which the supply function becomes vertical will depend upon whether any new entrants' reservation prices are greater than the price at the "kink" at Q^{MAX}.

11. The foregoing long-run adjustment scenario assumes that all the initial determinants of market-period demand and supply remain constant. We rarely, if ever, actually reach such an equilibrium, since the parameters we have assumed as constant are typically in constant flux in the real world. Nevertheless, the concept is useful in providing guidance as to the directionality of the numerous market adjustments occurring, given the prevailing conditions.

12. In downgrading, the *cost* is the potential loss of market valuation per unit; the *benefit* is the savings in upkeep expenditures.

13. This is an application of the conventional principle that cross-price elasticities are directly related to the degree of substitutability between the two goods in question.

Part Two: Applications of the Theory to Contemporary Urban Housing Issues

8 Housing Availability, Quality, and Affordability

The goal of this chapter is to assist the reader in gaining a better understanding of our model of housing markets in metropolitan areas by employing it in its simplified, graphic form. The model can elucidate the dynamics of some of the major phenomena currently being witnessed in urban America: the simultaneous processes of housing decay and renovation, and the juxtaposition of severe rent burdens and homelessness with the abandonment of dwellings (see, e.g., Burns and Grebler 1986; Hughes and Sternlieb 1987; Apgar 1988; Keyes 1988). The exposition will demonstrate the usefulness of our submarket approach not only in isolating the origins of phenomena, but also in unraveling the complex mechanisms through which causes prduce ultimate effects.

The theme here is "systematic nonuniformity." Housing submarkets respond to changes in demand or supply in their own and in other submarkets in systematic ways. But the pattern and magnitude of response are not uniform across quality submarkets. The size of the repercussions from a particular initial impact submarket to any other submarket decreases with increasing remoteness in terms of degree of substitutability—the size of the quality differential between the pair. Differences in cross-price elasticities for households considering switching occupancy to different submarkets and differences in supply responses (especially associated with upgrading versus downgrading costs and the mix between new construction and conversion) are the key sources of this nonuniformity.

8.1 Housing Downgrading and Upgrading: The Dynamics of Decay and Renovation

The stock of residential dwellings in any metropolitan area is constantly in a state of flux. While many owners continuously reinvest enough in their properties to maintain them at their current quality levels, others do not. The result is a complex pattern of transferrals of dwellings between submarkets, some involving downgrading of quality, others involving upgrading, and only partially overlapping in time.

Some owners make enough minimal repairs so that their dwellings do not visibly decay, but refrain from modernizing the mechanical, structural, or aesthetic features of the house. Eventually, such residences may become "obsolete" and drop to correspondingly lower-quality submarkets. Other owners, either because they choose not to or cannot afford to, are lax in making certain repairs or performing preventative maintenance in degree sufficient to offset structural wear and tear and weathering, whereupon their dwellings perceptibly deteriorate as they drop into lower submarkets. Still other owners intentionally modify dwellings through partitioning or subdividing, thus producing units of smaller size and fewer amenities that become categorized in lower submarkets than the original, undivided dwellings.

Yet in the same urban housing market there are undoubtedly other owners who are engaged in activities that serve to upgrade the quality of their dwellings. Mechanical systems may be modernized or augmented; more rooms may be created or added, with or without additional size; special features like swimming pools, garages, or enclosed porches may be built; interior and exterior features may be remodeled; occupancy tenure may be changed, with attendant physical changes, for example, numerous, smaller rental apartments may be consolidated into fewer but larger condominiums, with concomitant additions of amenities.

What lies behind this web of varied, seemingly random movements of dwellings between quality submarkets? What consequences do such movements produce for various segments of the housing market? Our theory of urban housing submarkets provides a simple yet powerful tool for arriving at answers to these questions.

8.1.1 Housing Downgrading

Prior to the analysis of why dwellings may drop into lower-quality submarkets (what we call *downgrading*), the concept of a *normal maintenance* must be introduced. Normal maintenance is defined as that minimum amount of periodic investment needed to maintain a dwelling in its current quality submarket and is specific to each dwelling. Put differently, it is enough upkeep, repair, replacement, and modernization actions adequate to ensure that the dwelling neither physically deteriorates in an absolute sense nor becomes relatively obsolete in terms of its mechanical and structural features. The point is that if and when owners fall below such a normal maintenance threshold, the inevitable result for their dwellings will be downgrading,[1] unless corrective adjustments are made.

What circumstances produce incentives for any owners to maintain their structures at a level below the normal maintenance thresholds? This section elucidates some (but by no means all) of these circumstances, through the use of our housing submarket model in a simplified, graphic format.[2]

For simplicity of exposition, assume we are considering a hypothetical urban housing market in which all dwellings may be categorized into one of three quality submarkets: low (L), middle (M), and high quality (H). We suppress distinctions between owner- and renter-occupied units. In each of the stylized scenarios below we begin by assuming that all submarkets initially are in general equilibrium, and that such is specified by the original market-period demand and supply functions as shown in succeeding figures by (D_{L1}, S_{L1}), (D_{M1}, S_{M1}), and (D_{H1}, S_{H1}), respectively, and by their corresponding equilibrium quantities (*Q*) and market valuations (*MV*). Then we perturb the equilibrium by introducing a factor that changes one of the exogenous determinants of a submarket demand or supply function, and examine the endogenous, medium-run demand and supply adjustments that are spawned, until the system again approaches a new equilibrium. Finally, we compare this new equilibrium with the initial situation in terms of changes in submarket quantities, market valuations, and the overall market valuation of housing in general. Even though for clarity we discuss these adjustments as if they occur sequentially, in reality many occur simultaneously or with partial overlapping.

Decreasing-Demand Scenario

Consider first what we would expect to occur in our hypothetical market if many households currently occupying high-quality dwellings were to move to another metropolitan area, perhaps due to searches for different jobs, transfers, or retirements. The initial consequence would be a reduction in the demand for high-quality housing, as shown by D_{H2} in figure 8.1.[3] As apartments in *H* were vacated, landlords would find it increasingly difficult to attract replacement tenants at the original market valuation MV_{H1}. Similarly, out-migrating homeowners would find that their homes remained unsold for long periods at initial market valuation levels. As market valuations in the *H* submarket fell to reflect the weakened demand, two responses would ensue simultaneously.

On the supply side, the absolute and relative rates of return to owners in *H* would fall. The absolute decline will discourage additional new construction

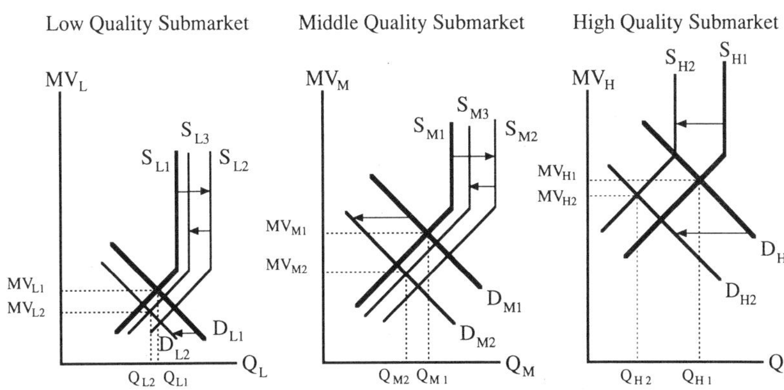

Figure 8.1. Downgrading submarket dynamics—decreasing-demand scenario.

by builders in *H*. From the perspective of owners of existing *H* units, the relative decline will produce an incentive for some to downgrade their dwellings to middle-quality submarket *M*. Some landlords in *H*, for example, may find that they can now attract only middle-income tenants (erstwhile inhabitants of *M*) and must offer correspondingly lower rents if they are to avoid excessive vacancies. Yet such relatively low rents may no longer justify the continued high levels of property upkeep investments previously necessary to maintain the apartments in the *H* submarket. As the intensity of repairs and the frequency of renovations and modernizations drop below the relevant *H* normal maintenance threshold, the apartments effectively would become downgraded to the middle-quality submarket *M*. Put differently, some apartment owners would find higher potential rates of return in *M* than in *H* because of the decrease in rents in *H*, and would allow their units to be downgraded to *M* via undermaintenance (thereby decreasing the level of normal maintenance). Owners most likely to convert in this circumstance are those whose units would experience the largest percentage decrease in operating costs associated with the undermaintenance, that is, those with the lowest conversion costs or highest conversion net gains (as explained in chap. 5).[4]

Some home sellers of existing units in *H* who have not downgraded may find that they must reduce their asking price so much that the buyers finally reached have considerably lower incomes than the previous owners, since these higher-quality units are now more affordable to them than heretofore. As these new owners make their optimizing decisions as to how much of their budget to allocate to home upkeep, they may be less willing to pay the higher maintenance costs necessary to keep the units at the original high quality, so they decide on strategies of undermaintenance that comprise a lower-quality / lower-quantity / lower-operating-cost stance more appropriate for their lower incomes. For example, as initially "luxury" furnishings, surfacing and structural materials, and other accoutrements wear out, they may be replaced by more pedestrian ones.[5] Even homeowners in *H* who would not attempt to sell immediately may become more pessimistic about the prospects of sustaining market values over time. As a result, they too would correspondingly choose to reduce their ongoing housing reinvestments in maintenance and improvements, since the marginal payoffs for such investments in terms of enhanced property values would be lower than previously.[6] The net result of all these aforementioned adjustments is that the supply of submarket *H* housing would decline and the supply of submarket *M* housing would rise, as shown by S_{H2} and S_{M2}, respectively, in figure 8.1.

Implicit in the above discussion is the new occupancy of *H* housing by households who previously could not afford more than *M* housing. This constitutes the initial demand adjustment. As households originally housed in submarket *M* see the market valuations of high-quality housing falling, some decide they can now afford to "move up" to better housing. As such moves occur the demand for housing in *M* drops correspondingly, as shown by D_{M2} in figure 8.1.[7] The degree to which this occurs depends on the size of the initial market valuation decrease and the cross-price elasticity of demand for the households considering whether to "move up" in quality.

As both these demand and supply responses occur in *H*, the net result is a reestablishment of market valuations (and rates of return) in the *H* submarket nearer to the original equilibrium level than to the initial, postdemand decline level. The exact relationship between initial and final equilibrium market valuations cannot be specified without more information about the medium-run supply function in *H* (see chap. 6). Nevertheless, given some plausibly—though not perfectly—elastic supply function for *H*, we predict that both the new MV_{H2} and Q_{H2} will be *lower* than initially. This means that the well-being of those consuming *H*-quality housing has improved, although the initial owners of *H*-quality housing may have suffered capital losses.

However, equilibrium has now been upset in the middle-quality submarket because demand has declined and supply has risen. The resultant weakening of market valuations and rates of return in *M* will now trigger a succeeding round of adjustments similar in kind to those previously described for *H*, but smaller in magnitude. In brief, although some households previously occupying submarket *L* housing may now be able to move up into the *M* submarket (producing demand shift to D_{L2} in fig. 8.1), owners in *M* will find a net worsening of their position due to the greater first-round increases in competition from the erstwhile *H*-quality dwellings that were downgraded.[8] Consequently, those owners in *M* who can gain the greatest cost savings by doing so will now downgrade their units over time to *L*, thereby raising supply in *L* while decreasing it in *M* (shown by S_{L2} and S_{M3}, respectively, in fig. 8.1). Similarly, some of the new homeowners in *M* who were previously in *L* may have an income level that calls for compromising their unit's quality through undermaintenance (relative to the new, higher normal maintenance threshold in *M* than in *L*) as a better overall budgetary strategy, thereby shifting units out of *M* into *L*.[9]

Finally, the lower market valuations in *M* will make that submarket a less attractive target for new construction, since the prospective rate of return has fallen. The decline in new construction is not due to a worsening of rate of return in this submarket *relative* to other submarkets. Indeed, the fall is less here than in *H*. It is a greater fall than in *L*, but little or no new construction occurred originally in *L* and is not likely to change significantly. The declines in *H* and *M* are *absolute* declines in the rate of return of new construction in housing relative to other forms of nonresidential construction and investment activity generally.

The above repercussions tend *toward* restoring an equilibrium in submarket *M*. Again, assuming a modestly upsloping middle-run supply function in *M*, we can deduce that the new stock Q_{M2} and the new market valuation MV_{M2}

would be somewhat less than originally in M. This, in turn, would produce the same welfare effects for households and owners in M as those described above for H.

These repercussions, however, will tend to generate further adjustments in L. These adjustments will undoubtedly be the smallest of all, because of the large differential in quality (substitutability) between the point of initial exogenous shock and the submarket in question. Some owners in L may not be able to attract enough tenants and revenues to cover the operating costs of the structure. If, in addition, there were no present or prospective buyers of the property at prices that exceeded transactions costs and outstanding property taxes, the eventual result will be dwelling abandonment.[10] In such cases the owner will have removed the dwelling from the housing stock[11] and, typically, will relinquish ownership rights by a continued failure to pay property taxes. Such abandonments would eventually reduce the supply in submarket L (shown by S_{L3} in fig. 8.1) to the point where surviving owners reap sufficient rates of return to remain in the business of operating such dwellings.[12] Similar qualitative comparisons between original and new quantities and market valuations as appertained above apply here in L, with the additional complication that residents and owners in L whose neighborhoods become blighted with more abandoned dwellings will suffer thereby. Inasmuch as the medium-run supply in L is probably the least elastic of all the submarkets, the relative decline in MV_{L2} will be large relative to the decline in Q_{L2}. Little or no effect of declining market valuations is to be expected on new construction in L, since we argued above that little or no such construction took place there prior to the original demand decline.

In summary, the initial demand decrease in H has been diffused across the submarket array, and changes in new construction and stock modifications have changed the absolute and relative distribution of supplies, decreasing them in declining degree from the point of initial impact—the degree of change being directly related to the degree of similarity of the given submarket to H. The decline in high-quality stock to Q_{H2} has led ultimately to the retirement of stock from the lowest-quality ranges (through abandonment) to Q_{L2}. The magnitudes of these sequences of supply adjustments here depend upon the nature of both the new construction supply function and the various submarket conversion supply functions. New construction rates of return have *decreased* unevenly across the submarkets. As for conversion, it cannot be overemphasized that the precise nature of the conversion supply functions depends upon the particular idiosyncracies of the existing housing stock and their distribution across submarkets. Also note that the *target* submarket of the initial demand decrease—its initial impact point—is crucial to the final outcome. If, for example, demand had initially declined in M instead of H, downgrading from M to L would still have occurred, but *not* downgrading from H to M—rather an upward shift from M to H.

The net results of these supply and demand repercussions which occur as a consequence of an initial decline in demand for H are then as follows. Final equilibrium market valuations in *all* submarkets are lower than originally, but unequally so. The differential degree of the reductions is directly related to the magnitudes of relative demand declines in all submarkets, that is, to the upward cross-price elasticities that induce households in L and M submarkets to move up to superior submarkets. The declines in H and M are inversely related to the differential decline in new construction (fed by differential declines in rate of return) and to the probability that the relevant owners of existing units will downgrade, that is, to the relative steepness of their conversion cost functions relative to that of the cross-submarket market valuation function. The valuation declines in L are in turn inversely related to the probability that owners in L will abandon units in response to weakening demand and intensified competition, that is, to their level of operating costs. The converse of the above considerations yields the predictions for the change in equilibrium housing stocks and occupancies in each submarket—a decline in H and graduated but more ambiguous changes elsewhere. There is increased abandonment (predominantly of stock originally in L). The lower market valuations across the quality spectrum lead to improved well-being for households as consumers of housing (with a caveat for those in neighborhoods which may be blighted by abandonment). This also has a redistributional effect among property owners and residents as differential capital losses are incurred.

Increasing-Demand Scenario

The second demand-change scenario to be illustrated involves the initial equilibrium in figure 8.2 being upset by an influx of low-income households into the given metropolitan area that boosts the demand for submarket L housing (as shown by D_{L2}). If the demand upsurge is strong and rapid enough, it could effectively swamp the existing low-quality submarket in the short term. Landlords would find that they could raise rents dramatically (to MV_L^*) and still retain 100% occupancy. Tenants, on the other hand, would be forced to deal with the tight L submarket in one of several ways. They could decide that the steep rise in MV_L has narrowed the difference with MV_{M1}, so, for only a bit more money, they could occupy middle-quality housing, whereupon they would switch their demands to M (shown as D_{M2} in fig. 8.2). They could double up with another household or relatives so as to share rents of apartments in L. Or they could be relegated some extramarket housing options, such as squatting, shelters, or life on the streets.[13] (These problematic options are discussed at more length later in this chapter.)

In any event, the low-quality submarket would send a strong signal of large potential rates of return to owners in other submarkets. Builders of new housing potentially might be interested in supplying for this submarket (as we saw in chap. 6), but building codes preclude doing so at appropriate costs. So the supply response is left to those who may wish to downgrade existing dwellings. Inasmuch as typical dwellings in M earn superior rates of return from downgrading to L than do dwellings in H (as we saw in chap. 5), the bulk of the initial response would lie here. As some owners actively subdivide their erstwhile M-quality dwellings or passively let them physically decay via undermaintenance, the supply would fall in M and rise in L (as shown by S_{M2} and S_{L2}, respectively, in fig. 8.2).

This initial supply response would tend toward restoring the initial equilibrium market valuations and rates of return in L. Given the presumed nontrivial elasticity of medium-run supply in L, however, we would expect the new equilibrium to be characterized by both higher quantities (Q_{L2}) and market valuations (MV_{L2}) than originally. This means an unambiguous reduction in the well-being of lower-income renters occupying the L submarket (either through higher rents or doubling up), especially if erstwhile occupants of L are rendered homeless.

The downgrading response from M to L would (in conjunction with demand shift 2) upset equilibrium in submarket M, thereby setting the stage for another round of adjustments. These would be similar qualitatively, but smaller quantitatively, than the aforementioned adjustments in L. Higher market valuations in M would induce some households in M to adjust their housing consumption. Some may find that H housing now represents a more optimal budgetary allocation. Such substitutions by households initially in M would raise demand in the H submarket (shown as D_{H2} in fig. 8.2). At the same time the now-improved rates of return in M would induce some owners of H submarket housing to downgrade. Assuming that new construction was legal in the M submarket, builders would respond here as well. The amount of new construction relative to the conversion of existing H units to M will be directly related to the elasticity of the construction industry's medium-run supply function versus that of marginal conversion cost in the array of conversion

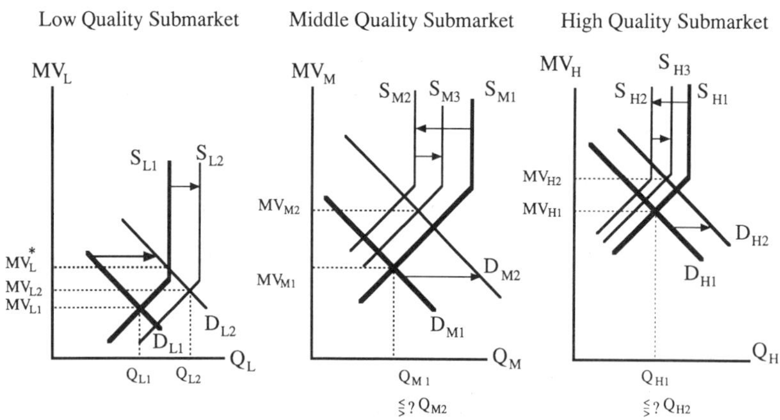

Figure 8.2. Downgrading submarket dynamics—increasing-demand scenario.

cost functions for existing units in H. The former is determined by the degree to which construction firms can increase output without concomitantly bidding up prices of construction inputs. The latter is a function of the types of units in H specified by age, structural features, and so forth which render them more or less easily malleable into M units (see chap. 5). The ultimate consequence would be an increase in supply of middle-quality housing back toward its initial level (S_{M3} in fig. 8.2),[14] and to the extent that downgrading occurred, a drop in supply in H (S_{H2} in fig. 8.2).

As before, this set of adjustments would tend toward reequilibrating the middle-quality submarket, but would have the opposite impact on the high-quality submarket. Presumably equilibrium would be restored there by an increase of H-quality new construction that would raise supply, as shown by S_{H3} in figure 8.2. As we saw in chapter 6, in higher-quality submarkets the predominant supply response is new construction, because it is the comparatively cheaper form. The resultant high elasticity of the medium-run supply would lead us to predict that MV_{H2} would be only modestly higher than MV_{H1}, and the stock in H would be substantially, but not wholly, replenished.

In summary to this increasing-demand scenario leading to downgrading, it can be seen that, once again, the stock has adjusted in light of altered relative rates of return available in the submarket array. Here rates of return initially were increased in L, so the stock there grew substantially (to S_{L2} in fig. 8.2) through downgrading from M. As such downgrading ensued (coupled with occupants of L moving up to M), rates of return were boosted in M, thus triggering a mix of downgrading and new construction responses that partially replenished the stock in M. Any downgrading from H generated a similar response. Thus the stock was "pulled" toward the L submarket, with partial replacements at higher-quality levels taking the form of new construction. As before, the target of the initial demand change was crucial in producing the direction of dynamic adjustment. If, for instance, the demand had risen in M instead of L, there would have been a net increase in the stock in M, some upgrading from L to M, some downgrading from H to M, and new construction in both M and H. An increase in demand for H would have led to no downgrading but rather to an upgrading response, as we shall see below, plus new construction.

The qualitative net results of the increasing-demand scenario are as follows. The stock and occupancy of low-quality stock rise. The change in middle- and high-quality stocks and occupancies cannot be predicted unambiguously without more detailed information about the conversion cost functions of the affected stock and the medium-run supply function of new construction. The equilibrium market valuation rises in all submarkets, but the precise degree cannot be determined without the aforementioned information about medium-run supply elasticities. Nevertheless, it is clear that housing prices overall are higher and housing consumers are worse off at the new equilibrium than initially.

The upshot of the two previous scenarios is that rather normal changes in the pattern of submarket demands (such as many cities have been experiencing) produce situations where it is rational (in terms of profitability) for owners to downgrade their dwellings from a higher-quality submarket to a lower. We have argued that, for properties in a given submarket, the fundamental precondition for downgrading is that (current or anticipated) rates of return in lower-quality submarkets exceed those in the given submarket. For owners of rental properties, this situation manifests itself when the prospects of lower rents coupled with lower-upkeep outlays in lower-quality submarkets produce a superior rate of return to that available in the current submarket. For homeowners, the situation is manifested by a change of ownership during a period when lower submarket valuations permit a unit to be occupied by owners with lower incomes than previously, whose incomes and weaker housing preferences make lower upkeep expenditures and a consequently lower-quality level more attractive overall than maintenance and its former quality level.[15] Concomitantly, continuing homeowners in the same submarkets with lowered rates of return will tend to become more pessimistic about the size of potential payoffs (in-market value) to continued home upkeep and reinvestments. In both situations, if the amounts and types of property upkeep and investments begin to fall consistently in net effect below the normal maintenance threshold appropriate to that dwelling and submarket, the dwelling will be downgraded. Additional complexities are created when the downgraded dwellings are spatially concentrated. The special features which arise from such neighborhood externalities are analyzed systematically in chapter 9.

Notice that in our theory it is the *relative* rates of return available across different submarkets that govern conversion supply dynamics, whereas it is these *and* rates of return in any housing submarket relative to those available in the nonhousing sectors that govern new construction. In the decreasing-demand scenario, the drop in demand in H leads to lower relative (and absolute) rates of return there. In the increasing-demand scenario, the higher demand in L leads to a lower *relative* rate of return in H. In either case, though, the existing stock gravitates away from H toward the submarket with the superior relative rate of return. From the perspective of a particular submarket, if relative rates of return are superior in lower-quality submarkets, some of its stock will be downgraded. If this downgrading (or demand upsurge) raises the absolute rate of return in this submarket compared to its original equilibrium level, and compared to returns from nonhousing investments, new construction will be induced so as to offset (at least partially) the downgrading.

Thus, in the context of our model it is not illuminating to talk simply about a "change in the demand for housing." As the above scenarios make clear, it is not only the *direction* of change but also its *point of initial impact* on the submarket array that crucially affect market response. We have seen that an increasing demand in the low-quality submarket, for example, draws the existing stock distribution toward it, inducing a sequential chain of downgrading *toward* it that, while largest in the "nearest," lower-middle quality submarket, can extend (though in progressively dampened magnitude) well up the quality spectrum. Yet a decrease in demand can also lead to systematic downgrading, in this case away *from* the submarket bearing the brunt of the decreased demand, and touching off subsequent downgrading from lower-quality submarkets whose magnitudes decline as the intersubmarket quality differential between the point of initial impact and the submarket in question increases. This is a clear demonstration of the efficacy of viewing urban housing markets from our segmented submarket perspective.

Increasing-Supply Scenario

A supply change conventionally believed to generate downgrading is an *excess of new construction,* that is, more dwellings built than net household formation. In the context of our model, it would indeed be probable that *if* such occurred it would lead to downgrading. To demonstrate, consider our hypothetical three-submarket urban area housing market and assume that an initial general equilibrium is upset by new, speculative construction of high-quality homes.

As shown by supply shift to S_{H2} in figure 8.3, these buildings would add to the stock of dwellings in the high-quality submarket, thereby raising vacancies and/or reducing market valuations for the older, presumably somewhat less competitive dwellings previously in this submarket. This submarket would reequilibrate through a combination of two simultaneous adjustments. Some households previously unwilling or unable to occupy high-quality housing would now do so, as shown by the increasing quantity demanded in H and a corresponding reduction in demand (shift to D_{M2}) in submarket M. Now because some of these "new" occupants have lower purchasing power[16] and/

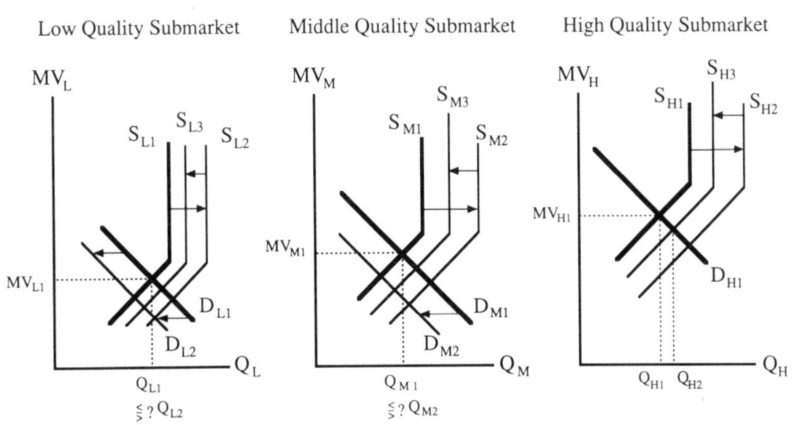

Figure 8.3. Downgrading submarket dynamics—increasing-supply scenario.

or because other owners in H perceive higher rates of return available in lower-quality submarkets, there would be some downgrading of dwellings from H to M (shift to S_{H3} and S_{M2}), as explained in the increasing-demand scenario above. As market valuations in H returned *toward* their initial levels, the "trading up" of households from M to H would be halted eventually and the new equilibrium would be reestablished.

As shown in figure 8.3, the foregoing changes would upset equilibrium in the middle-quality submarket, tending to depress market valuations and rates of return there. The consequence would be qualitatively similar to that just described: some "trading up" by households originally in the low-quality submarket L (shift to D_{L2}) and some downgrading of dwellings from M to L (shift to S_{M3} and S_{L2}). Corresponding results would then transpire due to the reduced rates of return in L: reductions in the stock of L via abandonment (shift to S_{L3}) until rates of return again reached minimally acceptable levels for "surviving" owners of units in L.

The overall medium-run result would be ambiguous net changes in the stocks and occupancies of all submarkets, with exact amounts depending on the relative magnitudes of new construction and gross downward conversions into each submarket versus gross downward conversion or abandonment out of it, and the cross-price elasticity of demand by households originally in it. The greater the net increase in stock and the reduction in demand, the lower is new equilibrium market valuation. Both supply and demand repercussions will be smaller the lower the quality of the submarket in question, that is, the more dissimilar in quality from the initial impact submarket it is.

Although the above supply-side scenario produces downgrading of dwellings within our model, this consequence only follows from a "pure" exogenous supply shock. Exogenous supply shocks do occur, as when construction technology or construction material costs exogenously change, but actual new construction is often a *response* to actual or imminent *demand* increases in one or more submarkets, for example, the result of increases in net household formations or real incomes or both. Where this is the case, pervasive downgrading will not occur since there is no initiating excess supply; but some *selective* downgrading may still occur as part of the complex of intersubmarket repercussions. Whether much "speculative" new construction occurs in the absence of both exogenous cost changes and either perceived or anticipated rising demands is empirically an open question.[17]

Decreasing-Supply Scenario

There are two scenarios involving *decreases* in supply that much popular and professional opinion credit with producing downgrading. Our belief is that the assumed linkages are either based on half-truths or represent situations that are comparatively rare in most urban housing markets. The initial, often-cited source of dwelling downgrading is structural aging, that is, it is alleged that aging necessarily means decay.[18] It seems to be the case that older dwellings do, on average, tend to demonstrate higher rates of deterioration and concomitant demands for repairs, replacements, and renovations. And, of course, by definition they will have a greater likelihood of possessing architectural and mechanical features that the contemporary market deems obsolete. All else equal, however, it has been observed that older dwellings elicit higher upkeep expenditures from their owners and that this upkeep, in a preponderance of cases, is sufficient to maintain these dwellings in their initial quality levels.[19] By implication, these older dwellings must still have the potential to provide rates of return commensurate with continuing them at the same quality level over time, even if the upkeep costs of doing so rise with age. To make the point differently, older dwellings do typically have higher normal maintenance thresholds than newer ones, but this alone does not imply that the higher requisite investments will necessarily not be forthcoming from their owners. Our model predicts that market conditions may well suggest superior rates of return in these submarkets for these dwellings if they are adequately maintained to remain there.[20]

A second conventional position is that raising the costs of supplying housing from the existing stock will lead to downgrading. A typical claim might involve increases in, for example, property taxes, insurance, utility rates, or dwelling maintenance and repair expenses. But in our model if any such costs increased proportionately in *all* submarkets, the optimal choice of submarket for maximizing rate of return may well remain unchanged for owners of existing units, as we saw in chapter 5.[21] Though it may now be more expensive to maintain any unit at its current quality level, it is now even more expensive to supply it at a higher level (the new upkeep cost there has risen also), and there is less savings involved in supplying it at a lower level for the same reason.

One possibility here could systematically induce some downgrading, however. Presumably, operating cost increases might raise reservation prices for individual owners, especially where the cost rises were believed to be temporary, thereby decreasing the market-period supply functions in each submarket.[22] Equilibrium market-period submarket valuations would thereby rise. Under these conditions, if demand elasticities were greater in higher- than in lower-quality submarkets, rates of return would become *relatively* more attractive in lower than in higher submarkets, thereby inducing net downgrading within the stock. The limited evidence reviewed by Quigley (1979) and Weicher (1979) suggests that tenants in lower-quality rental submarkets have only slightly lower housing price elasticities of demand than households in higher-quality owner submarkets.[23] Thus, while our model makes theoretically possible a downgrading spurred by across-the-board increases in housing costs, this possibility depends on very special empirical circumstances relating to expectations and relative demand elasticities. It is certainly not a guaranteed outcome.

8.1.2 Housing Upgrading and Gentrification

It is certainly not unusual for owners to invest sufficient funds in additions, alterations, modernizations, and other improvements so as to upgrade their dwellings to higher-quality submarkets. (Specific empirical evidence on this point is presented in chapter 13.) In the past decade, certain inner-city neighborhoods initially containing low- or moderate-quality dwellings have experienced such significant renovations on a spatially concentrated and dramatic scale—a dynamic popularly referred to as *gentrification.*[24] Not surprisingly, given our analysis above, we believe that housing renovation at both the individual dwelling and neighborhoodwide levels can be understood basically as responses to special demand conditions that indicate an increase in the potential rates of return if dwellings in the particular areas were upgraded.

To illustrate, consider again our hypothetical, three-submarket metopolitan housing market initially in general equilibrium, as shown in figure 8.4. Suppose that equilibrium is upset by dramatic improvements in the region's economic health such that numerous households originally housed in middle-quality submarket M have substantially higher real incomes. Presuming that many of these now better-off households would wish to improve on the quality of the housing they consume, this would result in an increased demand in submarket H and a correspondingly decreased demand in submarket M (shifts to D_{H2} and D_{M2}, respectively, in fig. 8.4). Market valuations and rates of return to owners in the H submarket would increase, vice versa in M.

These market signals would guide resulting supply adjustments. Supply would be added to H through both new construction and the upgrading of dwellings from M. Owners of rental dwellings in M would perceive the high rents and low vacancy rates implied by the foregoing demand increase in H, and some would beautify their units or add luxury features in an attempt to capture part of this stronger market. Dwellings with the lowest costs of up-

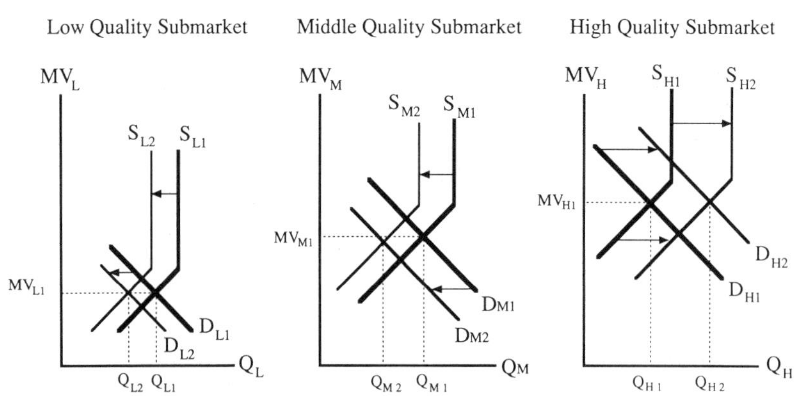

Figure 8.4. Upgrading submarket dynamics—increasing-demand scenario.

grading would be the ones most likely to be converted upward. Homeowners in M who now have higher incomes may choose to move from their original dwelling into one of H quality. Some, however, would likely have strong social-psychological attachments to their original home and neighborhood, and would prefer to improve their housing situation in place. Whether owners renovated in fact would depend on the particular structural transformation possibilities of their particular dwellings, prices of renovation inputs, and their ability to obtain requisite financing.[25] As renovations ensued from M to H, supply would grow in H and shrink in M (shifts to S_{H2} and S_{M2}, respectively). This adjustment would move toward reestablishing equilibrium in both submarkets.

However, we would predict that much of the initial demand increase in H was met with new construction because, as we saw in chapter 5, perfectly malleable new units are typically a cheaper form of supply here than modifying existing units. Thus there would be an increase in the number of dwellings relative to the number of households in the metropolitan area. As newly affluent households in M vacated their dwellings and market valuations accordingly fell, some households originally in L would find it advantageous and feasible to move up to M, thus stanching a bit the drop in M quantity demanded and helping to reestablish equilibrium there.[26]

This demand change (shift to D_{L2}) would necessitate further adjustments in low-quality submarket L to compensate for reduced rates of return there. This adjustment would likely take the form of abandonment (shift to S_{L2}).

Thus, to the extent that real-income increases produce a supply response of new construction instead of renovation of existing stock, the overall market will eventually adjust to the excess stock by accelerated abandonment. For any given demand increase that stimulates upgrading, abandonment will be minimized to the extent that (1) the initial demand increase does not come at the expense of a demand decrease in another, lower-quality submarket (i.e., it represents a net overall increase in demand); (2) the initial demand increase occurs in M as opposed to H (because more supply response in M will take the form of conversion instead of construction); and (3) the stock in M has characteristics such that the costs of upgrading are lower. Market valuations in the submarket affected by the initial demand increase will likely be inflated; those in other submarkets will be reduced. The change in the overall expense of housing compared to nonhousing goods cannot be predicted.

It is clear from our model that real household income increases can easily yield changes in the patterns of cross-submarket rates of return that induce a substantial amount of dwelling renovation, especially if new construction constitutes a smaller share of the response and renovation costs are not excessive. As shown in figure 8.4, the occupied stock in H has risen to Q_{H2} and the total stock to S_{H2}. Inasmuch as demand was assumed to decline in M (and eventually slightly in L as well), there was a corresponding supply decline to S_{M2} and S_{L2}, respectively. Of course, these results would have been modified if demand in *H* was assumed to rise as a result of, for example, an in-migration of upper-income households into the metropolitan area. In this case there would have been no resulting demand (and few, if any, supply) decreases in *M* or *L*. Most of the response in *H* would have taken the form of new construction instead of upgrading, because the relative differential in returns from upgrading from *M* to *H* would have been less.

What about gentrification? In the context of our model, gentrification can be viewed as the result of a confluence of several unique *demand*-shaping factors that over the past fifteen years or so have raised the potential rates of return from upgrading particular geographically concentrated subsets of the low-quality submarket's dwellings. In brief, these demand-shaping factors have been (1) demographic patterns producing unusually large numbers of childless, young-adult households; (2) economic changes leading to more multiple-worker households among this group, whose employment has been heavily located in the central business district; (3) increases in real commuting costs; and (4) growing preferences for the architectural features and style associated with particular sorts of older structures.

In concert, these demand factors have spatially focused the housing demands of such households, who normally would have occupied existing suburban middle- to upper-quality submarkets, upon particular centrally located neighborhoods having architecturally distinctive but often rundown structures, neighborhoods initially categorized as part of low- or sometimes moderate-quality submarkets. Either the "gentrifiers" personally arranged for the renovations after purchasing a dwelling or developers speculatively did so in anticipation of selling to such ultimate occupants. In either case, the parties involved perceived that the superiority of the dwellings' potential rates of return in a higher-quality submarket would justify the substantial upgrading renovation if such renovation became reflected in considerably higher market valuations, as would be likely to occur only if similar renovation were duplicated by large enough numbers to tilt the whole neighborhood character "upward."[27] But no such potential hordes of like-minded households existed, most of them only waiting for market clues as to *where* such anticipated cumulative renovations could best succeed. In such a climate a pioneering few speculative renovations could have disproportionate market influence in determining the location of gentrification activities. What makes gentrification especially noteworthy is that, because the demand has a definite *spatial* referent in already-developed central city locations, conversion of existing stock in these locations becomes the dominant supply mode. The normal superiority of new construction in supplying upper-quality submarkets is muted in this case by its high accompanying expense of having to demolish existing structures in these prime, central neighborhoods to make new construction possible.

In contrast to this demand-side impetus, we find no plausible recent changes on the supply side of urban housing markets that might explain either the large-scale or spatially concentrated pattern of gentrifying renovation. In principle, this might occur if the costs of dwelling upgrading were substantially reduced, given the context of strong neighborhood externalities (to be discussed in chap. 9). But short of the quite limited impact of a few modest public rehabilitation subsidy programs that we do not investigate here,[28] there does not seem to have been any sizable decrease in the real cost of renovation inputs over this period. Moreover, no cross-submarket relative variation in such costs of a magnitude anywhere sufficient to explain gentrification is evident. Nevertheless, our model is capable of handling such a theoretical possibility straightforwardly.

In summary, a given owner is encouraged to upgrade when the *relative* rates of return available from improving the dwelling to higher-quality submarkets are higher than those available both in the current submarket and in lower ones (and, of course, in nonresidential uses and abandonment). This typically occurs when demand falls in the given owner's submarket relative to that in higher-quality submarkets, in any combination of absolute or only relative changes. Whether upgrading will be profitable for any given market valuation differential among the submarkets depends on the costs of upgrading the unit in question in varying degrees. These normally will be higher (1) the older the unit, (2) the lower its initial quality, and (3) the larger the quality differential between origin and destination submarket. In aggregate, these features for the entire stock in any given submarket will help determine the total number of units that will be upgraded in different degrees in any particular scenario. Thus, once again, nonuniformities arising out of the idiosyncracies of the existing stock will generate nonuniform aggregate adjustments. Finally, potential upgrading as a response to higher *absolute* rates of return via increased demand will always compete with potential new construction to those submarket destinations for market shares. Generally, the higher the destination quality level, the greater the market share for new construction. In the case of inner-city gentrification, however, high land clearance and preparation costs associated with new construction but not with upgrading weaken the competitive power of the former and allow upgrading of the existing stock to dominate in these neighborhoods.

8.1.3 Combination of Upgrading and Downgrading

In the previous sections we sought to illustrate the basics of our model by considering highly simplified scenarios in which only one determinant of demand or supply was assumed to change and the pattern of ultimate stock conversions was unambiguous. Clearly, in most urban housing markets, several determinants of demand and supply in several submarkets are changing simultaneously and, perhaps, in countervailing directions. Our model can easily analyze such more complex scenarios, even though without precise information about the magnitudes and differential submarket locations of initial impact of the changes posited it is not always possible to derive unambiguous predictions. Nevertheless, even then the model highlights the key variables whose quantification is crucial for unambigous prediction. In particular, in emphasizing that even the *direction* of the outcomes of multiple exogenous shocks depends critically on the exact location of the initial impact of these shocks within the housing submarket complex, the model contributes an insight which is outside the boundaries of traditional housing market approaches. This nonuniform, multiple-shock scenario is exactly the kind of problem for which our segmented market, nonuniform intersubmarket repercussion emphasis was designed. Omission of such structural-functional features not only hampers proper analysis of such problems; it gives misleading answers by failing to appreciate that such concerns are important.

To illustrate, we consider three more complicated hypothetical situations—one in which unambiguous predictions about aggregate conversions can be made, and two others in which they cannot. For the first, consider what would occur if simultaneously there were upsurges in demand for both low-quality and high-quality submarkets. This could occur, for example, if the net in-migration stream for a metropolitan area consisted only of very poor and very rich households. Now, absolute rates of return in both *L* and *H* would rise, leaving owners in *M* with conflicting signals about which direction to convert. Since new construction is empirically effectively proscribed in *L* but not at all in *H*, and there is an asymmetry between upward and downward conversion costs for units in *M*, the primary result should be many downward conversions from *M* to *L*, since upward conversions, at higher real costs, would have to meet strong competition from new construction. However, those *M* units that are particularly malleable upward might well be able to compete with new construction there and so would be upgraded to *H*. Since both types of conversion would raise rates of return in *M* above their initial equilibrium levels because of the lesser *M* supply remaining, some new construction would be induced substantially to replenish the stock in *M*.[29] In the meantime, of course, new construction would be the major form of supply response in *H*. On balance, then, we can predict the following: (1) increases in the stocks of *L* and *H* through primarily downgrading and construction, respectively; (2) both considerable downgrading and lesser amount of upgrading from *M;* (3) new construction in *M* that returns the stock to or above its initial amount;[30] and (4) higher equilibrium market valuations in all submarkets, with corresponding decreases in the well-being of all housing consumers.

In the second scenario, suppose that simultaneously the demand in *L* rose (e.g., via in-migration of low-income households) but the market-period supply in *L* declined (e.g., due to large increases in operating costs related to, say, higher vandalism and insurance rates). These countervailing shocks would unambiguously increase the equilibrium market valuation in *L* (perhaps forcing some erstwhile *L* households to move to *M*, double up, or become homeless), but the net change in stock is unclear. If the *net* result were to *raise* the rate of return in *L*, downgrading would be induced from *M*, along with the intersubmarket downgrading dynamics noted above. If, on the other hand, rates of return declined in *L,* the stock would eventually decrease through upgrading out of *L,* or, more likely, through abandonment.

In the final scenario, suppose that simultaneously the demand for *H* rose (e.g., via in-migration of high-income households) and the market-period supply in *L* declined (e.g., via massive slum clearance, conversions to nonresidential uses, highway construction etc.). Then absolute rates of return would rise in both *L* and *H,* thereby creating conflicting conversion inducements for owners of dwellings in the *M* submarket. If the increase in D_H far outstripped the decline in S_L, *and* the costs of upward conversion from *M* were not too high to permit effective competition with new construction, some owners in *M* would upgrade. The opposite condition would tend to produce predominant downgrading. Clearly, different owners in *M* with dwellings possessing radically different conversion cost functions (especially their degree of upward-downward asymmetry) would tend to choose opposite conversion strategies. Thus, once again, although certain predictions hinge upon the specifics of the particular case, the model would predict (1) at least partial replenishment of the lost stock in *L* via downward conversion from *M,* but at higher equilibrium market valuations than previously; (2) conversions in both directions out of *M,* in relative numbers that depend on the relative size of the exogenous shocks in *L* and *H,* on the array of upward and downward conversion cost functions for the units in *M,* and on the strength of the inducement to new construction in *H;* (3) at least partial replenishment of the converted *M* dwellings with newly constructed *M* stock, but at somewhat higher market valuations; and (4) net increases in the *H* stock (through both conversion and new construction) and a higher equilibrium market valuation.

Thus, although qualitative predictions cannot always be made at this level of generality for scenarios in which an amalgam of upgrading and downgrading is produced, the model indicates that such predictions can be made once the initial shifts in demand and supply and the relevant conversion cost functions (i.e., the net changes in actual and prospective rates of return) are precisely located and quantified. This holds true for more complex scenarios as well.

8.1.4 Filtering Revisited

Now that the intersubmarket repercussions that lie at the heart of our model have been illustrated, a clearer perspective can be gained on the often-used term *filtering.* Unfortunately, the literature contains almost as many distinct definitions of filtering as analysts who employ the term.[31] It has been seen as everything from changes in dwellings' market valuations, to shifts of households across dwelling qualities, to changes in dwelling qualities. Fortunately, our model provides an encompassing framework within which *all* of the aforementioned repercussions can be comprehended and interrelated.

We do not espouse a particular, narrow definition of filtering. Indeed, given its ambiguity we question whether there remains much point in continuing its use. Rather, we note that our approach provides a straightforward means of identifying the conditions under which the various market valuation changes, household shifts across qualities, and dwelling-quality changes loosely associated with filtering will occur. While some of these tend to occur together, this is by no means assumed, and conditions can easily be specified under which the three kinds will diverge markedly. This is a further, and telling, reason for either attempting to pinpoint the definition of filtering or dropping its use altogether.

Submarket equilibrium market valuations are established through the interaction of market-period and medium-run demand and supply conditions and will change when any of the determinants of any of these functions are altered. As illustrated in the foregoing scenarios, when market valuations fall in a given submarket, some households previously occupying a lower-quality submarket may indeed be able to "move up" in quality; but also some households in *higher*-quality submarkets whose market valuations have risen may shift *downward* in quality. Falling market valuations will also induce some owners in this submarket to change the quality of their dwelling either upward or downward so as to improve rates of return, but these conversions may be either upward or downward. These medium-run demand and supply responses in any one submarket upset the equilibrium in other, especially near-quality submarkets, thereby triggering further "filtering-like" repercussions—market valuation adjustments, household moves, and dwelling-quality conversions. The adjustments thus spread throughout the submarket complex, in successively dampened degree with increasing substitutional remoteness, like the ripples in a pond radiating from the spot where the initial disequilibrating impact occurred. But the complex of such intersubmarket adjustments will often *simultaneously* show rising *and* falling market valuations, rising *and* falling dwelling-quality changes, and rising *and* falling household-quality shifts. The single directions of outcome loosely posited by the filtering concept are often violated in actual practice.

One frequent use of the term *filtering* in the literature is particularly noteworthy—price filtering, or the occupancy of relatively better-quality dwellings by households with constant real incomes.[32] Above we have considered circumstances that can reduce a submarket's market valuation and thereby induce a "moving up" of some households from a lower-quality submarket. It is a component of many dynamic scenarios, but not a uniquely inevitable one. For example, even aging units need not pass downward to lower-income households when (1) market conditions are generally tight—households may have to *lower* their housing standards; or when (2) such aging units become upgraded—they become occupied by *higher-income* households, as in the gentrification scenario above. This literature often goes beyond describing its theoretical *possibility* to argue both that it is in fact *inevitable* and that its deliberate acceleration is *desirable*. Indeed, many have suggested that our national housing policy should be centered on this goal, that in fact new construction should be seen primarily as an implement to bring this about. So, for example, substantial new construction in high-quality submarkets should be used as a policy tool for forcing the improvement of housing standards of lower-income groups by stimulating precisely this linked chain of downward price filtering. This important claim is the subject of a detailed policy analysis which we perform in chapter 11. We note at this point simply that we are skeptical of its alleged attractiveness.

8.2 Homelessness, Rent Burdens, and Housing Abandonment

It is easy to extend our analysis to consider the most prevalent and widely publicized triad of problems facing contemporary urban housing markets. At first glance, it might appear that homelessness, households paying excessive portions of their incomes toward rent, and the abandonment of usable dwellings could not all logically occur simultaneously in the same city. If so much unmet demand exists, and if housing is so "expensive," should there not be profit to be made from supplying more housing?

Such an impressionistic view fails to recognize the core that unites these problems into a coherent picture of woe: insufficient household purchasing power in the face of high market valuations of even minimally decent housing. Homelessness is fundamentally the result of people who are without enough money for rent to bid even the lowest market-period reservation price of any private dwelling owner (and still have enough left over for bare necessities), or to promise a high enough rate of return to induce substantial numbers of higher-quality units to be downgraded in the medium run, at a time when government policies are generating neither subsidized new construction nor rent subsidies in amounts necessary to meet this private shortfall.[33] Households with somewhat higher purchasing power can afford housing, though it is likely to be of very low quality. But such occupancy often requires paying a "burdensome" fraction of a household's budget, typically defined as 30% or more. Though purchases of other necessities may therefore be shortchanged, a household is capable of choosing among at least some gradations of housing quality, whereas the alternatives—living on the street or sharing quarters with another household—represent such radical declines in living standards as to justify the choice of the burdensome situation. Again, pervasive experience of such conditions means that government programs to subsidize such burdened households are inadequate or absent.

Although the problems of both homelessness and rent burdens thus far have been phrased in terms of the individual household's purchasing power, this begs the question of how far a dollar goes when expended on housing. Clearly, a given absolute income could be made to stretch farther if the equilibrium market valuations in the lower-quality housing submarkets were relatively lower.[34]

What makes the equilibrium market valuation in a submarket higher? Any factor which reduces supply and/or increases demand in this submarket. This chapter has provided several scenarios which potentially produce this result for the low-quality (*L*) submarket. Three particular scenarios, however, offer special empirical relevance for the contemporary urban scene: (1) increasing demand for *L;* (2) decreasing the stock of *L;* and (3) increasing the operating costs in *L*. Each is considered in turn.

As households who originally consumed middle-quality housing find themselves unemployed or underemployed (say, e.g., during the 1982–83 recession), or as various governmental housing or other subsidy programs for low-income households are decreased or ended, effected households are forced to switch occupancy to lower-quality, less-expensive submarkets. If these submarkets, in turn, are not being vacated at the same rate by upwardly mobile households, the net result will be an increase in demand in the lowest-quality submarkets (and a corresponding decrease in demand in the somewhat-higher-quality and the middle-quality ones). The consequent fillip in the rents of the former forces the original residents of these submarkets into even more burdensome rent outlays and lower housing qualities, or, what is worse, for those who could least afford the initial rent levels, into doubling up or actual homelessness. Recent trends in the purchasing power of many urban residents are suggestive in this regard. From 1974 to 1983 the number of renters earning under $10,000 annually (in constant 1983 dollars) rose from 8.9 million to 11.9 million. It has been projected that by 1993 the number will be 14.3 million (Clay 1987). Some of this demand-induced rent inflation at the low-quality end may be only a short-run phenomenon which persists until medium-run supply adjustments (like downgrading) can catch up. The extent to which this will occur depends on supply considerations. But the considerable duration of the affordability problem is not encouraging in this regard.

A second factor here is the rising opportunity cost of the dwelling and land parcel it occupies. In many cities the rates of return from continuing to supply housing to the lower-quality rental submarkets have shrunken in comparison with those prospectively available from upgrading the units to higher submarkets, or converting them to nonresidential uses (e.g., offices or stores), or demolishing the structures and replacing them with "higher," more-intensive residential uses (e.g., high-quality condominiums or high-rise luxury apartments). In metropolitan areas where the competition for central city land by high-income households and nonresidential users has grown most intense, the loss of lower-quality, lower-rent stock to alternative uses appears to be most severe. It has been estimated that the stock of "affordable" apartments[35] fell from 10.8 million to 8.8 million units from 1974 to 1983, and that it will fall an additional 1.3 million units by 1993 (Clay 1987:4). In terms of our model, this is represented by a shift leftward of the entire market-period *L* supply function, including its vertical segment. The accompanying increase in the market valuation of the remaining *L* stock serves to exacerbate the problems of homelessness and rent burdens, as before. Again, part of this stock reduction may be recouped over time, depending on the degree to which rates of return to nonhousing investments and in higher-quality submarkets decline and those in the low-quality submarkets rise in response to these trends. But yet another factor suggests that the latter rise will be minimal.

Real operating costs have been rising dramatically, especially in the lower-quality submarkets. Property taxes, utility rates, maintenance input prices, insurance premiums, and extraordinary repairs resulting from arson, vandalism, and "problem tenants" have combined to boost the reservation prices of many dwelling owners markedly.[36] From 1974 to 1984 real operating expenses have risen on average by 18%, whereas real rents have risen only 10% (National Association of Homebuilders 1986). In terms of our model, this means that the upsloping portion of the market-period supply function in *L* (but not necessarily the vertical segment) has shifted to the left. The resultant long-term increase in rents is thus a reflection of *lower* rates of return induced by higher costs, not of favorable returns that will eventually elicit medium-run supply adjustments to replenish the stock in *L*.

Finally, it is the further consideration of these operating costs of low-quality housing that brings into focus the remaining piece of the urban housing problem puzzle—abandonment. Even if, because of high rents, owners are receiving high gross returns in absolute terms, if operating costs are also high absolutely, the *net* returns may be negative. If, in addition, net returns are negative for all upgrading, demolition, and land-use conversion options, the loss-minimizing strategy will be abandonment. Of course as owners pursue this option, the available housing stock declines and the equilibrium rents are driven still higher.[37]

Thus our model makes it clear that homelessness, rent burdens, and abandonment are different manifestations of a confluence of demand-side and supply-side phenomena which have inflated rents yet deflated rates of return (both relatively and absolutely) in the lower-quality submarkets. The results are staggering. Even conservative estimates place the number of individuals who are homeless at any one time at over a quarter of a million. In 1983, 78% of renters who earned less than $7,000 paid over 35% of their income as rent. On average this group paid over 60% of their income as rent (National Association of Homebuilders 1986:10). Estimates of current abandonment rates are imprecise, but are likely above 100,000 dwellings annually.

8.3 Conclusion

In this chapter we have illustrated the power, applicability, and intuitive appeal of our approach to modeling urban housing markets. Our approach focuses on adjustments across the array of housing-quality submarkets guided by differential degrees of demand-side and supply-side substitutability and by prospective relative rates of return. Through a simplified graphic portrayal of the model we illuminated stylistically the mechanics of crucial housing market phenomena like slum formation, rent burdens, and homelessness by showing the pattern of dynamic, repercussive adjustments that ensue from changes in demand or supply in a particular submarket and the ultimate consequences that result across the entire array of quality submarkets.

We have shown how current or anticipated changes in the cross-submarket pattern of demands alters the array of potential rates of return to new construction and conversion of existing units, and how these induce changes in new construction and actions by owners of existing dwellings to alter their quality. We have also shown how particular exogenous supply-side changes can also generate such shifts. Weakened demands for housing of a given quality, for example, will tend to decrease new construction there relative to other submarkets and will encourage some owners in this submarket to upgrade, some to downgrade their dwellings in order to improve their rates of return. These initial adjustments, in turn, will tend to depress rates of return in submarkets into which shifted new construction and/or net conversions occur, thereby triggering subsequent selective upgrading and downgrading from them. Conversely, strengthened demands in a given quality submarket will induce additional new construction there, together with some owners in lower- and higher-quality submarkets upgrading and downgrading their dwellings to that submarket to capture some of the newly higher rates of return. These adjustments, in turn, improve rates of return in the submarkets from which the units converted, thereby encouraging more upgrading/downgrading from still lower/higher-quality ranges and, subsequently but competitively, new construction as selective replenishments. Whether impelled by increasing or decreasing exogenous forces, and whether of demand or supply, induced new construction and conversion make the housing stock gravitate toward the submarkets whose rates of return were made relatively higher by these exogenous shocks.

This is the fundamental systemic *regularity* in the dynamics of urban housing submarkets. But there are two important *nonuniformities* in this systematic pattern. The first concerns the differential magnitudes of adjustment depending on the quality differential (i.e., the degree of demand and supply substitutability) between the initially disequilibrated submarket and any other particular one in question, and on the direction of stock conversion. Any given shock that upsets general equilibrium in a particular submarket will produce progressively dampened consequences in submarkets of progressively higher or lower quality. And adjustments encouraging upgrading are likely to be smaller, ceteris paribus, than those encouraging downgrading, given the asymmetries of the two conversion cost functions.

The second nonuniformity concerns the extent to which submarket signals generate responses through conversions of existing dwellings as opposed to the construction of new ones. This will depend on conversion versus building costs and potential legal restrictions. For example, favorable rates of return in higher-quality submarkets will more likely generate a predominantly new construction response, given the comparative technological difficulties and higher costs associated with radically renovating existing, lower-quality structures. In certain cases where the existing structures have distinctive historical architectural features and centralized locational advantages, however, the cost comparison favors upgrading over construction. Favorable rates of return in lower-quality submarkets will, on the contrary, produce an almost exclusively downgrading response, since building codes, zoning restraints, and other legal strictures effectively boost minimal construction costs to the point where they are uncompetitive in these submarkets.

Our emphasis on *systematic nonuniformities* in the responses of urban housing submarkets also yields important implications for the well-being of various household groups, defined by either socioeconomic status or location. The less elastic the aggregate, medium-run supply response for a submarket, the more any (exogenous or endogenously induced) increase in demand there will result in higher equilibrium market valuations, with the resultant decrease in the welfare of those who normally choose that quality level. Such elasticities are likely to be especially low in lower-quality submarkets, where new construction is effectively proscribed. At the spatial level, abandonments produced by various scenarios are likely to be concentrated in neighborhoods comprised of lower-quality dwellings occupied by lower-income households. Similar welfare concerns are raised by dynamics spawning new construction with the concomitant downgrading of older stock, which penalizes existing neighborhoods with decay while encouraging the birth of new (typically suburban) developments. These implications of our model for neighborhood dynamics are the subject of the next chapter.

Our focus on dual-mode supply decisions guided by relative rates of return also informs the analysis of the tripartite contemporary problems of homelessness, rent burdens, and abandonment. The varied costs of supplying even inferior-quality urban housing set a floor level of market valuations that provide the requisite rates of return for these owners to remain in the market, as opposed to shifting their resources to nonhousing investments. Unfortunately, these market valuations are high in real terms when contrasted to what many can afford to pay. Those with the most limited means do not possess sufficient funds to bid on even the cheapest accommodations and hence are relegated to homelessness. Others opt to occupy a dwelling in the market, but do so only by allocating a burdensome fraction of their budget for this purpose. Ironically, the existence of an unhoused group and of others struggling to meet their rent payments is not always translated into acceptable rates of return for dwelling owners or builders. Indeed, even in contexts where there would appear to be an urgent "need" for housing, the costs of operating even minimal-quality dwellings may be so excessive that structural abandonment is the only rational means by which losses can be minimized.

Notes

1. Of course this is not the only means by which downgrading can occur; subdividing is another prime vehicle.

2. In our analysis we restrict ourselves to consideration of forces that initiate with the demanders or suppliers of housing. Other exogenous forces undoubtedly have potent impacts on urban housing markets and provide several contexts for downgrading (Grigsby et al. 1987). For instance, changes in the intrametropolitan location of jobs, in local public sector tax/service packages, in local land-use externalities, or in the technology of particular dwelling mechanical systems could, by definition, render dwellings in particular submarkets obsolete or of lower quality and necessitate their recategorization into a lower submarket. Such possibilities are omitted from the current discussion because they are not initiated by behaviors in the housing market but rather create downgrading tautologically.

3. None of the graphic shifts portrayed in this or succeeding figures is necessarily drawn to represent reasonable scales; they are meant to suggest qualitative dynamics only.

4. Some may now decide that L is the most profitable submarket, whereupon they actively downgrade by, e.g., subdividing units.

5. This "budgetary constraint" type of rationale has been most frequently cited in the literature; see Muth 1969:117; Grigsby and Rosenburg 1975:198–99; Ahlbrandt and Brophy 1975:5; Public Affairs Counseling 1975:12; Leven et al. 1976:38–39.

6. For a formal microeconomic theory of the homeowner's reinvestment decision and supporting evidence, see Galster 1987.

7. Note that this does not increase the entire demand function in H. Implicitly any D_H already embodies those households who switch to H from other submarkets or away from H to other submarkets, as its price (MV_H) changes relative to the prices of the other submarkets.

8. We have little evidence on the cross-price elasticity of demand for households in various income ranges, but see ch. 14 below.

9. Another possibility as market valuations fall is a conversion to nonresidential use.

10. A less extreme conversion would be to nonresidential use.

11. This removal often takes the form of boarding up the dwelling or, it has been alleged, of intentionally setting it on fire so as to collect insurance. Usually the structure is not demolished or the land cleared by the owner.

12. S_{L3} need not necessarily be greater than S_{L1}; it depends on the conversion costs and operating costs in L.

13. Conceivably some might even move out of the given metropolitan area.

14. Perhaps even greater than S_{M1}.

15. Or, similarly, if the same homeowner demonstrates a major change in preferences, income, or expectations, and remains in the dwelling.

16. And thus financial resources to devote to home repairs and maintenance; see Galster 1987.

17. Undoubtedly, builders have made mistakes and "overbuilt" in response to particular demand-generated signals, but we do not view such instances as endemic or as a prevalent, nontrivial cause of systematic downgrading in most housing markets.

18. See, e.g., Muth 1968:98; Public Affairs Counseling 1975:12.

19. For a review of the empirical evidence in this regard, see Galster 1987: ch. 9.

20. For a somewhat different analysis that reaches a similar conclusion, see Grigsby et al. 1987: ch. 6.

21. The one exception is owners who now earn insufficient returns to keep them in the market, whereupon they abandon their units.

22. But only the upsloping segment of the function would shift to the left; the vertical segment representing the total stock would not be affected.

23. Somewhat more complicated intersubmarket dynamics would occur if the hypothetical change affected costs (and hence rates of return) in only a selected subset of the submarkets. In such a case, only if the net effect was an initial increase in relative returns in lower-quality submarkets would the result be downgrading. We do not believe that such cases occur to any significant extent.

24. For detailed examinations of the extent, nature, origins, and consequences of gentrification, see Laska and Spain 1980; Palen and London 1984.

25. For a comprehensive theoretical and empirical analysis of upgrading by incumbent homeowners, see Galster 1987.

26. Such reequilibration in *M* may eventually require some downgrading from *M* to *L*, especially if most of the supply response in *H* took the form of new construction.

27. For more discussion of neighborhood inertia and change, see ch. 9.

28. For a review and evaluation of these programs, see Varady 1986.

29. The *M* stock might actually be overreplenished, since spillover demand to *M* due to the rising prices in both *L* and *H* would raise rates of return enough to support a net expansion of the stock there.

30. A quantification to this prediction is in order. The generally upward pressure on building resources due to new construction in *H* and *M* could, depending on long-run supply conditions, raise construction costs and, thereby, the equilibrium average level of housing market valuations. This could decrease average housing consumption and thereby, via complicated chains of doubling up and smaller numbers of households, *lower* the stock in *M* below its initial size.

31. For a review of these alternative definitions, see Weicher and Thibodeau 1988; Grigsby et al. 1987.

32. Ratcliff 1949:321–22; Ahlbrandt and Brophy 1975:9; Grigsby 1963:97; Lowry 1960:363; Leven et al. 1976:46.

33. We recognize that many homeless may be so mentally debilitated or chemically dependent that they cannot successfully search for, acquire, and/or regularly meet rental obligations associated with occupying housing (Keyes 1988). Our model cannot, of course, explain their plight. We also recognize that various governmental housing problems could exacerbate problems faced by low-income tenants and the homeless; see chs. 9–12 below.

34. We are abstracting here from issues concerning the separation of rental from ownership markets, assuming easy substitutability across the two. But important institutional constraints and incentives in fact exist, involving tax advantages, etc. These can create barriers or distorted incentives in supplying housing "to meet public needs."

For example, the substantial individual income tax gains from occupying condominium rather than rental units has created strong incentives to convert rental units into condominiums. This has contributed significantly to the drying up of housing supply to lower-income households in many metropolitan area markets, who depend overwhelmingly on the rental market.

35. Affordable is defined as under $250 rent monthly, the amount someone with a $10,000 income could occupy without rent burden.

36. For a fuller discussion of these issues, see Sternlieb 1966; Stegman 1972; Sternlieb and Burchell 1973; Grigsby and Rosenburg 1975; Clay 1987.

37. Of course, it should not be inferred from the foregoing that the only important cause of abandonment has been rising costs of supplying housing in modest-quality submarkets. On the contrary, as the graphic expositions above made plain, a wide variety of shifts in the cross-submarket pattern of demands can lead to abandonment. Primary suspects in this regard for many of the older, declining industrial cities would be reductions in the real incomes of many erstwhile middle- and working-class households and a net out-migration of many nonpoor households.

9 Neighborhood Decline

Neighborhoods have come increasingly to the attention of urban students both as a vital arena where critical urban problems are generated and played out and as an analytical unit for the understanding of these problems. We have the evidence before our eyes that some neighborhoods decline, sometimes so far that they become like battlefields, littered with bitter, wasted lives and physical structures—both abandoned, wrecked, and burned out. And more—that the waste does not stay in one place: it travels across the city. What causes this physical destruction? What can stop it?

This chapter is an attempt to throw some light on neighborhood decline, primarily by placing it within the larger context of the working of the urban housing market. We emphasize first that neighborhood decline does not arise solely from forces emanating from *within* a neighborhood, but also from those impinging upon it from *without* that involve dynamics of the metropolitan area's array of submarkets. We emphasize second that decline is not an unusual, traumatic event that happens *to* a city; rather, it is generally an integral aspect of a continuing process that is part *of* the city.[1] When viewed in this context, not all decline is socially undesirable. Indeed, much of it is a conveyance for social advantage. But some decline is dysfunction, and some, which would be useful if reasonably bounded, is carried to excess and results in serious waste of human and property resources. We try to distinguish the advantageous normal process from its dysfunctional counterpart, explain the source of the latter, and structure the problem for a productive discussion of public policy in the neighborhood arena.

This chapter also rectifies the scant attention paid in the theory chapters 4–6 to location-specific aspects of housing demand and supply. Specifically, here we focus on spatial externalities—both physical and social—that arise at neighborhood scale, and consider how they affect households' residential choices and welfare, and the supply behaviors of owners of existing dwellings as well as builders of new ones, and thereby, via both types of behavior, the process of neighborhood change.

The plan of the chapter is as follows. In section 9.1 we show how the concept and reality of neighborhood arise out of the provision of urban housing services and examine how neighborhoods influence the welfare of the urban population. In section 9.2 we relate neighborhood—as environment and actor—explicitly to important aspects of the urban housing sector and explain the mutually causal connections between submarkets and neighborhoods. Section 9.3 elaborates neighborhood changes as explicit aspects of the adjustment process of the housing submarket complex and discusses in more detail how the system furnishes housing for the urban poor. Scenarios involving metropolitan changes in population and in income distribution are described. This discussion of neighborhood change is specialized in section 9.4 to consider decline and the various components that comprise it. In section 9.5, distinctions between socially advantageous and disadvantageous forms of decline as an adjustment process are examined, and both the character and some contributing sources of the latter are discussed. Section 9.6 attempts to derive from the foregoing recommendations for appropriate public policy action. We argue that the goal should not be to halt all neighborhood decline, but rather to reduce inefficient dynamics of cumulative decline and encourage where possible housing upgrading in place.

9.1 Housing, Neighborhood, and Welfare

One of the most distinguishing features of *urban* housing is that it spatially *localizes* the consumption of housing services and other public and private commodities. A considerable amount of time must be spent in a single location at which the behaviors, attitudes, and values of others living, working, and investing nearby have significant consequences for individual residents (households) and property owners. Residents likely engage directly in various sorts of social, educational, economic interchanges with this array of other actors operating within the local area. But many behaviors of these other actors indirectly affect residents and owners whether they are actively involved in the particular transaction or not. The consequences which result from this sort of interaction may be termed *neighborhood externalities*. Their form can be aesthetic (e.g., the renovation or upkeep or mode of use of a nearby house, or its conversion into an office), social (the identity, social habits, and values of other residents in the neighborhood, e.g., their age, status, race, or ethnic membership), interventional (crime rate), public goods (shared public education, sanitary services, parks and other local government services), and commercial (colocational presence of private production and retail activities). Their impacts are sometimes good, sometimes bad.

Whether the form of the localized interaction be direct or indirect, the result is the same for those remaining in the area—accommodation. Thus, casual social encounters can deepen into friendships by repetition; shopping and recreational habits of importance can develop; a distinct character of public services can be absorbed and, eventually, become "needed." Perhaps most important of all, the style and substance of one's own attitudes, values, and behavior adapt with coherence to dependable expectations about the behaviors, values, and attitudes of others in the neighborhood. Both children and adults, but especially children, become socialized within the arena of repeated, customary, and dependable interactions with others. For children such socialization is especially deep and long lasting, forming a basis for fundamental lifetime personality development (Keller 1968; Suttles 1972; Hunter 1974, 1979; Hallman 1984).

Thus, *neighborhood* is the result of the stationary nature of the residential function that not only itself comprises a varied repertoire but acts as a selective magnet to the spatial provision of private and public goods. It not only anchors and shapes behavior as a "consumer" and as a "producer" of both market and nonmarket goods, but also creates, maintains, deepens, and sometimes modifies values and attitudes.

Because urban housing units are spatially fixed within a dense, multidimensional milieu, a household establishing itself in one buys or rents not only the physical structure with its sheltering services but also the location—the neighborhood. This comprises the people, with their local social interactions and networks (including positive socializing and criminal activity, among other aspects); the other housing structures and lots, and their upkeep and modes of use; the public infrastructure (streets, parks, lights, sanitation, etc.) and other spatially distinctive local public goods (public education, police and fire protection, etc.); the nearby sellers of private goods; and the natural environment. The value of different "housing packages" to the household is substantially affected by the neighborhood components of the packages, both because the physio-socio-politico-economic character of the closely surrounding area matters in itself by shaping choice options, attitudes, and active and passive receipt of experiences and also because different neighborhoods generally differ variously in performing these functions.

How important to a household's welfare is the neighborhood component of the housing package? The physical environment dimension can influence life, death, and morbidity via illness and security of person and property through fire hazard; the demographic dimension can influence security of person and property through crime, and some of the deepest human relationships via friendships; the political dimension can promote or retard the health and life chances of household members via education, health care, and so forth; the economic dimension can influence job selection, variety of consumption, and the level of real income via availability, accessibility, and prices of private goods and employment opportunities. Finally, neighborhood is the matrix of some of the most important values and attitudes of the individual and, as such, is at the base of much of the individual's valuation of nonneighborhood commodities and opportunities and of the degree of his or her own well-being.

The neighborhood is crucial to the property supplier as well as to the household demander. The capital values or rents owners of existing dwellings can hope to obtain depend only partly on their intrinsic characteristics; often the larger part depends on the current and expected future flow of externalities which the neighborhood provides. These prospective returns influence, in turn, the level of dwelling reinvestments these owners undertake for their properties. Realizing the sensitivity of the value of existing units to such location-specific factors, builders of new dwellings carefully choose where construction will take place. In sum, neighborhood conditions affect both conversion and new construction supplies and, in turn, are themselves affected by the actions of suppliers. These mutually causal interactions create significant capital gains for some property owners and significant losses to others.

So neighborhood is significant, and changes in the quality of a neighborhood can considerably influence for better or worse the well-being of its inhabitants and its property owners. This gives relevance to our enquiry concerning the nature, course, and consequences of neighborhood decline.

9.2 Neighborhoods and the Housing Submarket Complex

Neighborhoods and housing-quality submarkets have mutually causal connections between them. On the one hand, housing quality depends on neighborhood because the myriad attributes of the neighborhood are components of the housing package that help constitute the quality of the package. As we have seen, a dwelling's appropriate submarket can be designated only after its particular neighborhood context has been identified. Furthermore, alterations in the physical dwelling may be induced by owner expectations that are molded chiefly as a result of particular occurrences in the neighborhood. In the other direction, the neighborhood character depends on the character of individual houses. The intentional conversion of several dwellings might well change the physical character of the neighborhood, the effect being greater the larger the number of conversions and the more radical the change involved in them. As home seekers, investors, retailers, and other neighborhood actors adjust their behavior in light of these physical changes, other dimensions of the neighborhood will be altered subsequently (Grigsby et al. 1987).

Of course other causal factors impinge on both neighborhoods and housing quality. Housing-quality conversions, for example, may be stimulated by metropolitan-wide changes in income or demographic profiles which affect an entire submarket's demand, independent of local neighborhood conditions. Conversely, neighborhood changes can be induced, for example, by a deterioration of public services or by a local pollution source, independent of the behaviors of dwelling owners in the area. Thus, neighborhoods and housing-quality submarkets are related but not synonymous.

As we have seen in chapter 3, the approximately hierarchical structure of housing quality suggests that the housing market complex can be treated as a sequence of quality submarkets, each submarket comprising housing units concentrated in a narrow interval of quality levels and behaving like the market for a normal good having variously related substitutes. Neighborhood characteristics go a long way to determine which housing units will cluster in the same submarkets. Indeed, the empirical work we describe in chapter 13, and that of Kain and Quigley (1975), Segal (1979), Birch et al. (1979),

Grether and Mieszkowski (1980), and Galster (1982, 1987: chs. 5, 6) attest to the important contributions that neighborhood makes to housing quality and value. Thus, neighborhood conditions contribute tautologically to dwelling quality and hence to its submarket designation.

Neighborhood conditions contribute in more behavioral ways as well. They significantly influence the pattern of demand and supply, and the very configuration of types of housing units, in different spatial areas. On the demand side, the strong household desire for coherency in style of life translates into preferences for coherency in the mix of the several components that make up housing packages—the structural and neighborhood attributes. So the various structure components not only complement each other in important respects, but complement the neighborhood characteristics as well. Households are particularly sensitive to such characteristics as socioeconomic status, racial composition, and housing conditions of the surrounding area, a sensitivity which represents signals of real relevance to builders and property owners.

The nature of these neighborhood preferences—and aversions—deserves a more systematic elaboration. In discussing housing packages we have referred to both attribute mix and an overall quality level. How well does the concept of *overall quality* fit that of *neighborhood*? A critical implication of the concept of overall quality is that households generally should *prefer* higher-quality packages to lower-quality, regardless of their *actual choice* among packages. Some neighborhood attributes appear to have this character in large measure—more attractive is consensual, whatever specific preferences are. The presence of parks, good public schools, effective sanitation, and fire protection are some of these. Others depend more on specifics of preference, the most notable being the identity of living styles of the residents. Associated with this are zoning regulations, *style* of police protection, presence/accessibility of facilities dispensing welfare services, and others. The concept of neighborhood attractiveness may not be very closely related to that of neighborhood quality.

Let us examine neighborhood attractiveness more systematically. We divide neighborhood attributes into objective and subjective quality categories. Objective quality attributes are those which command approximately consensual ranking. They include many kinds of government-provided services, especially those not de facto related to the socioeconomic characteristics and lifestyles of its neighborhood population. Also included are certain inherent attractions of the physical environment, like air quality, panoramic views, conditions of structures, and aesthetic character of land use and vegetation.

Subjective quality characteristics are most notably the identity and lifestyles of the resident population, land-use mix, patterns of building, architectural style, government-provided services related to demographic identities, and socioeconomic status. Partly derived from some of the above characteristics are such expected responses from the resident populations as acceptance, moral approval, and friendliness.

Objective quality features would generate rather uniform preferences concerning neighborhoods among the overall urban population. All households would be willing to pay more for objectively "better" than for objectively less good neighborhoods. In the competition for location, higher bid prices would win the better neighborhoods, reflecting a confirmation of higher income and/or higher preference intensity for neighborhood quality (relative to other commodities, all competing for the household's limited purchasing power). The best neighborhoods would thus be inhabited by a set of households with combinations like very high income/resident intensity of preferences for neighborhood quality, through high income/moderate preference intensity combinations, to lower income/high preference intensity combinations. The result in the best neighborhoods, and thereby down the objective quality ladder in all neighborhoods, would be nontrivial forms of demographic heterogeneity, and thus, through the supply response to their housing preferences, nontrivial forms of housing structure heterogeneity as well (abstracting from the respect in which "objective" neighborhood features are endogenously linked to neighborhood demography).

But these locational tendencies are offset by the presence of subjective quality features as well. People are attracted to neighborhoods also because of features which appeal to some households but not to others. Any given mix of subjective quality features will be responded to in quite different ways by the overall population. Each household's net evaluation of any given neighborhood will depend on both the neighborhood's objective and subjective features. Therefore, two households with the same income and preference intensity for (objective) neighborhood quality may have very different evaluations of a given neighborhood, or of a comparison between two neighborhoods, if the subjective features of the neighborhoods in question appeal to them differently. So preference heterogeneity with respect to subjective attributes can substantially modify the bid-price ranking of neighborhoods derived solely from objective, consensual attributes.

We formalize this complication as follows. Each household has a utility function elaborated for neighborhood analysis as shown in equation (9.1):

$$U^i = U^i\,[H, N(Q, L^i), X], \tag{9.1}$$

where

U^i = household i's utility level;
H = the housing structure and lot components of its housing package;
N = the neighborhood component of the housing package;
X = the vector of nonhousing, nonlocational commodities;
Q = the index of objective neighborhood quality (thus, independent of the identity of household i); and
L^i = a neighborhood "likeness deficit" function as perceived by household i.

Function L^i is the expression of the (inverse) attractiveness of each particular neighborhood in terms of subjective quality features. We assume a vector of such indicators, $S_j = (S_{1j}, S_{2j}, \ldots, S_{mj})$ for each neighborhood j. Each household i has an ideal expression of each component of the vector, namely, $S^i = (S_1^{\,i}, S_2^{\,i}, \ldots, S_m^{\,i})$. L_j^i is then the vector distance of components of neighborhood j from the vector of ideal expressions:

$$(9.2) \qquad L_j^i = L\,[|S_{1j} - S_1^{\,i}|, |S_{2j} - S_2^{\,i}|, \ldots, |S_{mj} - S_m^{\,i}|].$$

In light of the preceding, we define household i's bid-price function for each overall housing package and time t_0 as

$$(9.3) \qquad B^i = B[H_k, N_k, Y_0^{\,i}, U_0^{\,i}] = B[H_k, N_k(Q^i, L^i), Y_0^{\,i}, U_0^{\,i}],$$

where

$$B_H^{\,i}>0,\ B_N^{\,i}>0,\ B_Q^{\,i}>0,\ B_L^{\,i}<0,\ B_Y^{\,i}>0,\ B_U^{\,i}<0.$$

We propose the following empirical regularities concerning these functions. Because of our perception that lifestyles have important coherences, there is likely to be a high degree of complementarity between N and H in U and B for each household. Moreover, both Q and H are likely to be positively related to household income Y. L, on the other hand, is not dependably related to Q or H or Y.

Empirical relationships like these in the model above suggest some important locational patterns. Insofar as Y is strongly related to H and Q, high-income population concentrations will tend to occur where objective neighborhood quality is high and where, in response to their housing demands, housing structures are of high quality. Similarly, low-income concentrations will tend to occur when objective quality is low and, through housing supply responsiveness, housing structures have low quality, and similarly for intermediate demographic concentrations. Suppose, moreover, that some forms of government-supplied services are endogenously responsive to neighborhood demographic concentrations. Now, suppose a moderate-income household has very intense preferences for objective neighborhood quality and thus, with respect to these components of the overall housing package alone, would have been willing to outbid a much richer, but lukewarm-preference household for locating in a very high quality (Q) neighborhood. But the above proposed empirical regularities suggest that the poorer household would also encounter there a supply of generally very high-quality housing structures, subjective government services tailored toward the rich, and a population with overall lifestyles very different from that of the household in question. These linked features of the neighborhood which are "unattractive" from the perspective of the poorer household would most likely lower the poorer household's overall housing package evaluation below that of the lukewarm but rich household. Instead, the poorer household would in all likelihood bid successfully in a neighborhood where the predominant housing structure quality, socioeconomically determined lifestyles, and endogenous government services fitted more closely with its own identity. The upshot of these forces is that neighborhoods are likely by self-selection of residents to be considerably more homogeneous than can be explained by housing structure quality alone, by objective neighborhood quality alone, or even by socioeconomic status alone. It is the empirical spatial linkage of these influences *together* in neighborhood markets that creates an extremely positive additional impetus on the demand side for neighborhood homogeneity. Of course these demand patterns have to be ratified by conditions of supply in order to be realized in the market. To this we now turn.

On the supply side we begin with an assumption which is reasonable in light of the empirical literature. Any given household group of a certain socioeconomic status would feel a reduction in its well-being if households of lower socioeconomic status moved in nearby in an otherwise status-homogeneous neighborhood. Moreover, the *absolute* amount the first group would be willing to pay to avoid such a situation could well exceed whatever premium a lower socioeconomic status group would be willing to pay to live near the higher-status group. If so, builders would gain by specializing dwellings to duplicate quality levels (and thus target status levels of residents) already dominant in each neighborhood, thereby contributing to the further consolidation of resident status/housing-quality homogeneity in each neighborhood. This holds for structures of all densities from single-family houses to large apartment complexes. The demonstration is straightforward if there is a single monopolistic owner of all structures since the dominance of premia for homogeneity maximizes total property values only via pure homogeneity. The argument confined to nonmonopolistic new building is more complex, since a specialist in low-quality structures could conceivably make a profit by building a high-quality neighborhoods. But such intentions would be frustrated by the more effective competition from would-be builders of high-quality structures—the low-quality building intentions would be squeezed out of every neighborhood other than those in which they were homogeneous.

But the supply incentives for homogeneity extend beyond new construction to management of the existing stock. For landlords, given the users' demand for homogeneity, maintenance and repair activities will be more profitable by prolonging the predominant homogeneity of the neighborhood. This does not mean that there are no incentives for change via conversion, but only that when there are they will usually favor relatively homogeneous shifts reestablishing a new uniformity.

For owner-occupiers the situation is more complex. Suppose an owner-occupier household experiences changed housing preferences after the passage of time—because of life-cycle changes, income changes, or other taste changes. It can modify its present premises to accord better with its new preferences. Or it can sell its present home and move to more acceptable premises elsewhere. If higher quality is what is wanted, the cost of the first option is often (but not always) likely to be much higher than the second because of the strong demand complementarity between housing structure characteristics and neighborhood.

If upgrading in place is desired, the indivdual structure can be upgraded, but not the entire neighborhood. So a desired overall improvement in housing quality would require a considerably larger structure improvement—in the absence of concomitant neighborhood improvement—than if both structure *and* neighborhood were improved side by side; a household is therefore willing to pay more for a structure improvement when it is accompanied by neighborhood improvement than when it is not, that is,

$$\partial B^{i2}/\partial H\, \partial N > 0. \tag{9.4}$$

The household would pay more by excessively modifying its present structure to achieve some predetermined increase in utility level. It would also pay more if it moved to a different house in a different neighborhood to achieve the same additional utility. But if neighborhoods are highly homogeneous in terms of housing structures *and* other neighborhood characteristics, then the competitive supply cost of producing structures of the necessary additional quality where both structure *and* neighborhood are better will be less than the excess modification cost of the present home because suppliers in the different neighborhoods do not have to overcompensate amenities in the structures for absence of amenities in the neighborhood. The latter are the natural by-product—a public good—of the separate structural supply actions of builders and owners. The result of these relative costs of upgrading is that owner-occupation households desiring upgraded housing will generally benefit by selling out and moving to different accommodations (in a different neighborhood) rather than by upgrading in place.

The case of desired downgrading differs. Here, downgrading in place reduces housing package quality *less than* the production cost of doing so (via maintenance or structural modification, like unit splits) because perceived quality (and so market values) will be held up by the unchanged but now *relatively* higher neighborhood quality. Moving to an overall lower-quality situation does not reap similar gains, since the neighborhood quality there is comparable to that of structure quality and does not, therefore, constitute an upward-quality subsidy. In such a situation, downgrading adjustments might well occur in place instead of leading to homogeneity-sustaining migration, and so *greater,* not less, heterogeneity might be introduced into neighborhoods over time. Such forces will be thwarted if the downgrading intention of our household is counter to the prevailing temporal changes in housing demands, that is, if it is truly idiosyncratic. With general population pressures for upgrading, positive neighborhood externalities make homogeneous houses (in comparable neighborhoods) more valuable than overstructured houses in less-than-comparable neighborhoods (as argued for upgrading)—*and* higher-quality units are rising in value relative to lower-quality units, so households moving against this tide gain financially by selling the former and moving to the latter, and thereby maintain homogeneity of both neighborhoods.

The mixed situation remains where the household's downgrading desires are not contrary to strong, contrasting mainstream market forces. The same, indeed, holds for landlords responding to prevailing downward market forces. Some heterogeneity may be induced, but this heterogeneity is probably self-limiting. If the downgrading is of considerable magnitude and/or pervasiveness, it constitutes a major negative externality to non-downgrading property owners. For reasons given above, beyond a certain point there will be an induced tipping of enough units to make a *new lower homogeneous* neighborhood the only new stable supply configuration possible. Homogeneity, via a quantum general downgrading, will be reestablished.

If the downgrading is nontrivial but only moderate in magnitude and/or pervasiveness, the negative externality remains without inducing general decline. So there is an uneven incidence of capital losses. Downgraders gain, maintainers lose. Because of the possibility of such asymmetrical loss patterns where no countervailing overall market forces exist, property owners often try to protect themselves against its occurrence by law. Formal zoning and sanitary and building code regulations attempt to prevent these idiosyncratic downgrading actions by effectively making them illegal. They are especially likely to be enacted in suburban jurisdictions where relative fewness and initial homogeneity of interests by property owners make single-minded direction of government action feasible. The presence of such protective regulations channels both subsequent new building and the maintenance and use of the existing stock into continued homogeneity. They do not, however, simply protect homogeneity; they maintain more homogeneity than market forces would have produced and often stifle market adjustments when even quantum changes are called for.

The neighborhood also affects dwelling quality through *alterations* in property owners' perceptions about alternative rates of return available from maintaining or converting their existing dwellings. Changes in both the physical and sociodemographic character of the area surrounding a given owner's dwelling will help form changes in the owner's expectations about the future stream of net returns that the dwelling may produce (Galster 1987: ch. 7). Such altered projections are inputs into the recalculation of optimal submarket destinations (as we saw in ch. 5) and the resulting induced conversion of the dwelling. Typically, these conversions will tend to ratify and intensify the qualitative change already underway in the neighborhood.[2]

As illustration, suppose the market has adjusted in such a way that most of the properties in a neighborhood recently have been downgraded in structural quality. Consider the situation of a property that has not yet been adjusted. Upgrading of this property is very unlikely because much of the overall attractiveness of the unit will be depressed by the downward drag of the surrounding downgraded neighborhood, so an investment in upgrading this unit alone would be unlikely to produce enough increase in market valuation to pay off. A compatible downgrading, on the other hand, is likely to give a higher return than either upgrading or remaining unchanged because the saving in maintenance expense or the investment in splitting units would likely be competitively protected by the similar predominant neighborhood response.[3]

Cases of neighborhood upgrading produce two possible responses. If only one or two dwellings are physically renovated amid an otherwise low-quality neighborhood, other nearby owners may be unwilling to follow suit. They may well believe that insufficient numbers of owners will renovate to change the overall character of the neighborhood. Without such overall improvement, existing neighborhood character will continue to hold market valuations down, preventing the particular upgraded units from commanding a higher enough price to justify similar investment. Nearby owners will "free ride" instead, reaping whatever modest windfall capital gains, if any, are spread from the minor upgrading already taken place. Thus approximately homogeneous use remains, and the neighborhoods remains of low quality, with the few original exceptions.

If, however, a sufficient fraction of a neighborhood's dwellings are upgraded at about the same time, the response may be different. Renovation activity may have reached a threshold at which other, more skeptical or pessimistic owners become convinced of the prospects of neighborhoodwide renewal. (See Taub, Taylor, and Dunham 1984 for this theory of threshold effects.) Successively more owners upgrade until the neighborhood again becomes homogeneous in dwelling quality, albeit at a higher level. Under what conditions will such a multiplicity of upgrading occur? One will be inauguration of a government policy that designates upgrading neighborhoods and makes available substantial aid for the upgrading (Galster 1987: chs. 9, 11, 12). Such strong signals may sometimes fail, but they significantly raise the probability of cumulative upward conversion. Another circumstance might be easily observable strong demographic/demand trends, punctuated by initial signs of upgrading by "pioneers" in conformity to those trends. Gentrification, as discussed above, is exactly of this nature.

Given such a structure of supply incentives, abetted by the closeness of housing substitutability in a neighborhood and the ease of perceiving discrepant adjustments, conformist supply behavior vis-à-vis stability and both downward and upward changes (save for the upward change qualification just noted) is most likely: the neighborhood tends to act and react as a unit. As we indicate below, the behavior of real estate agents, financial institutions, and even government tends to support and even increase this uniformity. So the neighborhood can be treated in analytically important respects as a behaviorally dependable unit.

Although a neighborhood *encourages* homogeneity, it does not necessarily follow that all (or even most) housing units within it fall in the same quality submarket. Indeed, the empirical congruence between submarket and neighborhood proves rather modest, as we shall see in chapter 13. Thus, we deem it inappropriate to treat the two as synonymous (cf. Grigsby et al. 1987). Besides its dubious empirical validity, to do so would implicitly require that a particular geographic scale of neighborhood be specified, and there are no compelling grounds for the choice of a unique spatial delineation (Galster 1986).

We avoid both pitfalls by simply avoiding the questions of what precisely the neighborhood *is* and how much submarket homogeneity there is within it. We assume only that within any given, unambiguously specified geographic area there are sets of dwellings that fall within one or more quality submarkets. The smaller the geographic area specified, the greater the probability that a smaller number of quality submarkets will exhaust the delineated set of dwellings. Insofar as marketwide dynamic forces induce conversion responses in a given submarket, individual neighborhoods will be affected to the extent that they are composed of dwellings in that submarket.

Since neighborhoods do not share the same market characteristics, they will not be affected in the same way or degree by metropolitanwide changes in incomes, preferences, or demographics. Changes that shift demands from middle- to upper-quality submarkets will, as we saw in chapter 8, encourage both upgrading and downgrading from the middle-quality submarkets. Middle-quality submarket dwellings located in better-quality neighborhoods will, for strategic reasons cited above, be more likely to upgrade compared to those in lower-quality neighborhoods. Thus, two formerly stable neighborhoods containing predominantly middle-quality dwellings may well evolve in different qualitative directions. Of course, neighborhoods originally containing only a few middle-quality dwellings will be little affected. Neighborhoods with a mix of middle- and upper-quality dwellings may well experience no net changes, since expectations generated by demand strength in one portion of the neighborhood's stock may be offset by demand weakness in the other portion. Thus, what happens in aggregate over a given urban space stems only partly from internal changes; probably the more important forces leading to neighborhood decline and renovation begin at the regional or metropolitan level (Grigsby et al. 1987). Those forces, by changing quality submarket demands and/or supplies, lead individual dwelling owners to modify their dwellings and residents to change their occupancies. These qualitative changes, in aggregate, shape the physical, socioeconomic, and demographic character of the neighborhoods in which they are concentrated. Whatever this initial irregularity of change within neighborhoods, however, subsequent reactions tend to render their characteristics more homogeneous over time.

9.3 Neighborhood Change as Market Adjustment

A neighborhood maintains or changes its character for reasons which stem from forces generated from within, from without, or from a combination of the two. Generally the repercussions generated from any initial impetus to change are adequately explained in terms of static (generally equilibrium) relationships belonging to the submarket analytic framework sketched in the previous chapters and so are self-limiting. The system is generally stable: exogenous shocks initiated in any part will generate a set of repercussions that converge toward a new general equilibrium resting place, with changes overall that are quite circumscribed. Under some circumstances, however, exogenous shocks *may* lead to cumulative changes. In evaluating the desirability or undesirability of neighborhood change, its self-limiting or dynamically augmenting character will be an important criterion.

We now consider systematically the source and character of neighborhood change. Under what conditions will a neighborhood maintain its character over time? The economic and demographic profiles of those moving out of the neighborhood must balance the profiles of those moving in, *and* the average quality of housing must be maintained. Complementary, supportive flows, like local public services and environmental attributes, must also remain constant if the *neighborhood* in its broadest sense is to maintain its character. Stability does not require an absence of change. As a result of normal life-cycle forces there is a continuous turnover of households out of present accommodations into different ones as their age, size, job location, income, and so forth change over time. Some houses in the same neighborhood may need repair while others are being renovated; some may be retired while others are being added. What is needed, then, is not an absence of change, but a balanced flow of changes.

Neighborhood stability involves balance in the aggregate flows of two sets of individual dynamic behaviors: mobility by households and property investments by owners and builders. While the two sets of behaviors are by no means perfectly correlated, they are interrelated in a complex of *mutually causal* relationships, but these connections extend beyond the focus of any *single* neighborhood in question. It is especially this latter aspect that distinguishes our approach to neighborhood change. Both household demanders and housing suppliers make their decisions not only by assessing the absolute conditions in one particular—their own—submarket and neighborhood, but by comparing them with the opportunities available in other submarkets and neighborhoods.

Mobility and housing investment flows for a given neighborhood occur against a backdrop of two relationships: (1) the competitiveness of the neighborhood in question with other neighborhoods that offer a highly similar typical housing package—neighborhoods consisting predominantly of dwellings in the samc or a very similar quality submarket; and (2) the relationship between this submarket and others currently subject to significant, exogenous changes. The first concerns the appearance and change of minor, possibly transitory, factors affecting the attractiveness of a neighborhood or the temporal sequence of market transactions. Slight aberrations may confer slight competitive edges or disadvantages among closely competitive neighborhoods, and these may form the basis for significant modifications in household perceptions.

It is in this connection that dynamic forces must be appraised. Some recent research (Goetze 1976; Taub, Taylor, and Dunham 1984; Varady 1986) has stressed that "neighborhood perception" by households, real estate agents, financial institutions, and local government has a vital effect on the stability of neighborhood character. All relevant actors are assumed to be making present decisions on the basis of expectations about the future of the neighborhood, and all of them are assumed to predict that future by examining very subtle, very slight changes in present circumstances. It is argued that even small stochastic events may be perceived by these actors as signaling quite substantial future changes, so such events may trigger larger systematic actions by them that self-fulfill their predictions. This is assumed to refer to both neighborhood upgrading and decline, but to be somewhat more likely for declines.

Such a view of market dynamics is contrary to the spirit of the theoretical model described in chapters 4–6. In terms of the latter, any small or temporary perceived realignments in relative attractiveness among neighborhoods will lead to behavior that is self-limiting, not self-augmenting. For example, a slight exogenous improvement for neighborhood A relative to B and C, all of which contained mostly housing in similar submarkets, will lead to increased relative household inflows to A. The higher demand-side competitiveness that results in A will raise housing prices in A relative to B and C. While perhaps signaling how much more attractive A is now than B or C in gross terms, these prices will, by equalizing the net attractiveness of representative units in the three markets, serve to shut off any further differential flows to A and thereby lead to a new equilibrium resting place. Only a slight mutual adjustment in A, B, and C need be involved in bringing about the shift from the initial to the final equilibrium.

The "neighborhood perception" approach might dispute this last judgment. It might argue that the price change, registering an initially perceived disparity, will itself constitute a further signal, both confirming and deepening the original conjecture, thus justifying stronger adjustments. Thus price changes, far from dampening the desire for further adjustment, will actually fuel those desires more strongly. The difference between the two theoretical treatments lies in how much information actors have about future attractiveness independent of market valuations. A world in which it is market price and transaction changes that constitute the source of expectations, and not the sources underlying those market changes, is a very unstable world indeed. Our model, in contrast, assumes the existence of a variety of informational sources of future forces, and therefore a less explosive formation and testing of expectations. Having said this, we admit that episodes of explosive expectation formation do sometimes occur. When they do, however, there are usually reasons for it. These are unusual and sometimes important phenomena; we attempt to suggest below some of the circumstances under which they are likely to occur.

The relationship of the neighborhood in question to changes in *other* neighborhoods is a more important exercise of our model. Both outflows and the potentially balancing inflows of households may be due to normal turnover driven by life-cycle processes. Then, so long as the overall metropolitan population is economically and demographically stable in size, age distribution, and income distribution, the flows may well balance for all neighborhoods. But if there are considerable changes in any of these dimensions, they will have the effect of changing the absolute and/or relative demand for accommodations in some initial set of submarkets and in the neighborhoods thereby involved. These changes will generate market adjustments there—prices, quantities occupied, induced qualitative conversions, new construction—that transmit repercussions into other sets of submarkets. Such indirect effects in a second generation of impacted submarkets and their constituent neighborhoods will in turn transmit repercussions to a third generation of submarkets/neighborhoods, and so on. Our original neighborhood in question will be swept by one or more of these generations of repercussions, the strength of which will be directly related to the proportion of the neighborhood's dwellings that have high substitutability with the submarkets receiving the initial impact. The same scenarios are true of large-scale, exogenous changes in supply-side variables.

Stability of a particular neighborhood therefore essentially depends on the macro-stability of both housing demand- and supply-side variables in the urban area as a whole. Failure of the latter stability will produce changes in generally more than one neighborhood. Some types of macrochange will result in mixed, indecisive, idiosyncratic types of change across neighborhoods. Others of some importance will produce a much more distinguishable pattern of changes. Among these latter, major currents of population, income, and transportation change generate highly characteristic configurations.

9.3.1 Adjustment to Population Change

Strong population growth, especially concentrated within the lower half of the income distribution, was one of the most important and pervasive experiences for U.S. cities from 1945 to 1970. Its schematic effect, taken by itself, is as follows.[4] For illustration, we focus on three sets of neighborhoods that (for simplicity) are comprised exclusively of dwellings differing only modestly in quality submarket: sets A, B, C ranked from lowest to highest quality. Suppose that the lowest-quality submarkets (say neighborhood set A) experience increased demand. Prices and rents are bid up, and as a result some current rental residents find it more advantageous to move to higher-quality submarkets, or some to decrease quality in the same neighborhoods, while many newcomers to the impacted neighborhoods find it desirable to occupy a lower quality of housing in those neighborhoods than they originally intended at the old lower prices. Some original residents who were owner-occupiers find it more profitable to sell their houses and move to somewhat superior-quality areas with prices as yet less inflated (e.g., neighborhood set B). As noted above, renters find that the now higher rents make the overall accommodation/rent package in the impacted neighborhood set A less a bargain than slightly higher-quality housing at less inflated rents in neighborhood set B. It is likely that both homeowners and renters who thus choose to move upward come from the upper portions of the original resident income distribution in neighborhood set A, whereas those moving in are less likely to be such. Thus an imbalance in the economic profiles of in- and out-movers occurs in set A.

Meanwhile the increased demand in set A for even lower-quality housing than typically supplied there initially induces some A owners (especially of rental units) to modify the quality of their structures downward—by splitting, by lowering the level of maintenance and repair, by shifting from owner-occupier to rental status, and so forth. In addition, if homeowners leaving set A have, on an average, somewhat higher incomes than those entering, the absolute flow of upkeep in investment is likely to decrease, thereby lowering quality there gradually. (For quantitative estimates of this effect on neighborhoods, see Galster 1987: chs. 9, 10.) Another complicating factor is how homeowners would adjust further if they expected the inflation of their homes' values to continue. Galster (1987: chs. 9, 10) argues that there would not be a further noticeable impact on home reinvestment behavior except in the lowest-quality homeowner submarkets. To summarize the set A supply adjustment, the present scenario is one in which demand-side alterations in net flows precede the supply responses there.

But supply adjustments relevant to set A are not exhausted in set A alone. The risen prices and rents there raise prospective rates of return relative to those in other neighborhoods for owners of units in those other neighborhoods. This induces downward conversions of quality in set B, thereby easing excess demand pressure in A and ending price rises there. These downgraders seek to supply a clientele who previously did not register demand in set B. So this supply response precedes the demand shift in its neighborhood.

The first wave of demand and supply adjustments leads to further waves. Demand inflows from set A to B raise prices and rents in the latter. This induces downward quality conversions from set C to the quality levels originally provided in set B. Original set B residents now face both higher valuations for dwellings remaining at their initial quality, and other dwellings in the neighborhood set that have been downgraded, thereby lowering the neighborhoods' overall attractiveness. This sours the evaluation of some households for continued residence there. So some of them now move to a slightly higher-quality submarket in neighborhood set C, thereby spreading the increased demand to higher and higher quality neighborhoods. The successive household spillover waves flow to higher and higher quality submarkets and bring with them rising prices and rents, and thereby induce downward quality conversions there from still higher submarkets. At some reasonably higher submarket level the spreading demand shifts induce not only conversion supply adjustments but also new construction. Since new construction competes with converted units, the increasing presence of augmented new construction decreases the share of conversions in supply adjustments at progressively higher-quality submarkets and their respective neighborhoods. This changed mix may give additional impetus to turnover within affected submarkets, perhaps even to some additional upward migration. The increasing domination of supply response via new construction culminates at the highest quality levels where it is almost entirely new construction that furnishes the net additional units demanded by household upflows. This stems from the absence of higher levels from which downward conversions can occur. An important implication of the strength of new construction in this process is that, unlike conversion responses, large-scale new construction typically involves the creation of new neighborhoods.[5]

Overall, then, the adjustment process to growing low-income population involves a required increase in numbers of units necessary to support the larger household population. This is furnished predominantly by downward conversion of the existing stock at lower quality levels, by mixes of such conversions and new construction at higher levels, and predominantly by new construction at the highest levels. Accompanying all this is a general, but damped, increase in market valuations throughout—highest at the initial impact submarkets and progressively less at higher and higher quality levels. The degree of price and rent inflation will be determined by the medium-run supply function in each submarket, as explained in chapter 5. The graduated inflation and pattern of conversions lead to substantial turnover of existing residents to previously higher-quality neighborhoods now downgraded through considerable downward conversions.

This process results in a decline in the quality of some dwellings in every impacted submarket and thus, implicitly, in every original neighborhood.[6] The incidence of decline is graduated, being greatest in the neighborhoods that contain dwellings most similar in quality to those initially demanded by the growing low-income population. Similarly, the socioeconomic profile of residents in all original neighborhoods will be lower than previously to a degree depending on the similarity with the initial impact neighborhoods. These two aspects of decline—physical and socioeconomic—are related in bidirectional ways. A decline in the socioeconomic profile of occupants in a given neighborhood leads owners there to adjust their properties' quality downward to meet the demands of the in-movers. But increased market valuations (due to both demand increases and supply declines) in submarkets of *lower* quality than represented in the given neighborhood will induce downgrading of dwellings to the latter, which in turn encourages a lower-income clientele to move into the area.[7]

So population changes can induce widespread neighborhood declines. Are these to be deplored or applauded? In this case they result from a particular form of supply adjustment to meet an initial need for more low-quality dwellings, fed by existing residents' adjustments in occupancy and existing owners' adjustments in their units' quality. Ought the real price of housing not rise at all as a result of population growth? For nonhousing commodities, we would expect an increase in demand to call forth increased production at higher prices due to upward-sloping supply functions. In addition to reflecting more costly production, such price increases moderate the size of the original demand pressures. This is an integral part of an efficient allocational process, and therefore desirable for those commodities. Why not then for housing also? So long as supply for low-quality housing comes predominantly by means of downward conversion of existing units originally built at higher qualities, and neighborhood externalities are important, quantum changes in the number of such units demanded will come via considerable numbers of such conversions that are at the same time spatially clustered. This means neighborhood change. The linked intersubmarket behavior of users and owners, moreover, will spread changes considerably beyond the neighborhoods initially directly impacted. So neighborhood change will be widespread as well. Since the process constitutes the market's effective adjustability, it may in fact be required for reasonably efficient resource utilization. As such, it may not be deplorable but the cost of meeting changing exogenous forces operating in the market. This surmise is examined further below.

9.3.2 Adjustment to Income Changes

Similar waves of shifts are generated by significant, sustained changes in per capita income. Income increases also raise housing demands, but now they are demands for *higher*-quality dwelling packages by households experiencing income increases, rather than a demand for more total units. Assume the income increases are widespread and proportional to existing incomes. Then demand for higher quality will generally affect all neighborhoods. A combination of two types of supply response may now occur. The large attempted upward shifts into better submarkets and, presumably, better neighborhoods by many households across most of the quality spectrum lead to excess demands and, thereby, to higher market valuations throughout, except in the lowest-quality submarkets.

In each neighborhood some owners may wish to upgrade their property, especially if they want to enjoy higher quality without changing occupancy.[8] If not enough owners are of the same mind, the combination of neighborhood externalities and close physical contact may deter many of these owners from carrying out this desire, as discussed earlier (since the property will therefore look dubious as a market investment, and their own desired higher consumption standards can be more safely attained financially by moving to a higher-quality neighborhood). Yet some few owners with high attachment to their existing home and neighborhood will nonetheless upgrade and remain (Galster 1987: ch. 9). An important reason for many owners not wanting to upgrade in these circumstances is that they can expect a higher demand for their unaltered property from occupants of lower-quality units/neighborhoods whose higher incomes induce them to seek better housing by moving to a better neighborhood. This is not true for owners in the lowest-quality neighborhoods, of course. The value of their assets will fall absolutely if they do not upgrade, because of the widespread demand for higher quality. Since such attempted upgrading will be seen as fighting against strong market currents in the neighborhoods, credit will not be easily forthcoming. Dependent, therefore, largely on their own resources and especially where they themselves have low—despite rising—incomes, they will find upgrading extremely burdensome, so only a modicum is likely to occur. Upgrading here could become even more problematic if some neighboring owners resort to abandonment to stem their losses under the circumstances.

As in the preceding scenario, at some sufficiently high-quality submarket the intensified demand for higher quality will elicit new construction, above which an increasing proportion of upward-household-shift behavior takes the form of moving into new dwellings. In large measure this involves creation of new neighborhoods at quality levels paralleling older, comparable-quality neighborhoods.

Overall, the pattern induced by income increases is a widespread movement by households into better dwellings and neighborhoods. At progressively higher-quality levels, increasing percentages of moves are into new units (and neighborhoods). While consumption improvements will come mostly by means of turnover into better units that already exist or are newly created, some improvements will also occur in existing units, especially in spatial clusters. Some existing neighborhoods will also experience upgrading, but this will not be general. It will not occur in the lowest-quality neighborhoods, where an opposite movement will occur. The overall supply response to general income increases is basically an upward interlocked turnover into existing and new units, resulting in more total housing units for the same-sized population. This will generate increased net vacancies, the size of which is mitigated by an income-increase inducement to create more households via splitting. These vacancies will be clustered at the lowest quality levels—the poorest-quality neighborhoods—whose demands have decreased but whose supplies are mostly locked in. Nontrivial clustering of vacancies there sets the stage for significant abandonment. So while each neighborhood experiences high turnover, the replacement flow of users essentially duplicates the original (absolute) socioeconomic status of the outflow in all but the lowest-quality neighborhoods. Thus there is little qualitative net socioeconomic or physical change in most neighborhoods. The major exception is in lowest-quality neighborhoods, where decline occurs. The secondary exception is clustered upgrading in a few moderate-quality neighborhoods, where households' strong attachment to their homes garners critical mass proportions to make a difference in the neighborhood as a whole. Thus, while population increase widely affects neighborhood quality, income increases largely leave it intact.

Suppose that instead of generally increasing incomes, the population suffers generally falling incomes. Then households generally will want lower-quality housing. (Since this is a long-run analysis, we exclude the case of households trying to maintain original housing standards because they believe the income declines are temporary.) They can adjust in two ways: move out and into lower-quality units in inferior neighborhoods, or continue their present occupancy and gradually allow housing quality to decline. Relative market assessment of these two options intimately involving the market relationship between unit and neighborhood could well differ in the downward direction rather than the upward direction. Depending on the individual unit, both options would likely be chosen. The first—downward turnover of households—would generate the same kind of musical chairs chain of population shifts, but from the top down, which we saw in the income-rise scenario. Since returns to especially high-quality units would decrease, significant numbers of these would convert downward to be competitive. This would in turn induce units at these lower submarkets to downgrade as well, leading in turn to the same kind of successive downgrading adjustments along the whole quality spectrum. Thus neighborhoods would generally experience considerable physical downgrading—existing-neighborhood decline.

In contrast to the effects of the upward waves, new construction could not be counted on here to mitigate these physical changes. Some new construction would be elicited. Households generally are demanding less (quality of) housing, but not fewer units. Given the unevenness of households and units over their respective incomes and quality arrays, there is no necessary coordination between the number of households at any particular quality level and the number of units initially available at the slightly lower level they now want. It is thus quite conceivable there would be considerable random disparities along the quality spectrum. Where these disparities produce excess demands at moderate and high quality levels, new construction could well be competitively favored over downward conversions from distant submarkets. So considerable, though randomly situated, new construction could occur, even though the market as a whole is declining.

Random demand-supply disparities along the spectrum would generate positive and negative changes in vacancies. Where new construction was induced, vacancies would likely increase. As both the original site of net demand decline and the most likely location of fill-in new construction, the highest-quality submarkets would be most likely to experience considerable increases in vacancies.

The second major household adjustment strategy, continued present occupancy with gradual use downgrading, is likely to be important because of the high costs of changing occupancy. Where a household's attachment to the present home and/or neighborhood is strong, it is especially likely to be chosen. This choice will generate market repercussions that may differ from those of the first option. Existing structures will be downgraded generally, although possibly more slowly, as under the first option. So neighborhoods generally will physically decline from this source as well. The socioeconomic identity of neighborhoods may, however, be affected somewhat differently, and through this, the decline may be less uniform. Stayers now represent a lower income level than previously, via the assumed exogenous income decline. Insofar as all or most units in the neighborhood are downgraded, it is quite possible that the original socioeconomic group will continue to occupy these units, that is, that the neighborhood will retain the same relative socioeconomic status as heretofore.[9] Whether the present occupants are newcomers or holdovers will make little difference. If, however, only some units are downgraded, then the new occupants for nondowngraded units will be only the turnover households from previously superior neighborhoods who now have the higher incomes of the original occupants of this neighborhood. Holdovers will now matter, creating the possibility of heterogeneity in housing quality and different relationships between the quality of individual units and that of the neighborhood. The issue depends on the empirical uniformity of income changes, the costs of changing occupancy, and of course the differential costs of downward conversions. Our earlier strong suggestions about neighborhood uniformity are based on long-run comparative static conditions that ignored the latter two factors.

Notice therefore the dramatic asymmetries in impacts on neighborhoods that arise from different kinds of changes in income. Generally rising incomes lead to basic stability in the physical quality of all but the lowest-quality existing neighborhoods, a modest amount of physical improvements through upgrading in some of them short of really high-quality neighborhoods, and significant abandonments in the worst neighborhoods. Much of the rising housing demand is siphoned off into newly constructed units in new neighborhoods. Generally falling incomes, on the other hand, lead to significant physical decline in most neighborhoods by means of downgrading, with little or no abandonment and only random clusters of new construction. The *relative* socioeconomic character of neighborhoods remains significantly unchanged, however, under both kinds of income change.

Scenarios of widespread wavelike shifts can be drawn for other exogenous impulses, like important changes in the urban transportation system (with differential neighborhood impacts based on their spatial accessibility), but they will resemble the configurations already drawn. The message in all of them will be similar: some form of deterioration—socioeconomic/demographic status or housing quality—will afflict some or most or all neighborhoods. Yet in all of the scenarios the neighborhood deterioration is not necessarily bad in itself. It is not even invariably associated with lowered welfare for some, let alone all, groups, either on its own or as a reflection of other forces. Sometimes it is indeed the mechanism by which some groups *improve* their welfare. Rather it represents an aspect—generally not the most important aspect—of the complex resource allocative adjustment by the housing market to changing exogenous forces. The demand side of the adjustment is responsible directly for making socioeconomic/demographic shifts and indirectly for giving signals to suppliers to adjust. Stock modification is responsible for quality deterioration (and enhancement) and further signals for subsequent household adjustments. New construction is responsible for creation and clustering of vacancies as well as new neighborhoods. So all elements of the adjustment share responsibility for instances of neighborhood deterioration.

9.3.3 Low-Income Housing and Neighborhood Decline

One final scenario, concerning how lower-income groups are housed in U.S. cities, is especially important. We have referred in the earlier scenarios to a lack of uniformity in the appearance of new construction at different-quality submarkets. This is neither arbitrary, accidental, nor inevitable, but rather the result of special institutional features in U.S. cities. In each quality submarket, new construction must compete with stock modification to supply units demanded there. How are the low-quality dwellings demanded by low-income households supplied? In many nations they are newly constructed expressly at the targeted quality submarkets. This is the character of the innumerable shantytowns that mushroom on the outskirts of cities in many parts of the world in response to heavy urbanization by the poor. In U.S. cities, on the other hand, low-quality units are supplied almost entirely by downward stock modification of older housing units originally built at much higher levels, the so-called filtering process discussed in chapter 8.

As we saw in chapter 6, the dominance of quality-downgraded units for lower-income households stems heavily from the fact that various building and health codes and zoning regulations make it either literally impossible or prohibitively expensive to build housing units of qualities relevant to the demand of approximately the lower half of the income distribution.[10] The lowest level permitted cannot be afforded by the very poor, and even the lowest levels that are permitted cost so much to produce that they can be easily undercut by competition from modified units which are converted downward, especially old units for which downgrading generally has low opportunity costs.

This form of supply for lower-income households inherently involves lowering the quality of existing housing units (1) by investing in the multiplication of lower-quality units via splitting, or (2) by disinvestment out of existing quality via undermaintenance. Neither of these options inherently involves a waste of existing assets, only a change in the quality distribution of the existing stock. Given the social valuation implied by the existence of the code and zoning regulations that elicit this supply pattern, it may well represent an efficient market adaptation to the existence of low income generally. If one deplores the significant intentional—noninevitable—downgrading of property involved and the associated downward socioeconomic drift of particular neighborhoods over time, it is in fact either the presence of a low-income population or the presence of building and land-use constraints (or both) that one is deploring. That filtering may be an efficient dynamic adjustment process does not, however, imply that such a dynamic should be deliberately chosen as a most advantageous public policy instrument. On the contrary, we analyze filtering as a policy option at length in chapter 11 and conclude that it is not, in general, a comparatively efficacious strategy.

The above case has been made deliberately provocative to underscore the fact that neighborhood decline should not be considered in a vacuum, but rather as part of a larger complex response by households, builders, property owners, financial and real estate agents, and others to market conditions, exogenous forces, and institutional constraints.

Within such complex processes, neighborhood changes may well represent the key *desirable* aspects of the system's response. The poverty scenario has been designed primarily to make this point. Further implications must be held in abeyance until we delve into additional features. We now discuss below some of the *disadvantages* of depending on this kind of pattern for meeting the housing demands of the most disadvantaged population groups.

9.4 Further Considerations in the Analysis of Neighborhood Decline

9.4.1 Internal versus External Sources of Decline

A neighborhood may well remain qualitatively stable *absolutely,* with all its myriad features maintained. But it may eventually become beset by downgraded structures and/or lower socioeconomic status residents if the housing submarket(s) represented within it become *relatively* more or less attractive to particular demanders and suppliers, compared with other submarkets and their constituent neighborhoods. Such alterations in the neighborhood's relative attractiveness may well stem from outside the given neighborhood and be typically beyond the control of the neighborhood's actors.

In the last section we saw that, with a widespread income decrease, most neighborhoods would become relatively *less* "attractive" (because they are now less affordable) to their original residents than less-expensive ones. This readjustment of demands toward lower-quality submarkets would induce downgrading of dwellings and the concomitant deterioration of neighborhoods containing them. But we also saw that a neighborhood may decline if it becomes relatively *more* attractive to households of lower socioeconomic status, because the latter can then bid away accommodations from present residents even if present residents feel as much attracted as before. This pattern is abetted especially if property owners in the neighborhood find that large-scale splitting of existing units and other means of accommodating higher-density land use would strongly enhance profitability. In this case, then, the neighborhood declines not because of failure to attract but because of spectacular success in attracting a different (lower socioeconomic status) kind of clientele. But in either case above, the "fault" of decline does not lie within the neighborhood but in the existence of large systemwide forces outside it. A number of research treatments of neighborhood decline emphasize the internal failure case, but we consider the external case to be more pervasive and hence more important.

9.4.2 The Importance of In-Migration versus Out-Migration Flows

Both of the above decline scenarios concern the relative paucity or poverty of in-migrants to a neighborhood. But some researchers argue that an important source of the trouble is the character of the population outflows. If U.S. households did not improve their housing consumption by moving out to better neighborhoods, they argue, but instead upgraded in place, this would avoid much of the neighborhood transition and prevent some of the consequent deterioration that accompanies it (Ahlbrandt and Brophy 1975; Ahlbrandt and Cunningham 1979; Clay 1979; Downs 1981).

For example, if a group of households occupying middle-quality submarkets and neighborhoods got richer, they would demand higher-quality housing packages. If they fulfilled these demands by moving out to different neighborhoods where higher-submarket dwellings were available, market valuations would be deflated in the areas they left. This, in turn, would make the latter areas more attractive to households with lower incomes than theirs and would thereby induce a different stream of in-migrants to the vacated neighborhoods than previously. The downgrading scenario described earlier would then ensue.

If, instead, the newly rich fulfilled their demands by upgrading their dwellings in place (or equivalently, having a third party do so), no incentives for downgrading would result—quite the contrary. Furthermore, the upgrading of such property in a neighborhood might tend to encourage other owners (of unaltered incomes) to do so too, because it might signal either that a critical threshold for overall neighborhood uplift could be achieved or at least that other property owners would be deterred from downgrading their property because of a perception that decent housing quality now pays off (Taub, Taylor, and Dunham 1984; Galster 1987: ch. 3). Frequent upgrading in place might generate a pattern of more heterogeneity of housing qualities in neighborhoods (as we remarked above about downgrading by stayers in a decline scenario).

Significant neighborhood heterogeneity has historically been found mostly in racial ghetto areas, where minority households of diverse income levels have been forced to live near one another because discrimination bars entry of their better-off members into other areas. It occurs in some ethnic neighborhoods as well (e.g., Greek and Chinese), where strong ethnic identification exceeds income-induced desires for separation by different lifestyles which are supported in distinct, homogeneous neighborhoods. Finally, it occurs in a few neighborhoods that possess special amenities (e.g., an urban university) that are very important to a self-selected assortment of households differing from one another in many respects.

These limited circumstances provide only a narrow incentive base for heterogeneity. The alternative pattern of upgrading one's housing consumption by moving to a different neighborhood rests on the formidable strength of the influence of neighborhood externalities on the character of lifestyles *and* on the fact that social mobility in the United States is quite high, so locational change is socially acceptable and is a highly visible way to change status identification. Upgrading housing as part of lifestyle upgrading requires a *homogeneous* higher-quality environment that reflects that lifestyle (Birch et al. 1979). To achieve a comparably adequate consonance of environmental components via upgrading in place is far more costly at best, and even fundamentally problematic, because it depends upon sufficiently numerous other residents, owners, banks, real estate agents, and government agencies taking comparable upgrading actions as well—something that cannot be guaranteed by any single household faced with the choice of the two options. So inter-neighborhood flows, with their resulting neighborhood transition phenomena, are likely to remain the dominant mode of *household upgrading*. This in turn means that both inflow and outflow dynamics will be crucial sources of neighborhood decline.

9.4.3 Expectations and Dynamics

Households' inflow and outflow decisions and property owners' reinvestment decisions for a given neighborhood depend, whatever the internal or external forces operating, on expectations about the future character of this and other neighborhoods. These expectations explicitly or implicitly refer to the behavior of other households, other owners of residential and commercial properties nearby, and other relevant decision makers. This dependency arises for households because the costs of changing occupancies are high in money, time, effort, and in emotional expenditure (few people want to develop a deep attachment to a neighborhood only to have to terminate it shortly and abruptly). Households cannot afford to make mistakes about the continued congeniality of their surroundings over a "decent interval." Similarly, once owners invest in a particular form of housing capital it becomes "sunk" and imperfectly malleable, so presently available information must be processed to form appropriate expectations (Galster 1987; chs. 7–8).

In highly stable times, or in situations pregnant with strong, unambiguous forces, most indicators are dependable and judgments are accordingly nearly objective. But widely changing or ambiguous circumstances make predictions more difficult. Familiar—yet still unresolved—problems about expectations abound here. Information will be unavailable, inadequate, confusing, and may be processed faultily. People's actions based on such shaky expectations may lead to inadvertent outcomes.

Neighborhood behavior can be strongly influenced by flawed expectations during complex situations. Interested parties read disparate signs and take nonrandom samples because complete information is not available to them. They are likely to project the individual case into the representative, perceiving the particular as the general. So the characteristics of individual transactions and of particular in- and out-movers, changes in the external upkeep and appearance of specific properties, incidents involving public services, applications for mortgage loans, and so forth sometimes take on disproportionate significance. Where currents are genuinely uncertain, these specifics are likely to contain a high chance content, so they are undependable for generating predictions about the future. Yet people act on them—households by moving in or out, owners by converting their dwellings to different quality levels, financial institutions by accepting or rejecting mortgage applications, real estate agents by shunting "the right kind of people" away from the neighborhood and channeling "the wrong kind" there, or by government agencies allowing sanitation services or police protection or code enforcement to slip there. All these set in motion self-fulfilling processes. Thus, predictions of decline will lead to some decline-oriented adjustments; these lead to a few instances of actual decline; these justify the original predictions, make them more credible to more people, thereby strengthening them and leading to further rounds of adjustment by others, which in turn justify the predictions with wider instances of decline, and so on in a cumulating movement of scope and intensity well beyond the validity of the original predictions. Galster (1987: ch. 9) has found that expectations about the quality of the neighborhood have the structural property of the self-fulfilling prophecy described here. Expectations about decline in property values, on the other hand, sometimes generate contrary behavior: in low-priced areas, such expectations may actually lead to dwelling *improvement* activity by homeowners. A theory of "threshold capital gains" has been forwarded to explain this behavior (Galster 1987: ch. 3). It is the absence of a strong unambiguous force, together with the concern that important stakes are involved, that both promotes the vicious circle in the first place and prevents effective testing of the premises along the way.

The impact of the vicious circle is especially abetted by the neighborhood externalities we have emphasized frequently. Even agents who do not themselves believe the original predictions are trapped in the currents whipped up, because the attractiveness of their own options is tied to the behavior of the larger group. These individuals are swept away by the behavior of the group. Their conforming adjustments, given the externalities, are rational despite the possibly irrational behavior of the larger group (Galster 1987: chs. 2, 10, 14). Neighborhood homogeneity is thereby exacted.

The dynamics of the adjustment process itself, then, fed in certain circumstances by unstable expectations, can sometimes determine outcomes. Our theoretical mainstay has hitherto been situations in which expectations were assumed simply to mirror highly discernible real forces. This assumption has been necessary to permit comparative static analysis. But the unstable expectations case must now be considered as well. In the next section we consider under what conditions it is likely to arise.

9.4.4 Components of Decline

We have alluded to, but never made explicit, the characteristics of deteriorated neighborhoods or the elements that contribute to decline. This is not an accident. There is such a variety of types of decline that features which fit some do not fit others (Grigsby et al. 1987). Thus, attributes of weak demand are present in some forms of decline, but not in those where it is the superabundance of demand for lowered quality that powers decline. The purpose of this section, then, is not to present *the* picture of a deteriorating or deteriorated neighborhood, but to indicate briefly different aspects of a neighborhood that may contribute to the decline process or state.

Physical Structures

In most forms of decline the structural quality of housing in the neighborhood decreases. The main exception is where dwelling quality is maintained but the new occupants are of lower status (and the society is status conscious when evaluating the neighborhood environment). This may occur if strong price declines in this general part of the market complex relative to elsewhere make higher-quality dwellings available to lower income groups than heretofore. Again, this may result either from relative weakness of the neighborhood in question or from larger forces like population decline, a building boom, or changes in accessibility patterns. However, even here, as we saw in chapter 8, such socioeconomic changes are likely *eventually* to be associated with dwelling-quality decline as the new systemic general equilibrium is reached.

Two forms of housing-quality decline occur in the usual cases. One is a deterioration in maintenance and repair or accelerated wear and tear attendant on overcrowded or abusive use of property. Often this is a consequence of pessimistic expectations about the competitive viability—the income-earning potentialities—of the property. The other form involves considerable increases in land-use density. Property is modified to accept more housing units per structure, more individuals per unit. This is usually attendant not on a loss of competitive viability, but rather on a change in the kind of population for which the property can now be most profitably used.

An additional dimension is sometimes associated with physical decline, especially in structures which are owner-occupied. It is a situation where simple aging of the structure brings about a cumulative physical deterioration or obsolescence that requires extensive repair or modernization to offset or moderate. The owner attempts to borrow money on mortgage for rehabilitation but is rejected by financial institutions. Except for tight overall credit conditions, this is most likely to stem from perceptions of neighborhood weakness by financial agents. Rejection because of the perception of the occupant population as a bad risk suggests population status decline as well.

Owner versus Rental Tenure

Tenure has a significant effect on owners' decisions about the level of maintenance and repair. In the presence of actual or expected market weakness, landlords of rental premises may well allow structure condition to decline by skimping on upkeep. It is a calculated strategy to maximize profits. Owner-occupiers have different motives and are subject to different forces. Since they consume the services of their own premises, they are less likely to accept lower consumption standards just because of commercial weakness afflicting other people's property. In addition, their residence in the neighborhood makes them susceptible to their neighbors' social sanctions and collective solidarity sentiments designed to maintain housing upkeep and neighborhood quality generally. Their maintenance standards are thus likely to be and to remain higher than those of rental units (Galster 1981b, 1983, 1987: chs. 3, 13).

Another difference between the two tenure types is that an owner-occupier is somewhat more likely than a renter to obtain improved housing conditions by upgrading in place rather than moving to a better neighborhood. This is due to a higher cost of changing occupancy, a potentially stronger allegiance to the neighborhood as a result of longer residential duration (i.e., renters are likely to be more transitory residents in general), and owner-occupiers' ability to tailor the exact form of upgrading they want, and at moderate cost (where the present structure permits), to their own house.

So the mix of tenures in a neighborhood influences the vulnerability of upkeep decisions to even temporary changes in market conditions. A high owner-occupier ratio helps insulate the neighborhood against physical declines that might be triggered by only slight weakness. One of the symptoms and predictors of physical neighborhood decline is therefore a significant shift of structures from an owner-occupier to rental status.

Demographic Character

We have mentioned before that one of the dimensions of neighborhood quality is the status of its residents, which really means the perception by residents of how desirable other actual or potential residents are as neighbors. While researchers often treat this subjective perception as having an objective representation in socioeconomic status, it is not always so. The actual or anticipated habits, mores, values, even appearance of different groups may influence perceptions of their desirability, over and above their education, occupation, or income. The case of racial prejudice is especially important and widespread. Whites of any social class may view blacks of every social class with suspicion, fear, and hatred, regardless of the latter's actual behavior. Inflow of any blacks into an otherwise white neighborhood will often be considered an unmistakable sign of neighborhood decline and provoke responses appropriate to decline—like panic, flight, or defensive behavior (Vandell 1981).

Another population type especially important to neighborhood deterioration is the so-called multiproblem population (Downs 1981; Grigsby et al. 1987), made up of individuals and households with very high incidence of welfare dependency, illness and/or disability, crime, violence, and other antisocial behavior toward one another and other groups. Their presence in significant numbers in a neighborhood is both itself a dimension of the low quality of neighborhood social status and cohesion and a trigger for defensive adjustments (like flight) by others that further weaken the social fabric of the neighborhood.

Although the individuals who make up this group constitute a special concern for society whatever their location within the urban area, there is some belief (though little hard evidence) that the levels of negative externalities generated by them are partly a function of their spatial clustering in critical masses. This is due to the greater (often fiscal) difficulty of using public services effectively to mitigate the problem as well as to the greater likelihood of deviant behavior when critical masses exist to provide quasi-legitimate deviant value systems to support such behavior.

An important difference exists between the demographic character of a neighborhood and the other factors that bear on its quality. As we noted early in this chapter when discussing neighborhood externalities, some factors can be effectively ordered in a noncontroversial way, while others are inherently subjective. In the first class, for example, nearly everyone knows that neighborhood A is better than B, and B better than C, with respect to these factors—even though the observers would differ over which represents the best choice for them (considering their different degrees of preference among A,

B, and C, and their budget constraints). But in the second class, which includes demographic features, there is not even near unanimity that group A is more attractive to live near than group B, or B more attractive than C—nor that A's lifestyle is more desirable for a neighbor than B's, or B's more desirable than C's. Observers will in fact differ markedly; differences will depend on each observer's degree of likeness or unlikeness to the various groups being ranked. Some degree of consensus will probably exist as to the generally nondesired status of multiproblem groups, or of a racial/ethnic group broadly discriminated against in the society, but little else is likely to be broadly agreed upon.

This means that market reflections of neighborhood demographic quality via price premia and discounts will heavily reflect the relative numbers of different groups—and therefore of different preferences—which are active in the market at one time. Insofar as nonconsensual characteristics of demographic structure are important, neighborhood *differences* will compete with neighborhood "quality" in determining relative prices and occupancies across neighborhoods.

Real Estate Agents

Real estate agents are important to the functioning of the housing market complex. In the presence of the considerable heterogeneity of housing and the less than 20% turnover of accommodations in each period, realtors are the richest sources of information about the characteristics of dwelling units and their availability on the market. As such they have great power to influence the match between households and housing units and, thus, the character of inflows into neighborhoods.

In carrying out their functions it has been argued that real estate agents both evince a concern to act as agent for their clients' welfare and share many of the attitudes and prejudices of at least some of their clients. The first leads them to try to fit buyers into neighborhoods "suitable" for them; the second help to define what is a suitable match in majority, stereotypical ways. Thus, on the one hand, they will steer the "right people" away from poor, worsening, or prospectively declining neighborhoods, permitting only less desirable clients, if anyone, to be placed there. On the other hand they are likely to match white with white, black with black, thereby helping to maintain stringent racial segregation in housing while fueling the dynamic of neighborhood racial "tipping" (Helper 1969; Pearce 1979; Yinger et al. 1979).

An exception to this careful separation policy is blockbusting, where deliberately provocative "mismatches" by the above standards are made for the purpose of inciting large-scale flight and thereby speculative gains and heavy property sales for real estate agents and their investor associates. Blockbusting generates unstable, pessimistic expectations out of shock and fear, which can induce deep, prolonged disinvestments that contribute to substantial decline in the physical condition of the area (Galster 1987: ch. 10).

Real estate agents can aggravate an incipient decline by acting on negative predictions so as to change the character of population inflows negatively. They can trigger rapid population turnover and physical deterioration by blockbusting. The formation of their expectations about the future of different neighborhoods is thus a very important influence on neighborhood transitions.

Financial Institutions

Financial institutions play a role in neighborhood transitions by determining which applicants for mortgage credit will be successful. Availability of credit for upgrading, new construction, maintenance, and market turnover sometimes decisively affects whether or not those activities take place. Allegedly decided on "objective" grounds of whether the project is a good credit risk, the decision is often a judgment on the credit worthiness of the applicant and the quality of the neighborhood. Low-status, deteriorated neighborhoods are likely deemed poor credit risks because the negative externalities operating there effectively doom the market success of upgrading or even of market turnover investments. The institutional response may be redlining—a general policy to withhold mortgage finance from such neighborhoods (Schafer and Ladd 1980). Clearly this practice contributes to a worsening of any small declines already begun (Bradford and Rubinowitz 1975; Urban-Suburban Investment Group 1977). It is one of the ingredients of the cumulative self-fulfilling prophecies that power the vicious circles discussed above.

Local Government

Even local government is a contributing actor in the deterioration of some neighborhoods. The quality and variety of public services provided in badly deteriorated neighborhoods are likely to fall significantly for various reasons. The inhabitants of such areas are likely to be politically weak. It may be believed that police and fire protection, for example, are too difficult or dangerous to provide in such areas, or that school room conditions are too chaotic because of the problem population to warrant serious attempts to maintain, let alone upgrade, the quality of schooling. The worsening of public services adds to the lowering of neighborhood quality both directly in itself and indirectly by triggering additional flight by the portion of the remaining population that might have helped to prevent further deterioration. Insofar as the government devises its service-quality differentiation on the basis of population change stereotypes rather than the evidence of actual decline, it should be characterized as an initiator of decline and therefore an integral participant of some of the worst vicious circles.

9.5 Neighborhood Decline and Social Welfare

9.5.1 The Social Costs of Neighborhood Transition

In an earlier section we argued that neighborhood change is often a major component of the process by which the housing market adjusts to large exogenous changes and that, subject to particular institutional constraints placed on that adjustment as a reflection of social values, it may well be an efficient form of adjustment in the sense that so long as the exogenous changes must be experienced, alternative kinds of adjustment may well involve less overall social advantage. Having presented a number of the elements associated with neighborhood decline in the last section, we are now in a better position to examine certain features of the neighborhood transition process more closely, to discover welfare issues that were not discussed earlier.

The first issue is the link between what we have called the comparative static (medium-run) transition process as a stable adjustment and dynamically unstable processes. Under what conditions are individual perturbations likely to generate cumulative self-fulfilling vicious circles instead of coming to closely circumscribed rest? The most important conditions seem to be associated with racial discrimination in housing.

Truly idiosyncratic perturbation may indeed, in the absence of broader information, be read by some individuals as a harbinger of some larger movement to come. But other individuals are likely to read the same instances differently. Then their respective adjustments are likely largely to cancel one another out. The individual instances are likely to be perceived in the same way only if there is some common frame of reference held by most of the group within which the kind of instance in question is conventionally treated the same way.

Racial discrimination and its consequences provide just such a common perceptual framework. The following seems to be the crucial chain of reasoning underlying the common perception: racial discrimination in housing exists; it generates a dual housing market with white neighborhoods and black neighborhoods;[11] black households are effectively excluded from white neighborhoods, not primarily by their own choice or relative lack of income, but by the choice of others (unlike whites, who can *choose* whether or not to live in black neighborhoods); so overall opportunities are not equalized, and black neighborhoods may harbor a pent-up demand by households to "escape" that reflects adverse differentials facing them; in the face of this, neighborhoods that are all white are so because of the existence of effective barriers against blacks (Yinger 1979; Yinger et al. 1979; Galster 1988a; Galster and Keeney 1988). Given this background, if an all-white neighborhood experiences a black household moving in, whites in the neighborhood may well reason that this shows that the erstwhile barrier is no longer so effective and that seeing this, blacks with pent-up demand, having very few other nonghetto housing options, will concentrate their efforts at "escape" to this "penetrated" neighborhood (the hole in the dike through which the whole sea tries to pour in). Regardless of the blacks' percentage in the overall city population, they typically will be capable of totally filling up the given neighborhood—so long as current white residents and/or owners behave in such a way as to let this happen.[12] But these white owners, in turn, are likely to do just that, inasmuch as each one may well reason that, seeing the penetration and anticipating the blacks' concerted efforts, his or her unwillingness to sell out to blacks and/or move away will only be effective if all the others originally in the neighborhood do likewise. Yet there is no way to guarantee that they *will* do likewise, especially since all of them also will reason that their own uncoordinated efforts will be ineffective. Since coordinated exclusionary behavior stronger than their initial barrier is illegal,[13] the reasonable conclusion can be drawn by the individual that the other residents/owners will cave in and the neighborhood will be transformed completely, so the sooner the owner adjusts to the inevitable the better off he or she will be from a financial point of view.

It is clear that the above mind-set is conducive to a homogeneous reading of small signs and a rapid adjustment to it (called *tipping*), so contrary perceptions have little chance to register before the observed larger consequences of first-round adjustments to these expectations take over and the cumulative self-fulfilling process is under way (Schelling 1972; Taub, Taylor, and Dunham, 1984; Galster 1987: ch. 2). The scenario drawn here applies to other types of unwanted "neighborhood invasion" as well as that relating to black-white relations. The key elements in all of them is this shared sense of impending larger forces held at bay by a precarious barrier, coupled with the belief that the individual is helpless in the face of these dangerous forces, part of which consists of the inability to secure coordinated action by the neighborhood's "defenders."

The neighborhood-invasion-and-spasmodic-transition pattern is most likely to be present when larger intersubmarket shifts occur in response to heavy low-income in-migration to the city. As we saw earlier, the price-raising, demand for lower-quality character of these shifts augurs neighborhood decline in both socioeconomic status and housing quality. This is exacerbated when the in-migrants are blacks or other nonwhite groups (because of their easy recognizability).

Another invasion-type scenario, although less marked, occurs where the worst neighborhoods have become concentrations of antisocial, "problem" groups because of self-selected out-migration by the relatively better-off residents, or because of a general thinning out due to urban population declines. Their concentrated presence is accompanied by a rising incidence of crime, violence, vandalism, housing abandonment, and arson, all of which serve to drive out still more of the mobile households, forcing them to cope with higher-priced accommodations in better neighborhoods. This centrifugal impulse can provoke the same sequence of quality-lowering invasions into these other neighborhoods.

The discussion suggests that market adjustment processes are capable of triggering destabilizing downward spirals in neighborhood quality. A main characteristic of such spirals is that they typically carry adjustments beyond the degree called for by comparative static relationships. In efficiency terms, there is an inadvertent excess—an inefficient outcome—due to the confluence of localized externalities and strategic gaming behaviors among residents and owners alike.

A second welfare issue relates to the first. Intersubmarket shifts of residents and dwellings are a constituent of equilibrating market adjustments. In effect, if lower-socioeconomic-status group A is dissatisfied with its present residency relative to other alternatives, it adjusts by moving into submarkets/neighborhoods occupied by somewhat higher-status group B—or attempting to do so. But group A's adjustments make group B worse off than before. If group B attempts to remain in the present neighborhood, it faces inflated housing costs as well as the discomfort and reduced gratification associated with proximity to group A. If group B moves it will incur substantial out-of-pocket, time, and psychological costs of occupancy change and face as well more expensive housing in its new location (although if members are homeowners they may reap compensating capital gains from the sale of their original home). Insofar as group B is induced to adjust by moving into neighborhoods occupied by those of still-higher status, it makes group C there worse off, and some of them, in turn, move, thereby spreading (albeit with progressively less impact) the impulse of "coerced" adjustment. Thus, neighborhood invasions, beginning at either quality extreme, produce a string of (ever-damped) adjustments by making each successively impacted group *worse off*, especially if the invading group is one of low status. Only groups more extreme than the initiating site of the disequilibrium (and *opposite* the intersubmarket direction of resident adjustment) find themselves induced to move because they are now *better off* (i.e., their initial occupancy is no worse for them than before, but they now have better alternatives than previously.)

In most conventional commodity markets, an initiating disequilibrium produces a string of linked adjustments primarily by making participants no worse off in their present consumption situation but better off by shifting to a different pattern. They are induced to change by the potential of improving their situation. But housing market adjustments proceed by compelling people to change in order to escape worse damage. The former proceeds largely by allocating gains, the latter by allocating losses. The difference stems from the strong neighborhood externalities, by which an action by A, involving no exchange with B, can nevertheless make B worse off, with no chance for B to gain redress from A and thus potentially to deter A's action.

Neighborhood turnover is thus a socially very expensive form of market adjustment. Each adjustment by one group generates a whole sequence of adjustments by other groups instead of being confined to the initial point of impact. There is a high social cost to these adjustments. Not only is each household's move both financially and psychologically costly, but established neighborhood institutions are disrupted through large-scale neighborhood transformation and can be reconstructed, if at all, only with large investments of human and nonhuman resources.

How can housing market adjustments be made less socially costly? The culprit is the strength of the many neighborhood externalities which are based on attitudes. With weaker preferences for very high degrees of neighborhood socioeconomic and demographic homogeneity, a whole family of out-migration behavior can be more nearly decoupled from interneighborhood shifts. Many households interested in upgrading would be more likely to do so on site, and financial institutions would be less pessimistic about the security of loans on such ventures. Similarly, modest changes in degree of heterogeneity in a neighborhood stemming from inflow-outflow discrepancies would not necessarily be perceived as destructive of attractiveness or property values.

A special source for the intensity of the distaste for mixing is ethnic/racial prejudice. The taste for similarity is likely to be less virulent than the distaste of particular differences. Indeed, the former may be at least partly developed as a respectable facade for the latter. A more understandable genesis of strong neighborhood externalities is the presence of actual, flamboyantly antisocial behavior. This is heavily concentrated in, but not exclusive to, very poor neighborhoods, especially where occupied by disadvantaged minority groups. It has the double disadvantage of worsening the welfare of residents in those neighborhoods and spreading the stereotyped association of any member of such groups with antisocial behavior. So a mentality of incipient invasion from various potential threats is engendered in neighborhoods considerably above the lowest.

The American ethos of social mobility, with its emphasis on housing and neighborhood status as overt validations of household status, is thus partly responsible for the high social cost of market adjustment. But there is no reason to believe that the valuation of neighborhood quality must perpetually insist on as much homogeneity as it apparently does today. Since some of the actual fear or hatred of particular differences is objectively excessive, efforts to inject stereotype-eroding situations into actual neighborhood contexts are to be recommended. The abundant evidence of a reduction in racial prejudice attendant upon increased interracial contact by equal-status residents is instructive and encouraging in this regard (Simpson and Yinger 1972). In addition, insofar as dislike of heterogeneity stems partly from its anticipated association wth the aforementioned uncontrollable cataclysmic transition process, efforts to defuse such downward spirals are to be commended. Potential public policy options for undercutting the conventional wisdom about the disadvantages of diversity per se and its unavoidable connection with neighborhood transition are discussed below.

9.5.2 The Social Costs of Very Poor Neighborhoods

In the last section we spoke of welfare problems associated with quality-decreasing neighborhood transitions generally. We did not refer specifically to very poor neighborhoods. In the general discussion we were concerned simply about declines in quality levels; in speaking about very poor neighborhoods we must be concerned as well with the absolute level of quality.

There are several reasons why the demographic and physical profiles of the very poorest neighborhoods represent a source of special concern. First, there are threshold levels of structure quality below which further downward conversions by dwelling owners result in noticeably more severe negative externalities for the neighborhood. For example, structures become visibly deteriorated only after a sustained period of deferred maintenance; they become unsafe only when key repairs are not made; they become unhealthy only when certain internal densities are exceeded and/or sanitary facilities function inadequately or not at all. The negative externalities associated with adjustments leading to dwelling abandonment are especially severe and are likely to be concentrated in the poorest areas (Sternlieb and Burchell 1973).

Second, these neighborhoods typically serve as the "ports of entry" to new, low-income in-migrants to the urban area. Even if these in-migrants do not lower the average income of the area (which they often do), they are likely to have especially inelastic demands for housing due to their lack of familiarity with the urban area and their limited access to formal sources of housing market information. As exploitable pools, they thus provide added incentives for owners to supply relatively costly, high-density structures in these neighborhoods, with their concomitant risks of health, safety, and social-psychological problems.

Third, the typical residents of these lowest-quality neighborhoods teeter on the brink of housing crisis. Any minor increase in the cost of supplying minimal-quality units (taxes, utilities, repairs, etc.) or decrease in the residents' income will lead to the unsavory options of homelessness or housing multiple households within a single unit, as we explained in chapter 8. Both options have severe social costs.

Fourth, residents of the poorest neighborhoods who do succeed in improving their economic means will likely try to move out rather than upgrade in place, both because they are unlikely to be homeowners and because the owners of their rental units will be loath to upgrade in the deteriorated environment. Even if they gain no real income increase, the more peaceable remaining residents are victimized and repelled by various antisocial behaviors of the highly concentrated, and highly visible, violent groups. They try to flee to better neighborhoods to avoid worse losses to their well-being, just as in the general neighborhood invasion pattern. The neighborhood location of the poor is therefore to some extent inadvertent as a result of this form of "poverty flight." That such flight induces subsequent reverberatory exodus by higher-income groups from these flight sanctuaries, and so on, serves to exacerbate the inefficiency.

These four neighborhood dynamic factors lead to real social problems involving both inefficiencies and inequities which go beyond the mere poverty of the population. At least three main facets should be mentioned.

Social Costs of a Concentrated Problem Population

The population here is likely to be heavily welfare-dependent, demoralized, and influenced by deviant subculture values, resulting in a high level of violent and other antisocial behavior. Property often is abused and worn out prematurely. Owners cannot hope to rent their property profitably under these conditions, so they avoid upkeep or abandon the property altogether. Resulting vacancies and absence of custodianship lead to vandalism and arson. The consequence is high rates of major inadvertent housing disinvestment and deplorable neighborhood conditions (Sternlieb 1966; Stegman 1972; Sternlieb and Burchell 1973). More generally, social interactions approach jungle ferocity. The absolute quality of the social and physical environment is reduced far below what can be explained in comparative static terms by poverty alone. Thus there is a disastrous inadvertent welfare loss for the very poor as a result of neighborhood dynamics. This is both an efficiency and an equity concern.

Nonrecyclability of Unused and Underused Land

Neighborhoods suffering from high vacancies, vandalism and demolition by violence, and abandonment suffer as well considerable wastage of land. In the presence of high urban land prices generally, such wastage would seem a strong invitation to "neighborhood recycling," especially in changed land uses. But the land can rarely be used productively because so long as demographic, social, and physical remnants of the higher deteriorated neighborhood are present, they cast an environmental pall over prospective new uses. Unless there is comprehensive demolition to achieve a critical mass of homogeneous new use, the land is an economic liability. And large-scale land assembly remains difficult, given an ecology of scattered unused parcels amid used ones and a fragmented pattern of land ownership wasted over extended periods—a clearly inefficient use of scarce resources.

Fiscal Problems of the Central City Government

Interneighborhood shifts have the effect of concentrating most of the problem population of the metropolitan area within the jurisdiction of the central city municipality. These problem neighborhoods provide few tax revenues to the city, but they clearly require an exorbitant allocation of public services. By contrast, relatively few suburban jurisdiction neighborhoods are of the lowest quality, yet their often substantial property tax bases are out of reach of the central city government. Thus, for many metropolitan areas there is a growing city/suburbs disparity—a jurisdictional mismatch—between needs for public services and the fiscal base to meet them (Pohlmann 1986). Local government becomes a more and more ineffectual instrumentality for meeting even the basic needs of the local population, let alone for moderating poverty. Its fragile imbalance of needs and means leads to fiscal crises. Both the actual experience of these crises and fears of new ones lead to lowering the quality of public services, raising effective tax rates, and disproportionately cutting programs with redistributional purposes. Suburban jurisdictions offer services at considerably higher quality levels and at lower effective tax rates. And often their zoning, code, and other regulations prevent establishment of low-income neighborhoods there to take advantage of the more attractive government tax/service packages being offered. This superimposition of problem neighborhoods upon local political jurisdictions least able to deal with them raises crucial equity concerns.

9.6 The Problem of Public Policy and Neighborhood Decline

The goals of public policy vis-à-vis neighborhood dynamics clearly should not be to halt neighborhood deterioration. This would be both inefficient and inequitable to lower-income households, to say nothing about impractical. Rather, the basic policy problem seems to be how to allow or promote a highly decentralized urban housing market to operate efficiently and equitably in the presence of social values reflected in high-minimum-quality housing construction and occupancy standards, and against a backdrop of high social and geographic mobility, with status expressed in neighborhood lifestyles. Add to this a very unequal income distribution and a federal system of government in which local public services are decided on and financed by decentralized fiscal bases which are to an important extent self-separated to maintain high degrees of neighborhood homogeneity.

Without a doubt, some basic values, economic conditions, and demographic changes are not readily manipulated by policies originating at any level of government. Yet there are a variety of actions that both local and higher levels of government clearly could undertake that would be appropriate tools for reducing the inefficiencies and inequities associated with neighborhood dynamics. Most crucial to this effort would be not a housing policy, but rather the widespread reduction of urban poverty and "problem subpopulations" (Varady 1986: ch. 9; Grigsby et al. 1987).

But even in the absence of effective antipoverty efforts, governments could enact a variety of initiatives that could effectively (1) reduce the destructive, self-fulfilling prophecies that result in spasmodic transitions and cumulative declines of neighborhoods, and (2) encourage residents with improved economic means to attain higher housing quality by an upgrading in place instead of out-migration to better neighborhoods. Attaining the former goal can be aided by efforts to reduce the degree of interneighborhood segregation of socioeconomic, ethnic/racial, and social groups, since such segregation is a precondition to the fear that "invasion" inevitably leads to "succession" (Grigsby et al. 1987). Vigorous enforcement of fair housing laws, affirmative marketing for racial integration, and extensions of "fair share" initiatives to deconcentrate low-cost housing opportunities are thus suggested (Galster 1988b). For neighborhoods where some mixing of groups has already been achieved, the defusing of stereotypical flight/disinvestment scenarios can be abetted by antiblock-busting laws, integration management plans, and owner-lender-local government coordination of reinvestment activities as embodied in the Neighborhood Housing Services approach (Ahlbrandt and Brophy 1975). As for the latter goal, policies designed to intensify commitment to neighborhood social networks, relationships, and institutions (Ahlbrandt and Cunningham 1979) and to subsidize owners whose property renovations would produce strong positive externalities for the neighborhood are recommended (Galster 1987: chs. 11, 14).

Furthermore, there is a strategy that warrants special consideration because it not only works toward meeting the aforementioned two goals, but also offers additional equity benefits and broader social externalities as well—encouraging homeownership. As we have seen, in a steady state owner-occupiers engage in greater home upkeep efforts than absentee owners of comparable properties. Moreover, homeowners in a dynamic scenario are more likely to upgrade in place and are less likely to fall prey to the self-defeating gaming strategies that can lead to either stalled upgrading or cumulative quality declines. Both benefits result from the enhanced social cohesion, cooperation, and commitment in the neighborhood engendered by the spatial congruence of residence and ownership of a significant asset (Galster 1987: ch. 14).

9.7 Conclusion

Implicit in the occupation or ownership of housing in urban areas is the fact that the dwelling in question is spatially fixed in a complex neighborhood milieu having social-interactive, psychological, demographic, political, and economic dimensions. Through the vehicles of local externalities and strategic interactions between actors, the behaviors and values of proximate others impinge strongly on the well-being and on the decision calculus of individual residents and property owners. Individual housing choice and reinvestment decisions by these actors, and by those outside a given neighborhood as well, will in turn affect the flows of households and resources over space which determine the future demographic, socioeconomic, and physical character of neighborhood.

Neighborhoods typically are not identical with housing-quality submarkets, but the two concepts are connected in mutually casual ways. On the one hand, because myriad dimensions of the neighborhood are important to the housing consumer, a dwelling's appropriate submarket only can be specified after its particular neighborhood context has been identified. On the other hand, exogenous changes in the metropolitanwide, intersubmarket array of demands or supplies will trigger changes in the composition of a neighborhood's population and the upkeep of its housing stock, to an extent that varies directly with the degree to which the neighborhood's structures are substitutable with those in the submarket where the initial impact occurred.

The qualitative stability of a neighborhood involves, therefore, particular aggregate outcomes of three key sets of individual behaviors: mobility by households into and out of the area, reinvestments by owners of residential property in the area, and new construction there by builders. This result is complicated by the fact that the three sets of behaviors are mutually interactive, and their connections extend beyond the focus of the given neighborhood. Both demanders and suppliers of housing assess not only the absolute conditions in the particular submarket/neighborhood, but judge these relative to the opportunities available to them in other submarkets/neighborhoods. This means that the seeds of change are typically not sown within the particular neighborhood, but rather outside it, in the form of demand or supply shifts in quality submarkets that initially may be substitutively quite remote. As households move, builders build, and owners convert their properties, the initial exogenous impulses eventually are propagated to the dominant submarket(s) represented in the neighborhood in question. Neighborhood change is, therefore, typically a result of metropolitanwide adjustments via the housing submarket complex.

In many contexts this adjustment process is reasonably efficient, even when it involves neighborhood decline. Given the implicit social values reflected in minimum housing codes and zoning regulations, neighborhood decline is the only way to meet, for example, the housing demands of a growing lower-income population in a metropolitan region. However, in some important contexts the extent of neighborhood decline is much greater than would otherwise have been called for by an efficient adjustment. The culprit in these contexts is the high U.S. cultural value accorded to neighborhood status. Destabilizing downward spirals of cumulative decline may be triggered by an "invasion" of lower-status or racial minority households into a higher-status or majority neighborhood, resulting in an extreme spasmodic "tipping" process often accompanied by radical disinvestment and physical decay. The mobility response of the fleeing group generates a sequence of adjustments by other groups in turn that incur high financial, social, and psychological costs overall. Thus the system adjusts to exogenous changes in the demand or supply for various submarkets by generating significant loses through negative externalities and strategic gaming behaviors which induce locational and housing-quality adjustments. It generates wasteful waves of population flight, a continuation of approximately all-or-nothing neighborhood turnover, and a strengthened retention of suspicion and fear about invasion by "undesirables." It makes stable residential mixing of various sorts extremely difficult by discouraging gradualism.

In addition to these general properties of the market adjustment processes, they disproportionately exacerbate the overcrowded, unsafe, unhealthy living conditions of the poorest groups by spatially and jurisdictionally overconcentrating them, denied the presence of more socially stable, economically mobile groups with deeper community ties. This leads to a highly destructive environment in which to live. It is an environment which local government can provide only minimal help to ameliorate because spatial separation is accompanied by jurisdictional separation whereby the central city jurisdiction is left with the problem population and the suburban jurisdictions with the stronger fiscal base.

From a public policy perspective, a variety of initiatives could be implemented to strike at the nexus of inefficiency and inequity associated with spasmodic neighborhood decline and concentrations of low-income populations in neighborhoods of poor absolute quality. In addition to the reduction of poverty in general, the instrumental goals should be the reduction of racial and socioeconomic class segregation (a final goal as well), the defusing of self-fulfilling prophecies that result in rapid transition, and the encouragement of upgrading in place instead of interneighborhood mobility.

Notes

1. Much of the viewpoint of this chapter as well as many of the details are similar to the argument of Downs 1981 and Grigsby et al. 1987. We have come to this confluence independently.

2. There are some empirical exceptions to this generality. In lower-valued neighborhoods some owners have increased their housing reinvestments in the face of falling neighborhood property values; see Taub, Taylor, and Dunham 1984 and Galster 1987: ch. 9.

3. In neighborhoods predominantly comprised of homeowners, however, informal social pressures and homeowners' sense of solidarity and identification with neighbors can often blunt incentives for downgrading responses; see Galster 1987: chs. 3, 9.

4. A graphical portrayal of this scenario is given in ch. 8.

5. Due to land costs these new neighborhoods typically have been located at the fringe of metropolitan areas (Grigsby et al. 1987). Some high-density new construction occurs in redevelopment projects in urban cores as well.

6. Again, assuming limited "infill" of new construction amid otherwise downgraded neighborhoods.

7. This view is in strong contrast to other views that focus only on absolute market conditions in the given neighborhood and emphasize either comparative numbers of demanders and sellers (Goetze 1979; Goetze and Colton 1983) or the comparative income profiles of in-and-out-movers (Grigsby et al. 1987).

8. This especially is likely for incumbent homeowners who hold strong social attachments to the neighborhood; see Clay 1979; Galster and Hesser 1982; Galster 1987: ch. 9.

9. Whether this should be termed "income succession" or not is a matter of debate; cf. Grigsby et al. 1987.

10. This is stressed in Downs 1981.

11. This exaggerates a bit. Racial mixtures appear in both types of neighborhood, but rarely approaching 50–50; one group generally predominates (McKinney and Schnare 1986).

12. The likelihood that one or a few in-migrants will be viewed as harbingers of an incipient invasion—indeed, as its trigger—depends on specific situational features relating to the particular neighborhood and recent history. One of the most important situational features is the neighborhood's nearness to other neighborhoods that are alredy mostly black or are currently undergoing transition in that direction. Both physical nearness and rates of transition in nearby neighborhoods are influential (Leven et al. 1976; Vandell 1981; Galster 1990.)

13. Yet this tactic may be tried nevertheless; witness the shape of harassment directed against blacks who have moved into white neighborhoods in some cities.

Part Three: Analysis of Urban Housing Policies

10 Urban Housing Policy: Demand-Side Approaches

Our model of urban housing submarkets is not only useful in understanding the impacts wrought by various changes in the demographic and socioeconomic character of the population, as shown in the previous two chapters, but also in analyzing the consequences of a wide spectrum of public policies designed to improve housing market performance. Indeed, because most housing policies have notably nonuniform initial impacts across the urban housing complex, it is *only* through our submarket approach that one can clearly comprehend the differential consequences across the housing-quality spectrum, and thereby evaluate these policies on both efficiency and equity grounds.

To illustrate the efficacy of our approach as a vehicle for policy analysis, we consider here and in the next two chapters three alternative categories of housing policy intervention—demand-side, supply-side, and market-regulation approaches. We have selected as archetypes of each category those that most frequently enter the contemporary urban housing policy debate: rental vouchers for tenants, rehabilitation and construction subsidies, and rent controls, respectively (Weicher 1988; Schwartz, Ferlauto, and Hoffman 1988; Keyes and DiPasquale 1988; Sullivan 1990; ch. 14). In our analysis of each policy option we employ the conceptual tools developed in chapters 4–6 and the more heuristic, graphic analysis introduced in chapter 7. Thus we intend to provide analyses that are both rigorous from the perspective of the academic specialist and intuitive from the perspective of the practicing planner or public official. A detailed summary of our findings concludes each chapter. Finally, at the end of chapter 12 we comparatively evaluate the three policy approaches in light of alternative criteria.

We believe that our submarket model represents a unique tool capable of incisive policy analysis. It is unique in its special ability to address short- and longer-run efficiency and equity issues. Because our approach pays attention to the conscious decisions of dwelling suppliers to maintain or alter quality in response to market signals across the submarket array, it easily permits us to analyze whether a policy "holds on" to its initial gains or whether they are negated over time by the endogenous market responses. In analogous fashion it permits comparative equity analyses for those who are direct policy recipients, nonrecipients who also reside in affected submarkets, and those residing in other submarkets. As we demonstrate below, the model can be used readily to illuminate how and why policies frequently produce unintended consequences, even ones that confound conventional wisdom. For example, a fiscally conservative rent voucher policy that severely limits the quality of the submarkets in which the vouchers can be used results in fewer dwellings being upgraded, more dwellings being downgraded, and less new construction than a program with more flexible benefits. Tying rehabilitation subsidies to limitations in subsequent rent increases ultimately harms lower-income tenants by hastening the deterioration of their units which were upgraded originally. Subsidizing construction of new units earmarked for low-income occupancy is a less efficacious means of assisting the bulk of the needy population in the long run than subsidizing the general construction of higher-quality dwellings. A policy putatively designed to help lower-income households afford decent housing by holding down rents in lower-quality submarkets actually makes these households worse off than a broader policy that attempts to control rents across the entire quality spectrum. The rationale of these and other surprising conclusions follows in the next three chapters.

10.1 Principles of the Demand-Side Approach

One alternative for dealing simultaneously with the problems of excessive rent burdens for tenants and their inability to consume decent housing is directly to augment tenants' purchasing power when they search for housing. The earliest federal experience with such a strategy was the 1965 enaction of rent supplements to tenants occupying section 221(d)(3) interest-subsidized buildings. In 1974 similar principles formed the basis of the section 8 program. Both of these approaches subsidize renters only if they occupy particular dwellings. More recently, a scheme wherein the subsidy is tied to the tenant instead of the dwelling has been widely supported and has been instituted on a trial basis in several metropolitan areas across the country. When first introduced in the 1970s it was called the housing allowance, in its more recent reincarnation the rent voucher plan.[1] Although there are many variants, these demand-side, rent subsidy approaches work fundamentally as follows.[2]

Renter households deemed eligible for the program search for accommodations in the local housing market as usual. But their ability to pay market rents is supplemented by the public policy authority.[3] Specifically, the government subsidizes eligible tenants for the difference between what they can afford to contribute toward the rent and the actual market rent for decent dwellings. What *affordability* conventionally means is 30% of gross monthly income. "Actual market rent for decent dwellings" is operationalized by establishing a fair market rent (FMR), which is the equilibrium valuation in the moderate-quality rental submarket.

To illustrate how a rent subsidy policy might work, consider a hypothetical renter household with a monthly income of $600. Suppose that the current market rents for the low-, middle-, and high-quality rental submarkets in the given city are \$300, \$400, and \$500, respectively. Without the policy the household will consume the lowest-quality (least expensive) unit, but still pay 50% of its income to do so. If, in addition, the low-quality submarket is associated with substandard housing quality, the household simultaneously may be subjected to the dual problems of rent burden and slums.

But with a rent subsidy plan that, for example, permits a maximum FMR at \$400 and requires a 30% household contribution, the household can afford to occupy a unit in the middle submarket. The household will pay .30 × \$600 = \$180 in rent, and the government will contribute the remaining \$400 − \$180 = \$220. Thus it appears that by supplementing lower-income renters' housing purchasing power the government can alleviate both their problems of burdensome rents as well as inadequate dwellings. In principle, even those who are homeless could be aided in this fashion and thereby participate once more in the housing market.

Whether these preliminary conclusions are valid can be tested by applying our theory of urban housing markets and submarkets. Initially we examine how a rent voucher scheme utilizing minimum tenant contribution and housing-quality requirements will affect owners of existing rental dwellings. Impacts on builders of new rental units are considered next. A three-submarket graphic analysis is employed to explore the aggregate net results of the policy. Finally, other issues relating to the particulars of how the policy should be formulated are analyzed. Specifically, the consequences of altering the FMR, instituting rent-savings reimbursements, and adopting an unrestricted allowance scheme are investigated.

10.2 Impacts on Owners of Existing Rental Housing

The situation that will confront owners of existing rental dwellings when a rent voucher program is enacted can be analyzed with the aid of figure 10.1, which shows some representative revenue and cost functions. The prepolicy revenue possibilities are shown as MV_1; four units' cost functions are shown as C_{H1}, C^{*}_{H1}, C^{**}_{H1} and C_{H3}.[4] Maximization of net returns implies that the owners of the three units with the C_{H1} functions will choose quality submarket H_1, and the owner of the unit with costs given by C_{H3} will choose H_3 as the initial position.

Now suppose a rent voucher policy is enacted that establishes an FMR corresponding to the current market rent in submarket H_F: MV_{HF}. It grants eligible tenants a voucher equal to the difference between FMR and 30% of tenant income, but is applicable to dwellings only in (or slightly below) submarket, H_F. As explained above, the policy enables participant households who presumably were renting initially in the lowest submarkets to now demand better-quality housing, in submarkets at least as high as H_F. (The degree to which demand is augmented will depend, of course, on the recipients' price elasticity of housing demand.)[5] As a result, the revenue function will shift so

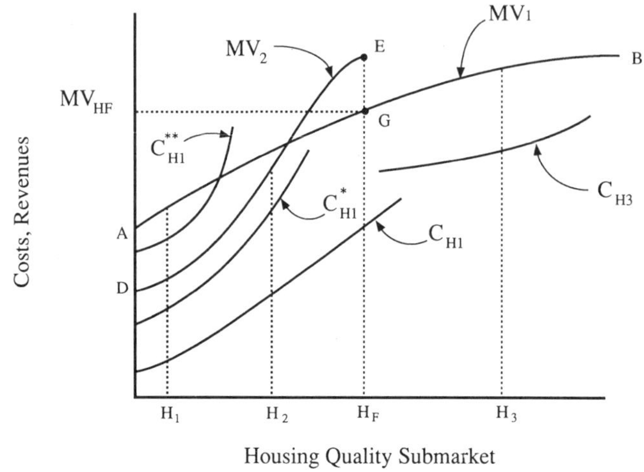

Figure 10.1. Rental housing cost and revenue functions with rent subsidy policy.

as to register demand decreases in lower-quality ranges and demand increases in ranges nearer H_F, as shown by MV_2 in figure 10.1. The locus of revenue opportunities across all submarkets is now shown by DEGB.

With the cross-submarket pattern of revenues distorted, some owners of existing units in various submarkets will be induced to convert their dwellings toward the submarkets where revenues have increased. For instance, the owner having C_{H1} will now find it profitable to upgrade to H_F. The owner having C_{H3} will now find it profitable to downgrade to H_F. The owner having C^*_{H1} will upgrade more modestly to H_2, since upgrading costs rise more quickly. Of course the owners of rental units initially at H_F will have no incentive to alter their units' qualities.

Another sort of adjustment will ensue—housing abandonment. Take the case of the owner having C^{**}_{H1}. This owner will have little incentive to change submarket; although net returns are now negative in H_1, the prospects are probably even more dismal at all possible destination submarkets. No buyer is likely to be found unless a change of ownership somehow drastically reduces costs (by, for example, the tax savings created by depreciation allowances).[6] Over time the lower rents and/or higher vacancy rates will continue to keep revenues less than operating costs. Drastic measures such as becoming delinquent on property tax assessments may postpone the inevitable. But eventually the least competitive owners in the lowest-quality submarkets will be forced to abandon their dwellings so as to cut their continuing losses.

10.3 Impacts on Builders of New Rental Dwellings

As explained in chapter 5, new construction is a minor source of the supply of units for the lowest-quality rental submarkets, even more so in the presence of stringent building codes. But with the onset of rent subsidies, demand systematically is shifted upward from these lowest-quality submarkets to those near H_F—those which more likely can be served by new rental construction. In addition, if any downgrading from submarkets above H_F occurs, these stock reductions can be replenished through building new rental dwellings.

The aforementioned new construction in the moderate and above rental submarkets may for a period divert resources that would have been intended originally for the owner sector. But since this rental construction was stimulated by an increase in the absolute rates of return there (and not, e.g., by a decline in the absolute returns in the owner sector), the long-term effect on construction in the owner sector should be minimal. On net, more resources from nonhousing investments will end up being allocated to the production of new rental housing as a result of the rent subsidy policy.

10.4 Aggregate Impacts of Rent Subsidies on Rental Submarkets

We can usefully illustrate the aggregate effects of the rent voucher policy on rental households, owners of existing rental units, and builders of new rental units with our simplified, three-submarket graphic analysis first introduced in chapter 7. Figure 10.2 shows the three hypothetical rental submarkets in initial equilibrium generated by the functions with the "one" subscripts. Before continuing, some additional comments about the nature of this equilibrium and its relationship to housing policy analysis are in order.

Even though we portray this equilibrium as if it were static, in reality it is but a static picture of a dynamic flow. The stability of the aggregate submarket

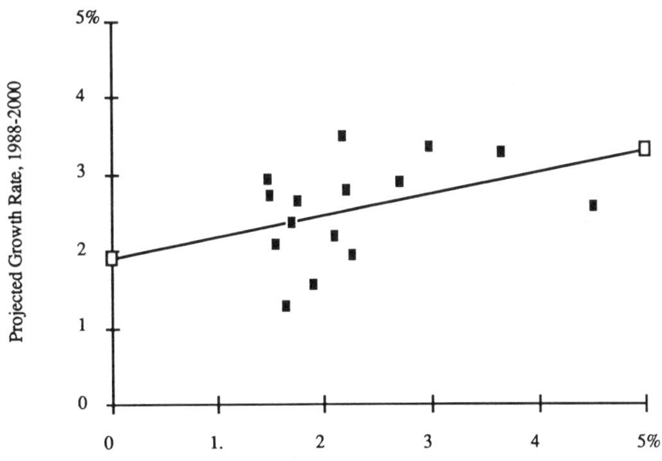

Figure 10.2. Rental submarket dynamics with rent subsidy policy.

demand and supply functions should not mask the reality that individual households are entering, exiting, and moving among submarkets and that individual dwellings are being converted, built, or abandoned. Indeed, as we show in chapters 5 and 6, as dwellings age their cost functions tilt so as to bias conversions toward downgrading. We would thus expect in equilibrium a general pattern (though by no means inexorable) of many dwellings moving downward in quality as a response to their aging, and some even moving out of the market, to be replaced by new construction at higher quality levels.

Our analysis of the aggregate market impact of a housing policy consists of contrasting the aforementioned equilibrium flow with another which has been altered by an ongoing injection of policy inputs, which indefinitely alters the cross-market patterns of demand, supply, or market valuations. Our method consists of (1) specifying the initial, prepolicy equilibrium, (2) showing the policy's short-run disequilibrium impacts, (3) describing the endogenous adjustments leading to the new, postpolicy equilibrium, and (4) enumerating the characteristics of this new equilibrium in comparison to the initial one, with attention paid to efficiency and equity concerns.

Consider now our hypothetical, three-submarket rental sector as shown in figure 10.2. The initial pattern of market valuations, occupied stocks, and total stocks is shown by MV_1, Q_1, and the vertical segment of S_1, respectively. Suppose the rent subsidy policy in question sets an FMR such that $MV_{M1} \leq$ FMR $< MV_{H1}$; that is, recipients can occupy units in the middle-quality submarket but not in the high-quality one.

The initial impact of the enactment of the policy will be to simultaneously decrease demand in the low-quality submarket to D_{L2} and increase it in the middle-quality submarket to D_{M2}.[7] In the short run these shifts push down occupancy rates in the low submarket and reduce rents there to MV_{L2} while simultaneously raising occupancy rates and pushing rents up to MV_{M2} in the middle submarket. Experience with rent vouchers both in the United States and abroad indicates, however, that occupancy rates absorb most of the short-run impact, not rents (Howenstine 1986; Kennedy and Finkel 1987).

Any changes in cross-submarket rent differentials produce subsequent adjustments on the demand-side of the market. Some households initially in the middle-quality submarket (who may not qualify for the rent subsidy) may be forced to move to the low-quality submarket if MV_{M2} rises too far. Some homeless may be able to reenter the low-quality submarket if rent (MV_{L2}) falls sufficiently, even if they are not direct recipients of a rent subsidy. The same could be true for doubled-up households initially in the low-quality submarket who now can afford separate quarters at MV_{L2}. The net effect of all three responses would be to temper both the ultimate demand increase in the middle-quality submarket and the decrease in the low-quality submarket. (For simplicity these adjustments are not drawn in fig. 10.2.)

An alteration in the cross-submarket pattern of net returns also generates medium-run supply responses. There will be net conversions into the middle submarket (through upgrading from the low and downgrading from the high submarket) and new construction there as well, producing an increase in supply to S_{M3}. Assuming the long-run supply function of middle-quality dwellings is not perfectly elastic, MV_{M3} will be greater than MV_{M1}. Downgrading from high to middle submarkets will produce initially a decline in high-quality stock to S_{H3}, but—due to its highly elastic supply—the replacement new construction should return the stock (and rent) to approximately its original level. Upgrading to the middle will lower the stock available in the low-quality submarket to S_{L4} until rents rise from MV_{L2} enough so that all owners of surviving low-quality rental units earn sufficient returns to keep them in business. Again assuming a supply function with a positive elasticity, this new rent (MV_{L3}) should be below MV_{L1}.

As these supply-induced adjustments in rents occur, households will of course further modify their consumption behaviors. These demand readjustments will tend to offset the changes they originally made in response to the short-run rent differentials, as described above.

At this point it should be stressed that a key feature of our approach can only roughly be portrayed in our simplified analysis embodied in figure 10.2—the "ripple effect" of cross-submarket responses. The ripple effect uses the analogy of a stone dropped into a pond, which creates over time an ever-expanding but ever-smaller ripple centered on the point of initial impact. So, too, with an array of quality submarkets: initial disequilibrating impacts create larger market repercussions in submarkets relatively similar in quality to that bearing the initial impact than in those more dissimilar in quality. This can be traced to the behavior of demanders and suppliers of housing, as explained in chapters 5 and 6. Households are less likely to change occupancy in response to a price decline in a submarket which is highly dissimilar in quality, because it represents a relatively poor substitute for the current submarket. Owners of existing dwellings face progressively different costs when contemplating conversions involving progressively larger quality changes. The upshot is that the ripple effect can best be seen in a more finely differentiated array of quality submarkets (as undoubtedly exists in urban housing markets), not in the tripartite simplification employed here.

As a result of the policy the new equilibrium clearly is associated with a comparative decrease in the number of inhabited, low-quality rental dwellings and an increase in the number of middle-quality rental dwellings. The precise quantitative nature of the supply response induced by the rent subsidies will be jointly determined by several factors. The greater the price elasticity (or, more correctly, the cross-price elasticity) of demand for housing by subsidy recipients, the greater the short-run demand shifts which trigger the initial disequilibrating rent differentials. The greater the elasticity of market-period supply from the existing stock in the middle submarket (e.g., the greater the vacancy rate and the more pessimistic the owners' expectations about future rents), the smaller the short-run fillip in returns as subsidy-induced demand intensifies, and thus the smaller the longer-run increment in middle-quality stock. The cheaper it is to renovate the initial stock in the low submarket compared to the costs of downgrading higher-quality stock, the more will the middle-quality supply response take the form of upgrading, and less abandonment will transpire. The lower the costs of new construction of middle-quality dwellings relative to their conversion supply costs, the more will the supply response in the middle submarket take the form of new construction, and the greater will be the amount of abandonment in the low submarket. The efficiency of the rent subsidy thus depends on a host of factors which likely vary across metropolitan areas: the life-cycle and demographic characteristics of the recipients (which affect demands); the characteristics of owners of the existing stock (which affect short-run supply functions); the vintage, structural, and qualitative characteristics of the stock (which affect aggregate conversion supply functions); and the technological, input-price, and industrial organizational characteristics of the local construction industry (which affect new construction supply functions). In spite of this ambiguity the strength of our approach should be manifest; indeed, this emphasis on the "contextuality" of policy response is a prime analytical contribution. We not only provide unmistakable qualitative predictions about the sorts of repercussions which would transpire throughout the market complex, but also point to the key parameter estimates which would be needed in order to make quantitative efficiency evaluations for particular urban housing markets.

Next consider equity implications for direct recipients of subsidies, indirect recipients, and others. The well-being of direct recipients clearly has been improved. They now occupy a superior quality of dwelling (presuming they so choose) but spend a lower fraction (30%) of their budget doing so. Nonparticipants may be affected appreciably through policy-induced rent changes, especially in the short run. The smaller the elasticity of short-run supply in the low-quality submarket, the greater the rent decline associated with the initial, policy-induced demand decline. This means greater welfare gains for tenants originally occupying the low-quality submarket and for the homeless who can move back into this submarket as a result. The degree to which these welfare gains to other low-income people who are not direct recipients will persist depends on the elasticity of the medium-run supply function in the low submarket.[8] Conversely, those originally occupying middle-quality dwellings are harmed in the short run as their rents are bid up by subsidy recipients. Those in high-quality housing are harmed as well, to the extent that downgrading from the high to the middle submarkets occurs and is not quickly offset by new construction. These losses are less likely to persist into the longer run, given our arguments about the relatively higher supply elasticities associated with better-quality submarkets.[9]

It therefore appears that, at least at a qualitative level, a rent subsidy policy would on balance have positive efficiency and equity consequences. Program participants would be aided with little likelihood of severe, unintended housing market repercussions. Some "slum" dwellings would be improved, and fewer people would be forced to live in them (or on the streets). Some downgrading of dwellings initially above FMR submarkets would be predicted, as would be new construction at these quality levels and higher. Rents in the middle-quality (FMR) submarkets would be inflated somewhat in the short run, but rents in the lower-quality submarkets would be deflated. These changes in rents would mean some losses in welfare for middle- and upper-income groups, coupled with gains for lower-income groups that did not participate in the program directly. It is likely that these initial welfare effects would be moderated as the stock adjusted over time.

Abandonment is the one unfortunate supply consequence likely with rent subsidies. It is clear that abandonment imposes undesirable externalities on neighboring residents and can create destructive, pessimistic expectations on the part of nearby property owners. Without knowing the precise spatial distribution of low-quality rental units in a city adopting rent subsidies, it is impossible to ascertain whether certain neighborhoods consisting of these units will be characterized predominantly by upgrading, abandonment, or a mixture. It can be suggested, however, that an aggressive public program of demolishing abandoned units[10] can minimize their negative impacts and pave the way for wholesale land use changes in affected areas. Another alternative would be to couple a rent subsidy program with one providing upgrading subsidies to property owners, but a fuller analysis of such a supply-side subsidy must await the next chapter.

10.5 Other Issues in the Formulation of Rent Subsidy Policy

Up to this point we have discussed a rent voucher policy that utilizes minimum tenant contributions and housing-quality requirements. Here we analyze variants on this policy approach. For more comprehensive discussions, see Lowry (1983: chs. 3–5), Howenstine (1986: chs. 3–7), and Weicher (1988).

10.5.1 Establishing Fair Market Rent Levels

What should be the highest rent that will qualify for reimbursement under the policy? The choice depends upon the policymaker's tradeoffs among budgetary allocation, the number of households targeted for assistance, and the minimum level of housing quality for which affordability by participants is guaranteed. Although our model provides no guidance as to the "correct" choice, it does help trace the consequences that will result, depending on the choice.

The crux of the prediction is that (1) downward conversion will predominate over upward conversion, and (2) the conversion response will predominate over the new construction response, the lower the FMR that is set. We showed above that with a rent voucher policy there is a tendency for the existing stock to gravitate toward the submarket corresponding to the FMR so as to meet the expected cluster of demand upsurges there. Thus, the lower the FMR that is set, the greater the number of dwellings that will be downgraded—some from submarkets immediately above the FMR, others from still-higher quality submarkets to replace those that were downgraded from the former. Just the opposite will be the case for upgrading: there will be fewer total units that will have the potential to upgrade profitably to the FMR submarket.

The lower the FMR, the smaller the likelihood that builders of new rental units can profitably (or legally) compete with converters of existing units to meet the swelling demands in the FMR submarket. However, because in this scenario there will be intensified chains of downgraded units from higher submarkets, there will be an enhanced stimulus for new construction at these latter quality levels. The ultimate distribution of new, converted, and unconverted stocks across these submarkets above FMR cannot be predicted without knowing more about the size distribution of dwellings there and the precise nature of their relevant conversion cost functions and ownership characteristics.

The foregoing suggests implications for changes in the spatial patterns of housing qualities. Assume that new rental construction will not occur predominantly in the same neighborhoods where some dwellings are being converted as a result of the subsidy policy. Then a lower FMR means that more existing neighborhoods will experience a decline in housing stock quality, fewer will experience an upgrading of quality, and the new neighborhoods built will consist of higher-quality dwellings, all else equal. These are additional factors to be considered, along with the other efficiency and equity concerns, when FMRs are set for a rent voucher policy.

10.5.2 Incentives for Reducing Policy Costs

One aspect of the rent voucher plan under consideration builds in inefficiently high budgetary outlays. If the government issues a voucher that defrays 100% of the difference between FMR and 30% of the participant's income, there are no incentives for participants to occupy dwellings costing less than FMR.[11] In other words, since tenants must contribute 30% of their income in any event, it is in their interest to gain the greatest value of additional subsidy beyond their contribution. As a consequence, landlords of units somewhat below FMR submarket quality have an incentive to raise rents to FMR, even if they do not upgrade. The result is both that some participants are induced to consume more housing than is optimal (given their preferences) and that rents for dwellings near and at such quality levels are unnecessarily inflated (at least in the short run).

To weaken these perverse incentives several schemes have been proposed. The simplest stipulates that for every $10 below FMR the recipient's rent is, the government will reduce by only $5 the subsidy that would have been paid if the rent were FMR. Put differently, if the participant can find a unit below FMR, the scheme will split the savings evenly between participant and government.[12] The key result is that all participants will not automatically occupy units of FMR, and participants will have a vested interest in obtaining less expensive lodgings, thus tempering landlords' inflationary incentives.

To illustrate how this scheme is intended to operate, consider the following hypothetical scenario. There are four renter households A–D who are eligible for a rent voucher policy. They currently occupy three submarkets: H_1, H_2, H_3, which have rents at \$300, \$400, and \$500, respectively. The particulars of the initial situation are given in table 10.1, panel 1.

Now assume that a conventional rent voucher policy is enacted, wherein FMR is set at \$500 and a 30% participant contribution is required. All the above households will likely participate, since they can now consume H_3 quality and (with the exception of household C) simultaneously devote a lower fraction of monthly income to housing. If they did so, the situation would be as shown in panel 2 of table 10.1. In this case the total subsidy required monthly from the government would be \$980, or an average of \$245 per recipient.

But consider what might occur if the rent voucher policy included a 50-50 cost-saving clause whereby the recipient could keep 50% of any rent savings below FMR. Now the recipients have a financial incentive to moderate their

Table 10.1 Illustrations of Alternative Rent Voucher Plans

	Household			
	A	B	C	D
Panel 1				
Income	\$600	\$800	\$1000	\$1000
Original submarket	H_1	H_2	H_1	H_2
Market rent	\$300	\$400	\$300	\$400
Rent/Income	50%	50%	30%	40%
Panel 2				
Submarket	H_3	H_3	H_3	H_3
Rent	\$500	\$500	\$500	\$500
Tenant share	\$180	\$240	\$300	\$300
Government share	\$320	\$260	\$200	\$200
Rent/Income	30%	30%	30%	30%
Panel 3				
Submarket	H_1	H_2	H_2	H_3
Rent	\$300	\$400	\$400	\$500
Tenant share	\$180 − 100*	\$240 − 50*	\$300 − 50*	\$300
Government share	\$120 + 100*	\$160 + 50*	\$100 + 50*	\$200
Rent/Income	13%	24%	25%	30%

*Denotes the refund to the recipient based on the cost savings from occupying housing costing less than FMR.

housing demands. The situation could well be as shown in panel 3 of table 10.1. In this case the total subsidy cost to the government would be only $780 (an average of $195 per recipient).[13] In addition, the well-being of recipients would be improved because the rent-saving reimbursement reduces household expenditures on housing (and rent/income ratios) even more and permits recipients to allocate more funds to nonhousing goods.

There will be several housing market impacts from such a plan as well. Since the incentive for all recipients to consume at FMR is reduced, the policy-induced increases in housing demand will be more diffused across rental submarkets. This, in turn, means that necessary modifications in the existing stock will, on average, involve a smaller absolute change in quality and, therefore, a lower-cost, more elastic supply response. The benefit of this in terms of moderating policy-induced, short-run rent inflation and minimizing program budgetary allocations could be substantial. In addition, some owners who might have opted for abandonment rather than remaining in the deflated low-quality submarket or upgrading to the FMR submarket may now find it profitable to upgrade more modestly.

A less salutary result would be that there would be less upgrading of the rental stock under the rent-savings reimbursement scheme. Because the demand will not be directed, on average, to as high a quality submarket, there will be less incentive overall for owners of units originally below FMR to improve their dwellings. Therefore if a primary goal of a subsidy policy is to abet neighborhood revitalization, such a variant would be less helpful.

10.5.3 Unrestricted Allowances

Finally, consider a rent subsidy plan that is less restrictive than the scheme discussed above: a housing allowance that does not require tenants to consume a minimum quality of housing and allocates to each recipient a cash allowance equaling the difference between 30% of tenant income and FMR. It is, in effect, a pure income supplement that is connected with housing only inasmuch as its size is based on FMR.

There are several appealing features to this unrestricted variant. Administrative costs are reduced and recipient freedom of choice is enhanced. Because households are free to use the allowance as they please, they will have the strongest possible incentive to search for the best value in the market that represents their optimal housing consumption. The need for a rent-savings reimbursement scheme is thus obviated. Reductions in tenant rent burdens can be expected.[14] Finally, because presumably recipients' housing preferences will differ, the demand upsurges induced by the policy will be spread over a wider range of submarkets than under a voucher/minimum-quality requirement plan.[15] In terms of figure 10.1, the MV_2 function would not be as depressed in the range of H_2, would not be so great at H_F, and would not fall discontinuously above H_F. As explained above, this has the advantage of minimizing short-run rent inflation and permitting a less-costly conversion response, but the disadvantage of reducing the net aggregate improvements in the existing rental stock.[16]

Consequences that follow from varying the size of the allowance payments can be elucidated similarly to the above analysis regarding setting FMR. The larger the subsidy, the greater will be the net improvements in the existing stock, as owners adjust their dwellings to demand upsurges in somewhat higher submarkets. Similarly, as demand is spurred to higher rental submarkets, the contribution made by new construction to the net stock increase will grow.

10.6 The Impacts of Rent Subsidies: A Summary

In this chapter we have illustrated the unique perspective that our model of urban housing submarkets contributes to an analysis of the efficiency and equity aspects of housing policy. Our analysis indicates that the institution of any of a variety of ongoing rent subsidy policies would do the following:

1. Decrease the number of occupied, substandard-quality rental units, reduce the rent burdens of recipients, have minimal adverse impacts on nonrecipient households occupying FMR-quality levels and (especially) higher, and have favorable impacts on nonrecipient households who are homeless or occupying lower-quality submarkets, especially in the short run;
2. Induce owners of existing rental units to convert units toward the "impacted" rental submarkets (i.e., where FMR prevailed or, equivalently, where most of the allowance-induced demands were directed), thereby producing both upgrading and downgrading of various segments of the rental stock;
3. Generate new construction primarily at and above the effected rental submarkets, with negligible impacts on construction in the owner sector;
4. Induce abandonment of the least competitive units in the lower-quality rental submarkets;
5. Stimulate relatively more downgrading and less new construction the lower the FMR level or allowance amount established; and
6. Provide greater benefits to recipients, smaller budgetary outlays, and tempered short-run rental inflationary pressures, but less overall upgrading of the stock, if rent-savings reimbursement schemes were adopted as part of an FMR-style subsidy policy or if an unrestricted voucher policy were adopted.

How these conclusions comport with those of other policy options is discussed at the end of chapter 12.

Notes

1. As early as 1968 the section 236 program subsidized the rents of households in qualifying projects, but unlike the schemes discussed here the subsidy was tied to the particular apartment. The same was true of the subsequent section 8 program. The

section 235 program provided a precedent for supplementing the purchasing power of low-income home buyers by reducing mortgage costs. See Weicher 1979, 1988 and Sullivan 1990: ch. 14 for a review of these policies.

2. For comprehensive descriptions and evaluations of variants of this strategy, see Struyk and Bendick 1981; Bradbury and Downs 1981; Lowry 1983; Friedman and Weinberg 1983; Howenstine 1986; Hartman, Meyerson, and Bratt 1986; Kennedy and Finkel 1987; and Schwartz, Ferlauto, and Hoffman 1988.

3. Typically the program would be administered by a local housing authority but funded by the federal government. In principle, however, any level of government could fund it.

4. Recall from ch. 5 that market valuation and cost functions are assumed to be expressed in opportunity terms, i.e., relative to the cost of capital.

5. A review of the evidence suggests that this elasticity is slightly below unity; see Quigley 1979. For variants of the demand-side approach that effectively represent income transfers, the recipients' income elasticity of demand becomes relevant; see Struyk and Bendick 1981: chs. 6–7.

6. This is much less likely given the 1986 federal tax law revisions.

7. This transferral of demand need not be one for one. If some program participants were not originally households, e.g., if they had lived in another household or were homeless, the increase in D_M would exceed the initial decrease in D_L.

8. Evidence from the Experimental Housing Allowance Program suggests that rents in the low submarket will eventually climb to approximately their original level; see Struyk and Bendick 1981; Bradbury and Downs 1981; Lowry 1983; and Friedman and Weinberg 1983.

9. The limited evidence on long-run supply elasticities for new construction of single-family homes supports this proposition; see Quigley 1979.

10. Or recycling them through a program such as Urban Homesteading.

11. Although they do have an incentive to search for the highest-quality unit available at FMR.

12. In fact in the case of the section 8 program, such a rent-savings reimbursement scheme has been implemented.

13. In general, the monthly subsidy savings per recipient is $(1 - n)(FMR - R)$ where n is the percentage of the rent savings reimbursed to the household and R is the rent of the dwelling occupied by the recipient.

14. The Housing Allowance Demand Experiment found that the average recipient rent burden fell from 40% to 25%, and the vast majority of the subsidies were allocated to nonhousing consumption (especially in sites having a tight housing market) when no minimum housing-quality standards for participation were enforced and when the grant took the form more of a general income supplement than a rent reduction; see Struyk and Bendick 1981: chs. 6–7 and Lowry 1983. European experience with such an unrestricted strategy is summarized in Howenstine 1986.

15. Based on the Housing Allowance Supply Experiment, Lowry 1983: ch. 6 estimates that the program-induced demand increases for the middle one-half to two-thirds of the rental stock were 4.6–5.6%; corresponding demand decreases in the lower-quality submarket were 3.5–6.0%.

16. The Housing Allowance Supply Experiment found that few landlords made repairs over $100 in response to the program over five years; homeowner participants on average invested $75–100 more annually. This minimal supply response was due to the

fact that relatively few eligible households participated and perhaps because landlords did not expect the program to be permanent; see Struyk and Bendick 1981. Lowry 1983: ch. 6 estimates that the broad, middle-quality submarket would grow by 4–5% if the experiment were continued for ten years; the corresponding decline in the lower-quality stock would have been 3–5%. Experience with rent supplement approaches in Europe suggests that the impact on both rehabilitation and new construction has been considerable (Howenstine 1986).

11 Urban Housing Policy: Supply-Side Approaches

11.1 Principles of the Supply-Side Approach

The demand-side approach discussed in the previous chapter focuses its subsidies on households and lets their resultant behaviors produce signals across the housing submarket array which ultimately lead to a hopefully efficacious supply response over time. By contrast, the alternative approach to urban housing policy analyzed here initially directs its efforts toward the supply side of the market. The central tenet of the supply-side approach is that if owners and/or builders can be encouraged to produce more decent-quality units by reducing their costs, the relevant housing supply will be augmented and equilibrium prices and rents will fall. This means that more households will be able to escape from homelessness or substandard conditions and/or their rent burdens will be reduced. Unlike the demand-side strategy, this approach pays subsidies directly to the suppliers of particular dwellings.

All levels of government have sponsored such production-subsidy programs. The public housing program, the section 221(d)(3) below-market interest rate program and the section 236 program for rental-sector construction subsidies, and the section 8 substantial rehabilitation grants for improving the existing rental stock in Neighborhood Strategy Areas are representative of federal efforts. More recently, the Tax Reform Act of 1986 provided tax credits for those who built or rehabilitated structures housing specified fractions of lower-income tenants. States have frequently issued general credit obligations in order to provide low-interest loans and grants to lower-income homeowners and landlords for property repairs and improvements. Localities have often allocated their Community Development Block Grant funds to similar rehabilitation subsidy programs. Indeed, such supply-side initiatives have constituted the overwhelmingly predominant form of public intervention in the private housing sector in the United States. In addition, private, nonprofit, and community-based organizations have made significant efforts to supply low-cost dwellings.[1]

In this chapter we again employ the analytical devices introduced in earlier chapters. Three distinct archetypical variants of the supply-side approach are considered: subsidies to rehabilitate existing dwellings, "shallow" subsidies for the construction of high-quality dwellings that ostensibly trigger "filtering" of units to lower-quality levels, and "deep" subsidies for the construction of dwellings intended directly for occupancy of low-income households. For each variant we analyze impacts on individual owners of existing dwellings, as well as the aggregate consequences across the array of submarkets, so as to draw conclusions about policy efficiency and equity.

Again, our approach stresses that it is not merely the initial, short-run impact of the policy which must be considered. Of even greater importance are the longer-run consequences that occur endogenously as both suppliers and demanders adjust among submarkets. These adjustments tend to counteract the initial policy impetus and will be greatest in the submarkets that bear the brunt of the initial policy impact, somewhat less in those of relatively similar qualities, and still less in those of substantially different qualities. This "ripple effect" of policy-induced repercussions is a central proposition which yields not only distinctive conclusions about program efficiency, but also ones about differential impacts on various groups of households and property owners that inform equity judgments. Put more bluntly, conventional analyses of supply-side subsidies often overlook how the market responds in ways that offset the original subsidy. They fallaciously consider a newly built unit as a visible addition to supply and ignore the reactions across submarkets that invisibly create other losses in the stock.

11.2 Subsidizing Rehabilitation of Existing Dwellings

Consider first an archetypical supply-side policy that compensates owners for the capital costs of rehabilitating their dwellings. Specifically, assume here that the policy pays 100% of the landlords' costs of repairing or replacing those items in rental units that constitute code violations.[2] Once repairs are made, assume initially that there are no subsequent restrictions on the rent that may be charged or on who may be an eligible tenant in these rehabilitated structures. As before, our analysis considers the impacts on owners of existing rental units, on builders of new units, and aggregate impacts on the set of submarkets. Variants of this basic scheme are then investigated in the same manner.

11.2.1 Impacts on Owners of Existing Units

The hypothetical situation facing owners of several rental units is portrayed in figure 11.1. Given a revenue function MV_1, owners of the units with cost functions C_1 and C_1^* find that their initial optimum submarket is H_1; the corresponding submarket for the units with cost functions C_2 and C_2^* is H_2. Suppose that the unit with C_1 has code violations eligible for subsidized repair.

Now with the adoption of the aforementioned rehabilitation grant program, the owner of this unit discovers that the cost function for upward conversion has been reduced. If all such violations were repaired, suppose that the dwelling could move from submarket H_1 to H_2. Thus in this quality range *AD* the new conversion cost function rises only to the extent that operating costs in these higher-quality ranges grow progressively.[3] Beyond the point where all eligible repairs are made (point *D*) the new cost function will rise parallel to the original one, to indicate that further upward conversion costs are not subsidized. Downward conversion costs remain unaffected. In sum, the new conversion cost function facing the owner, C'_I, is shown in figure 11.1 as *GADJ.*

With these reduced costs it clearly makes sense for this owner to make the repairs and, consequently, to upgrade the unit to H_2. But what rent will be charged? In order to match the initial return $B - A$, the owner would only need to charge the rent corresponding to point *E*, thereby earning return $E - D$. But because the unit is now indistinguishable from other H_2 units, there is no reason why the owner cannot also charge what the market will bear—the rent corresponding to point *F.*

Of course the exceptionally high returns $(F - D)$ earned by the first set of owners to upgrade cannot persist indefinitely, as new upgraders and owners of units originally in H_2 compete down the rent in H_2 and in the other submarkets to which the magnitudes of their quality improvements destine them. Conversely, as the stock available in H_1 (and other origin submarkets of the upgraders) declines due to the upgrading, the rents will rise there. This is portrayed by the dashed modifications of the revenue function—MV'_I in figure 11.1.

These relative rent changes may encourage some households to switch their demands from H_1 to H_2, thereby tempering this change in revenues. Simultaneously, the alteration in the cross-submarket pattern of returns will induce some owners of units originally in H_2 to downgrade (although presumably not in a fashion which would lead to code violations). This is illustrated in the case of the owner facing C_2^* and MV'_I in figure 11.1. Thus, to the extent that any reduction in real rents in H_2 produces fewer households switching demands from H_1 to H_2 then the number of units upgraded between these two submarkets,[4] the policy likely will produce some "compensatory downgrading" to replace at least partially the upgraded stock.

Note that upgrading through participation in the rehabilitation grant program is not necessarily the optimal strategy for all owners having code violations. Even with costless repairs of code violations, the intersubmarket differential in *operating* costs (perhaps in conjunction with the new rent differential) may be sufficient to warrant refusing the subsidy and remaining in H_1. This nonparticipation would be minimized to the extent that code violations resulted in swift, certain, and substantial legal penalties for the owner.

But even if all owners of dwellings which were in violation when the policy was initiated chose to upgrade, this does not necessarily mean an elimination of low-quality units. So long as all the erstwhile occupants of code-violating dwellings were not willing and able to move to a higher submarket and pay the associated rent, some effective demand for low-quality, unimproved

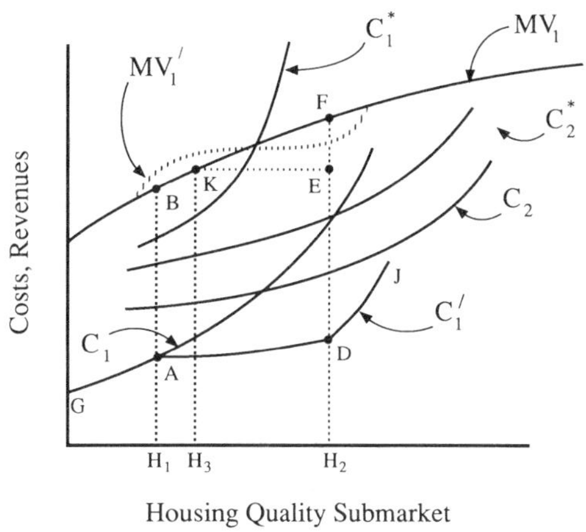

Figure 11.1. Rental housing cost and revenue functions with rehabilitation subsidy policy.

dwellings will persist. This, in turn, means that profit potentially can be earned by owners of units initially in that submarket and those who downgrade to it, so long as they can do so at sufficiently low operating cost and without violating codes. (And, since in the real world code enforcement is far from perfect, some below-code units will almost certainly be present.)

11.2.2 Impacts on Builders of New Units

The rehabilitation subsidy policy would affect the new construction sector only insofar as some new construction would have been forthcoming in the submarkets that serve as destinations for the subsidized upgraders. That is, if building was going to occur in H_2 before the policy, the subsidizing of certain upward conversions into H_2 encourages that form of supply instead of new construction. The magnitude of this effect will be smaller, the lower the quality implicit in H_2, however. Insofar as the aforementioned compensatory downgrading originates in submarkets of higher quality than H_2, the net impact on new construction in these origin submarkets will be positive.

11.2.3 Aggregate Impacts of Rehabilitation Subsidies on Rental Submarkets

Consider next the ultimate impacts on the rent and housing stock patterns across rental submarkets which will result in the long run after the enactment of a rehabilitation subsidy policy. These impacts will depend on the cost functions of the dwellings that participate in the rehabilitation program and the cost functions of the dwellings in the submarket to which the rehabilitated units are destined, as well as those of dwellings in other, higher submarkets that may convert downward as a response to these shifts. It is these cost functions which, in aggregate, specify the relevant conversion supply functions into and out of the various submarkets, as explained in chapters 5 and 6. To explain this we employ our previous, three-submarket graphic model. We assume for simplicity that the rehabilitated units are in the low-quality submarket originally and are converted into the middle-quality one (see fig. 11.2).

Consider, on the one hand, the extreme situation in which the units that upgrade happen to have comparatively low costs of operating at the destination submarket (like those represented by C_1 in fig. 11.1), and the lower-cost units originally in the destination submarket have the least cost savings by downgrading (like those represented by C_2 in fig. 11.1). As a result of these assumptions, rents in H_2 initially will be competed down to a relatively low level after the initiation of the policy (i.e., near point E in fig. 11.1). In terms of figure 11.2, this low-cost group of upward converters shifts the middle-quality submarket supply S_{M1} to S_{M2} and simultaneously shifts the low-quality submarket supply from S_{L1} to S_{L2}. Owners originally in H_2 find it more profitable to compete in H_2 than to convert, given their assumed cost functions, so S_{L2} and S_{M2} persist. Rents in the middle submarket fall correspondingly to MV_{M2} and rise in the low to MV_{L2}.

As a result of these new rent differentials, some of the erstwhile residents of H_2 submarket units will be willing and able to move up to H_2, and demands will adjust accordingly, as shown by D_{M2} and D_{L2} in figure 11.2. (Note that from the perspective of either submarket the price of a substitute good has changed absolutely; hence both submarket demands shift in their entirety.) The magnitude of these shifts will depend on the idiosyncratic cross-price elasticity of housing demand between these two submarkets in the given metropolitan area.

Whether this sequence of upgrading, rent deflation in the middle-quality submarket, and low-income renter demand increases (decreases) in the middle (low) submarket produces incentives for large-scale downgrading of units

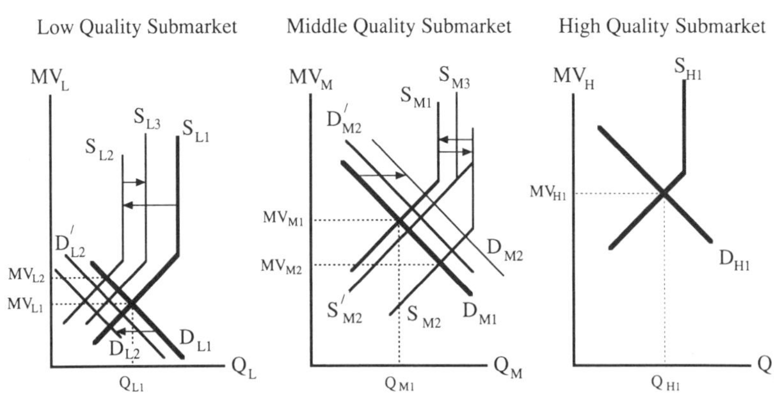

Figure 11.2. Rental submarket dynamics with rehabilitation subsidy policy.

from the middle- or even high-quality rental submarkets depends on several factors. Downgrading from the middle submarket will be minimized to the extent that the original units in this submarket save little in costs by downgrading, yet can still compete effectively in the middle with the newly upgraded units because the formers' *level* of costs is relatively low. The same can be said about compensatory downgrading from higher-quality submarkets. Under these contingencies the initial supply shifts shown in figure 11.2 will approximate their long-run position. The extent of downgrading will also be inversely related to the cross-price elasticity of demand by occupants in lower-quality submarkets. With an ideal confluence of conversion cost functions and demand elasticities, it is theoretically possible for a rehabilitation subsidy policy to expand the middle-quality stock and deflate its rents for an indefinite period.[5] Some erstwhile low-quality dwellings (and the neighborhoods in which they were located) thus would be improved, and the future downgrading of dwellings below middle quality would be discouraged, without sizable adverse unintended consequences. These are promising efficiency implications indeed.

From an equity standpoint, households originally living in the low-quality submarket but who were able to move up to a preferable submarket clearly will benefit from the policy. Occupants remaining in low-quality submarket units will not be adversely affected if rents are little changed from initial absolute levels. This is likely the case in both short and long run when the number of upgraded units approximates that of households who subsequently choose to consume in the middle submarket.[6] Occupants of the middle-quality submarket will be better off under the policy because the real cost of the housing they occupy has been reduced. Property owners reap capital gains in the areas where the number of low-quality (presumably substandard) rental dwellings has been reduced. Owners of middle-quality dwellings which now face stiffer competition from rehabilitated units suffer some capital losses. Households who are "doubled up" in the low submarket and the homeless are not likely to be strongly affected one way or the other.

On the other hand, the results are not nearly as salutary if the configuration of cost functions proves to be quite different. Suppose subsidized units happen to be those with relatively high middle-quality operating costs, such as the unit with cost C_l in figure 11.1. Also suppose units originally in the middle not only have relatively high costs, but costs that drop rapidly when downgrading occurs, as shown in figure 11.1 as C_2^*.

In this case the initial upgrading response can be portrayed in figure 11.2 as supply function S'_{M2}, which generates little reduction in middle submarket rents from MV_{M1}. Fewer renters in the low-quality submarket can afford to move up to middle quality (whatever their cross-price demand elasticity), so the demand changes will be modest, as shown by D'_{L2} and D'_{M2}. As a consequence of the new rent differential, some owners of middle-quality units will downgrade their dwellings.[7] This tends to drive the stocks in both low and middle submarkets back toward their initial levels, as shown by S_{L3} and S_{M3} in figure 11.2.

Thus, if the subsidized stock is costly to maintain at higher quality levels and/or the original stock in the destination submarkets of these upgraded units (and/or the stock in even higher submarkets) can reap large cost savings through downgrading, a rehabilitation subsidy policy will have comparatively little efficiency.[8] The physical or financial housing conditions of few households will be enhanced. And there will be little net improvement overall in the rental stock, because compensatory downgrading will offset the units with rehabilitation subsidies. The importance of the particular housing market context in which a rehabilitation subsidy policy is implemented is thus manifest.

11.2.4 Variants of the Rehabilitation Subsidy Policy

In the previous section we analyzed a policy aimed at rehabilitating rental units with no subsequent controls on permissible rents. Here we consider how our conclusions need to be modified if our policy for rental units attempted to control rents of the upgraded units, and if our policy was directed toward owner-occupants instead of the rental sector.

Suppose initially that a policymaker tried to ensure that the original tenants could afford to remain in their dwelling even after it had been rehabilitated. An obvious means for doing so would be to stipulate that owners receiving rehabilitation subsidies must accept limitations on their postrehabilitation rent levels. Several sorts of limitations are conceivable, and each has its particular drawbacks.

The most extreme limitation would be to freeze real rents in perpetuity at prerehabilitation levels (or perhaps to permit increases only in line with inflation of operating costs). These limitations would also apply to the potential buyers of such dwellings. In such a scenario it is doubtful that many owners would voluntarily participate. Even if a 100% subsidy of rehabilitation capital costs were involved *and* there were no differences in operating costs between origin and destination submarkets, the owner would still gain no extra net returns by participating.[9] And if either of the prior two conditions were not met, the owner's returns would drop by participating. In either case participation would need to be induced by coercion, for example, by swift, uncompromising code enforcement coupled with stiff penalties for violations.

A less extreme limitation would be to permit rent increases in the rehabilitated units that would cover incremental operating costs between origin and destination submarkets plus some added profit. In such a case the problem of participation would be overcome, but with the concomitant tradeoff in the resultant affordability of the rehabilitated units. In addition, unless the original owner were restricted from selling the unit for some period, some owners would find it more profitable to realize their capital gains, and the purchaser would be free to raise rents to market levels. Finally, the problem associated with any form of rent control would emerge—downgrading over time. Suppose, as illustration, the owner of the rehabilitated dwelling in submarket H_2 was permitted to charge the rent associated with point E in figure 11.1. But since costs C'_l decline to the left of H_2, the owner would find it profitable to let the dwelling deteriorate to H_3 while holding rent at level E (equal to K). This adjustment, of course, would offset to some extent the impact of the rehabilitation subsidy. Although certain features were repaired, other features (which presumably did not violate code) would be allowed to deteriorate. (Rent control is analyzed more fully in the next chapter.)

Many of the aforementioned concerns are obviated by a policy that directs subsidies toward owner-occupied, single-family dwellings. Because there is a more direct link between ownership and occupancy, the correspondence between housing stock upgrading and the switch of demand to the higher submarket will be greater. Furthermore, this ability of recipients to consume an enhanced quality of housing will be perpetuated in the future, because the capital gains provided by the repairs that are captured at the time of home sale can be applied subsequently to the purchase or rental of another dwelling. Rehabilitation subsidies to homeowners therefore are fundamentally different from those to absentee owners, because the fillip to dwelling quality is eventually capitalized as additional wealth to the occupant. In this sense they represent an amalgam of supply-side and demand-side approaches.

As a result of the close correspondence between supply and demand increases in middle-quality submarkets, there will be much less incentive for owners of middle-quality homes to consider compensatory downgrading. The net effects more likely would be the salutary ones described above in the context of functions S_{M2}, D_{M2}, S_{L2}, and D_{L2} in figure 11.2. There are two clear shortcomings, however. First, a large fraction of low-income households are not homeowners. Second, the implicit demand-side subsidy is attached only to the owner of the dwelling when it is rehabilitated. When the unit is sold and the rehabilitation is capitalized, the buyer will receive no benefit and the dwelling will be subject to the potential pressures to downgrade described above.

In conclusion, our analysis of policies to subsidize the rehabilitation of rental dwellings reveals the potential problem of downgrading of the stock originally in the target submarkets into which the subsidized dwellings upgrade. This unintended consequence will be minimized to the extent that operating/maintenance costs of the rehabilitated dwellings do not increase, existing dwellings in target submarkets have comparatively low operating costs and save little on such by downgrading, and low-income tenants have substantial cross-price elasticities of demand. Insofar as this unintended "compensatory downgrading" consequence is avoided, the policy would provide welfare gains to low-income tenants who choose to move up to target submarkets and to original households in those submarkets. Other low-income households and the homeless would not be affected noticeably in any case. Variants of the basic policy which restrict rents on the upgraded dwellings face a dilemma. Unless there is stringent code enforcement which coerces participation, and postrehabilitation prohibitions on selling or downgrading rehabilitated properties, there will be little efficiency in the long run. On the other hand, such restrictions would be expensive to enforce and would impose substantial welfare losses on the original owners of rehabilitated dwellings. A variant of the policy which subsidizes rehabilitation of owner-occupied dwellings would minimize the potential problem of compensatory downgrading and finesse the dilemma associated with rent restrictions. Such a policy would provide welfare gains to participating low-income homeowners, losses to homeowners in target submarkets, and have virtually no impact on low-income renters or the homeless.

11.3 Subsidizing High-Quality New Construction and Filtering

A widespread belief, indeed the foundation of much of our postwar national housing strategy, is that by encouraging the construction of higher-quality dwellings we can hasten the process by which lower-income tenants can occupy decent, if older, units and the least-habitable units are removed from the stock. The conventional, though ill-defined, term for this process is *filtering*.[10]

To evaluate the consequences of this supply-side approach we first assume that a policy has been adopted that effectively reduces the cost of building new, middle- to upper-quality rental dwellings. (A similar strategy's impact on the owner sector is considered later.) Conceivably the particular policy could involve such "shallow" subsidies as below-market interest rates for builders, alterations in the tax status of the properties, or direct grants to defray the cost of land acquisition, site preparation, and construction. We assume that beyond the terms of these subsidies the policy imposes no restrictions on new buildings' owners.

11.3.1 Impacts on Builders of New Rental Dwellings

The initial impact of the construction subsidy policy will be a reallocation of resources from the nonhousing sector to the rental housing sector, because the returns available from the latter will be enhanced. With lower costs, builders of new dwellings find that they can more easily compete with owners of existing units in the middle- to upper-quality submarkets where new construction is a significant form of supply.

As usual, builders will compare the expected streams of revenues and (now reduced) costs of supplying units at various alternative submarkets and will build in those submarkets where expected net returns are maximized. Of course, with reduced costs more such units will be constructed at any given quality level before net returns are competed down to make them comparable to those from nonhousing investments.

11.3.2 Impacts on Owners of Existing Rental Dwellings

The intensified competition from builders that owners of existing units will confront as a result of the policy can be portrayed with the help of figure 11.3. Consider the owner of a unit in the high-quality submarket H_3, with cost function C_3. It may now be the case that many newly constructed units in H_3 have considerably lower costs, such as is portrayed by C_3'. As more such new units enter the market, rents in H_3 will be competed down and vacancies will increase. As a consequence the revenue function will dip, as shown by MV_1'. This dip will be ameliorated to the extent that households who previously were unwilling to occupy H_3 now become so and switch their demands out of some lower submarket.

Now some owners may find that, although their net returns have fallen, they can do no better by modifying their units, given the nature of their conversion cost functions. But other owners, such as the one with the dwelling characterized by cost C_3, will have an incentive to downgrade their units to, say, submarket H_2 as shown in figure 11.3.

As such downgrading of dwellings ensues, it will depress rents in the submarkets into which they converted (and simultaneously will raise them in those from which they converted). This depressing effect will be intensified by any new, subsidized construction that occurs there as well. For the same reasons as noted above, some owners in these somewhat lower-quality submarkets also will choose to downgrade their units, and simultaneously some households will move up to the submarket from which they are converting. This process of simultaneously restoring equilibrium at the origin submarket(s) but disrupting it at the destination submarket(s) continues through additional rounds.

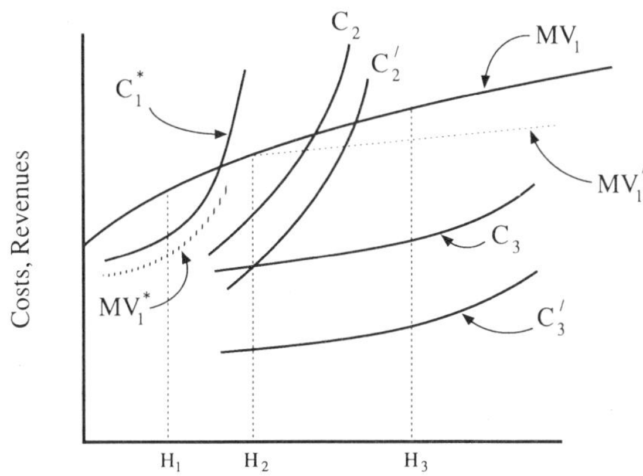

Figure 11.3. Rental housing cost and revenue functions with high-quality construction subsidy policy.

It must be emphasized, however, that each successive round represents a progressively smaller disruption, because in each submarket the gross additions to the stock will be greater than the gross losses via downgrading. That is, it is probable that price (rent) and vacancy rate adjustments will bear some of the brunt of the reequilibrium process. To suggest that net conversions would be zero throughout the submarket array would be to make unrealistic assumptions about the set of conversion cost functions extant at each submarket.

This ripple effect of successive but ever-damped waves of downgrading from high- to ever-lower-quality submarkets eventually, in principle, affects the lowest rental submarket H_1 and depresses rents there. Let this be illustrated as MV_I^* in figure 11.3. Given this effect, some owners will inevitably be forced to abandon their dwellings if they have intolerably high costs, such as C_I^*.

11.3.3 Aggregate Impacts of Subsidizing High-Quality Construction on Rental Submarkets

The aggregate consequences of the aforementioned process can be analyzed with the aid of the three-submarket graphic scenario portrayed in figure 11.4. We assume for simplicity that the incentives for new construction result initially in increasing the stock in the high-quality rental submarket from S_{H1} S_{M2}.

As a result, the rents in the high submarket are competed down to MV_{H2}, and some demanders originally in the middle-quality submarket now find it desirable to consume in the high submarket. This switch to a substitute submarket is portrayed in figure 11.4 as an increase in quantity demanded to Q_{H2} and a decrease in demand to D_{M3}.

The depressed rents in the high submarket trigger some downgrading from high-to middle-quality submarkets, thereby reducing the former's supply S_{H4} toward its original level and expanding the latter's to S_{M4}. This stock adjustment drives rents in the high-quality submarket back toward their initial equilibrium level and lowers still further those in the middle submarket to MV_{M4}. These rent reductions may induce some tenants originally consuming in the lowest submarket to move up to the middle one, thereby increasing the quantity demanded in the latter and decreasing the demand in the former to D_{L5}.

With depressed rents in the middle submarket, a second (albeit smaller) wave of downgrading is generated. This wave reduces supply in the middle submarket back toward its original level (S_{M6}) and simultaneously increases supply in the lowest submarket to S_{L6}. As equilibrium is thereby reestablished in the middle-quality submarket, so too is it further upset in the low-quality one. Demand has slackened at the same time that owners of erstwhile middle-quality units have intensified the competition on the supply side. Owners with noncompetitive low-quality units will be forced to abandon them. This re-

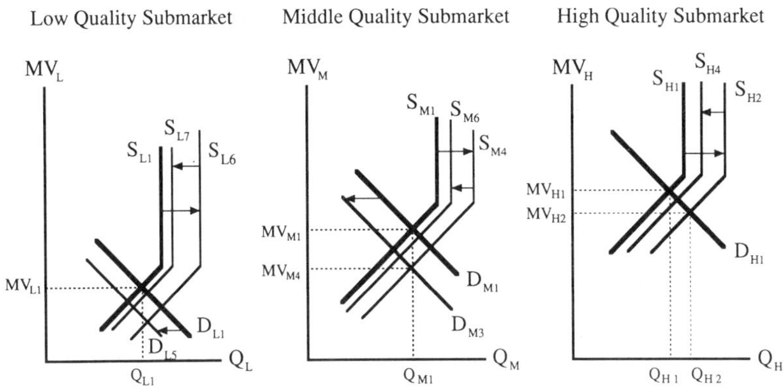

Figure 11.4. Submarket dynamics with high-quality construction subsidy policy.

duces supply to S_{L7} until an equilibrium is reestablished wherein owners of all surviving units are making returns adequate to keep them in the industry.

The crucial empirical question here is the degree to which short-run rent decreases translate into long-term equilibrium ones and across how wide an array of quality submarkets this occurs. If the long-term rents in all rental submarkets are substantially lower than those prevailing in the absence of the construction subsidies, then this reduction in the real price of housing permits all renters to consume superior housing than they could have otherwise. From the perspective of a given group of tenants, they have been able to "filter up" to better dwellings. From the perspective of a given quality submarket, it has "filtered down" not in physical quality but insofar that it is occupied by tenants with lower incomes than previously. And from the perspective of an individual dwelling that was downgraded, it has "filtered down" both in terms of its absolute quality and in terms of the relative economic status of the clientele it now serves.

What determines the degree to which these attractive aspects of filtering will occur? The answer revolves around whether and to what extent in the filtering process (1) tenants' cross-price elasticities of demand are substantial, (2) the older, less competitive stock in each submarket is replaced by newly constructed stock and/or by newly downgraded stock, and (3) this replacement results in lower costs of operating dwellings, on average, in each submarket.[11] For example, if cross-price elasticities are low for all sorts of tenants and downward conversion cost functions from each origin submarket are not steep, a large construction "splash" in the high submarkets will cause few, if any, supply-response "ripples" in the lowest submarkets.

Even if downgrading into the lower-quality submarkets proves substantial, resulting operating costs must fall if rent reductions are not to prove ephemeral.[12] For instance, should the typical new dwellings in submarket H_3 in figure 11.3 have costs like C_3' and ultimately replace the original dwellings with costs like C_3, rents in H_3 will be reduced for an extended period. Similarly, if downgraded units have costs like C_3 and those originally in H_2 have costs C_2, the result will be long-run rent reductions in H_2 as well. But there is no necessary reason why this should be so. It is just as likely in principle, for example, that the units being replaced in H_2 have costs like C_2'. In this case the newly downgraded units can supply housing services in this submarket no more cheaply than the original stock, and long-run equilibrium rents should be no lower as a result of the filtering process.

The foregoing has considered longer-run equilibrium rents, which would be relevant if the construction subsidy policy was continued for a limited duration. This becomes less relevant if, on the other hand, the policy under consideration re-created an "excess supply" of high-quality dwellings in perpetuity. In this case the gross conversions into any given submarket might so surpass gross conversions out of it that, for any finite period, the submarkets might accurately be portrayed by the "short-run" functions S_{L6}, S_{M4}, and S_{H2} in figure 11.4. Of course such an ongoing policy of filtering stimuli would trade off the desirable result of reducing housing prices or rents with the undesirable result of accelerated decay and ultimate abandonment of valuable housing resources and the concomitant disruption of existing neighborhoods—topics we consider further below. In addition, as the character of the stock radically changed over time as a result of accelerated filtering, we have little assurance what forms the associated aggregate operating cost and supply functions would assume, either in the short or the longer run.

Empirically, the degree to which rents are reduced and, thus, some households are able to move up to better-quality housing through the filtering process appears to be nontrivial in the short run (at least historically) but marginal in the long run. Weicher and Thibodeau (1988) found that new construction (in excess of net household formation) replaced the most dilapidated units in the stock on a one-for-one basis during the 1960s; the comparable ratio for a broader range of low-quality units was three for one in the 1970–75 period. From a longer-run perspective their estimates suggested that there was one fewer dilapidated unit in 1970 for every four additional new units built during the 1950s, but that subsequent new construction did not significantly reduce the number of lower-quality units after 1970. Vitaliano (1983) found no statistically significant relationship between the amount of new private construction in a metropolitan area and changes in the inhabited slum-quality stock five to fifteen years later.[13]

The evidence thus suggests that encouraging filtering by subsidizing high-quality new construction is a comparatively inefficient way to aid lower-income households. This is precisely what follows from our model of a segmented urban housing market: repercussions dampen progressively the further in quality one moves from the submarket bearing the initial impact. In fact, the policy confronts an efficiency dilemma. On the one hand, to obtain substantial and persistent reductions in the rent of decent, modest-quality housing one must have a massive, ongoing commitment of resources to new, high-quality buildings and a concomitant downgrading of a substantial number of dwellings of all qualities (with its associated attenuation of their usable lifetimes). But this would waste valuable housing resources which are clearly cheaper to maintain than to build. On the other hand, if no wasteful downgrading were to occur there would be no impact of the policy beyond the original, high-quality submarket. In such a case the programmatic benefits would accrue only to occupants of the high-quality submarkets. The aforementioned evidence of the decreasing efficacy of this approach over time suggests this dilemma is becoming more constricting. This finding is consistent with the hypotheses that (1) less conversion from the initially impacted submarkets has occurred per unit of new construction due to the changing nature of the aggregate downward conversion cost function associated with the existing stock, (2) dwellings converted downward into lower submarkets have had similar operating costs to those originally there, and (3) lower-income households' cross-price elasticity of demand has fallen.

The spatial impacts of subsidizing higher-quality new construction are crucial to consider as well. Because the filtering process ultimately speeds the replacement of older stock with newer stock, it means that the physical decline of neighborhoods containing these existing units also will be exaggerated. Those neighborhoods containing the least competitive, lowest-quality units will suffer from intensified abandonment. New construction typically will not occur to a large degree in these same neighborhoods unless wholesale demolition and parcel consolidation efforts are undertaken. As a result, the filtering policy exacerbates suburbanization and the attendant decay of more centralized neighborhoods. This raises important concerns about inefficiencies in land-use and transportation patterns and about inequities vis-à-vis lower-income and racial minority households.

11.3.4 Subsidizing Construction of Owner-Occupied Dwellings

The previous discussion focused on a policy that encouraged the construction of rental units. Here we consider what modifications in the analysis are needed if the building of single-family, owner-occupied dwellings is to be subsidized. The central distinction is in the mechanism by which the existing stock is downgraded in response to the intensified construction in upper-quality submarkets.

Above we saw that owners of some existing rental units will find it more profitable in a filtering scenario intentionally to downgrade their dwellings, either through passive undermaintenance or subdivision of the dwellings. By downgrading they must reduce rents, but they save even more on operating expenses. By contrast, the owner-occupants of existing single-family dwellings typically react to an upsurge of new construction in their submarket only when they decide to sell their homes.[14] At this point they realize that the real price of their homes has decreased.

As a result, the home may be purchased by a buyer of somewhat lower income than would have occurred without the intensified filtering. Over time this lower resource base of the owner-occupant will be translated (on average) into lower expenditures on repairs, alterations, and additions, as has been proven in over a dozen empirical studies.[15] It is thus only after the home changes hands that quality decline becomes more likely, whereupon the dwelling passes into a lower submarket.

When, in turn, owner-occupants in these destination submarkets try to sell their homes they will find an intensified competition from the newly downgraded homes. They, too, will have to reduce their asking prices, thereby paving the way for still lower-income owner-occupants to occupy these homes. Given the more constrained reinvestment choices of these new owners, the process of passive downgrading continues into another submarket, albeit at a smaller magnitude.

As in our analysis of the rental sector, the central empirical issue here is whether the real housing price declines are significant enough and sufficiently long lasting to warrant the adoption of the policy. The answer again will depend on the conversion cost functions of existing dwellings in owner submarkets.

Suppose, for illustration, that initially a homeowner could afford to buy the home in submarket H_2 with cost function C_2, as shown in figure 11.3. But now as a result of the construction subsidy policy, prices of homes in H_3 have dropped so that this homeowner can afford to buy the home with cost C_3. For as long as this owner's dwelling remains in H_3, his or her well-being clearly will be improved. But even if reduced upkeep efforts eventually drive the home into H_2, the cost of keeping it there will be less than originally. Thus, once again, the owner's well-being will be enhanced.

Such a felicitous outcome can by no means be guaranteed, however. If in the above scenario the original home's costs were like C_2', the longer-run savings in the real price of occupying H_2 quality homes would be voided. In such a case the only welfare gain would be of a temporary nature—only until the reduced upkeep efforts of the owner succeeded in downgrading the erstwhile H_3 home to an H_2 one.

In addition, there is new evidence that even this short-run gain will be voided in the lowest-quality owner submarkets. Galster (1987: ch. 9) has found that homeowners in lower-quality neighborhoods respond to expected reductions in their property values by *increasing* their home upkeep efforts.[16] This means that the *absolute* price of these improved homes may not fall if the incremental value of their improvements offsets the general deflation in the submarket. If so, few renter households will be able to enter the homeownership sector, and the putative improvements in well-being for higher-income homeowners will be truncated at the lower end of the income distribution.

In conclusion, our analysis suggests in general that any sort of supply-side policy relying on stimulating new construction and concomitant filtering will be a relatively inefficient device for improving the well-being of lower-income households, because the initial programmatic impact is far removed in the submarket array from the desired range of ultimate impact. The precise consequences of "one-shot" injections of additional construction will depend on the empirical nature of households' cross-price elasticities and the slope and level of dwellings' conversion cost functions across the array of submarkets. A massively scaled, ongoing subsidy policy would hold more potential for impact on lower submarkets, but would inherently incur the waste of housing resources through accelerated downgrading and abandonment, with its associated spatial inefficiencies and welfare losses imposed on residents of older, inner-city neighborhoods.

11.4 Subsidizing New Construction Targeted for Low-Income Occupancy

Instead of subsidizing construction in middle- and upper-quality submarkets and then relying on the filtering process to improve the well-being of low-income tenants, an alternative policy approach is to tie the construction subsidy directly to the provision of units at below-market rents which are affordable to the target population. Such a strategy can subsidize the private sector, as in the federal government's section 236 program of the 1970s and in Massachusetts' new State Housing Assistance for Rental Production policy. Or it can subsidize dwellings to be retained under public ownership, as in the public housing program. As illustration for our analysis, suppose that the government subsidizes the costs of building privately owned, middle-quality apartment projects that set aside a minimum proportion of units for occupancy by low-income tenants.[17] We will note any distinctions which must be made if publicly owned properties are considered.

11.4.1 Impacts on Builders of New Rental Dwellings

The situation facing builders after the adoption of this illustrative policy can be explained with the help of figure 11.5. Suppose that the subsidies offered by the policy would reduce any participating builder's cost function by some given amount X (so long as the construction was in submarket H_3), and that the allowable rent that could be charged on these subsidized, middle-quality units is A ($= D$)—what low-income households originally in H_1 are paying. Without the subsidy the builder would have cost E to build middle-quality, submarket H_3 units and could charge market rent F. If the net returns $A - (E$

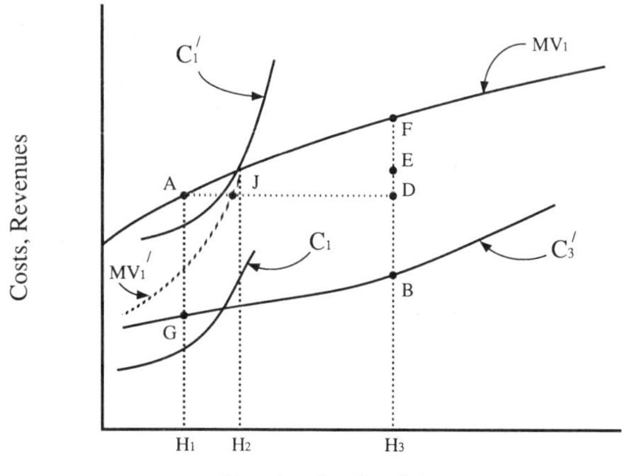

Figure 11.5. Housing cost and revenue functions under subsidized construction for low-income occupancy.

$- X$) under the policy are greater than nonpolicy returns $F - E$, the builder will choose to participate.[18]

Because the absolute level of net returns available in at least one submarket has been enhanced (for at least some builders), the aggregate level of construction activity across the submarkets should be higher. Of course some of the activity in the middle-quality submarket probably would have occurred in the absence of the policy, and some has merely been diverted from production in other submarkets (at least in the short run). Empirical estimates have indicated that past federal schemes to encourage construction of moderate-quality, low-rent units have resulted in only fifteen net additions to new construction for every hundred subsidized units built (Swan 1973; Murray 1983b).

11.4.2 Impacts on Owners of Existing Rental Dwellings

Suppose the tenants who are deemed eligible to occupy the newly built, subsidized units originally were consuming in submarket H_1. With the completion of the new subsidized units in H_3, the owners of H_1 units will find some of their tenants "siphoned off." As a result, the revenues gained in the low-quality submarket are reduced, as shown by MV'_l in figure 11.5. Some owners in H_1 having costs like C_1 will opt to upgrade to H_2, but of course net returns will be lower than before the policy's inception.[19] Others with costs like C'_l will be forced to abandon. Still others will choose to remain in H_1 but tolerate lower returns.

Owners in other submarkets are likely to be affected by the policy as well if the cross-submarket pattern of unsubsidized new construction is grossly altered in the long run by the policy. If the hypothetical construction subsidy policy were continued indefinitely, there would be an ongoing bias toward allocating construction resources into the targeted (middle-quality) submarkets. In the short run this could detract from unsubsidized construction which otherwise would have occurred in these and in other submarkets, given the limited production capacity of the building industry. But in the long run there is no reason to believe that the building industry would be incapable of expanding capacity sufficiently so as to relieve this short-run "substitution effect." The issue then becomes one of the long-run industry supply function. If the function is upsloping, the aforementioned expansion of production will be associated with higher construction costs. This, in turn, means that it will no longer be profitable for all the unsubsidized dwellings to be built that would have been in the absence of the policy. To the extent that such would occur, owners of existing dwellings in the submarkets to which this construction formerly would have been directed will experience weakened competition and, consequently, improved returns.[20]

There is, however, a countervailing impact on owners of unsubsidized units in the targeted, middle-quality submarkets. They may face stiffened competition if many erstwhile dwellings from H_1 are upgraded to H_3. The competition is not, however, intensified by the new H_3 apartments which have been set aside for low-income occupancy. Although the nominal stock of middle-quality units has increased by the amount of subsidized, set-aside construction, there has been a corresponding increase in the demand (occupancy) of these units by erstwhile H_1 tenants. The net effect upon the competition faced by (and thus returns earned by) owners in the targeted submarkets is ambiguous, therefore.

11.4.3 Postconstruction Impacts on Builders of Subsidized Units

Once the builders have constructed the subsidized dwellings a new supply dynamic becomes relevant. These private owners may have an incentive to allow their units to deteriorate, unless there are policy contingencies for avoiding it. Publicly owned units are also likely to deteriorate, but for different reasons.[21] The process is shown with the aid of figure 11.5.

Suppose after construction the private owner of the subsidized unit faces conversion cost function C'_3. There is a clear incentive to downgrade this unit to H_1 while still charging rent D ($= A$), thereby improving net returns by the amount $B - G$. Even assuming that demands in the lower submarkets have fallen as a result of the policy to MV'_1, there is still an incentive to downgrade to the submarket corresponding to point J. Insofar as this downgrading occurs it will dilute the initial gain in well-being obtained by the tenants of the subsidized units and will render the long-run distribution of the stock less distinguishable from that before the policy was instituted.[22] Avoiding this problem would require an ongoing program of governmental inspections to insure that the set-aside dwellings remained in the H_3 submarket, although this has its attendant costs as well. The problem would also be avoided if the policy is both massive and permanent enough that virtually all those housed originally in below-target submarkets would be housed in newly constructed subsidized units. In such a case the downgrading incentive would be removed because there would be no demand for such downgraded units.

11.4.4 Aggregate Impacts of Subsidized Construction for Low-Income Occupancy

The aggregate consequences of the individual behaviors noted above can be examined through the three-submarket graphic analysis portrayed in figure 11.6. We assume initially that the subsidy policy encourages the production of (or, in the case of public housing, directly produces) middle-quality rental units which are then rented to tenants originally in the low-quality submarket at rents currently prevailing in that low submarket. Because this new construction is prohibited from serving the normal middle submarket clientele, it is portrayed in figure 11.6 as a distinct stock S_{MS2}. Simultaneously, the demand represented by the low-income tenants obtaining these subsidized units, D_{MS2}, leads to a decrease from D_{L1} to D_{L2} in the low-quality submarket. Of course the apparent rent reduction in the middle submarket to MV_{L1} is relevant only for the eligible low-income tenants; the situation confronting the original demanders in this submarket is unchanged.

The supply response in the low-quality submarket will be some combination of upgrading and abandonment, the mix to be determined by the profile of the conversion cost functions of the stock in the low submarket. Either response will decrease the stock to S_{L3} until rents recover sufficiently to provide adequate returns for owners of surviving low-quality rental units. The speed and degree to which this supply adjustment returns rents to their original level will affect the gains in well-being accrued by low-income tenants who were unable to obtain the subsidized units. Of course this long-run con-

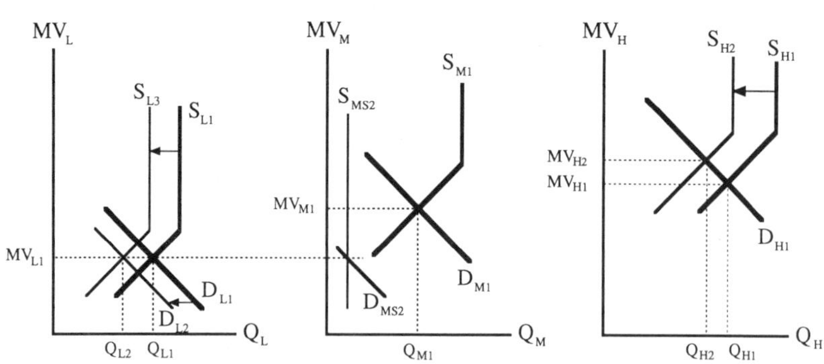

Figure 11.6. Submarket dynamics with subsidized construction for low-income occupancy.

sideration would be rendered moot if the policy were a large-scale, ongoing one which continued to reduce the demand for the low-quality submarket faster than the upgrading/abandonment supply adjustment.

If, as explained above, the subsidy policy were to distort permanently new construction toward the middle-quality submarket and were to result in a long-term reduction in new construction elsewhere, it might be shown in figure 11.6 as a decrease from S_{H1} to S_{H2}. We are unable to make any unambiguous predictions about the net changes in the unsubsidized middle-quality stock and therefore portray S_{M1} as unchanged.

In the absence of a massive, ongoing policy and/or programmatic provisions for ongoing inspections of subsidized dwellings, the private owners of the newly built, subsidized units will have an incentive to downgrade them over time, as explained above. (Downgrading through undermaintenance is a typical, though not necessary, result for public housing.) This would mean that supply S_{MS2} (and the corresponding demand D_{MS2}) effectively will be transferred to the lower-quality submarket, which could be portrayed in figure 11.6 as shifts to the right of S_{L3} and D_{L2} toward their original positions and correspondingly opposite shifts in S_{MS2} and D_{MS2}. The extent and speed at which this downgrading adjustment occurs will determine the gains in well-being that the occupants of the new subsidized dwellings will receive. Thus our theory clearly suggests that if the subsidized units are subject to little or no inspection, the program will produce only minimal reductions in real rents and in the incidence of substandard units in the long run.[23]

In fact, the limited empirical evidence on past policies (all of which fit this description) supports this prediction. Davis, Eastman and Hua (1974), Hirsch and Law (1979), and Weicher and Thibodeau (1988) find no evidence that the supply of subsidized, newly constructed private units has led to any long-run reductions in the incidence of substandard units in U.S. metropolitan areas. Vitaliano (1983) and Weicher and Thibodeau (1988) found the same for public housing.[24] Thus, ironically, it appears that previous incarnations of construction subsidies for below-market rent dwellings have been totally ineffective as a means of assisting low-income tenants in the long run. Our analysis suggests, however, that this need not be inherent if the former program were of larger scope, longer duration, and/or possessed more rigorous postconstruction inspection requirements.

As for equity effects, consider first program beneficiaries. Low-income tenants who obtain the newly built, middle-quality dwellings at below-market rents clearly are made better off. Unlike the filtering policy where tenants can move up to higher-quality submarkets only so far as these submarkets' rents fall in response to additional supplies of downgraded units, here affordability of the target quality level by the target population is assured in advance.[25] Unlike either the rehabilitation or filtering options, here low-income tenants occupy new dwellings which are more likely to be located in the suburbs than either the upgraded or downgraded existing dwellings they would occupy under the other options (although such is less likely if public housing is contemplated). This potential for deconcentration of lower-income households would be further abetted to the extent that some of the subsidized units are built within large complexes which also contain unsubsidized apartments. The potential detraction from this is the aforementioned incentives present in certain formulations of the policy which lead to downgrading of the new subsidized stock.

Other low-income households may also reap benefits, even if they do not occupy a subsidized unit. Analogous to our discussion of demand-side policies, this policy has the immediate effect of reducing the demand for low-quality submarkets and, thereby, the competition for and rents of dwellings there. Residents and property owners in the neighborhoods which contain the lower-quality stock will further gain or lose as the policy-stimulated supply response takes the form of upgrading or abandonment, respectively.

Households in other submarkets will lose from the policy (in the form of higher rents) to the extent that the stock in their submarket is reduced below what it would have been otherwise due to the new construction substitution effect. The opposite can be said for owners of dwellings in these submarkets. As we explained above, these effects can be predicted unambiguously only in the higher-quality submarkets, but we cannot predict where their magnitude will be the greatest.

Finally, as with all policies which encourage new construction, welfare effects stemming from the potential location of such construction must be considered.[26] These spatial issues have already been discussed above in the context of filtering and will not be revisited, other than to note that subsidized construction for lower-income tenants is likely to be more centralized in metropolitan areas than that for higher-income groups. Suffice it to reemphasize, however, that the policy under consideration here has the distinct feature of moving low-income tenants into the newly constructed, not rehabilitated or downgraded, dwellings. Thus the *potential* for spatial deconcentration of lower-income tenants is better here than with the other two supply-side alternatives.

11.5 The Impacts of Rehabilitation and Construction Subsidy Policies: A Summary

On the basis of our analysis we can conclude the following:

1. Subsidies to landlords to rehabilitate their dwellings can in principle reduce the long-run equilibrium rents in the submarkets to which the rehabilitated dwellings are destined, which will permit some renters to improve their well-being. However, the extent to which this improvement occurs depends on (*a*) the level of operating costs of the upgraded dwellings, (*b*) the cost savings that dwellings at these destination (and higher) submarkets can accrue by downgrading, and (*c*) low-income tenants' cross-price elasticity of de-

mand. Consider an extreme case wherein all three aforementioned parameters were disadvantageous. If upgraded dwellings were expensive to maintain at their new quality, the original dwellings in higher-quality submarkets could save greatly by downgrading, and tenants would not move to better-quality dwellings in response to small rent changes, the rent differentials generated by the policy would trigger significant compensatory downgrading. The degree to which this occurred would offset in aggregate the improvements in the rehabilitated stock and result in decreased program efficiency.

2. If rent controls accompany the rehabilitation subsidy, there will be problems of nonparticipation and either the selling (with subsequent loss of rent controlled-status) or downgrading of dwellings subsequent to the repairs originally made on them. Program strictures against said responses will be expensive to enforce and will impose welfare losses on original owners of rehabilitated dwellings.

3. Rehabilitation subsidies to owner-occupants of single-family dwellings will produce more salutary consequences than subsidies to landlords because there is a perfect correspondence between demander and supplier. Recipient homeowners reap short- and long-term welfare gains because the increment in dwelling quality is eventually capitalized as added wealth, thereby enhancing their continuing ability to consume higher-quality housing. Low-income renters and the homeless are not aided by this variant, however.

4. Subsidies to spur new construction of middle- to upper-quality dwellings will replace existing stock with new stock at targeted-quality submarkets, create some incentives to intensify downgrading, and ultimately perhaps encourage abandonment of the least-competitive stock. In the short run this filtering process will deflate price/rent levels in submarkets which have a net increase in stock through conversion and construction, and thus will allow some households to afford better housing there. The extent to which this will occur across the submarket array will depend upon households' cross-price elasticities of demand and the slope and level of dwellings' conversion cost functions. Relatively flat but low-level cost functions in a submarket, coupled with low elasticities for occupants of lower submarkets, will tend to stifle any subsequent transmission of response below the given submarket.

5. Whether households in a submarket permanently gain from a filtering-enhancement policy depends on whether the new long-run equilibrium rents/prices are lower there than originally. For a "one-time-only" policy this will depend on whether the cost of newly downgraded dwellings are less than those originally comprising the submarket, on average. A massive, ongoing policy which re-creates a perpetual excess of supply in all submarkets can achieve such a rent/price reduction only with the associated waste of valuable housing resourcces through accelerated downgrading and abandonment, and the spatial inefficiencies and inequities associated with suburban-oriented construction patterns.

6. Subsidies for middle-quality dwellings set aside for low-income occu-

pancy will encourage the abandonment and/or upgrading of some low-quality stock insofar as demand is siphoned off into the new, subsidized dwellings. The mix of abandonment and upgrading will be determined by the nature of the conversion cost functions associated with the dwellings in the low submarkets. Private owners of the newly built subsidized dwellings will have an incentive to let them deteriorate; different factors are likely to lead to deterioration of public housing. There is likely to be some reduction in the rate of unsubsidized new construction in higher-quality submarkets, as construction resources are shifted into subsidized projects in target submarkets by the program. The degree of this substitution effect in the long run will be influenced by the scale of the subsidy program and the long-run supply function of the construction industry. Net changes in the unsubsidized stock of the middle-quality submarkets cannot be predicted unambiguously.

7. Compared to filtering there is a better correspondence with the set-aside new construction between target population and target-quality submarket; new supply is implicitly tied to the desired demander group by programmatic rent limitations. The benefits to recipients will be eroded over time, however, unless the policy includes provisions to deter postconstruction downgrading. There is, in addition, an enhanced potential for spatial deconcentration of participating low-income households compared to the other supply-side approaches, especially if private market-rent units are interspersed with subsidized ones. Nonrecipient low-income households may reap somewhat lower real rents as a result of the policy, assuming that the reduction in demand for the low-quality submarket outweighs the loss in its stock through abandonment and upgrading. However, highly elastic long-run supply and the consistent record of past new-construction policies suggest strongly that these benefits will approximate zero in the long run. Households in higher-quality submarkets are likely to suffer a welfare loss to the extent that their stocks are smaller over time due to the construction substitution effect into subsidized projects.

The foregoing conclusions suggest comparisons with those drawn from the previous analysis of demand-side policies. These comparisons are considered explicitly at the end of chapter 12.

Notes

1. For descriptions and evaluations of these programs, see Weicher 1979, 1988; Varady 1986: ch. 1; Galster 1987; ch. 12; Hartman, Meyerson, and Bratt 1986; Clay 1987; Mayer 1988; and Stegman 1988.

2. This is not assumed to be a "one-shot" policy, but rather an ongoing one. Thus in the future, instead of an owner allowing a unit to become substandard because of excessive expenses for necessary repairs and replacements, the policy would provide the funds to forestall this eventuality.

3. If only a fraction of repair costs were reimbursed through the policy, the conversion cost function would pivot downward only to the extent of these reimbursements.

4. This will occur unless MV'_l is lower for H_2 than H_1 or the two rents are equal.

5. The policy's success in doing so in the long run depends on the precise formulation of repairs eligible for subsidy. That is, once all code corrections are made to the stock existing at the policy's inception, what sorts of repairs are eligible as these dwellings age in the future? If "prophylactic" sorts of repairs and replacements are eligible for units in the middle submarket before they downgrade to lower-quality submarkets (whether codes are thereby violated or not), then the aforementioned effects on the middle submarkets will more likely be perpetuated.

6. Even if upgrading exceeds demand changes (thereby yielding short-run rent increases), in the longer term the downgrading from middle submarkets should ease this pressure, as is explained below. A possible vehicle whereby nonparticipants are affected is through neighborhood effects. As some properties in the neighborhood are rehabilitated, other landlords may raise rents to reflect the real improvements in their units' quality. If tenants in these nonrehabilitated dwellings value the improved residential environment more or less than the incremental rent, they will reap welfare gains or losses, respectively, assuming that residential mobility is not free; see Bartik 1986.

7. In principle, downgrading could also come from even higher quality levels, although for simplicity this is not drawn in fig. 11.2. Should such be the case, a large portion of the downgraded stock would be replaced by new construction in the origin submarket.

8. Remember that these conclusions apply to a policy which subsidizes the capital costs of major dwelling repairs and replacements. A policy which also subsidizes the operating expenses of the dwellings once they are rehabilitated would be less subject to these criticisms (although possibly subject to others). Such an option has not, to our knowledge, been employed in any large-scale housing policy initiative.

9. Unless the repairs were such that the useful lifetime of the dwelling was extended and/or current operating costs were reduced. Remember, because it is assumed that rent limitations apply to prospective buyers, current owners cannot reap capital gains from the rehabilitation.

10. For a critical review of the various meanings and theories of *filtering,* see Grigsby et al. 1987 and Weicher and Thibodeau 1988.

11. This is the key distinction among theoretical models of filtering. Lowry 1960 and Olsen 1969 argue that if the stock were perfectly malleable, filtering would be impossible in the long run. With malleability the prices in all submarkets would be driven back to their original value level—the minimum long-run average costs of producing a unit of housing services. By contrast, numerous recent theoretical treatments which embody imperfect stock malleability demonstrate that filtering is possible in the long run. See Sweeney 1974b; Ohls 1975; Braid 1984; Schall 1981.

12. Recall that the *slope* of the downward conversion cost function will influence whether a dwelling is downgraded; the *level* of the function will determine at any given submarket whether net returns will be positive (and thus can preclude some potential downgrading options if returns prove to be negative).

13. The "chains of moves" literature provides evidence that lower-income households eventually move in response to construction of housing originally occupied by higher-income households. Clifton, Lansing, and Morgan 1969 found, e.g., that for every 1,000 new units constructed, 3,500 moves were generated, 333 of them by low-income households. This literature has several methodological weaknesses, however, central of which for our purpose is that the quality of the unit being occupied is not

controlled for. For a fuller discussion, see National Association of Homebuilders 1986:20–21.

14. Careful empirical tests of whether homeowners in middle- and upper-quality neighborhoods reduce home upkeep investments when they perceive falling property values have proven negative; see Galster 1987: ch. 9.

15. For a review, see Galster 1987: ch. 9.

16. Galster has developed a theory based on "threshold levels of home capital gains" to explain this behavior (1987: ch. 3). A similar empirical observation of the inverse relationship between expected property value inflation and upkeep expenditures has been made by Taub, Taylor, and Dunham 1984.

17. Although our illustration considers apartments, there is no reason in principle why the strategy could not be employed in the ownership sector. For example, at this writing Massachusetts' Homeownership Opportunity Program encourages municipalities to establish linkages whereby zoning variances, land write-downs, or other enticements are provided in exchange for a commitment that 30% of the new homes in the subdivision will be affordable to low/moderate-income first-time buyers. In addition, the policy provides state-funded subsidies so that the buyers' mortgage rates are reduced to 5.5%.

18. Or, equivalently, if the government provides, e.g., zoning variances without which the builder could construct no units, the decision rule becomes whether the permitted construction (with low-rent unit set-asides) offers positive profit compared to other opportunities.

19. Note the key difference between this scenario and the upgrading induced by demand-side rent subsidies described in ch. 10. In that case upgrading was encouraged not only by a reduction in demand for the low submarket, but concomitantly by an increase in demand by the newly subsidized tenants in the middle submarket. Here the newly constructed supply exactly equals the induced demand by low-income tenants, leaving owners who upgrade to compete with owners of the original dwellings in the middle submarket for the same pool of demanders. This latter circumstance is clearly less profitable for the upgraders than the former.

20. Thus far the analysis would also be applicable to a traditional public housing policy.

21. Although local public housing authorities (PHAs) are not subject to the same profit motive, a similar downgrading response has occurred frequently. Due to an unforeseen combination of factors (e.g., building type and materials quality, excessive wear and tear and vandalism of apartments, low tenant incomes), PHAs have found that their revenue streams (from tenant rent contributions) have fallen short of the expenditures necessary to maintain the apartments at their original quality level. Mismanagement in some PHAs has also played a role. The resultant deterioration and even abandonment of some public housing projects has been well documented (Stegman 1988; President's Commission on Housing 1982: ch. 2).

22. The extent of downgrading would also be limited if the subsidized units were sprinkled among unsubsidized ones in the same buildings.

23. Previous theories have come to differing conclusions here. Olsen 1969 comes to the same conclusion as we do, but for different reasons. Schall 1981 predicts that new construction in submarkets "nearer" to those occupied by the poor should lead to reductions in substandard units and rent levels. The model of Sweeney 1974b implies that lower-income nonparticipants are harmed by the policy, paying higher rents and

living in lower-quality units than they would otherwise. Somewhat different conclusions follow when public housing programs are evaluated theoretically; see Sweeney 1974b and Ohls 1975.

24. Our analysis in ch. 15 comes to similar conclusions.

25. This match between target populations and submarkets here would also be superior to that achieved with the aforementioned rehabilitation subsidy policy which did not subsequently control rents.

26. The likelihood that public housing will be spatially deconcentrated as much as privately owned complexes which contain set-asides of below-market rental units is obviously less.

12 Urban Housing Policy: Market-Regulation Approaches

12.1 Principles of the Nonmarket Approach

If one believes that the unfettered actions of the urban housing market complex will not produce rents or prices that are equitable, a possible programmatic response is administratively to constrain prices within a configuration that is perceived as more fair. For instance, if it is believed that rents of modest-quality dwellings will inflate to the point where lower-income households will be forced to spend burdensome fractions of their incomes on rent, consume even less-expensive, lower-quality dwellings, double up with another household to share rent, or move to the streets, one seemingly straightforward solution would be to freeze rents of such dwellings at their current levels. Such a policy, and others that legally limit prices that can be charged in one or more housing-quality submarkets, can be termed rent control (Gilderbloom and Appelbaum 1988; Downs 1988).

The typical historical circumstance under which rent control policies are enacted occurs when there is a considerable excess demand for housing, especially rental housing, due to heavy net in-migration and/or sharp constraints on new housing construction. Thus, for example, during World War II there was a large influx of rural in-migrants to urban industrial centers, yet building materials and skilled construction labor were in short supply. Laws stipulating permissable increases in rents were passed to avoid the predicted escalation of rents in these cities.

With a return to a peacetime economy, virtually all cities dismantled their rent control statutes, with the prominent exception of New York City. Only recently has the strategy regained widespread acceptance, typically as a response to unusually inflationary housing price trends in comparatively localized metropolitan areas or regions. Santa Monica and Berkeley, California, and Cambridge, Massachusetts, are representative of communities that have adopted rent control in the past two decades for this reason.[1]

The consequences of rent control are analyzed below for two typical variants of the strategy: where rents in all quality (renter) submarkets are controlled, and where controls are extended only to a limited number of lower-quality submarkets. For both variants we first consider the initial impacts on individual owners of existing rental housing and on potential builders of new rental housing. Second, secondary impacts on the owner submarkets are analyzed. Third, we consider the aggregate impacts across the array of rental submarkets, using the three-submarket graphic exposition introduced in chapter 8. Finally, an overall assessment of the policy's consequences for the quantity and price of dwellings in different submarkets is made.

For ease of analysis we make the simplifying assumption that the hypothetical city in question is confronted by strong increases in housing demands across the quality spectrum such that revenues are expected to rise by the same proportion in each rental submarket. That is, we assume the original function $MV_1(H)$ relating the array of (rental) quality submarkets $[H_i]$ and market evaluations (rents) of that quality MV_{1i} will rise to a new level $MV_2(H)$ such that $\log (MV_2) - \log (MV_1)$ is constant for all H_i. (None of the general conclusions that follow is dependent on this simplifying specification.)

12.2 Rent Control in All Rental Submarkets

For illustration we assume a form of rent control approximating that of New York City and several other urban areas. In this form, (1) all existing rental units of all qualities are regulated; (2) all newly constructed rental units are exempted; (3) increases in apartment costs, whether from making capital improvements or carrying out higher levels of maintenance (but assuming away rising input costs), are allowed to be exactly compensated for by higher rents, but no higher.

12.2.1 Impacts on Individual Owners of Existing Rental Dwellings

Consider first the effect of such a rent control policy on individual owners of existing rental units. Given that owners seek the quality submarket where their rate of return is maximized, the imposition of rent control increases the potential returns available to owners if they downgrade their dwellings to lower-quality submarkets. This crucial proposition can be explained with the aid of figure 12.1, which shows the conversion cost function facing the owner of a particular rental unit currently in submarket H_1, C_{H1}. Before the upsurge in demand, the schedule of equilibrium market evaluations (rents) available across the rental submarket spectrum is shown as MV_1. Recall from chapter 5 that rate-of-return maximization implies seeking the submarket where the difference $MV_1 - C_{H1}$ is maximized; hence the location of our given unit in H_1 (with associated rent MV_0) is optimal under initial conditions.

Now with the presumed upsurge in housing demand, rents can be predicted to rise (at least before any supply adjustments) so that the new revenue function can be shown in figure 12.1 as MV_2. If there were no rent control, our representative owner would scan the opportunity set represented by the MV_2 and C_{H1} functions so as to identify the H yielding the greatest rate of return. As a result the owner would maintain the dwelling at H_1, given our assumption that MV_1 and MV_2 are parallel, and charge rent MV_{00}. But under rent control the owner cannot raise rents to this level.

The set of opportunities available to the owner is now quite different. If the owner chooses to upgrade the dwelling, rents can rise only to compensate for higher costs. In other words, because allowable rents in submarkets above H_1 must reflect upward conversion (including incremental operating) costs, the new revenue function from upgrading *AFK* is parallel to C_{H1} between the points *A* and *F* in figure 12.1. (Beyond *F,* it is not the rent control board but demand that constrains the rent charged.) If we assumed that, as is typical, there are no proscriptions against downgrading the dwelling,[2] the owner can do so but continue to charge the original rent MV_0, so long as the market is willing to pay at least that amount for the implicit quality that the downgraded unit embodies. This set of opportunities is shown in figure 12.1 as the horizontal line *AB*. Should the owner downgrade below submarket H_2, rents would need to be lowered corresponding to the MV_2 function (segment *BD*), not because of rent control strictures but because of market demand constraints on prices in these lower submarkets.

In sum, the revenue opportunities available to the owner of an existing rental unit after the imposition of rent control are shown in figure 12.1 by the function MV_2^*, or segments *DBAF.* At what submarket will the rate of return be maximized? Consider each segment of the new returns function separately. Because by definition segment *AF* is parallel to upgrading cost function C_{H1}, the gap between the revenues and costs will be constant for all submarkets higher than H_1 and thus equal to the net rate of return at the original submarket H_1: $A - E$. On segment *BA*, downgrading to lower-quality submarkets is associated with an ever-increasing rate of return because revenues remain constant and costs decline. For segment *DB* the answer will depend in general on the relative rates of decrease in the cost and revenue functions. If the former

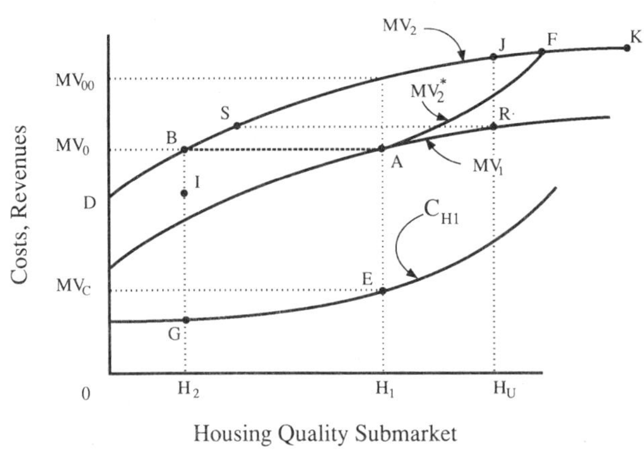

Figure 12.1. Rental housing cost and revenue functions with rent control policy.

declines faster than the latter, the maximum return submarket will be somewhat lower than H_2. If vice versa, returns at H_2 will be superior to those at lower quality levels. In our case of a parallel shift upward in the revenue function, the second condition holds, and the owner will attempt to downgrade the dwelling to H_2 in order to maximize returns.

But the central point here is that, regardless of the exact nature of the upsurge in housing demand presumed to stimulate the policy response of rent control, owners of existing rental dwellings will be encouraged to downgrade them so as to improve their rate of return. In most cases this quality downgrading will not be accompanied by a reduction in nominal rent; thus the *real* price of such downgraded dwellings rises. Each rental submarket will experience a loss of dwellings through downward conversion as a result of this systematic, policy-generated inducement. This theoretical prediction has been confirmed by empirical work.[3]

Of course not all dwellings from a given H_i will be downgraded. As more and more units downgrade to, for example, submarket H_2, the aggregate supply there will increase and competition between converters will force down prices from their initial, preadjustment level MV_0. This diminution of initial, short-run inflation will act eventually as a brake on further downward conversions.

Thus, from the viewpoint of a given submarket, a certain fraction of its initial stock will be lost through downgrading. But simultaneously it will experience as well a gain of units insofar as those from initially higher submarkets are converted down to it for the same reason.

What net pattern of conversions can be predicted? The net change of units through conversion for any quality submarket depends on the number of units originally located at relevantly higher levels relative to the number at this submarket, and the differences in those factors that influence the percentage of units that will actually convert in response to the returns differentials available.[4] The only systematic hint we can offer about net changes here is that the higher-quality submarkets will tend to have fewer units at submarkets relevantly higher. Lower submarkets will tend to have many more units at relevantly higher submarkets, probably disproportionately so to the number of units at each of those lower submarkets itself. While predictions depend on actual data about the quality distribution of dwellings in the city enacting rent control, some presumption exists on the basis of the general character of housing submarket distributions that very high quality submarkets will experience net conversion declines while moderately low and very low quality submarkets will experience net conversion increases. Nothing a priori can be surmised about the large middle range of qualities.

In summary, at this first impact stage, rent control across the quality spectrum will induce general disinvestment in existing rental housing capital through systematic, downward conversions throughout the quality spectrum, while holding nominal prices virtually constant. This will raise the real prices on those rental units that have been converted. The size of the net conversion additions to any submarket H_i will depend on (1) the number of rental units at relevantly higher levels than H_i; (2) the number of units in H_i; (3) the percentage of owners in these higher submarkets who will respond to these market signals; and (4) the relative increases in rents across the quality spectrum that would have been observed in the absence of rent control—larger putative increases at lower submarkets increase the incentive to downgrade.

12.2.2 Impacts on Individual Builders of New Rental Dwellings

Despite not being covered by rent control, the construction of new rental dwellings is affected indirectly in two ways. For the first, although the new unit is uncontrolled when it first comes into the market, the existence of rent control as a policy raises the possibility that controls may be extended to it at some later part of its life. Such subsequent extensions of control have been experienced in the real world, so it is not an idle surmise. If that occurs, the unit would from then on be constrained in its ability to take advantage of new market opportunities. Thus in its overall lifetime it would represent a less valuable asset than without this possibility. Anticipation of such a decline in lifetime value makes the unit less valuable to its builder because it will be less valuable to its next owner (in anticipation of it being less valuable to its next owner, etc.). So its expected rate of return to the builder is less for every current set of prices at which comparable units sell (or rent). Therefore, the number that will be built decreases since fewer rental housing projects will command rates of return that are superior to those available from alternative, non-rental-housing investments. This construction decrease is true at every prospective quality submarket in which new construction is economically feasible and legally permissible. In sum, the first effect of rent controls on the existing market is a reduction in the willingness of builders to supply new rental dwellings across the quality spectrum.

The second impact stems from the fact that new construction and the existing stock (converted and unconverted) are competitors in supply. As we have seen above, rent control changes the pattern of the existing rental stock by encouraging systematically the downgrading of the existing stock and thereby increasing the stock at lower-quality submarkets while simultaneously decreasing it at higher-quality submarkets. This, in turn, means stiffer competition (and lower rents) for builders originally contemplating construction of lower-quality units and just the opposite for those building higher-quality units. Of course nothing more definitive can be stated about the pattern of these construction disincentives and incentives without knowing the factors that generate a precise intersubmarket pattern of net conversions, as noted earlier.

In summary, rent controls have an overall depressing effect on the construction of new rental dwellings, even if they are not directly subject to rent control. In addition, rent control skews the distribution of whatever new construction does occur toward higher-quality submarkets, as a competitive response to the net downgrading of the existing stock from those submarkets. The ultimate additions to the stock in any rental submarket H_i from new construction thus depend on (1) the intensity of investor worries about the future extension of rent controls to newly constructed rental units; (2) the absolute rise in demand (and price for new rental units) in H_i; (3) the relative rise in demand and prices in all other submarkets; (4) the net additions or losses to the stock in H_i due to conversion; and (5) the rate of return to non-rental-housing construction (i.e., ownership housing and nonhousing investments).

12.2.3 Impacts on Renters and on the Owner Market

Besides its impacts on individual owners and builders of rental units, rent control also affects renter households and the distribution of units between rental and owner-occupied tenures. For renter households, the primary effects noted above lead to a situation where we can distinguish three types of rental housing units at each quality submarket: existing units that did not convert to the given submarket as a result of rent control; units that were converted to that submarket as a result of rent control; and units that were newly constructed in the submarket after the imposition of rent control. Both new units and converted units will have higher real (uncontrolled) rents as reflected in the MV_2 function in figure 12.1;[5] unconverted existing units will have the lower, controlled rent as reflected in the MV_1 function. This shows that the downward conversion of units effectively decontrols them. The dual rent situation between new and converted units on the one hand and unconverted units on the other persists because of the constraints imposed by rent control.

Since all three types of units have the same quality if they are in the same submarket, the existence of two rents leads consumers to have significant preferences among them. The controlled, lower-rent units are highly preferred. They come to have extremely low vacancy rates, long waiting lists, and low turnover. Present tenants cannot expect to obtain so good a bargain in the uncontrolled portion of the market, so they may remain in the controlled, unconverted units even long after their desired *type* of housing has changed markedly. The match of tenant characteristics and housing characteristics can come to decline appreciably as household characteristics change over time, while the households feel frozen into controlled units. Turnover and vacancy rates for the uncontrolled units are considerably higher.

This argument raises serious concerns about both efficiency and equity aspects of the policy. The aforementioned lack of correspondence between housing needs and the currently occupied dwelling suggests that an especially scarce resource is being used especially inefficiently: encouraging significant overall mismatches represents heavy waste.[6] The artificially reduced turnover of these units may well also increase search costs for households who do search for rental accommodations. Furthermore, there is no horizontal equity in the resulting situation: households occupying the same quality of housing differ in the amount they are paying for it, and the differences bear no appropriate relationship to need or deservingness. Those households simply fortunate enough to be occupying a unit that, for whatever reason, was not downgraded as a consequence of rent control are granted a lower real cost due to the vagaries of the policy. It is quite possible that these households have much higher incomes than those living in more expensive units, thus violating norms of vertical equity as well. There is no normative reason a priori why such households deserve to be so favored by the public through the auspices of a rent control policy.

Up to now we have been focusing only on the occupants and owners of rental units. But just as new construction and conversion are substitute forms of supply, so rental and owner-occupancy (hereafter "owner") units are substitutes as well. The described events in the rental market will have an effect on the owner market. More importantly, the existence of the owner market as a reasonably close substitute use of resources will significantly affect the events in the rental market that ultimately result from rent control.

The effect on new rental construction is probably more marked. We have noted that the expected lifetime rate of return on new rental units is likely to decline as a result of the onset of rent control and that this would decrease the number of such new units built. The original tradeoff noted in this decline was between rental housing and non-rental-housing use of funds. The closest tradeoff here is between rental and owner housing, not rental housing versus nonhousing uses altogether. Moreover, the supply cross-elasticity between rental and owner housing is very high. The rate of return on new owner units is not impaired by rent control, so funds that would have gone in the direction of rental construction shift heavily to the owner sector. The closeness of substitutability between the two sectors suggests a much larger decline in rental construction, other things being equal, than in the overall housing-nonhousing shift. However, because the systematic downgrading of the existing rental stock will likely create additional opportunities for profitable new construction in higher-quality rental submarkets, the net impact on new rental construction in these submarkets cannot be predicted unambiguously.

There is a similar effect on existing rental units. In addition to the different rental quality-submarket options open to any existing rental unit, there is for some a very real option to be converted to the owner part of the market. This is so especially for single-family houses, where the lesser expected return from a rent-controlled status can be bypassed by converting the property to owner-occupancy, its own or that of a new buyer, since excess demand probably obtains in the owner market as well, but without the profit-dampening operation of rent control. Shifts of units into the owner market are likely to occur at all submarkets, but especially at middle- and higher-quality ones, since this is where household wealth typically makes ownership feasible. For single-family homes the shift is easy. But it is not impossible for multifamily dwellings, given the relatively new tenure possibilities of condominium or cooperative ownership.[7]

Finally, there may be cross-tenure switches in households. Some renter households may be unable to locate the particular configuration of rental dwelling they seek, given the aforementioned reduction of turnover rates in the unconverted rental stock. Alternatively, they may assess the real price of the new or converted rental units as higher than that of comparable-quality units in the owner market. As a result, erstwhile demanders in the rental sector will join the ranks of homeowners. In the aggregate such switches will provide further incentives for new construction in the owner market and more conversion of formerly rental units there.

12.2.4 Aggregate Impacts of Rent Control on Rental Submarkets

The submarket graphic analysis introduced in chapter 8 provides a means for tracing the aggregate market results of all these individual adjustments that follow from the imposition of rent control. For simplicity we focus only on the rental sector and assume that the rental stock has been exhaustively partitioned into three quality submarkets—low, middle, and high quality (see fig. 12.2). We begin by assuming that the housing market is in equilibrium throughout, with initial, market-period submarket demand D_{i1} and supply S_{i1} functions producing equilibrium market valuations (rents) and occupied stocks in each submarket indicated by MV_{i1} and Q_{i1}, respectively. Our scenario assumes that an across-the-board increase in demands to D_{i2} is anticipated when rent control is enacted, which freezes prices at original levels.

As explained above, owners of existing rental units will have an incentive to downgrade while keeping nominal rent constant. So some owners origi-

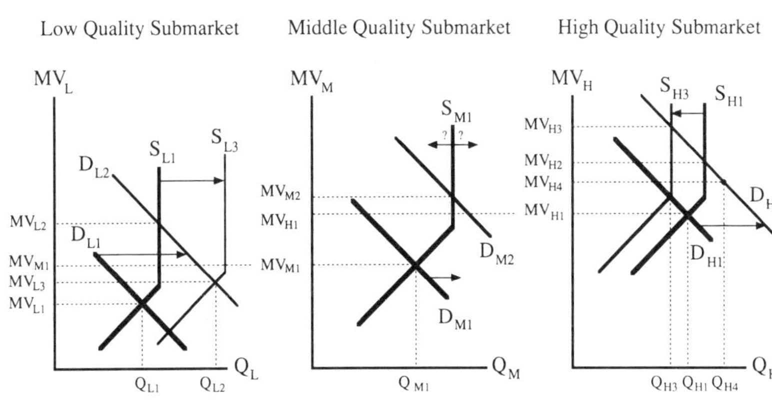

Figure 12.2. Rental submarket dynamics in the case of complete rent control.

nally in the high submarket will convert their units to middle (or even low) quality, but retain their rents at MV_{H1}. Similarly, some owners in the middle submarket will downgrade to the low, but keep their rents at MV_{M1}. As net additions to the stock of low-quality rental units occur, as shown by S_{L3} in figure 12.2, the rents that downconverted units can command will fall from the initial, transitory level MV_{L2} toward MV_{L3}. Conversely, as net reductions in the high-quality submarket occur (S_{H1} shifts toward S_{H3}), rents (for uncontrolled units) rise even farther than MV_{H2} toward MV_{H3}. Converters into the middle initially will charge MV_{H1}. After complete supply adjustments, these converters will charge more than the (controlled) MV_{M1} being charged by nonconverters in the middle, but the net change in the stock (from both conversion and construction) cannot be predicted with certainty.

Although their expected rate of return is dampened by the prospect of rent control eventually being extended to their newly built units, some entrepreneurs will construct new rental housing. The amount of new construction here will be greatest in the high-quality submarket, because it has the least competition from owners of existing units. That is, there has been a net loss of existing units from the high submarket due to downgrading, resulting in enhanced revenue possibilities for new construction there. This new construction will arrest the decline in stock due to downgrading and eventually stabilize rents in the high-quality submarket.

Concurrent with the above adjustments, some of the existing rental stock and perhaps a few of the renter households as well will be diverted into the owner sector of the market. In concert these dynamics will eventually reestablish a new, long-run equilibrium as shown in figure 12.2 by the set of demand functions having the 2 subscript and supply functions having the 3 subscript.

What can be said about such an equilibrium compared to what would have been generated by an unconstrained rental market's adjustment to the identical demand shifts? In the high-quality submarket there is the unambiguous prediction that the rental stock will be lower in the rent-controlled equilibrium. With rents rising from MV_{H1} to MV_{H2}, we would expect an unfettered market to produce an increased stock, both through new construction and, perhaps, by upgrading. This, in turn, pushes rents back toward their equilibrium level, as we demonstrated in chapter 8. But just the opposite occurs in the rent control scenario. The policy-induced downgrading siphons off much of the initial stock in the high submarket, leaving comparatively few unconverted, controlled units (shown as a shift to the left of S_{H1} in fig. 12.2). The ensuing new construction in this submarket may be more than would have occurred in the unfettered scenario, but it is not sufficient to compensate completely for the stock lost to downgrading, given our arguments about eroded expected returns for builders, that is, the new S_{H3} will end up less than the original S_{H1} in figure 12.2. Furthermore, those that do build under rent control can expect higher rents in equilibrium than builders obtain in the unfettered scenario, since there is markedly less competition from the existing rental stock. There is no contradiction in these two results. If rent MV_{H4} is the new equilibrium in the unfettered scenario it means that, on the margin, builders would be willing to produce one unit at that rent. But under rent control the willingness to build at any given rent is reduced; hence the rent control equilibrium stock must be less than that in the unfettered equilibrium, and the rent for new units under rent control must be higher than equilibrium rents for new and existing stock in an unfettered equilibrium. Of course, because the unconverted high-quality stock rent is frozen under rent control, the *average* rent for both existing and new units may or may not be higher than under the unfettered market. The particular relationship will depend on that myriad of aforementioned factors that determine the pattern and magnitude of conversions among submarkets, as well as the shape of the unfettered long-run supply function for the relevant submarket.

In the middle-quality submarket the differences in the net equilibrium stocks are less dramatic. It is probable, but not definite, that there is a smaller final equilibrium stock here too under rent control than without it, but of course a smaller decline than in the high-quality submarket. In the unfettered adjustment process we predict unambiguously that the stock of middle-quality rental housing would increase through a combination of net conversions and new construction, in response to the growing demand. But in the rent control scenario the net result of new construction and conversions into and out of the middle-quality submarket is unclear. Using the same logic as above, however, it is unlikely that the stock will expand to the same extent with rent control as without it. As before, an unambiguous prediction about *average* rents in the two scenarios cannot be made.

Finally, a demand upsurge in the lower-quality submarket normally would elicit a large downgrading response, especially from the owners of erstwhile middle-quality housing. Under rent control there is likely to be even more net downgrading, because the policy constrains returns available from maintaining or improving quality.[8] In the unfettered scenario the demand increases across all quality submarkets would provide more attractive options for potential returns for those owners who might otherwise consider downgrading to the low submarket. These higher-quality submarkets might prove so attractive that even some owners of low-quality units may be induced to upgrade. Thus, by limiting the ability of owners to take advantage of demand-induced improvements in returns to be gained by maintaining or upgrading rental units, rent control will magnify the size of net additions to the low-quality stock (shown as a shift from S_{L1} to S_{L3} in fig. 12.2). As a result, rents of units converted into the low submarket will be somewhat lower than the new, long-run equilibrium price evidenced in the comparable unfettered market scenario. And, of course, because unconverted units remain at rent MV_{L1}, the average rent in the lowest submarket will be lower under rent control.

12.3 Rent Control in Selected Low-Quality Submarkets Only

Suppose the chief purpose of rent control were to protect lower-income renters during a period of housing price inflation rather than to control the entire rental market. Toward this end it may be believed that only the units inhabited by this group should be subject to rent control, so the regulation imposes controls only on some particular fraction of the (lowest-quality) rental stock. In addition, suppose it is stipulated that (to avoid losing units affordable to the poor) a unit originally in a controlled submarket cannot escape control by upgrading beyond the control boundary submarket. Within the controlled submarkets the regulations are assumed to be identical to those discussed above.

12.3.1 Impact on Owners of Existing Rental Units

Within the controlled, low-quality submarkets the opportunities faced by owners are identical to those explained for the across-the-board rent control program analyzed above. Suppose that the boundary separating the controlled from the uncontrolled submarkets is given as H_U. Thus, if the owner in question has a unit below H_U, say at H_1, the constraints faced will be identical to those in the complete-control scenario: *DBAF* in figure 12.1.[9] As a result, the same sorts of systematic downgrading within all submarkets below H_U would be predicted.

Outside these controlled submarkets, owners of rental units face a very different set of revenue opportunities. As long as they choose a submarket above H_U they can reap the new, higher rents implicit in the inflated MV_2 function in figure 12.1. Where they find their optimum will, as usual, depend on the precise nature of the demand increases (that is, the shape of MV_2) and on their conversion cost functions. But if they consider downgrading to a destination submarket that is below H_U, they must confront the imposition of rent controls. Thus, their potential revenue function falls discontinuously at H_U from what uncontrolled units slightly above H_U can charge to what controlled units slightly below H_U were charging before the demand upsurge. From that point on, the opportunities become indistinguishable from those faced by owners of units originally in the controlled range. In sum, the revenue function faced by owners outside of the controlled sector is shown by *DSRJK* in figure 12.1.

As a consequence, for owners of rental units originally outside the controlled submarkets there will be no systematic tendency for downgrading of their units. On the contrary, the discontinuous drop in revenues that would be associated with downgrading across the boundary submarket delineating the controlled sector would provide a strong deterrent to such actions. Thus compared to a universal rent control policy, the partial rent control scheme will produce, all else equal, fewer net conversions out of higher-quality (above H_U) submarkets into lower-quality (controlled) ones. There will be, however, comparatively more downward conversions of units initially at the upper-quality ranges within the controlled sector. Because there will be less competition from units downgrading to low quality from origin submarkets above the controlled sector, more owners within the controlled sector must downgrade before rates of return in the destination submarkets are competed down to be comensurate with those in the origin submarkets. Put differently, some owners initially above H_U with conversion cost functions that would render downgrading below H_U very profitable would, under the partial rent control policy, refrain from doing so. This, in turn, paves the way for some owners below H_U with somewhat higher downward conversion cost functions to compete profitably in lower submarkets.

12.3.2 Impact on Builders of New Rental Units

The central distinction between universal control and a partial control policy is that, in the latter, builders of new units in the uncontrolled rental sector likely have less fear that controls may someday be extended to their units. To the extent that this is the case, the expected lifetime rates of return on new units built in controlled levels fall not only relative to new owner sector units and nonhousing investments, but also relative to an even closer substitute—new rental construction in higher-quality, uncontrolled submarkets. The result could be a substantial percentage shift of construction away from controlled to uncontrolled submarkets (although the absolute number will be small, because little absolute new construction normally occurs in the submarkets likely to be controlled here), as well as some to the other two alternatives. New construction of housing overall, or even rental housing overall, need not be much affected by partial rent control; only its distribution across rental-quality submarkets will be much affected.

12.3.3 Aggregate Impacts

The aggregate results of the partial rent control policy, contrasted to those of an unfettered market, can be seen with the aid of figure 12.3. We assume again the across-the-board demand increases as shown by shifts from D_{i1} to D_{i2}. Partial rent control is assumed to cover only the low-quality rental submarket portrayed.

In the uncontrolled (middle- and high-quality) rental submarkets, the rental increase to MV_{M2} and MV_{H2}, respectively, will elicit a supply response (primarily new construction) under either the unfettered market or the partial control policy, thereby increasing the respective stocks toward S_{M3} and S_{H3} and moderating over time the initial rent increase. But the policy will have the effect of boosting equilibrium stocks and lowering equilibrium rents even more than in the unfettered market case, since downgrading is discouraged and some new rental construction that would otherwise have occurred in controlled submarkets is deflected into the uncontrolled one.

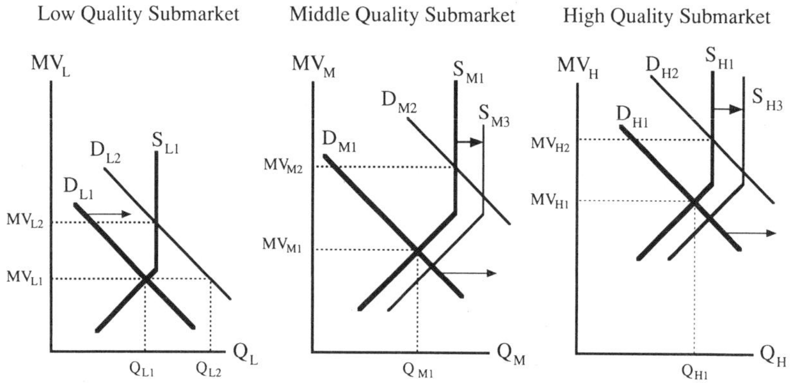

Figure 12.3. Rental submarket dynamics in the case of partial rent control on low submarket.

Very different results and rationale pertain to the situation in the lower-quality submarkets that fall under the rent controls. Consider first the case in which only a single quality submarket is controlled, as is implicit in figure 12.3. A shortage of $Q_{L2} - Q_{L1}$ dwellings would be created if rents were frozen at MV_{L1}. In the short run this creates all sorts of horizontal inequities among the potential occupants of the lowest submarket: the neediest do not necessarily get the units but nevertheless must bear higher search costs. With little incentive to downgrade from the uncontrolled submarkets, this shortage is likely to persist indefinitely. The inequities arising from the growing mismatch of household needs and incomes with the rent and type of low-quality housing they occupy will therefore grow.

If we allow several lower-quality submarkets (with distinct quality levels) to be rent controlled, there will be an incentive for owners in the higher tiers of the controlled sector to downgrade (while attempting to charge rents commensurate with their original quality).[10] This would tend to make the rent-controlled stock "pool" at the lowest of the controlled submarkets, creating there the two-tiered system of rents and associated inequities explained earlier under the complete rent control scenario. Conversely, persistent shortages would be created in the submarkets from which the dwellings were downgraded. An unambiguous prediction about comparative average rents in the lowest controlled submarkets in the partial-control scenario and the unfettered market scenario cannot be made. It is true that rents of the original, lowest-quality units are controlled at levels below what the equilibrium would have been in an unfettered market.[11] But the real rents of units converted downward into this submarket could well be higher than in the unfettered scenario. Whether the weighted average of rents for these controlled and effectively uncontrolled tiers of dwellings in the lowest submarket represents an increase or decrease over the unfettered equilibrium will depend on all the particular factors outlined above that govern the pattern of conversions in a particular housing market context.

12.3.4 Comparative Impacts of Partial versus Complete Rent Control

The following comparative consequences can be predicted for the two types of rent control. The partial control policy, by discouraging systematic downgrading of higher-quality units and by encouraging builders to switch construction out of controlled sectors, will result in comparatively larger rental stocks in the higher-quality (uncontrolled) rental submarkets and smaller stocks in the controlled submarkets. Overall this should make average real rents higher here than under complete control, but the exact pattern depends, again, on the weighted average rents of the unconverted (controlled) and the converted and new (uncontrolled) units under the complete control policy, and their distribution.

For submarkets in the upper-quality ranges of the controlled sector there will be smaller equilibrium stocks under the partial control policy, since owners there are encouraged to downgrade but both builders and converters are discouraged from adding to the stock there. As a result, rents for the stock consisting of converted and new units will be higher. Rents for the original stock will be at the same, controlled level.

Finally, in the lower-quality (controlled) submarkets there will be slightly fewer units under the partial control policy, because many units (from uncontrolled sectors) that potentially could have inexpensively downgraded are deterred from doing so. Although the slack at the lowest submarket is partially filled by downgrading within the controlled sector, undoubtedly some of these units convert at comparatively higher cost, and thus the resultant equilibrium rent for converted units is somewhat inflated over that under a complete control policy. Since the number of original, lowest-quality units is approximately the same under either policy, the *average* rents here will be higher under the partial control policy. More shortages (at least in the upper-quality ranges of the controlled stock) are created in the lower-quality submarkets under the partial control policy.

Thus, although the inefficiencies of any rent-control policy are reduced to the extent that controls can be limited to only certain submarkets, the effects of limited controls have perverse, unintended redistributional effects. Because equilibrium stocks are higher (and rents thus lower) in uncontrolled sectors under partial control than under an unfettered market, the (presumably middle- and upper-income) occupants of these submarkets gain indirectly by partial control. Conversely, because there are fewer units downgraded into the controlled sectors but potentially many downgraded within these sectors, real average rents in the lowest-quality submarkets may be higher than in the unfettered market, and certainly more than in a complete control system. The similar arguments about the costs associated with shortages can be made for the upper ranges of the controlled sector.

Even more perverse equity effects arise if we let more time pass than our middle-run perspective. Over an even longer run, maintenance becomes more expensive for aging dwellings, so conversion cost functions come to decline more steeply for these units. Thus owners will want to downgrade beyond the original degree, increasingly as structural aging progresses further. Under a complete control policy, units moving ever-farther downward in quality are replenished by continuous downward conversions from submarkets all the way to the highest—and there they are replenished by new construction. So a net distribution not very different from that of the original adjustments persists. But under a partial control policy this continuing downward pressure in the controlled sector is not replenished by conversions from higher submarkets or by much new construction. Above the controlled level, units are more zealously maintained over time to avoid falling into the controlled sector. So the diminution of stocks there due to dwelling retirements increases, eventually affecting all parts of the controlled sector. Even the very low quality sectors become progressively starved for dwellings. Thus over time a partial rent control hurts even the very poor—ostensibly the chief clients of the policy—much more so than general control, and very probably more than no rent control at all.

It is clear that a partial rent control policy with the putative goal of protecting lower-income renters would be notably inefficient and inequitable, and likely even counterproductive. Compared to allowing the rental market to adjust freely to demand upsurges, the partial rent control policy (1) *may,* at first, product lower average rents in the lowest-quality controlled sectors, but not necessarily; (2) *may* (not necessarily) produce lower average rents in the higher-quality controlled sector, but at the cost of severe shortages that force erstwhile households in this submarket to consume housing elsewhere at potentially higher real rents; and (3) will produce lower average rents in the uncontrolled, higher-quality rental submarkets. Compared to a policy that completely controls all rental submarkets, the partial control policy (1) produces higher average rents in the lowest (controlled) submarkets; (2) produces lower average rents but more severe shortages of less expensive units in the higher-quality controlled submarkets; (3) produces in the longer run severe shortages, and thus higher real rents, throughout the entire controlled sector; and (4) produces an unpredictable effect on uncontrolled, higher-quality submarkets.

12.4 The Impacts of Rent Control: A Summary

Our housing submarket analysis of two types of rent control policies reveals that several general consequences follow from their imposition, in contrast to what would transpire in an unfettered market adjustment process:

1. Although nominal rents are frozen (in the absence of upgrading) at original levels in all controlled submarkets, the average *real* rents in such submarkets rise absolutely due to the downgrading of units in which quality depreciation exceeds rent depreciation. Whether these average real rents are lower than would be produced in an unfettered equilibrium cannot be ascertained in general, although it is likely that they will be somewhat lower in the lowest submarkets under a policy of rent control which includes all submarkets.

2. There is a more rapid depreciation of the controlled existing rental stock through widespread downward conversions induced by rent control. Each successive upsurge in demand results in a further repetition of this downgrading dynamic.[12] The situation worsens with time and the aging of the existing stock. Thus the policy induces owners to disinvest in an especially scarce resource at a substantial rate rather than invest in it.

3. A two-tier rent system is created in the controlled submarkets. Unconverted units have nominal (and real) rents frozen at original levels, but converted and newly constructed units of the same quality have higher real rents. These rents will be higher to the degree that new construction shifts out of the controlled rental submarkets. Because there is no programmatic system for allocating households to rent-controlled units, serious horizontal and vertical inequities are created.

4. The two-tiered rent system drastically reduces household turnover in the controlled units with the lower real rents. Over time this leads to increasing mismatches between household needs, their financial resources, and dwelling features. This, in turn, implies that even larger inefficiencies and inequities result from the policy in the long run.

5. The effective extent of controls in considerably smaller than the legal extent, either through conversions of existing controlled rental units downward in quality or through their conversion to owner units.

6. The mix of new construction and net conversions will be altered throughout the spectrum of rental submarkets. New construction will become a higher share of net stock additions in the higher-quality and/or uncontrolled submarkets, and net additions through downward conversions into the submarket will assume a larger share in the others, compared to the unfettered equilibrium.

7. A partial rent control policy results in larger (smaller) rental stocks and lower (higher) real rents in the uncontrolled, higher-quality (controlled, lower-quality) submarkets, compared to a complete control policy or the unfettered market, especially in the longer run.

12.5 Urban Housing Submarkets and Policy Analysis: Comparing Alternative Policy Options

Our theory of the behavior of demanders and suppliers of heterogeneous, imperfectly malleable housing dwellings in a segmented market context provides a robust vehicle for analyzing urban housing policies. We have demonstrated that many conventional nostrums about the impacts of various policies have little or circumscribed validity. Although we have not attempted here a detailed benefit-cost analysis of a variety of specific programmatic options, we believe some general conclusions can be drawn from our analysis that provide crucial implications for future formulations of urban housing policy.

In this final section of our policy analysis we first note that any judgments made about the comparative efficacy of one approach or another depend critically upon the goals of the policymaker and the idiosyncracies of the particular metropolitan housing market for which the policy is designed. In other words, each form of policy we have analyzed has its own comparative advantages and disadvantages for meeting certain ends; optimal strategy thus depends on programmatic goals specified. The efficacy of a strategy will be influenced by the particular metropolitan context in which it is implemented; characteristics of the individual area's housing stock, housing market, households, construction industry, and preexisting social welfare policies matter. After considering these factors in more detail below, we conclude by arguing for the general superiority of demand-side strategies in meeting the most important consensual goals in most urban contexts.

12.5.1 Goal-Setting and the Comparative Advantages of Different Policies

We recognize that there are many potential goals for urban housing policy and numerous constituencies whose interests can be weighted and evaluated differentially.[13] Our point here is not to advocate particular goals, but rather to indicate which policies would be most (and least) likely to meet whatever goals have been established. For each of the nine goals considered below we draw upon our earlier conclusions which followed from our housing submarket–based analysis.

1. *Maximizing the well-being of low-income recipients.* Clearly an unrestricted housing voucher would best achieve this goal, for it provides the maximum flexibility for recipients to allocate budgetary expenditures in ways which best satisfy their preferences. Other policy options either would reduce the price of housing (filtering, rent control) or require the consumption of a particular quality of housing (rehabilitation or new construction targeted for low-income households). In either case the recipients' consumption would be distorted in favor of more housing than they otherwise would have chosen. A policy of partial rent control would severely harm most of the low-income tenantry in the long run.

2. *Maximizing the quality of housing consumed by recipients.* Logic opposite that used in (1) applies here. New targeted construction at an appropriate-quality submarket (with provisions deterring subsequent downgrading), substantially rehabilitating dwellings and subsequently limiting their rents, and rent supplements using high FMRs with no cost-saving provisions all would

be appropriate. On the contrary, rent control would be least effective in this regard. Only in the short run are real rents of superior-quality units reduced, and the resulting shortage makes it unlikely that lower-income tenants can benefit.

3. *Minimizing housing payment burdens on recipients.* Demand-side subsidies, rehabilitation (with subsequent rent limitations), and targeted new construction would be recommended. Rehabilitation with no rent limitations and filtering policies might provide progress toward this goal, but with less certainty. Rent control would only reduce real rents for those occupants lucky enough to occupy a controlled unit that was not downgraded. Other tenants in downgraded units within the controlled sector may not realize significantly lower real rents than those they would face absent controls. Tenants unable to find any controlled units because of the induced shortages may be forced to consume even more expensive housing than originally.

4. *Maximizing benefits (minimizing harms) to nonrecipient, low-income households.* Demand-side subsidies (especially if high FMRs or voucher amounts were issued and upgrading rather than abandonment were the predominant supply response) and targeted new construction would provide reasonably certain benefits to nonrecipients because they would reduce the demand (from recipients) for the low-quality submarket. Rehabilitation might have this impact if many of the erstwhile occupants of the low submarket (the policy recipients) could afford to move up to the rehabilitated units' target submarkets. The least efficacious policy in this aspect would be partial rent control. Due to the shortages induced, some erstwhile tenants of the controlled submarkets would be forced to consume more expensive, uncontrolled housing, to double up with another household, or even to become homeless.

5. *Maximize horizontal equity among low-income households.* Because ideally it would depress rents of moderate-quality submarkets in such a way that all low-income households could gain, filtering offers the greatest potential here. Although rent control similarly would have marketwide impacts, the resultant two-tier system of real rents in the controlled sector and the shortages would create clear winners and losers among low-income households. All other policies make explicit distinctions between policy recipients (those who receive rent supplements or reside in rehabilitated or newly built dwellings) and nonrecipients, assuming that these policies were of insufficient scale to provide universal coverage of low-income households.

6. *Maximize spatial deconcentration of low-income households.* If targeted new construction could be built in a variety of suburban areas it would offer the greatest potential for deconcentration. Demand-side subsidies apparently offer only minimal incentives for significant relocations, although this might be improved if more generous FMRs were specified so that a wider spatial array of dwellings presented feasible choices for participants. Rent control, filtering, and rehabilitation would be comparatively inferior vehicles for achieving this goal.

7. *Maximize upgrading of the substandard housing stock.* Clearly the most effective means to maximize upgrading would be the rehabilitation subsidy policy. Demand-side policies could also encourage rehabilitation, especially if rent supplements were large and tied to high FMRs, and if much of the low-quality stock was comparatively inexpensive to upgrade. Equally as clearly, filtering and rent controls would counter this goal, as they both encourage downgrading.

8. *Minimize the deterioration and abandonment of the existing housing stock.* Rehabilitation would be unlikely to generate much abandonment response. It could, however, encourage some downgrading of units from the submarket into which dwellings were upgraded to the extent that the number of upgraded dwellings exceeded the number of lower-income households who could afford to move up. Targeting new construction with set-asides for low-income households would lead to abandonment insofar as demand was siphoned away from the low-quality submarket by the policy. Downgrading responses from unsubsidized sectors should prove minimal, however. Rent supplements, if they produced any substantial supply response at all, would simultaneously encourage the upgrading of some low-quality dwellings, the downgrading of others initially of higher quality than the submarket in which the subsidized tenants would be demanding, and some abandonment of the least competitive stock. As noted in (7), filtering and rent control would prove antithetical to this goal on both scores.

9. *Maximize political feasibility/attract widespread public support.* If policymakers were concerned about providing programmatic benefits (or at least minimizing costs) to the middle and upper classes, filtering would prove the most appealing. A rent control plan which set regulations over a wide spectrum of quality submarkets and rehabilitation subsidies for homeowners likely would as well. Targeted new construction and rent supplements would provide the least net benefits to these groups.

No single policy represents the preeminent means for attaining all possible programmatic goals. Some, however, demonstrate a wider range of goals over which they demonstrate comparative advantage. Although in our analysis we have considered various policy options as if they were mutually exclusive, we recognize that an amalgam of options might represent a superior strategy to any "pure" approach in a particular context. For example, suppose a policymaker was faced with a particular urban area with the following characteristics: (1) a low-quality stock which was very expensive to upgrade and to maintain at an improved level; (2) a low vacancy rate in the moderate-quality submarket; and (3) low-income tenants having high demand elasticities. Suppose in addition that the two preeminent policy goals are to improve the well-being of low-income tenants and to preserve and improve existing neighborhoods. In such a case a combination of unrestricted rent vouchers and rehabilitation subsidy policies would be suggested. The point of our analytical approach is not to suggest *the* correct strategy. Rather, our approach provides a vehicle for understanding the general consequences which will occur across the submarket array as a result of alternative policies and shows the particular features of the given urban context which must be assessed before more quantitative estimates of policy outcomes can be made. Then the optimal policy or policy mix can be selected based on its comparative advantage in achieving the goals of particular importance to the policymaker.

12.5.2 Policy Formulation and the Metropolitan Context

A key result of our analysis is that the consequences of any given policy, indeed the optimal policy choices, depend in large measure on the particular features of the urban housing market for which it is being considered. These contextual features involve characteristics of the existing housing stock (age, structural features, distribution by quality submarket and tenure), local housing market conditions (vacancy rates), the low-income households to be targeted for assistance (incomes, preferences), the area's construction industry (nature of the long-run supply function), and other welfare policies which already might be in place. Key contextual elements are considered below.

1. *Costs of upgrading the existing stock in low-quality submarkets.* If the features of the low-quality stock in general were such that the aggregate upgrading conversion supply function was only gradually upsloping, the beneficial supply responses associated with a demand-side approach would be larger. Similarly, a given commitment of resources devoted to a rehabilitation program would produce a greater extent of upgrading.

2. *Costs of downgrading the existing stock in middle- and upper-quality submarkets.* If the features of these submarkets were such that large cost savings could be gained through downgrading, demand-side policies would result in more downgrading responses into the submarkets where the new demand was focused. As a result more new construction would be induced to replenish this downgraded stock. Rehabilitation policies would be more likely to generate compensatory downgrading from the unsubsidized stock with which the rehabilitated units competed. Finally, the cross-submarket filtering waves of downgrading triggered by new, unsubsidized construction in high-quality submarkets would be larger in magnitude and affect a broader range of quality levels.

3. *Costs of operation after conversion.* If the operating/maintenance costs of dwellings which were upgraded were low, rehabilitation policies would yield lower long-run rent levels in the submarkets into which participating units were converted, thus obviating the need for associated rent limitations. If these costs were to fall relatively quickly and consistently across the quality spectrum, filtering would more likely keep rents depressed for longer periods.

4. *Market conditions.* If the low-and moderate-quality rental submarkets were to have high vacancy rates, rent supplements would generate small short-run rent increases and correspondingly small conversion supply responses,

inasmuch as the policy-induced perturbations were absorbed by the existing stock. Such market "softness" over a wider array of submarkets would produce a more significant filtering response to new, high-quality construction. It might also postpone the appearance of shortages under a rent control policy, although such a market scenario is typically not that which produces the political momentum for enacting such controls.

5. *Demand elasticities.* If lower-income households had higher cross-price elasticities of housing demand, a rent supplement policy would result in the recipients occupying higher submarkets than otherwise. Under this circumstance a rehabilitation policy would induce more occupants of low submarkets to move up in quality, even without rent restrictions on the rehabilitated dwellings. Similarly, filtering would produce a more powerful and widespread pattern of households choosing to occupy superior-quality submarkets in response to narrowing intersubmarket rent differentials if all households demonstrated such a higher elasticity.

6. *Construction industry.* If the resources needed for the expansion of the local construction industry within an urban area can be drawn upon with little increase in input costs, the long-run supply function of the industry will be highly elastic and the marginal costs of building new dwellings will not increase appreciably. This would mean that a policy to stimulate new construction targeted for low-income occupants would not permanently deflect construction away from unsubsidized sectors and, therefore, not impose welfare losses on the occupants of these sectors through higher long-run housing prices.

7. *Preexisting welfare policies.* If, for example, a broad-gauge rent control policy were already in place in a metropolitan area (such as New York City), the efficiency of various additional housing policies would be affected. Most obviously, demand-side policies would make little sense in an environment already experiencing shortages. Filtering is rendered pointless. Given the rent control constraint, only rehabilitation and construction options would make sense. Other considerations might involve a wider array of social welfare policies such as income maintenance, health care, and so forth. Certain eligibility rules for housing entitlements, in conjuction with those for the others noted, might create perverse disincentives for recipients to increase their earned incomes. This danger typically is associated with tenant allocations to new or rehabilitated subsidized dwellings, but also could involve rent supplements.[14] Rent control and filtering options would finesse these considerations.

12.5.3 Demand-Side versus Supply-Side and Market Regulation Approaches: A Final Comparison

We have just finished making the point that there is no unambiguously "best" housing policy in all circumstances. Every policy has its own comparative advantages to a degree as determined by the particular urban housing market context and by the goals of the particular policymaker. Nevertheless, our analysis clearly shows that, in general, demand-side approaches are by far superior on most efficiency and equity grounds typically considered. The reasons follow from our unique submarket approach to urban housing market analysis. Demand-side approaches are fundamentally different from either supply-side or market-regulatory approaches because they do not engender conflicting adjustments across submarkets which counteract policy intents.

Demand-side approaches directly attack the root of the problem in most markets—the inability of some households to afford decent-quality housing at current rents for such. When rent supplements are provided to these households, the market responds so as to supply more housing to the quality level at which these augmented demands are concentrated. Although downgrading responses from submarkets above these target submarkets may not be as socially desirable as upgrading responses from those below, nevertheless both sorts of responses benefit the policy participants by lowering market valuations in the target submarkets. In addition, no counterproductive market adjustments adversely affect other low-income households who are not direct subsidy recipients.

By contrast, all the other approaches set in motion market responses which tend to erode the efficiency of the policy. Rehabilitation and targeted new construction require such additional programmatic stipulations as rent limitations on rehabilitated units, inspections to prohibit downgrading, and participation coercions. Rent control causes systematic downgrading tendencies in the controlled submarkets. Filtering achieves its desired impact only through the wasteful acceleration of the downgrading of a wide range of housing-quality levels.

We thus conclude our policy analysis by returning to our recurrent theme. Urban housing markets should be viewed as an interconnected system of submarkets. What occurs in one will create repercussions in others in predictable ways and of a magnitude inversely related to the quality differential between the submarkets. The ultimate (as opposed to transitory) efficiency and equity of a particular policy will be crucially affected by the form taken by the inter-submarket repercussions which are induced.

Notes

1. For more details about the rent control systems in New York and California, see Niebanck 1985: chs. 3 and 4, respectively. The Canadian experience is described in Miron and Cullingworth 1983 and Marks 1984. Also see Gilderbloom and Appelbaum 1988 and Downs 1988 for alternative treatments of rent control.

2. Or at least there is no effective administrative machinery to monitor and punish or roll back such downgrading, which will be essentially universal under this plan.

3. The effects in New York City were tested by Moorhouse 1972. Niebanck 1985: ch. 6 estimates that after a decade about two-thirds of the average amount of the rent

decrease generated by the Los Angeles rent control laws will be offset by its degree of average decline in dwelling quality resulting from downgrading. Vitaliano 1985 found that the flow of housing services declined about 25% due to rent control in upstate New York during 1942–49.

4. These factors include whether the owner is "market oriented" and continuously seeks to maximize returns through marginal adjustments, the costs of market information, tolerance for risk, and access to financing.

5. These are the initial prices; after full supply adjustments the price will be moderated somewhat, but still undoubtedly will be above the rent-controlled level.

6. It has been estimated that 20% of all renter households in New York City are misallocated to dwelling type (Niebanck 1985: ch. 3).

7. Stegman 1985, found that from 1981 to 1984 the New York rent-controlled stock declined 24%, mainly due to conversions to cooperatives and condominiums. Similar supply decreases in Vancouver have been estimated by Marks 1984.

8. Even if it were legal to build new, low-quality units here it would be an unlikely response given the likely superiority of conversion as the cheaper mode of supply, as argued in ch. 5.

9. The only minor difference here is that higher rental compensations for upgrading costs only extend to the H_U boundary.

10. This distinction cannot be easily portrayed with our simplified, three-submarket diagram as in fig. 12.3.

11. Assuming an upward-sloping long-run supply function for this submarket.

12. That the New York City rental stock has not depreciated more than it has can partially be attributed to the fact that a large portion of the units are located in buildings containing commercial properties, for which rents are not controlled; see McCain 1987: sect. 8, p.1.

13. For discussions of these issues, see Bradbury and Downs 1981: 67–93; Howenstine 1986: ch. 10; Gilderbloom and Appelbaum 1988; and Keyes and DiPasquale 1988.

14. See Newman and Schnare 1988.

Part Four: Empirical Explorations

13 Estimating the Structure of Housing Submarkets

13.1 Empirical Issues in the Estimation of Hedonic Indexes and Housing Quality

In a large metropolitan area there can be literally hundreds of thousands of somewhat different housing commodities, and many dimensions along which such dwelling units differ—for example, number of rooms, square footage, heating, bathrooms, architectural styles, structure type, lot characteristics, and neighborhood characteristics. And since structures are usually highly durable and have significant, but not unlimited, possibilities of conversion, their precise nature during any period is a major determinant of the character and magnitude of housing supply as well as occupancy and prices in subsequent periods.

For these reasons we require a scheme of market segmentation that characterizes and orders the degree of substitutability among units, both actual and potential. Substitutability defines functional "nearness" for consumers and for builders of new dwellings or converters of existing ones, and this in general suggests the direction and size of intersubmarket repercussions arising from each exogenous impact originating in any part of the market complex.

For any individual agent operating in the market, as we saw in chapter 3, the gradations of substitutability are given by utility differences (insofar as they can be consistently and transitively ordered by consumers) and transformation possibilities (for builders and converters). For any household, these utility differences can define a single-dimensional index of *quality,* or quantity of housing services. Similarly, for any builder or converter, these transformation possibilities and costs define a single-dimensional index of quality, or

Portions of chapter 13 were originally published in the *Journal of Regional Science* 20, no. 4:439–53 (© 1980 by the Regional Science Research Institute) as "Cross-Sectional Variation in the Hedonic Relationship for Urban Housing Markets," by Richard V. Butler, and in *Land Economics* 58, no. 1:96–108 (© 1982 by the Regents of the University of Wisconsin System) as "The Specification of Hedonic Indexes for Urban Housing," by Richard V. Butler. Permission to reprint this material has been granted by the Regional Science Research Institute and the University of Wisconsin Press, the respective copyright owners, and is gratefully acknowledged.

quantity of housing services. However, households differ markedly in their taste for housing; production possibilities and relative costs also vary widely among builders and converters. The members of each group are likely to disagree among themselves about the patterns of substitutability. Obviously, no "quality" index would be unanimously valid for the two groups taken together.

To recapitulate our central claim of chapter 3, our procedure is to take advantage of an important form of market consensus which, while not complete, represents a promising convergence for our purposes. Although average tradeoffs among the several components of the housing package may differ among both demanders and suppliers, a market equilibrium implies that each participant equates the marginal rate of substitution (in consumption or production) for any two such components to the (implicit) common market-clearing relative prices of those components: in other words, that everyone has the same *marginal* tradeoffs among components. These common marginal tradeoffs should be observable in the average clearing prices of components as implied by the observed market prices for housing packages.

Average implicit component prices in the market can be approximately derived by regressing observed market valuations (rents for apartments, prices for sales units) on constituent components of the package: size, condition, architectural features, land, neighborhood accessibility, and so forth. Such an index gives a one-dimensional use value for every housing unit. Degrees of substitutability are given simply as the size of differences in use—or hedonic—value. Moreover, these degrees are in principle as relevant for supplier as for demander options, inasmuch as they also reflect transformation possibilities.

Once estimated, we employ our hedonic indexes in two crucial empirical tasks. First, we array the existing housing stock in the sampled metropolitan area(s) according to the quality (i.e., hedonic value) implicit in their packages of dwelling components—subdivisions of this array represent our empirical operationalization of *housing-quality submarket*. Second, we use the hedonic index to estimate both submarket prices and the potential gross returns earned by suppliers who place a dwelling with particular characteristics on the market. The index thus becomes a device for generating important explanatory variables in our market-period demand and supply model (ch. 14) and in our medium-run stock change models (chs. 15, 16).

Given the centrality of the hedonic index to our empirical work, it is crucial to explore its features, its alternative forms and applications, and its potential flaws. In particular, we investigate in this chapter several questions dealing with our empirical application of hedonic indexes. Is the hedonic relationship stable across metropolitan areas? What happens when certain dwelling characteristics must be omitted from the hedonic regression, due to data limitations? Can a hedonic index estimated for a sample of recently-sold dwellings be representative of the overall housing stock? How sensitive is the explanatory power of the index to various functional forms of the hedonic regression? Put differently, these represent questions about aggregation bias, omitted-variables bias, sample-selection bias, and functional-form specification bias. The former two issues are discussed below in the context of our cross-SMSA model, the latter two in the context of our single-SMSA model.

Even if the hedonic indexes which underlie them prove not to be subject to severe biases, are the estimated housing-quality submarkets reasonable? Do the clusters of dwellings which they contain appear intuitively pleasing? Do intersubmarket price correlations correspond to a priori expectations? Do quality submarkets have distinct geographic analogues (with geographic areas defined by census tracts, by travel zones, or by racial composition) characterized by a large degree of dwelling homogeneity? Again, these are fundamental questions in our empirical applications of housing submarket theory. We attempt to provide answers in both cross-SMSA and single-SMSA models discussed below.

This chapter contains two major subsections, corresponding to the cross-SMSA and single-SMSA applications of our theory. Within each subsection, the data base employed is first described. Then the particular hedonic index(es) estimated for the given application is presented and potential biases in the index are investigated. Finally, the sample's housing stock is subdivided into quality submarkets (based on the hedonic index), and the characteristics of these submarkets are probed.

13.2 Cross-SMSA Model

13.2.1 Data Base

Our cross-metropolitan area empirical analyses are based on two samples of standard metropolitan statistical areas (SMSAs) relevant for two different periods. For 1960, a sample of thirty-six SMSAs (about 15% of the SMSAs defined by the 1960 Census) was randomly selected with a stratified procedure which attempted to achieve a balance by region, SMSA size,[1] and SMSA growth rates.[2] For 1975–76, a sample of thirty-eight SMSAs was employed, which corresponded to the combined samples of the 1975 and 1976 Annual Housing Surveys. A complete listing of the specific SMSAs used in the 1960 and 1975–76 samples is given in the bottom panels of tables 13.1 and 13.2, respectively.

The reason for choosing the 1960 Census over more recent ones was the unavailability of structural condition measures in the latter. Since the 1975–76 Annual Housing Survey data also lack such measures, we felt it was important to test one cross-SMSA model with condition being controlled for.

The nature of the dwelling characteristics available from the 1960 (Census) and 1975–76 (Annual Housing Survey) data bases is different. The former notes the number of rooms, condition (sound, deteriorating, dilapidated), inadequate plumbing, and structural vintage (pre-1940, 1940–49, 1950–54,

1955–59). The latter adds to the above list: type of heating equipment, structure type, kitchen facilities, and (for renters) numbers of units in structure, number of stories in structure, and whether there was direct access to the unit. The 1975–76 survey contains no information about structural conditions, however.

Finally, the nature of the observations in each sample is different. The 1960 decennial census data do not delineate characteristics of individual dwellings, as the 1975–76 Annual Housing Survey data do. Rather, they give a set of two-way cross-tabulations of structural characteristics of various sorts with corresponding rent and price categories. These cross-tabulations can be used to generate *mean* values of the necessary structural and financial data for dwellings classified in each category. Thus, within each sampled SMSA there are seventeen such "observations" of average rent or price and corresponding average values of each of the aforementioned structural features.[3] As we shall see below, such "observations" have implications for estimating procedures.

13.2.2 Estimated Hedonic Indexes

For both cross-SMSA samples, the general form of the hedonic index estimated may be expressed symbolically as

$$\text{(13.1)}\quad \text{Log}\, MV = a_0 + a_1 ROOMS + [a_i][PL_i] + [a_j][CN_j] + [a_k][AGE_k] + [a_l][STR_l] + [a_m][HT_m] + [a_n][D_n] + e,$$

where:

- Log MV = natural logarithm of the unit's market price (if owner-occupied) or monthly contract rent (if renter-occupied);
- a_0 = a constant term;
- $[a]$ = row vectors of estimated coefficients;
- $ROOMS$ = number of rooms in the unit;
- $[PL_i]$ = column vector of dummy variables describing i plumbing features of the unit;
- $[CN_j]$ = column vector of dummy variables describing j condition features of the unit (available only for 1960);
- $[AGE_k]$ = column vector of dummy variables denoting k different vintages of unit construction;
- $[STR_l]$ = column vector of dummy variables denoting l different structural features of the unit (available only for 1975–76);
- $[HT_m]$ = column vector of dummy variables denoting m different possible types of heating systems in the unit (available only for 1975–76);
- $[D_n]$ = column vector of dummy variables denoting each different SMSA in our sample of size $n + 1$; and
- e = a random error term with the usual assumed properties.

We employ the semi-log functional form here not only because it is conventional, but because it implies interactions between structural features in producing quality. That is, it is intuitively pleasing that the marginal increment in hedonic value associated with one additional room is not constant, but rather depends on its age, condition, associated plumbing facilities, structure type, and so forth.

Separate equations like equation (13.1) were estimated for owners and renters. While recognizing the deep connections between owner and renter submarkets (see our tenure-choice analysis in ch. 4), we believe that the two types of tenure involve both primary and induced differences in the nature of housing services. Not only do the psychological as well as legal experiences of the tenures per se differ, but they induce some specialization in the types of units that come to be predominantly used for each. Since we do not possess explanatory variables that capture these differences, we treat them as different commodities, commensurable only in terms of the comparisons between estimation fits and corresponding coefficients. In effect, we have parallel modes of segmentation in the different tenures, and direct transitive comparisons of quality can only be made within each mode.

Climatic variation, which is expected to affect the coefficients of the housing characteristic variables systematically, is the basis for stratifying the SMSAs into two separate categories. Gross differences in climate are expected to exert a major impact on market tradeoffs among characteristics. For instance, lack of central heat should detract little from value in warm areas. Older units may deteriorate more slowly in warm areas, thereby reducing the effect of structural age on value. Thus, in both years four hedonic indexes like equation (13.1) were specified and estimated: cold-renter, cold-owner, warm-renter and warm-owner. These regional breakdowns are shown in tables 13.1 and 13.2

Differences between SMSAs are also allowed for by the inclusion of SMSA-specific dummy variables. These dummies are intended to reflect inter-SMSA variations in forces which impact equally on all qualities of housing units, for example, land prices.

For the 1975–76 sample (23 "cold" and 15 "warm" SMSAs), the data permit the straightforward use of ordinary least squares (OLS) for parameter estimation. For the 1960 sample (20 "cold" and 16 "warm" SMSAs), however, the categorical average nature of the data suggests a different estimating technique. If OLS were to be used with such data, the weighting of observations implicit in the grouping process would lead to heteroscedasticity (Prais and Aitchison 1954). Thus, generalized least squares (GLS) is a more appropriate estimator. However, as Haitovsky (1973)[4] has pointed out, not all of the seventeen categories can be used to form the GLS estimate. The problem is that the pooled grouping matrix (call it G) used to transform the original observations into grouped data does not have full rank; thus GG' will be singular and

Table 13.1 1960 Hedonic Index Estimates and Sampled SMSAs

COLD SMSAs

Variable	Owners	Renters
Rooms	.1629	.09409
Sound, lacking plumbing	−.5761	−.3826
Deteriorating, all plumbing	−.3400	−.1167
Deteriorating, lacking plumbing	−.7110	−.4256
Dilapidated	−.6155	−.3070
Built before 1940	−.5770	−.3300
Built 1940–49	−.2452	−.2423
Built 1950–54	−.1950	−.09617
R^2	.9728	.9727
d.f.	239	239

SMSA	Owner Dummy	Renter Dummy	SMSA	Owner Dummy	Renter Dummy
Buffalo	8.901	4.172	Springfield, IL	8.896	4.258
Chicago	9.161	4.422	Trenton	8.815	4.339
Detroit	8.821	4.251	Utica	8.728	4.101
Minneapolis	9.003	4.314	Topeka	8.836	4.281
Omaha	8.833	4.297	Denver	8.880	4.266
Philadelphia	8.657	4.182	Portland, OR	8.712	4.138
Pittsburgh	8.762	4.130	Seattle	8.864	4.173
Syracuse	8.786	4.263	Pueblo	8.733	4.120
Duluth	8.772	Excluded*	Spokane	8.671	4.105
Scranton	Excluded*	3.924	Tacoma	8.666	4.077
			MEDIAN	8.815	4.182

WARM SMSAs

Variable	Owners	Renters
Rooms	.2087	.1061
Sound, lacking plumbing	−.4991	−.3853
Deteriorating, all plumbing	−.3171	−.1565
Deteriorating, lacking plumbing	−.5776	−.4732
Dilapidated	−.5029	−.4500
Built before 1940	−.4246	−.2675
Built 1940–49	−.2649	−.2450
Built 1950–54	−.1327	−.1335
R^2	.9798	.9705
d.f.	187	200

SMSA	Owner Dummy	Renter Dummy	SMSA	Owner Dummy	Renter Dummy
Atlanta	8.524	4.174	Knoxville	8.262	3.949
Jacksonville	8.498	4.286	Raleigh	Excluded*	4.061
Louisville	8.473	4.130	Savannah	8.407	4.065

Table 13.1. continued

WARM SMSAS					
SMSA	Owner Dummy	Renter Dummy	SMSA	Owner Dummy	Renter Dummy
Miami	8.815	4.523	Phoenix	8.434	4.141
Oklahoma City	8.353	4.059	San Diego	8.832	4.269
Tampa	8.566	4.334	San Jose	8.742	4.262
Austin	8.530	4.101	Albuquerque	8.538	4.155
El Paso	8.514	4.077	Tucson	8.504	4.094
			MEDIAN	8.514	4.135

Note: The coefficients of all of the characteristics are significant at the 1% level (1-tail test).
*Three SMSAs were dropped from one tenure because of an unusual market situation at the time of the 1960 Census.

$(GG')^{-1}$will fail to exist.[5] To obtain a modified G matrix which does have full rank, Haitovsky suggests deleting (arbitrarily) one row from all but one of the separate grouping matrices that go to make up G. Since the corresponding rows must also be deleted from the data matrix, the seventeen census categories must be reduced to fifteen for estimation purposes.[6] It must be emphasized that numerous alternative deletions meeting Haitovsky's criterion are possible; deletion of a different pair of categories would presumably lead to somewhat different results. However, since there is no strong reason to choose one such estimate over another, this poses no serious problems.

The method used in this estimation diverged slightly from that proposed by Haitovsky. Since GG' is not diagonal in this case, use of his technique would have required the computation of $(GG')^{-1}$for each of seventy-one different subsamples. This would have imposed an unreasonably large computational burden, so (following suggestions by Haitovsky 1973 and Maddala 1977) weighted least squares (WLS) was employed instead. The resulting estimator is likely to have a considerable advantage in efficiency over ordinary least squares, since the differences in the variances (represented by the diagonal elements of $(GG')^{-1}$, which are used as the weights) are taken into account. Since the off-diagonal elements are left out, WLS estimates are not Best Linear Unbiased. The coefficient estimates will still be unbiased, though, and Haitovsky's experimental results suggest that WLS estimates can be quite close to those generated using GLS.[7]

The estimated coefficients for the 1960 and 1975–76 samples are shown in the upper panels of tables 13.1 and 13.2, respectively. At the outset we note that the goodness of fit and significance levels are substantial and that the pattern of coefficients of characteristics, when compared both within and across equations, is reasonable.

Although the 1960 and 1975–76 hedonic indexes are somewhat different in variables (i.e., the 1960 lacks measures of structural features, heating, and

Table 13.2 1975–76 Hedonic Index Estimates and Sampled SMSAs

COLD SMSAs

Variable	Owners	Renters
Rooms	.129	.129
Lacking plumbing	−.515	−.216
Built 1960–69[a]	−.092	−.111
Built 1950–59	−.193	−.210
Built 1940–49	−.300	−.347
Built before 1940	−.549	−.398
Single-family attached	−.385	−.118
No. units in structure	—	.002
Stories in structure	—	−.007
No or shared kitchen	−.276*	−.241
Heating equipment[b]		
Steam	.067	−.071
Electric	−.053*	−.054
Floor furnace	−.160	−.204
Room heater, flue	−.352	−.216
Room heater, no flue	−.677	−.182
None or fireplace	−.423	−.290
No direct access	—	−.079**
R^2	.39	.30
d.f.	7184	4751

SMSA	Owner Dummy	Renter Dummy	SMSA	Owner Dummy	Renter Dummy
Chicago	10.20	5.11	Springfield, MA	9.92	4.92
Cincinnati	9.93	4.81	Allentown	10.07	5.01
Columbus	9.91	4.85	Baltimore	10.14	5.02
Hartford	10.15	5.10	Buffalo	9.98	5.01
Kansas City	9.74	4.86	Cleveland	10.13	4.95
Madison	10.04	5.03	Denver	10.04	4.99
Milwaukee	10.08	5.02	Grand Rapids	9.78	4.89
Paterson, NJ	10.42	5.34	Indianapolis	9.82	4.92
Philadelphia	9.98	4.94	New York	10.29	5.80
Portland, OR	9.90	4.95	Omaha	9.83	4.88
Rochester, NY	9.95	5.09	Providence	10.04	5.00
			Seattle	10.05	5.05

WARM SMSAs

Variable	Owners	Renters
Rooms	.172	.133
Lacking plumbing	−.247	−.211
Built 1960–69[a]	−.072	−.120
Built 1950–59	−.172	−.210
Built 1940–49	−.232	−.302
Built before 1940	−.374	−.278
Single-family attached	.051**	−.031**

Table 13.2. continued

Warm SMSAs		
Variable	Owners	Renters
No. of units in structures	.000**	−.000**
Stories in structure	—	.005**
No kitchen	—	−.201
No or shared kitchen	−.087	—
Heating equipment[b]		
Steam	.032**	−.249
Electric	−.092*	−.152
Floor furnace	−.261	−.260
Room heater, flue	−.383	−.442
Room heater, no flue	−.531	−.333
Fireplace only	−.271	−.369
None	−.423	−.339
R^2	.43	.36
d.f.	5202.	3796

SMSA	Owner Dummy	Renter Dummy	SMSA	Owner Dummy	Renter Dummy
Atlanta	9.72	4.82	Honolulu	10.95	5.56
Miami	10.15	5.30	Houston	9.74	5.07
New Orleans	9.74	4.80	Las Vegas	9.85	5.16
Newport News, VA	9.71	4.94	Louisville	9.48	4.75
San Antonio	9.48	4.81	Oklahoma City	9.57	4.84
San Bernardino	9.73	4.98	Sacramento	9.86	5.03
San Diego	10.10	5.15	St. Louis	9.51	4.82
San Francisco	10.12	5.26			
Birmingham	9.61	4.75			

Notes: All coefficients statistically significant at 1% level unless noted. Honolulu was dropped from the sample after trial estimation of the hedonic index.
*Significant at 5% level.
**Significant at 10% level.
[a]Reference category for vintage variables is 1970.
[b]Reference category for heating equipment is central forced air.

kitchens while the 1975–76 lacks condition) and are estimated for different periods and samples of SMSAs, there is a good deal of similarity among comparable variable coefficients. All the hedonic indexes demonstrate an increasing value decrement associated with an additional decade in structural age. Increments in values associated with more rooms are larger for owners than renters, as are decrements associated with lack of complete plumbing facilities. Two interesting differences emerge between the samples, however: the magnitude of coefficients for the rooms and lack of plumbing variables decrease from 1960 to 1975–76 for owners, but increases for renters. This may be partly an artifact of the differences in data format: in 1960, values are the medians of categories, whereas in 1975–76 they are actual values for specific units. This difference also explains the lower R^2 in the 1975–76 hedonic regressions.[8]

13.2.3 Geographic Stability of Hedonic Indexes: Tests for Aggregation Bias

Conventional wisdom and empirical practice have for the most part restricted econometric studies of housing markets to a single metropolitan area. A principal reason for concentrating on individual cities is that it seems most natural to include only households and housing units which arguably "compete" with each other. If this is done, the market under analysis arguably corresponds to a meaningful economic market. Cross-sectional studies, by pooling markets in which the underlying behavioral relationships differ, could thus seriously misrepresent the nature of these relationships in the constituent markets. If, however, the relationship in question is basically similar across housing markets, pooling carries few risks.

This section examines the cross-sectional stability of the relationship between housing characteristics and the market prices of bundles of these characteristics. While the results of this inquiry are themselves of interest, they also have broader implications. Hedonic indexes, as we have argued, can be used in housing market models as a means of representing in one dimension the multifaceted quality of housing units with varying amounts of many distinct housing characteristics. If it could be shown that the price-characteristics relationship is essentially similar across housing markets, a major obstacle to the construction of cross-sectional market models would be removed.

The theory of hedonic indexes presented in chapter 3 provides some basis for skepticism about the likelihood of pervasive cross-sectional similarity in the hedonic relationship. Recall that the hedonic function is the envelope of a family of bid functions (of households) and another family of offer curves (of sellers) which represents marginal market tradeoffs among housing characteristics in competitive equilibrium. An implicit assumption of this theory is the existence of a single market in which all households and suppliers interact. Since the hedonic relationship is the product of equilibrium in one market, and since housing units (and customers) in other metropolitan areas are irrelevant alternatives for the vast majority of participants in that market, it would be surprising if the same hedonic function also characterized the equilibrium achieved in the other markets. Systematic cross-sectional differences in the underlying influences on either the supply or the demand for housing characteristics could lead to a distinct equilibrium in each area. If the variations are sufficiently great, any pooling of markets would be undesirable.[9] It must be emphasized, however, that it is the size of differences in the marginal market tradeoffs characterizing equilibrium, not simply variations in the determinants of supply or demand, which determines whether or not aggregation of markets is desirable. While it may seem unlikely that housing markets possess the necessary degree of cross-sectional similarity, similar stability assumptions are made routinely in other applications of the hedonic technique.[10] Whether these assumptions are credible in the case of housing can only be resolved empirically.

In studying this question, it is important to distinguish between two possible sources of observed intermetropolitan variation in housing prices. Differences in the structure of housing prices arise when supply and demand forces in some housing markets give rise to a characteristics equilibrium with different implicit tradeoffs among attributes than those which characterize equilibrium in other markets. In this case, the estimated coefficients for particular attributes will vary significantly across markets so that pooling is inadvisable. If, on the other hand, the structures of household preferences and supply characteristics are sufficiently similar for marginal valuations of characteristics to be the same everywhere, some factors with metropolitan-area-wide effects could still cause variation in the level of housing prices across markets.[11] In the latter case, the appropriate model is a pooled equation with separate intercepts for each city in the sample.

Whether intermetropolitan housing price variations are due to structural differences in the hedonic relationship or to variations in SMSA-specific conditions can be determined by testing separately the homogeneity of the intercept terms and the structural coefficients. Such tests are reported below.

In evaluating the empirical results below, it is important to keep in mind that measures of statistical significance tell only part of the story. The importance of the observed cross-sectional differences depends on the use to which the estimated hedonic index is to be put. A divergence which has great practical significance for one application might be of little consequence in another. Accordingly, while the emphasis in the discussion to follow is on measures of statistical significance and goodness of fit, drawing the implications of the statistical findings for many potential uses requires further interpretation and judgment.

The costs of aggregation can be measured in two ways. First, an F test can be constructed to determine whether the coefficients of the hedonic relationship differ significantly among the individual SMSAs which make up the sample. Note that this is a test of the equality of the four structural coefficients as a group over the nearly three dozen sample SMSAs. The appropriate n-way F test differs slightly from the usual two-equation test; details and a derivation may be found in Dhrymes (1971:142–47). An alternative (but related) approach is to compare the standard errors of estimate for the pooled and unpooled relationships. This measure of the impact of coefficient differences on the explanatory power of the equation is computed as the absolute (and proportional) excess of the standard error of the constrained (pooled) regression over that of the unconstrained (unpooled) estimate. The latter is calculated as a weighted average of the standard errors of the individual SMSA regressions for the cities in the sample.[12] Both measures are presented here because, as noted above, aggregation can significantly affect coefficient magnitudes without having much impact on the explanatory power of the regression.

At the outset it must be noted that the tests reported here and in the next section employ a more parsimonious version of equation (13.1). This specification collapsed the vintages into a single *AGE* variable, and combined both deteriorating and dilapidated dwellings into a single dummy variable—*POORCOND*. Units that are sound but lack plumbing facilities are denoted by the dummy variable *SNDNPL*.

The *F* test requires the estimation of hedonic regressions for each metropolitan area and for the entire pooled sample. These regressions are far too numerous—seventy in all—to reproduce here. Although detailed commentary on each equation is not possible within reasonable space constraints, some general observations are in order.

The explanatory power of the regressions is quite high, with the owner results slightly stronger than those for renters. Among the owner equations, all save one (Utica-Rome at 0.83) have adjusted R^2 in excess of 0.91. The adjusted R^2 for the renter equations are generally lower, with a value less than 0.8 for four cities. However, more than half the equations have adjusted R^2 greater than 0.90, and the smallest value (for Raleigh) is a still healthy 0.75. The statistical significance of the individual coefficients is equally impressive. Only a handful fail to be significant at the 10% level or above; the *ROOMS* coefficient, in particular, is significant in each of the seventy equations. In addition, all coefficients have the expected sign: positive for *ROOMS*, negative for the other three independent variables. By and large, then, the results are consistent with a priori expectations and are statistically quite strong.

Looking more closely at the coefficients in the individual SMSA owner equations, we see some indications that the hedonic relationships might differ across metropolitan areas. All coefficients save four (those of sound units lacking plumbing for Tacoma, Trenton, San Diego, and San Jose) are significant, most at the .1% level. *ROOMS* and *AGE* perform particularly well, with five coefficients significant at the 1% level and the remaining sixty-three at the .1% level. However, these coefficients take on a rather wide range of values. For each of the four variables, the magnitude of the largest coefficient is more than twice that of the smallest coefficient. The wide range of coefficient values suggests that pooling may involve significant distortions, a supposition which is supported to some extent by an examination of confidence intervals for these coefficients. Even 99% confidence intervals fail to overlap for the largest and smallest *AGE* coefficients, while the 95% confidence intervals are distinct for the largest and smallest *ROOMS* coefficients. The 90% confidence intervals for *POORCOND* just barely fail to meet, and they overlap noticeably for the *SNDNPL* coefficients. However, the significance of the variations in the *SNDPL* coefficients and *POORCOND* coefficients is in doubt. The confidence intervals thus indicate that (at worst) significant cross-sectional variation in *ROOMS* and *AGE* coefficients is likely[13] but that the observed differences in the remaining coefficients are probably not of great importance. Whether the coefficients as a group vary significantly across SMSAs will be tested shortly.

A somewhat similar pattern appears in the individual SMSA equations for renters, though the estimation results are not quite as strong as for owners. In addition to the lower adjusted R^2 noted above, the significance levels of individual coefficients are generally somewhat lower than for owners. With the exception of *ROOMS*, few attain the .1% level of significance; all told, 22 (half of them *AGE* coefficients) of the 140 coefficients are insignificant even at the 10% level. The range of values is wider than in the owner equations for all variables except *ROOMS;* indeed, the largest *AGE* coefficient is nearly ten times the size of the smallest. However, when confidence intervals are constructed around these coefficients, the wide range of values is put into perspective. Only for the *AGE* coefficients do even the 90% confidence intervals fail to overlap; in that case, the gap is not extensive. Thus, in contrast to the owner equations, the individual coefficients of the SMSA renter regressions do not appear to differ significantly from one another. Whether this is true for coefficient packages as well will now be explored.

The individual and pooled regression estimates can be used to construct the F tests and standard error comparisons described earlier.[14] The results show[15] that the null hypothesis of an identical hedonic relationship fares better in renter markets than among owner-occupants. For renters, the F test indicates—as the initial check of confidence intervals suggested—that the coefficients of the four structure characteristics do not vary significantly across SMSAs. The standard errors of estimate are virtually identical (0.0827 versus 0.0837). The only noteworthy differences across renter markets are in the constant terms. The hypothesis that the intercept for each individual SMSA is the same as that for Detroit (holding the coefficients of the other variables constant) is rejected (by a t test) at the 10% level in all but four cases; twenty of the rejections are at the .1% level. Geographic variations in the structure of rents, then, appear to arise not from differences in the underlying hedonic relationship but rather from differences in the overall level of rents.

Owner markets, as the exploration of confidence intervals suggested, appear to be somewhat more heterogeneous. The null hypothesis of uniform *ROOMS, AGE, SNDNPL,* and *POORCOND* coefficients is strongly rejected, as the test statistic has a value of 3.74 compared to the 1% critical value of 1.41 for F (132,306). The constant terms also vary markedly, as nineteen SMSAs have intercepts significantly different from that of Detroit (fifteen of these at the .1% level). Pooling the owner markets causes a 35% increase in the standard error of estimate; however, since this represents the difference between one standard error of 0.06 and another of 0.08, it is unlikely to have much practical significance for the prediction of housing prices.[16] Thus, even though the coefficients of the hedonic relationship appear to differ significantly across owner housing markets, they do not differ enough to have a serious impact on the explanatory power of the regression.

The major impact of complete pooling, then, is on the coefficient values among owners; for neither tenure is explanatory power greatly affected. Individual constant terms in the pooled regressions seem to absorb most of the cross-SMSA variations in housing prices and rents. Given that there is every reason to expect a lack of uniformity across markets,[17] the broad similarities apparent in these results are quite remarkable. The absence of any significant differences (except in the intercepts)[18] across all renter markets is especially striking. Presumably this is so because renter households are significantly more mobile than are owners, which in turn requires that rental housing units be less idiosyncratic so that they can satisfy a much larger number of households during their useful lives. More frequent participation in the market by both suppliers and demanders, then, seems to produce rental units which are relatively homogeneous (with respect to tradeoffs among characteristics) across markets as well as within them.

In an attempt to discover the underlying causes of the heterogeneity which apparently characterizes owner housing markets, some further explorations of aggregation across these markets were undertaken. As previously noted, the nature and sources of intermetropolitan variation in the hedonic relationship are not well understood. Of necessity, then, the results of this investigation are suggestive rather than conclusive; however, they do provide some useful insights into the ways in which owner housing markets are differentiated.

The hypothesis to be tested was, in effect, whether the coefficients of the hedonic relationships for individual owner markets varied systematically with some identifiable cross-sectional determinant(s) of the demand or supply of housing characteristics. Five such determinants were selected for testing: climate (as measured by heating degree days per year, 65°F base), SMSA population, the average age of the SMSA's owner-occupied housing stock, the median family income of owners in the SMSA, and the distribution of this income (as measured by a Gini coefficient). The costs of aggregation at different levels were investigated using two different procedures. First, the coefficients estimated for each characteristic in the individual SMSA equations were tested for systematic cross-sectional variation by regressing them (one at a time) on the five "splitting variables" just identified. If, for example, *ROOMS* coefficients tended to be lower in cold areas and higher in large cities, the regression of the *ROOMS* coefficients across the sample would have a negative climate coefficient and a positive size coefficient. Significant coefficients in these regressions presumably indicate the existence of strong relationships between splitting variables and characteristic coefficients among the sample SMSAs. A second test examined the extent to which coefficient variations across SMSAs could be captured by a lesser degree of aggregation. The sample was divided into two groups[19] according to the values of each splitting variable, and hedonic regressions over these two subgroups were compared (using the *F* test and standard error comparison described above) to determine whether the relationship as a whole—not just individual coefficients—differed between the subgroups. By examining the results of this experiment for each of the five splits, the splitting variable providing the greatest differentiation could be identified. Dividing the sample along this axis, the need for still further disaggregation was determined using the tests described earlier.

The results of these tests reveal some underlying regularities among the owner markets, thus suggesting that even here a degree of aggregation is possible at negligible cost. An initial split into warm and cold climate groups was clearly indicated by the tests; indeed this provided our motivation for the stratification reported in tables 13.1 and 13.2. This division appeared to reflect important distinctions among markets in a consistent way. For example, the *ROOMS* coefficients were generally smaller and the intercepts greater in cold SMSAs, reflecting the greater proportion of total structure value invested in the "overhead" components of shelter (heating, sturdier construction, insulation, etc.) in colder climates. However, an *F* test indicated that significant differences remained among the SMSAs within the warm and cold subsamples, so further disaggregation was examined. Beyond the first split, however, the meaning of homogeneity darkens somewhat. The high discriminatory power of the division by climate greatly narrowed the range of coefficient variation within the subsamples, and the cross-SMSA differences which remained seemed for the most part to reflect the heterogeneity of packages of coefficients and not a consistent set of effects upon particular characteristics considered singly.

A second stratification, by age of the owner-occupied housing stock, was chosen. *F* tests revealed no significant differences among the SMSAs with older housing stocks in each climate class, but the newer SMSAs appeared sufficiently heterogeneous to warrant further exploration. These subsamples were split by income dispersion; here, as in the second-level splits, consistent patterns of coefficient magnitudes characterizing the resulting subsamples were difficult to find. Finally, the homogeneity of these subsamples was tested, again with mixed results. The high Gini coefficient SMSAs in each class displayed no significant intermetropolitan differences, while the opposite was true of the low-Gini cities.

The explorations just discussed are only the first step toward a full understanding of the dimensions of heterogeneity in the hedonic relationship across owner housing markets. The finding that grouping SMSAs by their values of certain cross-sectional determinants permits pooling into groups sometimes as large as a quarter of the sample suggests strongly, however, that some broad similarities among owner housing markets in fact exist. It is hoped that further exploration will illuminate more clearly the nature of these differences and similarities. The need for such exploration seems less pressing in the case of renter markets, whose homogeneity has been demonstrated earlier.

13.2.4 Specification of Variables in the Hedonic Index: Tests for Omitted Variables Bias

In principle, all characteristics relevant to the determination of market price—that is, those that both yield utility to residents and are costly to produce—should be included in the hedonic index. In practice, this cannot be done because the number of such characteristics is unmanageably large. Data on many of these are either unavailable or of exceedingly poor quality. Even without data constraints, the intrinsic clustering of characteristic combinations into a relatively small number of configurations[20] leads to considerable multicollinearity in estimates employing a generous selection of the relevant variables. For these reasons, any estimate of the hedonic relationship will have to be misspecified because some of the relevant independent variables must be omitted. Since all estimates are to some extent "incorrect," differences among them must be attributed at least in part to differences in adaptation to the specification problems common to all.

The empirical strategy here is to compare the results of the (condensed version of the) cross-SMSA hedonic index specification (equation 13.1), which has few structural characteristics and none for location or lot size, to those of a "benchmark" hedonic index, which is otherwise comparable except that fewer variables are omitted. Both of these specifications—*restricted* and *benchmark*—are estimated using data obtained in a survey of approximately fifteen hundred individual households in the city of St. Louis; the survey was conducted in 1967 for the St. Louis Community Renewal Program's Survey of Residential Blight. With the addition of some variables and some households in suburban areas outside the city of St. Louis, the survey was used as the basis for a number of studies by Kain and Quigley (1969, 1970, 1975). After a final revision to include further descriptions of land use, the sample available for this study consisted of some 380 owner-occupied single-family units and 594 renter units (approximately 16.5% of the sample units were located outside the city limits). More than a hundred characteristics were available for each unit, assuring a wide range of choice for the selection of independent variables. The following were chosen as representative measures of the housing-quality aspects not found in the census:

AMILES Distance (in miles) to the central business district; the most commonly used accessibility measure.

PAREA Lot size (in thousands of square feet). This measure was used only for owner-occupied units as it is not very meaningful for units in multiple-unit structures.

DENSITY Estimated population per acre of usable nonindustrial, noncommercial land in the transportation zone surrounding the unit.

COUNTY A dummy variable; = 1 if the unit is located in St. Louis County (outside the city limits); = 0 if it is within the city proper. This variable proxies the aspects of suburban location not adequately represented by *AMILES*, *DENSITY*, and the neighborhood variables.

BPSP Percentage of structures on the same block face as the units that are in deteriorated-obsolete-neglected-poor condition (a direct measure of the structural dimensions of neighborhood quality).

PSAA Median arithmetic achievement test score for sixth-grade students at the local public elementary school. Measures of this sort have been widely used in other studies as proxies for both school quality in particular and the quality of public services in general.

The St. Louis data set includes information sufficient to construct equivalents to the census variables *VALUE*, *ROOMS*, *AGE*, *SNDNPL*, and *POORCOND*. However, since the survey collected contract rent rather than gross rent, the independent variable *STR*(= 1 if a stove was not included in the rent; = 0 otherwise) was included in the renter equations to provide the needed correction.[21] Also, since the original sample was drawn disproportionately from low-income census tracts, the observations were weighted by the inverse of the sampling ratios used so that the results would more accurately represent the distribution of housing units present in St. Louis at the time of the survey.

How can the specification bias from using the restricted specification be measured? As it happens, this is a somewhat unusual question to ask. In general, investigators either have data on all the variables they believe should appear in the proper specification, in which case they use the data, or they lack data on some of the variables, in which case they theorize about the effects of the missing variables on the equations they can estimate.[22] Only rarely is one in a position to compare alternative specifications empirically. The strategy employed here is in the spirit of what Leamer (1978) calls a "simplification search," that is, an inquiry into the costs and benefits of using a restricted specification when the true model is quite complex. This procedure is not a "test" of specification in the sense of distinguishing a "true" model from alternatives, since it is clear a priori that the restricted model is misspecified.

The received theory of specification does offer a few insights into the problem at hand. If the true model is

$$Y = Xb + Zd + e_1 \qquad (13.2)$$

and instead

$$Y = Xa + e_2 \qquad (13.3)$$

is estimated, the resulting coefficients of equation (13.3) have expectation

$$E(\hat{a}) = b + Cd, \qquad (13.4)$$

where $C = (X'X)^{-1}(X'Z)$[23]; *a, b,* and *d* are vectors of coefficients; and e_1 and e_2 are random error terms. The estimated coefficients of the included variables will thus be influenced by the excluded variables so long as the latter indeed belong in equation (13.2) (that is, $d \neq 0$) and are not orthogonal to the included variables ($C \neq 0$). What statistical tests can be used to determine the significance of this specification bias? One possibility is to test whether $d = 0$, that is, whether the *Z*s belong in the equation at all. If the null hypothesis is not rejected, the problem of specification bias vanishes since the *Z*s are then irrelevant variables that serve only to reduce the efficiency of equation (13.2). But if the hypothesis is rejected (as it is with the St. Louis data), this test gives no indication of the extent or significance of any biases that may arise from the exclusion of *Z* in equation (13.3). More helpful would be a test of the hypothesis $a = b$. But if $d \neq 0$, e_2 must include the effects of the excluded *Z*s. That being the case, the assumptions that e_1 and e_2 are independent and have the same variance—necessary for the *F* test to be valid—are violated. So we are left without a direct statistical test of whether $a = b$, and other indicators of the extent and seriousness of bias must be used.[24]

Specification bias also affects predictions made with the misspecified equation. It can be shown (Leamer 1978) that predictions from equation (13.3) will, in general, be biased unless the relationship between *X* and *Z* is the same in the prediction set as in the sample (as, for example, when the prediction set is the sample). However, in this case, a strong relationship between *X* and *Z* may improve the accuracy of predictions since the biased *X* coefficients would then contain "proxy effects" of the *Z*s. Of course, if prediction is to be done over data other than the sample, these proxy effects will be beneficial only to the extent that the relationship between *X* and *Z* is the same in the two data sets. Under these circumstances, high correlation between *X* and *Z* may be helpful for prediction outside the sample because of the distortion in coefficient magnitudes it causes. It must be stressed, though, that the resulting coefficients do not accurately represent the relationship between the included explanatory variables and the dependent variable. Instead of assuming that the excluded variables can be neglected, the biased model assumes that they can be compensated for via their relationship with the included variables. This can lead to erroneous interpretations of the model (Leamer 1978: ch. 6).

What follows is an attempt to portray the magnitude of the specification bias resulting from the use of a severely restricted model. As previously noted, this inquiry does not reveal the "true" specification bias but rather the bias relative to a benchmark model which is representative of the models other researchers have estimated using extensive survey data bases. While many other specifications for the full model might be suggested, the intrinsic collinearity among characteristics and the impossibility of estimating the true model suggest that there are few grounds for preferring one such benchmark to another. Alternative choices of representative variables would most likely have led to results very similar (qualitatively) to those reported below.

The first step in the inquiry is to estimate both the restricted model and the benchmark model using the St. Louis data set. These estimates are presented in table 13.3. The results seem reasonable in light of theoretical expectations and previous research, with two exceptions: the positive coefficient of *SNDNPL* in the owner equations (probably the result of some idiosyncratic data in this sample)[25] and the positive coefficient of *AMILES* in the renter equation (also related to a quirk of the sample).[26] The remaining coefficients and the adjusted R^2 all fall within expected bounds.

Table 13.3 Hedonic Equation with and without Extra Variables

	Owners [Dependent Variable = Log (Value)]		Renters [Dependent Variable = Log (Rent)]	
Variable	Restricted Model	Full Specification	Restricted Model	Full Specification
INTERCEPT	9.094	8.962	4.382	3.9851
	(169.937)***	(20.823)***	(94.620)***	(19.262)***
ROOMS	.15690	.15957	.13984	.13240
	(18.454)***	(18.705)***	(14.484)***	(14.291)***
AGE	−.0098718	−.010707	−.0092142	−.0069989
	(−15.273)***	(−12.223)***	(−18.554)***	(−12.228)***
SNDPL	.22232	.22142	−.41418	−.33158
	(1.911)*	(1.990)*	(−5.516)***	(−4.531)***
POORCOND	−.46280	−.14253	−.17070	−.12586
	(−4.210)***	(−1.144)	(−5.791)***	(−4.205)***
AMILES	—	−.021789	—	.019821
		(−3.653)***		(3.328)***
PAREA	—	−.0000091404	—	—
		(0.204)		
PSAA	—	.056027	—	.030625
		(1.193)		(1.319)
BPSP	—	−.034079	—	−.012833
		(−4.245)***		(−4.308)***
COUNTY	—	−.063286	—	−.011193
		(−1.447)		(−.253)
DENSITY	—	−.0066229	—	−.00055593
		(−2.397)*		(−.506)
STR	—	—	−.30297	−.29394
			(−10.960)***	(−11.066)***
R^2 (adj.)	.6104	.6448	.6894	.7183
SEE	.2579	.2462	.2678	.2550
SSR	24.94	22.37	42.16	37.92
n	380	380	594	594

Note: t-statistics are in parentheses.
*Indicates significance at 10% level.
**Indicates significance at 1% level.
***Indicates significance at .1% level.

In the absence of a definitive statistical test for specification bias, it is necessary to use a variety of measures in order to gain a perspective on the biases that may arise and on their practical consequences. The indicators used here include the one feasible significance test described in the previous section and several measures of the size and importance of the biases in the restricted model.

Joint F *Test*

The joint F test is a test of whether the coefficients of the nonstructural variables are jointly equal to zero (i.e., whether $d = 0$ in equation 13.2). If this hypothesis is not rejected, the implication is that the coefficients of the structure variables in the restricted specification cannot suffer bias as a result of excluding the remaining dimensions of housing quality.

In the case of the owner equation, the test statistic has a value of 7.065. Since it is distributed as F (6,369), this value is highly significant (the 1% critical value of F—6,369—is approximately 3.86). For renters, the test statistic, distributed as F (5,583), has a value of 13.038. Once again this is highly significant, the 1% critical value of F (5,583) being approximately 3.05. As expected, then, the null hypothesis is rejected for both owners and renters. Because the structure and nonstructure characteristics are hardly orthogonal, some specification bias in the coefficients of the restricted model is inevitable.

Magnitude of Bias

How big are these biases? A comparison of the coefficients of the structure variables in the benchmark and restricted models provides an estimate. It must be noted that these coefficient differences are only approximations to the true biases, both because the "full" specification used here is but one of many possible empirical approximations to the true model and because measurement error (highly likely in the nonstructure variables) may have biased the estimated coefficients of the full model. Also, as noted above, the statistical significance of the estimated biases cannot be tested. Still, the comparison of coefficients provides the most direct indication of the extent to which the restricted model is affected by specification bias.

In the owner market, *ROOMS, AGE,* and *SNDNPL* seem relatively unaffected, whereas a more substantial bias appears in the coefficient of *POORCOND*.[27] For *ROOMS* and *SNDNPL,* the bias is vanishingly small: less than 2% of the coefficient magnitude and an insignificant proportion of the standard error (less than 1% for *SNDNPL* and for *ROOMS*). For *AGE,* the difference between coefficients is larger—about 7.8% of the coefficient magnitude and a bit less than one standard error—but still quite small by either measure. The bias in *POORCOND,* though, is substantial by both measures. The principal source of this bias appears to be the high correlation (.55) between *POORCOND* and *BPSP*, a relationship that should appear consistently across cities and over time. Since the returns to expenditures on structural maintenance and improvement depend heavily on the extent to which one's neighbors maintain their properties, a neighborhood containing one structure in poor condition is likely to include many more poorly maintained properties.[28] Accordingly, the coefficient of *POORCOND* in an equation without BPSP will reflect both neighborhood quality and structure quality. Such a stable relationship, though it changes substantially the magnitude of the *POORCOND* coefficient in the reduced specification, should have little adverse effect on predictions made with that equation. The owner equation, then, survives the loss of lot size, accessibility, and neighborhood variables with few adverse effects of consequence.

The story is somewhat different in the rental market. Once again, the impact on *ROOMS* is minimal; dropping the added variables raises the *ROOMS* coefficient by less than 6% (.80 of a standard error). *SNDNPL*, too, is not greatly affected; its coefficient increases in absolute value by about 25% (or slightly more than one standard error). The *POORCOND* coefficient also rises in magnitude, by a somewhat larger amount (36% or 1.5 standard errors). This is a smaller bias than was apparent in the owner equation, though again an association with BPSP is probably the principal cause (simple correlation = .32). The change in the *AGE* coefficient is of similar size (32%) but probably more significant since this amounts to nearly four standard errors. This last bias appears to come from many sources. *AGE* has correlations ranging (in absolute value) from .39 to .57 with the excluded variables, suggesting the existence of many associations strong enough to cause bias. Accordingly, it is unlikely that this bias is stable or predictable as a dependable proxy effect of a single excluded characteristic; it could well cause bias in predictions with the restricted equation, since the relationship between *AGE* and the excluded variables is likely to change from sample to sample.

Standard Errors of Estimate

A comparison of standard errors of estimate and adjusted R^2 for the two specifications provides two (related) measures of the misspecification's effect on the equation's explanatory power.[29] If the differences are sufficiently small, it can safely be said that whatever the biases in individual coefficients, their practical impact on the equation's efficiency (and accuracy of prediction over the sample) is minor.

In both tenures, the standard errors of estimate differ by only .01, an increase of 4.75% for owners and 5.02% for renters.[30] The nonstructure variables, then, have a negligible impact on the accuracy of the regression. The comparison of adjusted R^2 presents this finding in different terms: the excluded variables account for less than 10% of the unexplained variance in the restricted model. These results imply that whatever biases arise from excluding other housing characteristics have little practical impact.

It is worth noting at this point that investigators using specifications much more complete than the full model of this study realize little gain in explanatory power from so doing. Kain and Quigley (1970), for example, using essentially the same data base but many more variables, achieved adjusted R^2 of .71 for both owners and renters.[31] Indeed, most studies using survey data report values of R^2 between .6 and .8. This observation lends credence to the full specification used here as a representative approximation to the true relationship.

Rank Order Correlations

Because the ordering of units implied by the hedonic index is the basis for stratifying the housing market into quality submarkets, the degree to which the index reproduces the market's ordering is a useful measure of its explanatory power and accuracy. The correlation between the market's rankings and those produced by the two versions of the hedonic equation provides a check on the degree to which the biased equation can predict accurately over the sample.

The results indicate that there is little difference between the rankings produced by the two estimates. Those from the full equation are marginally closer to the actual rankings (0.7834 versus 0.7459 for owners; 0.8115 versus 0.7707 for renters), but the rank order correlations between the sets of predicted values are so high (0.9559 for owners; 0.9627 for renters) that these rankings must be virtually identical. The nonstructure characteristics apparently do little to affect the market's ranking of housing units, so an equation limited to structural components can be used to reproduce that ordering with a high degree of confidence.

13.2.5 Quality Submarket Partitioning

Since our cross-SMSA hedonic indexes evidently do not suffer severely from aggregation bias or omitted variables bias, we are confident in employing them to array each sampled SMSA's housing stock according to predicted hedonic value, or quality. That is, for each dwelling in each SMSA we generate a hedonic value, *HV*, which is predicted by substituting the values for the structural characteristics of that dwelling into the appropriate hedonic index presented in tables 13.1 and 13.2.

In particular, the 1960 index is used to generate hedonic values for all dwellings in both tenures in the thirty-six SMSA sample for both 1960 and 1970. Note, however, that structural condition was not recorded in the 1970 Census. The 1970 values for the (*CN*) vector of variables were assumed identical to those in 1960 in each of the corresponding cells of cross tabulations of structural features by condition. This means that our quality distributions in 1970 are estimated purely on the basis of number of rooms, lack of complete plumbing, and age of structure.[32]

The 1975–76 index is used to generate hedonic values for all dwellings in both tenures in the thirty-eight SMSA sample for both 1970 and 1975–76. The series of three-way cross-tabulations found in the 1970 Census is used to estimate the number of dwellings with the particular characteristics employed in the 1975–76 hedonic: age, heating equipment, plumbing, and rooms. As before, some variables in the 1975–76 hedonic (lack of kitchen and/or direct access, number of stories) are unavailable in the 1970 Census cross-tabulations, and estimates of *HV* in both years therefore are made without them.

Given the aforementioned data idiosyncrasies associated with using 1970 Census data to estimate the quality of the housing stock for one year in both of our samples, certain limitations of our cross-sectional analysis must be recognized. Foremost, changes in structural condition (e.g., those typically associated with passive undermaintenance) are not reflected in our estimates of housing stock changes in either 1960–70 or 1970–1975/76 periods. The same is true of any qualitative changes associated with the neighborhood characteristics, local public service features, and accessibility associated with the array of dwellings, in so far as these are uncorrelated with changes in variables included in the hedonic index. What the cross-sectional model does capture are changes in dwelling quality which result from either splitting or consolidating units or making additions to them (changing numbers of rooms), adding plumbing fixtures to those which previously lacked complete facilities, and (for 1970–1975/76) altering the type of heating system. (A richer array of housing stock modifications is analyzed in our single-SMSA model.)

The particular method of partitioning hedonic values into quality levels (or submarkets) used in the model presented here is as follows. All units in each SMSA in our census sample were given hedonic values and arrayed by hedonic value. Four such distributions were, in fact, calculated for each tenure category, j (= owner, renter), in each SMSA: all occupied units in 1960 (H_1); all vacant, available units in 1960, those for sale only being classified as ownership and those for rent or sale being classified as rental (H_2); all units, occupied and vacant, standing in 1970 that were built in 1960 or later (H_3); and all units in 1970 that were built before 1960 (H_4). Each H_1 is a vector of many (small) hedonic value/rent intervals ranging from 0 to the maximum observed *HV* in each tenure. Similar calculations were made for 1970 and 1975–76.

To arrive at partitions, H_1 and H_2 were summed for owners and renters separately across SMSAs and, in turn, summed to give H_5 for both tenures: an array of hedonic value (quality) ordering *all* the units collectively in the sample SMSAs on the same scale. The resulting aggregate frequency distributions were then partitioned at the *15th, 30th, 50th, 75th, and 95th deciles* to define five bounded and one open-ended, highest-quality submarket in both tenures. These same *HV* boundaries applied to each sample SMSA, thus permitting inter-SMSA variation in the distribution of the housing stock across quality submarkets. The partitions were chosen so as to provide a reasonable clustering of implied substitutability without thereby creating great discrepancies in the average number of units in different quality levels on the one hand, or in the implied relative degrees of substitutability across quality levels on the other hand. We have confined our cross-SMSA modeling of the housing market, described in chapters 14 and 15, to the ten closed quality-level submarkets so defined, because the upper tails of the hedonic distributions are long and exceptionally heterogeneous.

Do housing-quality submarkets, so defined, have any meaningful empirical content? We believe that they do, first because they correspond closely to intuitive notions about what constitutes "close substitutability" and second because of the distinct, intersubmarket patterns of price correlations.

Consider the first reason with the help of table 13.4, which displays the partitioning of the housing stock in our cold SMSAs. It shows for each category of dwelling forming the basis for the 1960 hedonic index (tenure, number of rooms, vintage, plumbing, and condition) its estimated hedonic value and its quality submarket designation, given the partitioning scheme above (where 1 designates lowest quality). Notice how dwelling types that fall within a particular submarket do appear indeed to be plausible substitutes. For instance, the renter 4 submarket consists of all sound units with complete plumbing facilities which have either two rooms and were built in 1955–59, three rooms and were built in 1950–54, four rooms and were built in 1940–49, or five rooms and were built before 1940. The submarket also consists of those sound units which lack plumbing but have, as compensation, four more rooms than units of comparable vintages having all plumbing. Similarly reasonable substitute combinations are illustrated in owner submarkets. For example, owner 5 submarket consists of all sound units having complete plumbing, six or more rooms, and built since 1940. Deteriorated units with complete plumbing are of comparable quality only if they have eight rooms and were built since 1955. Lack of some or all plumbing facilities disqualifies a unit from this submarket, regardless of condition. The least-clear combinations of substitutes occur in the lowest quality levels in both tenures. This is to be expected, of course, since they are more open-ended and, as a result, encompass dwellings of a larger *HV* range (from 33.79 to 52.93 in renter 1 and 2,190 to 9,330 in owner 1) than shown in submarkets 2–5.

As can also be seen from table 13.4, similar quality levels in the different tenure classes do not necessarily signify comparable characteristics. Thus, for example, owner quality level 3 units have hedonic characteristics similar to renter quality level 5 units. However, it should be noted that renter and owner units differ in other respects not measured by the hedonic characteristics, for example, accessibility, type of structure, and services provided. In general, though, it is clear that corresponding quality-level numbers (i.e., relative sub-

Table 13.4. Hedonic Value and Quality Level in Cold SMSAs, 1960, by Characteristics of Unit

	RENTERS (HV in $1)							
	Number of Rooms							
Year Built	1	2	3	4	5	6	7	8
Sound Units with All Plumbing Facilities								
1955–59	71.94	79.04	86.84	95.41	104.92	115.16	126.52	139.01
	(3)	(4)	(5)	(5)	(*)	(*)	(*)	(*)
1950–54	65.33	71.79	78.88	86.66	95.21	104.60	114.92	126.26
	(3)	(3)	(4)	(5)	(5)	(*)	(*)	(*)
1940–49	56.46	62.03	68.15	74.88	82.27	90.38	99.30	109.10
	(2)	(2)	(3)	(4)	(5)	(5)	(*)	(*)
Before 1940	51.72	56.83	62.43	68.59	75.36	82.79	90.96	99.53
	(1)	(2)	(2)	(3)	(4)	(5)	(5)	(*)
Sound Units Lacking Some or All Plumbing Facilities								
1955–59	49.07	53.91	59.23	65.08	71.50	78.55	88.30	94.61
	(1)	(1)	(2)	(3)	(3)	(4)	(5)	(5)
1950–54	44.57	48.97	53.80	59.11	64.94	71.35	78.39	86.12
	(1)	(1)	(1)	(2)	(3)	(3)	(4)	(5)
1940–49	38.51	42.31	46.49	51.07	56.11	61.65	67.73	74.41
	(1)	(1)	(1)	(1)	(2)	(2)	(3)	(4)
Before 1940	35.28	38.76	42.58	46.78	51.40	56.47	62.04	68.16
	(1)	(1)	(1)	(1)	(1)	(2)	(2)	(3)
Deteriorating Units with All Plumbing Facilities								
1955–59	64.02	70.34	77.27	84.90	93.27	102.48	112.59	123.70
	(3)	(3)	(4)	(5)	(5)	(*)	(*)	(*)
1950–54	58.15	63.89	70.19	77.11	84.72	93.08	102.26	112.35
	(2)	(2)	(3)	(4)	(5)	(5)	(*)	(*)
1940–49	50.24	55.20	50.65	66.63	73.20	80.43	88.36	97.08
	(1)	(1)	(2)	(3)	(4)	(5)	(5)	(5)
Before 1940	46.03	50.57	55.55	61.04	67.06	73.67	80.94	88.93
	(1)	(1)	(1)	(2)	(3)	(4)	(4)	(5)
Deteriorating Units Lacking Some or All Plumbing Facilities								
1955–59	47.01	51.64	56.74	62.34	68.49	75.24	82.67	90.82
	(1)	(1)	(2)	(2)	(3)	(4)	(5)	(5)
1950–54	42.70	46.91	51.54	56.62	62.21	68.35	75.09	82.50
	(1)	(1)	(1)	(2)	(2)	(3)	(4)	(5)
1940–49	36.89	40.53	44.53	48.92	53.75	59.05	64.88	71.28
	(1)	(1)	(1)	(1)	(1)	(2)	(3)	(3)
Before 1940	33.79	37.13	40.79	44.82	49.24	54.09	59.43	65.30
	(1)	(1)	(1)	(1)	(1)	(1)	(2)	(3)
Dilapidated Units								
1955–59	52.93	58.15	63.88	70.19	77.11	84.72	93.08	102.25
	(1)	(2)	(2)	(3)	(4)	(5)	(5)	(*)
1950–54	48.07	52.82	58.03	63.75	70.04	76.95	84.94	92.88
	(1)	(1)	(2)	(2)	(3)	(4)	(5)	(5)
1940–49	41.54	45.64	50.14	55.08	60.52	66.49	73.05	80.26
	(1)	(1)	(1)	(1)	(2)	(3)	(4)	(4)
Before 1940	38.05	41.80	49.93	50.46	55.44	60.91	66.92	73.52
	(1)	(1)	(1)	(1)	(1)	(2)	(3)	(4)

Note: Quality levels are shown in parentheses; (*) indicates open-ended, high-quality submarket 6 (not modeled). (*Table continues on next page.*)

Table 13.4. continued

Year Built	Owners (HV in $1000)							
	Number of Rooms							
	1	2	3	4	5	6	7	8
Sound Units with All Plumbing Facilities								
1955–59	7.93	9.33	10.98	12.92	15.21	17.90	21.07	24.9
	(1)	(1)	(2)	(3)	(4)	(5)	(*)	(*)
1950–54	6.52	7.68	9.04	10.63	12.52	14.73	17.34	20.4
	(1)	(1)	(1)	(2)	(3)	(4)	(5)	(*)
1940–49	6.20	7.30	8.59	10.11	11.90	14.01	16.49	19.4
	(1)	(1)	(1)	(2)	(3)	(4)	(5)	(5)
Before 1940	4.45	5.24	6.17	7.26	8.54	10.05	11.83	13.8
	(1)	(1)	(1)	(1)	(1)	(2)	(3)	(4)
Sound Units Lacking Some or All Plumbing Facilities								
1955–59	4.46	5.24	6.17	7.26	8.55	10.06	11.84	13.9
	(1)	(1)	(1)	(1)	(1)	(2)	(3)	(4)
1950–54	3.67	4.32	5.08	5.98	7.03	8.28	9.74	11.4
	(1)	(1)	(1)	(1)	(1)	(1)	(2)	(3)
1940–49	3.49	4.10	4.83	5.68	6.69	7.87	9.27	10.9
	(1)	(1)	(1)	(1)	(1)	(1)	(1)	(2)
Before 1940	2.50	2.95	3.47	4.08	4.80	5.65	6.65	7.8
	(1)	(1)	(1)	(1)	(1)	(1)	(1)	(1)
Deteriorating Units with All Plumbing Facilities								
1955–59	5.64	6.64	7.82	9.20	10.83	12.74	15.00	17.8
	(1)	(1)	(1)	(1)	(2)	(3)	(4)	(5)
1950–54	4.64	5.46	6.43	7.57	8.91	10.48	12.34	14.5
	(1)	(1)	(1)	(1)	(1)	(2)	(3)	(4)
1940–49	4.42	5.20	6.12	7.20	8.47	9.57	11.73	13.9
	(1)	(1)	(1)	(1)	(1)	(2)	(3)	(4)
Before 1940	3.17	3.73	4.39	5.17	6.08	7.16	8.42	9.9
	(1)	(1)	(1)	(1)	(1)	(1)	(1)	(2)
Deteriorating Units Lacking Some or All Plumbing Facilities								
1955–59	3.89	4.58	5.39	6.35	7.47	8.79	10.35	12.1
	(1)	(1)	(1)	(1)	(1)	(1)	(2)	(3)
1950–54	3.20	3.77	4.44	5.22	6.15	7.23	8.51	10.0
	(1)	(1)	(1)	(1)	(1)	(1)	(1)	(2)
1940–49	3.05	3.59	4.22	4.97	5.85	6.88	8.10	9.5
	(1)	(1)	(1)	(1)	(1)	(1)	(1)	(1)
Before 1940	2.19	2.57	3.03	3.56	4.20	4.94	5.81	6.8
	(1)	(1)	(1)	(1)	(1)	(1)	(1)	(1)
Dilapidated Units								
1955–59	4.28	5.04	5.93	6.98	8.22	9.67	11.38	13.4
	(1)	(1)	(1)	(1)	(1)	(1)	(3)	(4)
1950–54	3.52	4.15	4.88	5.75	6.76	7.96	9.37	11.0
	(1)	(1)	(1)	(1)	(1)	(1)	(1)	(2)
1940–49	3.35	3.95	4.64	5.46	6.43	7.57	8.91	10.4
	(1)	(1)	(1)	(1)	(1)	(1)	(1)	(2)
Before 1940	2.41	2.83	3.33	3.92	4.02	5.43	6.39	7.5
	(1)	(1)	(1)	(1)	(1)	(1)	(1)	(1)

Note: Quality levels are shown in parentheses; (*) indicates open-ended, high-quality submarket 6 (not modeled).

market rankings) reflect higher real quality for ownership units than for rental units, as would be expected.

Consideration of intersubmarket price correlations yields additional evidence that our submarkets are meaningful. Recall that it is our claim that these partitions represent agglomerations of housing units that have rather close, but not perfect, substitutability for buyers and sellers, on the average, in market transactions. Moreover, a general transitivity is likely to hold: units in adjacent quality submarkets are likely to be more closely related—and therefore more similarly affected by market events—than units in different nonadjacent submarkets. If this is so, it means that there will be a gradation of impulse propagation among submarkets like the widening circles of waves made by a stone dropped into a body of water: the closer the submarket to the initial point of impact, the greater the intensity of repercussion. Thus, a price change originating at one submarket may well disturb an initial set of relative prices among submarkets because it will tend to generate a set of lesser, and graded, price changes in the others.

Table 13.5 suggests that this implication is, indeed, manifested. It gives the zero-order (Pearsonian) correlations among the actual mean "prices per unit of quality" (market price or rent, *MV,* divided by hedonic value, *HV*) in each of the ten submarkets for the 1960 and 1975–76 samples, respectively. The table shows that the correlations, all of which are high, decrease monotonically with the quality differential between the two submarkets being compared.

13.3 Single-SMSA Model

13.3.1 Data Base

In order to investigate different applications of our model, we sought comprehensive data which would be indicative of changes in individual units comprising the housing stock of a particular metropolitan area. Our desire to be detailed and comprehensive led us to consider only moderately sized SMSAs (i.e., under 500,000 population), where the central city dominated the market. Exploratory phone calls to numerous cities revealed only one that demonstrated a bureaucratic willingness to share individual property information gathered within a ten-year period—Des Moines, Iowa.

The basic source of data was the property record cards filed in the office of the Tax Assessment Department of the city of Des Moines.[33] These cards indicated for each parcel a wide variety of qualitative and quantitative structural features, as determined by on-site inspections by field listers in both 1963 and 1971. They also included sales price(s) if the property was sold during this period. During the period of fall 1974 through summer 1975, research assistants under the supervision of John Pitkin examined these property record cards for sampled properties and transcribed in code the desired information. Census tract data were later appended to the records of individual properties.

Table 13.5 Sample Correlations among Prices (MV/HV)

			1960		
Owners					
	PO1	PO2	PO3	PO4	PO5
PO1	1.000	0.9693	0.9727	0.9670	0.9504
PO2		1.000	0.9970	0.9848	0.9569
PO3			1.000	0.9941	0.9727
PO4				1.000	0.9878
PO5					1.000
Renters					
	PR1	PR2	PR3	PR4	PR5
PR1	1.000	0.9850	0.9702	0.9550	0.9382
PR2		1.000	0.9929	0.9784	0.9467
PR3			1.000	0.9936	0.9823
PR4				1.000	0.9943
PR5					1.000
			1975–76		
Owners					
	PO1	PO2	PO3	PO4	PO5
PO1	1.000	0.938	0.917	0.888	0.823
PO2		1.000	0.951	0.925	0.897
PO3			1.000	0.962	0.844
PO4				1.000	0.913
PO5					1.000
Renters					
	PR1	PR2	PR3	PR4	PR5
PR1	1.000	0.938	0.937	0.913	0.854
PR2		1.000	0.950	0.913	0.836
PR3			1.000	0.956	0.890
PR4				1.000	0.938
PR5					1.000

Note: 1960 SMSAs = 36; 1975–76 SMSAs = 38.

The properties were selected for analysis on the basis of a multistage stratified/cluster sampling procedure. First, all forty-seven (1960) census tracts within the city of Des Moines were sampled. Second, within each tract a number of "neighborhoods" as defined by the tax assessors' "field maps" were randomly selected.[34] The number of maps selected per tract was directly related to tract vacancy rates, population turnover, and the amount of new construction.[35] A priori, we suspected that such areas might have unusually high incidences of structural conversions and hence warranted closer examination.

A total of 136 maps were selected. Third, within each field map every *second* "residential" property was sampled,[36] and *every* residential property that was sold during 1962–69 also was sampled (if it was skipped by the former procedure).[37] As a result, for a series of 136 "neighborhoods" scattered across Des Moines we obtained a 50% sample of residential properties with their structural characteristics measured for both 1963 and 1971 and a 100% sample of residential properties which sold during the period of 1962–69, with their structural characteristics measured at the time of sale(s).[38]

13.3.2 Estimated Hedonic Index

The hedonic index for our single-SMSA application took the following form:

$$(13.5)\quad MV^{1/2} = a_0 + [a_i]\,[STRUC_i^{1/2}] + [a_j][LOC_j^{1/2}] + [a_k][MKT_k^{1/2}] + e,$$

where

MV = sales price of single-family dwelling;
a_0 = constant;
$[a]$ = row vector of regression coefficients;
$[STRUC]$ = column vector of eighteen structural attributes of the dwelling;
$[LOC]$ = column vector of five locational attributes of the dwelling;
$[MKT]$ = column vector of three market conditions when the dwelling sold; and
e = a random error term with the usual assumed properties.

The particular explanatory variables and the functional form of equation (13.5) are discussed below.

All variables describing the property were taken from the assessor's property record card. Eighteen such [*STRUC*] variables were employed in the final form of the hedonic equation, and most are objective and self-explanatory (see table 13.6). Three, however, provided by the assessor are subjective and unusual, and require explanation: *Grade* of construction is a measure of the quality of the original construction of the building, having to do with the type of materials used and level of workmanship. By definition, it is not subject to later alteration, and it is coded on a scale from 0–280, with 100 defined as average. Structural *condition,* coded on a scale from 0 to 100% good, measures the physical depreciation of the structure relative to its condition when new. The listers attempted to estimate directly the relationship between physical condition and value in this variable. Structural *obsolescence,* also coded on a scale from 0 to 100% good, describes the degree of conformity with current technology, conditions, and fashion, irrespective of physical condition. The degree of obsolescence may vary for structures of a given vintage. In addition, five locational attributes of each parcel were included in the hedonic. Each assessor's map sampled was examined to ascertain which dwelling that sold had the worst condition (defined above). This variable was coded as a proxy for neighborhood structural upkeep levels (with better condition of the "worst" property signifying better neighborhood quality). The one-way travel time (in minutes) from the centroid of each map to the central business district (*CBD*) was estimated based on actual roadway distance[39] and served as a proxy for accessibility of each parcel in that map. Census tract data for median income, and percentage of black and of single-family structures were also added as controls for neighborhood status, demographic composition, and physical environment. Interpolated figures from the 1960 and 1970 Censuses were used to obtain 1965 estimates for the above three variables.

Finally, three variables were employed as proxies for idiosyncratic market attributes that may have influenced observed selling price. Land contract (i.e., seller-financed) sales were denoted by a dummy variable, as were sales occurring during the "credit crunch" years 1965–66. Finally, a time trend was included to control for any general housing inflation tendencies during the 1962–69 era.

Values for the parameters of the hedonic index (equation 13.5) were estimated using OLS by regressing sales price on the aforementioned structural, locational, and market characteristics, employing the double square-root specification. Since it is presumed that single-family (primarily owner-occupied) properties demonstrate a different hedonic relationship than do multifamily (renter-occupied) properties, only observations of the former are employed for the analysis. In the Des Moines sample this represents an $N = 1360$. The estimated parameters and associated t-statistics are presented in table 13.6. Twenty-one are statistically significant at the 5% level or better, and all have the expected signs. About two-thirds of the variance in prices is explained by the model. This highly satisfactory estimated hedonic gives us confidence that it can be employed in subsequent analyses to both partition the Des Moines housing stock into quality submarkets and estimate returns from various housing improvements.

13.3.3 Sample Selection Bias: Tests for Specification Error

In contrast to a census- or an Annual Housing Survey–based sample that includes estimates of value for the entire stock of owner-occupied housing, the Des Moines sample contains prices only for those houses that were actually sold during the observation period. In order to make inferences about the entire stock of owner-occupied, single-family housing, it is necessary to assume that the houses sold were a representative sample, or sample selection bias would occur. An attempt to control for this was made through use of a PROBIT analysis using a sale as the binary dependent variable. Such a procedure is described by Heckman (1979).

The logic of this approach is that the regression error e in equation (13.5) is not independent of the sample selection rule. Therefore, not including that sample selection rule results in a specification error in the regression. Heck-

Table 13.6. Coefficients (t-statistics) of Hedonic Index for Des Moines, 1962–69

Structural Attributes			
Finished attic (sq.ft.)	.4365 (4.87)[a]	Modernity (% new)[2]	4.443 (3.74)[a]
Unfinished attic (sq. ft.)	.0178 (0.19)	Central air conditioning (1 = yes)	.7887 (0.37)
Finished basement (sq. ft.)	.6374 (6.26)[a]	Lacks central heat (1 = yes)	−8.087 (1.55)[c]
Unfinished basement (sq. ft.)	.3986 (5.69)[a]		
		Locational Attributes	
Living area[1] (sq. ft.)	.8533 (7.47)[a]	Travel time to CBD (min.)[3]	−.1.512 (4.00)[a]
Open porches (sq. ft.)	.1775 (2.03)[b]	% Black in tract	−.0291 (0.09)
Enclosed porches (sq. ft.)	.1313 (1.32)[c]	Median income in tract	.3227 (5.00)[a]
Garages (# spaces)	3.265 (3.78)[a]	% Single-family units	.9508 (2.27)[b]
Lot size (sq. ft.)	.0461 (2.12)[b]	Condition of worst house in area[4]	2.132 (3.79)[a]
Fireplaces (#)	6.009 (4.36)[a]		
Brick construction (1 = yes)	4.071 (2.56)[a]		
		Market Attributes	
Plumbing fixtures (#)	7.866 (3.61)[a]	Land contract sale (1 = yes)	.1288 (0.13)
Structure age (years)	2.422 (5.14)[a]	Sold during 1965–66[5] (1 = yes)	2.800 (2.80)[a]
Condition (% good)[2]	2.644 (2.50)[a]	Time trend (1962–69)	.6189 (3.19)[a]
Grade of construction	8.660 (6.99)[a]		
		Constant	−146.2 (8.05)[a]*

R^2 = .651
R^2 (adj.) = .647
N = 1360
F (26,1333) = 93.57

Notes: Double square root model; single-family units only.
*Two-tail test.
[1]Total interior finished area, less finished attic and basement areas.
[2]Scale established by assessors.
[3]Computed by authors based on actual roadway distances.
[4]Area = assessors' tax map; computed by authors.
[5]The years 1965 and 1966 were "credit crunch" years.
[a]Coefficient statistically significant at 1% (one-tail test).
[b]Statistically significant at 5% (one-tail test).
[c]Statistically significant at 10% (one-tail test).

man offers a solution to this problem through a two-stage estimator. First, a PROBIT analysis of the full sample is performed to estimate the probability that an observation will have a value for the dependent variable. From this, the inverse of the Mills ratio is calculated. This is the density over the distribution function of an observation, assuming a standard normal distribution, and is a monotone decreasing function of the probability that an observation with particular values of dependent variables is selected into the sample. This is then used as a regressor in the subsequent hedonic regression to eliminate the specification error.

To use this technique required that a sample selection rule be specified. This rule would identify what types of houses are more likely to have changed hands and would use variables that would not properly enter the hedonic index, that is, the sample selection rule says nothing about the value of the houses, just their probability of having a sale during the time period. After considering several different specifications, the following variables were chosen for the PROBIT analysis: (1) proximity to Interstate 35 (now 235), which was under construction during the sample period; (2) a dummy variable for whether the house was newly built or not (since new houses tend to be sold by developers, one would expect to see a higher proportion of new houses sold than older houses); (3) the fraction of sales in the area that are land contract sales; (4) the proportion of residents in the census tract that have lived at the same residence for twenty years or more; and (5) the change in the percentage of black population in the census tract from 1960 to 1970.

These last two measures were interacted with two dummy variables dividing the city into white and black areas since different effects were expected in the two areas. The results of the PROBIT analysis were quite significant and indicated that there was, indeed, sample selection bias. However, the resulting PROBIT variable in the hedonic regression was found to be statistically insignificant and eventually was dropped. This is reassuring since the hedonic index was intended to represent the equilibrium values of the attributes of the housing stock. These results indicate that even though the housing which is sold is a biased sample of the total stock (the significant PROBIT analysis), it represents strong pressure on neither the demand side (those houses sold being high priced) nor on the supply side (only the lower-priced houses being bought).

13.3.4 Functional Form of the Hedonic Index: Tests for Specification Error

Given the rich, detailed data about individual home sales in the Des Moines sample, it becomes especially important to consider the question of functional form of the hedonic equation. Our previous cross-sectional investigation was based on a limited set of characteristics of groups of properties. Thus, in part, we were forced to argue implicitly that a hedonic functional form wherein dwelling characteristics were interactive (e.g., a semi-log form) was necessary to measure, by proxy, the effect of characteristics omitted from the model. In part, of course, such a specification may be supported on less pragmatic grounds: as we saw in chapter 3, interactiveness is an inferred property of the surface of tangencies of the housing bid and offer functions—the surface estimated by the hedonic. Put differently, there is strong intuitive appeal to the notion that the hedonic value of, for example, an added room will depend on the age of the dwelling, its lot size, and neighborhood quality.

In our Des Moines empirical investigations we no longer need the former, pragmatic justification for a particular specification. But we add another crucial one: since the Des Moines hedonic equation is to be used ultimately to predict potential capital gains from undertaking various alternative dwelling alterations, the specification implicitly should embody diminishing returns. To recap the theoretical arguments of chapters 4 and 5, successive increments in a particular dwelling feature are likely to produce simultaneously both diminishing marginal utility for current or future occupants and marginally increasing costs as the basic structural/mechanical features of the dwelling are required to become progressively more distorted by the change in question. The net result: attempts to drastically upgrade a dwelling by undertaking alterations of structural characteristics which contribute to its hedonic value are likely to be subject to diminishing returns in market value.

The upshot is that there are compelling theoretical reasons for adopting a functional form in the Des Moines application of the model which embodies both interactive effects between characteristics and diminishing return effects for a single characteristic. The general functional form that incorporates all others of interest as special cases (Halvorsen and Pollakowski 1981) may be written as

$$P^{(c)} = a_0 + \sum_{i=1}^{m} a_i Z_i^{(b)} + 1/2 \sum_{i=1}^{m}\sum_{j=1}^{m} d_{ij} Z_i^{(b)} Z_j^{(b)} \tag{13.6}$$

where P is price, the Z_i are attributes, $d_{ij} = d_{ji}$, and $P^{(c)}$ and $Z_i^{(b)}$ are Box-Cox transformations,

$$\begin{aligned} P^{(c)} &= (P^c - 1)/c & c &\neq 0, \\ &= \ln P, & c &= 0, \\ Z_i^{(b)} &= (Z_i^b - 1)/b & b &\neq 0, \\ &= \ln Z_i, & b &= 0. \end{aligned}$$

Unfortunately, given the large number of independent variables we employ, we are forced to make the additional restriction of $d_{ij} = 0$ when $i \neq j$, that is, there are no separate pair-wise interaction variables. This restriction, in turn, means that our aforementioned criteria of interaction and diminishing returns can only be met by restricting both c and b to less than unity.[40]

The obvious empirical question becomes What is the loss of explanatory power associated with such constraints on functional form? To obtain an answer we employ a version of the Box-Cox technique first employed for hedonic indexes by Halvorsen and Pollakowski (1981) and now used conventionally in hedonic index research. In the technique, different values for c and b are chosen, dependent and independent variables are transformed, regressions are estimated, and that version evidencing the highest explanatory power is selected as the "best" form. For computational feasibility, we confine our search over forms of equation (13.6) where $d_{ij} = 0$ with permutations of b and c values of zero, one-half, and one.[41]

The comparative explanatory power of three alternative hedonic regressions (each employing twenty-six independent variables) is presented in table 13.7. As found in previous work (Linneman 1980; Halvorsen and Pollakowski 1981), results appear more sensitive to the transformation of the dependent variable (the c parameter) than of the independent variables (the b parameter). Unfortunately for our purposes, the highest R^2 (= .694) is present in the linear specification, which violates both our assumptions of interaction and diminishing returns. However, the double square-root form ($b = c = 1/2$) does fulfill our assumptions[42] and produces only 6% less explanatory power than the "best" form.[43] In addition, signs and levels of statistical significance of coefficients are very insensitive to choice of functional form.

These results are similar to those of other researchers (esp. see Grether and Mieszkowski 1974; Kain and Quigley 1970; Schnare and Struyk 1976), who have found little empirical basis for choosing one functional form over another. Dhrymes (1971: 96) suggests the following explanation—that clustering of combinations of dwelling characteristics can so restrict the range of the sample that it covers only a relatively small portion of the (hypothetical) equilibrium price surface. If such is the case, it would not be unreasonable for many functional forms to be equally good approximations to the true (and more complex) surface over that limited range. In short, choice of hedonic functional form seems more a matter of theoretical propriety than practical importance.

Table 13.7. Comparative Explanatory Power (R^2) of Alternative Functional Forms (Des Moines Sales Sample, 1962–69)

Independent Variables Transformation (b)	Dependent Variables Transformation (c)		
	0	.5	1
0	.542	.636	.673
.5	.555	.651	.691
1	.563	.656	.694

Table 13.8. Distribution of Des Moines Single-Family Dwellings by Quality (Sales Sample, 1962–69)

Hedonic Value (1,000s)	Frequency	Percentage
2–3	5	.4
3–4	20	1.5
4–5	24	1.7
5–6	48	3.5
6–7	111	8.1
7–8	90	6.5
8–9	98	7.1
9–10	73	5.3
10–11	119	8.6
11–12	87	6.3
12–13	87	6.3
13–14	115	8.3
14–15	125	9.1
15–16	97	7.0
16–17	61	4.4
17–18	48	3.5
18–19	55	4.0
19–20	32	2.3
20–21	22	1.6
21–22	12	.9
22–23	9	.7
23–24	7	.5
24–25	4	.3
25–26	5	.4
26–27	1	.1
27–28	1	.1
28–29	3	.2
29–30	1	.1
Total	1360	100

Notes: Mean hedonic value = 12.66; standard deviation = 4.63.

13.3.5 Quality Submarket Partitioning: Specifying Submarket Definitions

The predicted value for each observation (generated by substituting values for all twenty-three property characteristics—excluding market attributes—into the hedonic equation reported in table 13.6) is equivalent to the given dwelling's estimated real quality or hedonic value, extracted from transitory market forces. The distribution of such hedonic values for the 1962–69 Des Moines sales sample is presented in table 13.8. Sold properties ranged in hedonic value from 2,000 to 30,000 and were arrayed along a slightly positively skewed distribution. This in itself provides little guidance as to where submarket partitions should be specified, since there are clearly no "natural" breaks in the quality array of single-family home sales in this sample.

Fortunately, such guidance is provided by a consideration of submarket prices. Our theory suggests that a submarket could be identified by common prices within it and (at least potentially) dissimilar prices outside it. Here, as before, *price* is defined as observed market value of property divided by estimated hedonic value, that is, *market price per "hedon."* When such prices were computed for each property and then arrayed by hedonic value, a distinct pattern of prices emerged that strongly suggested a stock partitioning scheme producing six submarkets. That is, a wavelike price pattern was observed across the hedonic array; submarket boundaries were suggested between the "crests" and "troughs." This scheme distinguishes the extreme upper and lower tails of the quality distribution, then approximately divides the remaining stock into quartiles. Coincidentally, this partitioning closely matches that employed earlier in our cross-SMSA analysis, which was selected purely on the ground of a priori rasonableness.

The precise hedonic value boundaries of the submarkets, the distribution of the Des Moines sales sample across them, and the price statistics for each are shown in table 13.9. Examination of the mean submarket prices suggests that, during the 1962–69 period in question, the market for lower-quality (submarket 1 and 2) single-family dwellings in Des Moines was comparatively strong, that is, relatively high submarket prices per unit of hedonic quality. The same could be said of high-quality, submarket 5 dwellings. By contrast, weaker price signals were evidenced in moderate-quality (3 and 4) and highest-quality (6) submarkets.[44] The cross-submarket pattern of standard errors/deviations is also revealing. It suggests that the hedonic was less efficacious in predicting values at both extremes of the quality spectrum, undoubtedly due to the increased likelihood of idiosyncratic structural or neighborhood features which were absent from the hedonic index.[45]

Table 13.9. Des Moines Quality Submarket Specification (Single-Family Sales Sample, 1962–69)

Submarket Boundaries	*N*	%	Submarket Price per Hedon: Mean	Standard Error	Standard Deviation
1. Under 6,000	97	7.1%	1.149	.060	.589
2. 6,000–8,999	299	22.0	1.036	.024	.423
3. 9,000–11,999	279	20.5	0.996	.015	.249
4. 12,000–14,999	327	24.0	1.010	.012	.212
5. 15,000–19,999	293	21.5	1.033	.010	.177
6. Over 20,000	65	4.8	1.003	.029	.232
TOTAL	1360	100.	1.027	.009	.313

Note: Submarket boundaries are measured in units of hedonic value.

Table 13.10. Distribution of Des Moines Single-Family Dwellings by Quality (Stock Sample, 1963)

Submarket	*N*	%
1. Under 6,000	187	9.1
2. 6,000–8,999	423	20.6
3. 9,000–11,999	410	20.0
4. 12,000–14,999	326	15.9
5. 15,000–19,999	464	22.6
6. Over 20,000	242	11.8
TOTAL	2052	100.

Note: Submarket boundaries are measured in units of hedonic value.

When the same submarket definitions and hedonic index are applied to larger "stock sample" (containing both sold and unsold single-family units in Des Moines), we obtain the distribution shown in table 13.10. It closely corresponds with the submarket distribution for sold units shown in table 13.9, although their comparison suggests that 1962–69 sales represented a somewhat smaller proportion of the sampled 1963 stock in the two extreme submarkets (1 and 6), and a larger proportion in submarket 4 than in the others. It is our assumption, then, that the submarket prices observed for the sales sample (table 13.9) are also applicable for the stock sample as partitioned in table 13.10.

In order to demonstrate the reasonableness of our partitioning by indicating what sorts of dwellings are actually contained in these six submarkets, we provide in table 13.11 the mean values of selected characteristics in each. Not surprisingly, there are monotonic direct relationships between submarket and mean levels of total living area, plumbing fixtures, lot size, brick construction, air conditioning, construction grade, median tract income, and tract percent white. There are slight deviations from monotonicity in the upper submarkets for age, condition, garages, and the condition of the worst house in the area. Somewhat more surprisingly, lower-quality dwellings are not exclusively concentrated near the central business district.

In sum, we believe a plausible and intuitively appealing way to partition the single-family housing stock in Des Moines is to define six quality submarkets using roughly the 10th, 30th, 50th, 70th, and 90th percentiles as boundaries, that is, about 3,000 hedons per submarket. These submarkets also best capture the essence of intersubmarket hedonic price differentials, the role of which we explore empirically in chapter 16.

13.3.6 Qualitative versus Spatial Dimensions of Submarkets

As we have seen in chapters 2 and 3, several uses of the term *submarket* in the housing literature embody spatial definitions: neighborhood (e.g., one census

Table 13.11. Selected Characteristics of Single-Family Dwellings, by Submarket (1963 Mean Values)

	Quality Submarket						
Characteristic	1	2	3	4	5	6	Total
Area (sq. ft.)	772	914	979	1091	1221	3254	1288
Plumbing fixtures	3.28	4.02	4.23	4.47	4.63	6.12	4.45
Age (years)	58.1	51.3	39.9	30.0	13.9	20.6	34.2
Lot (sq. ft.)	7402	7406	8409	8886	9755	12857	9015
Brick construction	1.1%	0.5%	2.7%	7.7%	13.4%	36.8%	9.3%
Garages	.22	.50	.78	.87	.71	1.12	.71
Air conditioning	0.0%	0.7%	0.7%	1.2%	11.2%	16.9%	5.0%
Grade	84.6	92.7	98.1	101.7	104.6	118.4	100.2
Condition	45.0	51.8	61.9	68.7	83.7	79.9	66.4
Time to CBD (min.)	11.4	9.0	5.7	5.6	7.0	5.8	7.2
Median tract income ($)	6326	6790	7706	8765	9172	10715	8246
Tract % black	21.0	16.5	8.7	3.0	1.1	0.5	7.9
Condition of worst house	37.2	42.6	47.2	50.8	70.8	67.1	53.6

tract versus another), metropolitan subregion (e.g., central city versus suburbs), and area of distinct racial composition (e.g., ghetto versus all white). In this section, our view of submarket (as a quality metric defined for a common structure type/tenure grouping) is contrasted to these others in order to assess their degree of correspondence.

The distribution of single-family dwellings in the 1963 Des Moines sample across census tracts is presented in table 13.12. What is most noteworthy is that, even though only selected areas within each tract were sampled, there is substantial variation of quality within each. Indeed, only one tract (#36) had all its dwellings in one quality submarket. By contrast, 80% of the tracts[46] had four or more different submarkets represented within them: 19 tracts had four of six, 10 had five of six, and 7 had all six represented.

There also appears to be an interesting pattern of intratract variation according to overall quality of dwellings in the tract: tracts with dwellings of higher mean quality have greater variation in quality. Specifically, 9 tracts had standard deviations in quality within them that were larger than the standard deviation of the entire sample. The 6 tracts with the highest mean hedonic value[47] are included in this group of 9. Of these 6, 5 (83%) have 4 or more submarkets represented. At the other extreme, only one of the 20 tracts with quality standard deviations below 3,000 have a mean quality above the sample mean of 13,200.[48] Of the 17 tracts with mean hedonic value below 10,000, only 70% had 4 or more submarkets represented. Thus, we conclude for this Des Moines sample, at least, that there is little homogeneity of housing quality at the tract level and that homogeneity is weakly inversely related to mean

Table 13.12. Quality Distribution of Single-Family Dwellings by Census Tracts, City of Des Moines, 1963

1960 Tract Number	Quality Submarkets							Hedonic Value	
	1	2	3	4	5	6	*N*	Mean	SD
1	2	4	13	3	134	5	161	15.8	3.0
2	0	0	0	0	21	12	33	18.9	2.3
3	1	0	4	3	16	5	29	16.9	5.6
4	0	2	55	57	7	1	122	12.5	2.4
5	1	8	38	22	2	1	72	11.5	2.5
6	0	6	31	16	8	0	61	11.9	2.7
7	2	6	15	26	50	62	161	12.3	7.5
8	0	3	14	19	41	34	111	19.2	7.8
9	0	0	1	8	5	3	17	17.7	6.4
10	0	1	7	14	5	4	31	15.0	6.2
11	0	4	10	5	0	1	20	11.1	2.7
12	6	50	65	17	6	0	144	9.9	2.6
13	1	42	7	1	0	0	51	8.0	1.5
14	1	6	10	3	0	0	20	9.1	2.4
15	0	1	2	17	11	4	35	15.3	3.2
16	1	1	3	1	0	1	7	12.9	9.6
17	21	27	9	2	1	0	60	6.6	3.0
18	2	20	8	3	2	0	35	8.9	2.6
19	0	3	2	4	23	13	45	17.3	4.1
20	0	3	1	0	2	0	6	11.1	4.8
21	7	43	7	2	1	0	60	8.0	2.0
22	11	25	2	0	1	0	39	6.9	2.2
23	8	3	0	2	15	0	28	11.7	5.2
24	24	11	2	0	0	0	37	5.5	1.9
25	3	0	1	0	0	0	4	6.3	2.5
26	0	5	4	0	0	0	9	8.8	1.4
27	11	28	4	1	0	0	44	7.0	2.1
28	0	1	0	5	5	1	12	15.3	3.3
29	0	0	4	3	4	5	16	18.5	9.4
30	0	0	2	19	14	7	42	16.2	4.5
31	0	0	1	7	19	33	60	23.5	8.1
32	0	0	1	0	2	19	22	28.0	8.4
33	0	1	0	0	0	0	1	6.3	0.0
34	3	13	10	2	0	0	28	8.7	2.0
36	12	0	0	0	0	0	12	2.3	1.4
37	11	4	1	0	0	0	16	5.5	2.6
38	21	9	3	1	0	0	34	6.0	2.5
39	1	0	1	0	1	0	3	10.1	7.7
40	0	2	0	4	7	8	21	19.6	9.1
41	1	2	2	5	3	7	20	18.5	10.3
42	14	11	14	3	1	0	43	8.0	3.1
43	4	12	17	20	25	6	84	13.2	4.3
44	0	20	10	12	6	0	48	11.1	3.5
45	7	19	12	8	7	2	55	10.2	4.3
46	10	22	10	9	19	8	78	12.1	5.8
47	1	5	7	2	0	0	15	9.4	2.6
TOTAL	187	423	410	326	464	242	2052	13.2	6.8

Notes: Tract 35 had too few single-family homes to be sampled. The hedonic value is in 1,000s

tract quality. We stress, however, that we have no direct evidence as to whether these findings may be generalized to larger metropolitan areas.

Another spatial aspect of the Des Moines single-family dwelling market can be investigated by considering distance from the CBD, that is, areas defined roughly as concentric circles. Table 13.13 presents quality submarket distributions for such areas. As in the case of census tracts, there is substantial variation in dwelling quality within travel time zones. Fully fourteen of the sixteen zones (88%) contain four or more submarkets. There appears to be no discernible relationship, however, between mean hedonic value for each zone and its internal variation in quality.

Finally, space can be defined in terms of racial composition. We have grouped Des Moines tracts into four classifications according to their estimated 1965 percentage black: under 1%; 1–9.9%; 10–49.9%; and over 50%. The quality submarket distributions of single-family dwellings for these racial classifications is shown in table 13.14. Not surprisingly, lower-quality dwellings have higher proportional representations in areas with larger proportions of black households. Nevertheless, both substantially integrated and majority black areas manifest dwellings in all but the highest-quality level. And of course all submarkets are heavily represented in predominantly white areas. Thus, it is inaccurate to use neighborhood racial composition as a proxy for dwelling quality, at least for this sample.

Table 13.13. Quality Distribution of Single-Family Dwellings by Travel Time Zone, City of Des Moines, 1963

Estimated Minutes Travel to CBD	Quality Submarket							Hedonic Value	
	1	2	3	4	5	6	*N*	Mean	SD
0	2	15	60	61	99	96	333	17.9	7.5
1	1	8	38	22	2	1	72	11.4	2.5
2	0	0	1	8	5	3	17	17.7	6.4
3	1	3	66	70	27	9	176	13.5	4.1
4	0	0	0	0	21	12	33	18.9	2.3
5	1	5	13	6	0	2	27	11.6	5.2
6	34	122	81	25	15	8	285	9.5	4.7
7	6	33	25	27	28	7	126	12.1	4.6
8	20	37	18	4	2	0	81	7.9	2.9
9	4	11	22	10	136	12	195	15.5	4.7
10	3	39	27	29	21	24	143	14.2	7.7
11	14	54	22	31	51	23	195	13.2	6.7
12	0	4	6	14	30	18	72	17.1	5.7
13	21	9	3	1	0	0	34	6.0	2.5
15	68	83	28	18	27	27	251	10.6	7.5
17	12	0	0	0	0	0	12	2.3	1.4
TOTAL	187	423	410	326	464	242	2052	13.1	6.8

Note: Hedonic value is in 1,000s.

Table 13.14. Quality Distribution of Single-Family Dwellings by Tract Racial Composition, City of Des Moines, 1963

Estimated 1965 Tract % Black	Quality Submarket							Hedonic Value	
	1	2	3	4	5	6	*N*	Mean	SD
Under 1%[a]	36	155	214	253	411	229	1298	15.5	6.8
1–9.9%[b]	41	71	99	51	45	13	320	11.0	5.0
10–49.9%[c]	75	170	81	20	6	0	322	8.0	3.0
50% or more[d]	35	57	16	2	2	0	112	6.9	2.6
Total	187	423	410	326	464	242	2052	18.1	6.8

Note: Hedonic value is in 1,000s.
[a]Tract numbers 1, 2, 4, 6–10, 15, 16, 19–21, 30–32, 39–41, 43–47.
[b]Tract numbers 3, 5, 11, 14, 18, 23, 28, 29, 33, 34, 37, 42.
[c]Tract numbers 12, 13, 24, 27, 36, 38.
[d]Tract numbers 17, 22, 25, 26.

13.4 Conclusion

This chapter has investigated issues relating to the estimation of hedonic indexes as measures of housing quality, and their use as devices for partitioning an SMSA's housing stock into quality submarkets. We considered two types of contexts in which indexes may be estimated and employed for this purpose—cross-SMSA, where data are derived from the census or Annual Housing Surveys, and single-SMSA, where data are derived from assessors' records or special purposive surveys. In both contexts, our investigations indicate that hedonic indexes can be estimated which are not seriously confounded by various sorts of econometric difficulties and which produce reasonable qualitative arrays of housing by hedonic value (quality)—the bases for partitioning into submarkets.

In the cross-SMSA application, our tests for aggregation bias demonstrate that the hedonic relationships across different metropolitan areas are considerably more alike than has generally been thought. The greatest homogeneity is to be found among renter markets, where the structure of tradeoffs among characteristics is quite stable; the observed cross-sectional differences in rents appear to result solely from variations in the overall price level. Owner markets seem somewhat more diverse, with small but significant differences in coefficients evident across SMSAs. Even so, substantial aggregation of owner markets is possible at low cost in terms of coefficient accuracy and explanatory power. It is important to note that the distortions from aggregating owner markets appear to reflect the heterogeneity of packages of coefficients and not a set of consistent effects upon particular characteristics considered singly.

These results serve as a reminder to students of urban housing markets that ownership and rental markets are subject to separate influences. Housing market models, if they are to represent accurately the nature of market interaction, must reflect the unique nature of the forces driving each of these sectors.

The findings shed some light on the practicality of constructing cross-sectional models of housing markets. This demonstration of substantial homogeneity across markets suggests that at least some degree of aggregation is both possible and practical (although complete national pooling in the owner-occupied sector is probably inadvisable). For purposes other than housing market modeling, the "optimal" amount of aggregation indicated by these results depends on the use to which the resulting hedonic index is to be put. If the investigator's main interest is in accurate projection of overall package prices, the findings suggest that the costs of even high degrees of aggregation are minimal in both tenure classes; for this purpose, a totally aggregated model is a reasonably efficient and tractable tool. The picture is somewhat different for researchers desiring to make use of the values of particular structural coefficients. Here the gains in tractability and comprehensiveness from having a more highly aggregated model must be balanced against the statistically significant geographic variations shown here to exist in some cases, the final judgment depending upon the researcher's desired standard of accuracy. Note that even in this case there is a significant advantage to some degree of pooling, since otherwise the scope of research effort needed to produce generalizable results becomes very large. Our understanding of urban housing markets in general will be impeded if the importance of idiosyncratic features in local markets is held to require the establishment of effectively separate "disciplines" of Pittsburgh housing economics, St. Louis housing economics, and so on. There are sizable returns to achieving an understanding of the broad similarities among housing markets as well as an articulation of the specific local factors which differentiate them.

There is no "perfect," fully complete set of housing attribute variables which can be used feasibly in estimating a hedonic index. Any realistic hedonic index, therefore, suffers from some degree of omitted variables. Our work suggests, however, that the practical impact of these biases is small. Even the severely restricted hedonic specification, using 1960 Census data on four independent variables, appears to suffer only limited coefficient biases, with a negligible impact on the explanatory and predictive powers of the equation. This finding, if confirmed by further tests, could enable both housing market researchers and others (such as property tax assessors) who use the hedonic technique to economize considerably, since it suggests that the costs of inaccuracy to misspecification are (for many purposes) smaller than has up to now been presumed. However, these results should be considered with three caveats in mind.

First, like any econometric estimate, a hedonic regression provides a far better reflection of the market evaluation for ordinary housing units than for truly idiosyncratic ones. If the ability to predict accurately for unusual units is especially important to an investigator, a more complete specification that captures some of the expected idiosyncrasies would probably be required. For use over the housing stock as a whole, though, the results indicate that a small number of variables will generally suffice.

However, it must be stressed that the apparent insensitivity of the coefficients of dwelling structural variables to specification changes does not necessarily carry over to other dwelling characteristics. Indeed, since nonstructure characteristics are typically highly intercorrelated (within the St. Louis sample, approximately half the simple correlation coefficients between pairs of these variables exceed 0.4 in absolute value), sizable specification biases from many sources are likely to distort their coefficients unless a fairly complete variable list is used. For example, an attempt to determine the effect of race on rents by estimating an equation containing only structure variables and a measure of neighborhood racial composition would in all likelihood yield a seriously biased coefficient for the latter variable.

The results of tests for omitted-variables bias presented here have been calculated for a single metropolitan area (St. Louis) at a single point in time (1967). It is possible that the relationships that lead to bias and the magnitudes of bias present are different in other cities and/or in other years. With one exception, the biases evident for St. Louis either result from relationships that are likely to be relatively stable or are quite small. This suggests that the outcome for other samples should at least be qualitatively similar to that reported here.

In our single-SMSA application, we found that hedonic indexes estimated for Des Moines from data on properties which sold were not significantly biased. Although such properties are not a representative sample of the entire housing stock, they do not skew the resulting hedonic in any particular fashion.

Our tests for "best" functional form revealed, as have other studies, little empirical bases upon which to choose. Complete searches over the entire possible set of Box-Cox transformations are simply infeasible when a robust number of independent variables are employed in the hedonic. Even if feasibly estimated, the form with the best fit may have neither intuitive appeal nor match theoretical prerequisites. Experiments with our Des Moines hedonic index (using twenty-six independent variables) revealed minimal differences in explanatory power among nine conventionally employed functional forms. We argue, therefore, that the hedonic specification should be made on a priori theoretical grounds. Two such grounds we deem critical are interactive effects among dwelling package attributes and diminishing returns (in market value) for increments in a given attribute.

In both cross-SMSA and single-SMSA applications, the quality array of dwellings generated by the hedonic index yields a reasonable basis for segmenting the market into submarkets. The types of dwellings which constitute individual submarkets appear to be plausible substitutes. The pattern of correlations of submarket prices (obtainable only in the cross-SMSA model) is also supportive of the hypothesis that degree of substitutability between any pair of submarkets is inversely related to their quality differential.

Finally, various spatial conceptions of "submarkets" serve as poor proxies for (single-family dwelling) quality submarkets in Des Moines. There is substantial variation in quality within the vast majority of areas defined either by census tract, travel-time zone, or racial composition. While these spatial concepts may be useful for many analytical purposes, they are unlikely to be helpful when the focus, like ours, is on understanding the dynamics of housing-quality alterations.

Notes

1. SMSAs under 100,000 population were excluded because some key cross-tabular data on their housing stock were not published by the Census Bureau.

2. Inclusion of housing markets significantly out of equilibrium in 1960 could have seriously distorted the results. Accordingly, anecdotal sources such as FHA Housing Market Analyses were searched for evidence of disequilibrium. On the basis of these findings, the renter market in Duluth-Superior and the owner markets in Scranton and Raleigh-Durham were excluded from the appropriate hedonic regressions.

3. That is, for each average rent or price there is a corresponding average value in each of seven categories of number of rooms, five categories of when the structure was built, and five categories of condition and plumbing.

4. The method described here was originated by H. S. Houthakker but never was published by him; Haitovsky's account (1973) is the standard reference.

5. For details, see Butler 1980: n. 8.

6. For the estimate reported here, the modal rooms category and the "sound with all plumbing facilities" category (to which the vast majority of units belong) have been deleted.

7. The estimated standard errors of the coefficients will also be biased, probably toward zero (Maddala 1977:283), as a consequence of using WLS instead of the correct GLS technique. The source of this bias is the correlation among observations resulting from the use of information from each unit up to three times (i.e., in each of the three cross-classifications). However, by eliminating two of the categories containing large numbers of units (see n. 6), this bias has been reduced to the greatest extent possible.

8. It should be noted in passing that these values of adjusted R^2 (and the corresponding standard errors of estimate) are probably affected by the transformation of the original household-by-household data into the grouped data published in the census. Since we do not have access to the original ungrouped data from the census questionnaires of individual households, it is impossible to tell how great this effect might be in the present case; however, past studies have indicated that grouping may substantially increase R^2 (see Cramer 1964).

9. The assumption that any pooling of housing markets is unwarranted underlies much of the existing economic literature on housing markets. See Hirsch and Margolis 1977, in which this assumption is made explicit; see also DeLeeuw and Struyk 1975 and Ingram, Kain, and Ginn 1972, two modeling efforts in which the assumption is

implicit but clearly central to the conception of the housing market employed in the models.

10. For example, the studies of automobile prices which heralded the revival of the hedonic technique in the early 1960s (see, e.g., Fisher, Griliches, and Kaysen 1962) pooled all types of cars sold in all areas of country. Hence the authors implicitly assumed stability of the hedonic relationship over space and "submarkets."

11. Such factors might include intermetropolitan variations in the supply prices of inputs to housing production (e.g., land prices, prevailing construction wages, transportation costs for essential building materials), which might be called "true price" differences; areawide components of housing quality (such as cultural or architectural uniqueness, levels of taxes and public services, "status" of the area, and the like) which, if omitted from the specification, will influence the constant term; and areawide disequilibrium in some housing markets at the time the data were collected, which would make the observation unrepresentative of the underlying hedonic relationship. In practice, distinguishing among these sources of price-level variation will be difficult if not impossible.

12. For details, see Schnare and Struyk 1976, in which this measure is suggested and explained.

13. Recall that the use of WLS introduced a downward bias into the estimated coefficient standard errors (see no. 7). For this reason, the confidence intervals calculated here are probably narrower than the true confidence intervals. Accordingly, the hedonic relationships of the various markets are probably more homogeneous than these results indicate.

14. When using weighted least squares, it is customary to normalize the weights so that they sum to the number of observations, as this produces a standard error of estimate commensurate with that of an unweighted regression. For the comparison reported here, the normalization for the individual SMSA standard errors was done using the average weight for the entire sample so that the constrained and unconstrained standard errors would be comparable.

15. Recall that the comparisons are based on a condensed version of equation (13.1). For complete regression results of the pooled model for this condensed version and for aggregation test statistics, see Butler 1980.

16. Schnare and Struyk, discussing a similar result, agree that a difference of this size "is of limited economic significance" (1976:151).

17. Recall that since the hedonic relationship in each SMSA is a reflection of the equilibrium determined by demand and supply forces within that housing market, we would generally expect different equilibria (and different hedonic relationships) in different SMSAs. For a complementary analysis of cross-sectional housing prices, see Ozanne and Thibodeau 1983.

18. Note that since the intercepts are so significantly different from each other, the hypothesis that all coefficients including the intercept are stable across markets would clearly be rejected, even for renters.

19. This was accomplished by ranking the SMSAs according to their values of the five splitting variables, and then dividing the sample into groups with high and low values of each splitting variable. When a gap in the distribution of splitting variable values was evident, the sample was divided at the gap rather than arbitrarily using the median value or the midpoint of the range as the separating value.

20. Some examples to illustrate this point: one cannot put a house with 5,000 square feet of first-floor on a 4,000 square-foot lot; one seldom finds units with fourteen bedrooms that have only one bathroom (or vice versa).

21. Actually, the survey collected data on most of the possible items of difference between gross rent and contract rent (heat, utilities, furniture, etc.), but since all were very highly correlated with STR the correction is effectively accomplished by adding just this one variable.

22. Indeed, such theorizing *is* specification analysis, as that term is conventionally understood. See, for example, Theil 1971:540–43.

23. For a derivation of this result, see Goldberger 1968:35–37.

24. Note that from a practical perspective, what matters most about the bias is its size, not its statistical significance. If either d or $c = 0$, no bias exists; if both are nonzero, a test of the $a = b$ hypothesis would not help to answer the central question of how big the bias is. Hence, the absence of such a test imposes few real hardships.

25. Only 10 of the 380 owner units are classified as *SNDNPL*. One of these units is located in St. Louis County, so it was weighted 6.5 times more heavily than the units within the city limits to compensate for sampling ratios. The *SNDNPL* coefficient of a separate estimate for city units only was indeed negative, suggesting rather strongly that the one idiosyncratic county unit was the source of the distortion in the pooled city-county estimate.

26. The renter observations within the city were drawn disproportionately from inner city low-income neighborhoods. For this reason, the *AMILES* coefficient reflects not only the effects of accessibility but also (and, evidently, more strongly) the superior neighborhood amenities in the areas surrounding the suburban observations. This association with suburban amenities probably also affects *COUNTY* and *DENSITY,* which are highly correlated with *AMILES* (simple correlation of 0.80 and -0.67 respectively).

27. For complete statistics on the magnitude of bias, see Butler 1982.

28. For a more detailed explanation of this phenomenon, see Rothenberg 1967 and Davis and Whinston 1961.

29. This comparison has been used by other authors interested in the effects of intrametropolitan aggregation on explanatory power (see, for example, Schnare and Struyk 1976). Note that a statistical test of the significance of the differences in adjusted R^2 would not be especially informative, since a directly related magnitude has already been tested in establishing that $d \neq 0$.

30. For details, see Butler 1982.

31. Calculated from the R^2 and number of observations reported in their article.

32. In calculating the predicted, or hedonic, value for the housing units in a particular metropolitan area, the median value of the constant term for the relevant tenure/climate index was used rather than the individual constant term estimated for the particular SMSA. This was done because a careful study of the magnitudes of these coefficients yielded no evidence that they measured aspects of housing quality not reflected by other components of the hedonic index. Thus we concluded that these terms indeed embodied areawide, area-specific effects on the level of housing prices. Intermetropolitan variations in land prices are one obvious and important source of these differences.

It should also be noted that, in calculating hedonic values as of 1970, temporal effects were added to the vintage dummy coefficients to allow for normal depreciation between 1960, when the index was estimated, and 1970. The adjustments used allow for depreciation at an annual rate of 1% for rental units and 1.5% for ownership units built in 1940 or later, and at half those rates for units built prior to 1940.

33. The cooperation of the Department is gratefully acknowledged. The patient assistance of Andrew Regis, Chief Assessor, and Lyman Ellars, Field Assessor, was invaluable.

34. There are typically twenty assessor's field maps per census tract, so the former represent neighborhoods somewhat larger than a block.

35. Sampling ratios in Des Moines are as follows:

	Parcels Sold during 1956–72	Unsold Parcels
Basic sampling ratios	.10	.05
If high population turnover in tract, then (Defined as Number of households moved in pre-1960/Number of housing units built in pre-1960 [as of 1970 Census] is less than or equal to .3.)	add .10	add .05
If high rate of housing disuse then (Defined as Proportion of housing units found vacant in *both* 1971 and 1972 [according to the R. L. Polk street directory] is .02 or greater.)	add .10	add .05
If high rate of new construction, then (Defined as proportion of stock built 1965–70, as of 1970 Census, is .2 or greater.)	add .10	add .05
	to maximum of .3	to maximum of .15

36. The properties were selected based on their order in the assessor's file. *Residential* is defined as a structure with four or fewer units, with no retail/commercial space in the structure.

37. In addition to files at the assessor's office, Board of Realty records and People's Abstract Company title records were also searched so as to insure a complete listing of sales. The sample included all recorded, "arm's length sales," including those involving land contracts (i.e., seller financed) and assumed mortgages. In the latter instances where the outstanding amount of the mortgage could be determined it was added to the stated price; if not, such a sale was excluded from the sample.

38. Note that every time a property in one of the selected neighborhoods sold during 1962–69, it was included in the sample used for the hedonic index regression an additional time.

39. A speed of 20 m.p.h. for surface streets and 50 m.p.h. for main arterials was assumed in the calculation.

40. Any value of b between zero and one will produce a partial derivative of dwelling price with respect to the (transformed) independent variable which is inversely related to the magnitude of the given characteristic variable. A similar range for c is equivalent to a specification wherein the aforementioned partial derivative of a given characteristic variable is related to the magnitude of other characteristic variables. The degree of interaction is inversely related to c.

41. Such a "constrained search" is conventional in more complex hedonic models, e.g., Linneman 1980 and Sonstelie and Portney 1980.

42. Take a simplified form of the double square-root equation:

$$P^{1/2} = h + fA^{1/2} + gB^{1/2}.$$

Thus,

$$P = h^2 + f^2A + g^2B + 2(hfA^{1/2} + hgB^{1/2} + fgA^{1/2}B^{1/2})$$

and

$$\partial P/\partial A = f^2 + (hf + fgB^{1/2})/A^{1/2}.$$

Thus the marginal returns from A are directly related to B and inversely related to A, as desired.

43. The square root transformation of the dependent variable was also selected as the "best" form of Sonstelie and Portney 1980 and by Goodman 1978. Cassel and Mendelsohn 1985 argues that strict adherence to "best fit" using Box-Cox criteria is inappropriate and can lead to serious bias in applications of hedonic indexes (such as ours) where accuracy of prediction is crucial.

44. In a pairwise comparison, only the mean prices in submarkets 1 and 3 are significantly different from each other at the 5% level of statistical significance.

45. For the lower end of the distribution it is also likely that more sales occurred which were not "arm's length" transactions.

46. There were forty-five tracts with more than one observation.

47. These tracts (numbers 8, 29, 31, 32, 40, 41) all have average quality in the fifth or sixth submarket; mean hedonic value for the group is 21,600.

48. As a group, those tracts with standard deviations below 3,000 had a mean hedonic value of only 9,125.

14 Cross-SMSA Model: Market-Period Demand and Supply

Previous chapters have presented our theoretical model of urban housing submarkets and how such submarkets may be defined operationally using a hedonic index of housing quality to partition the stock. As explained in chapter 13, one such segmentation of housing submarkets was conducted for two samples of SMSAs—one for the 1960–70 period and the other for the 1970–1975/76 period.[1] The next two chapters utilize these submarkets as a basis for formulating and empirically estimating behavioral relationships. Chapter 14 focuses on market-period (short-run) housing submarket demand and supply relationships. Chapter 15 deals with medium-run (five- to ten-year) changes of housing stocks in various submarkets. In a broad, behavioral sense the cross-SMSA model describes the interplay of the forces of demand, which are motivated by aggregate changes in population and incomes, and the forces of supply, which are motivated by the costs of inputs to the production of housing capital and the cross-submarket spectrum of market valuations.

Before beginning the particulars of the models, two introductory points should be made. First, our primary rationale for undertaking these estimations was to discern whether our theory of housing submarkets could be rendered operational in a way having meaningful empirical content. As such, our specifications are evaluated in terms of the light they cast on our theory. They should be interpreted as exploratory probes into a new field of housing market modeling, not as definitive models currently suitable for housing market predictions or policy-scenario simulations. Second, we estimate our empirical specifications at different periods using different SMSA samples in an attempt to test the robustness of our approach. While, of course, we hope to learn that the thrust of our logic is not dependent on the particular circumstance, we would be surprised to find intertemporal invariance of estimates in all our estimations. During our period of analysis we witnessed the following: unprecedented growth followed by stagflation and recession; the coming of age of the baby-boom generation, with their unique lifestyle choices and housing preferences; the genesis of a host of income-support and housing subsidy programs under the Great Society aegis and the subsequent phasing out of urban renewal and public housing programs; and a variety of innovations in housing technology, perhaps most visible in the mobile home spurt. The consequences of these changes on the stability of particular parameters are considered further below.

14.1 Overview

The segmentation of the housing market into tenure-quality submarkets structures the market-period (short-run) demand and supply sector. Existing dwellings in the various submarkets are allocated among households, and submarket valuations (rents or sales) and vacancy rates are determined by this sector. In the market period both the number and attributes of existing housing units and the number and characteristics of households are fixed. The households move (substitute) among the tenure-quality submarkets in response to differences in the market valuation relative to housing attributes of dwellings in the different submarkets, net of search and moving costs. For their part, owners of housing units decide whether to make each unit available for occupancy at a given market valuation rather than hold it vacant in the expectation of receiving a higher valuation in the near future. The cross-submarket spectrum of aggregate demand and supply functions (i.e., spectral demand and supply) determines market-clearing submarket valuations and vacancy rates. Our goal here is the specification and empirical estimation of the parameters of these market-period demand and supply functions. But before proceeding, the data limitations, simplifications, and assumptions which underlie our cross-sectional approach should be explicitly noted.

The single most important constraint on the scope of our cross-SMSA empirical work is the paucity of appropriate cross-sectional data. This limitation is not a small factor in the sketchy state of empirical knowledge in the field. At the outset of our project in the early 1970s, comparable data on the stock and occupancy of housing units were obtained only at the times of the decennial censuses; data for intermediate periods were limited mainly to surveys on the conditions of occupancy and to counts of new housing units constructed. Later during the course of our work, Annual Housing Survey (later, American Housing Survey) data became available. Hence, our cross-sectional empirical investigations have been limited to one sample of SMSAs in the 1960 and 1970 Censuses and another sample delineated by Annual Housing Survey SMSAs in 1975 and 1976 and their counterparts in the 1970 Census.

While such data hold the advantage of being generally and easily accessible, they unavoidably leave untouched the locational and dynamic areas of our theory and lump together most of the variant forms of stock investment and housing adjustment activity. It was such data shortcomings that led us to obtain a much richer empirical base by surveying housing in Des Moines, as described in chapter 13. But here the limitations on our cross-sectional empirical models imposed by census and Annual Housing Survey data have required us to make a number of theoretical simplifications. The empirical cross-sectional model does not, therefore, have the richness of reference of our theoretical framework, but this has been necessary to permit focusing on the paramount issues. We do not believe this seriously distorts the empirical illumination of these issues, namely, the market stratification and measurement of demand and supply in terms of intersubmarket relationships. In light of these simplifications, however, the model must be viewed as exploratory rather than as a definitive empirical realization.

The following are some important simplifications: First, the model is comparative-static, not dynamic. The resulting assumption is that secular market forces dominate dynamic effects. Second, all forms of stock-supply activity other than new construction are treated as a single activity, called *net conversions*. The implicit assumption is that the coefficients of the behavioral relationships involving different forms of conversion activity are identical. Third, there is no segmentation of the market by size or structure type of housing unit. The resulting assumption is that the effects of these aspects for both demanders and suppliers are parametrized by the single hedonic quality measure.[2] Fourth, the aggregate data offer only a limited range of structural characteristics and no information on the locational and neighborhood characteristics of housing units within each SMSA. The implicit assumption is that all of the omitted characteristics of housing units are highly complementary with one another and with the included ones.[3] Fifth, it is not possible to measure meaningfully persistent differences in capital market conditions across SMSAs. The resulting assumption is that finance costs and availability are the same in all areas (and at the same time, specific to the data period(s)). Sixth, to incorporate endogenously the determination of the number of households and size of population into the model would have increased the complexity and demographic data requirements so substantially as to be infeasible. Our operating assumption is that the number of households and total population are exogenous.

Besides these simplifications, in order to permit the cross-sectional estimation it must be assumed that SMSAs are members of a homogeneous population. Despite the obviously vast differences among the metropolitan areas defined by the Census Bureau, differences which tend to undercut this assumption, this diversity results mainly from different blends of the same elemental ingredients. All large cities in the United States have a central business district, a stock of old, poor-quality housing, new suburban developments, and different groups of residents who each share common tastes, incomes, and so forth. The diversity that matters most, of course, is the relative mix of the different population types and housing characteristics. These we explicitly incorporate into our model to the extent the data permit. In this connection it should be recalled from chapter 13 that the model explicitly treats differences in building technology due to gross climatic differences by estimating separate hedonic indexes for the SMSAs categorized into warm and cold regions. (Tests for further bases of gross differentiation were much less persuasive.) With this important qualification, then, the assumption of SMSA homogeneity seems tenable.

Finally, and perhaps most importantly, all the empirical models in our work share a key assumption: the observed capital characteristics of the housing unit are assumed to serve as proxies both for the services provided by the unit to its occupants and for the (marginal) costs to the owner of providing these services. In other words, current housing operating/maintenance inputs are assumed to play *no independent* role relative to capital (i.e., structural) inputs in the production of housing services. We assume, essentially, approximately fixed proportions between capital and current inputs.[4] Our discussion of component complementarity above suggests, for example, that high levels of housing service will not normally be provided to the occupants of dilapidated tenement buildings, nor will service levels be subnormal in luxury apartment buildings. (This does not, however, imply that the *costs of maintaining* a given level of service are necessarily constant or proportional to other characteristics.) This assumption of constant proportionality between housing capi-

Table 14.1. Variable Names and Definitions for Market-Period Demand and Supply

Name	Definition
STijk	Proportion of all households in SMSA *k* occupying units in submarket *ij*; that portion of all SMSA's *k*'s occupied units which are in *ij*.
Pijk	Market value/hedonic value ratio in submarket *ij*, deflated by an index of price of nonhousing goods in SMSA *k*, where "value" ≡ "sales price" for owner-occupied units, ≡ "rent" for rental units.
PUijk, *PLijk*	Average market value/hedonic value ratios in upper (lower) adjacent submarkets of same tenure as *j*, relative to market value/hedonic value in *ij*.
*PAj*ijk*	Average market value/hedonic value ratios in the five submarkets of the tenure opposite of *j*, relative to that ratio in *ij* (in SMSA *k*).
IVijk	Reciprocal of vacancy rate in submarket *ij* (in SMSA *k*).
IVUijk	Reciprocal of average vacany rate in upper adjacent submarkets in same tenure as *j* (in SMSA *k*).
Yijk	Proportion of families in SMSA *k* with current money income in a range corresponding to that typical of housing consumption pattern, in the *ij* submarket.
NWk	Proportion of all households with nonwhite head in SMSA *k*.
A034k	Proportion of all households with head under 35 years old in SMSA *k*.
A65Pk	Proportion of all households with head over 64 years old in SMSA *k*.
DPjk	Absolute change in the average market value/hedonic value ratio of units in the same tenure as *j*, relative to price of nonhousing goods, during the decade* prior to the market period in question; both market and hedonic values calculated on basis of SMSA *k* median of dwelling characteristics.
DPOPk	Proportional change in population in SMSA *k* during the decade* prior to the market period in question.
TTijk	Total number of units (occupied plus vacant) in submarket *ij*, divided by the number of households in SMSA *k*.

*For 1975–76 sample the period 1970–1975/76 is used instead of prior decade.

tal and housing services does not seem unreasonable for the 1960s decade, since this was a period of approximate stability in relative costs of housing inputs. It would be less reasonable past the mid-1970s, however, which experienced considerable increases in the price or energy, a major input in the production of housing services.

14.2 Specification of Market-Period Demand Equations

In order to specify market-period demand we must assume that demanders (households) adjust their housing consumption immediately to changing conditions and that all house prices and rents adjust to reflect current transactions. The lags caused by out-of-pocket and psychic search and moving costs and by other behavioral and institutional frictions are assumed here to be insignificant. As a behavioral proposition these assumptions are very strong for reasons given in our demand theory (ch. 4), but as an aggregate, statistical proposition they are less heroic for the following reason. Market prices and rents in our data bases are reported by households and are not actual "spot" market valuations. Average submarket valuations therefore reflect perceptions of market transactions made in the recent past as well as in the present period, and may in fact approximate the average market valuations prevailing when current occupancies were determined much more nearly than do current transactions valuations. During periods of relative stability or smooth (and possible anticipated) change in housing valuations such as the late 1950s and 1960s, there will be an especially close correspondence between reported valuations and those on which (lagged) consumption decisions were made.

14.2.1 Dependent Variables

There are ten market-period demand equations, one for each *ij*th tenure-quality submarket (j = owner/renter, $i = 1, 2, \ldots, 5$ quality level.) The variable names used in these demand equations are summarized and defined in table 14.1. The dependent variables in the market-period demand functions are the proportion of households in the *k*th SMSA *occupying* units in the different *ij* submarkets, ST_{ijk} (k = SMSA 1, 2, . . . ; n = sample size).[5] Thus, our econometric specification of market-period demand is not an individualistic, behavioral one in the sense of our theory presented in chapter 4. Rather, our dependent variables here represent the *probabilities* that a randomly selected household in a given SMSA housing market will occupy housing in a given submarket. (The sum of the probabilities predicted in the separate equations was not constrained to sum to one.)

14.2.2 Right-Hand Endogenous and Exogenous Variables

Further divergencies between our empirical demand equations and the theoretical paradigm occur in the right-hand variables. Some, but by no means all, divergencies are due to the definition of the left-hand variable. Others stem from constraints imposed by data availability and statistical problems. In other words, given the aggregate nature of the left-hand variables, the right-hand variables must describe *distributions* of the relevant characteristics on the population of demanders and the array of submarkets; yet such attempts are quickly met with confounding degrees of multicollinearity.

The endogenous right-hand variables include housing submarket valuations (rents for renter submarkets, prices for owner-occupied submarkets) and vacancy rates (both measures of housing costs). The *housing market valuations* used in the demand equation for each market are as follows:

P_{ijk} The "price" (proportional market premium or discount relative to the hedonically explained value of the structural attributes in question) in the given *ij* submarket, deflated by an index of the price of nonhousing goods in SMSA *k;* that is, P_{ijk} = (actual market valuation/estimated hedonic value) divided by price index of nonhousing goods. Valuation is defined in terms of either sales prices or rents, depending on tenure. P_{ijk} thus is a proxy for the price per unit of housing quality in the given submarket *ij* relative to other goods.

PU_{ijk} (PL_{ijk}) The average price of housing in "upper" ("lower") adjacent submarkets in the same tenure, relative to price in given submarket *ij;* that is, $PU_{ijk} = (P_{i+1,jk} + P_{i+2,jk}) / 2P_{ijk}$; $PL_{ijk} = (P_{i-2,jk} + P_{i-1,jk}) / 2P_{ijk}$. For submarkets at the ends of the hierarchy the appropriate truncations occur, for example, $PU_{4jk} = (P_{5jk} / P_{4jk})$. Thus, these "relative price in same tenure" terms serve as proxies for the cost of substituting up or down in the housing-quality hierarchy.

$PA_{j^*ijk} \equiv \sum_{j^*}^{5} P_{ij^*k} / 5P_{ijk}\ j^* \neq j$. Thus, these "relative price in opposite tenure" terms serve as proxies for the cost of switching tenures. As above, "prices" involve either sales prices or rents, depending on tenure.

High sample correlation among the submarket prices within each SMSA (see ch. 13) precludes the inclusion of prices for all submarkets in each equation. The above limited selection of price terms is appropriate because demanders are more likely to substitute housing in adjacent (similar-quality) submarkets. The *vacancy rate terms* are as follows:

IV_{ijk} The reciprocal of the vacancy rate (= 1-occupancy rate) in the given submarket *ij*.

IVU_{ijk} The reciprocal of the average vacancy rates in "upper" adjacent submarkets in the same tenure.

Search costs, it is assumed, increase more than proportionately as the vacancy rate falls. Hence the vacancy rate terms are specified in reciprocal form. These terms are included only in the (lowest-quality) renter submarket 1, where supply is likely to be especially inelastic due to legal constraints on the construction of new, low-quality dwellings. (Preliminary tests indicated that these search-costs proxies were only statistically significant in this submarket.)[6]

The exogenous right-hand variables in the demand equation are proxies for the distribution of income and relevant demographic characteristics in the population of SMSA k. The *income distribution terms* are Y_{ijk}, the proportion of families in SMSA k with money income in an interval which "typically corresponds" to the particular housing-quality level ij, that is, families with income which, when multiplied by the median market-valuation of housing consumed/income ratio for that income group yields a market valuation placing it within the ij submarket. Such correspondence is determined by mapping the quality-submarket (HV hedonic value) bounds from the cross-SMSA total distribution of housing units on to the real income distribution for all households in the same tenure in the sample. A single set of dollar bounds for each tenure is applied to the income distribution in all SMSAs. We define the (real, current) income distribution function in a given year for households by tenure, $\pi_j^T(Y)$, and select income bounds Y_{i*j}, $Y_{i*} = 1,j$, for each submarket so that

$$\sum_{n=i*}^{i*+1} \pi_j^T(Y_n) = \sum_{n=i*}^{i*+1} \beta_j^T(HV_n).$$

Then,

$$Y_{ijk} = \sum_{n=i*}^{i*+1} \pi_T^k(Y_n),$$

where π_T^k is the income distribution function for all households in both tenures in SMSA k. The variables can be conceptualized as an "income-determined" demand.

The *demographic characteristics* terms[7] are as follows:

NW_k The proportion of SMSA k households with a nonwhite head, a proxy indicator of net housing consumption differentials induced by a lower ratio of wealth to current income for minorities, by racial discrimination and, perhaps, by interracial differences in housing tastes.[8]

$A034_k$ The proportion of SMSA k households with a head under age thirty-five, an indicator of consumption differentials induced by a lower wealth-income ratio and, perhaps, age-specific taste differences associated with younger life-cycle stages.

$A65P_k$ The proportion of SMSA k households with a head over age sixty-five or older, an indicator of consumption differentials induced by a higher wealth-income ratio and, perhaps, age-specific taste differences associated with older life-cycle stages.

The market-period demand equations for the ten tenure-quality submarkets are thus specified in general, as[9]

(14.1) $$\underline{ST}_{ijk} = f_{ij}\,(\underline{P}_{ijk}, \underline{PU}_{ijk}, \underline{PL}_{ijk}, \underline{PA}_{j*ijk}, Y_{ijk}, NW_k, A034_k, A65_k).$$

(The underlined variables in this and subsequent equations are endogenous, e.g., $\underline{ST}_{ijk}$). In addition, the $\underline{IV}_{ijk}$ and $\underline{IVU}_{ijk}$ terms are included in (lowest-quality) renter submarket 1. Note, also, that the $\underline{PU}$ ($\underline{PL}$) terms are not defined for the highest- (lowest-) quality submarket in each tenure.

14.2.3 Cross-Submarket Differences in Demand Relationships

To conclude the description of our specification of demand, some of the less-obvious linkages between it and our theory should be pointed out, as well as our predictions about coefficient signs and magnitudes across submarkets.

The submarket "price," P_{ijk}, measures in part the price of housing *relative to nonhousing goods* (relative prices among the submarkets in the same tenure held constant), and in part the relative price among submarkets. And because the ascending submarkets include progressively "larger," more expensive bundles of housing, our theory indicates that estimated demand, ST_{ijk}, may respond *positively* to this "price" in lower-quality submarkets and negatively, as is more usual, in higher-quality submarkets. With higher housing prices relative to nonhousing prices, "more" consumption of low-quality housing is the likely result, meaning "less" consumption of housing in the aggregate.

The demographic variables, reflecting life-cycle and minority status, embody an intermingling of income, wealth, taste, and price effects. For example, wealth and, thus, permanent income are negatively associated with youth and minority status, and minority status is associated with higher prices and search costs due to discrimination.[10] Housing preferences have been shown to vary systematically across both life-cycle and racial groups.[11] Clearly, the correspondence between our theoretical concepts and available statistical measurements is not one to one, and the coefficients of the demographic variables thus become difficult to predict and interpret.

Thus, from the wealth effect we would predict that *A034* should be negatively correlated with *ST* in owner submarkets and positively correlated with *ST* in renter submarkets; but the within-tenure patterns of occupancy remain ambiguous. The same ambiguity is present for *A65P*, except that its predicted relationship with *ST* in owner and renter submarkets would be opposite that of *A034*, of course. The effect of minority status is different. The effects of discrimination and lower minority wealth lead to the expectation of *NW* being negatively correlated with *ST* in owner submarkets, and vice versa in renter submarkets.[12] But discrimination (and resulting inflation of minority housing prices) should also lead to a reduction in the quality of housing consumed *within* any given tenure. Thus the combined effects should produce a positive correlation in lower-quality renter submarkets and a negative correlation in higher-quality owner submarkets; correlations in others remain unpredictable.

Our other independent variables yield less ambiguous predictions. The income distribution variable, Y_{ijk}, should be directly related to ST_{ijk} in all submarkets, as it serves as proxy for the housing purchasing power existing for the relevant quality range. Similarly, conventional microeconomic theory would predict a direct relationship between the prices of "substitute" quality levels in the same tenure (PU_{ijk}, PL_{ijk}) and in the opposite tenure (PA_{j*ijk}) and occupancy (demand) in the given *ijk* submarket. In the lowest-quality rental submarket (1), the inverse of the vacancy rate (IV_{1R}) should be inversely related to ST_{1R}, whereas that in the upper adjacent submarkets (IVU_{23R}) should be directly related to ST_{1R}.

The expected positive correlation between average relative prices in the opposite tenure (*PA*) and demand in a given submarket is not likely to be manifested strongly in all submarkets, however. The impact of relative tenure prices is undoubtedly asymmetric across current owners and renters. Owners face no downpayment constraint on switching tenures. But the sizable tax and other benefits associated with homeownership mean that few homeowners become renters simply because "apartments are so cheap." More often it is due to reasons of age or health. On the other hand, many renters are prevented from becoming homeowners primarily by the downpayment constraint. And the size of this constraint is affected by the relative real price existing in owner submarkets. It is likely, though, that only those renters occupying middle- to upper-quality rental submarkets have the economic wherewithal to become homeowners as a result of price signals of the magnitude demonstrated in our sample. Analogously, it is probably not the most expensive, highest-quality owner submarkets to which those erstwhile renters would switch. Thus, the coefficient of *PA* should be largest in the higher-quality renter submarkets and the moderate-quality owner submarkets.

14.3 Specification of Market-Period Supply Equations

The theory and specification of the *short-run supply equations* require considerably less explication than the demand equations. As the size of the housing stock in each tenure/quality submarket is fixed in the short-run market period and as owners do not usually hold large fractions of their units vacant, most of the variation in the number of units supplied for occupancy in a given submarket can be accounted for by variations in the size of the standing stock. However, vacancy rates do, in fact, vary, and this variation is an issue of considerable theoretical and empirical interest.

Why do not the owners of the existing housing stock simply supply all their units to households for whatever price (rent) they will fetch? We have argued in chapter 5 that the answer is that a rate-of-return maximizing owner of housing units has at all times a "reservation price," below which he or she will not sell, or rent, a particular house or apartment. Therefore, the market-period supply curve has an upward-sloping segment; it is not vertical throughout.[13]

The level of reservation prices is determined, first, by the owner's estimate of how much can be gotten for the housing unit in the future if he or she does not sell (rent) it today (i.e., primarily by expectations) and, second, by the costs of not selling or renting it today (holding costs). In other words, maximization of expected rate of return by owners normally entails some amount of speculative behavior.

14.3.1 Dependent Variables

As there are ten market-period demand equations, there are also ten market-period supply equations, one for each *ij* tenure/quality submarket. Each predicts the proportion of households occupying units in the *ij*th submarket in the *k*th SMSA, ST_{ijk}. Given a fixed (in the short run) stock of housing units in each submarket, these equations relate the share of units actually occupied (i.e., share of quantity supplied) to current submarket prices and suppliers' expectations of future submarket prices. Measures of the fixed costs of holding a vacant dwelling unit and the variable costs of operating an occupied unit (e.g., interest rates, real estate taxes, and rental operating costs) are not included because measures of interarea variation in them are not available. Analogous to the demand equations, the market-period supply equations require assumptions about adjustments in occupancies and valuations: first, that actual occupancy levels are equal to owner-desired occupancy levels; and second, that reported prices and rents have fully adjusted to current market conditions. The same considerations that tend to provide an empirical basis for the assumptions about demand also support the assumptions about supply behavior. Also, since the price data embody demanders' perceptions, it must be assumed that suppliers' perceptions of submarket prices correspond to those of demanders.[14]

14.3.2 Right-Hand Endogenous and Exogenous Variables

The right-hand variables in the market period supply equations are the following:

- P_{ijk} The given submarket "price," as defined in the demand equations (endogenous).
- DP_{jk} The absolute change in the average price of housing in same tenure (controlling for differences in attributes), relative to the price of nonhousing goods, during the decade prior to the market period under study (exogenous or predetermined). This serves as a proxy for expectations of relative rates of return to housing investments.
- $DPOP_k$ The proportional change in population during the decade previous to the market period under study in SMSA *k*. This is another expectational variable (exogenous or predetermined).

TT_{ijk} The total number of units occupied and vacant in the submarket ij, divided by the number of households (or total occupied units) in SMSA k (exogenous or predetermined).

Though a measure of relative holding costs of vacant housing is desirable on theoretical grounds, none could be found for inclusion in this model. Thus, the resulting ten market-period supply equations are specified as[15]

$$(14.2) \qquad \underline{ST}_{ijk} = g_{ij}\,(\underline{P}_{ijk}, DP_{jk}, DPOP_k, TT_{ijk}),$$

where underlined terms are endogenous.

14.3.3 Cross-Submarket Differences in Supply Relationships

Our theory of owners' expectations and perceptions of holding costs is too imprecise to allow us to predict whether or how the signs or significance of the coefficients of the above variables might vary across quality levels or tenure submarkets. We have no reason to believe that any particular submarket group of owners should respond differently to forces measured by these variables. Thus, we would expect that DP_{jk} and $DPOP_k$ should be inversely related to ST_{ijk} in all submarkets. In other words, past favorable trends in housing prices and population growth should buoy expectations about the continuation of such trends and thereby raise owners' reservation prices. TT_{ijk} serves as proxy for the total capacity of the given submarket; that is, the vertical segment of the market-period supply curve is where the physical quantity constraint has been reached (no vacancies) and it becomes perfectly inelastic (see fig. 7.1). Another reason TT_{ijk} should be directly related to ST_{ijk} is that it serves as proxy for the opportunity costs of speculatively holding a unit vacant or unsold.

14.4 Empirical Results

Market-period demand and supply equations as specified by linear forms of equations (14.1) and (14.2) above were econometrically estimated using two-stage least squares (TSLS) techniques. Parameters of the same specifications[16] were estimated for all five renter submarkets and five owner submarkets in 1960 (using a sample of thirty-six SMSAs) and again in 1970, and in 1975–76 (using a different sample of thirty-eight SMSAs). The results closely corresponded with our a priori expectations: of the statistically significant coefficients for which strong priors were held, over 92% were of the predicted sign in the demand equations, and 100% were so in the supply equations. The market-period demand equations showed a great deal of coefficient stability across the three samples, while the supply equations demonstrated more of the expected variability. On average, each submarket demand equation explained half the variation in the dependent variable; the comparable figure for the supply equations was 99%. The complete results of the demand estimates are presented in table 14.2, and those for the supply estimates are presented in table 14.3.

14.4.1 Demand Estimations

Our variables which measured perhaps the most powerful determinant of housing demand—income distribution of households—consistently proved the most statistically significant correlate of occupancy proportions in the given submarket, ST_{ijk}.[17] The coefficient of Y_{ijk} was the expected positive sign and significantly different from zero in at least half of all the submarket market-period demand equations for all three samples/periods.

Our attempts to capture the spirit of cross-SMSA differences in housing preferences was less successful: few coefficients of the age-composition variables ($A034_k$, $A65P_k$) were statistically significant. They clearly represent a much too crude measure of preferences, especially in periods when longer-term relationships between age, preferences, life-cycle stage, and permanent income expectations become disrupted, as they likely were in 1970–76.

The proportion of nonwhite households (NW_k) did, however, perform close to expectations, demonstrating consistent negative coefficients for owner submarket demands and positive coefficients for renters. This suggests that some amalgam of wealth differentials and/or discrimination associated with race was influential in shaping cross-tenure patterns of housing demand during the sampled periods. In addition, within the owner sector it appears that those forces have more severely reduced nonwhite occupancy of higher-quality submarkets, at least since 1970.

Of particular interest to us are the variables unique to our study which try to measure "prices" in the given submarket and in various "substitute" housing submarkets. We were most gratified to find that P_{ij}, the price per unit quality of housing in the given submarket relative to nonhousing goods' prices, performed as predicted, with statistical significance in about half the submarkets in all three samples. Note how there is a distinct pattern of *positive* coefficients in lower-quality submarkets within that tenure. This provides clear support for the proposition that lower-quality housing can be considered a "Giffen good." The higher the ratio of inferior-quality housing prices to prices of other goods, the more people will want to substitute toward the latter, and the way households substitute is precisely by consuming "less" (i.e., lower-quality) housing. But since some minimal amount of housing consumption is a necessity, the substitution possibilities are constrained in the lower-quality submarkets and quantities demanded thereby rise. Elasticities are large here: from 1 to 2 in renter submarket 2 and from 2 to 3 in renter submarket 1. In highest-quality submarkets, where greater possibilities for substitution exist, the conventional negative price effects are demonstrated. Elasticities are largest in owner submarkets 3 and 4—from -.4 to -1.0. Our second component of "price" in lowest-quality renter submarket 1, a proxy for search costs

Table 14.2. Market-Period Demand Equation Coefficients

	1960 Market Period									
	Owner Submarkets					Renter Submarkets				
	1	2	3	4	5	1	2	3	4	5
P	−.049	−.003	.016	−.059	−.100	.135	.037	.049	−.022	−.095
	(.87)	(.08)	(.42)	(.89)	(2.35)[b]	(2.27)[b]	(1.15)	(1.49)*	(.73)	(1.80)[b]
PU	.134	.364	−.061	.184	—	.519	.087	−.120	−.182	—
	(1.04)	(2.40)[b]	(.46)	(.56)		(3.08)[a]	(.58)	(.86)	(.87)	
PL	—	−.028	−.146	.453	.116	—	−.084	−.079	−.053	−.271
		(.36)	(.86)	(1.41)[c]	(1.00)		(1.06)	(.88)	(.47)	(1.61)[c]
PA	.108	.010	.086	.123	.116	.092	.057	.128	.192	.138
	(.77)	(.19)	(1.68)[c]	(1.59)[c]	(1.90)[b]	(1.60)[c]	(2.05)[b]	(3.59)[a]	(6.08)[a]	(3.67)[a]
Y	.338	−.242	.218	.164	1.31	2.19	.255	.519	−.239	.646
	(2.06)[b]	(.93)	(1.04)	(.36)	(3.03)[a]	(2.00)[b]	(.84)	(1.72)[b]	(.80)	(2.55)[a]
NW	−.220	−.119	−.001	.087	−.070	.143	.136	.108	.055	.004
	(1.72)[c]*	(1.83)[c]*	(.02)	(.72)	(.83)	(1.32)[c]	(2.59)[a]	(2.66)[a]	(1.08)	(.06)
*A*034	.065	.102	.050	−.278	−.042	.109	−.144	−.249	−.099	.044
	(.26)	(1.04)	(.40)	(1.14)	(.27)	(.48)	(1.29)	(2.54)[b]*	(.99)	(.33)
A65P	−.045	.126	.235	.010	−.057	−.002	−.050	−.163	−.081	.124
	(.13)	(1.12)	(1.68)[c]	(.04)	(.29)	(.01)	(.39)	(1.55)[c]	(.84)	(.73)
IV	—	—	—	—	—	−.003	—	—	—	—
						(1.22)				
IVU	—	—	—	—	—	.004	—	—	—	—
						(1.56)[c]				
C	.058	.122	.025	.223	.117	−.232	.032	.062	.178	.042
	(.56)	(1.53)*	(.30)	(1.69)*	(1.66)*	(1.91)[c]*	(.92)	(1.52)*	(2.28)[b]*	(.72)
R^2	.43	.49	.46	.16	.55	.29	.49	.63	.76	.51

Table 14.2. continued

	1970 Market Period									
	Owner Submarkets					Renter Submarkets				
	1	2	3	4	5	1	2	3	4	5
P	.038	.079	.041	−.144	−.065	.173	.037	.047	−.019	−.020
	(.94)	(1.55)*	(.75)	(2.01)[b]	(1.38)[c]	(5.57)[a]	(2.62)[b]*	(2.62)[b]*	(.52)	(.76)
PU	.245	−.277	.265	.455	—	.223	−.066	−.068	.06	—
	(1.42)[c]	(3.35)[a]*	(3.47)[a]	(3.19)[a]		(1.45)[c]	(1.17)	(1.05)	(.47)	
PL	—	.111	.066	.203	.064	—	.126	.038	−.133	−.106
		(.68)	(1.16)	(1.61)[c]	(.77)		(2.61)[a]	(.52)	(.98)	(1.06)
PA	.062	.041	−.013	−.160	−.143	−.057	.076	.089	.217	.041
	(.86)	(.61)	(.24)	(2.12)[b]*	(2.42)[b]*	(.81)	(2.73)[a]	(2.78)[a]	(3.69)[a]	(.93)
Y	.011	.004	.007	.011	.004	.022	.011	.007	−.001	.002
	(3.44)[a]	(1.14)	(2.24)[b]	(2.51)[b]	(1.71)[b]	(4.61)[a]	(3.72)[a]	(3.06)[a]	(.04)	(1.01)
NW	−.133	−.078	−.103	−.354	−.155	.038	.069	.039	−.123	.008
	(1.17)	(.79)	(1.21)	(3.24)[a]	(2.23)[b]	(.42)	(1.79)[b]	(.82)	(1.46)*	(.12)
A034	−.456	−.006	.081	−.021	−.181	−.188	−.093	−.142	−.089	.190
	(1.59)[c]	(.03)	(.43)	(.08)	(1.08)	(.82)	(.79)	(1.26)	(.43)	(1.21)
A65P	−.758	.319	.230	−.355	−.314	−.503	−.163	−.027	−.104	−.344
	(1.49)*	(1.02)	(.87)	(.85)	(1.20)	(1.39)[c]	(.87)	(.17)	(.36)	(1.44)[c]
IV	—	—	—	—	—	−.018	—	—	—	—
						(2.11)[b]				
IVU	—	—	—	—	—	.000	—	—	—	—
						(.12)				
C	−.242	.006	−.488	−.260	.332	−.356	−.156	−.076	.078	.125
	(1.28)	(.021)	(2.39)[b]*	(.76)	(3.01)[a]*	(2.16)[b]*	(1.69)*	(.74)	(.31)	(.82)
R^2	.52	.43	.63	.60	.30	.69	.68	.62	.41	.44

1975–76 Market Period

	Owner Submarkets					Renter Submarkets				
	1	2	3	4	5	1	2	3	4	5
P	−.012	−.002	.034	−.067	−.095	.110	.083	.020	−.008	−.012
	(.24)	(.08)	(.82)	(1.85)[b]	(3.25)[a]	(4.27)[a]	(3.72)[a]*	(.64)	(.16)	(.41)
PU	.127	.139	.098	.353	—	.253	.387	−.289	.099	—
	(.86)	(1.41)[c]	(.87)	(3.63)[a]		(2.82)[a]	(2.80)[a]	(2.12)[b]*	(.77)	
PL	—	−.017	.017	.235	.132	—	.048	.096	.065	.040
		(.38)	(.26)	(2.32)[b]	(2.33)[b]		(.85)	(.98)	(.31)	(.56)
PA	.055	−.026	.013	−.017	−.076	.007	−.027	.084	.197	−.024
	(.44)	(.59)	(.18)	(.26)	(1.68)*	(.13)	(.72)	(1.64)[c]	(2.24)[b]	(.53)
Y	−.001	.003	.009	.007	.006	.009	.013	.000	.002	.001
	(.18)	(1.33)[c]	(2.23)[b]	(2.86)[a]	(3.40)[a]	(3.33)[a]	(4.11)[a]	(.03)	(.53)	(.82)
NW	.031	−.121	−.115	−.157	−.083	.078	.129	.001	−.135	.117
	(.24)	(2.50)[b]*	(1.23)	(2.42)[b]	(1.71)[b]	(1.19)	(3.13)[a]	(.01)	(1.55)*	(2.24)[b]*
A034	.102	−.366	.186	−.149	−.057	.400	−.201	−.098	−.211	.255
	(.31)	(3.09)[a]*	(.88)	(.88)	(.48)	(2.36)[b]	(1.60)*	(.68)	(.92)	(1.78)[b]
A65P	.436	.023	.575	−.005	−.361	.499	−.541	.224	−.166	−.390
	(.77)	(.12)	(1.77)[b]	(.01)	(1.94)[c]*	(1.79)[c]*	(2.33)[b]	(1.10)	(.51)	(1.76)[b]
IV	—	—	—	—	—	−.011	—	—	—	—
						(2.24)[b]				
IVU	—	—	—	—	—	.029	—	—	—	—
						(1.17)				
DUM76	−.011	−.003	−.002	.005	−.003	.003	.004	−.005	−.001	.086
	(.61)	(.52)	(.18)	(.60)	(.44)	(.29)	(.59)	(.63)	(.04)	(.81)
C	−.146	.067	−.374	−.403	.176	−.629	−.429	.139	−.197	.032
	(.50)	(.47)	(1.46)*	(1.41)*	(1.66)*	(3.85)[a]*	(2.82)[a]*	(.65)	(.54)	(.22)
R^2	.18	.67	.53	.59	.63	.64	.55	.45	.27	.68

Note: t-statistics are in parentheses.

[a]Coefficient statistically significant at 1% level (one-tail test).

[b]Coefficient statistically significant at 5% level (one-tail test).

[c]Coefficient statistically significant at 10% level (one-tail test).

*Two-tail test if opposite predicted sign or no predicted sign.

Table 14.3. Market-Period Supply Equation Coefficients

	1960 Market Period									
	Owner Submarkets					Renter Submarket				
	1	2	3	4	5	1	2	3	4	5
P	.003	.002	.002	.002	.003	.002	.001	.007	.013	.006
	(1.68)[b]	(1.89)[b]	(1.01)	(.92)	(1.56)[c]	(.45)	(.20)	(1.29)	(2.26)[b]	(1.12)
DPOP	−.002	−.002	−.004	−.009	−.006	−.001	−.004	−.003	−.005	−.004
	(1.98)[b]	(3.11)[a]	(3.74)[a]	(6.16)[a]	(6.97)[a]	(.77)	(2.19)[b]	(1.62)[c]	(3.81)[a]	(2.76)[a]
DP	.000	−.001	−.001	−.008	−.001	.003	.007	−.004	−.011	−.010
	(.14)	(.24)	(.42)	(2.07)[b]	(.53)	(.54)	(.81)	(.50)	(1.55)[c]	(1.63)[c]
TT	.975	.964	.944	.999	.989	.929	.914	.959	.953	.926
	(178.)[a]	(112.)[a]								
		.001	.004	−.003	−.003	−.002	−.002	−.008	−.010	−.002
	(1.00)	(.70)	(1.12)	(1.01)	(1.31)*	(.91)	(.49)	(1.59)*	(2.14)[b]*	(.47)
R^2	.99	.99	.99	.99	.99	.99	.98	.98	.99	.99

	1970 Market Period									
	Owner Submarkets					Renter Submarket				
	1	2	3	4	5	1	2	3	4	5
P	−.001	.001	.002	.001	.000	.010	.003	.002	.004	.004
	(.28)	(.56)	(1.76)[b]	(.63)	(.24)	(3.27)[a]	(1.50)[c]	(.51)	(1.16)	(.66)
DPOP	−.000	−.001	.001	−.007	−.005	.000	−.005	−.001	−.004	−.004
	(.34)	(.84)	(.63)	(7.43)[a]	(6.16)[a]	(.02)	(2.48)[a]	(.43)	(1.09)	(.99)
DP	.002	.003	−.000	.003	.002	.002	.001	−.000	.005	−.010
	(1.34)*	(1.85)[c]*	(.01)	(1.43)*	(.99)	(.27)	(.26)	(.01)	(.66)	(.88)

TT	.989	.991	.993	.993	.998	.902	.954	.990	.973	.927
	(338.)[a]	(283.)[a]	(267.)[a]	(298.)[a]	(185.)[a]	(95.1)[a]	(67.9)[a]	(56.5)[a]	(75.3)[a]	(34.1)[a]
C	.000	.000	−.002	.001	−.000	−.011	−.004	−.005	−.007	−.003
	(.24)	(.03)	(1.66)[a]	(.53)	(.22)	(3.38)[a]*	(1.72)[c]*	(1.66)*	(1.88)[c]*	(.42)
R^2	.99	.99	.99	.99	.99	.99	.99	.99	99	.98

1975–76 Market Period

	Owner Submarkets					Renter Submarkets				
	1	2	3	4	5	1	2	3	4	5
P	.002	.001	−.002	−.000	.001	.002	.001	.002	.005	.002
	(1.59)[c]	(.82)	(1.42)*	(.22)	(.72)	(.79)	(.68)	(1.10)	(2.79)[a]	(.40)
DPOP	.001	−.002	−.013	−.013	−.011	.006	.002	−.008	−.002	−.011
	(.27)	(.89)	(4.04)[a]	(4.03)[a]	(3.62)[a]	(.77)	(.58)	(1.43)[c]	(2.67)[a]	(.71)
DP	.003	−.001	−.000	.002	.001	.008	.002	.004	.003	.001
	(1.34)*	(.96)	(.15)	(1.11)	(.58)	(1.65)*	(.74)	(1.30)	(.95)	(.10)
TT	.984	.989	.985	.987	.984	.905	.957	.939	.952	.853
	(182.)[a]	(155.)[a]	(167.)[a]	(142.)[a]	(133.)[a]	(67.2)[a]	(92.3)[a]	(66.2)[a]	(99.9)[a]	(33.6)[a]
DUM76	.000	.001	.001	.001	.001	.001	.000	−.000	.001	.004
	(.65)	(2.94)[a]*	(2.42)[b]*	(1.68)*	(1.96)[c]*	(.60)	(.12)	(.45)	(.83)	(2.27)[b]*
C	−.004	−.001	.002	.000	−.001	−.004	−.003	−.002	−.006	.004
	(2.45)[b]*	(.88)	(1.46)*	(.16)	(.75)	(1.58)*	(2.00)[c]*	(.93)	(2.54)[b]*	(.51)
R^2	.99	.99	.99	.99	.99	.99	.99	.99	.99	.99

Note: t-statistics are in parentheses.
[a]Coefficient statistically significant at 1% level (one-tail test).
[b]Coefficient statistically significant at 5% level (one-tail test).
[c]Coefficient statistically significant at 10% level (one-tail test).
*Two-tail test if opposite predicted sign or no predicted sign.

(IV_{ijk}), proved statistically significant only in 1960, although the comparative costs of search in renter submarkets 2 and 3 (IVU_{ijk}) showed the expected relationship to ST_{1Rk} in both 1970 and 1975–76. As a whole, these results indicate dramatically different price sensitivities in different sectors of the market, thereby challenging previous works that have attempted to estimate "the" elasticity for an unstratified market (see ch. 2).

The coefficients of variables denoting relative prices between adjacent quality submarkets within the same tenure (PU_{ijk}, PL_{ijk}) were statistically significant with the expected positive sign in only a minority of the submarkets for all samples.[18] However, a noteworthy pattern of results occurred for upper-quality (4, 5) owner submarkets, where statistically significant positive coefficients were demonstrated in all periods, and suggested cross elasticities to prices in higher and lower submarkets of about 2 and 1, respectively. A consistently significant coefficient (and usually with the largest magnitude) for *PU* occurred in the lowest-quality renter submarket and indicated a cross-price elasticity of over 3. Together these results suggest that there is indeed some degree of intersubmarket price sensitivity on the part of housing demanders, at least at the extreme ends of the tenure/quality submarket spectrum. This confirms our theoretical prediction that occurrences in one submarket are transmitted to others through the altered behaviors of households, but with the strength of the transmission nonuniform across submarkets.

While this evidence about own-price and cross-price sensitivities provides strong support for our theory, a caution must be forwarded. A consistent difficulty we faced was the persistent lack of substantial variation on our measures of housing prices, either across submarkets or across SMSAs, as well as high degrees of intercorrelations between submarket prices. However, that any price coefficients emerged statistically significant under these circumstances of suspected multicollinearity provides testimony to the power of the approach.

The results of the variables serving as proxies for cross-tenure price differentials proved most stable in the renter submarkets. In all three periods, a curvilinear pattern across quality levels emerged: *PA* coefficients (and their t-statistics) grow larger with quality level, reach a maximum at submarket 4, then decline. This suggests that households who most likely occupy renter submarket 4 are those who have the economic wherewithal to be on the margin of homeownership; they are most sensitive to relative price changes in owner submarkets (a cross-tenure price elasticity of approximately 2). By contrast, most potential occupants of the more expensive, level-5 renter submarket probably can afford to own, but choose not to do so for nonfinancial reasons; they are thus less sensitive to cross-tenure changes in affordability. Potential renters in lower-quality submarkets are similarly less sensitive, but only because homeownership is typically beyond their means, regardless of typical variations in relative prices of owner-occupied homes.

From the perspective of owner submarkets, the converse arguments were not supported. Lower-quality owner submarket occupancies were not sensitive to relative rents in rental submarkets, and inconsistent results emerged for upper-quality owner submarkets over the three sample periods. One possible explanation is that the *PA* variable may have been picking up a growing influence of *asset* demands for housing, as opposed to the *pure* consumption demands. In 1960, with little home price inflation, actual (and potential) owners may have been more sensitive to the pure consumption price of both tenures. The 1970s witnessed the inception of unprecedented inflation of owner-occupied home prices and subsequent stronger demands for owner-occupancy as a vehicle for reaping capital gains. Comparatively higher prices of units in high-quality owner submarkets compared to those in renter submarkets thus might signal to current owners here enhanced possibilities for such capital gains (see ch. 4). This could conspire to produce the observed negative coefficient in 1970 and 1975–76 upper-quality owner submarkets.

14.4.2 Supply Estimations

As expected, the total housing stock in the given submarket relative to the total number of households (TT_{ijk}) dominated the market-period supply estimates, leaving little residual variation in ST_{ijk} to be explained by the other variables (see table 14.3). It is not surprising, then, that our holding cost variable, the price of housing in the given submarket relative to nonhousing goods (P_{ijk}), demonstrated the expected statistically significant positive sign in only about a third of the submarkets in all samples. Even in these cases, the implied supply elasticities were very low—all renter and owner submarkets below .2 and .02, respectively.

Also disappointing (though not unexpected) was the performance of our expectational variables. The proportional changes in SMSA population during the prior medium-run period ($DPOP_k$) proved to have the predicted negative coefficients in 80% of the submarkets in the 1960 sample, but this number dropped dramatically in the latter periods' samples. We interpret this as resulting from the radically different suppliers' expectations vis-à-vis demography which arose from the entrance of the baby boomers into the housing market in these latter periods. Of course, $DPOP_k$ is a crude proxy of the more particular, disaggregated demographic trends that may influence suppliers in different submarkets.

More confounding was the switch in coefficient signs for the previous period's change in housing versus nonhousing prices: from the expected significant negative sign in upper-quality submarkets in 1960, to no negative and several modestly significant *positive* signs in lower-quality submarkets in 1970 and 1975–76. Inasmuch as this variable deals with only the hypothetical dwelling unit having the SMSA median characteristics, it is undoubtedly a weak proxy for suppliers' future price expectations in particular submarkets. Further, whatever expectations might be conveyed by this variable are likely confounded by the fact that each of our "snapshot" observations of market periods represents a distinctive period of general economic activity, especially in the housing market. Some of the key items for comparison are summarized in table 14.4. The year 1960 culminated a noninflationary, modest growth period; prior upward trends in the relative returns from housing probably conveyed the hypothesized expectation of continued stable appreciation and hence higher current reservation prices (and thus lower supplies). On the other hand, 1970 capped off a period of unprecedented growth and incipient inflationary pressures. Higher relative prices for *average* units in an SMSA may have been interpreted as a sign of growing household affluence, whence suppliers in lower-quality submarkets would have less incentive to withhold units for speculative purposes. Stagflation and ultimately recession occurred during the period 1970–75, and much of the boost in average house prices was fueled by the aforementioned asset demand for high-quality, owner-occupied units. Once again, suppliers in lower-quality levels must have interpreted such inflation as a sign of further weakness in their submarkets. These conjectures are not completely satisfying, of course, since they should also imply strongly negative coefficients for DP_k in upper-quality submarkets which were not, in fact, observed.

A final suggestion of the difficulty in modeling suppliers' expectations is provided by the results of the dummy variable denoting 1976 in the pooled 1975–76 sample (*DUM76*). The coefficient of this variable was significantly positive in almost half of the submarkets (especially owner tenure). From certain data one could judge that, compared to 1975, 1976 was a good year for housing: starts were up 380,000 units; public housing was being phased out; and vacancy rates were falling generally (see table 14.4). Yet apparently, sup-

Table 14.4. Selected Data for Market Periods Analyzed

	1960	1970	1975	1976
Starts of new privately owned structures (millions)				
Total	1.25	1.43	1.16	1.54
Single-family	1.01	.82	.90	1.17
Multifamily	.24	.61	.26	.32
% Multifamily	20%	43%	33%	24%
Starts of new publicly owned structures (thousands)	44	35	11	10
Boeckh index of construction costs (small residential structures); 1967 = 100	81.8	122.4	183.5	198.6
Vacancy rates in SMSAs				
Renter	6.5%	4.9%	6.1%	5.7%
Owner	1.2%	1.0%	1.3%	1.2%

pliers of existing units, especially owner-occupants, were more pessimistic or less inclined to speculate. Two possible lines of reasoning seem plausible. One is that suppliers have adaptive expectations, that is, their perceptions are altered with a substantial lag. This would mean that 1976 expectations were shaped by the disastrous economic performance of 1974–75, not the contemporaneous upturn. The other argument is that suppliers perceived the strong resurgence of single-family home construction (up 30% from 1975–76; see table 14.4) as an indicator of intensified competition and a looser future resale market. In any event, the only clear result is that suppliers' expectations are extremely difficult to model, and our specification did not prove very robust in its attempt to do so.[19]

14.5 Conclusion

Our exploration into the market-period demand and supply relationships in a cross-section of SMSAs provided strong support for our theory. Short-run supply decisions were, as expected, overwhelmingly dominated by the size of the existing stock. But current submarket prices were often statistically significant as well, suggesting that although supply is very inelastic there is some distribution of reservation prices across owners. We could discern little convincing evidence on the role of expectations, undoubtedly due to our crude proxies for such. It is, perhaps, beyond the capabilities of such an aggregate model employing five- or ten-year data intervals to capture the intertemporal pattern of dynamic forces that produce particular sorts of owner expectations.

Estimates of market-period demand functions offered especially provocative insights into cross-submarket relationships. Distribution of demands across the quality spectrum depended not only upon household income distribution and racial composition of the SMSA, but also on the array of submarket prices. Prices in a given submarket, relative to the price of nonhousing goods, generally were inversely (and strongly) related to the proportional share of demands allocated to that submarket. But this relationship was reversed in lowest-quality renter submarkets, indicating that such dwellings can be considered Giffen goods. For households consuming in the upper-quality owner submarkets and those in the lower-quality renter submarkets, prices of units in near-quality submarkets proved to be directly related to demand shares in the given submarket, as would be predicted for substitute commodities. Finally, average prices of rental submarkets were directly (and strongly) related to occupancy levels in (especially middle-quality) owner submarkets, suggesting that many households' tenure choices are, indeed, affected by short-term market conditions which alter the relative tenure costs.

The central conclusion is that our tests have demonstrated the undesirability of suppressing housing-quality differences and aggregating submarkets into a single, undifferentiated market for "urban housing." Especially, there is not a single demand function for housing that gives a relationship between occupancies and "the" price of housing services. Rather, there are dramatically different demand relationships across the housing quality/tenure spectrum. These are characterized by own-price, cross-submarket price, and cross-tenure price relationships that are distinct in both direction and magnitude. These findings support our theoretical proposition that submarkets are linked in systematic but nonuniform ways through the responses of demanders to prices in their own and in other submarkets.

Notes

1. In order to obtain an adequate sample size, observations for SMSAs sampled in both 1975 and 1976 in the Annual Housing Survey were employed as our "end period" data.

2. Which is itself specified in terms of rooms, condition and age, stratified by tenure and region; see ch. 13.

3. These assumptions are investigated empirically in ch. 13.

4. Theoretical models where owners choose various mixes of capital and operating inputs have been developed by Ingram and Kain 1973 and Ingram and Oron 1977.

5. Alternatively, ST_{ijk} is that portion of all SMSA k's occupied units which are in submarket ij.

6. Empirical findings by Weinberg and Atkinson 1979 and Weisbrod and Vidal 1981 attest to the importance of search costs for low-income households.

7. Other potentially important demographic characteristics, especially family size, are not included due to the lack of statistical significance in preliminary estimates of aggregate demand equations.

8. For evidence on the above differentials, see Kain and Quigley 1975; Galster 1979; and Yinger et al. 1979.

9. In the combined 1975–76 sample demand equation, a dummy variable was added to denote 1976 observations.

10. See Wienk et al. 1979; Yinger et al. 1979; Newberger 1984; and Galster 1988a for evidence.

11. See Wheaton 1977; and Galster 1979, 1980 for evidence.

12. For reviews of a variety of empirical studies which have arrived at this conclusion, see Yinger et al. 1979.

13. It does become vertical, of course, at that quantity where the entire stock has been offered for occupancy.

14. This assumption is supported by a study in the 1950s that found no systematic differences between the property values reported by owners of single-family houses and valuations of the same houses by professional appraisers; see Lansing and Kish 1954.

15. In the 1975–76 supply equations, a dummy variable denoting 1976 observations was also included.

16. The one exception being the 1975–76 runs where an added dummy variable, *DUM*76, was added to distinguish 1976 observations in the pooled 1975–76.

17. Overall explanatory power of the demand equation regressions was generally in the $R^2 = .4 - .7$ range. Exceptionally low R^2 were obtained for renter 1 and owner 4 submarkets in 1960, owner 5 in 1970, and owner 1 and 4 in 1975–76.

18. Two emerged with the opposite sign and were statistically significant.

19. This difficulty in adequately modeling suppliers' expectations is endemic in the housing literature; see Galster 1987: ch. 7.

15 Cross-SMSA Model: Medium-Run Supply

This sector of our cross-SMSA model attempts to describe somewhat longer-run (five- to ten-year) changes in the demand for and resulting supply of housing units in each submarket than the market-period (short-run) model of chapter 14. Two such "medium-run" periods are considered here—1960–70 and 1970–1975/76. Our task is to model the forces which determine how the stocks of units in different tenure/quality submarkets are altered by suppliers over such medium-run periods—what we have called the stock adjustment process. More specifically, we seek to explain both the total changes in stocks of all ten tenure/quality submarkets from 1960–70 and from 1970–1975/76 due to new construction and net conversion modes of supply response, and the composition of such changes in terms of those modes.

15.1 Overview

In brief, our model sees end-of-period stocks as jointly determined by within-period demand changes, beginning-of-period housing capital stocks, and the economic, technical, and institutional forces which shape the production, modification, and destruction of residential structures. Changes in strength and submarket distribution of demands are determined by changes in the (number and composition of) population and in the distribution of income. The stock of housing units in each submarket is altered by removals of existing units, conversions of existing units to and from other submarkets, and the construction of new units. The supply changes, other than new construction, are strongly shaped by the number and attributes of the beginning-of-period stock. Also, there are strong interactions among the submarkets due to the conversion flexibility of the existing stock and the competition among submarkets for new construction inputs—land, capital, materials, labor, and so forth.

15.1.1 Alternative Supplying Groups

The stock adjustments occurring are the result of actions by two groups of potential suppliers, as we saw in chapter 5. One *builds new units* at various tenure/quality levels and the other *converts existing units* from one tenure/

quality level to another. While both groups would respond in broadly similar patterns to perceived differences in rates of return, there are some systematic differences between the two that produce empirical implications for us here.

Builders of new dwellings compare expected rates of return on total construction costs in different tenure/quality levels to those which can be had in nonhousing investments, that is, the cost of capital to the housing industry. Potential converters (i.e., owners of existing units) compare these rates of return to that expected by maintaining their units in the same submarket and also to those in nonhousing investments, but only for the incremental capital costs of any contemplated conversion. The greater the positive differential between a destination and origin submarket rate of return, the greater the probability that any member of the original group will transform capital from the origin to the destination submarket. While, in general, builders must obtain a positive differential in rate of return between that in the target housing submarket and that in nonhousing investment to produce an adjustment response, this need not be the case for converters. Owners may convert their units to a submarket which promises a smaller negative return than either maintaining or abandoning their property, as long as the net gain outweighs the opportunity cost of any conversion capital required.

For both types of suppliers the expected revenue component of an expected rate of return is the same: a composite of expected price (or capitalized rental stream) and expected vacancy rate. But the expected cost component differs for the two. The cost to a builder for any target type of unit is simply the cost of constructing it with presumably the least-cost input combination. But to a converter, the cost for the same target type depends not only on the prices of conversion inputs but also on the nature of the converter's *existing* unit, which technologically determines the magnitude and the composition of the inputs which must be committed. The past exerts constraints, therefore, on the present conversion adjustment processes through its legacy of the imperfectly malleable stock of capital embedded in existing units. Faced with the same market adjustment signals, converters may well make different adjustment choices than builders because the former's relative costs for given destinations will generally differ from the latter's.

15.1.2 On the Nature of Medium-Run Supply Adjustments

Although the period of stock adjustments in this model is five to ten years, an interval that is long enough for most industries fully to adjust their stocks of capital assets, the housing supply relationships in our model are not true long-run supply functions. They are, rather, a form of medium-run function because the great durability and almost total immobility of residential structures effectively prevent suppliers, as a group, from completely adjusting their "fixed" costs over a decade (full adjustability of all costs being an essential attribute of a true long-run supply relationship). They are to be distinguished from the market-period supply functions discussed in chapter 14, in which stocks are fixed. We refer to them as medium-run stock supply functions to emphasize their length and distinctness from short-run or market-period supply functions.

In the period of five to ten years the adjustability of supply to changing market circumstances is constrained in a number of ways. First, while existing housing units can be physically modified by conversion processes, they effectively cannot be moved to a different neighborhood or location. The attempt to have them offer housing services at particular different quality levels or various nonhousing services (i.e., to retire them from the housing sector) incurs costs that depend not so much on the target submarket—as with new construction—as on the discrepancy between that target level and the quality and character of the preexisting unit. The ease of different patterns of conversion thus *depends on the nature of the existing stock.*

Second, both new construction and most forms of conversion are often limited in the aggregate by resource limitations. Sometimes this involves supply bottlenecks in construction materials and labor. More frequently, it involves a quantity limitation of funds available to be loaned for construction, conversion, and ownership tenure (i.e., building and improvement loan funds). So all forms of supply activity *compete* with one another for resources that may be sticky in forthcoming or absolutely limited. Moreover, new construction requires empty land. This can only come from preexisting vacant areas or by demolishing existing structures to create vacant areas. Preexisting vacant acreage does not normally replicate supplier-desired neighborhood and locational characteristics, and demolition is quite costly.

In sum, the preexistence of durable housing units embeds capital in forms that are not as malleable as uncommitted capital, and which compete with the latter for the scarce resources being bid away from nonhousing used in adjusting to changed market conditions. New construction generally requires more new inputs per housing unit than conversion. On the other hand, the conversion more usually simply shifts existing units from one quality submarket to another. This judgment is not inevitable: new construction can decrease the size of the housing stock if it causes the demolition of more preexisting units than it adds; conversion can increase the stock if it takes the form of subdividing large existing units into a greater number of smaller units.

Because of the cost constraints in conversion and the limitations on availability of key inputs necessary to produce housing in particular submarkets or in the market as a whole during the decade, economic rents can accrue to holders of housing assets over significant periods. Because of the durability of housing assets, these returns can be gained from speculative holding of assets in the present in anticipation of attractive future prospects, as well as by supplying appropriate new units when that future comes. So speculative as well as "current" motives can figure importantly in suppliers' decisions to alter their present holdings of housing stock. Our model must therefore take account of the role of present and anticipated capital gains in determining the medium-run behavior of both types of suppliers.

In view of the role of expectational aspects of supplier behavior it is, perhaps, unfortunate that our model does not include some direct measures of rents, prices, and quantities demanded *during* the period. Such measures were not available for all of the sample SMSAs. Instead, we measure demand pressures on the market over the period (and, implicitly, changes in these price variables) by the horizontal shift in the demand function for each submarket for the whole medium-run period. This is discussed in detail below. While we believe that shorter-term dynamics may affect the ultimate supply response, it seems reasonable to assume that, to a first approximation, dynamics do not matter very much so long as *sustained* demand pressures are included, that is, that shorter-term variations in prices and quantities net out over the course of a decade. Inasmuch as suppliers themselves are interested primarily in anticipated longer-term demand prospects because of the great durability of their assets, this assumption does not seem to be overly strong or restrictive.

For any given market forces signaling a stock adjustment to generally higher quality, new construction and conversions are competitive modes of securing the desired change. Thus the response of one supply mode in a given submarket depends partly on the response of the other mode that is forthcoming. While strictly speaking there may be different response lags across modes, these become blurred when viewed from our five- or ten-year change perspective, and it may be more reasonable to treat the medium-run responses as being simultaneously determined. This proved unsuccessful in earlier trial estimations of our model using two-stage least squares, however. Our final adjustment response equations are, therefore, modeled without (endogenous) opposite-mode response variables, so the specter of omitted variable bias must be recognized.

Similarly, the theory would suggest that new construction and conversion supply responses in *all* ten tenure/quality submarkets should be modeled simultaneously. While in principle this may be an attractive notion, in fact limitations of our data base resulting in the under identification of such a system made it impossible to do so in practice.

15.2 Specification of Stock Supply Equations

15.2.1 Dependent Variables

Two equations are modeled for each of the ten tenure/quality submarkets. One is a stock supply equation, discussed here; the other is a stock-supply-mode mix equation, considered in section 15.3 below. The former has as *dependent variable* the *proportional net change* in the total (occupied and vacant) stock in the given *ij* submarket during the medium-run time period under consideration, $PSTK_{ijk}$ (a period either 1960–70 or 1979–75). This is our measure of medium-run "stock supply." The net change here refers to within-period new construction in *ij* (NEW_{ijk}) plus net conversions (CON_{ijk}), where CON_{ijk} is conversions of units into *ij* less conversions of units out of *ij* to another submarket, plus demolitions, mergers, losses to nonresidential uses, and abandonment. That is, $PSTK_{ijk} = (NEW_{ijk} + CON_{ijk})/STK'_{ijk}$ where STK'_{ijk} is the total beginning-of-period stock in the market. (For convenience, these and all other variable names are defined in table 15.1).

15.2.2 Right-Hand Exogenous Variables: Expected Revenues

The first key set of right-hand variables common to all stock supply equations is designed to measure the revenue dimension of the expected rate of return as perceived by suppliers during the period. This is modeled in each of the $PSTK_{ijk}$ equations by a series of exogenous "proportional demand shift" variables which were constructed as proxies for the general degree of market tightness (i.e., high prices, low vacancy rates) in the various tenure/quality submarkets during the period. More specifically, these variables represent the *predicted, exogenous,* within-period changes in demand, as a proportion of the initial stock in the given submarket. They are generated using the estimated coefficients of the appropriate short-run demand equation presented in chapter 14, when all endogenous price and vacancy rate variables are held constant at their beginning-of-period levels, but end-of-period values are inserted for the exogenous income and demographic variables.

Clearly, some measures of actual prices in different submarkets during the decade would have been desirable, but none was available. Furthermore, we believe the observed short-run prices observed at both end points of the decade provide highly misleading signals of revenues expected and actually received during the decade. We have, therefore, constructed these "proportional demand shift" variables out of variables that would more adequately reflect the strength of exogenous demand pressures (and hence revenue expectations) in the market over an extended period.

Thus the proportional medium-run demand shifts, X_{ijk}, are defined as

$$X_{ijk} = [\hat{f}_{ij}(P'_{ijk}, PU'_{ijk}, PL'_{ijk}, PA'_{j*ijk}, Y_{ijk}, NW_k, A034_k, A65P_k)H_k - STK'_{ijk}]/STK'_{ijk},$$

where $\hat{f}_{ij}$ is the estimated market-period demand function (see ch. 14), H is the total number of households in SMSA k at the end of the period, STK is the housing stock at the beginning of the period, and the prime (′) denotes a beginning-of-period observation; all other variables are measured at the end of the period. The first term within the brackets provides an estimate of the proportion of all households in SMSA k who would choose to occupy submarket *ij*, given beginning-of-period prices in *all* submarkets and end-of-period household characteristics. It gives an estimation of the within-period (horizontal) demand shift in the submarket due purely to *exogenous* changes. These proportional demand shifts are designed to reflect average submarket demand conditions during the period. This is a desirable property for empirical modeling purposes. In contrast to these shifts, actual submarket prices and vacancies are, of course, determined jointly by supply and demand adjustments. The shift variables, on the other hand, are a measure of "pure" demand variations and as such indicate the profit opportunities available to suppliers in different submarkets, on average.

Various modifications and combinations of this set of X_{ijk} variables are specified as right-hand variables in the $PSTK_{ijk}$ equations:

XU_{ijk} (XLi_{jk}) Average proportional demand shift in upper- (lower-) adjacent submarket(s), relative to demand shift in given submarket *ij*, that is,

$$XU_{ijk} = (X_{i+1,jk} + X_{i+2,jk})/2X_{ijk} \text{ and}$$
$$XL_{ijk} = (X_{i-2,jk} + X_{i-1,jk})/2X_{ijk}.$$

(For submarkets at the ends of the quality hierarchy the appropriate truncations occur.) *XU* and *XL* attempt to measure the relative attractiveness of submarkets most likely to serve as substitutes within the same tenure. The proxy for relative attractiveness of cross-tenure supply substitutions is

$$XA_{j^*ijk} = \ldots X_{ij^*k}/5X_{ijk}, \qquad j^* = /\mathrm{j}.$$

Also included in the $PSTK_{ijk}$ equations to serve as proxies for prospective revenues are beginning-of-period "market-tightness indicators": P'_{ijk}, PU'_{ijk}, PL'_{ijk}, PA'_{j^*ijk}, where all are defined as in market-period demand equations. These are assumed to be predetermined (exogenous) variables for the periods in question (see table 15.1).

Finally, the revenues that can be expected by private housing suppliers, given a particular (X) vector, will be affected by the degree to which the *public sector* intervenes competitively in the market. These effects are complex and vary according to both the tenure/quality submarket and type of supply mode being considered. They are discussed in detail below.

Our measures for such public sector activity in the housing market vary slightly depending on the time period in question, due to varying data constraints:

PUB_{ijk} The number of public housing unit contracts let in SMSA *k* in 1959–67, relative to the 1960 total stock of housing in submarket *ijk*. For the 1970–75 period: the number of public housing units built in 1970–75, as a proportion of the 1970 total stock in *ijk*.

SUB_{ijk} The number of subsidized housing units (privately owned units built with federal subsidies)[1] that were constructed in SMSA *k* in 1970–75, as a proportion of the 1970 total stock of housing in submarket *ijk*.

The allocation of public and subsidized units to quality submarkets was based on our hedonic index applied to characteristics of the dwellings. This is, of course, risky inasmuch as it is doubtful that the parameters of the he-

Table 15.1. Variable Names and Definitions for Medium-Run Stock Supply

Name	Definition
CONijk	Conversions of units into submarket *ij*, less conversions of units out of *ij* to other submarkets, less demolitions, mergers, and losses to nonresidential uses of *ij*, less abandonment of *ij* units during medium-run period, i.e., net conversions in SMSA *k*.
NEWijk	Numbers of units built in *ij* during medium-run period, i.e., new construction in SMSA *k*.
STKijk	Total stock of units (occupied plus vacant) in submarket *ij* at beginning of period in SMSA *k*.
PSTKijk	Proportional change in total stock of units in *ij* during medium-run period, i.e., stock supply in SMSA *k*.
PMODEijk	Difference between new construction and net conversions in *ij* during period, relative to total stock in *ij* at beginning of period in SMSA *k*.
Hk	Number of households in SMSA *k* at the end of medium-run period.
Xijk	Estimated end-of-period excess of units in *ij* demanded over beginning-of-period stock in *ij*, expressed as a proportion of beginning-of-period stock, i.e., proportional demand shift in SMSA *k*.
XU'ijk, XL'ijk	Average of proportional demand shifts in upper (lower) adjacent-quality submarket(s), relative to proportional demand shift in submarket *ij* (in SMSA *k*).
*XA'j*ijk*	Average of proportional demand shifts in the five submarkets of the tenure opposite of *j*, relative to proportional demand shifts in *ij*.
P'ijk	Market value/hedonic value ratio at beginning of period in submarket *ij*, deflated by price of nonhousing goods in SMSA *k*; where value is defined appropriately as sales price or rent, according to tenure.
PU'ij, PL'ij	Average market value/hedonic value ratios in upper (lower) adjacent-quality submarket(s) in same tenure as *j*, relative to that ratio in *ij* (in SMSA *k*).
*PA'j*ijk*	Average of market value/hedonic value ratios in the five submarkets of the tenure opposite of *j*, relative to that ratio in *ij*.
PUBijk	Number of public housing units (contracts let during 1959–67 for 1960–70 period, actually built for 1970–75 period) added in medium-run period, relative to beginning-of-period stock in *ij* (in SMSA *k*).
SUBijk	Number of subsidized housing units (either interest, rent subsidies, or direct loans) built in 1970–75 relative to beginning-of-period stock in *ij* (in SMSA *k*).
SV'k	Median value of sites of newly constructed housing financed by FHA under sect. 203 at beginning of period (in SMSA *k*), in $1000.
CC'k	Dodge index of residential construction costs at beginning of period (in SMSA *k*).
DN'k	Population density; thousands of inhabitants per square mile in SMSA *k* at beginning of period.
SU'ijk, SL'ijk	Ratio of total housing stock in the upper (lower) adjacent-quality submarket in total stock in *ij* at the beginning of period (in SMSA *k*).
AGED'jk	Proportion of all units in same tenure as *ij* built before 1940 (in SMSA *k*).

donic index estimated from the whole range of private housing market data are appropriate for the type of structures typically involved in public sector interventions. Our delineation of public and subsidized units by quality thus represents a crude attempt to distinguish only large differences in their quality. Such governmental housing supply is assumed exogenous to our mode.

15.2.3 Right-Hand Exogenous Variables: Expected Costs

A variety of right-hand variables were used to measure the cost constraints faced by builders and converters in the medium-run stock adjustment period:

SV'_k Median value of sites of newly constructed housing financed by FHA under section 203 at the beginning of the period in *SMSA k;* a proxy for land acquisition costs for builders.

CC'_k Dodge index of residential construction costs at beginning of period in SMSA *k*.

DN'_k Population density; inhabitants per square mile for urbanized area at beginning of period in SMSA *k*; a proxy for site availability and/or cost.

SU'_{ijk} (SL'_{ijk}) The ratio of housing stocks in upper adjacent $i+1, j$ (lower adjacent $i-1, j$) submarkets to given submarket *ij* at beginning of period in SMSA *k;* a proxy for the availability of units that can be most easily converted into *ij*.

$AGED'_{jk}$ The proportion of *all* units in tenure *j* built before 1940 in SMSA *k;* a proxy for the relative costs of downgrading versus upgrading the stock.[2]

Since all these cost variables are defined for the beginning of the period in question, they are treated as predetermined (exogenous) right-hand variables. Thus, our general stock supply equation is specified as

$$(15.1)\quad \underline{PSTK}_{ijk} = h_{ij}\,(P'_{ijk}, PU'_{ijk}, PL'_{ijk}, PA'_{j*ijk}, X_{ijk}, XU_{ijk}, XL_{ijk}, XA_{j*ijk}, PUB_{ijk}, SUB_{ijk}, SU'_{ijk}, SL'_{ijk}, CC'_k, DN'_k, SV'_k, AGED'_{jk}),$$

where only the underlined variable is endogenous, and SUB_{ijk} is only available for the 1970–1975/76 period.

15.2.4 Cross-Submarket Differences in Supply Responses

Landlords and homeowners have important differences in both incentives and constraints with regard to their housing investment decisions, but these can be well characterized by differences in the influence on the two of them possessed by an essentially common set of explanatory variables (defined in equation 15.1 above), rather than by different variables operating on the two. To organize and explain these divergences we develop below separate models of rental and homeowner stock supply. Since these include stock adjustments in both new construction and conversion-demolition supply modes, we supplement these equations by a second set that determines the split between these two modes for each tenure/quality submarket. These latter equations are discussed in section 15.3 below. Before considering the idiosyncratic responses in both tenures, we provide an overview of the contrast in motivations and behaviors between them.

Our paradigm of *rental market stock supply* is that of builders and landlords who combine existing residential structures and land, construction inputs, and equity and borrowed capital to produce either new or converted housing stock in given rental submarkets sometime during the period. Each such supplier seeks to maximize the returns on the investment in a new structure or a conversion of an existing structure. These returns consist of the present capitalized value of expected returns derived from rents (net of operating costs) and expected future capital gains or losses. The opportunity cost for investment in one submarket is the return obtainable from other submarkets or from nonhousing sectors. In equilibrium, this equals the cost of obtaining loanable or equity funds for this submarket. In the aggregate, the suppliers who invest in a particular rental submarket during a period determine the number of dwelling units, or stock, in that submarket at the end of the period.

The *homeowner market supply* adjustment is similar to that for the rental market with respect to *new construction*. The capital subject to commitment in both is unspecialized and highly mobile, and the expected returns and costs are similar: all based on purely commercial considerations. With respect to conversion, however, they differ. The owners of rental property already in existence consider it solely as an asset in their portfolio indeed, and expect it to be occupied during their tenure of ownership by several households, who perhaps have significant differences in tastes. So the property is likely to be dealt with flexibly, with alert attention to changing market opportunities and a strong penchant for rapid and substantial adjustments in its use (via occupancy or quality level) to meet those changes. It is even likely to be physically formed to permit easy conversion in a variety of directions as conditions warrant, that is, it is likely to be quite standardized rather than idiosyncratic and custom-tailored.

The homeowner of an existing unit, on the other hand, has a double use of the property: it is both a portfolio asset and the source of the owner's current housing (see ch. 4). Conversion often requires that the homeowner move elsewhere to live, usually selling the first unit. But such a move and capital transaction are disruptive, costly, and time consuming. Moreover, the intimate relationship between ownership and owner consumption is likely to foster closer physical conformity of the dwelling to the particular preferences of the owner, and therefore to render the unit somewhat more difficult to convert easily to suit a projective buyer's tastes. This imposes an extra constraint or cost in conversion.

Renter-Submarket Responses

In analyzing predicted rental supply responses, we first consider the effects of *costs* on expected rates of return, and thus desired stocks. It must be noted at the outset that all these variables serve as proxies for inter-SMSA differences in costs at the beginning of the period. We were unsuccessful in our attempts to model these factors as endogenous variables.

Land prices (SV'_k). Insofar as land size utilized varies proportionally with housing unit size, there will be a near proportionality of impact across submarkets within the conversion supply mode. Since landlords who convert units already own their relevant land, this effect operates by changing the opportunity cost of land; that is, it changes the attractiveness of land uses that require demolition of the existing structure relative to those in which the existing structure can be retained, albeit converted. Changed supply decisions here are likely to be infrequent. For new construction, however, land must be acquired by the builder, and this increase in direct costs is probably a more powerful influence on action. Lack of proportionality between land and structures (in quality terms) will, of course, further differentiate the impact of land costs on the different quality submarkets, but this is not expected to be major. Thus, higher land prices should be inversely related to $PSTK_{ijk}$ in stronger magnitudes in higher-quality submarkets, that is, those relying more heavily on the new construction mode of response.

Availability of units that can be most inexpensively converted to the given submarket (SU'_{ijk}, SL'_{ijk}). For any given array of relative rates of return, larger proportional numerical dominance of the stock in adjacent submarkets should increase the likelihood of units being converted into the given submarket. But since this form of supply response is more dominant in lower-quality submarkets, the magnitude of this direct relationship should be larger there.

Construction costs (CC'_k). Rising construction costs should decrease the attractiveness of housing investment generally. But their effects on new construction, upward conversion, and downward conversion differ appreciably. Upward conversion entails much less construction inputs per affected housing unit than does new construction; so the former is placed at a competitive advantage relative to the latter in penetrating markets that look especially attractive on revenue grounds. Because they are dominated by new construction, higher-quality submarkets are more depressed by these cost increases than lower-quality submarkets. However, downward conversion usually entails only modest amounts of construction inputs. Thus, it becomes a more attractive option than upward conversion for owners of existing units as input costs rise. This means that higher construction costs should encourage an overall shift in the existing stock toward lower-quality levels. In sum, the foregoing implies that CC'_k should be inversely related to $PSTK_{ijk}$ in upper-quality levels, directly related to it in lower-quality levels, and have an unpredicted relationship with it in middle-quality levels. The composite of the absolute and relative effects results in the prediction of a stronger magnitude of inverse relationship between construction costs and increases in the stocks in higher-quality submarkets.

Costs of downward versus upward conversion among quality levels within a tenure is proxied for by the proportion of pre-1940 units ($AGED_{jk}$). Structural age is presumed to be directly associated (in a nonlinear way) with the costs of upward conversions and inversely associated with the costs of downward conversions. Thus, higher proportions of older stocks are expected to increase the likelihood of stock increments (see ch. 5) in submarkets below the median quality level and decrease them in submarkets above the median quality level, ceteris paribus.

Scarcity of sites available for new construction is proxied for by *population density* (DN'_k). Its initial impact differs somewhat among quality levels, but more sharply between the tenures taken as a whole. Higher densities are expected to be strongly inversely related to increments in stocks in submarkets requiring large land inputs—high-quality, single-family homes and large apartment complexes. The former clearly fall in our higher owner submarkets, but the new, larger complexes may be spread over a somewhat wider range of rental submarkets.

We turn now from cost to revenue considerations. The *price* and *quantity-demanded* components of the landlord's rate-of-return calculus for a given *ik* rental submarket are measured by (1) the real price in the *i*th rental-quality level at the beginning of the period, P'_{ik}; (2) the proportional demand shift in the *i*th rental-quality level during the period, X_{ik}; (3) the relative beginning-of-period real prices and the relative proportional demand shifts in other, competing rental submarkets different from i, PU'_{ik}, PL'_{ik}, XU_{ik}, XL_{ik}; (4) the ratio between the beginning-of-period average price in all *owner* submarkets and the price in the given *i*th rental submarket, PA'_{j*ik}; and (5) the average of the within-period demand shifts in all *owner* submarkets, XA_{j*ik}.

The first variable above serves as proxy for revenues obtainable by landlords in submarket *i* at the beginning of the period. The greater these revenues, the greater the likelihood of an ensuing supply response serving to augment the stock in *i*, occurring primarily in the first several years within the period. Unfortunately, we have no within-period prices to use at this point as predictors of subsequent responses. So here is where the *proportional demand shift* term comes into play, measuring for demand-induced changes in prices, quantities demanded, and thus revenue opportunities within the period. We expect both these terms to be directly related to $PSTK_{ijk}$, and we have no a priori expectations that the size or statistical significance of their coefficients should vary across rental submarkets.

The relative price and proportional demand shift variables in other rental submarkets (PU', PL', XU, XL) serve as proxies for intersubmarket competitive pressures. We expect that these variables will be inversely related to $PSTK_{ijk}$, since higher values will be associated with increased likelihoods that

(1) current landlords in *i* will convert their units into these other, more profitable submarkets; (2) fewer landlords in these other submarkets will deem it wise to convert into *i;* (3) builders of new dwellings will not find *i* the most profitable of all alternatives.

As we noted in the discussion of a market-period demand in chapter 14, we believe for considerable numbers of households that rental and owner tenures are reasonable substitutes. Relatively few owners, however, shift to rental tenure purely on the basis of relative prices. Thus, we would expect cross-tenure price/substitution elasticities to be primarily the result of current renters' responses, not those of current owner-occupants. From the perspective of household demands, therefore, we would predict that the fourth and fifth variables cited above (PA', XA) should be directly related to $PSTK_{ijk}$. That is, higher beginning-of-period owner prices and stronger within-period owner demand pressures should preclude more renters from becoming owners and thus provide a fillip to rental submarket demands.[3] This effect is only likely in higher-quality rental submarkets, however, inasmuch as households in other rental submarkets typically do not have the financial resources to consider owner-occupancy feasible at any of the relative prices being analyzed.

From a different perspective, however, the owner-tenure price and proportional demand shift variables may serve as proxies for conflicting elements in the *suppliers'* choice calculus. Higher values of these variables would be indicative of improved gross returns derived from selling units for owner-occupancy. This should mean that some builders of new dwellings who otherwise might have constructed rental units may be induced instead to construct ones for owner-occupancy. Analogously, some owners of existing rental units may be tempted to try to convert them to owner-occupancy. In the 1960–70 period under consideration, such tenure conversions were probably confined to the rental stock of single-family, duplex, or triplex units; in 1970–75, condominium conversions of larger, multiunit (formerly rental) structures were more common. These arguments would lead one to predict an inverse relationship between owner-tenure prices and demand shifts and renter $PSTK_{ijk}$. The strength of this relationship should be related to the ease of cross-tenure conversions of the stock within the given rental submarket. Unfortunately, we have no way of knowing this structure-type composition by quality submarket, and hence no exact prediction can be forthcoming.

Finally, our measures of public supply intervention in the housing market (PUB, SUB) are also expected to have two conflicting influences that, in combination, have a net impact that differs substantially among rental-quality levels. Landlords, particularly in lower-quality levels, should see governmentally supported construction as lowering their expected rates of return by diverting demand that would otherwise have occupied (their) private units (see ch. 11). But since the data on stock supply ($PSTK_{ijk}$) do not distinguish between privately owned and publicly owned units, public-supported units also appear on the *left-hand side* of our equations, primarily in the mid to upper rental-quality levels. In itself, the diversion of demand from private to public units should have no net aggregate effect on the total end-of-decade stocks. But there should be a diversion of demand, attracted by subsidized rents, from *lower renter* and to a lesser extent *all owner* levels to the *mid to upper* rental stocks, and a corresponding differential pattern of $PSTK_{ijk}$.

Owner Submarket Responses

As we previously mentioned, while the specification of variables for the owner-occupied stock supply functions is analogous to the renter-occupied functions, the underlying theory is quite different and so behavior may diverge significantly. The owner-occupier's intimate linking of consumption and investment in housing differs from the rental landlord's more univalent motivations. These differences necessitate fundamental alterations in our empirical paradigm before it can be applied to homeowner-investors.

First, the absolute linkage of housing consumption and investment makes meaningless the concept of a fixed population of investors altering their holdings of housing units, as used in the rental tenure. For this reason we instead conceptualize the homeowner's stock supply functions as determining changes in the numbers of *households* owning and occupying units in a given submarket. In this paradigm, then, the proportional shift of demand in the given owner submarket, X_{ijk}, measures the incremental number of households that would prefer, ceteris paribus, to *own and occupy* housing in the given submarket and not, as in the rental markets, simply an incremental quantity of services demanded.

A second discrepancy between the two paradigms lies in the difference between our measures of prices in the two tenures, that is, rents and expected sale prices. Economic theory tells us that rents are directly related to the rate of return on an asset and that the capitalized value of expected *future* returns is *an* important determinant of the *demand* for an asset and the price at which it can be sold. However, the actual price of an asset is a function of *all* of the factors which influence *both* supply and demand in the market for the asset and bears no fixed relationship to the rate of return. Since investors of both types, landlords and homeowners, are believed to make their investment decisions on the basis of maximizing expected rates of return, and since the paradigm of landlord behavior is based on rents, which most closely proxy for rates of return, it has not been necessary previously to draw this distinction between their responses to rents and prices. In the paradigm of homeowner behavior, however, it is necessary to describe the probable consequences of possible empirical variations in the relationship between sale prices and rents. As explained below, other variables in our model closely reflect the rates of return expected by homeowners in all submarkets. Therefore, our behavioral model must take account of the influence of variations in the price of houses in different owner quality levels while the rate of return is held constant.

What partial effects do we expect these variations to have? (1) For a given rate of return, the higher the own (beginning-of-period) price relative to non-housing goods, P'_{ijk} ($i=1, \ldots, 5$), the greater will be the incentive to bid resources away from other users and thus more households will owner-occupy stock in the given quality level; and (2) for given rates of return, the higher the own price relative to the price of housing in other owner submarkets, PL'_{ijk} ($i=2, \ldots, 5$) and PU'_{ijk} ($i=1, \ldots, 4$), the more attractive it will be to convert units from these other submarkets (and the less attractive to convert *away* from the given submarket). Because the rates of return in the different owner submarkets are held constant, by assumption, these adjacent-submarket price effects should be weaker than the effects of the corresponding renter-price variables (which are much more closely related to rates of return) in the renter equations.

As previously mentioned, rates of return are not reflected in the observed prices for owner-occupied housing stock, and this leads to a third alteration in the paradigm of investor behavior, namely, the calculation of returns to a homeowner investment in the housing stock. Of what do the returns to an investment in home ownership consist? They are comprised, first, of the rent not spent on an equivalent rental housing unit, and second, of a prospective future capital gain (or loss) when the house is eventually sold. The role of capital gains may be somewhat enhanced, moreover, because of the large proportion of a homeowner's portfolio that typically consists of equity tied up in the home; that is, the risk of capital loss is not spread among a number of diversified assets. The level of the rent-saving component of the calculation at the beginning of the period is measured by the ratio of the average rents in all renter submarkets and in the *i*th owner submarket, PA'_{j*ijk} ($i=1, \ldots, 5$); the average of the proportional demand shifts in all renter submarkets, XA_{j*ijk}, serves as proxy for the changes in this component. We thus predict that both variables would be directly related to owner $PSTK_{ijk}$. The prospective capital gains component is measured for by the beginning-of-period prices in the given submarket, P'_{ijk}, and by the demand shift in that submarket, X_{ijk} ($i=1, \ldots, 5$). The X term also measures, however, the number of households that are likely candidates to invest in a submarket. So this variable represents an intermingling of effects that operate in the same direction: greater demand shifts tending to increase anticipated capital gains *and* the likelihood that a given household will occupy and own a unit in a particular submarket. Nevertheless, both these measures of prospective capital gains in the submarket should be directly related to owner $PSTK_{ijk}$.

Opposite expectations hold for variables measuring beginning-of-period prices in other owner submarkets, PU'_{ijk}, PL'_{ijk}, and trends in these prices during the decade, XU_{ijk}, XL_{ijk}. As these terms serve as proxies for alternative prospective capital gains from homeowning in other submarkets, they should be inversely related to $PSTK_{ijk}$ in the given owner submarket.

Our econometric specification of owner *cost* variables differs trivially, if at all, from the specification of the landlord stock supply function above. Though the distribution and even the types of units and structures typically owned by landlord and homeowner investors are technically dissimilar, the production functions for housing units have the same general form and interpretation. Like the landlord, the homeowner combines inputs or buys from an entrepreneur who combines existing structures, land, construction inputs, capital, and equity to produce a housing unit that exists at the end of the period. The cost variables on which the homeowner's stock supply depend are the same as the cost variables in the renter-occupied model, as are our predictions about differential impacts across quality submarkets.

The final variable set included in the owner stock supply equations acts as a proxy for governmentally assisted housing supply, as defined earlier. These variables are intended to measure the number of probable homeowning families induced to occupy subsidized rental housing rather than own and occupy another unit. It seems likely that it is those households that would occupy units in lower-quality owner levels for whom subsidized housing is a viable substitute. Therefore, the government housing variables' (PUB, SUB) strongest inverse relationships should be shown with these submarkets, $PSTK_{ijk}$.

15.3 Specification of Stock-Supply-Mode Mix Equations

The previous section described factors which we feel influence the proportional net change in the housing stock in a submarket over the medium run, $PSTK_{ijk}$. Here we are interested in trying to uncover the determinants of the *composition* of these net changes: Were they accomplished primarily through new construction or, rather, net conversions into the given submarket?

To help understand the interactions in the model of supply adjustment, it may be helpful to view them as describing a two-stage sequential process in which the first stage determines the total end-of-decade stock in each submarket and the second stage the relative amounts of new construction and net conversion carried out by suppliers in order to achieve a given change in their stocks. In fact, as will be explained, the two processes are jointly determined. The *total (absolute)* change in the stock in the *i*th submarket, STK_{ijk}, equals the sum of *new construction*, NEW_{ijk}, and *net conversion* to that submarket, CON_{ijk}. We note that net conversions, in turn, equal the sum of gross conversions to a submarket minus the sum of gross conversions from a submarket, demolition, abandonment, and other losses. There is reason to believe that these flows should be modeled separately. This, however, is not possible with census or Annual Housing Survey data since they do not allow individual units to be tracked through time.

Our reasons for exploring the mix of supply modes are twofold. First, the amount of new construction called forth to produce a given total change in supply under various circumstances is of intrinsic interest. The total resource requirements needed to bring about a given change in supply, for example, are directly related to the proportion of new supply produced by new construction rather than by conversion. Second, both modes have distinct spatial impacts—conversion on existing neighborhoods, and new construction typically on undeveloped fringe areas. Third and most importantly, because the marginal costs of supply through new construction and conversion are generally different, the balance between the two affects both the returns to be gained from supply and the total amount of additional supply called forth by a change in market forces. Thus, by studying the determination of the mix of supply modes, we can expect to gain valuable insight into the determination of overall supply changes (see ch. 6).

The production of end-of-period stocks can be viewed as being performed either by the owner-suppliers themselves or by competitive construction and conversion industries. We assume that, as a group, landlords and homeowners are indifferent between holding newly-constructed and converted units, ceteris paribus. Therefore, the split of supply production between the two modes is completely determined by the *costs of production*. If costs are increasing at the margin for both modes and if both are used to produce units in a given submarket, then the suppliers equilibrate the cost of producing a marginal unit by the two modes. Suppliers simply minimize production costs and are indifferent between both modes of production and to the identity of the producer.

For any given market forces signaling an upward stock adjustment toward enhanced quality levels, new construction and conversions are competitive modes of securing the desired change. Thus the response of one supply mode in some submarket depends partly on the response of the other mode that is forthcoming. While strictly speaking there may be different response lags across modes, these become blurred when viewed from our medium-run change perspective, and it may be more reasonable to treat these responses as simultaneously determined. An empirical modeling attempt to do this proved unsuccessful, however. New construction and net conversion in virtually all of our submarkets are highly positively correlated. And because we were unable to specify significant exogenous variables which are unique to either the new construction or conversion functions in a given submarket, the estimation of these relations by simultaneous equations methods was infeasible. It is for this reason that we model the combined response of the two supply modes and then, separately, model the split between the two modes of production.

For similar reasons, theory also would suggest that new construction and conversion production responses in all ten tenure/quality submarkets should be modeled simultaneously. While in principle this may be attractive, in fact liminations of our data base resulting in the underidentification of such a system made it impossible to do so in practice.

Under the circumstances, the specification of the model of medium-run stock supply adjustments represents a compromise between the most theoretically reasonable specification and the constraints dictated by limitations of the available data.

15.3.1 Dependent Variables

The dependent variables in the supply-mode mix equations are the *difference between new construction and net conversion* to submarket *ij*, expressed as a *proportion* of the stock in the submarket at the beginning of the period, $PMODE_{ijk}$, that is,

$$PMODE_{ijk} = (NEW_{ijk} - CON_{ijk})/STK'_{ijk}.$$

As the stock supply function is based on the *sum* of medium-run new construction and medium-run net conversion supply functions, so the supply-mode mix function for a submarket is based on the *difference* between this new construction function and the net conversion function. Behaviorally, the *PMODE* function shows the extent to which investors choose to produce a desired change in end-of-period stock by means of new construction rather than by preservation of an existing unit or by conversion of units from another submarket.

15.3.2 Right-Hand Variables

What determines the choice of supply mode? First, we expect that anything that affects the stock supply will affect the proportion of the two supply modes differently, because the production of new units is likely to be more elastic, or responsive, than the production of converted units above some modest level of supply change (except in low-quality submarkets, as explained below). Positive net conversions will be increasingly constrained by the availability in other submarkets of existing housing units that can be feasibly or profitably converted to the given submarket, and the marginal cost of units produced by this mode will rise increasingly as total "conversion production" increases (see ch. 5). In contrast, new construction costs will increase much more gradually with the amount of production in a particular submarket. Therefore, any force that affects the amount of total supply response is also expected to influence the choice of supply: as total supply adjustment increases, so will the difference between new construction and net conversion. For this reason then, the explanatory variables in the supply-mode mix equations are, with one trivial exception, the same as those in the stock supply function equations, although their interpretations differ.

Our second expectation is that the relative position of competing demand pressures—whether they are associated with higher- or lower-quality submarkets—will also affect supply-mode mix. This is because the cost of converting existing units is not symmetric for equal amounts of quality upgrading and downgrading: the latter is typically much less expensive. What this means is that signals of favorable gross returns emanating from a *lower*-quality submarket than the one in question will more likely produce conversions out of the given submarket that comparable signals emanating from a higher one. Of course, conversions out of *ijk* would lower $PMODE_{ijk}$. Thus, controlling for the total size of the stock supply response in submarket *ijk*, the pattern of market forces which produced this response will also affect supply-mode mix.

In sum, our supply-mode equation is specified as

$$PMODE_{ijk} = \begin{array}{l} m_{ij}(P'_{ijk}, PU'_{ijk}, PL'_{ijk}, PA'_{j^*ijk}, X_{ijk}, XU_{ijk}, \\ XL_{ijk}, XA_{j^*ijk}, PUB_{ijk}, SUB_{ijk}, SU'_{ijk}, \\ SL'_{ijk}, CC'_{k}, DN'_{k}, SV'_{k}, AGED_{jk}). \end{array} \tag{15.2}$$

15.3.3 Cross-Submarket Differences in Supply-Mode Responses

On the expected-revenue side, then, we would expect that both the beginning-of-period price (P'_{ijk}) and proportional demand shift (X_{ijk}) terms in the given *ij* submarket in the SMSA should, in general, be directly related to $PMODE_{ijk}$. That is, larger demand pressures for stock supply in submarket *ijk* should favor new construction over conversion responses in *ijk*, due to the comparatively superior supply elasticity of the former described above. This prediction is tempered in lower-quality submarkets, however. There strong demand pressures can be readily responded to by *downward* conversion of units in many other, superior-quality submarkets. If such conversions prove less costly compared to new construction (due to building and zoning codes), one would predict the predominance of the former, whereupon P'_{ijk} and X_{ijk} would be inversely related to $PMODE_{ijk}$ in lower-quality submarkets.

The arguments about the direct relationship between size of stock supply response and $PMODE_{ijk}$ would analogously lead us to predict an inverse relationship between $PMODE_{ijk}$ and proxies for the beginning-of-period levels and within-period trends in revenues in adjacent submarkets in the same tenure as *ijk* (PU'_{ijk}, XU_{ijk}, PL'_{ijk}, XL_{ijk}) and in the opposite tenure (PA'_{j^*ijk}, XA_{j^*ijk}). While this is the case for variables denoting returns in the upper adjacent (higher-quality) submarket in the same tenure, other offsetting elements must be considered in the case of the other variables. Stronger demand pressures in lower adjacent submarkets will magnify the incentives for owners of existing units in *ij* to downgrade, and these incentives will more likely produce conversions than comparable pressures in upper adjacent submarkets, due to the comparative costs of downgrading versus upgrading. Thus the predicted sign of the PL'_{ijk} and XL_{ijk} coefficients is ambiguous, since these variables suggest not only comparatively less new construction in the given submarket, but also less net conversions into it (i.e., more gross conversions out of it).

Asymmetries in cross-tenure conversion possibilities should also produce ambiguous predictions regarding the opposite-tenure terms. Given the comparative ease of converting owner-occupied units into renter-occupied ones, stronger average demand pressures in renter submarkets should elicit more tenure conversions from a given owner submarket than the opposite situation. This means that, once again, for owner submarkets the relationships between

$PMODE_{ijk}$ and PA'_{j*ijk} and XA_{j*ijk} cannot be clearly specified a priori, although the inverse relationships should still hold for rental submarkets.

The effects of the final expected revenue proxies, the numbers of public housing and publicly subsidized dwelling units, are also difficult to predict. Newly constructed public and subsidized units contribute to NEW_{ijk} in rental submarkets, of course, but insofar as they *substitute* for rental units that would otherwise have been built by private interests, the net effect on this component may be near zero (see ch. 11). On the other hand, if those public and subsidized units substitute for existing units that otherwise would have added to net conversions into a rental submarket, they would be directly related to $PMODE_{ijk}$. For owner submarkets, the effect of increased governmentally assisted housing production should be to siphon off some demands that otherwise may have been influencing lower- and modest-quality owner submarkets. For reasons given at the outset of this section, this should yield the expectation of an inverse relationship between the assisted-housing variables and $PMODE_{ijk}$ in owner submarkets.

On the expected cost side, the land cost, site availability, and construction cost variables (SV'_k, DN'_k, CC'_k) should all be inversely related to $PMODE_{ijk}$ in all submarkets. Higher costs in any such areas would encourage conversion instead of new construction model responses, ceteris paribus, since they utilize land and construction materials much less intensively in their "stock production" process. Higher proportions of older dwellings in the stock ($AGED_{jk}$) would favor conversion over construction in lower-quality submarkets (i.e., be inversely related to $PMODE_{ijk}$) and vice versa in upper-quality ones, given that the asymmetry in conversion costs is intensified with structural age (see ch. 5). Finally, larger proportions of stocks in adjacent submarkets (SU'_{ijk}, SL'_{ijk}) also should be inversely related to $PMODE_{ijk}$ for all *ij*, since it would signify a larger pool from which to draw potentially more easily convertible units.

This completes our specification of our cross-SMSA model of medium-run housing stock supply and supply composition. The next section presents our econometric estimates of parameters of these specifications and a discussion of their implications.

15.4 Empirical Results

Medium-run stock supply and supply-mode mix equations as specified in equations (15.1) and (15.2) were econometrically estimated using ordinary least squares techniques. In both sets of equations, in each submarket about three-fourths of the variation in the dependent variable was explained by the model. Parameters of the same specifications were estimated for all ten tenure/quality submarkets for the 1960–70 period (using the sample of thirty-six SMSAs) and for the 1970–1975/76 period (using the sample of thirty-eight SMSAs). As in the case of the market-period demand and supply equations, we feel the results provide convincing support for our general theoretical approach. There were, however, a few results that were not wholly explicable. The patterns of coefficients across tenure/quality submarkets and between samples were generally not as consistent as was the case with the market-period equations. As such we here consider only the most salient results.The interested reader will find the complete set of regression results for stock supply and mode mix equations in tables 15.2 and 15.3 respectively. The paucity of robust results is not altogether surprising given the theoretical shortcomings in the specification that were necessitated by data constraints. First, we argued in chapters 5 and 6 that idiosyncrasies in the existing stock involving age, type, condition, and structural attributes greatly affected aggregate conversion cost functions for the submarket array and, thereby, the amount and mix of supply response that would be forthcoming from any demand pressures. These stock idiosyncrasies were, however, poorly proxied for in the model. Second, our hedonic index used to estimate conversions did not include arguments involving the condition of the dwelling, thus upgrading or downgrading activities that only involved over- or undermaintenance would not have entered into our dependent variables. Yet their presence in varying degrees across submarkets and sample SMSAs might have influenced the sorts of conversions (and new construction) measured by our index, thereby possibly eroding and confounding the explanatory power of the predictor variables.

15.4.1 Stock Supply Equations

For introduction it should be noted that, although the overall degree of fit, R^2, was higher on average for the 1960–70 equations than the 1970–1975/76 equations, the number of statistically significant variable coefficients was greater in the latter set of equations. The difference appears to be due to a comparative lack of independent variation in the right-hand, demand-shift variables in the earlier period, that is, multicollinearity. The greater independent fluctuation of 1970–1975/76 demand terms could reflect either a fundamental change in growth patterns between the 1960s and 1970s or the suppression of processes that equilibrate SMSA growth patterns in the longer term but require at least a decade to reach completion. To the extent that the latter explanation is correct, individual coefficient estimates for shorter (five-year) periods will be more precise.

We consider first the variables proxying for the revenue side of suppliers' net-returns estimates. The beginning-of-period price of housing in the given submarket versus nonhousing goods (P'_{ijk}) proved a totally insignificant predictor of stock supply adjustments in all owner submarkets, perhaps because sales prices are less closely related to rate of return that are rents. This finding is also consistent with the hypothesis that the longer-term supply of single-family housing is perfectly elastic (Muth 1960; Follain 1979; Stover 1986). The variable was statistically significant in the higher-quality renter submar-

Table 15.2. Medium-Run Stock Change Equation Coefficients

	1960–70									
	Owner Submarkets					Renter Submarkets				
	1	2	3	4	5	1	2	3	4	5
X	.299	.125	.267	−.076	.071	−.038	−.030	.010	.137	1.160
	(2.95)[a]	(.88)	(1.52)[c]	(.33)	(.46)	(.24)	(.21)	(.05)	(.63)	(2.06)[c]
XU	.158	.551	−.074	.009	—	.038	.019	.145	.217	—
	(1.67)*	(1.96)[c]*	(.39)	(.11)		(.21)	(.09)	(1.15)	(1.73)[c]*	
XL	—	−.017	−.385	−.414	−.042	—	.073	−.136	.056	.436
		(.20)	(1.46)[c]	(1.12)	(.22)		(1.11)	(.63)	(.22)	(.51)
XA	−.151	.044	.092	.184	.180	.079	.233	.460	.515	.187
	(1.15)	(.32)	(.60)	(1.21)	(1.21)	(.41)	(1.39)*	(2.85)[b]*	(1.90)[c]*	(.23)
P′	.046	.005	−.006	.203	.111	.328	−.433	−.145	.518	1.865
	(.22)	(.03)	(.03)	(.66)	(.42)	(1.14)	(2.08)[c]*	(.78)	(1.90)[c]*	(2.19)[b]
PU′	−.279	.184	−.289	1.135	—	2.26	−1.780	−1.382	1.657	—
	(1.39)[c]	(.24)	(.43)	(1.28)		(3.49)[a]*	(2.06)[b]	(1.57)[c]	(1.41)*	
PL′	—	−.043	−.530	−2.379	−.518	—	−1.080	−.719	.728	−2.736
		(.15)	(.76)	(1.81)[b]	(1.06)		(1.75)[b]	(1.32)[c]	(.49)	(.76)
PA′	.210	−.056	.396	−.198	−.244	−.439	−.530	.078	.584	1.362
	(.28)	(.19)	(1.09)	(.53)	(.71)	(1.62)*	(1.80)[c]*	(.25)	(1.58)*	(1.40)*
PUB	−.271	−.259	−.026	.413	.692	.235	−.314	−.119	−.194	1.940
	(.54)	(.57)	(.04)	(.37)	(1.0)	(.69)	(1.26)	(.33)	(.40)	(1.36)*
SV′	.021	.001	.012	−.065	−.019	.100	.088	.031	−.053	−.361
	(.57)	(.03)	(.25)	(1.11)	(.36)	(1.91)[c]*	(2.06)[c]*	(.66)	(.90)	(2.01)[b]
CC′	.004	.003	.005	−.002	−.002	.005	.002	.001	.002	−.006
	(3.11)[a]	(1.93)[c]	(2.82)[b]*	(.94)	(1.10)	(2.89)[a]	(1.39)[c]	(.59)	(1.05)	(.93)
DN′	.026	−.032	−.069	−.084	−.151	−.065	−.090	−.022	.046	.279
	(.47)	(.53)	(.14)	(1.02)	(2.99)[a]	(1.03)	(1.45)[c]	(.41)	(.73)	(1.32)*

SU′	.199	.620	−.045	−.339	—	.377	.274	−.188	.081	—
	(1.99)[b]	(2.66)[a]	(.23)	(1.17)		(2.64)[a]	(1.18)	(.80)	(.31)	
SL′	—	.060	.069	.389	.346	—	.037	−.70	.286	.120
		(.57)	(1.28)	(.81)	(2.44)[b]		(.37)	(1.25)	(.97)	(.23)
AGED′	.511	.026	−.908	−.484	−.746	.170	.252	−.219	−.1085	−1.668
	(3.14)[a]	(.16)	(4.29)[a]	(1.46)[c]	(3.11)[a]	(.72)	(1.26)	(1.12)	(3.73)[a]	(2.16)[b]
C	−1.52	−1.63	−.321	2.93	1.57	−4.721	2.287	2.481	−3.584	2.666
	(3.35)[a]*	(1.51)*	(.23)	(1.34)*	(2.43)[b]*	(4.14)[a]*	(1.99)[c]*	(1.97)[c]*	(1.91)[c]*	(.69)
R^2	.86	.60	.80	.83	.90	.79	.85	.66	.86	.82

1970–75/76

	Owner Submarkets					Renter Submarkets				
	1	2	3	4	5	1	2	3	4	5
X	.323	.806	.513	.402	.734	.122	−.025	.210	.178	.322
	(2.50)[b]	(1.59)[c]	(2.27)[b]	(3.63)[a]	(3.22)[a]	(1.03)	(.21)	(2.21)[b]	(1.99)[b]	(1.43)[c]
XU	.439	.810	−.244	.243	—	.096	−.287	.346	.162	—
	(3.66)[a]*	(1.60)*	(1.71)[c]	(1.88)[c]*		(.93)	(1.42)[c]	(2.94)[a]*	(1.69)*	
XL	—	.145	.041	.136	.285	—	.024	.070	−.077	.089
		(1.13)	(.43)	(1.39)*	(.81)		(.41)	(.77)	(1.04)	(.40)
XA	.204	.298	.114	.117	.184	.219	.045	.192	.179	−.006
	(.65)	(.55)	(.48)	(1.23)	(.82)	(1.42)*	(.35)	(2.55)[b]*	(3.77)[a]*	(.03)
P′	−.667	.578	−.047	.128	.327	.142	−.585	.101	.501	1.18
	(1.05)	(.39)	(.12)	(.56)	(.65)	(.39)	(1.71)*	(.40)	(3.29)[a]	(2.29)[b]
PU′	−4.48	2.89	−1.97	−.144	—	.777	.888	−1.23	−.195	—
	(2.83)[a]	(1.02)	(3.19)[a]	(.38)		(.77)	(1.04)	(2.57)[a]	(.60)	
PL′	—	2.08	−.576	−.183	−.203	—	−.614	−.589	.822	2.28
		(1.04)	(1.00)	(.50)	(.17)		(.86)	(1.07)	(2.15)[b]*	(2.01)[c]*
PA′	.673	−.190	.673	.446	1.16	−.213	.045	.531	.732	−.121
	(.99)	(.19)	(2.04)[b]*	(2.04)[b]*	(1.82)[b]*	(.43)	(.49)	(1.06)	(.96)	(.73)

(continued)

Table 15.2. continued

	1960–70									
	Owner Submarkets					Renter Submarkets				
	1	2	3	4	5	1	2	3	4	5
PUB	−.534	2.60	−.464	.019	.578	.075	−.239	−.494	−.473	2.29
	(.57)	(1.60)*	(.70)	(.03)	(.80)	(.13)	(.54)	(1.36)[c]*	(1.91)[c]*	(2.69)[b]*
SUB	2.90	−2.10	2.75	−.117	−1.24	.543	.329	−.518	.808	−.485
	(2.31)[b]*	(.76)	(1.95)[c]*	(.07)	(.79)	(.63)	(.46)	(.89)	(1.45)*	(.26)
SV′	.010	.081	.020	−.008	.025	−.016	.009	−.014	−.036	.025
	(.13)	(.62)	(.46)	(.38)	(.49)	(.32)	(.22)	(.58)	(2.22)[b]	(.47)
CC′	−.008	.001	.003	−.002	−.006	−.005	−.002	.007	−.007	−.018
	(1.07)	(.06)	(.65)	(.82)	(1.02)	(.89)	(.45)	(2.36)[b]*	(3.00)[a]	(2.35)[b]
DN′	.022	.107	.034	.022	−.023	.006	.108	−.030	−.029	−.224
	(.24)	(.72)	(.64)	(.82)	(.31)	(.12)	(2.19)[b]*	(.94)	(1.32)[c]	(3.24)[a]
SU′	.806	.607	−.110	.380		.356	.364	.268	.048	
	(3.58)[a]	(3.38)[a]	(1.50)*	(1.11)	—	(2.16)[b]	(1.66)[c]	(4.09)[a]	(.76)	—
SL′		.488	−.110	.262	.147		.029	.285	−.008	.069
	—	(1.25)	(.66)	(1.74)[b]	(1.13)	—	(.39)	(1.26)	(.07)	(.40)
AGED′	2.03	.991	−.479	−.573	−1.79	.004	−.749	−.066	.020	−.558
	(2.30)[b]	(.60)	(.94)	(1.87)[b]	(2.24)[b]	(.09)	(2.17)[c]*	(.30)	(1.32)*	(1.00)
C	2.51	−7.78	2.07	−.522	−.410	−.830	−.058	.743	−.420	−.608
	(2.03)[c]*	(2.35)[b]*	(1.83)[c]*	(.73)	(.33)	(.73)	(.06)	(.67)	(.68)	(.48)
R^2	.84	.90	.74	.83	.84	.48	.42	.79	.76	.78

Note: t-statistics are in parentheses.
[a]Coefficient statistically significant at 1% level (one-tail test).
[b]Coefficient statistically significant at 5% level (one-tail test).
[c]Coefficient statistically significant at 10% level (one-tail test).
*Two-tail test if opposite predicted sign or no predicted sign.

Table 15.3. Medium-Run Mode Mix Equation Coefficients

	1960–70									
	Owner Submarkets					Renter Submarkets				
	1	2	3	4	5	1	2	3	4	5
X	−.273	−.076	.190	−.175	−.045	.038	−.002	.201	.378	1.40
	(3.29)[a]	(.74)	(.93)	(.75)	(.21)	(.24)	(.02)	(1.08)	(2.20)[b]	(3.08)[a]
XU	−.119	.344	.103	.007	—	−.038	−.030	.067	−.025	—
	(1.53)[c]	(1.69)*	(.46)	(.09)		(.21)	(.14)	(.54)	(.25)	
XL	—	−.114	−.064	−.582	.226	—	−.058	.086	−.177	.928
		(1.79)[c]*	(.21)	(1.56)*	(.87)		(.86)	(.41)	(.87)	(1.36)*
XA	.118	.119	−.037	.093	−0.010	−.079	−.240	−.419	−.289	−.916
	(1.10)	(1.20)	(.21)	(.60)	(.05)	(.41)	(1.41)*	(2.47)[b]*	(1.35)*	(1.39)*
P′	.023	.125	.074	.740	.371	−.328	.403	.364	.481	1.99
	(.13)	(.91)	(.27)	(2.38)[b]	(1.02)	(1.14)	(1.90)[c]*	(2.03)[c]*	(2.22)[b]	(2.90)[a]
PU′	.068	−.161	−.385	1.53	—	−2.26	1.12	2.08	3.80	—
	(.41)	(.29)	(.49)	(1.70)*		(3.50)[a]	(1.83)[c]*	(2.43)[b]*	(3.22)[a]*	
PL′	—	−.418	−.397	−2.38	−1.60	—	1.10	.577	.332	(−6.29)
		(1.98)[c]*	(.81)	(1.79)[c]*	(2.39)[b]*		(1.77)[c]*	(1.09)	(.16)	(2.18)[b]*
PA′	.097	.551	.420	.482	.067	.440	.467	.012	−.202	1.80
	(.44)	(2.59)[b]*	(1.00)	(1.27)	(.14)	(1.62)*	(1.56)*	(.04)	(.69)	(2.30)[b]*
PUB	.161	.154	−.008	−.610	−.170	−.235	.274	.325	.528	2.04
	(.39)	(.46)	(.01)	(.54)	(.17)	(.70)	(1.08)	(.93)	(1.39)*	(1.78)[c]*
SV′	.002	−.021	−.032	−.053	.026	−.100	−.083	−.054	−.017	−.400
	(.07)	(.74)	(.59)	(.89)	(.35)	(1.92)[c]	(1.92)[c]	(1.18)	(.37)	(2.77)[b]
CC′	−.003	.001	.004	−.005	−.002	−.005	−.003	−.001	.001	−.005
	(2.36)[b]	(.75)	(1.99)[c]*	(2.06)[b]	(.56)	(2.89)[a]	(1.66)[c]	(.45)	(.80)	(.89)
DN′	−.101	−.154	−.213	−.228	−.193	.064	.094	.006	−.043	.183
	(2.18)[b]	(3.55)[a]	(3.43)[a]	(2.75)[b]	(2.78)[b]	(1.02)	(1.50)*	(.12)	(.86)	(1.08)

(continued)

Table 15.3. continued

	1960–70									
	Owner Submarkets					Renter Submarkets				
	1	2	3	4	5	1	2	3	4	5
SU′	−.158	.229	−.358	−.354	—	−.377	−.266	.020	−.321	—
	(1.92)[c]	(1.35)*	(1.56)[c]	(1.21)		(2.64)[b]	(.96)	(.09)	(1.54)[c]	
SL′	—	−.010	−.669	−.813	−.167	—	−.014	.142	−.473	−.547
		(.13)	(1.17)	(1.67)[c]	(.86)		(.14)	(.26)	(2.02)[b]	(1.32)[c]
AGED′	−.900	−.907	−.969	−.458	−.911	−.170	−.295	−.206	−.589	−.509
	(6.72)[a]	(7.90)[a]	(3.95)[a]	(1.36)[c]	(2.76)[b]*	(.72)	(1.46)[c]	(1.09)	(2.56)[a]	(.82)
C	1.14	.214	1.02	2.74	2.70	4.72	−1.99	−2.40	−3.30	5.91
	(3.05)[a]*	(.27)	(.64)	(1.24)	(3.04)[a]*	(4.15)[a]*	(1.71)*	(1.96)[c]*	(2.22)[b]*	(1.89)[c]*
R^2	.93	.93	.83	.89	.83	.79	.84	.73	.89	.77

	1970–75/76									
	Owner Submarkets					Renter Submarkets				
	1	2	3	4	5	1	2	3	4	5
X	−.308	−.819	−.451	−.093	.603	−.125	.118	−.103	.300	.122
	(2.27)[b]	(1.63)[c]	(2.52)[b]*	(.89)	(2.74)[a]	(1.07)	(.93)	(1.23)	(2.20)[b]	(.63)
XU	−.421	−.822	.189	−.295	—	−.099	.474	−.219	.194	—
	(3.34)[a]	(1.63)[c]	(1.67)*	(2.45)[b]		(.96)	(2.33)[b]*	(2.11)[b]	(1.34)*	
XL	—	−.170	.204	.003	.291	—	−.030	.057	.107	.007
		(1.34)[c]*	(2.67)[a]*	(.03)	(.86)		(.47)	(.71)	(.95)	(.04)
XA	−.259	−.305	−.449	−.097	.537	−.224	.028	−.080	−.058	.067
	(.79)	(.57)	(2.41)[b]*	(1.07)	(2.50)[b]*	(1.46)*	(.21)	(1.21)	(.81)	(.44)
P′	.593	−.527	−.023	−.254	.887	−.141	.701	.129	.024	1.06
	(.89)	(.36)	(.07)	(1.17)	(1.84)[b]	(.38)	(1.93)[c]*	(.58)	(.12)	(2.36)[b]

PU′	4.17	−3.12	1.04	−.609	—	−.778	−.593	.963	−.478	—
	(2.51)[b]*	(1.11)	(2.11)[b]*	(1.70)[c]		(.78)	(.65)	(2.27)[b]*	(.98)	
PL′	—	−1.93	1.42	.675	−.635	—	.646	.523	−.297	.946
		(.97)	(3.13)[a]*	(1.96)[b]*	(.54)		(.85)	(1.07)	(.52)	(.96)
PA′	−.666	.325	−.401	−.221	.205	−.113	.207	−.053	.386	.436
	(.94)	(.33)	(1.53)*	(1.07)	(.33)	(.38)	(.58)	(.03)	(.97)	(1.10)
PUB	.500	−2.53	−1.34	−.533	.926	−.057	.322	.376	−.319	1.41
	(.51)	(1.58)*	(2.54)[b]*	(.83)	(1.34)*	(.10)	(.69)	(1.17)	(.86)	(1.93)[c]*
SUB	−2.63	2.26	.458	.061	−1.18	−.543	−.541	.076	1.12	1.96
	(1.99)[b]*	(.83)	(.41)	(.04)	(.78)	(.63)	(.72)	(.15)	(1.34)*	(1.23)
SV′	.005	−.056	−.069	.011	−.047	.017	−.009	−.003	.021	.031
	(.06)	(.43)	(1.98)[b]	(.51)	(.95)	(.34)	(.19)	(.15)	(.83)	(.67)
CC′	.008	−.000	.000	.002	.002	.005	.004	−.005	.004	−.020
	(1.04)	(.01)	(.07)	(.83)	(.36)	(.93)	(.75)	(1.78)[b]	(1.31)	(3.12)[a]
DN′	−.009	−.115	−.055	−.024	−.080	−.006	−.102	.032	.049	−.155
	(.09)	(.79)	(1.33)[c]	(.93)	(1.14)	(.11)	(1.96)[b]	(1.13)	(1.59)*	(2.60)[a]
SU′	−.787	−.597	−.027	−.853	—	−.362	−.304	−.232	−.059	—
	(3.32)[a]	(3.35)[a]	(.47)	(2.64)[a]		(2.21)[b]	(1.31)	(3.99)[a]	(.62)	
SL′	—	−.487	.522	.111	−.057	—	−.019	−.091	−.142	.308
		(1.26)	(3.91)[a]*	(.78)	(.46)		(.24)	(.45)	(.82)	(2.06)[c]*
AGED′	−2.24	−1.24	−.418	−.087	−.447	−.420	.610	−.280	−.074	−.531
	(2.63)[a]	(.76)	(1.03)	(.30)	(.58)	(.10)	(1.67)*	(1.41)[c]	(.32)	(1.10)
C	−3.14	7.64	−1.79	1.18	.635	.821	−.593	−.833	.357	.892
	(1.73)[c]*	(2.33)[b]*	(1.99)[c]*	(1.75)[c]*	(.53)	(.73)	(.57)	(.85)	(.39)	(.79)
R^2	.83	.91	.69	.48	.62	.49	.44	.85	.64	.75

Note: t-statistics are in parentheses.
[a]Coefficient statistically significant at 1% level (one-tail test).
[b]Coefficient statistically significant at 5% level (one-tail test).
[c]Coefficient statistically significant at 10% level (one-tail test).
*Two-tail test if opposite predicted sign or no predicted sign.

kets 4 and 5, with implied elasticities of .6 and over 1.0, respectively. Proportional demand shifts in the given submarket (X_{ijk}) demonstrated the expected, significantly positive sign in virtually all submarkets in the 1970–1975/76 period and were mostly positive, though less significant, in the equations for the 1960–70 period.

With the exception of the relative beginning-of-period price terms in the upper, adjacent-quality submarkets (PU'_{ijk}), the measures of relative returns in competitive, same-tenure submarkets (XU_{ijk}, XL_{ijk}, and PL'_{ijk}) did not provide consistent support for our theoretical predictions. The predicted negative coefficient pattern for PU'_{ijk} suggests that short-term differences in relative prospective rates of return earned by units in a given submarket and those in submarkets of somewhat higher quality do affect the likelihood of units being supplied in the former, in the expected, substitutive fashion. There appears to be less sensitivity to relative differences in lower-quality submarkets. The inconsistent pattern of coefficients for the relative proportional demand-shift variables is probably due to their failure to adequately measure true intersubmarket rate-of-return differentials. The relationship between demand shifts and these differentials is particularly problematic for owner-occupants, as explained earlier. In addition, for all submarkets the specification is additive between projected revenue ([X]) and (the admittedly weak) cost variables, and thus the differential costs of supplying to various submarkets are not appropriately matched with revenue differentials.[4] Finally, the variable specification implies a symmetrical behavioral effect regardless of the *direction* of demand shifts; that is, a given relative differential has the same impact regardless of whether demands in both are rising or declining.[5]

The variables proxying for returns in opposite-tenure submarkets (PA'_{j*ijk}, X_{j*ijk}) performed as predicted. The positive coefficient for relative average rental prices in the owner submarket equations is consistent with the hypothesis that such serve as proxies for the implicit rent-savings component of the homeowners' rate of return. It could also signify that lower absolute ownership prices permit substantial numbers of erstwhile renters to become homeowners. The positive coefficients for both PA' and X variables in the renter submarket equations suggest that (implicit) reductions in the affordability of homeownership serve to strengthen prospective rates of return in upper-quality rental submarkets, as predicted. This, in turn, provides a fillip to the growth of the rental stock here.

The final variable that serves as a proxy for returns, new public housing construction, PUB_{ijk}, had a negative correlation with stock supply in renter quality levels 3 and 4, and a positive correlation with it in level 5. This result is explained by reference to our hedonic index. Recall that it fails to distinguish new private from new public units, building type, floor area, neighborhood location, amenities, socioeconomic status, or public services. Thus the index categorized most newly constructed public housing units in the top rental-quality submarket, instead of submarkets 3 and 4 where we suspect they "truly" were. Had this correct categorization been done (and values of the dependent variables for these submarkets altered correspondingly), we suspect that all coefficients of *PUB* would have been statistically insignificant. Unfortunately, because we have no confidence in our hedonic index's ability to categorize public housing quality, we are unable to make any estimates of public stock/private stock substitution effects, as did Swan (1973), Murray 1983b), and Weicher and Thibodeau (1988). The government-subsidized construction variable (SUB_{ijk}), which was only available for the 1970–1975/76 period, surprisingly had significant positive coefficients in the bottom and middle owner submarkets and renter submarket 4, with insignificant coefficients in all rental submarkets. We can offer no cogent explanation for this wholly unexpected result. Nevertheless, like others we can note that the results provide no support for the hypothesis that either public or subsidized private construction reduced the lower-quality rental stock (Vitaliano 1983; Weicher and Thibodeau 1988).

Next we consider the excellent results for the cost variables. Higher land prices (SV'_k) and construction costs (CC'_k) apparently had the expected effect of discouraging stock supply in high-quality submarkets and encouraging it in lower-quality submarkets in both periods, as predicted.

Proxies for the availability of land (DN'_k) and for cost of maintaining a structure at a given quality ($AGED'_j$) also had the expected coefficient patterns in both periods, the latter being an especially significant determinant of flows of housing stock from higher to lower quality levels. Finally, the availability of stock (for prospective conversion) in adjacent upper- and lower-quality-level submarkets (SU'_{ijk}, SL'_{ijk}) had significant coefficients of the expected positive sign in nine cases in both periods combined. The strongest and most consistent results were for relative stock size in the upper adjacent quality level and on supply in the lowest-quality submarkets in both tenures. The result for the availability and age of existing stock provides further support for our contention that interconnections between submarkets, though systematic, will be nonuniform in strength because of differences in aggregate conversion cost functions between different submarket pairs.

15.4.2 Supply-Mode Mix Equations

Our attempts to estimate the mix of new construction versus net conversion modes of supply responses over the 1960–70 and 1970–1975/76 periods were the least successful and least capable of easy interpretation. Although overall R^2 were well above 0.8, individual coefficients of revenue proxies did not show consistent or easily explained patterns of sign and of statistical significance. This is not completely unexpected, of course, given that for many variables we predicted offsetting factors which rendered the expected relationship ambiguous.

Consider initially the price and proportional demand-shift variables which served as proxies for likely magnitudes of total stock supply as well as intersubmarket conversion responses: P'_{ijk}, X_{ijk}. These terms for the given submarket generally supported our expectations of an inverse relationship with $PMODE_{ijk}$ in lower-quality submarkets, becoming more of a direct relationship in higher-quality ones. That the coefficients of P'_{ijk} remained significantly positive in renter submarkets, however, suggests that new construction is a significant source of supply even in quite modest-quality submarkets.

Results for beginning-of-period price and within-period proportional demand-shift terms in adjacent and opposite-tenure submarkets were less satisfying. Coefficients of PU'_{ijk} and XU_{ijk} terms were expected to be inversely related to excesses of new construction over conversion in all *ijk*. Although they proved to be such in about one-third of the cases, in an equal number of cases they proved significantly positive in both samples. For PL'_{ijk} and XL_{ijk} our a priori predictions were ambiguous. For both variables, coefficients had no clear intersubmarket pattern of signs. Finally, relative opposite-tenure PA'_{j*ijk} and XA_{j*ijk} coefficients were statistically insignificant in all but one or two submarkets. These results, which mirror those of the stock supply equations, suggest that our aggregate variables have failed to measure adequately the perceived revenue prospects available to individual converters and builders in particular submarkets.

The proportion of beginning-of-period stock which new public housing units (PUB_{ijk}) and (in 1970–1975/76) new subsidized housing units (SUB_{ijk}) represented had the expected patterns of coefficient signs. Stronger relative impacts of governmentally supported housing construction were associated generally with larger excesses of new construction over conversion in upper-quality renter submarkets since, unlike in lower submarkets, such support augmented the new construction totals without producing offsetting pressures on net conversions into the submarket. For owner submarkets, a few of the predicted negative coefficients were found at the lower-quality levels, mainly during the 1970–1975/76 sample period. The outstanding anomaly was the inexplicable, significantly positive coefficient for PUB_{ijk} in the highest owner submarket; that government housing subsidies should have any effect at all here was surprising.

As for variables which served as proxies for the cost side of suppliers' rate-of-return calculus, the results were more satisfactory. Our estimated coefficients were almost always the predicted sign when they were statistically significant. One particularly interesting pattern of statistical significance emerged: whereas many of the cost variables were significant in owner submarkets during the 1960–70 sample period, few were during the 1970–1975/76 period.[6]

To be more specific, the beginning-of-period construction cost index (CC'_k) yielded coefficients of the expected negative sign in four submarkets in the 1960–70 sample, and two in the 1970–1975/76 sample. The SMSA population density variable (DN'_k) demonstrated the predicted significant inverse relationship with $PMODE_{ijk}$ in five of the submarkets in the 1960–70 sample, but this fell to three in the later period. In the 1960–70 sample, land site price (SV'_k) coefficients were significant in three submarkets in both samples, but only in one in 1970–1975/76. The proportion of the given tenure's stock built before 1940 ($AGED'_j$) was expected to be inversely related to $PMODE_{ijk}$, especially in lower quality levels. In fact, its coefficient turned out significantly negative in seven submarkets in 1960–70 and two in 1970–1975/76. And in each case, the reduction in explanatory power for the above variables in the latter period occurred in the owner submarkets. Finally, the proxy for easily converted existing stocks in upper-adjacent submarkets (SU'_{ijk}) demonstrated the predicted negative coefficient in half the submarkets in the combined sample periods. Given the asymmetries of conversion costs, the amount of existing stocks in lower adjacent submarkets (SL'_{ijk}) was not expected to prove as strong a correlate of $PMODE_{ijk}$. In fact it was not, as shown by variations of coefficient sign and lower levels of statistical significance.

We would hypothesize that the reduced ability of these conventional cost variables to predict the mix of supply responses for owner-occupants is related to the growing impact of asset demand considerations during the 1970–1975/76 period. Cost considerations (at least those captured by the specified variables) apparently played a minor role compared to less easily measured and unspecified variables related to expectations of capital gains. Another potential difference is that the conversion of rental units in multiple-unit structures to owner occupancy via condominiums only became a viable option in the 1970s. Although this could provide a possible source of response which breaks the traditional owner-occupancy/new construction link, condominium conversions were an insignificant portion of the stock adjustments in all but one of our sampled SMSAs.[7]

15.5 Conclusion

Our cross-SMSA, aggregative model of medium-run housing supply revealed much that is supportive of our theory of urban housing submarkets. Proxies for prospective revenues gained by and costs incurred by supplying units to a particular submarket consistently proved to be statistically significant predictors of five- to ten-year changes in the stock of that submarket. This suggests that our supplier behavioral assumption about rate-of-return maximizing is not inappropriate, even in owner submarkets. (This assumption is tested further in the next chapter.)

Higher costs of construction and conversion were associated with a shift in the cross-submarket distribution of the stock from higher to lower quality levels. Higher land and building costs also were correlated with a shift in the composition of stock supply from new construction to net conversion.

As predicted by our theory, the mix of supply response between construction and conversion appeared to be highly sensitive to quality level. The relative elasticity of construction supply response was greater in higher-quality submarkets, although our empirical estimates suggest that this superiority persists well down the quality hierarchy.

Characteristics of the standing stock at the beginning of the period apparently affect the nature of forthcoming responses as well. On average, an older stock was associated with a greater tendency for the stock to be more prone to downgrading as well as for net conversion to be a relatively larger fraction of any supply response. For any given submarket (especially if it was of low quality) the stock of dwellings in upper-adjacent submarkets proved directly related to the elasticity of supply response, and to the extent that conversion will exact a larger share of the response. The observed lack of comparable explanatory power of the stock in lower-adjacent quality levels attests to our view of crucial asymmetries between upgrading and downgrading in the conversion cost functions.

Market forces operating in one set of tenure submarkets appeared to influence suppliers in the opposite tenure. Higher relative prices in ownership markets were associated with greater stock increases in upper-quality rental submarkets, apparently due to the diversion there of would-be homeowners who could not afford such. Conversely, higher relative rental prices were associated with growth in the owner submarkets, apparently due to the increased rate of return seen by homeowners through their augmented savings in implicit rent.

Intersubmarket competitive influences on stock supply and mode mix do not, however, appear to be adequately measured by variables in our cross-SMSA model. Undoubtedly much of the shortcoming arises from the aggregative nature of the model—its inability to match the potential revenue gains to the costs incurred by undertaking a particular form of conversion on a particular dwelling. This shortcoming is remedied in the model presented in the next chapter. Nevertheless, there is much in these results that suggests that systematic, nonuniform patterns of responses between submarkets can be traced to supplier behaviors, as predicted by our theory.

Although our treatment of public policy interventions was necessarily crude, there was no support for the contention that public and subsidized private construction of housing effectively reduces slums. We could find no evidence that either form of public intervention in the housing market was associated with reductions in the stock of the two lowest-quality rental submarkets. This does not necessarily imply that they cannot in principle do so, but perhaps only that in our sample the degree to which they were employed seemed to produce no impacts on these submarkets.

Of course this result may be symptomatic of the more general lack of significance of *any* variables explaining medium-run supply behavior in the lower-quality rental submarkets. Perhaps minimal variations in dependent or independent variables here or multicollinearity were responsible. But the findings are also consistent with the hypothesis that supply changes in the lower-quality renter submarkets may be more of a "residual" of what is occurring in *other* submarkets than a reaction to signals transpiring within them. Given the importance of the operation of these submarkets to concerns of housing policy, this provocative hypothesis warrants further empirical testing.

Notes

1. Subsidized units are those so designated by the Annual Housing Survey, where some governmental body pays part of the construction cost, mortgage, or operating rent supplements, and direct loans for elderly housing.
2. More detailed breakdowns of age by submarket were not obtainable.
3. This cross-tenure effect could not, of course, be captured by the rental submarket $[X]$ terms since, by definition, they hold all prices constant.
4. This is a shortcoming we remedy in the single-SMSA model; see ch. 16.
5. Experiments to allow such differences to have separate parameter values quickly ran afoul of multicollinearity, unfortunately.
6. The exception being SL', SU' variables.
7. This SMSA was Chicago. Trial runs with Chicago eliminated from the sample did not noticeably alter the results.

16 Single-SMSA Model: Medium-Run Supply

This chapter describes and then analyzes the changes in the stock of single-family dwellings which occurred between 1963 and 1971 in Des Moines, Iowa. The sample which forms the basis of this study was described earlier in chapter 13. Here we explore in detail the various particular changes which took place in the stock (e.g., adding rooms, finishing a basement, installing air conditioning) and attempt to model econometrically the behavior which produced these changes. This contrasts with the analysis of medium-run stock changes presented in the prior chapter, which modeled dwelling modifications as defined only by the generic metric of hedonic value.

The comparative advantage of our microscopic view here is that both the incremental capital value and the incremental cost associated with particular modifications of particular houses in particular submarkets can be measured explicitly. Thus, the single-SMSA model holds more potential for adequately testing the significance of prospective rate of return as an explanatory variable in home alteration and improvement behavior. The disadvantage of this model is that the variation in submarket prices is much more limited (to only that between six submarkets) than in the cross-SMSA approach. It represents, therefore, a less-robust test of this feature of our theory.

The correlates of homeowners' actions to improve their homes have been the focus of several empirical investigations (for a review, see Galster 1987: ch. 9). These previous works analyze the behavior of a particular homeowner living in the same dwelling over a two- to three-year period. Key explanatory variables measure characteristics not only of the dwelling and the neighborhood, but also of the homeowner's household, so as to control for consumption-based demands for dwelling characteristics. Capital gains flowing from improvements are not measured, nor are particular types of alterations disaggregated. By contrast, our model considers changes in a given single-family dwelling over an eight-year period, during which different households may reside within and different owners (both absentee and occupant) may hold property rights. We view prospective rates of return associated with particular modifications of sampled dwellings as the main explanatory variable, regardless of characteristics of the occupant and owner.

Section 16.1 of this chapter describes the phenomena to be analyzed: improvements in the sampled Des Moines single-family dwelling stock during

1963–71. Section 16.2 presents our specification of econometric models designed to explain such modifications. The first, a disaggregated view, considers the choice of each of a variety of particular home alterations and improvements. The second aggregates these different alterations to discover the determinants of a total alteration (in money cost) function. Section 16.3 provides the results of our estimations and evaluates our theories in light of the findings.

16.1 Modifications in the Des Moines Single-Family Dwelling Stock

Between the two property assessments of 1963 and 1971 we were able to discern numerous objective alterations in the sampled dwellings. Of interest to us are those changes which are under the discretionary control of the owner, not those which arise out of inexorable structural aging or out of changes in the surrounding neighborhood. The overall consequences of these discretionary changes on the quality of the stock can be conveniently assessed through the use of our Des Moines hedonic index (see ch. 11). By inserting both 1963 and 1971 values of observed dwelling characteristics into the equation, while holding structural age and all neighborhood characteristics at their 1963 values and omitting all transistory market variables, one can easily estimate how the given dwelling's quality has been altered on net. This procedure yields hedonic value changes in individual dwellings as shown in table 16.1. It indicates that the discretionary actions or, in many cases, inactions by owners of single-family dwellings led to quality changes in over 97% of the observations. In 37.2% of the observations net quality rose; it fell in 59.6% of the cases. This is not to say that nominal sales prices of these latter homes fell or that their quality as measured by *all* characteristics (including neighborhood) necessarily fell. Rather, it shows that the net changes in hedonic value-producing *dwelling* characteristics which owners potentially could control led to a loss in real quality twice as often as it led to a gain. The magnitude of these changes is sizable: almost 18.0% of the dwellings experienced increases of 500 or more in hedonic value whereas almost 19.2% of the dwellings had declines of 500 or more. Expressed as a proportion of original quality, 15.8% of the dwellings rose by 5% or more and 19.2% fell by 5% or more in quality (see bottom panel in table 16.1).

The pattern of these discretionary alterations across quality submarkets is also interesting (see table 16.1). Note first that the frequency of improvements is not monotonically related to submarket quality, inasmuch as a relatively large proportion (41%) of owners initially in the lowest submarket achieved net improvements. Indeed, it is notable that net improvement activity occurred for at least a fourth of the single-family dwellings in each submarket. Of course, net quality losses outnumbered improvements in all but the highest-quality submarket.

The overall result of the above alterations was a change in the quality distri-

Table 16.1. Quality Changes in Des Moines Single-Family Dwellings, 1963–71

Change in Hedonic Value	Original-Quality Submarket, 1963						Total	
	1	2	3	4	5	6	#	%
Below −2,000	0	8	8	2	2	7	27	1.3%
−1,001 to −2,000	18	39	25	12	5	8	107	5.2%
−501 to −1,000	17	83	73	30	34	23	260	12.7%
−1 to −500	73	161	171	142	209	73	829	40.4%
0	2	15	19	21	5	3	65	3.2%
1 to 500	38	82	75	68	89	43	395	19.2%
501 to 1,000	17	15	13	24	50	23	142	6.9%
1,001 to 2,000	15	17	20	21	52	33	158	7.7%
2,001 to 3,000	1	1	1	3	12	16	34	1.7%
Over 3,001	6	2	5	3	6	13	35	1.7%
Total + Changes	77	117	114	119	209	128	764	—
% of Total 1963 Stock	41%	28%	28%	37%	45%	53%	—	37.2%

Change in Hedonic Value	Original-Quality Submarket, 1963						Total	
	1	2	3	4	5	6	#	%
Below −20%	21	15	6	0	1	2	45	2.2%
−10% to −20%	19	56	29	7	1	4	116	5.7%
−5% to −9.9%	30	108	63	18	9	4	232	11.3%
−1% to −4.9%	38	112	179	161	239	101	830	40.4%
0%	2	15	19	21	5	3	65	3.2%
1% to 4.9%	19	67	75	76	127	76	440	21.4%
5% to 9.9%	52	50	39	43	82	52	318	15.5%
Over 10%	6	0	0	0	0	0	6	0.3%

Note: Changes exclude those due to structural aging, changing neighborhood conditions, and transitory market forces.

bution of dwellings by submarket, as shown in table 16.2. Specifically, the number of dwellings in the lowest two quality submarkets (1, 2) rose by 10.6% and 5.4%, respectively; the number in the middle (3, 4, 5) submarkets fell by 9.0%, 2.8%, and 3.7%, respectively; and the number in the highest (6) submarket rose 9.5%. Thus it is apparent that modifications in the single-family housing stock which are deliberately undertaken by owners do, in fact, shape the character of the standing stock in nontrivial ways, assuming that we may generalize from the results in Des Moines.

In our analysis here we focus only on those additions, alterations, and modifications which tend to raise the quality of the dwelling. The particular quantitative and qualitative changes which served this end in our sample are itemized in tables 16.3 and 16.4. Table 16.3 shows that the most common way chosen by Des Moines owners to add to living space during the period was to finish a basement. Additions to the dwelling (both newly constructed and through conversion of existing features) and porches (both open and enclosed)

Table 16.2. Single-Family Dwellings by Quality Submarket, 1963 and 1971 (Des Moines Stock Sample)

Submarket	(1) 1963	(2) 1971	(3) [(2) − (1)]/(1)
1	187	207	+ 10.6%
2	423	443	+ 5.4%
3	410	373	− 9.0%
4	326	317	− 2.8%
5	464	447	− 3.7%
6	242	265	+9.5%

Note: For 1971, changes exclude those due to effects of structural aging, changing neighborhood conditions, and transitory market forces.

Table 16.3. Additions to Des Moines Single-Family Dwelling Stock, 1963–71

	Square Footage of Addition						
Type	Total	Under 100	100–199	200–299	300–399	400–499	Over 500
Living area*	134	49	36	10	10	9	20
via new construction	59	15	10	7	6	7	14
via porch enclosure	39	18	20	1	0	0	0
Finished basement	170	1	9	26	37	52	45
Unfinished basement	40	5	8	5	5	6	11
Finished attic	7	1	0	0	3	1	2
Open porch	136	38	44	32	13	4	5
via conversion**	28	11	10	3	0	1	3
Closed porch	111	44	48	15	1	1	2
via conversion**	87	30	44	10	1	0	2
Total additions	598	138	145	88	69	73	85

*Excluding finished basement and attic spaces.
**Involving loss of preexisting porch space.

were also relatively frequent improvements undertaken (4–5% of the sample). Table 16.4 indicates that central air conditioning was the most popular qualitative improvement, being undertaken by 12% of those not already possessing it. Over 8% of the dwellings showed the installation of more plumbing fixtures; over 5% added one or more garage spaces. Over 2% of dwellings without a fireplace added one and almost 8% of dwellings without central heat installed such during the 1963–71 period.

In summary, examination of the changes in the stock of single-family dwellings in Des Moines from the medium-run period 1963–71 convincingly supports a major premise of our work: owners' discretionary changes are frequent, and they significantly alter the character of their standing stock. Virtually all (96.8%) observed dwellings changed quality during the period as a

Table 16.4. Alterations and Modifications to Des Moines Single-Family Dwellings, 1963–71

Alteration/ Improvement	No. of Dwellings Not Having Feature in 1963	No. of Dwellings Installing Feature
Central air conditioning	1950	242
Central heat	65	5
Garage space		
(1)	933*	78
(2)	1721*	54
Total	—	132
Plumbing fixtures		
(1)	7*	107
(2)	36*	51
(3)	56*	4
(4)	93*	47
(5+)	1595*	2
Total	—	211
Fireplace	1757	38
Total alterations/improvements	—	628

*Dwellings having fewer than the given feature.

result of alterations in structural characteristics presumably under the control of owners. And over two-fifths of these changes were significant enough to change the initial dwelling by 500 or more units of hedonic value, that is, by 5% or more. The pattern of stock modifications was quite variable across original-quality submarkets, and the modifications were sufficiently large to alter the composition of submarkets at the end of the period by 3–11%. Particular sorts of dwelling additions, alterations, or modifications were individually, by contrast, comparatively rare over the eight-year period. Even the most frequently observed particular change (air conditioning) occurred in only 12% of the cases not originally possessing the desired feature. Most other specific changes were much less common. Such rarity of individual changes makes the modeling of specific change decisions very difficult. Nonetheless, we believe that there is enough systematic character to these decisions that our modeling effort described below will prove fruitful.

16.2 Specification of a Model of Home Alterations and Improvements

Home alterations by an owner-occupier represent a complex phenomenon to integrate into our analytical approach. An alteration by an owner-occupier is a supply-side action, but it is addressed to two markets that may or may not be dissimilar—the present consumer household (the owner-occupant's "inside market") and the larger metropolitanwide ("outside") market. If the owner household were perfectly mobile it would make whatever modifications seemed to promise the higher rate of return between the two markets. If the higher return were attainable in the outside market, the household would be prepared to move elsewhere—either to provide rental accommodations to others or by outright sale. Only if its own continued consumption occupancy (in the inside market) represented the highest rate-of-return opportunity would its ownership-occupancy continue.

The latter situation is often the more likely. The existing occupancy typically represents a deliberate pairing of house with household, the former approximately reflecting the special tastes of the latter. This means that the owner is likely to be the highest, or near-highest, bidder for the house. As the latter's life cycle flows, with its changing tastes, needs, and budget opportunities, certain changes in the housing become appropriate to improve the household's overall consumption situation. Given the original pairing, the same owner is likely to continue to be the highest or near-highest bidder for the modified house, so long as no radical structural changes are envisioned. For radical changes the aptness of the original pairing is largely lost, and so becomes irrelevant for differential hypothetical bids. But radical modifications are not likely to be frequently resorted to, because they are likely to be at a competitive cost disadvantage in the outer markets, as we argued earlier in chapter 5.

This kind of opportunity for the owner-occupier implies that many home improvements by owner-occupiers will be made primarily to enhance their own consumption, not to take advantage of immediate outer-market investment opportunities (i.e., not to provide consumption *for others* in the near future). Prediction of such improvements would therefore ideally require an understanding of the determinants of both outer-market and inner-market gains, namely, outer-market valuations for different housing attribute configurations, and the housing preferences–income situation (utility function) of each household involved, expecting that the latter of the owner-occupant would generally dominate.

While our theoretical treatment of modification supply explicitly incorporated this conflict between consumption for self and market investment (see chs. 5 and 6), our present empirical application is less able to cope with this broad a position. Our data base richly details housing characteristics, but lacks a pairing of these with characteristics of the occupying household. So we are unable to generate the consumption demand relationships for each house that would be necessary to measure the owner-occupant's consumption gains for different improvements to that house. We are therefore left with an empirical base that can generate the outer market's evaluation of different improvements, that is, the payoff to improvements as a market investment, but not their evaluation as an item of consumption. How good an approximation can this be to the more general model?

Three facts lend encouragement to the belief that an outer-market, investment-oriented model can tolerably serve as proxy for the more general investment-or-consumption model. First is the meaning of improvements as "an investment in owner-occupant consumption" for owner-occupiers. The lifetime of the investment is composed of two segments: (1) from the present to the end of the present occupier's occupancy; and (2) the remaining productive lifetime under the occupancy of others. Thus the personalistic tailoring of improvements to "inner-market" preferences is relevant only for the proportion of productive lifetime represented by the first segment. Since it antedates the second, the discounting process weights it more heavily than its successor (year by year). But household occupancies are not generally long relative to the total lifetimes of many improvements—and especially not expected *remaining* occupancies for households that have already inhabited the dwelling for substantial periods. Furthermore, remaining occupancies are not known with certainty. A household today may quite appropriately feel that its occupancy plans could change suddenly at any time in the near future as a result of life-cycle surprises. At that time the value of its improvement today would depend on the outer-market valuation, not the inner. A prudential investment strategy might well be conservative under these conditions, namely, that when the optimal pattern of improvements for owner-occupant consumption that would have dominated diverges considerably from outer-market directions, the actual improvements decided on represent a compromise between the two. The owner therefore moderates the risk of being left with a white elephant—and possibly at a time of family crisis—when the house must be sold quickly for liquidity reasons.

A second ground for expecting tolerable efficacy from the outer-market-oriented model is that the household may well be considering improvements as an explicit preparation for selling the house. Having allowed their own preferences, tolerances, and accommodations to govern stewardship of their home during their occupancy, now, on the brink of trying to sell on favorable terms, they find they must accommodate to the outer-market realities, that is, make changes apparently heavily favored by others which heretofore they spurned for themselves.

Where selling preparations include these outer-market accommodations, therefore, improvements will be dominated by the market investment motive. To the extent that this is a frequent situation, the market investment model should predict groups of housing improvements by owner-occupants tolerably well.

The third ground for modest optimism is that the discrepancy between the inner- and outer-market valuations may not be great in a large majority of cases. The U.S. housing market in metropolitan areas shows important degrees of homogeneity in housing standards on the basis of neighborhood, as we saw in chapter 9. The frequent turnover of residential property coupled with continued neighborhood homogeneity—although neighborhoods as a whole may well change in the course of this turnover—suggests a high degree of self-selection by households to experience similar housing lifestyles with their neighbors. But this implies that the preference valuation of different housing configurations held by each household is likely to be quite similar to that held in the neighborhood generally. Then the ability to measure valuations in the *neighborhood submarket* for different prospective improvements is likely to be a good predictor of the valuations of any particular household in that neighborhood. Our data base does include a set of neighborhood variables linked to individual houses that permits us to predict valuations in different neighborhood situations. This should strengthen our ability to predict what are in fact joint consumption-investment decisions by means of a model that appears to consider only the investment component of that decision.

In what follows, therefore, we model home improvements by owner-occupiers as though the improvement decision is approximately an investment in which the returns are calculable in terms of how the current (outer) market evaluates these improvements. Our specification of the hedonic valuation process—via a multiplicative function—reflects our conviction (not contradicted empirically) that not only the disembodied housing attributes (structural and neighborhood) but also their joint configuration contribute to the overall value of a house. Therefore, a given prospective improvement may well generate a different addition to value for different houses, depending on how well it complements what is already there. So the investment return to that improvement must be calculated separately for every house—and what may be a good investment for some may well be a bad investment for others.

In the above paragraph we indicated that our payoff mechanism is the current market valuation. If the properties being studied were landlord-owned rental units, the outer-market investment orientation would be directly appropriate: no consumption elements of the occupants would intrude in the improvements decision. Then the investment period would begin immediately, and it would be the current market situation that would be most relevant to evaluation. But our discussion of the relevance of an investment orientation for owner-occupiers suggested a somewhat forward delay in the inception of that investment period. Should not the appropriate market valuations therefore reflect a somewhat similar future market situation? Ideally yes, but the exigencies of data have forced on us a compromise procedure by which we have essentially treated the entire estimation period, 1963–71, as a single period of action. Some of the neighborhood variables are indeed measured after the period's beginning, but no explicit year-by-year matchup of home improvement action with explanatory variables has been attempted. This is, alas, standard estimation procedure in the housing field, generally forced by data inadequacies. In the present case, little damage is likely to result, given the complex, far from decisive theoretical delineation of timing perspectives in this kind of decision, as touched on above.

In what follows we specify two types of empirical models. The first, a disaggregated view, considers the choice of each of a variety of particular home alterations and improvements. The second aggregates these different alterations to discover the determinants of a total alteration (in money cost) function. These specifications are discussed in more detail below.

16.2.1 Disaggregated Model

The goal of the disaggregated model is to uncover those factors which explain the particular structural modifications in the single-family housing stock which were observed during the 1963–71 period and which were described in tables 16.3 and 16.4. Many of these modifications—central air conditioning, fireplaces, plumbing fixtures, garages—are by their nature relatively homogeneous and "lumpy," with discrete values possible only over limited ranges. Other modifications involve changes which are measured in square feet and thus are virtually continuous over a wide range of values. Inasmuch as such latter changes clearly are not all commensurate, they must be reduced to a smaller number of sets which are more so.

The technique employed here is to define "archetypical" changes. After examining frequency distributions of additions as in table 16.3, relatively narrow ranges of square footage were collapsed into categories, and the median square footage of each such range was specified as the archetype. Ranges were chosen broadly enough so that at least twenty dwellings (about 1% typically) which feasibly could have undergone the given archetypical change did, in fact, do so during the period.[1] In choosing archetypes we also were limited to the degree that unambiguous cost data were required for the given modification.[2]

The result was the specification of sixteen distinct archetypical home alterations and additions, which are listed and defined precisely in table 16.5. With five types of modifications—plumbing, garages, finished basement, open porches, new additions—there are multiple, mutually exclusive choices specified. The owner-occupant may choose, for example, to add either a one-car garage or a two-car garage, but not both. All other types of archetypical modifications are dichotomous, so the choice is viewed as either undertaking the given change or not. Choices across various types of archetypical modifications are dichotomous, so the choice is viewed as either undertaking the given change or not. Choices across various types of archetypical modifications are assumed not to be mutually exclusive. (The groupings within which choices are mutually exclusive are shown in table 16.5 by brackets.)

Our explanatory models here are probabilistic. Left-hand variables are the probabilities that each specified alteration will be made; right-hand variables are the explanatory factors.

Each archetypical change within a (bracketed, mutually exclusive) modification type is contrasted to making no modification of that given type, and the probability of each such dichotomous choice is the dependent variable. That is, let O_j be the choice of no modification of a given type j, and let i_j be the

Table 16.5. Archetypical Home Alterations and Additions Modeled (Des Moines Single-Family Structures, 1963–71)

Modification	Detailed Description	*N*
1. Plumbing	Adding 1 plumbing fixture, i.e., sink, toilet, shower or tub	107
2. Plumbing	Adding 2 plumbing fixtures of types above	51
3. Plumbing	Adding 3 or 4 plumbing fixtures of types above	51
4. Fireplace	Adding 1 fireplace	38
5. Garage	Adding 1 enclosed garage space (attached or unattached)	78
6. Garage	Adding 2 enclosed garage spaces (attached or unattached)	54
7. Basement	Finishing basement area of 50–350 ft² (median = 275 ft²)	73
8. Basement	Finishing basement area of 351–500 ft² (median = 425 ft²)	52
9. Basement	Finishing basement area of over 500 ft² (median = 600 ft²)	45
10. Porch	Add open porch area of under 200 ft² (median = 100 ft²)	69
11. Porch	Add open porch area of 201–600 ft² (median = 275 ft²)	53
12. Porch	Add new* enclosed porch area of under 300 ft (median = 100 ft²)	53
13. Cooling	Add central air conditioning	242
14. Addition	Build new* addition of 50–350 ft² (median = 200 ft²); not bathroom**	22
15. Addition	Build new* addition of 351–1300 ft² (median = 550 ft²); not bathroom**	20
16. Addition	Convert closed porch into year-round addition of 50–200 ft² (median = 100 ft²); not bathroom**	31

Note: Brackets indicate mutually exclusive options.
*New construction; not involving modifying existing porch(es).
**No additions with three or more new plumbing fixtures are included; additions must alter ground floor plan of home.

choice of a particular archetypical change i within type j, where $i = 1, \ldots,$ n possibilities. Then we can specify n equations which attempt to explain the relative probability $Pr(i/O)$, $i = 1, \ldots, n$. If the explanatory variables for these relative probabilities are specified in terms of the cumulative logistic probability function wherein the $Pr(i/O)$ term is the natural logarithm of the odds that the particular choice i has been made, then the model becomes the well-known multinomial LOGIT specification.[3] The disaggregated model involves estimating such LOGIT equations, one for each of the archetypes listed in table 16.5.

Explanatory variables for these LOGIT models follow from previous econometric studies of home upkeep behavior, especially those of Shear (1983), and Stewart and Hyclak (1986), who have distinguished between alterations and additions.[4] These studies suggest that features of the individual owner, the dwelling, and the surrounding neighborhood be controlled for. Unfortunately, the Des Moines sampling procedure did not permit the acquisition of data about the individual owner. Some attempt is made to minimize this omission by the inclusion of aggregate census tract demographic and socioeconomic characteristics, for reasons suggested above. From that discussion the reader should be aware that these tract variables serve as proxies for the owners of individual single-family dwellings in the tract primarily via their direct function of controlling for the socioeconomic status of the tract, but these two functions are not identical.

With this caveat in mind, the following census tract–based variables are specified, each estimated for 1965.[5] The percentage of the tract population aged 5–9 years (*AGE*5–9%) is used as a proxy for the likelihood that homeowners will have within the period children reaching the age where demands for extra bedrooms and bathrooms will increase. The percentages of the tract adult population (aged 20 and older) who are 20–34 years (*AGE*20–34%) and 35–64 years (*AGE*35–64%) are used as life-cycle stage proxies. Compared to those in the reference category (age 65 and over), younger owner-occupant households demonstrate higher demands for dwelling space and amenities, which might be met by home improvements, as shown by numerous studies. An estimate of the duration of tenure of owner-occupants in the tract is provided by the percentage of households who in 1960 resided in the same unit in 1955 (*PRE*-1955%). Longer-term owner-occupants seem less prone to make alterations and additions (Shear 1983; Stewart and Hyclak 1986), either because modifications eventually seem less necessary from a consumption standpoint or because crucial changes have already been made in earlier periods.

The socioeconomic status of the tract and, presumably, the economic wherewithal of sampled owner-occupants are controlled for by two variables—median income (*MEDINC*$) and the percentage of employees in professional, managerial, and technical occupations (*OCCUP*%). Other studies have found that the status of the neighborhood has only a weak impact upon home improvement behavior,[6] so the coefficients of these variables may be more tolerable proxies for individual household status. But in this role the predicted impact is unclear. Relative to other income groups, higher-income owner-occupants may have more financial assets with which to undertake home modifications, but they are more likely to respond to home inadequacies by moving to another dwelling instead of improving in place (Seek 1983).[7]

The peculiar investment dynamics which might occur in neighborhoods characterized by particular racial or class features are investigated with three variables. If a tract was adjacent to a majority-black tract in 1960 and the change in the percentage of blacks from 1960 to 1970 was 20 percentage points or more, it is denoted by the dummy variable *TIPAREA*. If a tract had a median income of $5,000 or less in 1960 and a percentage of single-family homes less than 30% and an increase in property values below 1% annually from 1960 to 1970, it is denoted by the dummy variable *BADAREA*. The 1965 percentage of black population is specified as the variable *BLACK*%. The conventional wisdom is that investors in "poverty neighborhoods" and in those of higher black concentrations (especially if threatened by racial "tipping") will be more pessimistic about the returns they expect to reap from home improvements (Taub, Taylor, and Dunham 1984). If this pessimism is abetted by a reluctance of financial institutions to make home improvement loans in such areas, the deleterious consequences for alterations and additions will be magnified. Insofar as the *BLACK%* measures for racial characteristics of sampled owner-occupants, it should also be inversely related to home improvement probabilities, insofar as black homeowners have less wealth and are more likely to be denied home improvement loans than comparable white homeowners.

The core of the model is the variables that directly reflect characteristics of the individual sampled dwellings. Foremost among these is an estimate of the market return the individual homeowner can expect from a given archetypical change *i* (*RETURNS*). This return is defined as the difference between the increment in hedonic (money) value generated by the given change (i.e., the capital gain) and the estimated marginal cost of that change. The gain term is computed using the hedonic index estimated in chapter 11, wherein all the other features of the dwelling and neighborhood which enter that index will affect the *marginal* hedonic payoff from the given improvement. The cost term is calculated using cost schedules supplied by the Assessor's Office of the city of Des Moines.[8]

So long as outer-market valuations have any effect, along with personal consumption preferences, in judging the desirability of prospective alterations, the *RETURNS* variable should be positively related to the probability of making each of the modifications. That is, an improvement which upgrades a dwelling's quality from *i* to *j* will be more likely the greater the differential rate of return between *i* and *j*. Recalling equation (6.7), this differential can be expressed as the market valuation differential between *j* and *i*, minus the (opportunity rate of return-inflated) differential between the costs of a unit upgraded from *i* to *j* and the costs of maintaining it in *i;* this is measured precisely by *RETURNS* (with the caveat noted below). But we argued above that some of the explanatory power of personal consumption preferences should be captured by outer-market considerations as well. So *RETURNS* should be the crucial variable reflecting net gains (positively) at the level of the individual house.

A central feature of our overall theoretical approach is our attention to market segmentation—the system of housing submarket interrelationships. That system is attended to here via two kinds of submarket variables—a pair of price variables, and a direct submarket dummy. As to the first, our net gains variable, *RETURNS,* abstracts from one element of net addition to house value—different submarket prices. Recall that total predicted market value of a housing unit is its hedonic value times its submarket price. *RETURNS* omits the latter factor. A composite net financial gain variable including this factor might have been constructed, but we decided to separate out the price factor in order to examine the effect of submarket price structure directly. Accordingly, we investigate the role of submarket price differentials with two variables. *PRICEP* takes the value of the ratio of destination and origin submarket prices if this ratio is greater than one, zero otherwise.[9] *PRICEN* takes the value of the ratio of destination and origin submarket prices if this ratio is less than one, zero otherwise. Here, *destination submarket* is specified for each individual case by adding the increment in hedonic value potentially produced by the given archetypical change to the initial hedonic value of the dwelling[10] and ascertaining in which submarket the dwelling would then be categorized. If there is a difference in origin and destination submarkets and the relative price ratio is positive (see table 11.9), theory suggests that the implied market strength in the destination submarket would provide an added fillip to the likelihood of undertaking the given change (because the total net financial gain from the improvement is thereby greater); thus, the coefficient of *PRICEP* should be positive. Just the opposite would be expected for *PRICEN:* a net financial gain less than shown by *RETURNS*—thus, a negative coefficient. Two separate price ratio variables are specified to see if the magnitudes of intersubmarket price differential effects are asymmetric depending on the sign of the differential.[11]

The second type of submarket variable is designed to test whether unmeasured, owner-related factors specific to different submarkets—for example, expectations, mobility—influence the modification decision. Since a number of the most likely of these influences have already been measured in other variables—for example, high covariance of submarket with neighborhood variables like median income, poverty, and black residents (*MEDINC$*, *OCCUP%* , *TIPAREA, BADAREA, BLACK%*)—it unclear what kinds or intensities of effect will be picked up. Influences here will be measured in terms of five submarket-specific dummies: $SUBMKT_k$, $k = 1, \ldots, 5$ (where submarket 6 becomes the excluded reference category). Each house is thus classified with at most one of these dummies equal to 1 and at least four equal to 0 (a house in submarket 6 has all dummies = 0).

Whether or not the dwelling is occupied by its owner at the beginning of the period is indicated by the dummy variable *OWNER*. Owner occupancy itself is likely to reflect conflicting forces. On the one hand, owner occupancy implies that motives of consumption will vie with market investment motives in determining the pattern of optimal modification, including zero modification, unlike the clear dominance of the latter in absentee ownership (with tenant). The most obvious direct effect should be to weaken the explanatory power of the *RETURNS* variable. On the other hand, owner occupancy gives two related but distinct grounds for making housing improvements instead of only market incentives. Moreover, when a household occupies its own house, the web of supportive social relations in the neighborhood in which it participates tends to generate social solidarity bonds: a sense of pride in, and responsibility to uphold, the values and standards of the neighborhood. So housing improvements not only add to the household's consumption standards; they also meet its desire to behave proudly and responsibly with respect to neighborhood enhancement. The result should be an increased probability of *any* improvement being made (Galster 1987: chs. 9, 13). Indeed, empirical evidence suggests that this contention is borne out for single-family homes (Galster 1983).

The dummy variable *OWNER*, therefore, should be associated positively with the probability of each of the various kinds of improvement. The strength of its influence on the different kinds of improvement ought to indicate the relative importance of neighborhood responsibility for these different improvements. Some are more overtly noticeable and hence socially relevant than others.[12]

Finally, three other variables are employed as controls for dwelling-specific features. If the dwelling sold during the 1963–71 period, the dummy *SOLD* is assigned the value one. The impact of *SOLD* on the probability of improvement is ambiguous. On the one hand, a household preparing to sell its home soon is not likely to make changes closely tailored to its own preferences inasmuch as they will not be enjoyed for long and may be "punished" by the market at sale time for being idiosyncratic. On the other hand, as suggested above, in preparing to sell their home a household that has tolerated major deficiencies (relative to what it perceives to be market preferences) may want to rectify such deficiencies to avoid being punished for *not* making a conventional change. Insofar as the propensity to make any change at all, even idiosyncratic, adds to the probability of making each particular change, the first factor would suggest a negative effect of the variable *SOLD*. On the other hand, insofar as preparatory rectification occurs, it adds to the probability of modification—a positive effect. The reality of the latter, indeed, would tend to strengthen the effect of market signals on modification, since it changes the relative weight of consumption and market investment in favor of the latter.

The variable *SOLD* reflects not only the situation of the incipient seller, but also that of the recent buyer. Anecdotally, it frequently happens that a new household occupant of a house makes a concentrated set of alterations to the house just after moving in—to "make the house truly theirs" by correcting various of its flaws from the point of view of their specific tastes. Indeed, for many households this may be the time of greatest modification activity over the household's tenure. Such postsale modification flurry, together with presale preparatory "corrections," probably outweighs presale conservatism, thus suggesting that if a house was sold anytime during our observation period there is a greater likelihood of alterations having occurred than if the house was not sold. So we expect *SOLD* to have a positive influence on the probability of modification.

The age of the dwelling (*AGEHOME*) is included as an additional variable to test for the possibility that different vintages of homes have peculiar technological constraints or opportunities for converting investments into home-quality increments, as discussed in chapter 5. Age here is controlling primarily for a set of discrete architectural styles and building materials. These are not necessarily linear with age; indeed, they may not even be monotonic. The variable may play an additional role, however. It could capture some age-related, monotonically increasing cost factors for any kind of upgrading (not captured in our cost indicators; see ch. 6). Similarly, it might reflect a systematic age-related drag on the market's valuation of improvements. Since such drag is presumably already basically measured in the hedonic index that enters into *RETURNS*, additional explanatory power from this source via *AGEHOME* rests on unmeasured systematic cost side factors, or a distinction between market valuation of existing attributes and that of modified attributes. For different ages, the latter may be seen as either aesthetically discordant or enhancing, so that the modification process itself is not necessarily neutral with respect to market valuation. Finally, since architectural discreteness, cost drag, and configurational coherence all seem decidedly nonlinear, we add the squared value of age ($AGEHOME^2$) as an additional variable. This should enable us to elicit the maximum distinctive explanatory power from home age, given the variety of its proxy roles.

A final feature is added in the equations for new additions involving extensions to the ground floor plan of the house. Here the lot size of the parcel (*LOT*) and its squared value (LOT^2) are included to see if this acts as a constraint on this particular sort of improvement.

In summary, the disaggregated model of home alterations and additions is specified as

$$(16.1)\quad Pr(i) = + AGE5\text{–}9\% + AGE20\text{–}34\% + AGE35\text{–}64\% - PRE-1955\% \pm ?MEDINC\$ \pm ?OCCUP\% - TIPAREA - BADAREA - BLACK\% + RETURNS_i \pm ?SUBMKT_k + PRICEP - PRICEN + OWNER \pm ?SOLD \pm ?AGEHOME \pm ?AGEHOME^2 + LOT \pm LOT^2.$$

Where all symbols are defined as in the text, *LOT* and LOT^2 are only used in the floor-area additions equations, signs indicate the predicted correlation between a given independent variable and the dependent variable, if any, and equation (16.1) is specified as a LOGIT functional form.

16.2.2 Aggregate Model

The aggregate model is more like a general investment model: no distinctions are made about kinds of modification, but only about whether or not they are made and their total cost. The disaggregate model more closely pinpoints configurational investment opportunities by pairing each particular type of modification with the specifics of a particular house. The aggregate model rests instead on an averaging of different opportunities and should therefore, in an ideal situation, give fuzzier predictions. In the present situation, however, the frequency of each kind of modification is very low (even though rate of return would suggest a much larger incidence), and so the absolute number of instances is small for our moderate-sized sample. A host of idiosyncratic chance factors would seem to be operative in the decision actually to make any alteration. As a result, the averaging of opportunities has much to recommend it as a way of coping with significant randomness. It is in this spirit that we specify our aggregate model. A comparison of empirical results between aggregate and disaggregate models will accordingly be most interesting in trying to understand the character of modification behavior.

The aggregate model of medium-run supply in Des Moines makes no distinction among particular types of home alterations and additions. Rather, all the aforementioned sixteen archetypical changes are considered as a whole, and a two-equation model is specified.[13] The first, analogous to the disaggregated probability model above, is a LOGIT model which predicts the log likelihood that one or more of the $m = 1, \ldots, 16$ archetypical changes will be undertaken during the 1963–71 period. The second predicts the estimated total expenditures on such archetypical additions and alterations (*IMPROVE$*) for those owners who do choose to undertake one or more.[14]

Explanatory variables for these aggregate models are identical to those for the disaggregated models, with the exception of the *RETURNS* variable. Here $\Sigma RETURNS$ is defined as the sum across all feasible i of all $RETURNS_i$, with only the highest return within each mutually exclusive set of archetypical changes being added and with all negative returns being assigned the value zero.[15] The logic of this procedure is that owner-occupants scan the entire array of potential archetypical changes and evaluate their respective potential outer-market rates of return and their potential consumption benefits. Owners may be dissuaded from undertaking improvements yielding substantial utility gains to the occupants if the market evaluates such changes harshly (i.e., negative returns), as our introductory remarks suggest. In the same spirit, certain improvements yielding high returns may be undertaken even if the current occupants have relatively weak personal demands for them. An owner is never forced to undertake any of the given archetypical changes, so if one or more are perceived as yielding negative returns they become irrelevant opportunities; hence the coding of negative returns as zero here. Similarly, within each set of mutually exclusive changes (i.e., plumbing, garages, open porches, finished basements, new additions), only the returns potentially available from the highest-return alternative in that set should be predictive of whether any improvement in that set will be undertaken.

In sum, the aggregate version of the single-SMSA, medium-run supply model can be expressed as

$$\begin{aligned}(16.2)\quad Pr(any\ m) = {} & + AGE5\text{–}9\% + AGE20\text{–}34\% + AGE35\text{–}64\% \\ & - PRE\text{-}1955\% \pm ?MEDINC\$ \pm ?OCCUP\% \\ & - TIPAREA - BADAREA - BLACK\% \\ & + \Sigma RETURNS \pm ?SUBMKT_k + PRICEP \\ & - PRICEN - OWNER \pm ?SOLD \pm ?AGEHOME \\ & \pm ?AGEHOME^2,\end{aligned}$$

where all the symbols are defined in the text, signs indicate the predicted correlation between a given independent variable and the dependent variable, if any, and equation (16.2) is specified as a LOGIT.

16.3 Empirical Results

Parameter estimates for the disaggregate LOGIT models (one for each of sixteen archetypical changes) are presented in table 16.6 and for the aggregate linear models in table 16.9. Before discussing them in detail it is important to understand exactly what hypotheses are being tested here.

Our application centers on the hypothesis that response to market profitability opportunities is both an important direct *and* proxy behavior incentive for deciding on alterations and additions. These opportunities are measured by rates of return generated via expected induced changes in market values for each house in question and the expected cost of the modification. Anticipated market value changes are measured by our hedonic index and the prices in different quality submarkets. Our basic assumption is that an index that predicts total market value for each house's already assembled configuration of housing attributes will also predict changes in market value for modifications of that configuration over time. This seems generally reasonable, but there are aspects of the modification process for which this assumption may be problematic, as we argue below. These market-opportunity decision incentives are qualified or augmented by fragmentary, suggestive information about housing consumption tastes of owner-occupiers of each house and about possibly special relevant features of the neighborhood and quality submarket in which the house appears. The qualifying variables concerning neighborhood and quality submarket are, however, significantly compromised and compromising in that they bear significant relations to the rate-of-return variable. Thus the significance of the estimates both for *RETURNS, PRICEP,* and *PRICEN* on the one hand, and the neighborhood and submarket dummy variables on the other, should be decreased through complex, multicollinear relationships.[16] Moreover, the affected variables should be interpreted not at face value, but as influences via their portions that are linearly independent of their "contaminating" counterparts.

As examples of this, the variables *MEDINC$*, *BADAREA*, *BLACK*, and *AGEHOME* are exact components of the hedonic index that generates *RETURNS; PRE*-1955%, *TIPAREA*, *SOLD*, and *OCCUP%* are related to it in varying degrees. Moreover, the submarket dummies $SUBMKT_1, \ldots, SUBMKT_5$ are variously related to *PRICEP* and *PRICEN*. Consequently, both the significance of their influence on the dependent variable and the identity of what aspect of them in fact has this influence must be interpreted with great care.

One final remark is appropriate in understanding the overall explanatory strength of each model. There are two major reasons for expecting only

Table 16.6. Coefficients of LOGIT Models for Individual Alterations and Additions

Independent Variables	Plumbing Fixtures 1	Plumbing Fixtures 2	Plumbing Fixtures 3–4	Fireplace 1	Garage 1	Garage 2
AGE5–9%	−.232	−11.3	5.10	−14.2	−4.03	9.37
	(0.05)	(1.97)[b]*	(0.85)	(1.41)*	(0.73)	(1.10)
AGE20–34%	−3.00	5.62	−3.02	8.17	6.69	−.272
	(1.05)	(1.62)[c]	(0.79)	(1.50)[c]	(2.12)[b]	(0.06)
AGE35–64%	−4.05	7.01	.424	6.81	7.19	−1.02
	(1.48)[c]	(2.14)[b]	(0.11)	(1.53)[c]	(2.49)[a]	(0.22)
PRE–1955%	−1.19	−.329	−3.01	4.10	.151	.540
	(1.32)[c]	(0.27)	(2.48)[a]	(2.88)[a]*	(0.14)	(0.38)
MEDINC$	−.07	.05	−.17	.13	−.09	−.15
($1,000s)	(0.86)	(0.49)	(1.45)*	(0.89)	(0.71)	(0.91)
BLACK%	−.005	−.011	−.005	−.004	−.001	−.004
	(0.68)	(0.98)	(0.51)	(0.17)	(0.08)	(0.38)
OCCUP%	.352	−1.17	2.02	−1.23	.883	2.01
	(0.24)	(0.53)	(1.00)	(0.50)	(0.48)	(0.82)
BADAREA	−.491	−.541	−.867	1.42	.182	.304
	(1.46)[c]	(1.26)	(1.57)[c]	(1.78)[c]*	(0.63)	(0.73)
TIPAREA	−.211	−.317	−.002	−1.68	.039	.203
	(0.80)	(0.67)	(0.01)	(0.67)	(0.14)	(0.51)
OWNER	.642	−.338	3.03	−.189	.166	.487
	(1.25)	(1.19)	(0.56)	(0.36)	(.453)	(0.93)
SOLD	.176	−.477	.024	−.023	−.096	−.403
	(1.62)*	(2.08)[b]*	(0.15)	(0.12)	(0.74)	(2.34)[b]*
AGEHOME	.009	.003	.011	−.034	−.009	−.001
	(0.98)	(0.25)	(0.98)	(2.18)[b]*	(0.84)	(0.08)
AGEHOME^2	−.06	.05	−.01	.47	.11	.01
(÷1,000)	(0.56)	(0.38)	(0.04)	(2.63)[a]*	(0.96)	(0.05)
SUBMKT1	−.273	.975	−1.81	−2.26	−.023	−.626
	(0.82)	(2.44)[b]	(2.53)[b]*	(0.81)	(0.06)	(0.93)
SUBMKT2	−.785	.054	−1.10	.756	.013	−.146
	(2.55)[b]*	(0.13)	(2.39)[b]*	(0.97)	(0.04)	(0.34)
SUBMKT3	−.801	−.611	−.829	.372	−.036	.032
	(3.10)[a]*	(1.46)*	(2.16)[b]*	(0.67)	(0.12)	(0.08)
SUBMKT4	−.699	−.312	−.854	−.182	.299	.254
	(3.08)[a]*	(0.94)	(2.47)[b]*	(0.40)	(1.16)	(0.74)
SUBMKT5	−.137	−.530	−.537	−.093	.243	.143
	(0.90)	(1.68)[c]*	(2.22)[b]*	(0.29)	(1.05)	(0.51)
PRICEP	.147	−2.87	−.317	.583	−.167	−.028
	(0.51)	(0.77)	(0.93)	(1.62)[c]	(0.52)	(0.10)
PRICEN	−.511	−.669	.197	.304	−.045	−.162
	(1.30)[c]	(2.12)[b]	(0.79)	(1.04)	(0.16)	(0.49)
RETURNS	2.08	1.29	.10	1.44	.39	1.89
($1,000s)	(2.90)[a]	(2.69)[a]	(0.21)	(3.53)[a]	(1.66)[b]	(5.80)[a]
Intercept	6.48		3.14	−4.61	−1.08	3.29
	(2.94)[a]*	(0.31)	(0.52)	(1.23)	(0.44)	(0.89)
Potential *N*	1951	1895	1894	2052	1998	1974
Actual *N*	107	51	51	38	78	54

(*continued*)

Table 16.6. continued

Independent Variables	Finished Basement 50–350ft^2	Finished Basement 351–500ft^2	Finished Basement 501 + ft^2	Open Porch 1–200ft^2	Open Porch 201 + ft^2	Closed Porch 1–350ft^2
*AGE*5–9%	−8.13	30.9	5.44	3.68	9.52	−10.8
	(1.54)*	(1.51)[c]	(0.42)	(0.52)	(1.02)	(1.19)
*AGE*20–34%	6.21	8.92	−5.72	7.48	−1.49	1.68
	(2.09)[b]	(1.35)[c]	(0.78)	(2.06)[b]	(0.29)	(0.24)
*AGE*35–64%	4.33	16.5	−7.63	9.32	−1.55	.500
	(1.57)[c]	(2.99)[a]	(1.06)	(2.78)[a]	(0.31)	(0.07)
PRE-1955%	.190	4.74	.818	2.51	1.12	1.09
	(0.21)	(2.07)[b]*	(0.41)	(2.10)[b]*	(0.75)	(0.52)
MEDINC$	.11	−.31	.05	−.19	−.29	−.48
($1,000s)	(1.18)	(1.20)	(0.26)	(1.55)*	(1.84)[c]*	(1.73)[c]*
BLACK%	−.014	−.029	−.008	.007	−.022	.002
	(0.56)	(0.54)	(0.36)	(0.92)	(0.92)	(0.19)
OCCUP%	−1.65	3.38	−2.15	2.76	5.94	6.98
	(1.12)	(0.83)	(0.60)	(1.50)*	(2.58)[a]*	(1.86)[c]*
BADAREA	−2.66	−.346	1.49	.508	−2.49	−.452
	(0.80)	(0.11)	(1.86)[c]*	(1.23)	(0.57)	(1.06)
TIPAREA	.72	2.47	.108	.000	−.071	−.189
	(1.06)	(1.40)*	(0.15)	(0.00)	(0.09)	(0.52)
OWNER	.67	2.09	−.171	3.24	2.60	.200
	(1.31)[c]	(0.49)	(0.30)	(0.59)	(0.55)	(0.38)
SOLD	−.01	−.02	.07	−.05	.42	−.10
	(0.12)	(0.09)	(0.32)	(0.33)	(2.44)[b]*	(0.42)
AGEHOME	−.009	−.011	−.004	.001	−.004	.034
	(0.71)	(0.43)	(0.15)	(0.03)	(0.21)	(1.60)*
AGEHOME^2	−.16	.06	−.22	−.05	−.01	−.32
(÷1,000)	(0.79)	(0.15)	(0.50)	(0.30)	(0.06)	(1.40)*
*SUBMKT*1	−2.38	−1.77	−2.47	−.416	.385	.241
	(0.73)	(0.40)	(0.40)	(1.08)	(0.70)	(0.34)
*SUBMKT*2	−.42	−1.94	−.891	−.456	.010	.144
	(1.19)	(0.83)	(0.92)	(1.42)*	(0.02)	(0.22)
*SUBMKT*3	−.60	−.300	.091	−.594	−.459	.261
	(1.96)[b]*	(0.29)	(0.11)	(1.97)[b]*	(1.10)	(0.43)
*SUBMKT*4	−.15	.261	−.168	−.229	−.140	−.354
	(1.23)	(0.33)	(0.25)	(0.96)	(0.45)	(0.48)
*SUBMKT*5	.21	.071	−.641	−.204	.062	.622
	(1.23)	(0.15)	(1.54)*	(0.99)	(0.25)	(1.10)
PRICEP	.57	−.05	−2.96	.457	.284	−2.37
	(2.68)[a]	(0.08)	(1.32)*	(1.52)[c]	(0.79)	(0.40)
PRICEN	.19	.45	.495	.692	−2.71	.362
	(1.25)	(1.45)*	(1.44)*	(2.59)[a]*	(0.63)	(0.89)
RETURNS	−.07	.64	.67	1.04	.67	2.44
($1,000s)	(.87)	(1.42)[c]	(2.23)[b]	(1.71)[c]	(1.21)	(2.21)[b]
Intercept	−.31	−14.3	6.83	−6.70	1.56	5.34
	(.13)	(2.16)[b]*	(1.26)	(1.09)	(0.26)	(1.06)
Potential *N*	1842	1573	1420	2012	1988	2052
Actual *N*	73	52	45	69	53	53

Table 16.6. continued

Independent Variables	Central A/C	Home Additions		Addition via Porch Conversion
		50–350 ft.^{2}	351 + ft.^{2}	
AGE5–9%	.095	−17.9	30.5	−5.25
	(0.03)	(1.72)[c]*	(1.56)[c]	(0.55)
AGE20–34%	1.62	13.9	2.82	−5.73
	(0.81)	(2.50)[a]	(0.40)	(1.11)
AGE35–64%	2.67	11.1	11.7	−7.02
	(1.39)[c]	(2.44)[a]	(1.91)[b]	(1.25)
PRE-1955%	.072	3.11	.818	1.28
	(0.11)	(1.68)[c]*	(0.38)	(0.70)
MEDINC$	.00	.30	−.63	.27
($1,000s)	(0.05)	(1.57)*	(2.28)[b]*	(1.45)*
BLACK%	.000	.008	−.040	−.005
	(0.01)	(0.72)	(0.73)	(0.46)
OCCUP%	.005	−4.95	8.86	−4.67
	(0.01)	(1.47)*	(2.23)[b]*	(1.38)*
BADAREA	−3.32	−1.55	−.778	−3.17
	(0.85)	(0.45)	(0.19)	(0.44)
TIPAREA	−.025	−1.89	−.626	.377
	(0.01)	(0.66)	(0.21)	(0.90)
OWNER	.529	−.284	−.213	3.35
	(1.70)[b]	(0.73)	(0.39)	(0.30)
SOLD	.022	−.295	1.06	.030
	(0.28)	(1.12)	(2.07)[b]*	(0.13)
AGEHOME	−.005	−.004	.039	−.015
	(0.63)	(0.18)	(1.57)*	(0.55)
AGEHOME2	−.02	−.10	−.48	.20
(÷1,000)	(0.20)	(0.40)	(1.30)*	(0.79)
SUBMKT1	−2.00	1.02	−1.90	.210
	(3.75)[a]*	(1.56)*	(1.71)[c]*	(0.29)
SUBMKT2	−1.11	.461	−1.04	−.344
	(5.31)[a]*	(0.72)	(1.37)*	(0.49)
SUBMKT3	−1.09	.089	−1.11	−.202
	(6.22)[a]*	(0.15)	(1.40)*	(0.31)
SUBMKT4	−.683	−.366	−1.13	−.034
	(4.91)[a]*	(0.65)	(1.56)*	(0.06)
SUBMKT5	−.494	−.125	−.66	.115
	(4.30)[a]*	(0.29)	(1.56)*	(0.30)
PRICEP	.145	.106	−.139	−3.32
	(0.57)	(0.24)	(0.20)	(0.21)
PRICEN	.507	−.506	.626	−3.37
	(1.93)[c]*	(1.05)	(1.63)*	(0.21)
RETURNS	.78	.02	.03	.97
($1,000s)	(1.75)[b]	(0.03)	(0.11)	(0.74)
LOT	NA	.06	−.05	NA
(in 1,000 ft^2)		(0.86)	(1.36)*	

(continued)

Table 16.6 continued

Independent Variables	Central A/C	Home Additions 50–350 ft.^{2}	Home Additions 351 + ft.^{2}	Addition via Porch Conversion
LOT^2	NA	−.001	.001	NA
		(0.79)	(1.97)[b]*	
Intercept	2.93	−7.64	−2.81	4.02
	(1.89)[c]*	(1.83)[c]*	(0.52)	(0.33)
Potential *N*	1949	2033	2025	621
Actual *N*	242	22	20	31

Notes: Dependent variable for LOGIT = $LN\ ((p/(1 - p))/2 + 5)$. Asymptotic t-statistics are in parentheses. NA = not applicable.
[a]Coefficient statistically significant at 1% (one-tailed test).
[b]Coefficient statistically significant at 5% (one-tailed test).
[c]Coefficient statistically significant at 10% (one-tailed test).
*Two-tailed test if no predicted sign or opposite predicted sign.

modest explanatory power overall and for individual variables. One is the aforementioned compromise forced on us by data limitations to proxy a combined investment-consumption decision by means of a closely targeted investment variable but only fragmentary, indirect suggestions concerning consumption tastes. Tolerability of explanation, reasons for which we surmised above, is not the same thing as comfortable explanatory power. We expect to pay a price here.

The second source of weakness stems from the fact that actual modifications make up only a very small percentage of total possible modifications in the observed stock. For each kind of change only a tiny percentage of the homes observed will have made it. An overwhelming proportion will register zero change, *despite great variety in housing and neighborhood attributes*. So our explanatory variables cannot be exhausting the ground for these decisions. Various private, individual, idiosyncratic, stochastic factors must be important in determining the action–no action decision, factors which are necessarily omitted here. Their importance—and omission—guarantee low overall fits, even where some of our included variables have explanatory significance.

These considerations are decisively reflected in the empirical results. But our purpose in this application, it must be reiterated, is not necessarily to create a powerful, dependable predictive instrument, but to test whether the structure of decision making for modification is at all shaped by our central notion of a supply responsiveness to ongoing market conditions—thus, to *changing* market conditions—on the part of owners of existing housing units. As we shall see, the results are quite encouraging on this score, despite all the limitations of data and the stochastic nature of the decisions themselves.

We discuss the empirical results separately for the disaggregate and aggregate models. We begin with the former and examine, first, the supply-side influences on all modifications; second, the demand-side influences overall;

third, the influence of market situation overall; and lastly distinctions in the configuration of model explanation for different kinds of modification.

16.3.1 Disaggregate Model

Detailed parameter estimates of the disaggregate model are shown in table 16.6. Summary results are shown in tables 16.7 and 16.8.

Supply Side: Rate of Return

The most striking result, and the most important for our purposes, is that *RETURNS* is statistically significant with correct (positive) sign for almost every kind of modification, and it is by far the only variable with such consistent influence. Among the few kinds of modification for which it does not have statistical significance, extensive plumbing, small additions to basement, and

Table 16.7. Lists of Significant Variable Coefficients for Improvement Categories, Disaggregate Model

Variable	(1) PL	(2) F	(3) Gar	(4) Base	(5) O Porch	(6) C Porch	(7) A/C	(8) Add	(9) PE
AGE5–9%	X	[X]	[X]	X	[X]	[X]		X	
AGE20–34%	X	X	X	X	X			X	[X]
AGE35–64%	X	X	X	X	X		X	X	[X]
PRE-1955%	X	X		X	X			X	
MEDINC$	[X]			[X]	X	X		X	[X]
BLACK%									
OCCUP%	[X]			[X]	X	X		X	[X]
BADAREA	X	X		X	[X]	[X]			
TIPAREA				[X]					
OWNER	[X]			X			X		
SOLD	X		X		X			X	
AGEHOME		X				[X]		[X]	
AGEHOME^2		X				[X]		[X]	
SUBMKT1	X				[X]		X	X	
SUBMKT2	X			[X]	[X]		X	[X]	
SUBMKT3	X			X	X		X	[X]	
SUBMKT4	X		[X]	[X]			X	[X]	
SUBMKT5	X		[X]	[X]		[X]	X	[X]	
PRICEP		X		X	X				
PRICEN	X	[X]		[X]	X		X	[X]	
RETURNS	X	X	X	X	X	X	X		
LOT	—	—	—	—	—	—	—	[X]	
LOT^2	—	—	—	—	—	—		X	
TOTAL X	13	8	4	9	10	3	9	9	0

Notes: *X* = significant at 10% level or better; [*X*] = $t > 1$.

Table 16.8. Actual/Potential Changes and Number of Significant Explanatory Variable Coefficients, Disaggregate Model

Archetype	Number Act./Pot.	Ratio Act./Pot.	Rank Act./Pot.	Number Sig. Var.	Rank Sig. Var.
*P*1	107/1951	.05	2	8	2
*P*2	51/1985	.03	6	8	2
*P*3	51/1894	.03	6	7	5
F	38/2052	.02	14	8	2
*G*1	78/1998	.04	4	3	11
*G*2	54/1974	.03	6	2	14
*B*1	73/1842	.04	4	5	8
*B*2	52/1573	.03	6	5	8
*B*3	45/1420	.03	6	2	14
*OP*1	69/2012	.03	6	7	5
*OP*2	53/1988	.03	6	3	11
CP	53/2052	.03	6	3	11
A/C	242/1949	.12	1	9	1
*A*1	22/2033	.01	15	4	10
*A*2	20/2025	.01	15	7	5
PE	31/621	.05	2	0	16

Notes: Excludes constant; 10% level of significance or higher.

large increments to open porches are cases where the other degrees of change in the same category *are* significant with appropriate sign. One can expect the existence of decisional rivalry—substitution effects—within each such category among the different degrees of modification. So a strong positive impetus to one or more degrees can well come partly *at the expense of* the other degrees, thereby weakening the apparent association between them and the *RETURNS* variable. The critical test for us is whether there is a significant net positive association between *RETURNS* and the category *as a whole*. It is thus appropriate to collapse results for mutually exclusive archetypes into overall results for the entire category of home improvements (see table 16.8). The relative sizes of the coefficients in each of these categories clearly show such a significant net positive association. Only area additions and additions via porch conversion fail in this sense, and of these only the former seem essentially unaffected. The impact on the latter *may* be nontrivial, but it is not dependable.

The impact of *RETURNS* on the whole set of modifications is not only highly dependable but also large in absolute size. The estimated parameters are near the highest among all variables for all modifications other than area additions and porch conversions, especially area additions. This performance assumes greater importance when it is realized that several other explanatory variables have multicollinear relationships with *RETURNS,* yet their presence in the regressions does not eradicate the explanatory power of *RETURNS;* rather, the effect seems to be the reverse. *RETURNS,* our central explanatory factor, strongly dominates all other influences. This represents considerable confirmation of our central approach.

The same cannot, however, be said about submarket prices, *PRICEP* and *PRICEN*. *PRICEP* is statistically significant with expected sign in only three of the nine improvement categories—for only three of the sixteen estimated parameters. For the remainder, the coefficients are nonsignificant. Results for *PRICEN* are even weaker. There are six of nine categories with significant or near-significant estimates (and ten out of sixteen parameters), but all but two of these—for moderate plumbing additions—have the wrong (positive) sign.

Submarket prices translate hedonic rate of return (*RETURNS*) into a *pecuniary* rate-of-return variable. Why do they perform so disappointingly while *RETURNS* performs so well? The most negative answer is that individual homes are simply not perceived as market peers of the collections allocated by our specification as belonging to the same quality submarkets. For the present results, however, special features of the case study suggest much more plausibly a different explanation.

The disaggregate model examines each modification one at a time. So an action is likely to change the hedonic index only a small amount, changing its submarket membership little, if at all. Thus, the variance of *PRICEP* and *PRICEN* will reflect, *at most,* differences in adjacent submarkets. But these are small in our sample. Table 11.9 shows these to be 1.149, 1.036, 0.996, 1.010, 1.033, and 1.003 for submarkets 1–6, respectively. The combination of modifications with no impact on submarket membership and those giving only a push to an adjacent submarket results in both too little variance and conflicting influence as obstacles to the two price variables showing much dependable additional impact on pecuniary rates of return beyond what is expressed through *RETURNS*.

The conflict occurs as follows. Submarket 1 has the highest price, 1.149; submarket 2 the next highest, 1.036. For hedonic changes that start *and* finish with submarket 1, the price multiplier is high, suggesting a positive impact; for modifications that start in 1 but end in 2, the price multiplier is lower (a large decline), suggesting a negative impact. The same is true between 2 and 3, and all subsequent pairs: a high initial price is linked to a lower adjacent price, a low initial price to a higher adjacent price. So modest and larger value shifts do not give monotonic but contradictory impacts on the dependent variable. This certainly would be expected to show confused results for the price variables, results stemming from the particular mix of actual changes that did and did not spill over into adjacent submarkets.

Some variance does exist, of course. But any impact this may have may well have been appropriated by the submarket dummies. Combinations of a particular kind of modification with an initial submarket membership could well serve as proxy for both the contradictory initial and spillover aspects of submarket prices, thus leaving the price variables with chaotic explanatory power.

The plausibility of this explanation is enhanced by the results of the estimates of the aggregate model. When the sum of all executed modifications is used as dependent variable, the total impact of some combinations of hedonic value can be considerable. Thus, a larger percentage of action cases in that model will shift a house to a different submarket, and the variance of such shifts can be much greater than under the disaggregate model. In such a situation the price variables should perform better, and they do—*PRICEP* moderately so, *PRICEN* resoundingly.

Of the remaining variables, *AGEHOME* and $AGEHOME^2$, *LOT* and LOT^2 (for living area additions alone) are the only ones that refer to supply-side influences for the individual house. Interpretation of the age variables must be done carefully. The conventional assumption is that older age depresses expected investment profitability by representing a combination of smaller remaining lifetime and possibly more expensive modification costs, due to greater collateral adjustments needed to accompany each particular modification. But there is an opposite side as well. Some of these variables represent unmeasured substitutive and complementary relationships with the specific forms of alteration-addition—size and character of basements, porches, plumbing and fireplaces, for example. The appropriateness of some of these modifications for two houses of very different age may be very different—and yet not be measured by our other variables, even by the hedonic index. The much older house may, for example, represent a far more fruitful base for particular investments than the younger, because of the former's particular features.

This is an instance of what we warned earlier, that a level of measurement detail adequate for predicting the market value of an already assembled configuration of attributes—a market statics question—may be inadequate for predicting incremental changes in that configuration over time—a market dynamics question. Individual modifications may rest more subtly on specific substitutive/complementary relations that require more complex specification than is contained in our hedonic functions.

The above is meant to convey that the age factor may have to carry a more complex burden here than in our hedonic index. It must serve as a proxy for changes in architectural styles as well as monotonic aging. It is for this reason, as well as to capture nonlinearities in its aging function, that we have introduced it separately, both in linear and squared forms, even though it is already directly included as well in the hedonic index component of *RETURNS*. Can its duplicate, separate appearance, augmented by squared form, really convey complications that appear to occur with discrete rather than continuous character?

The estimation results suggest that the repeat, separate appearance of age, in linear and squared form, is superfluous. The effect of age, in whatever complex of components, seems to be exhausted by its appearance in the hedonic index. It will be recalled that its influence there was *positive* and solidly significant, a strong suggestion that complexities beyond mere depreciation were being measured here. That very likely accounts for its failure as a duplicate variable here. Even addition of its squared form here seems to make no difference. Only one of sixteen coefficients is significant for both terms, and most parameters overall are estimated as negative (ten of sixteen for both). Moreover, no special relationship of signs occurs dependably between *AGEHOME* and $AGEHOME^2$, although of the one where both parameters are significant, *AGEHOME* is negative and $AGEHOME^2$ is positive. This lack of sign patterns is not really a surprise, however, since the special function of these variables as redundant with age in the hedonic index means that we simply do not have any strong a priori expectations about signs. In sum, the effect of structure age is solidly (although somewhat surprisingly) accounted for in the hedonic index component of *RETURNS,* and its separate, direct second appearance (linear and squared) is superfluous. It will take a more subtle proxy to enable detailed attribute configuration to capture what we only crudely attempted to examine here with the continuous age variables. And as a footnote, the dominance of age incarnated within *RETURNS* over its separate appearance provides additional confirmatory evidence about the salience of a rate-of-return conceptualization of the modification decision.

The lot size variables are expressly configurational variables. It is not a question of whether more lot adds or subtracts from market value. Lot modifications are not considered here at all. The only question is whether lot size (and its square) physically permits living area additions. Thus its inclusion as variables here may play a somewhat different function than its function in the hedonic index. In the latter it has a solidly positive effect on value. Here there is a notably significant positive sign for LOT^2 and a nearly significant negative one for *LOT,* with respect to large additions, and insignificant signs for small additions. The real test here would seem to be the effect of very small lots on large additions. For this situation, *LOT* would dominate over LOT^2. Our findings suggest that on balance there would be no deterrent effect on additions—indeed, there might even be a net encouragement effect. This result once again is probably due to the strong positive effect of lot size on hedonic value, masking the purely technical constraints sought for in this redundant use. Thus, the duplicate use of lot variables does not really clarify the overall explanatory pattern of the model beyond the contribution of lot in the hedonic index. The strength of the *RETURNS* variable is even further enhanced by this result.

The last supply-side variable is *SOLD,* a dummy variable that indicates whether or not the house was sold during our observation period. Our earlier discussion of it suggested that its overall influence would be composed of a presale conservatism against making large or idiosyncratic changes (negative), a presale desire to correct what the general market would consider flaws (positive), and an immediate postsale inclination to combine the correction of many flaws from the point of view of the specific tastes of the new buyers (positive). We predicted mixed influences but an overall positive impact.

The posited influences are not only mixed as to sign but also as to character. The first refers to large or idiosyncratic changes; the second involves smaller, more staple types of change; and the third probably involves large *and* small *and* idiosyncratic changes. This suggests that the empirical findings should show not only the effect of mutually canceling forces, but also a variety of outcomes for different kinds of alterations—by size and type of alteration.

The results are basically in the spirit of these expectations. The variable's hybrid character has given it weak overall predictive power. It has only four significant coefficients, spread over four modification categories, and they are as mixed in sign as it is possible to be: two positive, two negative. Moreover, in four of the five categories with more than one size option, the signs are mixed. Substitutive relationships within categories, of the kind we should expect, appear to be occurring.

We are also able to see some evidence of the three different influences working. Conservatism is reflected in the plumbing and garage categories: two-fixture modifications and two-car garages are discouraged. Yet major alterations (presumably postsale) also are reflected, for general area additions and open porches: in the former, large additions are significantly encouraged; in the latter, large, but not small, open porch additions are encouraged by a sale.

Thus, while the *SOLD* variable is not a strong one for predictive purposes, and the surmised net positive bent is not unambiguously forthcoming, its seemingly chaotic performance is in fact consistent with our interpretive approach to the modification decision. More detailed data, matching occupant characteristics, dates and kinds of modification, and time of sale would permit a more searching test.

Demand Side: Owner Consumption Tastes

The partition of explanatory variables into supply, demand, and market situation is imperfect. Our supply-side variables are cleanly so, referring to individual houses. But the remainder are aggregates, referring to clusters of individual houses. It is impossible to separate out these variables' characterization of the individual household linked to each house from the characteristics of the neighborhood—*external to that household*—in which the house is embedded. Any heterogeneity within the neighborhood, for example, between the particular household being considered and the rest, is therefore lost. Lost, too, is any ability to distinguish finely between the owner consumption tastes of that household and its perception of specific characteristics of that neighborhood that might qualify the expected value appreciation due to modification, as generated from a more general market predictor like the hedonic function.

Of the remaining explanatory variables, those that refer most purely to consumption tastes are owner occupancy (*OWNER*), the neighborhood population age distribution (*AGE*5–9%, *AGE*20–34%, *AGE*35–64%), its percentage of population with long occupancy (*PRE*-1955%), and its percentage of population in skilled professions (*OCCUP%*). Those most nearly market situation variables are *TIPAREA, SOLD,* and the five submarket dummies (*SUBMKT*1–*SUBMKT*5). The last three, black (*BLACK%*) median income (*MEDINC$*), and problem areas (*BADAREA*), seem to partake elements of both consumption tastes and market situation, but these are conventionally the most important neighborhood variables.

A mixed variable may reflect contradictory elements. A poor or black neighborhood, for example, may be stereotypically perceived from the outside as a poor investment locale. Yet its own inhabitants may share strong in-group feelings and/or be less able to move elsewhere when family circumstances change (for example, because of discrimination). The former would make for a negative impact on modifications, the latter possibly a positive impact. Thus, neighborhood minority composition, median income, and poverty circumstances mean one thing if one is trying to characterize a particular house via predictions from the group, but something quite different if one is trying to characterize the group itself as an environment for any particular household. Accordingly, we would expect better estimates from the "pure" demand and market situation variables than from the mixed variables, other things equal (e.g., their multicollinearity).

Population age distribution. Our consumption variables do certainly have explanatory power. The three population age variables are most notable: together, they have twenty-one significant coefficients, and for the middle- and upper-age variables the signs of these coefficients are overwhelmingly consistent (see tables 16.6 and 16.7).

The performance of the *AGE*5–9% is adequate, but least strong of the three. The variable was expected to capture the situation of young families with children aged 5–9. For them the life cycle brings rapid changes in housing needs: children in the age bracket mature quickly to need more bedroom, bathroom, and playing space. With multiple children per household, moving to larger quarters would be less attractive because either premature (changing requirements would come more than once) and/or expensive (because of the needed repetition). So modifying in place seems to represent a reasonable way for such families to cope.

The results generally confirm this picture for those modifications for which the variable is statistically significant. It is significant for modifications that add usable space—via general area additions and finishing basements. Moreover, the pattern in both displays a substitution effect: a smaller negative effect on small additions is offset by a larger positive effect on larger additions, indicating responses to needs for significantly larger living space. The significant negative coefficient on fireplaces is further consistent with this picture, since fireplaces would represent an unaffordable luxury given the urgent space needs.

The significant negative coefficient on two-fixture plumbing raises a different question. It is paired with corresponding significant positive coefficients for the *AGE*20–34% and *AGE*35–64% variables. There is reason to expect considerable multicollinearity of *AGE*5–9% with the *AGE*20–34% variable, since the latter is the age group of adults most likely to have children aged 5–9 in their family, and somewhat less multicollinearity with *AGE*35–64% for similar reasons. The sum of the positive coefficients on the two older age groups exceeds that of the negative one on *AGE*5–9%. It is tempting to believe that behavior of the families with children aged 5–9 is reflected in a mixture of the three groups, thereby possibly having an inconclusive net effect, and so thereby tempering the somewhat anomalous meaning of negative plumbing coefficient on *AGE*5–9% alone.

*AGE*20–34% is a stronger explanatory variable. It has seven significant coefficients instead of six for *AGE*5–9%; more important, however, they cover six categories of modification and, moreover, these are overwhelmingly of the same (positive) sign. This young adult family group is likely to have rapidly changing housing needs but wants to adapt to them without moving, because of both the rapid succession of changes that have to be adjusted to and an income level, still distant from lifetime highs, inadequate to do so via repeated moves. Young adulthood increases the probability of making plumbing additions, putting in a garage, adding living space via finishing basements, and constructing additional area as well as an open porch. Only central air conditioning, a closed porch, and conversion of porch area for additional interior space are not noticeably affected by greater incidence in the population of this young adult group.

Incidence of the stable population age group, *AGE*35–64%, is the strongest of the age distribution variables, and markedly so. Ten coefficients are significant and all but one positive. A positive impetus is given by increased incidence of this group to seven of the nine categories of modification. Only the closed porch and porch conversion for interior addition are exempted. Factors that could explain this pattern are a continued increase in family size, but with a slower dramatic sequence of changes, accompanied by incomes rising to lifetime maxima. Some of this, of course, favors housing upgrading by moving, but enough families toward both the lower and upper bounds of this wide age interval are likely to prefer to adjust in place to generate the statistically measurable positive impetus. The extra explanatory power of this variable also comes partly from its having less of a multicollinear relationship with *AGE*5–9%.

It may seem strange that all three population variables should impart a net positive effect on modification. Is there not some branch of the population relative to which these incidences are positive—an age group whose presence imparts a negative influence? Yes. It is the group 65 and older. Implicitly, as the reference group they should have a preponderantly negative effect on modifications. This is plausible, because (1) family size is declining, as grown children move away; (2) income levels fall; (3) older families are more modest in their housing needs and more conservative in making changes of various sorts; and (4) their houses are likely already to embody most types of modification, in either a long occupancy that progressively added what seemed desirable, or in a more recent move that self-selected for desired housing characteristics.

Other consumption taste variables. No other consumption taste variables approach population age in explanatory power. The best of them is the incidence of the skilled occupation groups in the neighborhood, *OCCUP%*. Unlike age, this is not a pure consumption taste variable. It is closely related to neighborhood median income and serves as a proxy for neighborhood and thus market situation. Furthermore, its close positive relationship with *MEDINC$* gives it also a close positive relationship with the hedonic index component of *RETURNS,* so the significance of its estimated parameters will be weakened. This expectation is borne out by the presence of only five significant coefficients—three positive, two negative—and covering only four types of modification. On the other hand, the distinctive aspects of both *OCCUP%* and *MEDINC$* do seem to have been factored out by the multiple regression, as evidenced by the remarkable fact that the two variables have a different coefficient sign in literally every archetype modification, whether the coefficient is statistically significant or not.

The occupational skill variable seems to focus on two kinds of consumption taste—porches and living space. The effect of all of the significant coefficients is either to build open and closed porches and avoid converting porches to general interior space, or to add general living space. The absence of basement additions, or other kinds of improvement very likely stems from the fact that, as well-paid workers, those families that decide to stay probably have chosen—or previously improved—a house that already embodies most of these other kinds of improvement. The latter may well be the more urgent or obvious first improvements to make in upgrading.

The long-term occupancy variable, *PRE*-1955%, would seem to avoid most of the inherent weaknesses of the occupational variable. It is not obviously related to neighborhood income level or other aspects of the hedonic index. Instead, it focuses on household mobility. In this regard it is most closely related to the (excluded) reference population age group, 65 and above, and thereby to some extent linearly related to the set of population age variables. But it reflects as well a specific set of household tastes not necessarily related to age, namely, preference for continuity, allegiance to house and neighborhood. As a reflector of elderly status the variable should show a negative impact on modification, for the various reasons given in the population age discussion. On the other hand, as a reflector of locational allegiance, the variable should show a positive impact because life-cycle changes will not result in moving away but in adjusting on the site. The net effect depends on the relative frequencies of the two types of households, but an additional negative tilt might be expected insofar as long-term occupancy suggests that many or most of the modifications at issue were probably already undertaken and are embedded in the house. The upshot is that the variable may well show only a weak association with the probability of modification, and there is no strong a priori case for either sign predominating.

The results do show a variable with only modest explanatory power. The pattern of signs for statistically significant coefficients is four positive and two negative. However, fully five modification categories have significant coefficients. Basement finishing, addition of open porch and general area, as well as addition of a fireplace are positively affected by length of tenure. Plumbing improvements concentrate the negative impacts, possibly showing here the effect of prior improvements over the long occupancy.

The final consumption taste variable is beginning-of-period owner occupancy.[17] This should have mostly an indirect effect on modifications, but little direct effect. We noted in the introduction to this chapter that the modification decision for owner-occupants involved a conflict between market investment and own-consumption goals. Primacy of the former would make *RETURNS* and the market situation variables more powerful relative to the consumption variables; primacy of the latter would reverse this. So modification for a house not owner-occupied should be decided predominantly on market gain grounds; hence, the market variables should be especially strong and all others weak. For a house that is owner-occupied the decision conflict is most notable, so the market variables should be weaker and the consumption variables stronger. This kind of influence can only really be tested by a model specification that uses *OWNER* interactivity with, especially, *RETURNS* and the population age variables. Unfortunately, due to the paucity of non-owner-occupants in our sample we could not run such interactive terms.

The direct effect of *OWNER%* is unclear. Market incentives may differ from own-consumption tests in various ways, making no general tilt for or against modification obvious. The results conform to this expectation. There are only two significant coefficients (positive, for modest basement finishing and installation of central air conditioning). The conventional thinking is that owner-occupancy should be positively associated with upgrading, but such expectations typically do not carefully consider the character of market rate-of-return goals and their conflict with own-consumption goals. The general weakness of *OWNER%* as an explanatory variable *is* consistent with our approach, but not with the conventional approach.

Market Situation Variables

Our market situation variables are *TIPAREA* and the submarket dummies $SUBMKT_k$. These differ from our so-called mixed variables in an important way. Unlike *BLACK%*, *MEDINC$*, and *BADAREA*, where the variable represents both the characteristics of the occupants of a given house as predicted from the characteristics of the census tract (loosely, neighborhood), in which the house is located, *and* the characteristics of the environment—again, neighborhood—of those occupants, the market situation variables represent only an aspect of the market environment as perceived uniformly by all of the residents of the tract. *TIPAREA* represents an expectation about the future demography of the neighborhood; the submarket dummies represent various otherwise unmeasured aspects of the different quality-level submarkets. The variables do not refer to the preponderant current inhabitants of the neighborhood; therefore, they do not represent the tastes of that population as linked to attributes of the sampled houses.

What aspects of market situation are supposedly captured by these variables? The *TIPAREA* dummy serves as proxy for expectations about a change in demographic situation, not as a predictor of how the market will value investments to property in a neighborhood that has the final anticipated demographic transformation. A market adjustment is anticipated because the population change is conventionally believed to involve not simply housing taste changes but also adverse neighborhood externalities like visible lifestyle, economic viability, prejudicial adjustments by present residents, and critical masses of poverty and crime. So *TIPAREA* should have a negative effect on the probability of dwelling improvement. *TIPAREA* seems a good proxy for such expectations, not being closely related to our other explanatory variables.[18] The submarket dummies presumably point to elements of submarket strengths and weaknesses, present and future, that are not measured in the submarket price variables. Such elements are presumably apprehended by the property owners through specifics of the situation that are understood as latent or incipient, but not now registered in differential market tightness. These variables can thus conceivably pick up a variety of special influences, whether monotonic or not, but accordingly their interpretation will rarely be simple and may even be inexpressible. Thus they may demonstrate nontrivial explanatory power without that power having any intuitive thrust.

Our expectations about *TIPAREA* are not realized. It has no perceptible explanatory power (no significant coefficients at all), and even the pattern of its coefficients is inconclusive (nine negative, but six positive—including the only nearly significant one). This is probably explained by noting that the *BLACK%* variable is similarly unproductive (for reasons discussed below), and the heavy cluster pattern of black percentages in the different census tracts makes *TIPAREA* closely related to *BLACK%*. The predictive failure of *BLACK%* is thus shared with *TIPAREA* (even the pattern of coefficient signs is quite similar for the two).

As predicted, the submarket dummies pick up a nontrivial degree of explanatory power. They have four, three, five, three, and three significant coefficients respectively. What is more, except for one coefficient in submarket 1, all these coefficients are of the same sign, negative. Finally, the significant coefficients cover from two to four modification categories, especially those involving plumbing and air conditioning.

What submarket forces are being reflected here? We suggested above that a general rationale might be difficult to discern for such a set of dummies. But the specific results here strongly suggest a simple interpretation: they are capturing the effect of differential submarket prices as a component of investment rates of return. Recall again that the submarket prices are as follows: (1) 1.149, (2) 1.036, (3) 0.996, (4) 1.010, (5) 1.033, and (6) 1.003. In our earlier discussion of the explanatory failure of *PRICEP* and *PRICEN,* we noted that both price difference for adjacent submarket (for investments which "spill over" submarket boundaries) and absolute price levels (for investments which do not) should influence modification attractiveness. The estimated coefficients for the *SUBMKT* variables are interpretable as the joint effects of these two factors. In none of the Des Moines submarkets do these effects work in the same direction, however. Submarkets 1, 2, and 5 have high submarket prices, both absolutely and relative to the next-higher submarket. Conversely, submarkets 3, 4, and 6 have low submarket prices, both absolutely and for the first two relative to the next-higher one.

Although no overall pattern of coefficient signs for the *SUBMKT* variables can thus be predicted, certain results can. First, submarket 1 demonstrates the highest absolute submarket price and the greatest differential between this price and submarket 2 price. This should mean, compared to other submarkets, the greatest comparative stimulus for modest reinvestments which keep dwellings in submarket 1, and the largest disincentive for major reinvestments which upgrade dwellings into submarket 2. This prediction is confirmed in table 16.6, with *SUBMKT*1 showing the only statistically significant positive coefficient (for adding 2 plumbing fixtures), and negative coefficients for three major improvements (3+ plumbing fixtures, air conditioning, 351+ square feet additions). Second, submarket 3 demonstrates both the lowest absolute price and the lowest relative price gain through upgrading. As would be expected given these facts, *SUBMKT*3 yields the largest number of statistically significant negative coefficients by far, suggesting that all sorts of improvements (plumbing, finished basements, open porches, air conditioning) are discouraged when both absolute and relative price signals are unfavorable.

The above strongly suggests that our submarket dummies are in fact reflecting submarket prices and are doing so better than the explicit price variables themselves, thereby robbing the latter of explanatory power. We have argued this in some detail because the proposition is very important to the use of this empirical application as a test of our overall theoretical approach. Financial rates of return on modifications have thereby been shown to reflect not only individual housing attribute impacts but also the effect of shifting the commodity as a whole within or across specific submarket concentrations—*where the relevant submarkets are defined by our conceptualization of quality.* That the submarket dummies have such a strong and a clear impact on improvement is especially promising.

Mixed Variables

Our mixed variables are *BLACK%*, *BADAREA*, and *MEDINC$*. Conventionally they would be considered the mainstay variables to express both owner tastes and budget constraints and neighborhood externalities affecting investment prospects. In our treatment they have a much more ambiguous role. For one thing they are all redundant in significant degree, being either directly or by close approximation already included in the hedonic index. This alone should considerably reduce their independent explanatory power. For another, as suggested in the previous section on market variables, they express both elements of occupant tastes and of market-relevant neighborhood externalities. What may be a sign of investment infeasibility to the outside market may represent to existing occupants a comfortable, homogeneous community which warrants loyalty, thereby promoting modifying in place instead of moving elsewhere to obtain more appropriate housing.

These qualifications are seen most dramatically for the variable *BLACK%*, classically expected to have a negative impact in upgrading investment. In fact, our results show no significant coefficients at all! Almost all are negative, but they are all nonsignificant. The substance of this variable is completely contained within the hedonic index, and it does not seem to have an impact on upgrading outside the explicit *RETURNS* context.[19] The owner-occupant's evaluation—as distinct from outside market's—seems to be especially important here. Moreover, it is very likely strongly abetted by the fact that racial segregation creates a "captive population": households who have outgrown their current premises cannot easily move to more appropriate accommodation because they are ghettoized. So the kinds of household-housing mismatch which in nonghettoized, mobile groups would result not in upgrading in place but in moving to better housing, thus leaving their present house unmodified, will here instead typically, for the artificially immobilized blacks, lead to upgrading in place—a positive modification force offsetting the negative neighborhood externalities. Thus the poor econometric performance of the *BLACK%* variable is not at all an anomaly.

Much the same is true of the *BADAREA* dummy. Tight budget constraints and bank unwillingness to lend for upgrading would certainly lead to the expectation of a strong negative impact on upgrading. Yet its content is substantially already included in the hedonic index, and some of the forced immobility of blacks applies here as well; indeed, "bad areas" as we have defined them are disproportionately black areas in Des Moines. The additional multicollinearity as well as the immobility weaken any further independent impact for this variable over and above its impact via the hedonic index. Indeed, they add randomness to its estimated performance. Thus, only four coefficients are significant, and two of them, a positive impetus to major basement finishing and to fireplaces, seem clearly anomalous. The other two, abetted by an almost significant coefficient for the third plumbing parameter, establish deterrence against any degree of plumbing improvement. This contrasts strangely with the near unanimity of negative signs for *BLACK%*, since the arguably stronger immobility of blacks but their greater income heterogeneity would lead one to expect more upgrading in place and hence some positive—even if nonsignificant—signs, while the more unremitting budget stringency of *BADAREA* occupants would lead one to expect few, if any, positive signs. In sum, *BADAREA* is a weak, unconvincing variable, but this is neither surprising nor damaging, since its influence is expressed through the hedonic index and is further blurred here by association with *BLACK%*. Its separate redundant appearance as another variable does not appear to capture additional facets of its influence.

The last variable to discuss is *MEDINC$*, census tract median income level. This is the most popular aggregate variable used to characterize tastes, budgets, lifestyles, education, housing tenure, social externalities, and many other group phenomena. It is usually a powerful predictor in many contexts, but the precise interpretation of its performance in different contexts is often highly debatable precisely because it has so many different dependable associations with preferences and behavior. This will be seen dramatically in its present use.

In our model *MEDINC$* has two facets: it reflects housing tastes of each owner-occupant household being linked to a particular house, and it portrays the socioeconomic ambiance of the neighborhood, that is, the environment of each such household—lifestyle, social responsibility, general property maintenance standards, tenure mix, crime, and so forth. Almost automatically it would be assumed that *MEDINC$*, given these facets, should have a positive impact on upgrading: richer people have tastes for higher housing quality and can more adequately afford to upgrade either through their own resources or through borrowing on a strong credit position. Moreover, the richer neighborhood would be likely to enhance, or at the very least sustain, market values built into property via investments. Indeed, our hedonic index shows a solid positive impact of median tract income on house market value.

Yet our empirical findings show that, while *MEDINC$* is a powerful predictor in our model, its direction of influence is predominantly negative! Of its five significant coefficients, three are negative; moreover, nine of the total sixteen coefficients are negative and only five are positive. Examined closely, this apparent anomaly in fact yields important new information about the modification process.

The first element in the interpretation is that exactly the same variable appears in the hedonic index component of *RETURNS*. Here, then, is the only occasion in our model where an explanatory variable has explanatory power in two separate incarnations—but the influence is exercised in opposing directions. The reason seems to be because two very different facets of this variable are being exposed in the two appearances. In the hedonic index, what is conveyed is that a house in a richer neighborhood will have a higher market value than the "same house" in a poorer neighborhood. This is a static relationship. As an independent explanatory variable in the modification model it conveys something different: a house in a richer neighborhood, with given prospective financial gains from various modifications and certain other socioeconomic neighborhood features, will have a lower probability of having certain upgrading changes made to it in our observation period than a house in a poorer neighborhood with the same gains and other neighborhood characteristics. This is a dynamic relationship.

At least two critical elements are different in the two cases—control over the identity of the house and the identity of the owner/dweller. In the hedonic index the identity of the house is statistically guaranteed, and the identity of the owner/dweller is not of great importance because the market price is established by a multiparty, two-sided competitive process. In the modification model, both are important and neither is controlled for. "The" house in the richer neighborhood may be significantly different than "the" house in the poorer neighborhood, and the start of period–end of period continuity may be significantly different as well between the two houses. Both types of differences have real relevance for the modification process.

First, differences in houses matter because an important portion of modification is to make up "deficiencies" in houses—factors recognizably making the house "inappropriately" of lower quality than it should be. Houses in poor neighborhoods are much more likely to possess deficiencies than those in rich neighborhoods, with gradations of the probability for intermediate neighborhoods. Some kinds of upgrading are simply not needed in the archetypical homes comprising richer neighborhoods, thus robbing *MEDINC$* of some of its potential positive impact via the association of higher income with better housing. Second, richer households are more likely to upgrade the quality of their housing consumption not by upgrading their present house but by moving to a better one. There are fewer financial or social obstacles to their mobility. Moreover, the importance of neighborhood as validating social status in U.S. urban areas makes upgrading by moving an especially efficient strategy, insomuch as dependence on better neighborhood externalities is often an cheaper way to obtain a desired overall quality gain than to try to build it into one's home—against the pull of worse neighborhood externalities. So upgrading is typically achieved by richer owner-occupants by a balanced mix of better house and better neighborhood, instead of by the unmixed route of improving the present house in place.

The effect of upgrading by moving is to improve the migrant household's quality of housing consumption but to leave the quality of the house from which they move unchanged. So if there is a systematic positive relationship between income level and probability of upgrading housing consumption by moving, normal life-cycle changes for households at all income levels will show a negative relationship between initial income level and the probability of the initially occupied house being upgraded.

Thus, the hedonic index embedded with *RETURNS* should reflect the positive, static relationship between individual and neighborhood income level and housing quality, and the separate *MEDINC$* variable should reflect the inversely related remaining needs or opportunities for modification for houses in different neighborhoods, and the positively related propensity for upgrading by moving by different income groups. So both the preponderant positive signs for *RETURNS* and the preponderant negative signs for *MEDINC$* are entirely consistent with this understanding. Examination of the detailed findings confirms this further. Negative (significant and otherwise) coefficients occur mostly for plumbing, garages, and porches (where architectural elements may be an additional factor), categories where "deficiencies" may be concentrated. The only significant positive coefficients occur for area additions—small general areas, and via conversion of closed porches. Larger area additions would conflict with an income-related propensity for upgrading by moving; the other additions are consistent with modest, ad hoc needs (never exhausted at any income level) for larger interior space not warranting moving.

Different Types of Modification

We conclude discussion of the results of the disaggregate, single-SMSA model with a brief glance at the pattern of explanation for the different kinds of modification.

The various kinds of upgrading differ greatly in the pattern of explanation/prediction accorded by our model: the number and identity of significant variables, the signs of the coefficients for each variable, the pattern of significant and nonsignificant variables, the signs of the coefficients for each variable, the pattern of significant and nonsignificant variables. Indeed, careful examination of the cluster of variables that are significant gives us the ability roughly to characterize the decision for each kind of modification as primarily market-oriented, own-consumption-oriented, or mixed.

Explanatory power of model. We may gauge roughly the explanatory relevance of the model for the different kinds of modification by counting the number of variables that have statistical significance for each. The range of numbers is wide, from zero to nine. Modifications with the most significant variables are air conditioning and one- and two-fixture plumbing. Those with the least are porch enclosures, two-car garages, and finished large basements.

Since some categories comprise more than one archetypical change, it may be more instructive to show the results for categories instead of individual archetypical changes. The change categories with the most significant variables (see table 16.7) are plumbing, open porches, followed by finished basements, air conditioning, and additions. The categories with the fewest are porch enclosures, closed porches, and garages.

We earlier noted that only a small fraction of our observed sample had any particular kind of change and that important idiosyncratic, stochastic considerations are likely to count heavily for the actual change–no change decision. Might the differences in explanatory relevance (number of significant variables) be accounted for by the relative paucity of each kind of change? If so, we would expect the smaller percentage of occurrence to accompany the smaller number of significant variables, since for such the stochastic elements would more likely overwhelm the systematic elements. Table 16.8 shows the ratios of actual to potential changes, their rank, the number of statistically significant variables, and their ranks.

Table 16.8 also shows a very small—surprisingly small—variance of ratios of actual to potential changes. There is a tight concentration between 3% and 5%. The variance in number of significant variables is considerably greater. Moreover, inspection shows no relationship between ratio rank and variable rank—Spearman's rho who was estimated to be only .08. So the pattern of explanatory relevance for the model rests on more specific factors relating to the categories themselves. Simple explanations, like change in "deficiencies" versus discretionary upgrading, or market-oriented versus own-consumption-oriented, as we shall see below, likewise appear wanting.

Not only does the explanatory relevance of the model differ substantially across change categories, but the identity of the statistically significant variables for each category differs markedly as well. Table 16.8 shows columns of significant variables for the nine change categories.

Table 16.7 shows that no two categories have even approximately similar patterns of significant variables. Probably the closest are the fireplace and area addition categories. The most uniform feature is the near-unanimous (seven out of nine) appearance of *RETURNS* across categories. Next is the frequent cluster of at least two population age variables along with *PRE*-1955% and *SOLD*. *BADAREA* and *SUBMKT*3 suggest a more tenuous membership in that cluster. The change categories affected by this cluster are plumbing, fireplace, open porch, and area additions, with basement more loosely associated. The pattern of category similarity is not especially suggestive of underlying uniformities: neither house deficiencies versus discretionary upgrading, nor alterations versus additions, nor any other easy latent characterization seem to fit. Inasmuch as the category variable similarities are loose anyway, this is not surprising.

Classification of categories: Consumption, investment, and mixed orientations. From the beginning of this chapter we have emphasized that modification decisions are a mix of owner's own-consumption and market-investment considerations, that the particular character of the mix depends on idiosyncratic specifics for each household-housing pairing, but that market-investment and own-consumption interests are often quite similar. While we believe it is not really possible to isolate the relative weight of these two influences on modification decisions, given the inadequacy of our household data, our findings make it possible at least to suggest very rough attributions for the different change categories on the basis of how we have characterized the individual variables and the clusters of these for the different categories. We repeat our disclaimer that what follows is only intended as rough suggestions.

Market-oriented investment variables are especially *RETURNS, PRICEP, PRICEN* and *TIPAREA*, less obviously the five submarket dummies, and still less obviously the two house age variables. Own-consumption variables are most nearly the three population age variables, *OCCUP%*, and *OWNER*. Mixed variables are *MEDINC$*, *BLACK%*, and *BADAREA*. Others, like *PRE*-1955%, *SOLD*, and the two lot variables, are more difficult to classify in this way.

Based on these variable characterizations and the significant variable distributions across categories as shown in table 16.7, we propose the following loose attribution. No categories seem to have a sole market-orientation, absent any own-consumptions orientation. The strongest of the former—plumbing, fireplace, basement, open porch, and air conditioning—are cases in point. Additions to the floor area of the home, on the other hand, appear more clearly influenced by own-consumption motives.

There seems, in fact, no clear a priori intuitive basis for anticipating in which group any particular modification will belong. Much more detail in household-house linkages will be needed before we have a more secure basis for categorizing modifications.

It may be noticed that central air conditioning was placed in the mixed category even though its significant variables are largely what we have considered market-oriented variables. This is because of some special factors that require careful consideration. Whereas for most archetypical changes a wide range of both positive and negative returns was generated across sampled dwelling, for central air conditioning all dwellings had estimated negative returns. We strongly suspect that this counterintuitive result was due to a hedonic function specification that suited most housing attributes but was inappropriate for air conditioning. In the double square root specification, the coefficient of air conditioning was small and statistically insignificant. But experiments with a linear, noninteractive hedonic equation yielded a much larger, significant coefficient, suggesting that air conditioning contributes a relatively constant amount of value ($685) to a dwelling, regardless of its other features. If this constant dollar payoff is used in estimating *RETURNS*, the expected distribution of both positive and negative returns emerges, although even the absolute value remains, at most, only $100.

This adjustment is important because installation of central air conditioning is by far the most frequent modification undertaken in our sample, affecting 12% of houses compared to 5% for the next highest category. If perceived returns were really uniformly negative, the positive significant *RETURNS* coefficient would imply that own-consumption motivations always initiated consideration of this modification and market forces only had a veto role, namely, to distinguish where the net cost of doing so was or was not prohibitively high. It is difficult to believe that comfort alone would induce so many owners to incur financial losses when comfort allied with financial gains do not elicit modifications at even half the rate for the other changes. In our adjusted treatment (not reported) a stronger, more balanced role emerges for *RETURNS,* so we have classified air conditioning as mixed orientation.

A similar anomaly appears to have afflicted area additions and additions via porch enclosure. Estimated rates of returns were negative for all observations. But here, experiments with other functional forms for the hedonic equation did not generate positive returns anywhere.[20] Perhaps this is why *RETURNS* is not a significant variable for these two categories, the only ones for which this is true. Yet the puzzle is deeper because while this financial drag is reflected in the lowest frequency of modification for floor space additions (1%), frequency of modification is one of the highest for porch enclosures (5%)—yet the former has the largest number of significant variables and the latter the smallest number. Notwithstanding this perplexity, own-consumption orientation variables are very strong for area additions and are the only ones nearly significant for porch conversions. It certainly seems as though own-consumption motives powered and targeted modifications here, with a general rather than directed (as under air conditioning) deterrence coming from the pervasively negative *RETURNS*.

16.3.2 Aggregate Model

We devised the aggregate model as a form of general investment function. Our disaggregate model gave us the opportunity to match each kind of modification with the particulars of each dwelling unit and, much more loosely, with owner-occupant household particulars. This provides, ideally, a close targeting of the investment for each behavioral unit sampled. Its weakness as a predictive/explanatory device, however, lies in the very small percentages of observations in which a given modification occurred—generally 1–5%. So our explanatory variables, despite their much greater variance than that of the dependent variables, were clearly an inadequate set to explain such behavior. It appears both that a variety of omitted household-idiosyncratic factors must bear a substantial explanatory power, and that a longer period of observation for following larger life-cycle and market changes might be required to derive maximum explanatory power from our included variables.

Understanding these difficulties, we formulated our aggregate model to decrease the power of idiosyncratic factors to obscure the effect of market forces. Averaging the prospective, most-profitable rates of returns from the whole set of possible modifications (Σ*RETURNS*) would, in principle, smooth out eccentric situations with respect to any particular modification, or house, or household. This would, of course, not add the missing power of the omitted household variables but should decrease some of the chaos of overspecificity surrounding the explanatory and dependent variables that are included. We looked to this model, therefore, to strengthen and clarify the explanatory power of the market situation variables. We did not expect much change in other variables, except insofar as they were mixed with elements of market situation or multicollinear with the market variables.

In order to italicize the power of the market variables we created a variant of the model for estimation as well as the basic model. As we noted at the end of the last section, air conditioning and area additions (and porch enclosures) always generated negative Σ*RETURNS* which, in the case of the former at least, was distinctly suspect. To search further whether market-investment influences are simply artificially suppressed or are genuinely minor relative to own-consumption considerations in the upgrading decision, we have, accordingly, specified a variant model that deals with all modifications other than air conditioning and area additions, but otherwise is unchanged. Results of the estimations of both variants are shown in table 16.9. We begin our discussion with the LOGIT model, determining, as in the disaggregate model, probabilities of engaging in modification. The total expenditure model (OLS) involves additional considerations, as discussed below.

Aggregate Improvement Choice Model

When account is taken of the two variants of the LOGIT model of whether any improvements have been chosen or not, our expectations about how the aggregate model would differ from the disaggregate model are basically realized. First, the explanatory variables have essentially the same direction and strength of effect as in the disaggregate model. There are two notable changes of sign: *PRICEN,* from a preponderantly positive to a negative, but nonsignificant, impact; and *SUBMKT*5, from a preponderantly negative to a significantly positive impact. There are four instances of a variable moving from indifferent strength to significance, with the same predominant impact direction: *OCCUP%*, *BADAREA*, *OWNER*, and *AGEHOME*. The strengthening is considerable for the last three.

If we compare variant B (excluding air conditioning and area additions) with variant A, we find that B tells essentially the same story, but there are four qualitative differences between the two, all of which favor variant B. *SUBMKT*1 shifts from a significant negative to a nonsignificant positive status; *SUBMKT*5 shifts from strongly significant to nonsignificant positive status; Σ*RETURNS* shifts from weakly significant to strongly significant positive status; and lastly, *PRICEN* shifts from nonsignificant to significant negative status. These four changes are closely interrelated and constitute, in fact, just the kind of outcome that motivated our resort to an aggregate model.

The key result is the significant negative coefficient for *PRICEN*. In discussing the disaggregate model, we argued that the important adjacent market price differentials were apparently ineffective because of internal impact conflicts and a particular pattern of submarket prices, and that its substantive impact was consequently taken over by the submarket dummies. The most relevant element here is that many individual upgradings fail to push housing hedonic value to a higher submarket, and for these it is the absolute origin submarket price level, not its relation to an adjacent level, that matters. This induces a "counterintuitive" effect opposite to the "intuitive" effect where higher submarkets are reached, thus confusing the overall direction of influence and weakening its size. When we aggregate all kinds of modification, the sum of all changes for any house is likely to push hedonic value to a higher submarket level in a considerably larger number of cases, and thus decrease the internal conflict for the price variables. Moreover, upgrading creates an action asymmetry between upward and downward submarket changes. So inasmuch as actual upward adjacent submarket price differentials happen to have been mostly negative in our 1963–71 Des Moines observation period, it is the *PRICEN* variable but not the *PRICEP* variable that is likely to bear whatever explanatory power submarket prices can possibly show in our particular application. Thus, in variant B, where the numerically important confusion of the misspecified air conditioning change is omitted, *PRICEN* is permitted a greater opportunity to show a more systematic, thoroughgoing market influence on upgrading. Its negative significant coefficient is an important confirmation of our overall theoretical emphasis and our interpretation of the empirical results.

This surmise is strengthened by attending to the other three changes between variant A and B. First, our main market variable, *ΣRETURNS*, increases markedly in explanatory significance, and the size of its effect on improvement probability is doubled. Second, *SUBMKT*1 and 3 become less significant—the first less negative toward zero, the second less positive toward zero. But this is exactly what we would expect if the submarket dummies were primarily, but indirectly, reflecting the influence of submarket prices. An increase in proper significance for submarket prices because more observed upgradings cross submarket lines makes the absolute characteristics of each origin submarket less influential on improvement probability. This is true for submarkets 1 and 3, but it is also true for submarkets 2 and 4. In every case, the other submarket coefficients lose considerably in statistical significance (for *SUBMKT*4 the coefficient, while remaining negative, actually goes from strong significance to nonsignificance). This patter of coefficient shifts, when market forces are given a real opportunity to show themselves in the data, is most striking.

It is worth reviewing the overall pattern of explanation in variant B. *ΣRE-*

TURNS seems the strongest variable. Greater prospective market profitability through hedonic improvement increases the probability of upgrading. The more the resulting submarket destination of any upgrading further increases expected financial market gains via differential submarket prices, the greater the probability of improvements. Various unspecified features of particular origin submarkets, including some residual reflection of absolute submarket price, also affect the probability, mostly negatively relative to the highest submarket.

The other supply-side market variables, *AGEHOME* and *AGEHOME*^{2}, perform as expected and more dependably than in the disaggregate model. Lumping different modifications together decreases the idiosyncratic housing attribute relationships that made *AGEHOME* too complex a variable in the disaggregate model. *AGEHOME* has a significantly negative impact, presumably reflecting the systematically rising real cost of various upgrading scenarios with increasing age of structure.[21] The significantly positive effect of *AGEHOME*^{2} means that there is a nonlinear relationship, partially capturing between the two variables the effect of considerable changes in architectural fashions as well as of pure aging.

The other nearly pure market investment variable, *TIPAREA,* continues to have a nonsignificant, barely negative effect. The mixed market consumption variables, *BADAREA* and *MEDINC$*, have sharper effects than in the disaggregate model—*BADAREA* in the conventional negative direction, and *MEDINC$* in the apparently counterintuitive same negative direction. In our more elaborate analysis, it actually confirms our belief that differential household mobility by income class is what is chiefly reflected. This is important for understanding the upgrading process, namely, the conflict between household upgrading and house upgrading, via the choice between upgrading on site and upgrading by moving. Another mixed market consumption variable, *BLACK%*, continues to show a very weak (though dependable, considering the uniformity of negative coefficients in the disaggregate model) negative influence. Its weakness is not a disconfirmation of conventional expectations; it only reflects the variable's redundancy in a model where the variable is already included, appropriately signed, in the hedonic index component of the dominant variable Σ*RETURNS*.

Our more nearly own-consumption demand variables are generally significant and in the expected direction. Two of the population age variables are significantly positive, appropriately suggesting periods of considerable life-cycle-generated changes in housing needs. The youngest population age variable shows a nonsignificant negative effect, but we argued earlier that the variable is a cloudy one because it is actually very closely linked to the two other age variables, which are probably carrying its life-cycle insight. *OCCUP%*, reflector of higher-quality housing demand, does show an expected strong positive effect on upgrading. The dummy *OWNER,* which suggests that own-consumption needs will be heeded as well as outside-market forces, and that a conventionally presumed greater interest by owner-occupiers in maintaining housing standards than either landlords or tenants extends to upgrading as well, indeed demonstrates a positive relationship with improvement probability (although our more extended analysis qualifies this). Such an implied effect is significantly present in our results and is stronger here than in the disaggregate model.

Finally, two variables, *PRE*-1955% and *SOLD* do not have intuitively obvious directions of influence. The first is insignificantly positive here, the second insignificantly negative. This is consistent with the expected mix of explanatory facets they represent.

Aggregate Improvement Expenditure Model

The aggregate home improvement expenditure model was formulated, as noted above, chiefly to counter the extreme clustering of observations in the zero modification cell for all types of modification, which suggested that our model was not capable of predicting the no-change decision. Corollary to this was the suggestion that our model *was* capable of differentiating modification behavior where it did in fact take place. To this end we specified an aggregate investment function only for houses that engaged in upgrading activity. Our model could presumably predict the relative sizes (by total upgrading expenditures) of overall upgrading activity: the greater the prospective net market gains for combinations of change, the larger and more extensive those combinations should be; the more unsatisfied own-consumption housing needs, the more separate kinds of upgrading, and at higher intensity, should occur. The same explanatory variables were used, and basically the same signs were expected of these variables as in the improvement probability model. The results are shown in table 16.9 for both variants A and B (all changes and all less air conditioning and area additions, respectively, as before).

In general, our expectations that our variables would predict actual improvement expenditures better than the probability of improvement were not fulfilled. Estimated equations (by ordinary least squares) under both variants have very low overall predictive power—with R^2 of .085 and .101, respectively. Whereas the LOGIT model has thirteen statistically significant variables for variant A and eleven for variant B, the OLS model has eight for A and only three for B. Moreover, the signs of many of these OLS-estimated coefficients are counter to expectation: variant A has ten sign turnabouts and variant B has seven. If we remember that the LOGIT models, and especially variant B, almost uniformly met our expectations about sign, these turnabouts represent inferior performance for the OLS model. Finally, the number of sign reversals where at least one coefficient in each pair is significant were five in variant A and three in variant B.

Our overall judgment, therefore, is that the aggregate improvement expenditure function is not successfully modeled by either variant A or B. It is easy

Table 16.9. Coefficients for Aggregate Models of Alterations and Additions

Independent Variables	A. All Alterations/Additions: Any Alteration or Addition? (LOGIT)	A. All Alterations/Additions: If Yes, Total Est. Expdt. $ (OLS)	B. Excluding A/C, Additions: Any Alteration? (LOGIT)	B. Excluding A/C, Additions: If Yes, Total Est. Expdt. $ (OLS)
AGE5–9%	−2.17	2523	−1.97	−1853
	(1.00)	(0.97)	(0.84)	(1.05)
AGE20–34%	2.67	2622	2.49	1193
	(2.02)[b]	(1.76)[b]	(1.75)[b]	(1.18)
AGE35–64%	2.66	3046	1.91	1115
	(2.10)	(2.13)[b]	(1.40)[c]	(1.14)
PRE-1955%	.082	654	.113	529
	(0.19)	(1.32)*	(0.24)	(1.55)*
MEDINC$	−.07	−66.6	−.09	1.37
($1,000s)	(1.70)[c]*	(1.35)*	(1.87)[c]*	(0.04)
BLACK%	−.004	−1.27	−.005	2.12
	(1.25)	(0.26)	(1.31)	(0.57)
OCCUP%	1.17	1013	1.50	−192
	(1.69)[c]*	(1.24)	(2.04)[b]*	(0.33)
BADAREA	−.386	196	−.236	267
	(2.63)[a]	(0.98)	(1.58)[c]	(2.18)[b]*
TIPAREA	−.069	26.9	−.042	96.3
	(0.60)	(0.16)	(0.33)	(0.80)
OWNER	.308	−92.8	.265	76.6
	(2.06)[b]	(0.46)	(1.62)[c]	(0.55)
SOLD	−.071	−89.8	−.051	−12.8
	(1.30)*	(1.38)*	(0.88)	(0.28)
AGEHOME	−.007	3.01	−.009	−5.96
	(1.72)[c]*	(0.56)	(2.06)[b]*	(1.64)[c]*
AGEHOME^2	.07	−56.4	.10	48.4
(÷1,000)	(1.31)*	(0.87)	(1.93)[b]*	(1.09)
*SUBMKT*1	−.364	−850	.042	−81.7
	(1.97)[b]*	(4.07)[a]*	(0.21)	(0.58)
*SUBMKT*2	−.576	−600	−.251	−53.1
	(3.74)[a]*	(3.38)[a]*	(1.53)*	(0.44)
*SUBMKT*3	−.632	−609	−.367	−149.0
	(4.03)[a]*	(3.16)[a]*	(2.15)[b]*	(1.10)
*SUBMKT*4	−.416	−545	−.193	−112.7
	(2.75)[a]*	(2.95)[a]*	(1.17)	(0.86)
*SUBMKT*5	.248	−235	.002	26.2
	(2.53)[a]*	(2.28)[b]*	(0.16)	(0.37)
PRICEP	−.058	152	−.015	90.2
	(0.50)	(0.99)	(0.11)	(0.85)
PRICEN	−.026	52.9	−.117	−50.1
	(0.34)	(0.61)	(1.50)[c]	(0.83)
Σ *RETURNS*	.05	−123.9	.10	75.9
($1,000s)	(1.43)[c]	(3.23)[a]*	(2.40)[a]	(2.84)[a]
Intercept	3.36	−687	3.22	−395
	(3.32)[a]*	(0.59)	(2.95)[a]*	(1.64)*

Table 16.9. continued

Independent Variables	A. All Alterations/Additions: Any Alteration or Addition? (LOGIT)	A. All Alterations/Additions: If Yes, Total Est. Expdt. $ (OLS)	B. Excluding A/C, Additions: Any Alteration? (LOGIT)	B. Excluding A/C, Additions: If Yes, Total Est. Expdt. $ (OLS)
Potential *N*	2052	706	2052	529
Actual *N*	706	NA	529	NA
R^2	NA	.085	NA	.101

Notes: Dependent variable for LOGIT = *LN* ((p/(l − p))/2 + 5). T-statistics are in parentheses.
NA = not applicable.
[a]Coefficient statistically significant at 1% (one-tailed test).
[b]Coefficient statistically significant at 5% (one-tailed test).
[c]Coefficient statistically significant at 10% (one-tailed test).
*Two-tailed test if no predicted sign or opposite predicted sign.

to believe that such an investment function needs a closer connection of household characteristics with dwelling characteristics (cf. Galster 1987: ch. 9), and that both detailed budget and liquidity factors, as well as availability of alternative nonhousing investments, must be considered. Our data sources simply did not permit any such close linkages. In addition, it should be recalled that expenditures for improvements (the dependent variable) were *estimated* for each dwelling, based on cost functions provided by the Des Moines Assessor's Office (used earlier in calculating the *RETURNS* variable). It is likely that these functions were insufficiently robust to capture sufficient detail of the actual expenditures made by owners on home improvements during the sample period. For all the aforementioned reasons it is not surprising that the resulting model estimations were weak in performance.

16.4 Conclusion

In sum, the single-SMSA version of our model offers considerable confirmation to our conceptualization of the home modification process and offers insights about an extremely complex, multifaceted decision process. It emphasizes the mixed consumption-investment nature of the home improvement decision, and the differences in kinds of change with respect to the initial configuration of the dwelling. In general, the decision is responsive to changing market situations, though in varying degrees for different changes. Modification *is* a form of market supply response, where market interrelationships are couched in the stratified terms of our fundamental housing submarket approach. These basic conclusions are borne out by the aggregate version of the model, with some greater clarification about the differential effects of different variables. The responsiveness of the home improvement decision to prospective investment opportunities in a segmented housing market is further confirmed and sharpened. That supply adjustments do respond to conditions in different quality submarkets further supports our central contention of systematic, if nonuniform, connections between submarkets.

Notes

1. This ruled out modeling finishing attics or installation of central heat, due to the paucity of such changes in the sample: seven and five instances, respectively.

2. For this reason we eschewed modeling open porch conversions into closed porches and vice versa.

3. For a complete discussion of the LOGIT model, see Pindyck and Rubinfeld 1981: 287–300.

4. Both these studies also employ the LOGIT specification, although neither disaggregate by particular type of modification, as is done here. For a complete review of these and other studies of home upkeep behavior, see Galster 1987: ch. 9.

5. The 1965 estimate was made by a simple interpolation between 1960 and 1970 tract data.

6. See Galster 1987: ch. 9.

7. Once having chosen to improve, of course, higher-income homeowners invest more; see Galster 1987: ch. 9.

8. The specific cost equations used for each archetypical change are available upon request.

9. Recall that *submarket price* is the average ratio of actual sales prices to estimated hedonic value; see table 11.9.

10. Estimated by the hedonic index.

11. Specification using the ratio of the two submarket prices if the differential was positive (or negative) was also tried, but with no success.

12. Of course, insofar as the probability of each sampled dwelling *remaining* owner-occupied *throughout* the period is not highly correlated with it being so at the outset, the explanatory power of *OWNER* will be reduced.

13. This two-equation model is commonly employed when a large number of observations are clustered at the origin; see, e.g., Mendelsohn 1977. In the present sample, 706 out of 2,052 dwellings had archetypical improvements during the period.

14. The expenditures are estimated by the cost equations provided by the city of Des Moines Assessor's Office. As such they are subject to error to the extent that a particular dwelling's modification is more or less expensive than the norm, due, for example, to architectural idiosyncrasies or owner-supplied renovating labor.

15. A "feasible" change is one that has not previously been made in the structure (e.g., air conditioning) or is not constrained by the existing dwelling features (e.g., impossibility of finishing a basement due to the absence of unfinished basement area).

16. Another possibility arises out of specification shortcomings with the *PRICEP, PRICEN* variables. Since they are estimated on the basis of sales transpiring throughout the 1962–69 period (instead of those only at the beginning of the stock supply period, 1963), they are not truly independent of observed medium-run supply adjustments. The unsatisfactory pattern of coefficients could, therefore, be the result of simultaneity bias.

17. Ninety-six percent of the sample consisted of owner-occupants in 1963.

18. It should be noted, however, that the more virulent cases of tipping seen in some larger cities were not present in Des Moines; making generalizations is thus risky.

19. The *BLACK%* coefficient in the hedonic index is negative but not significant. This could be due to ghettoization of blacks, since it both forced greater-income heterogeneity within a neighborhood than is usual for whites and also (during this period) raised housing prices above those of comparable units in nonblack areas (Galster 1977).

20. It is possible that costs are inflated here, since the possibility of "do-it-yourself" labor is excluded. However, such was also excluded from other archetypical change cost estimations as well, and these still produced numerous instances of positive returns. Furthermore, major structural additions seem least likely to involve substantial amounts of such types of labor.

21. This is consistent with the findings of Shear 1983 and Stewart and Hyclak 1986.

Part Five: Conclusions, Implications, and Future Directions

17 The Maze of Urban Housing Markets: What Have We Learned?

In this book we have tried to give the reader a better understanding of the maze of urban housing markets. This final chapter reviews our goals and assesses our explorations in each of the three areas of our subtitle—theory, evidence, and policy. We conclude by identifying some fruitful directions for future research.

17.1 Theory

Our theory is premised on the notion that housing is a special kind of commodity and, therefore, that a housing market is a special kind of market. Unlike many other theorists, we have not tried to make housing into some sort of generic good so that it could be treated in the conventional way. Rather, we have treated it on its own terms, taking its idiosyncrasies—spatial immobility, durability, heterogeneity, and modifiability—seriously. These idiosyncrasies have numerous important implications for modeling the housing market—including, among others, joint consumption-investment behaviors of owner-occupants; neighborhood externality effects; predominance of supply from the existing stock; substitutability among many attributes of the housing package; and active participation in the market of only small fractions of both demanders and suppliers during any given period. It is no small challenge to create a theoretical framework which is unified and consistent, robust enough to encompass these various unique complexities, and yet not intractably complex.

Our theoretical framework is founded upon the unifying assumptions of utility maximization by demanders and rate-of-return maximization by suppliers, with the associated key implication of graded behavioral sensitivity on both sides of the market to prices of dwellings with graded degrees of substitutability. Applying these assumptions to the idiosyncratic features of urban housing markets, we have developed a rich theoretical structure reflecting the segmentation of the market into interlocking quality submarkets. Within this market structure, we have modeled demand by both renters and owner-occupants, incorporating the portfolio and tenure-choice decisions which unavoidably accompany participation in the housing market; supply by owners of existing dwellings in the short-run market period; changes in the stock of housing due to conversions and new construction over a medium-run period;

market-period and longer-run general equilibrium; and intersubmarket dynamic adjustments. By integrating all of these features into a single unified model, we have produced a coherent theoretical apparatus for both comprehending and analyzing the maze of urban housing markets.

To explicate this theory in all its richness requires considerable rigor and theoretical formality; these we have supplied at length in chapters 3–6. But the theory has an intuitive thrust that makes it easy to grasp. The graphical summary of the model in chapter 7 and its application to a wide range of contemporary urban housing issues and policy questions in chapters 8–12 provide tangible proof of the model's usefulness. These chapters show how our model can be understood and applied by the nonspecialists to yield powerful insights for the understanding and policy modification of urban housing phenomena.

17.2 Evidence

Our theory is founded on two key propositions concerning the structure of urban housing markets and the behavior of housing demanders and suppliers. The first of these is that a stratified complex of interrelated submarkets is the appropriate representation of housing supply, demand, and market interaction and that a hedonic index is an effective way to capture this stratification. The second (and more conventional) assumption is that housing consumers behave as utility maximizers, and housing owners and suppliers as rate-of-return maximizers, when confronting the opportunities and constraints they face in the market for housing. These propositions are, of course, falsifiable. If there were no systematic variations in the behaviors of demanders and suppliers, or in the market responses across submarkets, then our fundamental notion of market stratification would be a needless complication; the simplifying notion of homogeneous housing services would be adequate. Similarly, if such variations existed but the market structure generated by our hedonic indexes of quality failed to capture them, our model would have proven inadequate. Given the central role of these propositions, our econometric work was designed primarily as a vehicle to explore the empirical plausibility of our approach; it is not, nor was it intended to be, the definitive econometric estimate of the entire model. Happily, the results are strongly supportive of our fundamental theoretical structure. Important systematic variations are apparent in several dimensions across submarkets, and our procedural definition of these submarkets as narrow ranges of hedonic value, as generated by hedonic indexes, captures them convincingly.

Consider first the relevant findings from our cross-SMSA modeling efforts. Perhaps most significantly, there was not a single "price" per unit of housing quality, but several; these prices varied across submarkets and were intercorrelated in ways consistent with their roles as substitute commodities. Over time the various segments of a given metropolitan area's housing market do not change to the same degree or even in the same direction. To speak of changes in "the" housing market is thus misleading. The mix of supply responses clearly varies, with new construction predominating in roughly the highest two quintiles and conversion predominating in the lowest two, in both tenures. The relevant elasticities also vary across submarkets. The responsiveness of demand with respect to own-submarket price becomes increasingly inelastic at lower quality levels until, at the lowest rental submarkets, housing behaves like a Giffen good. The elasticity of demand with respect to market valuations in substitute submarkets of higher quality is the greatest in the lowest-quality rental submarket, is insignificant in other renter submarkets, and is large across the entire array in the ownership tenure. The market-period elasticity of stock supply is less in owner than in renter submarkets, but in all except one it is extremely small. The medium-run supply function in all owner submarkets appears to be perfectly elastic over a three-year time horizon, while high-quality renter submarkets have somewhat less elastic responses. No consistent indicators of medium-run supply elasticities in the lowest-quality renter submarkets could be observed, but that is to be expected given the evidence that these latter submarkets function as "residuals" reacting primarily to events in other submarkets.

The results of our single-SMSA empirical investigations are equally supportive of our theory of market segmentation. In particular, we found that the submarket in which a dwelling originated substantially affected the probability that improvements would be made to it. This impact occurred through two routes: first, implicitly, because the initial characteristics of the dwelling interacted with the proposed improvement multiplicatively (through the hedonic index) so as to affect the prospective gain in market value; and second, explicitly, since submarket price differentials independently affected the prospective rate of return to improvements. The net result was that certain parts of the single-family housing stock in Des Moines were much more prone to upgrading than were others, and this pattern was not simply related monotonically to quality or current market value, but also to relevant submarket price differentials between the origin and destination submarkets.

Our second major assumption portrayed demanders as utility maximizers who choose the appropriate quality submarket to enter (i.e., their optimal amount of housing consumption) partly on the basis of intersubmarket price or rent differentials. The already noted sensitivity of demand to prices in substitute submarkets provides direct evidence that this view is correct. Similarly, our assumption that rate-of-return maximization motivates the behavior of housing suppliers is supported by the finding that proxies for the pattern of submarket prices/rents and excess demands across the quality array were strong predictors of medium-run supply responses in both tenures. In our single-SMSA application, we found that even owners of single-family dwellings (mostly homeowners), who would be expected a priori to be least likely to manifest such motivations, were, in fact, strongly influenced by the differences between expected returns and the expected costs of improvements, irrespective of their own households' consumption desires.

Bringing together all of our empirical evidence on market structure, demander behavior, and supplier behavior, the special implications about the dynamics of market adjustment which we posited in our theory—systematic nonuniformities—are apparent. What is systematic is that, indeed, the strength of intersubmarket repercussions appears to be inversely related to the quality differential between any two given submarkets, due to the implicit degree of substitutability perceived by both demanders and suppliers. Observed nonuniformities from several sources are superimposed on this systematic pattern. Own-price and cross-price elasticities of demand vary depending on the submarket. Similarly, the speed and extent of medium-run supply adjustment vary by submarket, especially if the age or quality distribution of the existing stock is also varied.

In sum, it is apparent that our fundamental theoretical constructs and assumptions have meaningful empirical support from the empirical results reported in chapters 13–16. This is not to say that our empirical efforts have been exhaustive. Later in this chapter we provide some suggestions for future empirical research.

17.3 Policy

We believe that our approach offers a versatile, powerful means of analyzing various urban housing problems and the policies designed to rectify them. Indeed, for many of the most important contemporary phenomena—rent burdens, homelessness, abandonment, slums, gentrification/displacement—*not* to view them in the context of a quality-segmented housing market is to gloss over most of their essence. Perhaps our most important finding (in contrast to previous work) is that the roots of these (and other) housing problems often can be found outside the lower-quality submarkets in which the consequences are manifested. Our theory shows how exogenous shocks to either the demand side or the supply side of any given submarket will eventually, through induced changes in consumption by demanders, induced conversions of the existing stock, and induced alterations in the destination of new construction, create repercussions in other submarkets (their magnitudes being inversely related to the quality differentials). Thus, for example, a widespread downgrading of erstwhile middle-quality stock might ultimately be traced not to shocks initially impinging on the middle-level submarkets but to events that have increased prices in lower-quality submarkets (increases in demand and/or decreases in supply there), decreased prices in higher-quality submarkets (decreases in demand and/or increases in supply there), or both.

This fundamental insight about intersubmarket adjustments carries over to policy analysis. Because most housing policies have notably nonuniform initial impacts across the submarket complex, it is only through our interlocking-submarket approach that one can clearly comprehend their ultimate effects. Both the shorter-run and longer-run efficiency consequences of a policy initiative can also be addressed because our approach pays explicit attention to how suppliers of existing and new dwellings respond to an initial pattern of policy-generated signals across the submarket array. It thus easily permits us to analyze whether the induced market repercussions augment a given policy action's initial impacts or offset them to a greater or lesser degree. In analogous fashion, our approach permits comparative equity analysis for direct policy recipients, nonrecipients who happen to reside in target submarkets, and those residing in nontargeted submarkets.

Thus, our model can readily be used to demonstrate theoretically how and why well-meaning policies frequently produce unintended and unwanted consequences. For example, a rent supplement policy that tightly limits the range of quality submarkets in which the supplement can be used will result in fewer dwellings being downgraded, and less new construction—and, hence, considerably less favorable market opportunities for the target population—than a program with more flexible and generous benefits. Tying rehabilitation subsidies to limitations in subsequent rent increases ultimately harms lower-income tenants by hastening the deterioration of the very units that were upgraded originally as part of the policy. A policy putatively designed to help lower-income tenants afford housing by holding down rents in lower-quality submarkets makes these households worse off than a broader policy that attempts to control rents across the entire quality spectrum.

We have stressed that the choice of an optimal housing policy (or combination of policies) depends crucially on the particular program goals sought and upon the particular metropolitan context in which the policies are to be implemented. Significantly, our theoretical analysis shows that, for most of the specific contexts evaluated, demand-side approaches appear superior to supply-side and direct market interventions on most efficiency *and equity* grounds. Demand-side approaches are fundamentally different from either supply-side or market-regulatory approaches in a way that only our approach makes plain: they do not engender conflicting endogenous adjustments across submarkets which counteract policy goals.

Our empirical analyses fully support this theoretical proposition. Recall at the outset the conventional proposition (Weicher 1979:483) that the comparative efficiency of demand- versus supply-side policies depends upon measured price and income elasticities of demand and on short- and medium-run supply elasticities. Consider now the implications of our findings for each.

Our demand elasticity estimates are especially compelling here.[1] Unlike other, aggregate studies that have estimated low price elasticities for housing as a whole,[2] we find that reducing the price of lowest-quality and/or moderate-quality rental dwellings would lead to dramatic *de*creases in low-quality housing consumption. Recall from chapter 14 that in the lowest-quality renter submarket the own-price elasticity was positive and greater than two, as was the cross-price elasticity. This implies that a policy which altered relative prices (between housing and nonhousing goods and/or between submarkets) would generate sizable demand shifts at this end of the rental submarket array. How would suppliers respond?

We have found market-period supply in all submarkets to be very inelastic, though not perfectly so. This means that the *initial* impact of stimulating demand via a rent supplement would be to inflate rents in the submarkets in which recipients' consumption would be focused (and deflate it in the submarkets from which they came). However, we have also found that this situation would likely persist less than five years, given the observed speed of response and the nearly perfectly elastic medium-run supply function in middle-quality rental submarkets. Indeed, although our finding of a nearly perfectly elastic medium-run supply for most submarkets is consistent with previous aggregate empirical estimates,[3] our measured speed of supply adjustment to precisely the sort of excess demands that a rent supplement policy might create is considerably more rapid than previously estimated.[4] Unfortunately, our results do not enable us to say much about supply elasticity or speed of adjustment in the bottom two renter quintiles. This is irksome, but understandable given the apparent "residual" status of these submarkets.

By contrast, our empirical findings prove almost uniformly *un*supportive of the efficacy of past or proposed supply-side policies. Our attempts to measure directly the impacts of past public housing initiatives, for example, revealed no convincing evidence that they had a net positive impact on the stock in any rental submarket,[5] and even less evidence that they reduced the occupancy of lower-quality rental submarkets.[6] Results for our subsidized housing variable were less discouraging, and were consistent with the hypothesis that section 235 programs in the early 1970s increased occupancy in the lower-quality owner submarkets (presumably by erstwhile renters). The aggregate nature of this variable makes interpretation difficult, however. Furthermore, there was a clear lack of relationship between this variable and the stock in the lower-quality rental markets, which is similar to the findings of Weicher and Thibodeau (1988).

Our results provide several pieces of strong indirect evidence that filtering is an inefficient device for improving conditions for lower-income households, especially if they are renters. Fundamentally, because medium-run housing supply throughout the owner submarket array and well down the renter array becomes highly elastic within a five-year period, any gains from additions to the stock (initiated by excess construction) which take the form of price or rent reductions will be transitory. Furthermore, there is doubt whether signals transmitted by excess construction at high-quality submarkets will create adequate repercussions throughout the quality array. Cross-price elasticities of demand appear substantial in all owner submarkets, but they are insignificant (or of the wrong sign) in middle-quality renter submarkets. This means that signals originating from construction in the highest-quality rental submarket will be truncated by tenant immobility in the middle-quality submarkets before they can have salutary impacts on the lowest-quality renter submarkets. This truncation of transmission may be even more general on the supply side. The mechanism by which increased supply in higher-quality submarkets impacts submarkets at lower quality levels is that filtering augments the stock in the latter. However, the coefficient of our variable measuring this effect is significantly positive only in the middle- and low-quality submarkets of both tenures; it is insignificant in the fourth-quintile submarket in both. As before, this implies that new construction in the highest quintile of quality of either tenure will generate only weak market signals for lower-quality submarkets. (Of course, these arguments would not apply to construction originating in middle-quality submarkets.) Finally, estimates of cross-tenure price elasticities indicate that, while they are nontrivial in middle-quality rental submarkets, they are very low in the lowest-quality rental submarkets. This means that a filtering policy of new construction designed for owner-occupancy will induce at least some middle-income renters to become owners. The concomitant reduction of rental demands could permit some lower-income renters to move up to better rental accommodations, but few (if any) of them would become homeowners.

There is, in short, abundant evidence that our approach yields important insights into urban housing problems and policies. Its unique theoretical approach has led us to undertake types of empirical investigations that previously had neither foundation nor justification. These investigations have, in turn, revealed important parameter estimates which have direct relevance for informing the contemporary debate over urban housing policy approaches.

17.4 Toward the Future

We see our theoretical and empirical efforts as more provocative than conclusive in the field of housing economics. Our hope is that this book will inspire subsequent investigations that dwarf by comparison our initial efforts as reported here. To this end, we now outline what we believe to be the most fruitful directions for future research—both theoretical and empirical—in the spirit of our work.

Perhaps the most obvious and immediate extensions are empirical ones. As we have noted repeatedly, our econometric analysis was designed not as the definitive estimate of our theoretical model but rather as a means of fleshing out the important empirical dimensions of that model. The data we used were appropriate for that purpose, but their limitations prevented us from addressing several questions of interest. Researchers who employ different data sets could most usefully pursue the following:

1. *A richer estimation of the demand parameters of the theoretical model.* Estimates of the full demand model, including the portfolio and tax variables, would be especially welcome. A less ambitious but still worthwhile project

would be to estimate a more restricted demand relationship with data that permit the calculation of income elasticities of demand. Having income elasticity estimates would permit the evaluation of a wider range of policy options within the segmented-submarket context of this model.

2. *The modeling of a wider range of supply behaviors.* In neither of our two empirical applications could we model conversions due to under- or over-maintenance, because neither hedonic index had any variable for upkeep that was measured consistently over time. The choices of individual homeowners to consolidate or partition their dwellings, to switch the tenure of occupancy, or to abandon their dwellings could be studied if better data were available. Even more helpful in this regard would be some empirical investigations into *rental* supply behavior using a micro–data base.

3. *Further empirical tests of the generality of our results,* both cross-sectionally and intertemporally. Our tests of various sorts of biases in the estimation and use of hedonic indexes, for example, were conducted with samples gathered in St. Louis in 1967 and in Des Moines in 1962–69. Similarly, our econometric estimates of behavioral relationships were based on two (different) samples of SMSAs in 1960–70 and in 1970–1975/76, and a 1960s sample in Des Moines. Replications with different geographic areas sampled more recently would clearly be of value. We especially encourage the use of data sets like our Des Moines sample, with extensive data on individual parcels, because they are uniquely well suited for capturing the rich variety of supply responses arising from the existing stock of housing.

A second set of extensions, with both theoretical and empirical components, would enrich the model by developing further its treatment of the following:

1. *Expectations.* Our theory of supply in both market-period and medium-run framework asserts that behavior is guided by expectations of future market valuations. We have attempted here no investigation of how these expectations are formed; indeed, this is a generally neglected topic in the field.[7] Devising variables which appropriately measure the essence of such expectations, especially at the aggregate level, is a related, and difficult, task.

2. *Neighborhood effects.* While we have incorporated neighborhood effects into our work by including them as a component of our hedonic equation and discussing their policy implications at some length in chapter 9, we believe that there is room for both theoretical and empirical extensions. A richer theoretical treatment of neighborhood effects would include not only their direct effect on property values through the hedonic index but also their influence on the decision-making calculus of both suppliers and demanders. In particular, suppliers' views of neighborhood quality may affect their behavior through a complex set of strategic games played out on a field of important spatial externalities, imperfect information, and volatile expectations. Integrating these complications into our formal theoretical model would be a rewarding (if

challenging) task. By the same token, an expanded empirical analysis of neighborhood effects would be highly useful (though such an effort would be constrained by well-known data limitations).

3. *Consumption-motivated home improvements.* Our formal theory of demand and tenure choice modeled the homeownership decision as one based on an amalgam of both consumption and investment motivations. It could be enriched by treating explicitly the home reinvestment behavior of those who have already made a commitment to homeownership. Specifically, what determines whether a homeowner seeking to increase housing consumption upgrades in a place or moves to a better dwelling? (Or, conversely, whether a homeowner facing economic exigencies passively undermaintains or moves to more modest quarters?)[8] The inclusion of variables measuring these homeowner consumption and mobility dimensions would doubtless improve the explanatory power of our empirical models of home improvement activity.

4. *Competitive interrelationships among alternative modes of supply.* We believe that all sorts of housing suppliers make their decisions based on some expectations of the forthcoming supply response from competitors. Modeling these empirically would require the development of complicated distributed lag or simultaneous-equation models of medium-run supply response integrating private conversion, private construction, and publicly sponsored conversion and construction behaviors. Ideally, observations of such responses could be made over shorter time intervals than we were able to use here.

5. *Institutional realities.* As any reader of chapters 8–12 can testify, our model as it stands is well adapted to analyze a wide range of real-world institutional realities and policy constraints. There are, of course, many others we have not discussed: examples include building codes, zoning redlining by lending institutions, the investment decisions made by owners of nonresidential properties, and the fiscal actions of the local public sector. Some of these phenomena could easily be incorporated into the framework of our model by treating them as constraints; in other cases, modifications to the objective functions would be necessary. With appropriate adaptations, our model can serve as a vehicle for exploring the consequences of virtually any force that impacts urban housing markets.

6. *The lower-quality rental submarkets.* Our empirical results suggest that the behavior of these submarkets is primarily a "residual" of events occurring in higher-quality submarkets. If this characterization is correct, researchers should place a high priority on developing an expanded theoretical treatment of these submarkets, one which views them as behaviorally distinct. This segment of the housing market has experienced a long period of "benign neglect" in economic research; it has been two decades since the last comprehensive empirical probes of it were conducted.[9] Given the concentration of significant social problems in these submarkets, a renewal of interest in their workings is long overdue.

17.5 Conclusion

Urban housing markets *are* a maze—a complex set of interlocking individuals, firms, markets, and constraints. Major issues of public policy and human welfare are at stake in society's attempts to find its way through this maze. We hope everyone concerned with housing can profit from the ideas and estimates presented in this book: academic researchers interested in an expanded theoretical and empirical understanding of the workings of urban housing markets; policymakers who seek to design efficacious and equitable public responses to housing (and related) problems; and suppliers of housing who desire a deeper understanding of the market context in which they work. We hope, in short, to have constructed a foundation upon which many may build in the years to come.

Notes

1. Unfortunately, the specification of our income variables does not allow the calculation of income elasticities of demand.

2. See the review in Quigley 1979: 397–99. Although Hanushek and Quigley 1979 found a low price elasticity of demand in low-quality ranges of the rental stock, their observed lack of response might be traced to the perceived transient nature of the Experimental Housing Allowance Program from which the data were gathered.

3. See Hirsch and Law 1979, Davis, Eastman, and Hua 1974; Quigley 1979.

4. By contrast, Muth 1960 sees 90% completion within six years; DeLeeuw and Ekanem 1971 sees 60% completion within three years; Rydell, Neels, and Barett 1982 sees 95% completion within fifteen years.

5. This is consistent with those studies which have found a substantial, if not total, long-run substitution effect of public housing for private construction that would otherwise have been forthcoming. See Swan 1973; Murray 1983b.

6. These results are identical to those of Vitaliano 1983 and Weicher and Thibodeau 1988.

7. For a review and an attempt at developing such a theory, see Galster 1987: ch. 7.

8. Some highly suggestive theoretical and empirical investigations into this joint mobility/reinvestment decision have been conducted by Galster 1987.

9. See Sternlieb 1966; Stegman 1972; Sternlieb and Burchell 1973.

References

Aaron, Henry O. 1975. *Who Pays the Property Tax? A New View.* Washington, D.C.: National Bureau of Economic Research.

Adelman, Irma, and Zvi Griliches. 1961. On an Index of Quality Change. *Journal of the American Statistical Association* 55: 535–48.

Adler, Moshe. 1987. The Location of Owners and Renters in the City. *Journal of Urban Economics* 21: 347–63.

Ahlbrandt, Roger S., and Paul C. Brophy. 1975. *Neighborhood Revitalization.* Lexington, Mass.: Lexington Books.

Ahlbrandt, Roger, and James Cunningham. 1979. *A New Public Policy for Neighborhood Preservation.* New York: Praeger.

Alonso, William. 1964. *Location and Land Use.* Cambridge: Harvard University Press.

Anas, Alex. 1978. Dynamics of Urban Residential Growth. *Journal of Urban Economics* 5: 66–87.

Anderson, Gary S. 1984. Characteristics of Discrete Housing Market Model Equilibria. *Journal of Urban Economics* 16: 125–48.

Anderson, R. J., Jr. and T. D. Crocker. 1971. Air Pollution and Residential Property Values. *Urban Studies* 8: 171–80.

Andrikopoulos, Andreas, and James A. Brox. 1984. Urban Housing Markets: A New Approach for Estimating Demand for Housing by Dwelling Type. *Journal of Urban Economics* 15: 230–43.

Apgar, William C. Jr. 1977. Census Data and Housing Analysis: Old Data Sources and New Applications. In Gregory K. Ingram, ed., *Residential Location and Urban Housing Markets.* Cambridge, Mass.: Lippincott, Ballinger for National Bureau of Economic Research.

———. 1988. The Nation's Housing: A Review of Past Trends and Future Prospects. Housing Policy Project Paper No. 1. MIT Center for Real Estate Development.

Arnott, Richard. 1980. A Simple Urban Growth Model with Durable Housing. *Regional Science and Urban Economics* 10: 53–76.

Arnott, Richard, Russell Davidson, and David Pines. 1986. Spatial Aspects of Housing Quality, Density and Maintenance. *Journal of Urban Economics* 19: 190–217.

Artle, R., and P. Vairaya. 1978. Life Cycle Consumption and Home Ownership. *Journal of Economic Theory* 18: 38–58.

Asmus, Karl, and Harvey Iglarsh. 1975. Dynamic Model of Private Incentives to Housing Maintenance: Comment. *Southern Economic Journal* 42: 326–29.

Bajic, Vladimir. 1984. An Analysis of the Demand for Housing Attributes. *Applied Economics* 16: 597–610.

Ball, Michael. 1973. Recent Work on the Determinants of Relative House Prices. *Urban Studies* 10: 213–33.

Ball, M., and R. Kirwan. 1977. Accessibility and Supply Constraints in the Urban Housing Market. *Urban Studies* 14: 11–32.

Bartik, Timothy. 1986. Neighborhood Revitalization Effects on Tenants and the Benefit-Cost Analysis of Government Neighborhood Programs. *Journal of Urban Economics* 19: 234–48.

Barton, D. M., and E. O. Olsen. 1976. The Benefits and Costs of Public Housing in New York City. Institute for Research on Poverty, Madison, Wisc.

Bender, Bruce. 1979. The Determinants of Housing Demolition and Abandonment. *Southern Economic Journal* 46: 131–44.

Birch, David, Eric Brown, Richard Coleman, Dolores Da Lomba, William Parsons, Linda Sharpe, and Sheryll Weber. 1979. *Behavioral Foundations of Neighborhood Change*. Washington, D.C.: HUD-PDR.

Birnbaum, Howard, and Rafael Weston. 1974. Homeownership and the Wealth Positions of Black and White Households. *Review of Income and Wealth* 20: 103–19.

Blomquist, Glenn, and Lawrence Worley. 1981. Hedonic Prices, Demands for Urban Housing Amenities, and Benefit Estimates. *Journal of Urban Economics* 9: 212–21.

Boehm, Thomas. 1981. Tenure Choice and Expected Mobility. *Journal of Urban Economics* 9: 375–89.

———. 1982. A Hierarchical Model of Housing Choice. *Urban Studies* 19: 17–31.

Boehm, Thomas, and Joseph McKenzie. 1982. Inflation, Taxes, and Demand for Housing. *American Real Estate and Urban Economics Association Journal* 10: 25–38.

Börsch-Supan, Axel, and Henry Pollakowski. 1990. Estimating Housing Consumption Adjustments from Panel Data. *Journal of Urban Economics* 27: 131–50.

Bradbury, Katherine, and Anthony Downs, eds. 1981. *Do Housing Allowances Work?* Washington, D.C.: Brookings Institution.

Bradbury, Katherine, Robert Engle, Owen Irvine, and Jerome Rothenberg. 1977. Simulation Estimates of Supply and Demand for Housing Location in a Multizoned Metropolitan Area. In Gregory K. Ingram, ed., *Residential Location and Urban Housing Markets,* 51–86. Cambridge, Mass.: Lippincott, Ballinger for National Bureau of Economic Research.

Bradford, Calvin, and Leonard Rubinowitz. 1975. The Urban-Suburban Investment-Disinvestment Process: Consequences for Older Neighborhoods. *Annals of the American Academy of Political and Social Sciences* 422: 77–86.

Braid, Ralph. 1981. The Short-Run Comparative Statics of a Rental Housing Market. *Journal of Urban Economics* 10: 286–310.

———. 1984. The Effects of Government Housing Policies in a Vintage Filtering Model. *Journal of Urban Economics* 16: 272–96.

Brown, Barbara. 1985. Location and Housing Demand. *Journal of Urban Economics* 17: 30–41.

Brown, L., and J. Holmes. 1970. *Search Behavior in an Intra-Urban Context.* Columbus: Ohio State University Press.

Brueckner, Jan. 1980. A Vintage Model of Urban Growth. *Journal of Urban Economics* 8: 389–402.

———. 1981. A Dynamic Model of Housing Production. *Journal of Urban Economics* 10: 1–14.

———. 1983. The Economics of Urban Yard Space: An Implicit-Market Model for Housing Attributes. *Journal of Urban Economics* 13: 216–34.

Brueckner, Jan, and Peter Colwell. 1983. A Spatial Model of Housing Attributes: Theory and Evidence. *Land Economics* 59: 58–69.

Brueggeman, William, and Richard Peiser. 1979. Housing Choice and Relative Tenure Prices. *Journal of Financial and Qualitative Analysis* 14: 735–51.

Burns, Leland, and Leo Grebler. 1986. *The Future of Housing Markets.* New York: Plenum Press.

Butler, Richard V. 1977. Hedonic Indexes of Urban Housing: Theory and Problems of Cross-Sectional Estimation. Ph.D. diss., Department of Economics, Massachusetts Institute of Technology.

———. 1980. Cross-Sectional Variation in the Hedonic Relationship for Urban Housing Markets. *Journal of Regional Science* 20: 439–53.

———. 1982. The Specification of Hedonic Indexes for Urban Housing. *Land Economics* 58: 96–108.

Butler, Richard V., George Galster, John Pitkin, and Jerome Rothenberg. 1974. A Second-Generation Microeconomic Model of Metropolitan Housing Markets. Paper presented at the Western Economic Association Meetings, Las Vegas.

Cagan, Philip. 1965. Measuring Quality Changes and the Purchasing Power of Money: An Exploratory Study of Automobiles. *National Banking Review* 3: 217–36. Reprinted in Zvi Griliches, ed., *Price Indexes and Quality Change,* 215–39. Cambridge: Harvard University Press, 1971.

Cameron, Trudy Ann. 1986. Permanent and Transitory Income in Models of Housing Demand. *Journal of Urban Economics* 20: 205–10.

Cassel, Eric, and Robert Mendelsohn. 1985. The Choice of Functional Forms for Hedonic Price Equations: Comment. *Journal of Urban Economics* 18: 135–42.

Chinloy, Peter. 1980. The Effect of Maintenance Expenditures on the Measurement of Depreciation in Housing. *Journal of Urban Economics* 8: 86–107.

Clark, W. A. V., ed. 1982. *Modelling Housing Market Search.* New York: St. Martin's Press.

Clay, Phillip. 1979. *Neighborhood Rehabilitation.* Lexington, Mass.: Heath/Lexington.

———. 1987. *At Risk of Loss: The Endangered Future of Low-Income Rental Housing Resources.* Washington, D.C.: Neighborhood Reinvestment Corp.

Clifton, Charles, John Lansing, and James Morgan. 1969. *New Homes for Poor People.* Ann Arbor: University of Michigan Survey Research Center.

Courant, Paul. 1978. Racial Prejudice in a Search Model of the Housing Market. *Journal of Urban Economics* 5: 329–45.

Court, Andrew. 1939. Hedonic Price Indexes with Automotive Examples. In *The Dynamics of Automobile Demand,* 99–117. Detroit: General Motors Corp.

Cowling, Keith, and John Cubbin. 1971. Price, Quality and Advertising Competition: An Econometric Investigation of the United Kingdom Car Market. *Econometrica* 38: 378–94.

Cramer, J. S. 1964. Efficient Grouping, Regression and Correlation in Engel Curve Analysis. *Journal of the American Statistical Association* 59: 233–50.

Crocker, Thomas. 1975. Cost-Benefit Analyses of Cost-Benefit Analysis. In Henry M. Peskin and Eugene P. Seskin, eds., *Cost-Benefit Analysis and Water Pollution Policy.* Washington, D.C.: The Urban Institute.

Davies, Gordon. 1978. Theoretical Approaches to Filtering in the Urban Housing Market. In Larry Bourne and John Hitchcock, eds., *Urban Housing Markets: Recent Directions in Research and Policy,* 139–63. Toronto: University of Toronto Press.

Davis, Otto, C. Eastman, and C. Hua. 1974. The Shrinkage in the Stock of Low-Quality Housing in the Central City. *Urban Studies* 11: 13–26.

Davis, Otto and Andrew Whinston. 1961. The Economics of Urban Renewal. *Law and Contemporary Problems* 26: 105–17.

DeLeeuw, Frank. 1976. The Demand for Housing: A Review of the Cross-Sectional Evidence. *Review of Economics and Statistics* 53: 1–10.

DeLeeuw, Frank, and Nkanta Ekanem. 1971. The Supply of Rental Housing. *American Economic Review* 61: 806–17.

DeLeeuw, Frank, and Raymond Struyk. 1975. *The Web of Urban Housing.* Washington, D.C.: Urban Institute.

Dhrymes, Phoebus. 1967. On the Measurement of Price and Quality Changes in Some Consumer Capital Goods. *American Economic Review* 57: 501–18.

———. 1971. Price and Quality Changes in Consumer Capital Goods. In Zvi Griliches, ed., *Price Indexes and Quality Change.* Cambridge: Harvard University Press.

———. 1983. On the Determination of the Probability of First Home Acquisition and Its Relation to Credit Stringency. In Ronald Grieson, ed., *The Urban Economy and Housing,* 59–104. Lexington, Mass.: D. C. Heath/Lexington.

Diamond, Douglas. 1980a. Income and Residential Location: Muth Revisited. *Urban Studies* 17: 1–12.

———. 1980b. Taxes, Inflation, Speculation and the Cost of Home Ownership. *American Real Estate and Urban Economics Association Journal* 8: 281–98.

Diamond, Douglas, and Barton A. Smith. 1985. Simultaneity in the Market for Housing Characteristics. *Journal of Urban Economics* 17: 280–92.

Dildine, Larry, and Fred Massey. 1974. A Dynamic Model of Private Incentives to Housing Maintenance. *Southern Economic Journal* 40: 40–48.

Doling, J. 1973. A Two-Stage Model of Tenure Choice in Housing Markets. *Urban Studies* 10: 199–224.

Downs, Anthony. 1981. *Neighborhoods and Urban Development.* Washington, D.C.: Brookings Institution.

———. 1988. *Residential Rent Controls: An Evaluation.* Washington, D.C.: Urban Land Institute.

Dynarski, Mark. 1985. Housing Demand and Disequilibrium. *Journal of Urban Economics* 17: 42–57.

Eberts, Randall, and Timothy Gronberg. 1982. Wage Gradients, Rent Gradients, and Price Elasticity of Demand for Housing: An Empirical Investigation. *Journal of Urban Economics* 12: 168–76.

Edel, Matthew. 1972. Filtering in a Private Housing Market. In Matthew Edel and Jerome Rothenberg, eds., *Readings in Urban Economics,* 204–15. New York: Macmillan.

Erekson, Homer O., and Anne Witte. 1979. The Demand for Housing: Comment. *Southern Economic Journal* 46: 640–48.

Evans, A. 1973. *The Economics of Residential Location.* London: Macmillan.

Färe, Rolf, and Bong Joon Yoon. 1985. On Capital-Land Substitution in Urban Housing Production. *Journal of Urban Economics* 18: 119–24.

Feige, Edgar, and Harold Watts. 1972. An Investigation of the Consequences of Partial Aggregation of Micro-Economic Data. *Econometrica* 40: 343–60.

Fisch, Oscar. 1977. Dynamics of the Housing Market. *Journal of Urban Economics* 4: 428–47.

Fisher, Franklin, Zvi Griliches, and Carl Kaysen. 1962. The Costs of Automobile Model Changes since 1949. *Journal of Political Economy* 70: 433–51.

Follain, James. 1979. Price Elasticity of Long Run Supply of New Housing. *Land Economics* 55: 190–99.

———. 1982. Does Inflation Affect Real Behavior: The Case of Housing. *Southern Economic Journal* 48: 570–82.

Friedman, Joseph, and Daniel Weinberg. 1981. The Demand for Rental Housing: Evidence from the Housing Allowance Demand Experiment. *Journal of Urban Economics* 9: 311–31.

———, eds. 1983. *The Great Housing Experiment.* Urban Affairs Annual Reviews, vol. 24. Beverly Hills, Calif.: Sage Publications.

Fujita, Masahisa. 1976. Spatial Patterns of Optimal Growth. *Journal of Urban Economics* 3: 193–208.

———. 1982. Spatial Patterns of Residential Development. *Journal of Urban Economics* 12: 22–52.

Galster, George. 1977. A Bid-Rent Analysis of Housing Market Discrimination. *American Economic Review* 67: 144–55.

———. 1979. Interracial Differences in Housing Preferences. *Regional Science Perspectives* 9, no. 1: 1–17.

———. 1980. *Consumers' Housing Satisfaction: Improvement Priorities and Needs.* Ohio State University Center for Real Estate Education and Research, Columbus, Ohio.

———. 1981a. A Neighborhood Interaction Model of Housing Maintenance and Quality Changes by Owner Occupants. *Regional Science Perspectives* 11, no. 2: 29–48.

———. 1981b. On the Motivation for Homeowners' Upgrading Behavior. Paper presented at the Mid-Continent Regional Science Association Meetings, Cincinnati.

———. 1982. Black and White Preferences for Neighborhood Racial Composition. *American Real Estate and Urban Economics Association Journal* 10: 39–66.

———. 1983. Empirical Evidence on Cross-Tenure Differences in Home Maintenance and Condition. *Land Economics* 59: 107–13.

———. 1986. What Is the Urban Neighborhood? An Externality-Space Approach. *International Journal of Urban and Regional Research* 10: 243–64.

———. 1987. *Homeowners and Neighborhood Reinvestment.* Durham, N.C.: Duke University Press.

———. 1988a. The Causes of Racial Segregation in American Cities: A Contrary Review. *Population Research and Policy Review* 7: 93–112.

———. 1988b. The Great Misapprehension: Federal Fair Housing Policy in the 1980's. Housing Policy Project Paper No. 5. MIT Center for Real Estate Development, Cambridge, Mass.

———. 1990. Neighborhood Racial Change, Segregationist Sentiment, and Affirmative Marketing Policies. *Journal of Urban Economics* 27: 344–61.

Galster, George, and Garry Hesser. 1982. The Social Neighborhood: An Unspecified Factor in Homeowners' Maintenance? *Urban Affairs Quarterly* 18: 235–54.

Galster, George, and Mark Keeney. 1988. Race, Residence, Discrimination and Economic Opportunity. *Urban Affairs Quarterly* 24: 87–117.

Gilderbloom, John, and Richard Appelbaum. 1988. *Rethinking Rental Housing*. Philadelphia: Temple University Press.

Gillingham, Robert, and Robert Hagemann. 1983. Cross-Sectional Estimation of a Simultaneous Model of Tenure Choice and Housing Services Demand. *Journal of Urban Economics* 14: 16–39.

Gillingham, Robert, and D. C. Lund. 1970. A Hedonic Approach to Rent Determination. *Proceedings of the Business and Economic Statistics Section of the American Statistical Association,* 184–92.

Goetze, Rolf. 1976. *Building Neighborhood Confidence*. Cambridge, Mass.: Ballinger.

———. 1979. *Understanding Neighborhood Change: The Role of Expectations in Urban Revitalization*. Cambridge, Mass.: Ballinger.

Goetze, Rolf, and Kent Colton. 1983. Dynamics of Neighborhoods: A Fresh Approach to Understanding Housing and Neighborhood Dynamics. In Phillip Clay and Robert Hollister, eds., *Neighborhood Policy and Planning*. Lexington, Mass.: Lexington Books.

Goldberger, Arthur. 1968. *Topics in Regression Analysis*. New York: Macmillan.

Goodman, Allen. 1978. Hedonic Prices, Price Indices and Housing Markets. *Journal of Urban Economics* 5: 471–84.

———. 1981. Housing Submarkets within Urban Areas: Definitions and Evidence. *Journal of Regional Science* 21: 175–86.

———. 1988. An Econometric Model of Housing Price, Permanent Income, Tenure Choice, and Housing Demand. *Journal of Urban Economics* 23: 327–53.

Goodman, Allen, and Masahiro Kawai. 1982. Permanent Income, Hedonic Prices, and Demand for Housing: New Evidence. *Journal of Urban Economics* 12: 214–37.

———. 1984. Estimation and Policy Implications of Rental Housing Demand. *Journal of Urban Economics* 16: 76–90.

Goodwin, Thomas H. 1986. Inflation, Risk, Taxes, and the Demand for Owner-Occupied Housing. *Review of Economics and Statistics* 68: 197–206.

Grether, David, and Peter Mieszkowski. 1974. The Determinants of Real Estate Values. *Journal of Urban Economics* 1: 127–46.

———. 1980. Effects of Nonresidential Land Uses on the Prices of Adjacent Housing. *Journal of Urban Economics* 8: 1–15.

Grieson, Ronald. 1973. The Supply of Rental Housing: Comments. *American Economic Review* 63: 433–36.

———. 1974. The Economics of Property Taxes and Land Values: The Elasticity of Supply of Structures. *Journal of Urban Economics* 1: 367–81.

Grieson, Ronald, and Richard Arnott. 1983. The Supply of Urban Housing. In Ronald Grieson, ed., *The Urban Economy and Housing,* 3–10. Lexington, Mass.: Heath/Lexington.

Grigsby, William. 1963. *Housing Markets and Public Policy*. Philadelphia: University of Pennsylvania Press.

Grigsby, William, Morton Baratz, George Galster, and Duncan Maclennan. 1987. *The Dynamics of Neighborhood Change and Decline*. New York: Pergamon Press.

Grigsby, William, and Louis Rosenburg. 1975. *Urban Housing Policy*. New Brunswick, N.J.: Center for Urban Policy Research, Rutgers University/APS Publications.

Griliches, Zvi. 1971a. Introduction: Hedonic Price Indexes Revisited. In Zvi Griliches, ed., *Price Indexes and Quality Change*. Cambridge: Harvard University Press.

———, ed. 1971b. *Price Indexes and Quality Change*. Cambridge: Harvard University Press.

Gross, David J. 1988. Estimating Willingness to Pay for Housing Characteristics: An Application of the Ellickson Bid-Rent Model. *Journal of Urban Economics* 24: 95–112.

Haitovsky, Y. 1973. *Regression Estimation from Grouped Observations*. New York: Hafner Publishing.

Hallman, Howard. 1984. *Neighborhoods: Their Place in Urban Life*. Beverly Hills, Calif.: Sage Publishers.

Halvorsen, Robert, and Henry Pollakowski. 1981. Choice of Functional Form of Hedonic Price Equations. *Journal of Urban Economics* 10: 37–49.

Hamilton, Bruce. 1982. Capitalization and Housing Demand Bias. *Southern Economic Journal* 49: 374–88.

Hanushek, Eric, and John Quigley. 1979. The Dynamics of the Housing Market: A Stock Adjustment Model of Housing Consumption. *Journal of Urban Economics* 6: 90–111.

———. 1982. The Determinants of Housing Demand. In J. Vernon Henderson, ed., *Research in Urban Economics,* 2: 221–42. Greenwich, Conn.: JAI Press.

Harmon, Oskar R. 1988. The Income Elasticity of Demand for Single-Family Owner-Occupied Housing: An Empirical Reconciliation. *Journal of Urban Economics* 24: 173–85.

Harrington, David E. 1989. An Intertemporal Model of Housing Demand: Implications for the Price Elasticity. *Journal of Urban Economics* 25: 230–46.

Harris, R., George Tolley, and C. Harrell. 1968. The Residence Site Choice. *Review of Economics and Statistics* 50: 241–47.

Harrison, David, and John Kain. 1974. Cumulative Urban Growth and Urban Density Functions. *Journal of Urban Economics* 1: 61–98.

Harrison, David, and Daniel Rubinfeld. 1978. Hedonic Housing Prices and the Demand for Clean Air. *Journal of Environmental Economics and Management* 5: 81–102.

Hartman, Chester, Ann Meyerson, and Rachel Bratt, eds. 1986. *Critical Perspectives on Housing*. Philadelphia, Penn.: Temple University Press.

Haurin, Donald R., and Kyubang Lee. 1989. A Structural Model of the Demand for Owner-Occupied Housing. *Journal of Urban Economics* 26: 348–60.

Heckman, James J. 1979. Sample Bias as a Specification Error. *Econometrica* 47: 153–61.

Helper, Rose. 1969. *Racial Policies and Practices of Real Estate Brokers*. Minneapolis: University of Minnesota Press.

Hendershott, Patrick. 1980. Real User Costs and the Demand for Single-Family Housing. *Brookings Papers on Economic Activity* 2: 401–44. Washington, D.C.

Henderson, J. Vernon. 1985. *Economic Theory and the Cities*. Orlando, Fla.: Academic Press.

Henderson, J. Vernon, and Yannia M. Ioannides. 1983. A Model of Housing Tenure Choice. *American Economic Review* 73: 98–113.

———. 1986. Tenure Choice and the Demand for Housing. *Economica* 53: 231–46.

———. 1987. Owner Occupancy: Investment vs. Consumption Demand. *Journal of Urban Economics* 21: 228–41.

———. 1989. Dynamic Aspects of Consumer Decisions in Housing Markets. *Journal of Urban Economics* 26: 212–30.

Hirsch, Werner, and C. Law. 1979. Habitability Laws and the Shrinkage of Substandard Rental Stock. *Urban Studies* 16: 19–28.

Hirsch, Werner, and Stephen Margolis. 1977. Habitability Laws and Low-Cost Rental Housing. In Gregory K. Ingram, ed., *Residential Location and Urban Housing Markets.* Cambridge, Mass.: Lippincott, Ballinger for National Bureau of Economic Research.

Houthakker, Hendrick. 1951–52. Compensated Changes in Quantities and Qualities Consumed. *Review of Economic Studies* 19: 155–64.

Howenstine, Jay. 1986. *Housing Vouchers: A Comparative International Analysis.* Center for Urban Policy Research, Rutgers University, New Brunswick, N.J.

Hufbauer, G., and B. Severn. 1974. The Economic Demolition of Old Buildings. *Urban Studies* 11: 349–51.

Hughes, James. 1974. The Dynamics of Neighborhood Decline. In James Hughes, ed., *Suburbanization Dynamics and the Future of the City.* Center for Urban Policy Research, Rutgers University, New Brunswick, N.J.

Hughes, James, and George Sternlieb. 1987. *Dynamics of America's Housing.* Center for Urban Policy Research, Rutgers University, New Brunswick, N.J.

Hunter, Albert. 1974. *Symbolic Communities.* Chicago: University of Chicago Press.

———. 1979. The Urban Neighborhood: Its Analytic and Social Contexts. *Urban Affairs Quarterly* 15: 267–88.

Ihlanfeldt, Keith. 1981. An Empirical Investigation of Alternative Approaches to Estimating the Equilibrium Demand for Housing. *Journal of Urban Economics* 9: 97–105.

Ingram, Gregory. 1979. Simulation and Econometric Approaches to Modelling Urban Areas. In Peter Mieszkowski and Mahlon Straszheim, eds., *Current Issues in Urban Economics,* 391–429. Baltimore: Johns Hopkins University Press.

Ingram, Gregory, and John Kain. 1973. A Simple Model of Production and the Abandonment Problem. *American Real Estate and Urban Economics Association Journal* 1: 79–106.

Ingram, Gregory, John Kain, and Royce Ginn. 1972. *The Detroit Prototype of the NBER Urban Simulation Model.* New York: National Bureau of Economic Research.

Ingram, Gregory, and Yitzhak Oron. 1977. The Production of Housing Services from Existing Dwelling Units. In Gregory K. Ingram, ed., *Residential Location and Urban Housing Markets.* Cambridge, Mass.: Lippincott, Ballinger for National Bureau of Economic Research.

Intriligator, Michael D. 1971. *Mathematical Optimization and Economic Theory.* New York: Prentice Hall.

Jackson, Jerry, Ruth Johnson, and David Kaserman. 1984. The Measurement of Land Prices and the Elasticity of Substitution in Housing Production. *Journal of Urban Economics* 16: 1–12.

Johnson, David Dale. 1982. An Alternative Approach to Housing Segmentation Using Hedonic Price Data. *Journal of Urban Economics* 11: 311–32.

Johnson, M. 1981. A Cash Flow Model of Rational Housing Tenure Choice. *American Real Estate and Urban Economics Association Journal* 9: 10–17.

Johnston, J. 1972. *Econometric Methods.* 2d ed. New York: McGraw-Hill.

Kain, John, and William Apgar. 1982. Revitalizing Central City Neighborhoods. Kennedy School of Government Working Monograph. Cambridge, Mass.

Kain, John, and John Quigley. 1969. Evaluating the Quality of the Residential Environment. *Environment and Planning* 2.

———. 1970. Measuring the Value of Housing Quality. *Journal of the American Statistical Association* 65: 532–48.

———. 1972. Housing Market Discrimination, Homeownership, and Savings Behavior. *American Economic Review* 62: 263–77.

———. 1975. *Housing Markets and Racial Discrimination: A Microeconomic Analysis.* New York: National Bureau of Economic Research.

Keller, Suzanne, 1968. *The Urban Neighborhood: A Sociological Perspective.* New York: Random House.

Kennedy, Stephen, and Meryl Finkel. 1987. *Report of the First Year Findings for the Freestanding Housing Voucher Demonstration.* Washington, D.C.: HUD/PDR.

Kent, R. 1983. Relationships between Income and Price Elasticities in Studies of Housing Demand, Tenure Choice and Household Formation. *Journal of Urban Economics* 13: 196–204.

Keyes, Langley. 1988. Housing and the Homeless. Housing Policy Project Paper No. 15. MIT Center for Real Estate Development, Cambridge, Mass.

Keyes, Langley, and Denise DiPasquale. 1988. Housing Policy for the 1990s. Housing Policy Project Paper No. 0. MIT Center for Real Estate Development, Cambridge, Mass.

King, A. Thomas. 1973. *Property Taxes, Amenities and Residential Land Values.* Cambridge, Mass. Ballinger.

———. 1976. The Demand for Housing. In N. Terleckyj, ed., *Household Production and Consumption.* New York: National Bureau of Economic Research.

———. 1977. The Demand for Housing: A Lancaster Approach. *Southern Economic Journal* 43: 1077–87.

King, A. Thomas, and Peter Mieszkowski. 1973. Racial Discrimination. *Journal of Political Economy* 81: 590–606.

King, M. A. 1980. An Econometric Model of Tenure Choice and Demand for Housing as a Joint Decision. *Journal of Public Economics* 14: 137–59.

Kristof, Frank. 1965. Housing Policy Goals and the Turnover of Housing. *Journal of the American Institute of Planners* 31: 232–45.

Krumm, Ronald. 1980. Neighborhood Amenities: An Economic Analysis. *Journal of Urban Economics* 7: 208–24.

Lachman, Leanne, and Anthony Downs. 1978. The Role of the Neighborhoods in the Mature Metropolis. In Charles Leven, ed., *The Mature Metropolis.* Lexington, Mass.: Lexington Books.

Lancaster, Kelvin. 1966. A New Approach to Consumer Theory. *Journal of Political Economy* 74: 132–57.

———. 1971. *Consumer Demand: A New Approach.* New York: Columbia University Press.

Lansing, John, and Leslie Kish. 1954. Response Errors in Estimating the Values of Homes. *Journal of the American Statistical Association* 49: 520–38.

Lapham, Victoria. 1971. Do Blacks Pay More for Housing? *Journal of Political Economy* 79: 1244–57.

Laska, Shirley, and Daphne Spain, eds., 1980. *Back to the City.* New York: Pergamon.

Leamer, Edward. 1978. *Specification Searches.* New York: John Wiley and Sons.

Lee, Lung-fei, and Robert Trost. 1978. Estimation of Some Limited Dependent Variables with Application to Housing Demand. *Journal of Econometrics* 8: 357–82.

Leven, Charles, James Little, Hugh Nourse, and R. B. Read. 1976. *Neighborhood Change: Lessons in the Dynamics of Urban Decay.* New York: Praeger Publishers.

Li, Mingche. 1977. A LOGIT Model of Homeownership. *Econometrica* 45: 1081–95.

Linneman, Peter. 1980. Some Empirical Results on the Nature of the Hedonic Price Function for the Urban Housing Market. *Journal of Urban Economics* 8: 47–68.

———. 1981. Demand for Residence Site Characteristics. *Journal of Urban Economics* 9: 129–48.

———. 1985. An Economic Analysis of the Homeownership Decision. *Journal of Urban Economics* 17: 230–46.

———. 1986. A New Look at The Homeownership Decision. *Housing Finance Review* 5: 159–87.

Lowry, Ira. 1960. Filtering and Housing Standards: A Conceptual Analysis. *Land Economics* 36: 362–70.

———. 1983. *Experimenting with Housing Allowances.* Cambridge, Mass.: Oelgechlager, Gunn and Hain.

Lucas, Robert. 1975. Hedonic Price Functions. *Economic Inquiry* 13: 157–78.

McCain, Mark. 1987. Rising Rents from Stores Subsidizing Apartments. *New York Times,* 1 Mar., sec. 8.

McDonald, John. 1979. *Economic Analysis of the Urban Housing Market.* New York: Academic Press.

McKinney, Scott, and Ann Schnare. 1986. *Trends in Residential Segregation by Race: 1960–1980.* Washington, D.C.: Urban Institute.

Maclennan, Duncan. 1977. Some Thoughts on the Nature and the Purpose of House Price Studies. *Urban Studies* 14: 59–71.

———. 1982. *Housing Economics.* London: Longmans.

MacRae, C. Duncan. 1982. Urban Housing with Discrete Structures. *Journal of Urban Economics* 11: 131–47.

MacRae, C. Duncan and Margery Turner. 1981. Owner-Occupied Housing Subject to Income Tax. *Journal of Urban Economics* 10: 338–56.

Maddala, G. S. 1977. *Econometrics.* New York: McGraw-Hill.

Margolis, Stephen. 1981. Depreciation and Maintenance of Housing. *Land Economics* 57: 91–105.

———. 1982. Depreciation of Housing: An Empirical Consideration of the Filtering Hypothesis. *Review of Economics and Statistics* 64: 90–96.

Marks, Denton. 1984. The Effects of Partial-Coverage Rent Control on the Price and Quantity of Rental Housing. *Journal of Urban Economics* 16: 360–69.

Mayer, Neil. 1981. Rehabilitation Decisions in Rental Housing. *Journal of Urban Economics* 10: 76–94.

———. 1985. The Impacts of Lending, Race and Ownership on Rental Housing Rehabilitation. *Journal of Urban Economics* 17: 349–74.

———. 1988. The Role of Nonprofits in Renewed Federal Housing Efforts. Housing Policy Project Paper No. 16. MIT Center for Real Estate Development, Cambridge, Mass.

Mayo, Stephen. 1981. Theory and Estimation in the Economics of Housing Demand. *Journal of Urban Economics* 10: 95–116.

Mendelsohn, Robert. 1977. Empirical Evidence on Home Improvements. *Journal of Urban Economics* 4: 459–68.

Meyer, Robert. 1980. A Descriptive Model of Constrained Residential Search. *Geographical Analysis* 12: 21–32.

Mills, Edwin. 1972. *Studies in the Structure of the Urban Economy.* Baltimore: Johns Hopkins University Press.

Miron, J. R., and J. B. Cullingworth. 1983. *Rent Control.* Centre for Urban and Community Studies, University of Toronto.

Miyao, Takahiro. 1978. Dynamic Instability of a Mixed City in the Presence of Neighborhood Externalities. *American Economic Review* 68: 454–63.

Moore, Eric, and Stewart Clatworthy. 1978. The Role of Urban Data Systems in the Analysis of Housing Issues. In Larry Bourne and John Hitchcock, eds., *Urban Housing Markets: Recent Directions in Research and Policy.* Toronto: University of Toronto Press.

Moorhouse, John. 1972. Optimal Housing Maintenance under Rent Control. *Southern Economic Journal* 39: 93–108.

Muellbauer, John. 1974. Household Production Theory, Quality and the Hedonic Technique. *American Economic Review* 64: 977–94.

Murray, Michael. 1978. Hedonic Prices and Composite Commodities. *Journal of Urban Economics* 5: 188–97.

———. 1983a. Mythical Demands and Mythical Supplies for Proper Estimation of Rosen's Hedonic Price Model. *Journal of Urban Economics* 14: 327–37.

———. 1983b. Subsidized and Unsubsidized Housing Starts. *Review of Economics and Statistics* 65: 590–97.

Musgrave, J. C. 1969. The Measurement of Price Changes in Construction. *Journal of the American Statistical Association* 64: 771–86.

Muth, Richard. 1960. The Demand for Nonfarm Housing. In A. C. Harberger, ed., *The Demand for Durable Goods.* Chicago: University of Chicago Press.

———. 1966. Household Production and Consumer Demand Functions. *Econometrica* 34: 699–708.

———. 1969. *Cities and Housing.* Chicago: University of Chicago Press.

———. 1973. A Vintage Model of the Housing Stock. *Papers of the Regional Science Association* 30: 141–56.

———. 1976. A Vintage Model of Housing Production. In G. Papageorgiu, ed., *Mathematical Land Use Theory.* Lexington, Mass.: D. C. Heath.

———. 1977. The Influence of Age of Dwellings on Housing Expenditures and Location. In Gregory K. Ingram, ed., *Residential Location and Urban Housing Markets,* 3–22. Cambridge, Mass.: Lippincott, Ballinger for National Bureau of Economic Research.

Myers, Dowell. 1975. Housing Allowances, Submarket Relationships and the Filtering Process. *Urban Affairs Quarterly* 11: 215–40.

———. 1983. Upward Mobility and the Filtering Process. *Journal of Planning Education and Research* 2: 101–12.

———. 1984. Turnover and Filtering of Post-War Single-Family Homes. *Journal of the American Planning Association* 50: 352–58.

National Association of Homebuilders. 1986. *Low and Moderate Income Housing*. Washington, D.C.: NAHB.

Nelson, Kathryn. 1978. Movement of Blacks and Whites between Central Cities and Suburbs in Eleven Metropolitan Areas, 1955–75. HUD, AHS Working Paper No. 2. Washington, D.C.

Newburger, Harriett. 1984. *Recent Evidence on Housing Market Discrimination*. Washington, D.C.: HUD/PDR.

Newman, Sandra, and Ann Schnare. 1988. Integrating Housing and Welfare Assistance. Housing Policy Project Paper No. 12. MIT Center for Real Estate Development, Cambridge, Mass.

Niebanck, Paul, ed. 1985. *The Rent Control Debate*. Chapel Hill: University of North Carolina Press.

Nourse, Hugh. 1963. The Effects of Public Housing on Property Values in St. Louis. *Land Economics* 39: 434–41.

Oates, Wallace. 1969. The Effects of Property Taxes and Local Public Spending on Property Values: An Empirical Study of Tax Capitalization and the Tiebout Hypothesis. *Journal of Political Economy* 77: 957–71.

Ohls, James. 1975. Public Policy toward Low-Income Housing and Filtering in Housing Markets. *Journal of Urban Economics* 2: 144–71.

Olsen, Edgar. 1969. A Competitive Theory of the Housing Market. *American Economic Review* 59: 612–21.

Ozanne, Larry, and Ray Struyk. 1976. *Housing from the Existing Stock*. Washington, D.C.: Urban Institute.

Ozanne, Larry, and Thomas Thibodeau. 1983. Explaining Metropolitan Housing Price Differences. *Journal of Urban Economics* 13: 51–66.

Palen, J., and Bruce London. 1984. *Gentrification, Displacement, and Neighborhood Revitalization*. Albany, N.Y.: SUNY Press.

Palm, Risa. 1978. Spatial Segmentation of the Urban Housing Market. *Economic Geography* 54: 210–21.

Parsons, George R. 1986. An Almost Ideal Demand System for Housing Attributes. *Southern Economic Journal* 53: 347–63.

Pearce, Diana. 1979. Gatekeepers and Homeseekers: Institutional Patterns in Racial Steering. *Social Problems* 26: 325–42.

Peterson, George, Arthur Solomon, Hadi Madjid, and William Apgar. 1973. *Property Taxes, Housing and the Cities*. Lexington, Mass.: Heath/Lexington.

Pindyck, Robert, and Daniel Rubinfeld. 1981. *Econometric Models and Economic Forecasts*. 2d ed. New York: McGraw-Hill.

Pitkin, John, and Jerome Rothenberg. 1978. Demand, Supply and Market Interaction in a Segmented Urban Housing Market. Paper presented at the American Economic Association/Econometric Society meetings, Chicago.

Plaut, Steven E. 1987. The Timing of Housing Tenure Transition. *Journal of Urban Economics* 21: 312–22.

Pohlmann, Marcus. 1986. *Political Power in the Post-Industrial City*. Millwood, N.Y.: Associated Faculties Press.

Polinsky, A. Mitchell. 1977. The Demand for Housing: A Study in Specification and Grouping. *Econometrica* 45: 447–61.

———. 1979. The Demand for Housing: An Empirical Postscript. *Econometrica* 47: 521–23.

Polinsky, A. Mitchell, and D. T. Ellwood. 1979. An Empirical Reconciliation of Micro and Grouped Estimates of the Demand for Housing. *Review of Economics and Statistics* 61: 199–205.

Potepan, Michael J. 1989. Interest Rates, Income, and Home Improvement Decisions. *Journal of Urban Economics* 25: 282–94.

Prais, S. J., and J. Aitchison. 1954. The Grouping of Observations in Regression Analysis. *Review of the International Statistical Institute* 22: 1–22.

President's Commission on Housing. 1982. *The Report of the President's Commission on Housing*. Washington, D.C.: GPO.

Public Affairs Counseling. 1975. *The Dynamics of Neighborhood Change*. San Francisco and Washington, D.C.: Public Affairs Counseling/HUD-PDR-108.

Quigley, John. 1976. Housing Demand in the Short Run: An Analysis of Polytomous Choice. *Explorations in Economic Research* 3: 76–102.

———. 1977. Comment on Bradbury et al. In Gregory K. Ingram, ed., *Residential Location and Urban Housing Markets*. Cambridge, Mass.: Lippincott, Ballinger for National Bureau of Economic Research.

———. 1979. What Have We Learned about Urban Housing Markets? In Peter Mieszkowski and Mahlon Straszheim, eds., *Current Issues in Urban Economics*. Baltimore: Johns Hopkins University Press.

———. 1983. Estimates of a More General Model for Consumer Choice in the Housing Market. In Ronald Grieson, ed., *The Urban Economy and Housing*, 125–40. Lexington, Mass.: Heath/Lexington.

Quinn, Michael, Donald Elliot, Robert Mendelsohn, and Jeffrey Thomas. 1980. Maintenance Effort and the Professional Landlord. *American Real Estate and Urban Economics Association Journal* 8: 345–69.

Rabianski, Joseph, and John Spitzer. 1978. A Two-Sector Cross-Section Econometric Model of the 1970 Housing Stock. *Growth and Change* 9: 2–8.

Ranney, Susan. 1981. The Future Price of Houses, Mortgage Market Conditions, and the Return to Homeownership. *American Economic Review* 71: 323–33.

Ratcliff, Richard. 1949. *Urban Land Economics*. New York: McGraw-Hill.

Richardson, Harry. 1977. *The New Urban Economics*. London: Pion.

Ridker, Ronald, and John Henning. 1967. The Determinants of Residential Property Values with Special Reference to Air Pollution. *Review of Economics and Statistics* 49: 246–56.

Robsen, Arthur. 1982. Comparative Statics of the Market for a Consumer Durable with an Age/Quality Structure: A Reprise of Models of Urban Structure. *Journal of Urban Economics* 11: 169–79.

Roistacher, Elizabeth. 1977. Short-Run Housing Responses to Changes in Income. *American Economic Review* 67: 381–86.

Rosen, Harvey. 1979a. Housing Decisions and the U.S. Income Tax: An Econometric Analysis. *Journal of Public Economics* 11: 1–23.

———. 1979b. Owner-Occupied Housing and the Federal Income Tax: Estimates and Simulations. *Journal of Urban Economics* 6: 247–66.

Rosen, Harvey, and Kenneth Rosen. 1980. Federal Taxes and Home Ownership. *Journal of Public Economics* 88: 59–75.

Rosen, Sherwin. 1974. Hedonic Prices and Implicit Markets: Product Differentiation in Pure Competition. *Journal of Political Economy* 82: 34–55.

Rothenberg, Jerome. 1967. *Economic Evaluation of Urban Renewal.* Washington, D.C.: Brookings Institution.

———. 1978. Urban Housing Markets and Housing Policy. In Samuel Bernstein and W. Giles Mellon, *Selected Readings in Quantitative Urban Analysis.* New York: Pergamon Press.

———. 1983. Housing Investment, Housing Consumption, and Tenure Choice. In Ronald Grieson, ed., *The Urban Economy and Housing,* 29–56. Lexington, Mass.: Heath/Lexington.

Rydell, Peter. 1976. Measuring the Supply Response to Housing Allowances. *Papers of the Regional Science Association* 37: 31–57.

Rydell, C. Peter, Kevin Neels, and C. Lance Barnett. 1982. *Price Effects of a Housing Allowance Program.* A final report of the Housing Assistance Supply Experiment, R-2720-HUD. Santa Monica, Calif.: Rand Corporation.

Schafer, Robert. 1977. Maintenance and Operating Behavior of Resident and Absentee Landlords. Discussion Paper D77–10. Department of City and Regional Planning, Harvard University.

Schafer, Robert, and Helen Ladd. 1980. *Equal Credit Opportunity.* Washington, D.C.: HUD.

Schall, Lawrence. 1981. Commodity Chain Systems and the Housing Market. *Journal of Urban Economics* 10: 141–63.

Schelling, Thomas. 1971. On the Ecology of Micro-Motives. *The Public Interest* 25: 59–98.

———. 1972. A Process of Residential Segregation: Neighborhood Tipping. In Anthony Pascal, ed., *Racial Discrimination in Economic Life.* Lexington, Mass.: Heath/Lexington.

Schnare, Ann, and Raymond Struyk. 1976. Segmentation in Urban Housing Markets. *Journal of Urban Economics* 3: 146–66.

Schwab, Robert. 1982. Inflation Expectations and the Demand for Housing. *American Economic Review* 72: 143–53.

Schwartz, David, Richard Ferlauto, and Daniel Hoffman. 1988. *A New Housing Policy for America.* Philadelphia: Temple University Press.

Seek, N. H. 1983. Adjusting Housing Consumption: Improve or Move? *Urban Studies* 20; 455–69.

Segal, David. 1980. A Model to Forecast Neighborhood Change. Paper presented at the Eastern Economics Association Meetings, Montreal.

———, ed. 1979. *The Economics of Neighborhood.* New York: Academic Press.

Shear, William. 1983. Urban Housing Rehabilitation and Move Decisions. *Southern Economic Journal* 49: 1030–52.

Shear, William, and Bruce Carpenter. 1982. *Housing Rehabilitation, Move Decisions and Neighborhood Change.* Washington, D.C.: HUD/PDR.

Shefer, Daniel. 1986. Utility Changes in Housing and Neighborhood Services for Households Moving into and out of Distressed Neighborhoods. *Journal of Urban Economics* 19: 107–24.

Simpson, George, and J. Milton Yinger. 1972. *Racial and Cultural Minorities.* 4th ed. New York: Harper and Row.

Smith, Barton. 1976. The Supply of Urban Housing. *Quarterly Journal of Economics* 90: 389–405.

Smith, Jeffrey W. 1989. A Theoretical Analysis of the Supply of Housing. *Journal of Urban Economics* 26: 174–88.

Smith, Lawrence B., Kenneth T. Rosen, and George Fallis. 1988. Recent Developments in Economic Models of Housing Markets. *Journal of Economic Literature* 26: 29–64.

Smith, Wallace. 1963. Forecasting Neighborhood Change. *Land Economics* 39: 292–97.

———. 1964. Filtering and Neighborhood Change. Center for Real Estate and Urban Economics Research Report, University of California, Berkeley.

Sonstelie, Jon, and Paul Portney. 1980. Gross Rents and Market Values. *Journal of Urban Economics* 7: 102–18.

Stegman, Michael. 1972. *Housing Investment in the Inner City: The Dynamics of Decay.* Cambridge: MIT Press.

———. 1985. *Housing in New York.* Office of Rent and Housing Maintenance, Department of Housing Preservation and Development, New York.

———. 1988. The Role of Public Housing in a Revitalized National Housing Policy. Housing Policy Project Paper No. 18. MIT Center for Real Estate Development, Cambridge, Mass.

Sternlieb, George. 1966. *The Tenement Landlord.* New Brunswick, N.J.: Rutgers University Press.

Sternlieb, George, and Robert Burchell. 1973. *Residential Abandonment: The Tenement Landlord Revisited.* New Brunswick, N.J.: Rutgers University Press.

Stewart, James, and Thomas Hyclak. 1986. Determinants of Household Expenditures for Additions, Alterations, Replacements, and Repairs to Owner Occupied Residences. Department of Economics, Pennsylvania State University. Photocopy.

Stover, Mark. 1986. The Price Elasticity of the Supply of Single-Family Detached Housing. *Journal of Urban Economics* 20: 331–40.

Straszheim, Mahlon. 1973. Estimation of the Demand for Urban Housing Services from Household Interview Data. *Review of Economics and Statistics* 55: 1–8.

———. 1974. Housing Market Discrimination and Black Housing Consumption. *Quarterly Journal of Economics* 88: 19–43.

———. 1975. *An Econometric Analysis of the Urban Housing Market.* New York: National Bureau of Economic Research.

Struyk, Raymond. 1976. *Urban Homeownership.* Lexington, Mass.: D. C. Heath.

Struyk, Raymond, and Marc Bendick, eds. 1981. *Housing Vouchers for the Poor.* Washington, D.C.: Urban Institute Press.

Struyk, Raymond, and Beth Soldo. 1980. *Improving the Elderly's Housing.* Cambridge, Mass.: Ballinger.

Sullivan, Arthur. 1990. *Urban Economics.* Homewood, Ill.: Irwin.

Suttles, Gerald. 1972. *The Social Construction of Communities.* Chicago: University of Chicago Press.

Swan, Craig. 1973. Housing Subsidies and Housing Starts. *American Real Estate and Urban Economics Association Journal* 1: 119–40.

Sweeney, James. 1974a. A Commodity Hierarchy Model of the Rental Housing Market. *Journal of Urban Economics* 1: 288–323.

———. 1974b. Housing Unit Maintenance and the Mode of Tenure. *Journal of Economic Theory* 8: 111–38.

———. 1974c. Quality, Commodity Hierarchies, and Housing Markets. *Econometrica* 42: 147–68.

Taub, Richard, Garth D. Taylor, and Jan Dunham. 1984. *Paths of Neighborhood Change*. Chicago: University of Chicago Press.

Theil, Henri. 1971. *Principles of Econometrics*. New York: John Wiley and Sons.

Triplett, Jack. 1969. Automobiles and Hedonic Quality Measurement. *Journal of Political Economy* 77: 408–17.

Urban-Suburban Investment Group. 1977. *Redlining and Disinvestment as a Discriminatory Practice in Residential Mortgage Loans*. Center for Urban Studies, University of Illinois–Chicago Circle.

Vandell, Kerry. 1981. The Effects of Racial Composition on Neighborhood Succession. *Urban Studies* 18: 315–33.

Varady, David. 1986. *Neighborhood Upgrading: A Realistic Assessment*. Albany, N.Y.: SUNY Press.

Vaughn, G. A. 1976. Sources of Downward Bias in Estimating the Demand Income Elasticity for Urban Housing. *Journal of Urban Economics* 3: 45–56.

Vipond, M. and J. Walker. 1972. Determinants of Housing Expenditure and Owner Occupation. *Bulletin of the Oxford University Institute of Economic Statistics* 34: 168–87.

Vitaliano, Don. 1983. Public Housing and Slums. *Urban Studies* 20: 173–83.

———. 1985. The Short-Run Supply of Housing Services under Rent Control. *Urban Studies* 22: 535–42.

Vousden, Neil. 1980. An Open-City Model with Non-Malleable Housing. *Journal of Urban Economics* 7: 248–77.

Webber, M. J. 1979. *Information Theory and Urban Spatial Structure*. London: Croom-Helm.

Weicher, John. 1979. Urban Housing Policy. In Peter Mieszkowski and Mahlon Straszheim eds., *Current Issues in Urban Economics*, 469–508. Baltimore: Johns Hopkins University Press.

———. 1988. The Voucher/Production Debate. Housing Policy Project Paper No. 13. MIT Center for Real Estate Development, Cambridge, Mass.

Weicher, John, and Thomas Thibodeau. 1988. Filtering and Housing Markets. *Journal of Urban Economics* 23: 21–40.

Weinberg, Daniel, and Reilly Atkinson. 1979. Place Attachment and the Decision to Search for Housing. *Growth and Change* 10: 22–29.

Weisbrod, Glen, and Avis Vidal. 1981. Housing Search Barriers for Low Income Renters. *Urban Affairs Quarterly* 16: 465–82.

Wheaton, William. 1977. A Bid-Rent Approach to Housing Demand. *Journal of Urban Economics* 4: 200–217.

———. 1979. Monocentric Models of Urban Land Use: Contributions and Criticisms. In Peter Mieszkowski and Mahlon Straszheim, eds., *Current Issues in Urban Economics*, 107–29. Baltimore: Johns Hopkins University Press.

———. 1982a. Urban Residential Growth under Perfect Foresight. *Journal of Urban Economics* 12: 1–21.

———. 1982b. Urban Spatial Development with Durable but Replaceable Capital. *Journal of Urban Economics* 12: 53–67.

———. 1985. Life-Cycle Theory, Inflation, and the Demand for Housing. *Journal of Urban Economics* 18: 161–79.

White, Michelle J. 1986. Property Taxes and Urban Housing Abandonment. *Journal of Urban Economics* 20: 312–30.

Wieand, Kenneth F. 1973. Air Pollution and Property Values: A Study of the St. Louis Area. *Journal of Regional Science* 13: 91–95

Wienk, Ronald, Cliff Reid, John Simonson, and Fred Eggers. 1979. *Measuring Discrimination in American Housing Markets*. Washington, D.C.: HUD/PDR.

Wilkinson, R., and I. Lau. 1978. A Model of Tenure Determination in a Local Housing Market. *Applied Economics* 10: 173–82.

Wilson, Franklin. 1979. *Residential Consumption, Economic Opportunity and Race*. New York: Academic Press.

Winger, Alan. 1973. Some Internal Determinants of Upkeep Spending by Urban Homeowners. *Land Economics* 49: 474–79.

Witte, Ann, Howard Sumka, and Homer Erekson. 1979. An Estimate of a Structural Hedonic Price Model of the Housing Market: An Application of Rosen's Theory of Implicit Markets. *Econometrica* 47: 1151–74.

Yinger, John. 1979. Prejudice and Discrimination in the Urban Housing Market. In Peter Mieszkowski and Mahlon Straszheim, eds., *Current Issues in Urban Economics*, 430–68. Baltimore: Johns Hopkins University Press.

Yinger, John, Howard Bloom, Axel Börsch-Supan, and Helen Ladd. 1988. *Property Taxes and House Values*. San Diego, Calif.: Harcourt, Brace, Jovanovich; Academic Press.

Yinger, John, George Galster, Barton Smith, and Fred Eggers. 1979. The Status of Research into Racial Discrimination and Segregation in American Housing Markets. *HUD Occasional Papers in Housing and Community Affairs* 6: 55–175.

Author Index

Subject Index